Understanding
International Economics:
Theory and Practice

Understanding
International Economics:
Theory and Practice

J. David Richardson
University of Wisconsin, Madison

Little, Brown and Company
Boston   Toronto

Library of Congress Catalog Card No. 79-89337

First Printing

Published simultaneously in Canada by Little, Brown & Company (Canada) Limited

Printed in the United States of America

To Karen

Preface

This book springs from repeatedly stimulating offerings of introductory international economics to undergraduates at the University of Wisconsin. My students in this course have always had a marked diversity of educational backgrounds: high-school training of variable quality; from one to four years of undergraduate experience; and majors that are as numerous in business, education, pre-law, political science, and history as in economics. The book reflects my (perhaps quixotic) attempt to educate and satisfy all.

Many excellent international economics texts are aimed primarily at students who have been exposed to intermediate microeconomics and macroeconomics. Only a few seem to be aimed at students who are less well-prepared or who would benefit from a more interpretative, less methodologically demanding course. And these latter texts go too far for my tastes toward jettisoning the unified analytical framework that is the strength of the logic called economics. The result is often a not fully satisfying potpourri of casual reflections on international economic policy, disparate glimpses at familiar economic models, and journalistic descriptions of international economic history and institutions. This book is not completely free of such shortcomings, but I have worked hard to develop a uniform approach and tone and to encourage students to think analytically about economic motivation, policy, and explanation—while still writing for students who cannot or choose not to master international economics at a comparatively abstract level.

AUDIENCE AND LEVEL

Students who have taken from twenty to thirty weeks of economics principles, covering both microeconomics and macroeconomics, should not feel strained approaching the central text. They are its primary audience. Students who have taken intermediate economic theory should be able to master the entire book, including those chapter supplements and footnotes that extend the central text in a more rigorous direction. I believe further that two students with the same economics preparation will comprehend the material comparably even when one is an economics major and one is not.

PURPOSE AND COVERAGE

The word *understanding* in the title conveys the book's principal purpose: to shed light on what is traditionally one of economics' most abstruse and arcane subdivisions, even to professionals. Some of its difficulty stems simply from subject matter. Much also stems from the lack of terminological clarity, from the frequency with which simple intuition and popular reporting is wrong, and from the occasional willingness of many private and governmental commentators to mislead out of self-interest or the pursuit of other goals. To encourage understanding of international economics, I have thus made a special effort to employ clear language, to explore apparent paradoxes at length, to explain in detail why some "received wisdom" is wrong, to highlight popular inaccuracies, and to reveal the economic incentives that underlie the statements and actions of the most prominent participants, including governments, in international exchange.

In this last endeavor, it helps greatly to emphasize income-distributional consequences of international economic transactions, in addition to their consequences for the nation as a whole. This dual emphasis sets the text apart from others, I believe, and characterizes both the macroeconomic part of the book (especially Chapter 3) and the microeconomic part (especially Chapters 10, 13, and 14).

Encouraging understanding has also prompted me to stress material that is relevant to modern policy and private decision-making; for example, a more complete treatment than is traditional of external-currency (Euro-) banking, multinational corporations, and the new international economic order. Less immediately relevant matters, by contrast, are addressed less completely than is typical; the historical working of the gold standard and empirical testing of international trade theories, for instance. The content of the last chapters of each part (Chapters 7 and 14) was chosen to be especially topical, and these chapters were written after the others to minimize their datedness.

My hope is that students who use this book will be more perceptive and incisive readers, critics, voters, and decision-makers. To that end, I have emphasized only a few familiar tools from the economist's toolbox rather than introducing a multiplicity of them. I have found that the latter approach diverts student attention toward mastering analytic techniques. Despite my self-imposed technical limitation, I have tried throughout to synthesize as well as summarize, drawing parallels among diverse themes when possible (the book contains numerous cross-references), and I have occasionally attempted to fill gaps in the existing literature or make subtle extensions to it. I hope that the result is a book that is more cohesive and coherent.

TECHNIQUES AND APPROACH

Most of the book's content is conveyed verbally, graphically, and by numerical example. There are almost no algebraic manipulations or demonstrations, and the number of *different* graphical and numerical approaches is minimized. The macroeconomic material on international finance relies principally on a supply-demand diagram of the foreign exchange market and on schematic diagrams that reveal exogeneity/endogeneity relationships and directional influences that come from IS-LM and "monetary approach" models. The microeconomic material on international trade relies principally on a two-country supply-demand diagram for a typical tradeable and on a two-country production-possibilities diagram. It is remarkable how far these simple tools can take us in understanding international economics.

There is no explicit textual dependence on Keynesian crosses, IS-LM diagrams, community indifference curves, offer curves, or Edgeworth-Bowley boxes. Extended footnotes, however, outline when and how these analytical constructs would provide an alternative way of understanding the text. Some footnotes also provide or point out analytically more advanced extensions, subtleties, and qualifications of the material in the text.[1] So do several of the chapter supplements.[2] Reliance on them enables this book to be used conveniently in courses with a more abstract orientation than I adopt at Wisconsin.

I have tried to fold liberal doses of data, real illustrations, and hypothetical examples into each chapter. Most come from recent economic history (post-1945). I have, by contrast, paid only slight attention to formal econometric work in international economics, feeling that its appreciation required skills beyond those of a large majority of readers.

The concerns of international economics often arouse heated controversy. I have made an effort to be fair to all well-taken conflicting viewpoints—without being bland. "Objective fairness" is, of course, unattainable. Fairness is subjective; my values and presuppositions shape my definition of *fair* (and my definition of *well-taken*). But the practical impossibility of objective treatment does not furnish me

---

[1] Examples are footnotes 1, 2, and 4 to Chapter 4, on the meaning of the *ceteris-paribus* approach; footnotes 3, 4, and 5 to Chapter 9, on the relationship of partial- to general-equilibrium diagrams; footnotes 16 to Chapter 9 and 1 to Chapter 12, on international economic transactions in a socialist system; and footnote 7 to Chapter 12 on factor-intensity reversals.

[2] Examples are Supplement 4A on price inelasticity of commodity demand and the foreign exchange market; Supplement 7A on Euro-currency banking; Supplement 9A on export taxes; and Supplement 11A on nontariff barriers and the terms of trade.

grounds for failing to move as close as I can to it. I apologize to the reader if the resulting discourse seems unduly indecisive. I think by contrast that we are altogether too quick to offer "the" answer as instructors and to insist on it as students.

ORGANIZATION

The macroeconomics of international finance precedes the microeconomics of international trade because I have always found students more receptive to the material presented in that sequence. Other instructors have no doubt found the opposite, and I have endeavored to oblige them. I believe that there would be very little awkwardness in a course which proceeded from the Introduction immediately to Part II and Chapter 8, continued through Chapter 14, and then turned to Part I.

Each chapter includes a summary. Some of them tie together and provide perspective on several chapters at once (the summaries to Chapters 4, 5, 9, and 11, for example). Each summary is followed by a list of key terms and key concepts for review. Suggestions for further reading will be found at the end of the book.

Most chapters contain from one to three chapter supplements— self-contained essays, almost mini-chapters. They furnish a second level of material to the text, in some cases providing additional detail, in others providing a more technically challenging treatment of similar material. I tried to avoid intrusiveness by placing supplements after chapters to which they relate most closely. I imagine that several of them could be shifted around. Flexibility is the principal aim of these supplements—flexibility in both content and length of the course.

LENGTH

The book contains more material than I cover in a typical fifteen-week (one-semester) course, in which I lecture two-and-a-half hours per week. Were I teaching a twenty-week (two-quarter) course, I would assign the entire text and most of the chapter supplements. Were I teaching a thirty-week (two-semester) course, I would assign the entire text (with supplements), along with outside readings (or an edited collection of them). Were I teaching a ten-week (one-quarter) course, I would rely on the central text alone, excluding almost all the chapter supplements.

TOPICAL HIGHLIGHTS

The following are highlights of both content and organization in addition to those already mentioned:
—The foreign exchange market (Chapter 1) is introduced before

balance-of-payments concepts (Chapter 2) in order to reveal why the latter are important.

—A glossary and schema of equivalencies is provided for alternative terminology relating to international capital movements (Supplement 1B).

—An entire chapter (3) is devoted to the fundamental and normative reasons why exchange rates and the balance of payments matter to the man or woman on the street and therefore also to governments; I have observed a striking need for such a discussion—most people care only because everyone else does, but there are better reasons than that.

—The special yet volatile position of the United States and the dollar in international monetary affairs is examined in depth in Chapters 2, 3, 5, and 7.

—Whether the United States has benefitted from this special position, and if so, whether at the expense of the rest of the world, is addressed in Chapter 3 and Supplement 3B.

—Chapters 4, 5, and 6 are parallel, harmonized treatments of interaction between international and domestic macroeconomic variables, drawing from both traditional and "monetary" approaches to the interaction: first, the impact of exogenous changes in domestic on international variables is discussed; then the impact of exogenous changes in international on domestic; and finally the impact of exogenous changes in one country on others.

—Material that is as up-to-date as possible is provided on International Monetary Fund reform, the European Monetary System, and external-currency (Euro-) banking.

—A sharp distinction is drawn between "normative" trade theory (Chapters 8 through 11) and "positive" trade theory (Chapter 12, with both normative and positive aspects to Chapters 13 and 14).

—There is minimal recourse to perfect competition or other restrictive assumptions in order to convey how unassailable certain conclusions are (for example, that some trade is nationally preferable to none, discussed in Chapter 8).

—The economics of real government reluctance to trade freely is revealed sequentially in Chapters 8, 9, and 10: allowing some trade is clearly beneficial (Chapter 8); but allowing free trade is less clearly so (Chapter 9 examines distortions, second-best considerations, and the terms of trade); and allowing freer trade is even less clearly so (Chapter 10 examines adjustment costs and income-distributional considerations).

—As much space is devoted to "modern" trade theories as to Heckscher-Ohlin, and each trade theory is introduced as a complement to the others, not as a competitor to them (Chapter 12).

—Considerable attention is paid to migration, the brain drain, and international trade in factors of production (Chapter 13).

—The treatment of multinational corporations (Chapter 13) is extensive, synthetic, and integrated with the rest of the book.

—An effort is made to explain the noneconomic motivation and objectives of the program for a new international economic order, as well as its economic aspects (Chapter 14).

ACKNOWLEDGEMENTS

Whatever credit my approach in this book receives is due in great part to my teachers and colleagues over the years, especially to Donald E. Kelly, H. Frank Carey High School, Franklin Square, New York; Robert M. Stern, University of Michigan; and Robert E. Baldwin, University of Wisconsin.

The content, organization, and style of the book has been improved immeasurably by a superb army of reviewers for Little, Brown. Noteworthy for their painstaking scrutiny of the entire manuscript are Richard E. Caves, Harvard University, and Judith Cox, University of Washington. The care with which they criticized and chided was much appreciated. They are not to be condemned for my stubborn reluctance to agree wholeheartedly. Other extremely helpful reviewers included: Thomas C. Anderson, Eastern Michigan University; Howard A. Bridgman, Southeastern Massachusetts University; Byron B. Brown, Southern Oregon State College; Dennis C. Duell, Wichita State University; H. Peter Gray, Rutgers University; Robert R. Johnson, Idaho State University; Gerald M. Lage, Oklahoma State University; Gilbert S. Suzawa, University of Rhode Island; Harold R. Williams, Kent State University; and Nancy Baggott, M. O. Clement, Arnold Collery, Richard Cooper, Alexander Garcia, Bernard Goodman, Kiyotoshi Iwanoto, Jerry Kingston, Steve Magee, Llewellyn M. Mullings, E. Wayne Nafziger, E. Dwight Phaup, Thomas Sears, Roger A. Sedjo, Donald Sternitzke, and B. H. Wilkins.

Not to be neglected are several generations of University of Wisconsin students, whose lively reaction to lectures and conscientious feedback shaped many parts of this book—the best parts, I trust.

This work was so long in the making that I think I exhausted even the extraordinarily patient Basil G. Dandison and Darrell R. Griffin, who both left the editor's position during its preparation. Gregory Franklin managed to hang on and to continue the praiseworthy Little, Brown tradition of long-suffering encouragement. The assistance of the publisher has been superb, and the Little, Brown staff, especially Al Hockwalt and Elizabeth Schaaf, deserve thanks.

Jean Arnold, Joneen Lee, and Kathy Monroe suffered my eccentricities with quiet acceptance while typing, pasting, drawing, and formatting with their usual grace. Jackie Forer, Jean Kennedy, Laurie Murphy, and Alice Wilcox shared their agony occasionally and should share their credit too.

Last but not in any way least, I want to thank my Christian brothers and sisters who upheld me continually in my labor, and especially Karen, Kris, and Laura for their love, patience, and support, to which I could return eagerly after each day of struggle over these pages.

Contents

Part II
International Trade 237

Introduction

International economics is concerned with exchange that takes place across national boundaries—with nation-to-nation purchases and sales.

Wheat, whisky, breeding bulls, chicken, copper, cosmetics, steel products, machine tools, auto parts, scientific equipment, blueprints, production manuals, management services, motion pictures, air travel, deeds to property, mineral rights, stock certificates, bonds, and even bank deposits—these are just a few of the goods that are bought and sold internationally. The only unique feature of such transactions is that the buyer is a resident of one country, and the seller is a resident of another. Except for that feature, international economics would be the same as everyday, garden-variety economics, and there would be no need of special courses and textbooks. Because of that feature, international economics emphasizes what makes countries economically different from each other—differences in such things as resource endowments, size, tastes, technology, education, growth, inflation, reliance on markets, systems of taxation, immigration laws, and national moneys.

Most such differences among nations are due to politically determined boundaries and policies. That is why governments and government policies have such a prominent place in this subject and book. Without government, there is *no* distinctive international economics, and no one can understand private international exchange without understanding the government policies that shape, structure, and sometimes try to suppress it. International economics, more than most other fields in economics, is necessarily "political economy."

The subject is traditionally divided into two distinct parts. *International finance* deals with the political economy of multiple world moneys. *International trade* deals with the political economy of natural and legal discrimination between foreigners and national residents. Because international finance focuses on money, many of its concerns and tools will be familiar from macroeconomics. Because international trade focuses on efficiency, equity, taxes, subsidies, government regulation, barriers to entry, and product differentiation, its concerns and tools will be familiar from microeconomics.

The opening of Part I of this book introduces international finance in more detail. The opening of Part II does the same for international trade.

Part I

International Finance

The economics called *international finance* is concerned with foreign exchange rates, the balance of payments, and the ways those interact with the domestic macroeconomy. Part I of this book focuses on international financial events and issues that are widely discussed yet imperfectly understood. For example, when the dollar "plunges to a new low" against the German mark, Japanese yen, or Swiss franc, the event is given considerable publicity. But what does this movement really mean? Why did it happen? And why should anyone care? Answers are not always readily available. Similarly, "good news" travels fast if the U.S. trade balance recovers from an unprecedented deficit. But many people do not know what the trade balance is; few know why it "recovered"; and still fewer know when or whether the recovery really is good news. Nor is it usually apparent why the world gold price, which has risen tenfold in a decade, has any special significance. Why is it quoted daily in radio and television reports, while the price of silver, platinum, or any other precious metal is not? Is there anything socially sinister about speculation in gold or in the markets for dollars, marks, or other world moneys?

Questions like these occupy the first part of this book. Another that is addressed (Chapter 2) is what governments typically *do* about uncertain exchange rates, unprecedented trade deficits, unpredictable gold markets, and uncontrolled speculation. Important related questions (Chapter 3) are *why* governments do what they do, and whether they should. Are variable exchange rates really a problem? Are they a problem for just foreign traders or for the whole nation? And what kind of national problem is a balance-of-payments deficit? Should governments always welcome balance-of-payments surpluses?

Answers to these questions for the United States have historically differed from the answers for every other nation. Since World War II, U.S. dollars have had a unique role in the international monetary system. This role freed the U.S. government from any legal obligation toward exchange rates and made U.S. balance-of-payments deficits less problematic than those of other countries. The asymmetric and advantageous position of the United States in the international financial system is remarked on frequently throughout Part I.

Many of the reasons for government policy toward exchange rates and the balance of payments are not at all as exotic as the terms sound. The international value of the dollar and the U.S. balance of payments have potentially dramatic *domestic* impacts: on U.S. jobs, growth, and wealth and on the U.S. cost of living (Chapters 3 and 5). These domestic impacts may not be directly apparent to doctors, lawyers, retail clerks, mechanics, owners of "Ma and Pa" stores, and Americans living in small towns and rural communities—but they exist nonetheless. For example, if Japan's government consciously holds down the international value of the yen, the result can be lower U.S. employment and growth in *all* sectors, not just in exportables and importables. On the other hand, the same Japanese yen policy can cause the cost of living for *all* Americans to be lower than otherwise.

It will also become clear (Chapter 6) that every country can "beggar its neighbors" by exporting unemployment, inflation, and sluggish growth to the rest of the world. Occasionally this results from deliberate government policy; more often it is a natural, inevitable consequence of international economic interdependence. Nations tend to suffer together, and prosper together, too, because of their international commerce. They also share both the benefits of sensible monetary and fiscal policies and the costs of misguided ones. It is no accident that many governments seek international cooperation in macroeconomic policy formation and look to historically successful countries such as the United States, Germany, and Japan to set the tone for global policy coordination.

But a deep-seated commitment to nationally independent policy still makes efforts at cooperation less than wholehearted. This same nationalism is really what makes foreign exchange markets (Chapter 1) necessary in the first place. And it sometimes forces governments to endure volatile exchange rates and their painful local consequences.

Policy nationalism also causes independent governments to chafe at interference in their domestic affairs by the globally constituted International Monetary Fund (IMF), to which most nations belong (Chapters 3 and 7). The IMF has always made responsible policy, as it defines it, a necessary condition for nations to obtain loans and other advantages of membership. Some governments have turned recently toward regional cooperation and toward loans from huge, rapidly growing, private commercial banks (Euro-banks) in order to circumvent IMF surveillance. This raises crucial questions for the future (Chapter 7). Is the IMF too powerful? Is increasing Euro-bank debt, especially that of the governments of less-developed countries, a threat to global financial stability? Should IMF rules and conventions be more favorable to less-developed countries? Should central banks try to regulate the international activities of private commercial banks more than they do now?

It is obvious from this introduction alone that international finance employs a unique terminology: exchange rates, balances of payments, surpluses, deficits, beggar-your-neighbor policies, Euro-banks, surveillance. Learning how to interpret initially puzzling events and statements is often simply a matter of "knowing the language." That is why we turn immediately to definition and description (Chapter 1) and even include a supplement on terminology.

Chapter 1

Foreign Exchange Markets

Exports, imports, the foreign exchange market, and foreign exchange rates are mentioned daily in financial commentary and in discussions of public policy. Many people know neither what these concepts are nor why they are important. Misinformation abounds, and the special vocabulary of international finance clouds attempts to correct it. Definition alone, therefore, is important to understanding international finance.

Key Terms and Concepts in Foreign Exchange Markets

All the concepts discussed in this book relate to the international exchange of *goods*, which include tangible commodities, intangible services, and something we shall call *assets*. Almost all goods are traded among countries. Among the few commodities *not* traded are used buildings and bridges—although the old London Bridge from the childhood song was moved to the Arizona desert as a sightseeing attraction a few years ago. Among services internationally traded are those provided by banks, insurance companies, and universities—for example, when a student receives an education abroad. Tourism is another important service that is traded. Among assets that change hands internationally are common stock, the bonds and IOUs of governments and private corporations, real physical property, bank deposits, and money itself. We will thus be using *assets* to mean financial claims on individuals, governments, and corporations, and ownership claims on property.

A broad definition of a country's *exports* is the value of all the goods it supplies to residents of foreign countries. A broad definition of

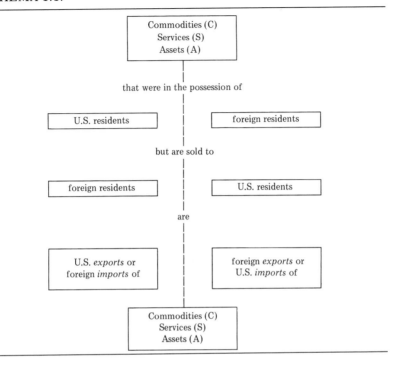

a country's *imports* is the value of all the goods it demands from residents of foreign countries. More precise definitions appear in Schema 1.1.

The most familiar exports and imports are those of commodities, described frequently as *merchandise* exports and imports. The international exchange of goods is more complicated than the exchange of merchandise, however. Modern economies are *monetary*: goods rarely are exchanged directly for other goods, a type of exchange known as *barter*. Instead, goods are exchanged almost always for money; money is therefore described as a *medium of exchange*. [1] What we call supply in monetary economies is the process of exchanging goods for money; what we call demand is the process of exchanging

---

[1] Economists mean something precise by *money* — they mean privately held currency (bills and coin) and demand deposits in commercial banks (checking accounts). They don't mean wealth or income, as we do when we colloquially speak of someone "having a lot of money stashed away" or "making a lot of money."

SCHEMA 1.2.

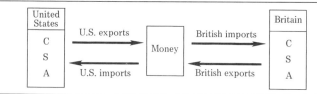

money for goods. Thus it might seem that Schema 1.2 is an accurate description of international exchange between two monetary countries, say the United States and Britain.

But this description omits the single most important characteristic that makes international finance interesting and important: different nations generally use different moneys. American exporters would like to receive American dollars for the goods they send abroad, but British importers of those same goods would rather pay in British pounds sterling. Similarly, British exporters want to receive sterling, but American importers prefer to pay in dollars. If international exchange is to succeed, some mechanism must be found for reconciling these conflicting preferences.

The mechanism that reconciles American and British desires to hold and use only local money in international exchange is a market, a place where one nation's money is exchanged (bartered) for another's. This colorful market is called the *foreign exchange market*. Its interaction with other markets in the domestic and world economies is the focus of most of Part I of this book.

Nations prefer to have their own national money partly for political and partly for economic reasons. (Both are discussed in Chapter 3.) This preference leads to a more realistic schema of how international exchange takes place (Schema 1.3).

Many aspects of the foreign exchange market are confusing at first—even its name. Since any country's money can be exchanged there for foreign money, why not call it the *foreign money market?* After all, the markets where money is exchanged for wheat, life insurance, and common stocks are called the wheat market, life-insurance market, and stock market. Unfortunately the term foreign money market describes another kind of market. *Foreign exchange,* however, is synonymous in the everyday sense with *foreign money.* And the word *exchange* therefore describes tangible objects, not activities.

Another point of initial confusion is that the foreign exchange market is not in a single location, as is the New York Stock Exchange and the Zurich gold market; it encompasses many locations in many countries. It is described as a single market because prices tend to be the same everywhere (see Supplement 1A). For example, it includes all the bureaus of exchange at international airports, where tourists can "buy" foreign money with their own. A more important part of the

SCHEMA 1.3

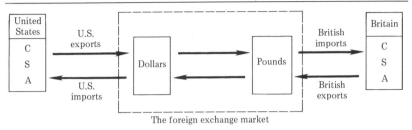

C = commodities
S = services
A = assets

foreign exchange market is made up of commercial banks. Foreign students at American universities who receive monthly scholarship checks from their home governments "buy" U.S. dollars when they cash them at local banks in their college town. In sum, the foreign exchange market is not really a place, but an interconnected group of banks and bureaus of exchange that are willing to exchange one country's money for another's. Today's interconnections consist of cable, telephone, and teletype lines that link all these institutions.

Money as "Nothing Special"

In examples above we described money as being "bought" by a tourist or a student and "sold" by a bureau of exchange or a bank. This is unusual terminology. We do not usually think of money as being bought and sold. Money is usually considered to be a special good, having unique features that differentiate it from other goods. It alone serves as a medium of exchange and as a unit of account.

In understanding the foreign exchange market it is helpful to disregard many of the unique features of money and to treat it as a good like any other.[2] Money shares at least three characteristics with other goods.

1. Money can be bought and sold. It is literally true that we almost always "buy" money when we sell goods. And it is equally true that we "sell" money when we buy goods. "Selling" money occasionally

[2] The Chicago Mercantile Exchange treats it this way, for example. Along with arranging and centralizing trade in familiar commodities such as live cattle, frozen pork bellies, russet Burbank potatoes, fresh eggs, butter, and turkey, the Exchange does the same for German Deutsche marks, Japanese yen, Canadian dollars, British pounds, Swiss francs, and Mexican pesos.

even requires salesmanship, as anyone knows who has tried to purchase goods on a trip away from home by writing the local seller an out-of-town check.

2. Money can be produced. For example, the U.S. Treasury oversees and controls the production of paper currency and coins, while the Federal Reserve System (the U.S. central bank) oversees and controls the total size of demand deposits in the commercial banking system.[3]

3. Money bears a price, or more accurately, a number of prices.

Let us look more closely at this third characteristic. Economists sometimes speak of the price of money being "one," or perhaps the interest rate. It is more revealing, however, to speak of the price of money as the number of goods you would give up to get a unit of money. Thus if the price of a pencil is 5 cents, one price of a dollar is 20 pencils. If the price of a shirt is $10, another price of a dollar is one-tenth of a shirt. If the price of one British pound on the foreign exchange market is $2, the price of a dollar is £0.5. (£ is the symbol for pounds sterling in the same way that $ is the symbol for dollars.)

The price of a dollar in terms of pounds sterling is called a *foreign exchange rate* or sometimes simply an *exchange rate*. Foreign exchange rates are defined as the price of one money in terms of another. "$2 per £" is a foreign exchange rate just as "£0.5 per $" is. It is important to perceive that a foreign exchange rate is just another price. There is no qualitative difference between the price "$2 per £" and the price "$10 per shirt." The world of international finance would be easier to fathom if we spoke more often about the dollar price of pounds or the pound price of dollars. Unfortunately, we use the term *foreign exchange rate*, which is somewhat like calling the price of shirts the "shirt rate." In this book we shall use the clear but unfamiliar terminology when it will help avert confusion. The obscure familiar language will no doubt continue to sit better with the media and the professionals in international finance.

Supply and Demand in the Foreign Exchange Market

Because money is in many ways not special or unique among goods, and because it is bought with, and sold for, foreign exchange (that is, foreign money) in a market that must exist for international exchange to take place, we can analyze the foreign exchange market in supply-and-demand terms. Many economic variables must be ig-

[3] For an engaging exposition of this process, see Robert Z. Aliber, *The International Money Game* (New York: Basic Books, 1979).

nored or held constant to make simple supply-demand analysis legitimate; these are taken into account in Chapters 4, 5, and 6. On the other hand, for a number of reasons the familiar supply-demand approach is *more* appropriate to the foreign exchange market than to many other goods markets. One reason is that money is one of the most homogeneous of all goods. That is, there is no such thing as a high-quality dollar. Nor are there bargain-basement dollars. Furthermore, developed foreign exchange markets serve large numbers of customers every day, and each transaction is usually small compared to the daily total. The foreign exchange market thus shares several of the characteristics of *purely competitive* markets, those for which economists and policymakers trust supply-demand analysis. However, governments are important noncompetitive participants in the market, as Chapter 2 demonstrates.

The foreign exchange market is depicted in Figure 1.1.[4] Several features of the diagram are notable.

1. Price is measured along the vertical axis and quantity along the horizontal axis, as is conventional. The fact that the price is an exchange rate, and the quantity is a number of units of money, does not affect the interpretation of the diagram.
2. The diagram, like the supply-demand diagrams applied to many commodity and service markets, has a time dimension. Horizontal distances measure quantities offered for sale, or being demanded, *per day*. Vertical distances measure the average price over the course of the day.
3. The curves are drawn with conventional shapes. It is virtually certain that the true demand curve for foreign exchange has a negative slope; it is not certain that the true supply curve of foreign exchange has a positive slope, as Supplement 4A shows.

Furthermore, if there were a market mechanism that could be relied on to bring the foreign exchange market to point C, we could draw the following descriptive conclusions about the market.

4. AB pounds were bought and sold today on the foreign exchange market.
5. The average price of the pound today was AD. That is, today's average exchange rate was AD. (This statement is analogous in every way to the statements, "The price of wheat today was . . . ," or "The Dow-Jones average today was . . . .")

---

[4] It will be convenient throughout this book to envision the world as divided into only two countries. This makes it easier to talk about the interaction of the domestic economy (us), and the international economy (the rest of the world), as though the latter were a homogeneous whole. Many of the conclusions we draw could be demonstrated in more complicated fashion for a multicountry world; a few could not, and an attempt will be made to point them out.

FIGURE 1.1. *The Foreign Exchange Market*

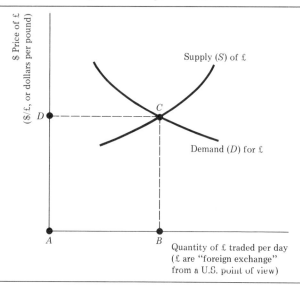

6. *ABCD* of dollars were bought and sold today on the foreign exchange market. (Hint: If Figure 1.1 described the wheat market rather than the foreign exchange market, the area *ABCD* would represent dollar revenues of wheat suppliers and dollar expenditures of wheat demanders.)[5]

The Source of Normal Foreign-Exchange-Market Supply and Demand

Figure 1.1 is a stylized picture of the foreign exchange market—an abstraction. But we can readily outline the economic behavior that underlies this market—that is, the economic activities and actors that produce a daily supply of and demand for foreign exchange in the real world. Two broad activities underlie the foreign exchange market:

[5] An April 1977 survey of forty-four major commercial banks trading foreign exchange in New York revealed that on average they bought and sold $5 billion per day in return for foreign money. Of that foreign money, 27 percent was German Deutsche marks, 19 percent was Canadian dollars, and 17 percent was British pounds. See the *Wall Street Journal*, July 12, 1977, p. 4. These figures, of course, understate total daily trade on the foreign exchange market, which is carried out all over the world by other banks as well as these forty-four.

international trade (the international exchange of commodities and services) and *international financial investment* (the international exchange of assets).

With respect to international trade, U.S. exports of commodities and services provide one source of the supply of pounds in Figure 1.1. For example, when Boeing sells an aircraft to British Airways, British Airways may decide to pay Boeing by forwarding a check written on its London checking account, denominated in pounds sterling. Since Boeing typically will want to receive dollars for its exports, it will usually send such a check to its own bank and have it converted to U.S. dollars. To call this a currency "conversion" masks the fact that Boeing has engaged in a foreign-exchange-market transaction. It has sold its pound-denominated check from British Airways to its own bank and has thereby bought dollars with pounds. In other words, Boeing has supplied pounds to its bank, which is a part of the foreign exchange market, and demanded dollars.[6] The impetus for the supply of pounds was Boeing's export to Britain.

United States exports lead to a supply of pounds even if they are paid for in a slightly different way. Boeing will more likely insist on receiving dollars directly from British Airways in payment for its aircraft export. British Airways will probably be forced to contact its own bank, convert pounds into dollars, and send a dollar check to Boeing. But British Airways' "conversion" is in fact the same as Boeing's—it supplies pounds to the foreign exchange market through a bank, and it demands dollars. The export of an aircraft from the United States to Britain thus leads to a supply of pounds, regardless of whether the exporter (Boeing) or importer (British Airways) makes the foreign-exchange-market transaction.

In similar fashion, U.S. imports of commodities and services provide a source of the demand for pounds in the foreign exchange market. When Beefeater ships gin to U.S. liquor wholesalers, the wholesalers may pay Beefeater by forwarding checks written on their New York checking accounts, denominated in dollars. By requesting its own bank to convert such checks into pounds, Beefeater effectively supplies dollars to the foreign exchange market and demands pounds. If the payment arrangements had been slightly different, and if Beefeater had required payment in pounds from the U.S. liquor wholesalers, then the wholesalers would have had to demand pounds from their local bank. Either way, the impetus for the demand for pounds was U.S. imports of gin from Britain.

---

[6] In reality, increasing numbers of corporations operate in many countries. If Boeing is one of these *multinational* companies (described in Chapter 13), then it might prefer to keep the pounds sterling. Boeing may, for example, have a London account out of which it pays its British subcontractors. If Boeing deposits British Airways' check directly in its London account, Boeing's aircraft export will have no effect on the foreign exchange market: no country's money is exchanged for any other's.

In much the same way, international financial investment leads to supply and demand in the foreign exchange market. When ownership of assets (for example, stocks and bonds) is exported from U.S. residents to British residents, a supply of pounds usually results. When ownership of assets is imported from British residents by U.S. residents, a demand for pounds usually results. While these statements are clear, their terminology is not what is conventionally used. United States exports of asset ownership are more conventionally described as "British investment in the United States." United States imports of asset ownership are more conventionally described as "U.S. investment in Britain."[7]

Let us look at two further examples. When British residents buy stock in Boeing from U.S. shareholders, they may decide to pay for it by sending pound-denominated checks to their U.S. stockbrokers. The stockbrokers supply these pounds to the foreign exchange market when their bank accepts the pounds and credits the brokers' accounts with a dollar equivalent.[8] When U.S. residents buy stock in Beefeater from British shareholders, British stockbrokers usually sell their dollar checks to their own bank and demand pounds.

In sum, U.S. exports of commodities and services and British financial investment in the United States normally lead to a supply of pounds on the foreign exchange market. United States imports of commodities and services and U.S. financial investment in Britain normally lead to a demand for pounds. Somewhat less exactly, U.S. exporters, British importers, and British investors in the United States are all suppliers of pounds. United States importers, British exporters, and U.S. investors in Britain are all demanders of pounds.[9] These conclusions are summarized in Figure 1.2. A more detailed arithmetic

---

[7] Often the former is described loosely as "foreign investment in the United States" and the latter as "U.S. foreign investment." The fact that the loose terms are so similar to each other, yet describe precisely opposite international exchanges of assets, is confusing. On the terminology of international financial investment, see Supplement 1B.

[8] The brokers' bank inherits a pound-claim on a British bank from the U.S. shareholders, as did Boeing's bank from Boeing in the aircraft-export example. The banks need not get stuck holding the pounds, though. They can generally sell them to (1) another customer who wants to buy pounds on that particular day, or to (2) another bank with customers who want to buy pounds, or, under circumstances to be made clear in the next chapter, to (3) the central bank of Britain or the United States.

[9] One reason this terminology is less exact is that when British investors are paid dollar dividends on their Boeing stock, they must become demanders of pounds to "repatriate" the dividends (bring them back to Britain). Similarly, when American investors repatriate pound dividends on their Beefeater stock, they become suppliers of pounds. Thus foreign investors are on one side of the foreign exchange market when they invest, and on the other side when they repatriate earnings. More generally, large multinational corporations engaged in both international trade and investment are usually simultaneously suppliers and demanders of pounds on the same day.

FIGURE 1.2. *Normal Determinants of Supply and Demand in the Foreign Exchange Market*

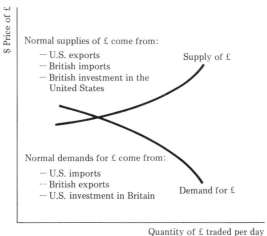

$ Price of £

Normal supplies of £ come from:

— U.S. exports
— British imports
— British investment in the
  United States

Supply of £

Normal demands for £ come from:

— U.S. imports
-- British exports
— U.S. investment in Britain

Demand for £

Quantity of £ traded per day

illustration of how exports, imports, and investment underlie supply and demand in the foreign exchange market is given in Supplement 4A.

Speculative Supply and Demand

The word *normal* is an important modifier in Figure 1.2 and in the preceding paragraph, because there is another important determinant of supply and demand on the foreign exchange market: speculative trade and financial investment, or simply *speculation*. Speculation is defined in general as buying or selling that is motivated by expected future prices (for example, buying a car this year instead of next year because you expect automakers to raise their prices substantially). Speculative international trade and investment is motivated by expected future exchange rates.

Suppose Boeing quite confidently expects the dollar price of pounds to fall dramatically in the next few months. Boeing will probably attempt to speed up any planned sales of aircraft or of newly issued Boeing stock to Britain. That is, it will attempt to make the sales immediately instead of in the future. If Boeing's expectations are correct, then the pounds it receives today for its accelerated sales will be worth more dollars than the pounds it would receive in the future by letting matters take their course. Boeing earns additional profit on its future sales, or possibly avoids a loss, by correctly anticipating the future movement of the exchange rate.

Expectations that the dollar price of pounds will fall may be quite widespread. If Beefeater confidently shares them, it will engage in a kind of speculative financial investment in the United States. Beefeater will sit on any dollar checks it receives today from U.S. liquor wholesalers and U.S. investors in Beefeater stock; it will not take them down to its bank for conversion into pounds. In fact, it may well open a New York bank account and hold them there. If Beefeater turns out to be right in its expectations, this action will earn additional profit or perhaps avoid a loss. The dollars or dollar assets that Beefeater sits on can be sold for more pounds in the future than today.[10] Of course, if Beefeater is wrong in its expectations, the dollars may "earn" less pounds in the future than today—possibly so many less pounds that Beefeater will be unable to cover its costs of gin production and will be forced to declare insolvency. Two large commercial bank failures of the early 1970s were due to ill-advised international speculative investment of exactly this kind. Speculation entails risk almost by definition.

Whether well advised or ill advised, speculation by Boeing and Beefeater on a fall in the value of the pound has a predictable effect on the foreign exchange market. Boeing's action leads to a greater-than-normal supply of pounds on the immediate foreign exchange market, because Boeing accelerates exports of goods for which it receives pounds in payment. Beefeater's action leads to a less-than-normal demand for pounds on the immediate foreign exchange market, because it defers the conversion of its dollar revenues from the export of goods to the United States into pounds. Figure 1.3 illustrates how speculative trade and investment alter the location of supply and demand curves in the foreign exchange market, when they are based on widespread expectations of a fall in the future dollar price of pounds.

Several conclusions can be drawn from this discussion and from Figure 1.3. First, widespread expectations of a future change in exchange rates are in part self-fulfilling. In Figure 1.3, if the forces of supply and demand are unencumbered, normal trade and investment in the absence of speculation establish AD as today's dollar price of pounds. Speculative trade and investment, motivated by expectations that the dollar price of pounds will decline, actually cause some decline. Normal and speculative trade and investment together establish AE as today's dollar price of pounds. Widespread expectations thus sometimes ratify themselves, even though there may be no underlying reason for the dollar price of pounds to fall. Widespread expectations that a price will fall can make it happen.

---

[10] Because expectations of a future exchange-rate change cause acceleration or deferral of normal international trade and investment, actions such as those undertaken by Boeing and Beefeater have come to be known as speculative *leads and lags* in international transactions.

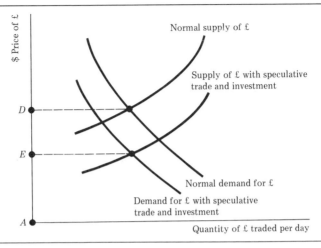

As an exercise, it is useful to demonstrate that the impact of the expectations described above would have been the same if Boeing had insisted on receiving dollars for its exports and Beefeater had insisted on receiving pounds. British Airways and American gin wholesalers would then be motivated to engage in exactly the same kind of speculative international trade and investment. The qualitative effects of their speculation on the immediate foreign exchange market would be the same as those of Boeing and Beefeater. It is also useful to consider the effects of widespread expectations that the future dollar price of pounds will rise rather than fall.

The economic agents who engage in speculative and normal trade and investment are usually one and the same. Despite misleading media accounts, there is not a distinguishable and nefarious group of international speculators or "gnomes of Zurich." Speculation is neither mysterious nor intrinsically evil, and it is carried out predominantly by the same persons, corporations, and financial institutions who export and import, and who invest and borrow abroad.

Concern about Exchange-Rate Variability

The potential for speculation, however, often causes concern among policymakers and experts that if the forces of supply and demand are allowed to rule, exchange rates will be subject to explosive swings up or down. The unpleasant consequences of such swings, discussed in Chapter 3, motivate governments to attempt to stabilize prices in the foreign exchange market by mechanisms described in Chapter 2. The concern is not universal, however. Many economists believe that an unencumbered (or "free") foreign exchange market usually shows a balance of expectations: about as many traders and investors expect the dollar price of pounds to fall as expect it to rise, and many expect no change. Therefore, the normal determinants of supply and demand predominate in establishing the exchange rate. These economists believe further that on those rare occasions when expectations of a particular change in exchange rates are widespread, the speculatively induced variability in exchange rates is no more pronounced or problematic than that caused by speculation in any other goods market (such as the stock market).

Table 1.1 casts some light on the issue. It records the average day-to-day change in the dollar price of four moneys during 1973, 1974, and 1975. Table 1.2 records the year-to-year changes in the same four exchange rates over a longer period. It is hard to reach conclusions from these tables about the variability of exchange rates under the unencumbered forces of supply and demand, because governments did make some efforts during this period to dampen the variability. Despite these efforts, the variability of the dollar price of all four moneys was quite large. In fact, in mid-1973, the dollar price of several European currencies changed 4 percent in a single day, and 10 percent over the course of a week![11] On November 1, 1978, the dollar prices of German marks and Japanese yen fell 5.7 and 3.5 percent respectively.[12]

We describe government intervention in the foreign exchange market in Chapter 2. Its merits are evaluated in Chapter 3.

Summary

What makes almost all international exchange unique is that buyers want to use one money and sellers want to receive another. Both can be accommodated in an unusual "market for money"—a market where foreign money can be bought and sold just like tomatoes and Treasury bills. This so-called foreign exchange market is organized by commercial banks worldwide, and the prices they quote for foreign money to buyers and sellers are known as foreign exchange rates.

Foreign exchange rates vary over time just like other prices. And they do so more predictably according to the forces of demand and

[11] International Monetary Fund, *Annual Report 1975*, p. 26.
[12] Federal Reserve Bank of Chicago, *International Letter* 383 (November 24, 1978): 4; 384 (December 8, 1978): 4.

TABLE 1.1. *Average Day-to-Day Percentage Changes (Plus or Minus) in the Dollar Price of Four Leading World Moneys, 1973–1975*

| Year | Percentage change in the dollar price of the money of | | | |
	Canada	Germany	Japan	Britain
1973	0.11	0.57	0.18	0.25
1974	0.11	0.52	0.28	0.33
1975[a]	0.12	0.48	0.28	0.27

[a] Figures based only on the first three months of 1975.
Source: International Monetary Fund, *Annual Report 1975*, Table 10, p. 26.

supply than most other prices. Demanders of, say, British pounds sterling from commercial banks on any day of the week are always connected with the merchandise, services, and property (stocks, bonds, land, bank accounts, and so on) whose ownership changes from British to non-British hands. These transactions are called British exports (or world imports from Britain). Suppliers of British pounds sterling in the foreign exchange market are, conversely, always connected with British imports (or world exports to Britain).

Frequently the decisions of demanders and suppliers in the foreign exchange market are altered by the pleasant expectation that they will be able to buy cheaper and sell dearer in the future, or by the painful fear that they will be forced to buy dearer and sell cheaper.

TABLE 1.2. *Year-to-Year Percentage Changes in the Average Dollar Price of Four Leading World Moneys, 1973–1978*

| From | To | Percentage change in the dollar price of the money of | | | |
		Canada	Germany	Japan	Britain
1973	1974	2.2	2.6	−7.1	−4.5
1974	1975	−3.8	5.2	−1.7	−5.1
1975	1976	3.1	−2.4	0.1	−18.8
1976	1977	−7.2	8.4	10.7	−3.3
1977	1978[a]	−5.7	16.0	41.4	9.3

[a] Percentage change from August 1977 to August 1978.
Source: Board of Governors of the Federal Reserve System, *Federal Reserve Bulletin*, various issues from 1976–1979, monthly table "Foreign Exchange Rates."

Speculative purchases and sales of foreign exchange can sometimes be huge, leading governments to fear that foreign exchange rates will suffer explosive swings. What governments do about speculation is described in Chapter 2. Why they fear it is described in Chapter 3.

Key Terms

exports
imports
money
foreign exchange

foreign exchange market
foreign exchange rates
speculation
leads and lags

Key Concepts and Review

Why foreign exchange markets are needed.
How money can be bought, sold, produced, and bear a price.
International trade; international financial investment.
"Normal" and "speculative" trade and investment.

Supplement 1A
The Foreign Exchange Market in Greater Detail

Only very simple foreign-exchange-market activities are described in the text. The activities that normal and speculative trade and investment generate are considerably more complex for two reasons: (1) Often an activity requires more than one simple transaction at the same time, such as a simultaneous purchase and sale in the foreign exchange market. (2) Often an activity requires transactions in a wholly different kind of foreign exchange market, the *forward* foreign exchange market. These points will be clarified in terms of four important foreign-exchange-market activities: exchange arbitrage, interest arbitrage, covering, and forward speculation.

EXCHANGE ARBITRAGE

Exchange arbitrage is the activity that unifies the foreign exchange market spatially. That is, it assures that the same exchange rates tend to rule at any moment in time, whether they are quoted by a London bank, a New York bank, or a Singapore bank. In fact, the existence of exchange arbitrage is what allows people to speak of "the" foreign exchange market instead of "the London" or "the New York" foreign exchange markets. Similarly, exchange arbitrage allows people to describe what happened to "the" dollar price of pounds today, without tacking on the words "in London" or "in New York." Exchange arbitrage insures that what happens in one place happens in the other.

Many markets feature the activity known as *arbitrage*. It is defined as buying a commodity where it is cheap and simultaneously selling it where it is expensive. For example, two cooperating scalpers at opposite ends of a football field will be able to engage in arbitrage if ticket prices happen to differ, and if they can communicate with each other, say via walkie-talkie. When 50-yard-line seats are being scalped by others more cheaply at the east end of the stadium than at the west, the east scalper-arbitrageur will buy them up, and the west scalper-arbitrageur will undercut the market at his end by offering to sell them for less than the going "west price." A "runner," perhaps a young nephew of one of the scalper-arbitrageurs, can run the bought-and-sold tickets quickly from east to west, and the difference between the cheap buying price and the dear selling price is pure riskless profit.

But arbitrage is self-limiting in any market. The east scalper-arbitrageur's purchases will tend to drive up the low east prices. The west scalper-arbitrageur's sales will tend to depress the high west prices. Prices of 50-yard-line seats will tend to equalize from east to west, and arbitrage profits will be reduced. It is precisely this tendency toward price equality that leads economists to talk about a *single* market for

50-yard-line seats. Any commodity market is spatially limited by definition—it is the geographical area in which one price tends to rule. A market can be equally well delineated as the geographical area in which arbitrage is prominent.

Arbitrage is rarely perfect. Not all 50-yard-line seats are equally good. Not all final buyers of west-end tickets are willing to wait for the runner to arrive, even though it would mean some financial savings. Thus, as a rule, ticket prices will not be fully equalized by arbitrage. But the more homogeneous the commodity, and the more quickly and cheaply it can be moved from location to location, the more perfect arbitrage will be, and the more pronounced the tendency for prices to be identical all over space. Money is one of the most homogeneous of commodities, as we have said. And it is also one of the most easily, quickly, and cheaply "transported." A large corporation can have money transferred from its New York bank account to its London bank account in a matter of minutes, and at almost no cost. As a result, the foreign exchange market is one of those in which arbitrage has a very prominent role. Its role is so prominent that it really *is* descriptively accurate to speak of the "world" dollar price of pounds. Exchange arbitrage tends to create a single worldwide market in which dollars are exchanged for pounds, and in which only one dollar price of pounds rules everywhere.

An example of exchange arbitrage that is fully analogous to scalping football tickets is easily understood. Suppose that by accident the dollar price of pounds quoted by New York banks was $1.98 per pound and the price quoted by London banks was $2 per pound. Profits would be huge and certain for all who phoned their bankers with orders to buy pounds in New York with dollars, sell them simultaneously to a London bank for more dollars than they started with, buy more pounds in New York, sell them for dollars in London, buy more pounds, and so on. If a single circular transaction took two hours, the arbitrageurs' dollar balances would be rising at the rate of 4 percent every business day! For the same reason, profits would be huge and certain if banks themselves did the same thing. And the pressure of dramatic pound demand in New York and dramatic pound supply in London would quickly drive the two exchange rates together. In fact, simply the *potential* for almost unlimited exchange arbitrage equalizes exchange rates between two moneys worldwide. No actual arbitrage is necessary to get this result. Commercial banks assure it by communicating with each other before they set prices.

Exchange arbitrage is not always so simple as the so-called "two-point" arbitrage just described. *Three-point* or *triangular* exchange arbitrage is more complex, as Table 1A.1 will reveal to the student who answers the questions below it. Even more complicated multipoint arbitrage opportunities exist and are seized in the actual foreign exchange market.

TABLE 1A.1. *An Opportunity for "Three-Point" ("Triangular")*
Exchange Arbitrage

Exchange rate	*Geographical location*		
	New York banks	*London banks*	*Paris banks*
Dollar price of a pound	2.00	2.00	No direct trades of dollars for pounds negotiated
Dollar price of a franc	.25	No direct trades of dollars for francs negotiated	.25
Franc price of a pound	No direct trades of francs for pounds negotiated	10	10

Questions:
1. Where is the opportunity for profit via exchange arbitrage?
2. How would an exchange arbitrageur realize the profit—what would be the mechanics?

INTEREST ARBITRAGE

Interest arbitrage is the activity that unifies the foreign exchange market temporally—that is, over time. It does not *equalize* present and future exchange rates; instead, interest arbitrage (or really a particular, risky variety of it) tends to establish a sensible relation (described below) between interest rates from country to country and expectations of future exchange-rate movements.

The simple variety of interest arbitrage that does this is called *uncovered interest arbitrage* (for reasons that will become clear in the next section). It is no more than speculative international financial investment of a kind similar to that carried out by Beefeater in the example in the text. Suppose that there were widespread expectations of stable exchange rates. There would then be a tendency for interest rates on similar assets to equalize worldwide. The tendency would be brought about by arbitrage of a kind very similar to that sketched above. Investors (asset holders) would sell assets with low rates of return and simultaneously purchase those with high rates of return. As a real example, some owners of U.S. Treasury bills that were paying 8 percent annual interest would sell them in order to buy British Treasury bills paying 10 percent annual interest. Large supplies of existing U.S. Treasury bills for sale by private holders would make it difficult for the U.S. government to sell new Treasury bills—unless it raised the interest rate. Large demand for British Treasury bills would make it possible for the British government to offer slightly less interest on their new offerings, yet still sell them. As a result, interest rates in the United States and Britain would tend to converge.[1] With enough convergence, one could talk about the single world market for short-term government debt.

What all this has to do with the foreign exchange market is clarified by several observations. First, almost all sales of U.S. bills to enable purchases of British bills will require a foreign-exchange-market transaction. The dollars received from the U.S. bill sales must be supplied on the foreign exchange market to demand pounds—which must be used in turn to buy the British bills. Such additional pound demands in the foreign exchange market lead to increases in the pound's value (see Figure 1.2). But this appreciation of the pound is necessarily unexpected—the example began by assuming stable future exchange rates. Prior expectations of exchange-rate stability will probably be altered. And as was demonstrated in the text, whenever expectations are altered, speculative trade and investment set in that tend to ratify those expectations, bringing about precisely the expected exchange-rate change. The circle is now complete. Uncovered interest arbitrage links future and present exchange rates because, when it occurs, it usually alters expectations of future exchange-rate change.

The importance of interest arbitrage for the temporal aspect of the foreign exchange market can be illustrated further by another example. Suppose expectations are that the pound will fall in value relative to the dollar by 5 percent per year. If so, then British Treasury bills at 10 percent will be less attractive investments than U.S. Treasury bills at 8 percent, even though they do pay higher interest. American investors would be foolish to hold British Treasury bills. They can increase the pound value of their wealth by 10 percent over the year, but the pounds they own at the end of the year will be worth 5 percent fewer dollars than pounds were at the beginning. The investors' true rate of return is close to 5 percent (10 − 5), not 10 percent. They would be better advised to hold U.S. Treasury bills yielding them 8 percent.

---

[1] A more important reason for convergence, but one that is harder to explain, is the inverse relationship that must exist between bond prices and their rates of return. Massive sales of U.S. Treasury bills will drive their price down but their rate of return up—even on the existing stock. The opposite will happen in Britain as a result of massive purchases of Treasury bills.

The upshot of such calculations will be a widespread tendency to sell British Treasury bills and to buy U.S. Treasury bills. Such activity will actually make interest rates *diverge*, although it is still called interest arbitrage. British Treasury bills will begin to pay more than 10 percent, U.S. Treasury bills less than 8 percent.

Furthermore, expectations of decline in the value of future pounds may be altered from 5 percent—this former expectation may not have taken into account the extra foreign-exchange-market supply of pounds that is a necessary transaction in moving from British Treasury bills into U.S. Treasury bills. The expected rate of decline in the pound's price may increase, say, to 6 percent at an annual rate.[2]

Regardless of whether expectations actually change, uncovered interest arbitrage tends to establish a curious link between interest rates and present and future exchange rates. If U.S. and British Treasury bills really are very similar (and they are), and if it costs little to transfer their ownership back and forth, then interest rates will tend to diverge by almost exactly the (revised) expected fall in the dollar price of pounds. That is, the British interest rate will tend toward becoming 6 percent higher than the U.S. interest rate. Otherwise, interest arbitrage would continue to go on—if it diverged by less than 6 percent, even more British Treasury bills would be sold in order to buy U.S. Treasury bills, and renewed pressure would be placed on interest rates and exchange-rate expectations.

Uncovered interest arbitrage tends thus to establish approximately the following relation, one representation of the so-called *interest parity condition*:

$$\begin{pmatrix} \text{U.S.} \\ \text{annual} \\ \text{interest} \\ \text{rates} \end{pmatrix} - \begin{pmatrix} \text{British} \\ \text{annual} \\ \text{interest} \\ \text{rates} \end{pmatrix} = \begin{pmatrix} \text{Expected annual rate of} \\ \text{change in the dollar} \\ \text{price of pounds} \\ \text{(percentage)} \end{pmatrix}$$

where the interest rates are measured on comparable assets from the point of view of liquidity, risk, and so on. The more comparable the assets, the more common and confident the expectations, and the less costly interest arbitrage is to carry out, the more closely this interest parity condition will hold.

COVERING

All the investors in the preceding example of interest arbitrage are accepting an exchange-rate risk. The risk is that they may be mistaken in their exchange-rate expectations. In the first example, an

---

[2] However, the expected rate of decline over the longer run, say the entire year, may remain at 5 percent. This is likely if all the funds that moved into American Treasury bills at the beginning of the year move back at the end—then there will be an extra foreign-exchange-market demand for pounds a year from now to counterbalance today's extra supply.

American who buys a 10 percent British Treasury bill expecting stable exchange rates, while the dollar price of the pound actually falls 5 percent over the course of the year, must take a painful capital loss. In the text, Boeing might similarly take a capital loss if the price of pounds unexpectedly fell after Boeing extended credit to British Airways on its 747 purchases—say by allowing British Airways to pay off the old pound value of the plane in installments, at a fixed interest rate. The pounds Boeing would receive toward the end of the debt would be less valuable than originally expected.

Both traders and investors often want to shield themselves from the risk of mistaken exchange-rate expectations. Many are "risk averse." That is, they want to avoid risk even though a mistake in the opposite direction—unexpected increases in the value of the pound—would be profitable. They can avoid exchange-rate risk through an activity known as *covering*, which is carried out in the *forward foreign exchange market*.

The forward foreign exchange market is not exactly a foreign exchange market. As a rule, neither domestic nor foreign money changes hands when a *forward transaction* is made. Forward transactions are really just the creation of contracts. They are promises to exchange dollars for pounds in the future, not in the present, and they are signed by both parties to the agreement. Thus *buying forward pounds* really means buying a contract that promises the holder receipt of pounds at some future date. *Selling forward pounds* really means drawing up and selling a contract that binds the contractor to supply pounds at some future date. The contract is "bought" and "sold" in the sense that the number of pounds to be supplied and delivered in the future is written into the contract, as is the number of dollars that the forward-pound buyer will give to the forward-pound seller on the same date. The number of dollars per pound that the buyer and seller agree to exchange in the future is called the *forward foreign exchange rate*.

The forward foreign exchange market is essentially a market that exists *today* for *future* foreign exchange. It is similar in many ways to *futures markets* that exist for some commodities. But it differs from the foreign exchange market discussed in the text: that market exists *today* for *today's* foreign exchange. To distinguish the two markets, we often call the latter the *spot foreign exchange market*. However, the institutional structure of the two markets is quite similar. Commercial banks, which handle most spot foreign-exchange-market transactions, also handle all forward transactions. And the forward foreign exchange market can also be suitably analyzed in the supply-demand framework that was applied to the spot market.

Covering is engaging in forward transactions in order to offset exchange-rate risk. For example, the interest arbitrageurs in the preceding section would not have had to worry about mistaken exchange-rate expectations if they had covered their arbitrage. For an American buyer of British Treasury bills, covering implies selling forward pounds. The number of pounds he would contract to *sell forward* would be exactly equal to the pound value of his stake in British Treasury bills, plus the interest he will earn on them. Operationally, on the very day he decides to buy, say, £1 million worth of British Treasury bills, he will call his commercial bank and (1) buy spot pounds, by instructing the bank to convert dollars from his account into £1 million, and to pass along the pounds to the seller of the British Treasury bills; (2) sell forward pounds, by instructing his bank to draw up a contract whereby the bank promises to accept £1.1 million (his investment with 10 percent interest) in a year's time, in return for crediting his account then with a number of dollars determined by the forward exchange rate.[3] Consequently, the investor is effectively sealed off from the effects of any change in actual spot exchange rates over the course of the year. No matter what the actual exchange rate is a year from now, whether expected or unexpected, whether more favorable or less, he will receive the number of dollars stipulated in his forward contract. He is said to be covered or *hedged against* unexpected changes in exchange rates. He is also said to have engaged in *covered interest arbitrage.*

Covered interest arbitrage is not subject to the exchange-rate risk of uncovered interest arbitrage. But its importance is similar. It tends to link spot and forward exchange rates in exactly the same way as uncovered arbitrage links present and expected future spot exchange rates. Suppose that the spot and forward exchange rates in the previous example are identical. As a result, covered interest arbitrageurs will be attracted to British Treasury bills. They pay a sure 10 percent compared to the sure 8 percent on U.S. Treasury bills. But the resulting covered interest arbitrage will tend to have four effects, three of which characterize uncovered interest arbitrage as well: (1) British interest rates will be pushed lower; (2) U.S. interest rates will be pushed higher; (3) the spot dollar price of pounds will be pushed higher (pounds are needed today to buy the attractive British Treasury bills); and (4) the forward dollar price of pounds will be pushed lower (there will be an excessively large number of attempts to contract to sell forward pounds to commercial banks). In light of effects (3) and (4), even if spot and forward exchange rates were equal to begin with, covered interest arbitrage would quickly end that. The spot price of pounds would rise above the forward price, and the pound would be

---

[3] If the bank doesn't want the £1.1 million a year from now, it can turn around and contract to sell £1.1 million forward to some bank that does want them. If no such bank can be found at current forward exchange rates, the forward dollar price of pounds will be bid down, and the bank will start offering dramatically fewer forward dollars in return for forward pounds. In normal times, a forward foreign exchange rate can generally be found that equates forward supplies of pounds to demands for them.

said to show a *forward discount*. (When the spot price of pounds falls below the forward price, there is said to be a *forward premium* on the pound.)

The rise in the spot pound price and fall in the forward pound price discourages further arbitrage. Arbitrageurs are increasingly forced to buy expensive spot pounds and sell cheap forward pounds—to buy dear and sell cheap, which is not the way to make a profit. As the percentage discount on forward pounds approaches 2 percent, the relative attractiveness of British Treasury bills vanishes, and covered interest arbitrage ceases. The extra 2 percent of interest (or somewhat less at the new interest rates) just compensates for the losses induced by the forward discount.

Covered interest arbitrage thus tends to bring about another relationship among interest rates and exchange rates, the most familiar *interest parity condition*:

$$\begin{pmatrix} \text{U.S.} \\ \text{annual} \\ \text{interest} \\ \text{rates} \end{pmatrix} - \begin{pmatrix} \text{British} \\ \text{annual} \\ \text{interest} \\ \text{rates} \end{pmatrix} = \begin{cases} \begin{pmatrix} \text{Premium on 1-year} \\ \text{forward pounds, if} \\ \text{positive (percentage)} \end{pmatrix} \\ \begin{pmatrix} \text{Discount on 1-year} \\ \text{forward pounds, if} \\ \text{negative (percentage)} \end{pmatrix} \end{cases}$$

where the interest rates are again measured on comparable assets. The more comparable the assets, and the smaller the transactions cost associated with covered interest arbitrage, the more closely this condition will hold in reality.

Unlike the interest parity condition associated with uncovered interest arbitrage, that associated with covered arbitrage contains observable economic variables. Table 1A.2 illustrates how closely the condition came to holding for Treasury bills during a period of considerable foreign-exchange-market turbulence. Such turbulence tends to raise many of the transaction costs facing covered interest arbitrage—for example, the cost of forward cover—and also heightens uncertainty about the true comparability of the assets—for example, the assets are not comparable if crisis-induced exchange control (Supplement 2A) inhibits some aspects of the arbitrage.

By contrast, the interest parity condition holds almost exactly in reality for dollar and pound bank deposits offered by the same commercial bank—even when there is considerable turbulence in the foreign exchange market. Banks that offer deposits and make loans in many different moneys, known as Euro-banks, are described in greater detail in Chapter 7; what is important here is that a particular Euro-bank's dollar and pound deposits are nearly identical. They are both liabilities of the same commercial bank and are not as subject to government control as other assets are.

In addition to its importance in linking spot, forward, and future foreign exchange markets, interest arbitrage also highlights the re-

TABLE 1A.2. *The Interest Parity Condition in Action, 1973*

Date	(1) Interest rate on U.S. Treasury bills[a]	(2) Interest rate on British Treasury bills[a]	(3) Discount on forward pounds[a]	Extent to which interest parity condition is inaccurate (absolute value[b])
Jan. 5	5.05	8.17	−3.29	.17
Jan. 12	5.19	8.15	−3.50	.54
Jan. 19	5.42	8.08	−3.66	1.00
Jan. 26	5.67	8.01	−3.65	1.31
Feb. 2	5.69	8.00	−4.04	1.73
Feb. 9	5.30	7.98	−3.00	.32
Feb. 16	5.31	7.96	−3.78	1.13
Feb. 23	5.44	7.95	−3.39	.88
March 1	5.68	8.01	−2.82	.49

[a] Ninety-one-day Treasury bill interest rates adjusted to assure comparability of quotation. Also discounts on 91-day forward pounds.

[b] Column (1) − column (2) − column (3). For each date, there was an incentive to move from British to U.S. Treasury bills.

Source: Board of Governors of the Federal Reserve System, *Federal Reserve Bulletin* 59 (July 1973): A93.

markable interdependence of foreign exchange markets and domestic financial markets. External shocks to foreign exchange markets, such as a change in speculative exchange-rate expectations, have important effects on domestic credit conditions, often driving domestic interest rates higher or lower. External shocks to domestic financial markets, such as a New York City default on its debt obligations, have important effects on foreign exchange markets. Exchange rates are not determined solely, or even principally, by exports and imports of tangible commodities. We return to these matters in greater detail in Chapter 4 and in footnote 10 to Supplement 7A.

Interest arbitrageurs are not the only foreign-exchange-market participants who cover. Covering by commodity exporters and importers is also common. For example, had Boeing extended credit to British Airways on its 747 purchases, it, too, could have covered itself from any exchange-rate risk. Suppose that British Airways will pay for its 747s in four quarterly pound installments, with suitable interest added to each payment by Boeing. Boeing faces the risk that the pounds it receives will have unexpectedly fallen in value in the foreign exchange market over the life of the installments. But it can eliminate

TABLE 1A.3. Gains to Boeing from Forward Cover under Declines in the Dollar Price of Pounds That Are More Rapid Than Is Generally Expected (Millions of Pounds or Dollars)

Period ending	British Airways installment payments in pounds	Presently expected dollar price of pounds[a]	Actual spot dollar price of pounds[b]	Present forward dollar price of pounds[a]	Without forward cover		With forward cover
					Expected dollar revenues to Boeing	Actual dollar revenues to Boeing	Certain dollar revenues to Boeing
Quarter 1	5	2.10	2.08	2.10	10.50	10.40	10.50
Quarter 2	5	2.09	2.06	2.09	10.45	10.30	10.45
Quarter 3	5	2.08	2.04	2.08	10.40	10.20	10.40
Quarter 4	5	2.07	2.02	2.07	10.35	10.10	10.35
Annual total	20				41.70	41.00	41.70

[a] "Present" denotes the beginning of the first quarter of the year. The four forward exchange rates are those quoted on "91-day," "182-day," "273-day," and "one-year" forward pounds. It is no accident that these four forward exchange rates are identical to those in the column that records presently expected future spot exchange rates. Forward speculation, defined in the next section, tends to make them so.

[b] These exchange rates are not known with certainty "at present" but are those that turn out to rule in the future.

the risk by selling forward each of British Airways' installment payments. That is, Boeing can contract *today* with its bank to deliver each of British Airways' installments to the bank on the day after Boeing receives them. The bank will contract in return to credit Boeing with a certain and known number of dollars each time, all determined by the appropriate forward exchange rate. Then, regardless of what happens to actual exchange rates over the life of the credit, Boeing will receive a known number of dollars.[4] Table 1A.3 illustrates exactly the kind of loss that Boeing can avoid by obtaining *forward cover*: $700,000 in this case. It also illustrates another important feature of this example and of forward foreign exchange markets: there are as many different forward foreign exchange rates as there are "periods" in the future.

FORWARD SPECULATION

Forward speculation, which also uses the forward foreign exchange market, is in a sense exactly the opposite of covering. It is the activity of engaging in forward transactions in order to gamble on exchange-rate expectations. Covering uses the forward market to avoid risk; forward speculation uses it to take on risk. Covering insures against mistaken expectations of future foreign exchange rates; forward speculation gambles on correct expectations of those rates.

From another perspective, forward speculation is just a particular kind of the speculative international financial investment discussed in the text. It is a purchase or sale of an asset that is motivated by expectations of future exchange rates—only in this case the asset is a forward contract.

Forward speculation exploits any difference between forward exchange rates and expected future spot exchange rates (see note a to Table 1A.3). Consider Boeing's covering in Table 1A.3. Suppose that a few days after making the credit-covering arrangements with its bank and British Airways, Boeing's corporate treasurer learns from a highly reliable source—a U.S. central banker, say—that the pound's value may decline over the course of the year "more than you think." If Boeing's corporate treasurer has confidence in his source, he will immediately revise his expectations of future exchange rates downward from the set 2.10, 2.09, 2.08, 2.07. And this opens an opportunity

---

[4] Why did Boeing not simply force British Airways to come up with four quarterly *dollar* payments, if it was so interested in eliminating exchange-rate uncertainty? That would be an entirely suitable alternative to covering for Boeing, but the alternative might well induce British Airways to cover instead. How does British Airways know that the dollars it must come up with every quarter will not unexpectedly rise in value? To solve this potential problem, British Airways could contract to buy forward dollars—by selling forward pounds, of course, which is exactly how Boeing would have covered under the original financing arrangements.

of immense potential profit, but equally immense risk as well. In the newly unclouded eyes of the corporate treasurer, forward exchange rates now "over-price" or "over-value" the future pound. By selling such overvalued pounds forward, and buying them back more cheaply on future spot foreign exchange markets, he could realize the dream of every speculator—buy cheap, sell dear.

Operationally, what he might decide to do is to sell *more* than British Airways' £5 million forward each quarter. That is, he might contract with his bank to sell £10 or £20 million forward. Or why stop there? Why not £105 million? But that, of course, would obligate Boeing to deliver £105 million to its bank in 3, 6, 9, and again in 12 months' time. Where would these £105 million come from? British Airways is sending only £5 million per quarter. The answer is simple: Boeing's corporate treasurer would buy them in future spot markets on the day of forward delivery, or slightly before. There would be no problem in doing so—*if he were right to have revised his expectations*. Table 1A.3 suggests that he would have been right. At the end of each quarter Boeing would deliver British Airways' check for £5 million to the bank and would also deliver £100 million more that had been bought on the spot foreign exchange market that very day for

$208 million at the end of the first quarter;
$206 million at the end of the second quarter;
$204 million at the end of the third quarter;
$202 million at the end of the fourth quarter.

All of the pounds would be delivered to the bank to honor the four forward contracts. For each of the deliveries of £100 million, the bank would credit Boeing's account with

$210 million for the first;
$209 million for the second;
$208 million for the third;
$207 million for the fourth.

And each of these deposits in Boeing's account would probably be made before Boeing's checks for $208 million, $206 million, and so on had cleared through the banking system. Boeing wouldn't even have had to have these sums in its accounts to start with, yet could still have written these checks. Boeing's profits on forward speculation would ultimately be $14 million (2 + 3 + 4 + 5)—a huge sum, and one that could have been doubled or trebled by contracting to sell £200 or £300 million forward. Furthermore, these profits were obtained without physically transferring any Boeing commodities or assets. The lure of forward speculation is that it requires no asset commitment, nor even any wealth at all. (Boeing's checking account could have been zero at the beginning of the year.) In principle, Boeing's corporate treasurer could have made the same $14 million, in exactly the same way, if he had been a penniless pauper to start.

In practice, paupers can't speculate in the forward market, and neither can even very rich individuals. Most banks will not engage in forward foreign-exchange-market transactions below a certain minimum size. And this minimum size is usually so large that individuals are completely shut out from the forward market. Furthermore, banks do not always trust even institutional forward contractors such as Boeing's treasurer. They will be suspicious of any offer to sell £100 million forward that is not backed up with £100 million worth of "accounts receivable." Their suspicions may lead them to turn Boeing down or, at the very least, to require Boeing to pledge £50 or £75 million *immediately* as a sign of Boeing's ability to deliver on each forward pledge. This is known technically as a forward exchange *margin requirement*.

What the bank worries about is exactly what should worry Boeing's corporate treasurer: what if he is wrong? The potential losses associated with forward speculation are as impressive as the potential profits. If Boeing's central-banker source is wrong (and why should he really know how to forecast any better than anyone else?), Boeing stands to lose big. The corporate treasurer stands to lose his job and his ability to get any other. And the bank may be saddled with a forward contract on which Boeing cannot or will not deliver.[5] The mechanics of losing in forward speculation are as simple as the mechanics of winning. If the actual exchange rates had turned out to be $2.12 per pound for the entire year, Boeing's corporate treasurer would have *lost* $14 million on his speculation.

Because the risks associated with forward speculation are so great, no corporation and very few financial institutions make it a regular practice. Commercial banks themselves generally cover all the forward transactions they arrange with their customers like Boeing. This often requires interbank forward transactions, since a single bank will usually have an imbalance between the number of pounds its customers want to sell forward and the number they want to buy.

Forward speculation does go on. Yet it is self-limiting in the same way as exchange and interest arbitrage are. Large forward sales of pounds, based on beliefs that present forward exchange rates "overvalue" the future pound, tend to drive down the present forward price of pounds. They may also affect expectations, but they will in any case bring about a narrowing of the gap between the forward price of pounds and their expected future spot price. As this gap is narrowed, the likelihood of profitability from forward speculation, and the poten-

---

[5] When the Franklin National Bank of New York collapsed in 1975, it left $750 million worth of forward contracts undelivered. Its own forward speculation losses were the immediate cause of its collapse. Source: Board of Governors of the Federal Reserve System, *Federal Reserve Bulletin* 61 (September 1975): 556. The Federal Reserve System ultimately made good on these contracts.

tial size of the profits, both decline. Less forward speculation will be carried out. To the extent that any persists, the gap between forward and expected future spot exchange rates narrows even further. In fact, the smaller the transaction costs associated with forward speculation (including margin requirements), and the less distasteful speculators find risk all by itself, the more closely the following "parity condition" will tend to hold in reality (and in Table 1A.3):

$$\begin{pmatrix} \text{Average or consensus} \\ \text{expected rates of change} \\ \text{in the dollar price} \\ \text{of pounds (percentage)} \end{pmatrix} = \begin{cases} \begin{pmatrix} \text{Premium on forward} \\ \text{pounds if positive} \\ \text{(percentage)} \end{pmatrix} \\ \begin{pmatrix} \text{Discount on forward} \\ \text{pounds if negative} \\ \text{(percentage)} \end{pmatrix} \end{cases}$$

That this relation is also suggested by the two interest parity conditions for covered and uncovered interest arbitrage should be no surprise. Uncovered interest arbitrage itself implies a kind of speculation—a willingness to bank on expectations in preference to covering.

Supplement 1B
Some International Financial Terminology

One of the most frustrating hurdles to clear in understanding the financial side of international economics is its terminology. Not only do some technical terms fail to parallel everyday usage (for example, foreign money is *foreign exchange*), but also some terms that are technically synonymous sound like opposites. Nowhere is this better illustrated than in international financial investment. What was described in the text as a "U.S. export of asset ownership to Britain" or as "British financial investment in the U.S." has a host of other names—most prominently, "capital inflow from Britain" and "capital import from Britain." As used in international finance, the word *capital* denotes financial resources. That is why when Boeing *exports* newly issued stock to British investors, it *imports* capital from them. That is, Boeing mobilizes the financial resources of the British investors and puts them to work for the corporation. In return for their capital, British investors receive ownership claims on Boeing, which we refer to in the text as *assets*. Familiar as the word *capital* is in international finance, it is studiously avoided in Part I of the text, because *capital* takes on a very different meaning in Part II.

From the U.S. perspective, *capital inflow* and *capital import* refer not only to British financial investment in the United States. They also refer to U.S. *dis*investment in Britain—for example, when American holders of Beefeater stock sell it back to British residents. While this is confusing, it is also sensible: the United States exports ownership of assets to Britain just as much when it sells a U.S.-owned share of Beefeater back to the British as when it sells them a share of Boeing.

The terminology of international financial investment may be summarized as follows:

A U.S. capital inflow
is
a U.S. capital import
is
a U.S. export of the ownership of assets.

And each of these three represents one of two activities. They represent either

British financial investment in the United States
which is sometimes called
an increase in U.S. indebtedness to Britain
or
an increase in U.S. liabilities to Britain
or
U.S. borrowing from the British;

or they represent

U.S. disinvestment in Britain
which is sometimes called
a decrease in U.S. ownership of British assets
or
a decrease in U.S. claims on the British
or
a liquidation of U.S. holdings of British debt.

It is symmetrically true that

A U.S. capital outflow
is
a U.S. capital export
is
a U.S. import of the ownership of assets.

Each of these three represents one of two activities. They represent either

U.S. financial investment in Britain
which is sometimes called
an increase in U.S. ownership of British assets
or
an increase in U.S. claims on the British
or
U.S. lending to the British;

or they represent

British disinvestment in the U.S.
which is sometimes called
a decrease in U.S. indebtedness to Britain
or
a decrease in U.S. liabilities to Britain
or
amortization of U.S. debt to Britain.

Chapter 2

Government Intervention in the Foreign Exchange Market

Much of what is interesting about international finance derives from attempts by governments to control it. Governments do not usually allow the forces of supply and demand free rein in the foreign exchange market. They believe it to be in society's interest to stabilize prices and perhaps even to restrict access to the market by private individuals. This chapter describes some of the most familiar ways in which governments intervene in the foreign exchange market. The next chapter explains why they intervene.

The Foreign Exchange Market without Government Intervention

We start with a description of the foreign exchange market in the absence of government intervention. The familiar forces of supply and demand can be expected to work, and the market behaves much like a competitive market for any good. Supply and demand interact to establish a particular price and a particular quantity that "clear the market"—a price and a quantity that are acceptable to both suppliers and demanders. The price and the quantity that clear the market are designated *equilibrium* price and *equilibrium* quantity, denoting the property that once established in the market, they tend to persist, since they satisfy both suppliers and demanders.

When the foreign exchange market is allowed to behave in this way, it is said that there are *floating exchange rates,* or that the market behaves according to a *floating exchange-rate system.* The terminology implies nothing more mysterious than that prices and quantities traded vary from day to day, and do so in response to the forces of supply and demand.

Figure 2.1 illustrates the foreign exchange market under floating exchange rates. When today's demand for pounds exceeds yesterday's, owing perhaps to increased U.S. imports of British gin, yesterday's exchange rate (OF) will no longer reconcile the supply of and demand for pounds. At yesterday's exchange rate OF, today's demand (OD) would exceed today's supply (OB), and some demands would be left unsatisfied (exactly BD). If any dissatisfaction of pound buyers vents itself in a willingness to bid more dollars for each pound, and if pound suppliers are willing to supply more pounds at higher prices, the foreign exchange market can and will be cleared at a higher price of pounds (OG). The quantity of pounds supplied and demanded will then be equal. Whereas the exchange rate OF was not an equilibrium exchange rate for today's market, OG is—all suppliers and demanders are satisfied.

When exchange rates do float (vary) in this fashion, news reports often carry the information. The news report to accompany Figure 2.1 might include any of several equivalent statements: the pound *appreciated* today (the technically correct description); the pound strengthened today; the pound advanced today; the pound rose in value today; the pound went up today. If tomorrow's supply and demand are as pictured in Figure 2.1, the equilibrium price and quantity established tomorrow will be OE and OA. News reports will include any of the following: the pound *depreciated* in light trading (indicating that the quantity OA is less than the quantity OC); the pound weakened . . . ; the pound fell . . . ; the pound fell back . . . ; or, for dramatic declines in its dollar price, the pound plunged . . . .

FIGURE 2.1. *The Foreign Exchange Market under Floating Exchange Rates*

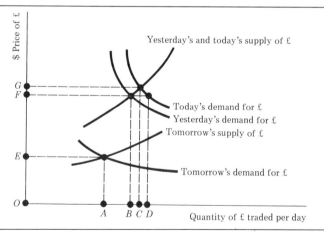

Chapter 2: Government Intervention

Government Intervention under the Adjustable-Peg Exchange-Rate System

Almost all governments, under certain circumstances, will allow their money to float on the foreign exchange market in the manner described. Typically, however, governments intervene in an attempt to eliminate pronounced variations in exchange rates. In fact, from late 1946 until 1971, most non-Communist governments adhered to a precise code of rules and procedures for stabilizing exchange rates, the *adjustable-peg exchange-rate system.*[1] This system has more than historical interest, because even today most governments intervene in the foreign exchange market in accord with its spirit.

The adjustable-peg exchange-rate system was an international agreement to keep exchange rates approximately constant. Responsibility for doing so rested with every government individually, but the mechanisms were standardized in an international code to which every country subscribed when it joined the international organization known as the *International Monetary Fund (IMF)*. Most countries did and do belong to the IMF, because of the advantages outlined in Supplement 2B. But membership also entailed commitments, of which the key commitment, say for Britain, was to establish a target value for the pound in terms of U.S. dollars on the foreign exchange market; and to guarantee that the dollar price of pounds never deviated by more than a small percentage from that target value.[2] The target price of the pound that Britain pledged itself to maintain was called the pound's *parity* with respect to the dollar. In fact, the pledge was only to maintain the exchange rate within 1 percent of the parity, and the implied range of permissible exchange rates was known as the *band*. Other terminology related to Britain's commitment is illus-

---

[1] The adjustable-peg exchange-rate system is also called the *pegged exchange-rate system*, the *gold-exchange standard*, and the *Bretton Woods* system (after the New Hampshire town where final plans for its structure were made in 1944).

[2] In fact, the commitment was slightly more complex than this. Britain and every other member of the IMF was obliged under the IMF's Articles of Agreement (IV, Section 1) to set and defend a *par value* for its money. The par value could have been either a U.S. dollar price of the pound or a gold value for the pound (the number of ounces of gold that could be bought with a pound). If Britain and the United States had each declared par values in terms of gold, the *parity* for the pound relative to the dollar would have been the quotient of (1) the dollar price of an ounce of gold, and (2) the pound price of an ounce of gold (see pp. 67–68). In practice, however, Britain and almost every other country that joined the IMF short-circuited this link by declaring par values and parities in terms of U.S. dollars *directly*. The United States, on the other hand, declared a par value for its dollar in terms of gold. Thus the dollar was pegged to gold, and almost all other moneys were pegged to the dollar. This asymmetry between the United States and other countries under the adjustable-peg system is discussed in greater detail at the end of the chapter.

FIGURE 2.2. *Acceptable and Unacceptable Exchange Rates under the Adjustable-Peg Exchange-Rate System*

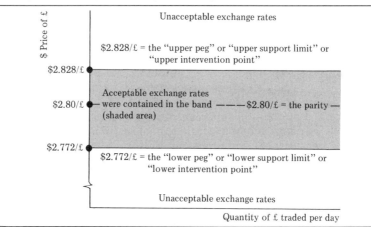

trated in Figure 2.2 for the parity of the pound in terms of dollars that existed through the 1950s and early 1960s, $2.80 per pound.

Governments honored their pledge by a buffer-stock price-stabilization scheme similar to those frequently encountered in domestic and world agricultural markets. Every government set up an agency whose purpose was to act as a residual demander or supplier in the foreign exchange market. These agencies were often known as *Exchange Stabilization Funds*, but we will describe them as a part of the central bank, because they usually are.

The ebb and flow of normal and speculative trade and investment often confronted the British central bank with days when the foreign exchange market was characterized by "oversupply" within the band, as illustrated in Figure 2.3. If the central bank had failed to intervene that day, the normal forces of supply and demand would have made the pound depreciate below the lower peg (to *OE*). The central bank intervened to avoid this, and to fulfill its adjustable-peg commitment, by actually becoming a foreign-exchange-market participant itself. It acted as the residual demander of the oversupply, "sopping up" the excess pounds at prices within the band by buying them from the commercial banking system. All the British central bank would have to buy was *AB* pounds, which, when added to the "private" demands for pounds by traders and investors, would make overall demand in the market just sufficient to establish the price *OF*, the lower peg.

But how would the British central bank "buy" pounds—that is, with what? Typically, it would buy them with dollars that came from buffer stocks of dollars owned by the British central bank. These stocks were a major part of what was (and still is) called British

FIGURE 2.3. *Central Bank Intervention under Conditions of Excessive Private Supply in the Foreign Exchange Market*

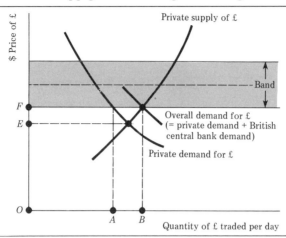

official reserves. Yet it is misleading to think of British central bankers hoarding U.S. currency in their vaults. Official dollar reserves are made up almost exclusively of bank accounts in the U.S. banking system and of short-term U.S. government bonds that are owned by the British central bank.[3] The British central bank bought pounds on the foreign exchange market either by writing checks on its dollar accounts or by selling off some of its U.S. government securities. Occasionally the British central bank might even sell off other parts of its official reserves—government-owned gold and special IMF assets, both described below—in order to get dollars to buy pounds.[4]

Once the British central bank intervened as in Figure 2.3, commercial banks and bureaus of exchange (the brokers of the foreign ex-

[3] More accurately, official dollar reserves are made up of two parts, the first of which is roughly one-quarter the size of the second: (1) demand deposits and time deposits owned by the British central bank, occasionally in U.S. resident commercial banks, sometimes in commercial Euro-banks (see Chapter 7), and most typically in U.S. Federal Reserve banks; and (2) U.S. Treasury bills (not technically bonds, although a few bonds are held) and several other short-term forms of U.S. government debt. (It is this portion of the U.S. national debt, along with that owned by private foreigners, that is generally agreed to be a "burden" on U.S. taxpayers.)

[4] In addition to dollars, gold, and special IMF assets, some countries hold German Deutsche marks (deposits and securities), and a few hold British sterling and French francs. At the end of 1977, the value of worldwide dollar-denominated official reserves was almost 12 times the value of mark-denominated reserves, 60 times the value of pound-denominated reserves, and more than 150 times the value of franc-denominated reserves. See International Monetary Fund, *IMF Survey,* May 22, 1978, p. 155.

change market) no longer felt any pressure to alter exchange rates. They were still faced with "long lines" of private customers such as Boeing who wanted to convert pounds into dollars (to supply pounds) and with only "short lines" of customers such as Beefeater who wanted to convert dollars into pounds (to demand pounds). But they were saved from being pressured to vary the price of pounds by one major government customer—the British central bank—who was willing to convert dollars from official reserves into pounds.

The ebb and flow of normal trade and investment could also produce the opposite situation. Figure 2.4 illustrates the foreign exchange market on a day characterized by excessive demand within the band. If allowed to go unchecked by the British central bank, this excessive demand would have forced the pound to appreciate above the upper peg (to OH). On these days, the British central bank remained faithful to the rules of the adjustable-peg exchange-rate system by becoming a residual supplier of pounds in the foreign exchange market. The bank "satisfied" the excessive demand by actually selling pounds to the commercial banking system in return for dollars, which the commercial banks were glad to give up. The commercial banks were being pressured by more (larger) requests to convert dollars into pounds than to convert pounds into dollars—more by customers like Beefeater than like Boeing. These banks were willing to accept the large quantities of dollars for conversion at existing exchange rates because they knew that they could pass the dollars on to the British

FIGURE 2.4. *Central Bank Intervention under Conditions of Excessive Private Demand in the Foreign Exchange Market*

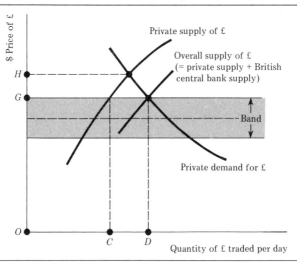

central bank. The minimum number of pounds that the British central bank supplied to keep its pledge was CD. When these were added to the private supply of pounds from traders and investors, overall supply in the market was just sufficient to establish the price OG, the upper peg.

On days such as these, when the British central bank acted as a residual supplier of pounds, it was simultaneously acting as an absorber of dollars from the foreign exchange market. It inherited claims on the U.S. banking system, such as the U.S. gin wholesaler's dollar check to Beefeater (which Beefeater cashed at its commercial bank and which its commercial bank in turn sold to the British central bank). The British central bank deposited these claims in its U.S. bank account. They thus became additions to British official reserves, and remained so even if at a later time the British central bank used them to buy U.S. government securities or gold.

One interesting implication of these examples was that stabilizing exchange rates could be profitable to the British central bank. As long as the parity was maintained, the British central bank found itself buying pounds only when they were inexpensive (at the lower peg) and selling them only when they were expensive (at the upper peg). The goal of every speculative investor is precisely this: to buy cheap, and sell dear. At times, therefore, under the adjustable-peg system, central banks did not have to stabilize exchange rates. Private speculators, motivated by potential profits, did so instead. Such private exchange-rate stabilization was even more prominent under another historical exchange-rate system, the *gold standard*, described in Supplement 2A. Potential profit notwithstanding, central banks often suffered huge losses under the adjustable-peg system (for reasons described later in this chapter). As a result, private speculators were reluctant to intervene in the same way that central banks did. Both central bank losses and private speculative reluctance are explained by the "adjustable" nature of this exchange-rate system.

Adjustability of the Peg: Devaluation and Revaluation

As we have noted, the overriding concern of the adjustable-peg exchange-rate system was to keep exchange rates stable. But the architects of the system recognized the impossibility of accomplishing this goal perfectly, especially over long periods. Economic developments that affected either normal or speculative international trade and financial investment could subject the foreign exchange market to indefinite excessive supply (Figure 2.3) or to indefinite excessive demand (Figure 2.4). Some of these developments had to do with domestic economic policy, others with foreign economic policy. Many are discussed in Chapter 4. Regardless of their source, such developments placed governments and central banks in a quandary.

When Figure 2.3 characterized the foreign exchange market day after day, Britain's quandary was the impending loss of all official reserves. For example, suppose in the diagram

$$OF = \$2.772 \text{ per pound};$$
$$AB = 10 \text{ million pounds};$$

Britain would be withdrawing approximately $28 million per day from its buffer stock of dollars in order to "defend the value of the pound." At that rate, a $16 billion stock of official reserves would be exhausted in a little more than a year. Foreign-exchange-market intervention would have to cease then, the pound would depreciate, and a number of unfortunate consequences would arise from the other roles that official reserves play (see Chapter 3).

The problems associated with steady losses of official reserves were due to the so-called *overvaluation* of the pound; the parity "valued" the pound more highly than the market did. To solve these problems, the adjustable-peg exchange-rate system allowed Britain to change its commitment to the International Monetary Fund—that is, to alter the parity it had pledged to defend. This feature made the system "adjustable." Britain could stem its loss of official reserves by *devaluing the pound*, by pledging a lower parity for the pound in terms of dollars. This would also obviously cure the pound's overvaluation. But to avoid one evil—the loss of all official reserves, Britain had to choose another—the temporary abandonment of stable exchange rates. Such was the real quandary.

The British devaluation of 1967 is illustrated in Figure 2.5. The word *devaluation* strictly describes an alteration of the parity and band and not necessarily a change in the exchange rate. However, under the adjustable-peg exchange-rate system, devaluation of the pound almost inevitably led to depreciation of the pound.[5] The supply and demand curves in Figure 2.5 illustrate what the British authorities may have believed about the foreign exchange market then. If they had been right, pound devaluation would have succeeded in eliminating the loss of official reserves. Furthermore, it would even have allowed Britain to rebuild lost reserves, since at the new parity and band, the pound would have been *undervalued*: the foreign exchange market would have been subject to excessive demand for pounds, as in Figure 2.4.

_____

[5] Hypothetically, a very small devaluation under the adjustable-peg exchange-rate system might not have implied any depreciation, but that is just a curiosity. Countries avoided devaluations if they possibly could. Note that depreciation of the pound under the adjustable-peg system did not necessarily imply devaluation either: the pound was free to depreciate and appreciate *within* the band.

FIGURE 2.5. *The British Devaluation of the Pound in 1967*

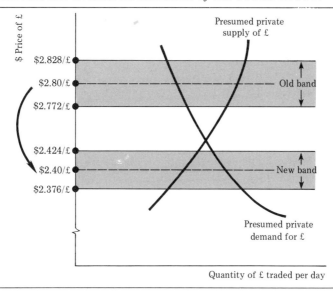

Historically, devaluations by developed countries under the adjustable-peg exchange-rate system were infrequent. Table 2.1 lists the more important ones until 1971. Both the International Monetary Fund and individual governments attached so much importance to stable exchange rates that they usually tried to stem official reserve losses by any means other than devaluation. For example, they instituted policies that affected traders and investors directly. Britain might attempt to discourage imports of commodities, services, and assets, all of which generated supplies of pounds; and it might attempt to encourage exports of goods, which generated demands. Before a country seriously contemplated devaluation, the pressure on official reserves had to be obvious, sustained, and large.

The quandary for countries whose money was *undervalued* (was in excessive demand on the foreign exchange market day after day, as in Figure 2.4) was very different, and the pressure on these countries was somewhat less severe. Instead of losing official reserves from buffer stocks, they were gaining them, and there was no technical limit to the number of days that countries could go on adding to official reserves. While at some point a country might decide that it "had enough," this can hardly be described as pressure.

In fact, the pressure on such countries generally came from another source: the British central bank's intervention illustrated in

TABLE 2.1. *Selected Devaluations, 1946–1970*

Year	Country	Percentage decline in dollar parity[a]
1949	Australia	30.5
	Belgium	12.3
	Canada	9.1
	Denmark	30.5
	Netherlands	30.2
	Norway	30.5
	United Kingdom	30.5
1958	France	17.5
1967	Denmark	7.9
	United Kingdom	14.3
1969	France	11.1

[a] [(Change in parity dollar price)/(Old dollar parity price)] × 100.

Source: International Monetary Fund, *International Financial Statistics*, any 1970 or 1971 issue, table on Par Values.

Figure 2.4 was potentially inflationary for the British economy.[6] By supplying CD of pounds to the foreign exchange market every day, the British central bank also tended to increase the stock of pounds in existence every day. That is, by selling CD of pounds to British commercial banks, the British central bank increased the number of pounds that British commercial banks had available for loans to customers by CD. The British money stock tended to rise by at least CD pounds per day, and possibly by even more, since most of the world's developed countries have commercial banking systems in which injections of "new money" such as CD are loaned, deposited, reloaned, and redeposited in such a way that the final increase in the money stock is a multiple of CD.

Yet inflation was not guaranteed for countries with an undervalued money. First, the inflationary effects were only tendencies. The British central bank was often able to offset ("sterilize") the inflationary impact of its exchange-rate stabilization on the British money stock by explicit, conventional, contractionary monetary policy. Second, some increase in the British money stock is often quite desirable, and not necessarily inflationary—especially if Britain is suffering from severe domestic unemployment. Finally, the money stock usually should rise in any growing economy just to finance the needs of

---

[6] Similarly, the intervention illustrated in Figure 2.3 was potentially deflationary. These matters are discussed in greater detail in Chapter 5.

growth. The requisite rises are not inflationary and might well be larger than *CD* per day, in which case the British central bank's stabilization of the exchange rate would not be inflationary.

Nevertheless, the potential for domestic inflation remained for countries regularly confronted by Figure 2.4. If the potential inflation became actual inflation, Britain was able and permitted to solve its problem by a *revaluation* of the pound—that is, by pledging a higher parity for the pound in terms of dollars.

A hypothetical revaluation of the pound is illustrated in Figure 2.6. By reducing or eliminating the need for the British central bank to intervene in the foreign exchange market, revaluation damped the tendency for the British money stock to rise. Revaluation was thus counterinflationary and a possible solution to the problems caused by excessive demand for pounds in the foreign exchange market.

However, as Table 2.2 shows, revaluations were even more infrequent than devaluations under the historical adjustable-peg system. And they were smaller in percentage terms, on average, than devaluations. This is explained by the unequal pressure faced by Figure 2.3 countries and Figure 2.4 countries. Central banks that were called on regularly to ward off depreciation by "supporting" (buying) their money on the foreign exchange market faced a clear and unalterable constraint: a fixed stock of official reserves cannot last forever. Central banks that were called on regularly to ward off appreciation faced uncertain, and not necessarily undesirable, consequences: potential increases in their domestic money stock. In a nut-

FIGURE 2.6. *A Hypothetical British Revaluation of the Pound*

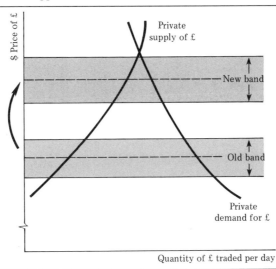

TABLE 2.2. *Selected Revaluations, 1946-1970*

Year	Country	Percentage increase in dollar parity[a]
1961	Germany	5.0
	Netherlands	5.0
1969	Germany	9.3

[a] [(Change in parity dollar price)/(Old dollar parity price)] × 100.
Source: International Monetary Fund, *International Financial Statistics*, any 1970 or 1971 issue, table on Par Values.

shell, it is probably fair to say that the countries in Table 2.1 were *forced* to devalue, but those in Table 2.2 *chose* to revalue. Undervaluation was not so severe a problem as overvaluation. This asymmetry is usually described as the *devaluation bias* of the adjustable-peg exchange-rate system: the system could be expected to have more devaluations than revaluations, because the pressures for the former were more certain and severe.

The Balance of Payments

The adjustable-peg exchange-rate system provided the rationale for the familiar concern about the state of a country's balance of payments. While the balance of payments may be defined and measured in a number of ways (see Supplement 2C), the most familiar of these relates directly to attempts to stabilize exchange rates.

The most familiar measure of the British balance of payments[7] is defined as follows:

$$\left(\begin{matrix} \text{The £ value of British} \\ \textit{exports} \text{ of} \\ \begin{cases} \text{commodities} \\ \text{services} \\ \text{assets} \end{cases} \end{matrix} \right) \textit{less} \left(\begin{matrix} \text{The £ value of British} \\ \textit{imports} \text{ of} \\ \begin{cases} \text{commodities} \\ \text{services} \\ \text{assets} \end{cases} \end{matrix} \right)$$

But in light of the discussion in Chapter 1 (see Figure 1.2), the pound value of British exports *is* almost exactly the demand for pounds on the foreign exchange market. The number of pounds that Beefeater demanded from its bank in exchange for the dollar check received

[7] The full technical name for this measure is the balance of payments *on official settlements basis* or *official reserve transactions basis*.

from U.S. gin wholesalers was precisely the pound value of the gin shipment. Similarly, the pound value of all British imports comes very close to equaling the supply of pounds on the foreign exchange market.[8] Thus the British balance of payments can be equivalently defined as:

$$\left(\begin{array}{c} \text{The private demand for £} \\ \text{on the foreign exchange} \\ \text{market} \end{array}\right) \text{ less } \left(\begin{array}{c} \text{The private supply of £} \\ \text{on the foreign exchange} \\ \text{market} \end{array}\right)$$

If British exports (of commodities, services, and assets) exceed imports, Britain is said to have a balance-of-payments *surplus;* if British imports exceed British exports, Britain is said to have a balance-of-payments *deficit.* From the second definition, an equally good measure of a British balance-of-payments surplus is any excessive private demand for pounds (private demand less private supply) on the foreign exchange market. An equally good measure of a British balance-of-payments deficit is an excessive private supply of pounds.

These statements illustrate several fundamental points about this measure of a country's balance of payments. (1) It is always zero under a floating exchange rate system without government intervention in the foreign exchange market. Exchange rates float until the private supply of pounds equals the private demand for pounds. When that occurs, the values of British exports and imports of commodities, services, and assets must be equal. No balance-of-payments surpluses or deficits exist, nor do balance-of-payments problems.[9] (2) Since balance-of-payments surpluses and deficits exist only when the government intervenes in the foreign exchange market, one can view them as the "price we have to pay" for having the government stabilize exchange rates. (3) The balance of payments can be identified with the amount of government intervention in the foreign exchange market.

---

[8] The equivalence is not exact. British Airways' import of a Boeing 747 may not lead to any immediate supply of pounds to the foreign exchange market. Not only may Boeing choose to hold the pounds in a London account (footnote 6 to Chapter 1), but Boeing may extend credit to British Airways, so that Boeing receives pound checks only in the future, as the debt is paid off. In principle, however, the British balance-of-payments accountant records Boeing's London bank deposit or its acceptance of British Airways' IOU as a British export of asset ownership to Boeing. Yet this British asset export leads to no demand for pounds. Thus, in this example, British imports would exceed the supply of pounds by exactly the same amount that British exports exceeded the demand for pounds. The difference between exports and imports—what we are really interested in—is unaffected by the inaccurate identification.

[9] Other balances that come from the balance-of-payments "accounts" (summarized in Supplement 2C) *may* still show surpluses or deficits under floating exchange rates. For example, a country may still have a *trade balance deficit* (exports of commodities less than imports of commodities), as long as it is offset by a surplus with respect to services and assets. Floating exchange rates do not "equilibrate" the trade balance, as is sometimes claimed.

This last conclusion deserves expansion. Under the adjustable-peg exchange-rate system, the only way in which private supply could differ from private demand was for the British central bank to be willing to act as a residual buyer and seller of pounds. In Figure 2.3, the British central bank was confronted with an excessive supply of pounds equal to AB — that is, with a balance-of-payments deficit equal to AB. Similarly, in Figure 2.4, the British central bank was confronted with a balance-of-payments surplus equal to CD. Thus, under the adjustable-peg system, still another way to measure the British balance of payments over a period of time was

$$\left(\begin{array}{c} \text{The number of pounds} \\ \text{sold by the British} \\ \text{central bank to the} \\ \text{foreign exchange market} \end{array} \right) \ less \ \left(\begin{array}{c} \text{The number of pounds} \\ \text{bought by the British} \\ \text{central bank from the} \\ \text{foreign exchange market} \end{array} \right)$$

Or, since the British central bank bought pounds with official reserves, and sold them for official reserves, the British balance of payments could be measured as follows:

$$\left(\begin{array}{c} \text{British balance of} \\ \text{payments in dollars} \end{array} \right) = \left(\begin{array}{c} \text{The change in British} \\ \text{official reserves} \end{array} \right)$$

British balance-of-payments surpluses obviously implied additions to the British stock of official reserves; deficits obviously implied official reserve losses.

All of these identifications can be illustrated in our diagram of the foreign exchange market. Figure 2.7 is an expansion of Figure 2.3, with different but equivalent labels.

We can now draw together all our conclusions about the adjustable-peg exchange-rate system, using more familiar terminology. Balance-of-payments-deficit countries were those faced continually with Figure 2.3. Deficits forced a country to use official reserves in order to keep its money from depreciating below the lower peg. Chronic deficits resulted from overvaluation. Devaluation was sometimes the only way out. Unfortunately, devaluations such as that in Figure 2.5 implied paper losses for central banks of deficit countries: before devaluation, they were buying their own money at a high price; after devaluation, they were selling it at a low price.

Balance-of-payments-surplus countries (Figure 2.4) were under less pressure. They were obliged to add to their stocks of official reserves in order to quell appreciation. Chronic surpluses resulted from undervaluation. If they were severe, surplus countries sometimes chose to revalue, sacrificing the goal of exchange-rate stability to anti-inflation policy. But even revaluation implied paper losses for central banks in surplus countries; before revaluation, they sold their money cheap; after, they were often forced to purchase it dear.

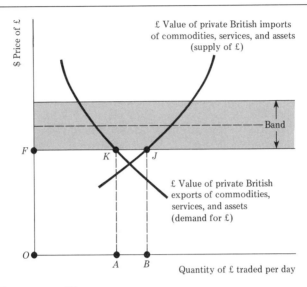

At the exchange rate *OF*:
(1) the *pound* value of daily British exports of commodities, services, and assets is approximately *OA*;
(2) the *pound* value of daily British imports of commodities, services, and assets is approximately *OB*;
(3) Britain's daily balance of payments is −*AB* pounds per day, a deficit;
(4) Britain's daily loss of official reserves is *ABJK* dollars per day.

The Special Position of the United States under the Adjustable-Peg Exchange-Rate System

The formal adjustable-peg exchange-rate system was characterized and eventually victimized by two fundamental asymmetries. One was the devaluation bias of the system discussed above, which generally left chronic balance-of-payments-deficit countries in dire straits compared to chronic balance-of-payments-surplus countries. The other was the special role played by the United States and by the U.S. dollar.

Much of what has been said about formal government intervention in the foreign exchange market did not apply to the United States. While every other country under the adjustable-peg exchange-rate system pledged and defended a parity dollar value for its money, this would have been meaningless for the United States. (The dollar value of a dollar must always be one.) Although every other country's central bank was obliged to act as a residual buyer or seller of its own money on the foreign exchange market, the United States could afford to maintain a hands-off attitude toward the market. This was possible because when every other country *did* successfully stabilize the dollar value of its money, then from a U.S. point of view, the value of the dollar in terms of every foreign money was stabilized, too. The United States did not have to intervene, because every other country intervened instead. Nor was the United States obliged, therefore, to maintain any official reserves for purposes of stabilizing exchange rates. (It did maintain official reserves for other reasons, made clear below.)

One important implication of this special position was that balance-of-payments deficits did not *require* the United States to undertake any kind of foreign-exchange-market policy. When private U.S. imports of commodities, services, and assets exceeded private U.S. exports, the rest of the world was obligated directly by their IMF commitment to "absorb" the U.S. deficit into their official reserves. The rest of the world had to act; the United States did not. The clarification of these assertions rests on a fundamental identity:

> *If the balance of payments were measured comparably worldwide, the size of any U.S. balance-of-payments deficit would match exactly the size of the rest of the world's balance-of-payments surplus with the United States.*

This identity springs from the primary definition of the balance of payments in the preceding section and from two other identities: U.S. exports are identically the rest of the world's imports, and U.S. imports are identically the rest of the world's exports (see Schema 1.1 in Chapter 1). When the United States had a deficit, the rest of the world had a surplus; and in light of Figures 2.4 and 2.7, when the rest of the world had a surplus, at least some foreign money was undervalued relative to its dollar parity. When foreign money was undervalued, foreign central banks were obligated to act as its residual supplier in the foreign exchange market in order to keep exchange rates within the band (Figure 2.4). They did so by absorbing (buying) official reserves into their buffer stocks—U.S. dollars in this case. To complete the linkage, these dollars were precisely the dollars that private U.S. residents "spent" on world goods in excess of what they "earned." That is, the number of dollars that foreign central banks had to absorb into official reserves when the United States had a balance-of-payments deficit was precisely the dollar size of that deficit. Unlike deficits for any other country, deficits in the United States had no immediate impact on U.S. official reserves under the adjustable-peg exchange-rate system.

Similarly, balance-of-payments surpluses in the United States typically led to *no* immediate increase in U.S. official reserves. Because the U.S. central bank, when confronted with a surplus, was not obli-

FIGURE 2.8. *An American Balance-of-Payments Surplus from a U.S. Point of View*

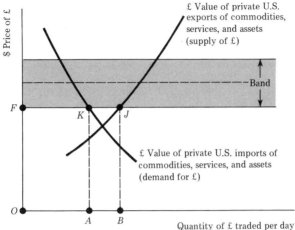

At the exchange rate *OF*:
(1) the *pound* value of daily U.S. imports of commodities, services, and assets is approximately *OA*;
(2) the *pound* value of daily U.S. exports of commodities, services, and assets is approximately *OB*;
(3) the U.S. daily balance of payments is *AB* pounds per day or *ABJK* dollars per day, a surplus;
(4) the U.S. official reserve position is unchanged by its surplus.

gated to sell dollars to the foreign exchange market, there was no potential inflationary impact of U.S. surpluses on the U.S. economy, as there was for surpluses in all other countries.[10]

This asymmetric position of the United States under the adjustable-peg exchange-rate system is illustrated in Figure 2.8. Figure 2.8 is Figure 2.7 relabeled and would be an appropriate depiction of a U.S. balance-of-payments surplus if Britain were the only other country in the world. The asymmetry rests in statement (4): no dis-

[10] When the United States ran a balance-of-payments surplus under the adjustable-peg exchange-rate system, foreign central banks were obligated by their corresponding deficits to draw down official reserves of dollars and sell them to commercial banks in the foreign exchange market. But this had no direct effect on the U.S. money stock, since U.S. demand deposits owned by foreign central banks as a part of their official reserves *are* part of the U.S. money stock. When these demand deposits are transferred or sold to private institutions or individuals, all that is changed is the owner's identity of that portion of the U.S. money stock, not its size. These matters are discussed at somewhat greater length in Chapter 5, but their full complexity, including some ways in which changes in the official reserves of foreign central banks *might* affect the U.S. money stock, is beyond the scope of this book.

tance or area in the diagram corresponds to any gain in U.S. official reserves, although *ABJK* still represents a loss of British official dollar reserves.

The discussion to this point gives the impression that the United States had an enviable position under the adjustable-peg exchange-rate system. It alone did not have to worry about establishing exchange-rate parities, intervening in the foreign exchange market, and holding official reserves. Nor was it subject, apparently, to the pressures that faced typical chronic balance-of-payments deficit and surplus countries. It had to fear neither the loss of official reserves that afflicted deficit countries nor the inflationary impulse that afflicted surplus countries. Nor should the United States' apparent inability to devalue or revalue the dollar—the United States did not declare an exchange-rate parity and hence could not alter one—necessarily be viewed as a disadvantage of its special role. Why should the United States have *wanted* to devalue or revalue if chronic balance-of-payments deficits and surpluses were innocuous?

In fact, of course, all these impressions are misleading. Only elements of truth are found in each. The United States did not escape all responsibility under the adjustable peg exchange-rate system, nor did it escape the quandary faced by typical chronic balance-of-payments-deficit countries. The nature of its responsibility and its quandary were different, relating primarily to gold.

Gold under the Adjustable-Peg Exchange-Rate System

The United States did in fact have to declare a target value for the dollar when it joined the International Monetary Fund. But unlike every other country, the United States chose to declare this "parity" for the dollar in terms of gold.[11] The United States then committed itself to maintain the gold value of the dollar, just as all other countries committed themselves to maintaining the dollar value of their own money. Why the United States chose to make this special commitment is explained in part by the huge accumulation of gold that it had amassed during the 1930s (by requiring private holders to sell it to the government) and during World War II (by being a major Allied supplier). The massive stock of U.S. gold made credible the U.S. pledge to back the dollar with gold.

This word *backing* is important. The demise of the adjustable-peg exchange-rate system began in August 1971, when the United States declared unilaterally that it was no longer prepared to back the dollar with gold (see Chapter 7). Until then, the entire adjustable-peg

[11] Technically, the United States was the only country to declare a par value relative to gold. See footnote 2.

exchange-rate system was founded in principle on gold. The United States stabilized the value of the dollar in terms of gold, and all other countries stabilized the value of their moneys in terms of dollars. The U.S. gold stock backed the dollar, and the gold and dollars held by foreign countries as official reserves backed their moneys.[12]

Yet the word *backing* is uninformative about the day-to-day implications of the U.S. commitment to the IMF. In reality, the gold value of the dollar that the United States pledged itself to defend was no more than the dollar price of gold in the world gold market. The "gold value of the dollar" is just the reciprocal of the "dollar price of gold." Throughout most of the era of the adjustable-peg system, the gold value of a dollar was 1/35 ounce of gold per dollar—precisely *because* the world price of gold was $35 per ounce of gold.

Thus, to be precise, what the United States established and defended from the late 1940s until the late 1960s was the world price of gold. To do so, it intervened in the world gold market in exactly the same way that other countries intervened in the foreign exchange market. It acted as the residual supplier and demander of gold. It bought gold when the world gold market was characterized by excessive supply at $35 ounce, and added such gold to the U.S. buffer stock of gold—U.S. official reserves. It sold gold when the world gold market was characterized by excessive demand at $35 per ounce, drawing down its buffer stocks of gold to sell to foreign buyers. These operations are illustrated in Figure 2.9, where the United States would successfully have stabilized the gold value of the dollar yesterday by buying *CD* ounces of gold from private foreign sellers, and today by selling *AB* ounces to private foreign buyers. (The figure refers to the period until 1968 for reasons discussed below.)

None of these U.S. responsibilities had anything *directly* to do with the foreign exchange market, foreign exchange rates, or the state of the U.S. balance of payments. But they indirectly placed the United States in a quandary wholly symmetric to that of other countries, in which U.S. balance-of-payments deficits *did* lead eventually to a loss of U.S. official reserves of gold. And U.S. gold losses eventually brought about the demise of the adjustable-peg exchange-rate system.

The gold foundation of that system had a fatal flaw. Because its price was fixed at $35 per ounce, the value of gold relative to other commodities fell steadily as their prices rose.[13] Industrial and ornamental uses of gold were stimulated. Yet world production of gold became progressively less profitable in comparison to production of

[12] In principle, balance-of-payments-deficit countries such as Britain in Figure 2.3 could have sold gold out of official reserves, bought dollars, and resold the dollars in the foreign exchange market for pounds, to keep the pound from depreciating. And balance-of-payments-surplus countries such as Britain in Figure 2.4 could have bought gold with dollars and then repurchased the dollars in the foreign exchange market, to keep the pound from appreciating. In practice, the former was almost never done, and the latter only rarely.

[13] The world price of gold remained constant at $35 an ounce from 1935 to 1968.

FIGURE 2.9. *The World Gold Market until 1968*

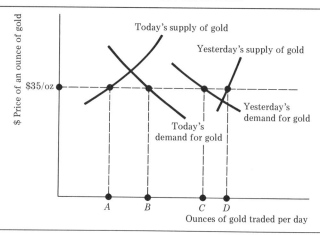

other commodities. Production steadily declined to the point where the world gold stock was growing at well below 1 percent per year toward the end of the 1960s. These trends had two unfortunate consequences. (1) The ratio of gold to dollars in foreign official reserves declined significantly. Almost none of the gold newly produced every year was purchased by foreign central banks. Yet regular and growing U.S. balance-of-payments deficits (see Table 3.5) forced them to purchase increasing numbers of dollars from the foreign exchange market. (2) The ratio of U.S. official-reserve gold to foreign official-reserve dollars declined even more rapidly.

Moreover, the decline in the first ratio aggravated the decline in the second. Most central banks preferred diversification to imbalance in their official reserves, especially when the imbalance was toward dollars. In their eyes, the dollar's value seemed less intrinsic than gold's: the dollar, after all, depended on gold to back it—that is, to guarantee its own value. Thus as their "diversification ratio" (1) fell, many foreign central banks attempted to arrest its decline by presenting dollar assets to the U.S. Treasury to be "converted" into gold. Private users and hoarders of gold indirectly did the same thing. Their demands, encouraged either by gold's relatively low price, or by the outside chance of a speculative gain,[14] had to be met out of U.S.

[14] As the world gold shortage became acute during the 1960s, there developed a real possibility that the United States and the IMF would declare a major increase in the parity dollar price of gold. France proposed doing so regularly and stridently, and in 1968 even Britain suggested doubling the gold price. The United States resisted these ideas, as it has ever since (see footnote 4 to Chapter 7). In U.S. eyes, such action would have represented a politically embarrassing devaluation of the dollar relative to gold, and it would have rewarded undeserving gold producers (South Africa and the Soviet Union) and gold hoarders.

TABLE 2.3. *Gold and Dollars in Global Official Reserves, Selected Years (Billions of Dollars)*

End of year	U.S. official reserves of gold	Global official reserves of gold (except U.S.)	Global official reserves of U.S. dollars[a]
1948	24.4	8.5	Approx. 3
1958	20.6	18.4	9.6
1963	16.0	24.2	14.6
1968	10.9	28.0	17.3
1969	11.9	27.2	16.0
1970	11.1	26.1	23.8
1971	11.1	28.0	50.7

[a] More exactly, U.S. liabilities to foreign official institutions. In the late 1960s some foreign central banks began holding official-reserve dollars in commercial banks *not* resident in the United States. These official-reserve "Euro-dollar" holdings are discussed in Chapter 7 and are not included in this column.
    Source: International Monetary Fund, *International Financial Statistics*, various issues, tables on Gold in official reserves and currency denomination of official-reserve foreign exchange.

gold stocks if world production was insufficient at $35 an ounce.

The result was that the U.S. gold stock decreased steadily, as illustrated in Table 2.3, and so did the "backing ratio" (2) for dollars already outstanding. This decline only heightened the concern of many dollar holders about the security of their assets, leading to still more pressure on the U.S. gold stock. The vicious circle culminated in a "run on gold" in March 1968, with private speculative purchases of gold estimated to have been as large as $3 billion.[15] Table 2.3 reveals that by that time the U.S. gold stock was already insufficient to redeem the stock of official-reserve dollars, to say nothing of the dollars being held by private foreigners. The system of *convertibility* between the dollar and gold was clearly in trouble.

Three efforts were made during the 1960s to alleviate the trouble. First, the United States developed a number of policies to shrink its balance-of-payments deficit, which was indirectly causing U.S. gold losses. These measures are described at appropriate places in subsequent chapters.[16]

Second, the United States and other major governments agreed

[15] Because they recognized the impending threat to dollar-gold convertibility, most foreign central banks became increasingly reluctant during the 1960s to make demands on the United States for gold. The March 1968 run on gold was brought on by private speculative pressure alone.
[16] See pp. 114, 146, and 230.

among themselves after March 1968 to divorce their own gold transactions completely from those carried out by commercial and speculative gold users. The United States continued to defend the $35 gold parity price among all official transactors (central banks and treasuries) who traded only with each other, not in the private world gold market. In the private "tier" (layer) the price of gold was allowed to float.[17] This segmented, *two-tier gold market* effectively squelched further speculative pressure on the U.S. gold stock, insuring its availability to meet the more limited and predictable requests for dollar-gold conversion from foreign central banks. A discreet request of just that sort in August 1971 is alleged to have prompted the United States unilaterally to withdraw from any further obligation to redeem dollars with gold, even when the dollars were held by foreign central banks. What followed this dramatic declaration of dollar *inconvertibility* is described at greater length in Chapter 7. Important for this chapter is that since 1971, there have no longer been even indirect links between the U.S. balance of payments and its official reserves, money stock, and inflation. Dollar assets have nevertheless remained the dominant component of foreign official reserves and have even grown in importance.

As a third and belated solution to the problem of gold, members of the IMF agreed in the late 1960s to create and distribute a new official-reserve asset that had all the characteristics of gold. This innovative asset was called *Special Drawing Rights* (*SDRs*, or in its early years, "paper gold"). SDR distribution was designed to reassure central-bank dollar-holders by restoring balance to their official reserves and by replenishing the U.S. gold stock with something just as good as gold. SDRs are described at greater length in Supplement 2B. Unfortunately, they were created in insufficient quantity, and distributed too late (in the early 1970s), to provide any relief for the problems that growing U.S. balance-of-payments deficits generated for U.S. gold reserves and for the entire adjustable-peg exchange-rate system.

This discussion begs still further the questions that we have deferred for the next chapter. Why are official reserves so important? If they are important only to maintain stable exchange rates and gold prices, why is the stability of these particular prices so paramount an objective? Before we turn to these questions, it is important to characterize the type of government intervention that ruled in the foreign exchange market through most of the early 1970s.

---

[17] The private world market price of gold rose above $40 per ounce almost immediately and remained there until 1970, when it fell back to $35. It climbed rapidly above $100 per ounce in the foreign-exchange-market crises of 1971 through 1973 (see Chapter 7), peaking just short of $200 per ounce in the mid-1970s. After declining in 1977 to just above $100, it rose again in mid-1979 to $290, and in late 1979 to $440.

"Managed Floating":
Individualistic Government Intervention
in the Foreign Exchange Market

Since the collapse of the adjustable-peg exchange-rate system, all governments have continued to seek exchange-rate stability. And most have continued to use the same mechanisms to bring it about. Primary reliance is placed on direct intervention in the foreign exchange market by central banks: official reserves are sold to keep a country's money from depreciating inappropriately and are bought to keep it from appreciating inappropriately. Countries that lose official reserves record balance-of-payments deficits; countries that gain official reserves record balance-of-payments surpluses. Chronic deficit countries are said to have overvalued money; chronic surplus countries, undervalued.

In contrast to the adjustable-peg exchange-rate system, many governments no longer stabilize exchange rates around a fixed (but adjustable) target value. Nor is it predictable in what way these governments will change their notion of an ideal target value from day to day or from month to month. Nor can conflict over exchange-rate goals necessarily be avoided. Britain may want the pound to depreciate relative to the dollar, but the United States may want the dollar to depreciate relative to the pound. It is impossible to satisfy both. Under the adjustable-peg exchange-rate system, the conflict was resolved by the strong presumption that the country with the balance-of-payments deficit (or more severe deficit) should be allowed the initiative.

This type of exchange-rate system is known as *managed floating*. A pejorative alternative is *dirty floating*. Exchange rates are allowed to float but not without some government nudging. The nudging may be infrequent, and the market forces of supply and demand may rule unencumbered for long periods. Or the nudging may be frequent, yet small, as if the central bank were daily bouncing its own idea for a desirable exchange rate off the head of the market. Or the nudging may be large and concentrated, as it was under the old system.

The International Monetary Fund is still a viable institution under managed floating. Yet instead of being the supervisor of a rigid, formal, and uniform code of behavior for government intervention in the foreign exchange market, the IMF has nurtured a flexible and purposely nebulous set of rules for good behavior in exchange-rate arrangements, rules that attempt to assure some comparability of behavior from country to country and to avoid conflict. These and other recent institutional changes are described at greater length in Supplement 2B and in Chapter 7.

Under managed floating, balance-of-payments deficits and surpluses have a more voluntary character than under the adjustable-peg exchange-rate system. Balance-of-payments-deficit countries are no longer *forced* by their international obligations to draw down official reserves in order to keep their money from depreciating. But they may *choose* to do so, for reasons outlined in the next chapter. The very existence of a country's balance-of-payments deficit implies that such a choice was made during the period to which the deficit applies. For the same reasons, such a country may be said to have chosen an "overvalued" money. Similarly, countries may choose to build up official reserves by buying dollars on the foreign exchange market with their own money. Such a choice holds down the foreign-exchange-market value of their money, implies "undervaluation," and creates a balance-of-payments surplus. Under managed floating, even the United States has abandoned its passive attitude toward the foreign exchange market and has intervened occasionally (usually in cooperation with foreign central banks) to keep the dollar from "excessive" depreciation or appreciation. Thus a part of even the U.S. balance of payments[18] is voluntary, determined by the U.S. central bank, just as it is for foreign countries. In fact, the United States has generally become more symmetric to all other countries under managed floating.

But full symmetry for the United States does not yet exist. Dollar assets are still the principal component of foreign official reserves, and the major part of U.S. balance-of-payments deficits still represents no voluntary U.S. action. Instead, it mirrors additions to dollar reserves that foreign central banks choose to make. Ever since 1971 these official-reserve dollars have had no gold backing, and the position of gold in the international monetary system has been cast into doubt. Yet at most, there has been only a minor collapse of confidence in the fundamental position of the dollar under managed floating.

Finally, under managed floating, countries that would have devalued in the past simply allow their money to depreciate on the foreign exchange market. Countries that would have revalued simply allow appreciation.

Managed floating is the most appropriate characterization of the exchange-rate system that rules among the largest countries or blocs of countries. A great many smaller countries, however, still maintain (adjustably) pegged exchange rates along the lines of the historical

---

[18] The U.S. compilers of statistics no longer even calculate the balance of payments as defined here. The IMF, however, still does, and so can anyone else who understands the process of *striking a balance*, described in Supplement 2C. The so-called balance on official reserve transaction basis was banished from U.S. statistics because its usefulness as a measure of pressure on exchange rates was diminished by the voluntary character of surpluses and deficits under managed floating. Its usefulness as a measure of pressure on the U.S. gold stock was made irrelevant by the 1971 abandonment of gold backing for the dollar.

TABLE 2.4. *Managed Floating and Adjustable Pegs as of mid-1975 and mid-1978*

Exchange-rate system for country's money	Number of countries as of midyear		Percentage share of total IMF trade for 1975 countries[a]
	1975	1978	
Managed floating relative to all other moneys[b]	15	31	48.4
Pegged to the U.S. dollar	54	42	12.4
Pegged to the French franc	13	13	0.4
Pegged to the British pound sterling	10	5	1.6
Pegged to other moneys[c]	23	35	12.4
European Community's mutual peg	7	6	23.2

[a] Percentage share of countries' commodity exports plus imports in total exports plus imports of IMF countries. Column does not sum to 100 because of omissions. Figures for 1978 not available.
[b] Includes countries that change a peg frequently according to a prescribed formula.
[c] Includes some moneys that are pegged to "composites" or "baskets" of other moneys.
Source: International Monetary Fund, *Annual Report 1975*, Table 9, p. 24; *Annual Report 1978*, Table I.1, pp. 90–93.

system. So do several European countries with respect to exchange rates among their own moneys. Table 2.4 records exchange-rate arrangements in mid-1975 and in mid-1978. Managed floating became more popular in the interim period and pegging to the dollar less popular. It seems certain that well over half of world trade in 1978 was carried out under managed floating arrangements. Even moneys that are pegged to the dollar still float up and down with the dollar against other moneys. Thus their being pegged does not necessarily keep them stable.

We began this chapter with the observation that no country allows the forces of supply and demand to remain unbridled in the foreign exchange market. In the next chapter we examine why this is so. We also examine the nature of the balance-of-payments problems that are the inevitable consequence of universal commitments to stable exchange rates.

Summary

Governments vary greatly in the scope they allow for price variation in the foreign exchange market. At times they allow the price of their money to be bid up and down, virtually without restraint, by the forces of individual and institutional supply and demand. Exchange rates are said to float freely at those times. At other times governments themselves enter the foreign exchange market as buyers and sellers. As buyers, they try to support the foreign-exchange-market value of their money at a level higher than it would otherwise have been; as sellers, they try to force it lower. In such periods of managed floating, the aim of governments is almost always to iron out unwanted fluctuations in exchange rates.

Many governments adopt rigid rules for their intervention in the foreign exchange market, and virtually all adopted a common set of rules from 1948 to 1971. These rules established target zones within which exchange rates relative to the U.S. dollar could vary permissibly, and beyond which they could not. The zones could be occasionally adjusted (by devaluation and revaluation). Otherwise governments were obliged to sell their own money when its price threatened to rise above the upper peg, and to buy it when its price threatened to fall below the lower peg. They would buy or sell in the foreign exchange market for U.S. dollars. For these purposes all governments owned stocks of dollars known as official reserves.

Government gold stocks were also a part of official reserves, because they too could be used to buy and sell domestic money. And until 1971 the U.S. government kept the dollar as good as gold by guaranteeing its gold value—in exactly the same way that other governments guaranteed the dollar value of their moneys. Natural economic forces, however, made the United States more frequently a buyer of dollars with gold than a seller of dollars for gold in the world gold market. Dwindling gold stocks led the U.S. government in 1971 to renounce its obligation to peg the dollar to gold. Other countries subsequently renounced their obligations to peg their moneys to the dollar. The adjustable-peg exchange-rate system was replaced by nationally determined rules for managed floating that differed greatly among governments.

Governments continue to this day to intervene in the foreign exchange market in order to stabilize exchange rates. Governments in countries that export more commodities, services, and assets than they import are always confronted with an excessive private demand for their money, which would drive its price up unless they became residual suppliers of it in the foreign exchange market (usually still in return for dollars). Governments of such balance-of-payments-surplus countries thus have strong (potentially appreciating) moneys and growing official reserves. Governments of balance-of-payments-deficit countries, by contrast, have weak (potentially depreciating) moneys and falling official reserves.

Chapter 2: Government Intervention

Key Terms

floating exchange rates
appreciation; depreciation
adjustable pegs
parity; band
intervention
official reserves
revaluation; devaluation
undervaluation;
  overvaluation

devaluation bias
the balance of payments
surplus; deficit
gold backing for the
  dollar
two-tier gold markets
Special Drawing Rights
  (SDRs)
managed or dirty floating

Key Concepts and Review

Exchange-rate systems.
Governments/central banks as residual suppliers and demanders in
  the foreign exchange market.
Connections between the balance of payments and the foreign exchange market.
The trade-off between accepting surpluses and deficits and accepting
  variable exchange rates.
The history and special position of gold and U.S. dollars in the international monetary system.

Supplement 2A
Other Exchange-Rate Systems

Floating exchange rates, the adjustable-peg exchange-rate system, and managed floating do not exhaust the possible market structures that can characterize the foreign exchange market. In this section we discuss three others. The first two are quite prominent methods of organizing foreign exchange transactions in nonmarket economies, in developing market economies, and during national emergencies. The third exchange-rate system is of historical interest—it ruled almost universally during peacetime from the beginning of organized banking until 1913.

EXCHANGE CONTROL

Exchange control is a foreign-exchange market structure that is really not a *market* structure at all. Even under the adjustable-peg system, government intervention was carried out primarily by market activity: the government itself became a market participant, supplying or demanding in the same way as other market participants. By contrast, exchange control is a system that suppresses the forces of supply and demand, channeling both through government authorities. Administrative decree and rationing replace price variation and buffer stocks as means of "clearing" the market.

Full and complete systems of exchange control are based on two rules:

Rule 1. All foreign money earned by domestic exporters of commodities, services, or assets must be surrendered to the exchange-control authorities. Foreign money cannot be sold (supplied) to a commercial bank in order to buy (demand) domestic money. Or if it can, it is only because commercial banks act as collection agencies for the exchange-control authorities. Exchange rates are legally or administratively fixed. They may, however, vary frequently with changes in the state of the economy, and they may also depend on the type of export that was the source of foreign-money receipts. In the latter case the system is known more precisely as a *multiple-exchange-rate* system; such systems are described below.

Rule 2. All foreign money that is required to pay for imports of commodities, services, or assets must come from the exchange-control authorities. It must be requested by application. Requests may be denied or exchange rates altered, depending on the state of the economy and the type of import. Providing foreign money for certain kinds of imports may be expressly prohibited—for example, for imports of luxury consumer goods or for imports of foreign bank accounts. Foreign money cannot be bought (demanded) from commercial banks by selling (supplying) domestic money to them. Or if it can, it can be bought only with the permission of the exchange-control authorities.

When a country's money is subject to exchange control, it is said to be *inconvertible*. The name is descriptive because domestic money cannot be freely converted into foreign money. Inconvertible currencies (moneys) are also known colloquially as *heavy currencies*. Examples of inconvertible currencies include many from developing countries, and most Communist-bloc money.

Exchange control is not always thoroughgoing. For example, when the exchange-control authority automatically grants requests by nonresidents to buy foreign money, the exchange-rate system is said to be characterized by *nonresident convertibility*. When the exchange-control authority automatically grants requests by traders of commodities and services to obtain foreign money, the system is said to be characterized by *current-account convertibility* (for the definition of the *current account,* see Supplement 2C).

Exchange control is an effective and flexible policy for dealing with balance-of-payments and exchange-rate problems for short periods. Huge short-run balance-of-payments deficits, with consequent losses of official reserves, can be avoided by resorting to stern rationing of the demand for foreign money (which is identically the foreign-exchange market supply of domestic money). Such means can even avert devaluation, at least temporarily.

Exchange control has also been used to alleviate temporarily large balance-of-payments *surplus* problems. Most European countries during the early 1970s used exchange control to ration the speculative supply of dollars being offered to buy European moneys whose value was almost certain to appreciate relative to the dollar. In this way they held down the size of their balance-of-payments surpluses and also moderated the size of their dollar absorption into official reserves.

Over long periods, however, exchange control in the foreign exchange market is subject to increasingly severe pressures, which are identical to those afflicting price controls and rationing in any goods market. Loopholes are discovered, cheating increases, *black markets* develop, rules must be revised, policing must be increased, and bureaucratic red tape becomes more cumbersome. When these pressures become severe enough, exchange control is usually abandoned, and market forces are allowed to reestablish their influence in the foreign exchange market. Then a new regime of exchange control may be imposed.

MULTIPLE-EXCHANGE-RATE AND DUAL-EXCHANGE-RATE SYSTEMS

Multiple-exchange-rate systems go several steps beyond exchange control, yet depend for their effectiveness on at least limited exchange control. By contrast, multiple-exchange-rate systems often include segments of the foreign exchange market where supply and demand rule and exchange rates float. *Segment* is the key word in understanding multiple-exchange-rate systems. They are administratively decreed divisions of the foreign exchange market. In each segment, different exchange rates rule: in some by administrative determination (exchange control), in others by the forces of supply and demand (floating), and in still others by official-reserve buffer-stock operations carried out by the central bank to defend a particular exchange rate (pegging). Policing and penalties for noncompliance are designed to keep everyone in his allotted segment of the foreign exchange market.

A simple example of a multiple-exchange-rate system is a *dual-exchange-rate system*. A typical dual system divides the foreign exchange market in two by requiring certain types of transactions to take place at the "official" exchange rate and other types at the "free" exchange rate. Domestic money is usually overvalued at the official rate, yet balance-of-payments deficits are avoided by rationing the demand for foreign money. Transactions that are forced or permitted to use the official segment of the market are often (1) imports of social necessities, investment goods, and intermediate inputs—they can be obtained more cheaply at the overinflated value of domestic money; (2) exports of items where the country faces few foreign competitors, such as tourism and vacation services (every country is unique)—foreign buyers will have to give up much foreign currency to buy the overpriced domestic currency that the domestic supplier requires. Transactions that are forced or permitted to use the free segment of the market, in which the price of foreign money is high compared to the official rate, and the price of domestic money is consequently low, are often (1) imports of luxury goods and other nonessentials (in the eyes of the bureaucrats); (2) exports of items facing stiff foreign competition, or that need subsidization for other reasons; (3) international financial investment in general.

On occasion, the official and free rates bear the opposite relation to each other. The official rate implies that domestic money is *undervalued* in the official segment of the market, compared to the free exchange rate. Such was the case with the dual-exchange-rate systems of France and Belgium during the early 1970s. Belgium, which has a long history of dual-exchange-rate systems, segments the foreign exchange market into a commodity trade part and a financial investment part. Trade in services is divided between the two. The exchange rate for the former segment of the market is called the commercial rate, and for the latter, the financial rate.

More complex multiple-exchange-rate systems segment the foreign exchange market still further, choosing exchange rates to penalize certain activities and reward others. This is the feature that makes these systems attractive to policymakers in highly centralized or socialized economies. They allow government planners considerable administrative flexibility to carry out overall development strategy, in addition to industry-by-industry planning. Ultimately, however, since these systems rest on exchange control, multiple-exchange-rate practices are subject to the same long-run pressures that gradually debilitate exchange control.

THE GOLD STANDARD

The *gold standard* bears no relation to exchange control or to multiple-exchange-rate systems. When it was in effect, it featured even less government intervention in the foreign exchange market than do current floating-exchange-rate systems. Thus it is something of a paradox that exchange rates under the gold standard remained exceptionally stable for long periods.

The gold standard "implied" the market organization of the foreign exchange market before the twentieth-century advent of discretionary government economic policy, with its simultaneous development of sophisticated systems of central banking. Instead of actively pursuing aggregate economic policy, governments under the gold standard pledged themselves to two simple promises: (1) domestic money would have a fixed, (almost) inalterable gold value—and, to back up this promise, (2) governments would provide gold out of their gold reserves to anyone who wanted to receive it by turning in domestic paper money. In other words, governments stood ready to sell gold to the public for domestic money. Similarly, they stood ready to buy gold from the public with domestic money.

These two promises had profound effects on the foreign exchange market. The first established almost inalterable exchange rates among countries of the developed world. It accomplished this because of the unique characteristics of gold. Gold was a universally accepted store of value, comparatively easy to hold and transport, and comparatively homogeneous in quality (even those differences in fineness that did exist could be cheaply assayed by a professional). Historically, gold was one of the very first commodities for which a world market existed (see Supplement 1A), so that the price of an ounce of fine gold tended to be the same everywhere in the developed world. If it was not, *gold arbitrageurs* (gold traders, completely analogous to the exchange arbitrageurs of Supplement 1A) would buy gold where it was cheap, ship it to where it was expensive, sell it, and make a clean profit. Their purchases would drive up the cheap price; their sales would drive down the expensive price; and prices would tend toward equality again. Under the gold standard, such international trading in gold was not circumscribed by governments, as it tends to be now.

The single worldwide gold market made exchange rates very stable around a *parity*, which was completely analogous to the parity of the adjustable-peg exchange-rate system. Suppose Britain had pledged that the gold value of one pound sterling was 2/25 ounce, and suppose the United States had pledged that the gold value of one dollar was

1/35 ounce. Then the domestic money price of an ounce of gold in each country would have been

£12.5 per ounce in Britain,
$35 per ounce in the United States.

Because only one price of an ounce of gold tended to rule throughout the world, 12.5 British pounds had to have approximately the same value as 35 U.S. dollars, or 1 British pound had to have approximately the same value as 2.80 U.S. dollars (2.80 = 35 ÷ 12.5). In other words, the price of pounds in the foreign exchange market (the exchange rate) had to be close to $2.80 per pound. If it was not and exchange rates differed too much from $2.80 per pound, profits would become available to gold arbitrageurs on trade in gold. Their resulting *arbitrage* operations would restore the exchange rate to the neighborhood of $2.80 per pound.

To see this, consider the incentives that would have been created if, owing to some fluke, the exchange rate in the foreign exchange market had been $2.50 per pound. Gold traders everywhere would jump! They would be able to sell gold to the U.S. government and receive $35 for every ounce that they sold. (British resident gold traders would have to ship it to the United States, of course.) Every $35 could be used to buy £14 in the foreign exchange market ($35 ÷ $2.50/£ = £14). The £14 could then be sold to the British government, which was committed by its promise to provide 1.12 ounces of gold for every £14 that the public turned in (£14 ÷ £12.5/oz = 1.12 oz). Gold traders would end up with 1.12 ounces of gold for every ounce that they originally sold to the U.S. government. (U.S. resident gold traders would have to ship it home, of course.) No gold trader would incur any expense except the cost of brokerage and one-way gold transport, yet would be able to transform 100 ounces of gold into 112 ounces in the short time it took to ship gold from Britain to the United States. Profits could be immense, since the process could be repeated again and again for as long as the price of pounds on the foreign exchange market remained at $2.50.

But the foreign-exchange-market price of pounds could not possibly remain at $2.50. Every ounce of gold sold to the U.S. government for $35 would be reflected in the foreign exchange market by an *additional* demand for £14. And, because of the arbitrage profits facing gold traders, the sum of all these additional demands would be huge. Huge additional demands for pounds would quickly drive the foreign-exchange-market value of the pound above $2.50 because of the absence of any change in supply. The exchange rate would usually rise to a price of pounds somewhat *below* $2.80 per pound—to a price where the profit derived from gold arbitrage, once the transport and brokerage costs were paid, was no greater than the profit derived from any other economic activity. With good reason, this *sub*-$2.80-per-

68   *Chapter 2: Government Intervention*

pound exchange rate was known as the *British gold export point* (price), or the *U.S. gold import point* (price).

For similar reasons, foreign-exchange-market values of the pound that were substantially above its parity, $2.80 per pound, could never last long. Gold traders would be only slightly less excited about the profits to be made when the exchange rate was $3 per pound than they were when it was $2.50 per pound. In this case, however, all the transactions would be reversed. Gold traders would sell gold to the British government (U.S. gold traders would have to ship it to Britain). They would receive £12.5 for every ounce they sold; they would then sell the £12.5 on the foreign exchange market in order to buy dollars, *supplying* pounds to demand dollars; and the $37.50 they would receive ($37.50 = $3/£ × £12.5) would be turned in to the U.S. government for slightly more than 1.07 ounces of gold (1.071 . . . oz = $37.50 ÷ $35/oz). (British gold traders would have to ship it back to Britain.) Gold traders would be able to increase their gold stock by 7 percent for no more than the costs of transport, brokerage, and the time it took to ship the gold! Furthermore, the process could and would be repeated for as long as the exchange rate remained at $3 per pound.

The process of gold arbitrage itself, however, would bring a quick end to the $3 price of pounds. The additional foreign-exchange-market supply of 12.5 pounds for every ounce of gold traded would exert supply pressure on the price of pounds to fall. It would fall to an exchange rate slightly *above* $2.80 per pound, at which gold arbitrage profits equaled those in alternative lines of economic activity. This *super*-$2.80-per-pound exchange rate was known as the *British gold import point* (price), or the *U.S. gold export point* (price).

In contrast to the cases analyzed above, during periods of normalcy, without gold flows, the foreign exchange market under the gold standard appeared as in Figure 2A.1.[1]

Typically, therefore, exchange rates were very stable under the gold standard. They varied only within the range determined by transport and brokerage costs in international gold trade. Yet such stability was *not* achieved through government intervention in the foreign exchange market. Governments maintained a hands-off at-

---

[1] Figure 2A.1 contains a puzzle. The demand-for-pounds curve stops at the British gold-import point. In fact, at dollar prices of pounds above the British gold-import price the demand for pounds should be zero—the demand curve should be coincident with the vertical axis. Why? Similarly, the supply-of-pounds curve stops at the British gold-export point. In fact, at dollar prices of pounds below the British gold-export price the supply of pounds should be zero—the supply curve should be coincident with the vertical axis. Why? A hint for solving this puzzle: the hypothetical supply curve (which assumes no gold arbitrageurs) has a southwest extension that has not been drawn; similarly, the hypothetical demand curve has a northwest extension that has not been drawn.

FIGURE 2A.1. *The Foreign Exchange Market under the Gold Standard*

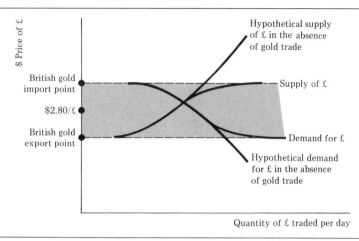

titude toward all foreign-exchange-market transactions. Instead, governments honored their pledge to intervene in the *gold* market in order to stabilize the gold value of their domestic money (that is, to back their money with gold just as the United States did in the early years of the adjustable-peg exchange-rate system). Their gold-market intervention led to *private* profit opportunities for gold arbitrageurs that brought about price stability in a wholly different market, the foreign exchange market.

Private stabilization of exchange rates under the gold standard was profitable just as long as parities never did change. The same is true of central-bank stabilization under the adjustable-peg system (see the text of this chapter). As a matter of fact, whenever there is widespread confidence in parities under the adjustable-peg system, private and profitable stabilization of exchange rates *does* take place within the band. Central banks then have very little need to intervene in the foreign exchange market, and they may not do so for weeks, or even months.

As a matter of historical accuracy, governments under the gold standard were not as passive as the discussion implies. Even before the twentieth century, governments frequently undertook discretionary policy action to keep their money from appreciating or depreciating on the foreign exchange market. But such action almost always centered on interest-rate policy and almost never involved direct intervention in foreign exchange transactions.

Finally, even though governments acted very differently under the gold standard than under the adjustable-peg exchange-rate system, there existed a similar linkage between the foreign exchange market and the domestic money stock. In particular, when the British government bought gold from gold traders, the British money stock in existence tended to rise—just as if Britain had had a balance-of-payments surplus. When the British government lost gold, the British money stock in existence tended to fall—just as if Britain had had a balance-of-payments deficit. However, under the gold standard, governments rarely tried to offset ("sterilize") these monetary contractions and expansions, as they do attempt to do under the adjustable-peg system (see Chapter 5).

Supplement 2B
The International Monetary Fund

The International Monetary Fund is an international financial organization that includes 137 of the roughly 150 countries of the non-Communist world (as well as Romania and Yugoslavia). In the text, it was depicted as a relatively passive supervisor of the adjustable-peg exchange-rate system and of managed floating.

In fact, the IMF's institutional role is more important and more active than the text implies. The IMF controls the creation of a specific type of official reserves, serves as the source of many countries' "borrowed" reserves, provides independent, professional advice to national policymakers on exchange rates and the foreign exchange market, and collects and analyzes large quantities of data relating to national economies and world trade. The IMF's importance may well grow in the future under a reformed international monetary system: a strong body of opinion supports its transformation into a formal "world central bank for central banks."

THE IMF AS A LENDER OF OFFICIAL RESERVES

Indeed, in a limited sense the IMF is already an international central bank. It "lends" official reserves to national central banks in much the same way that national central banks lend reserves to their commercial banks. A country faced with unwanted depreciation and massive losses in official reserves (owing to foreign-exchange-market intervention) is able to "borrow" dollars, pounds, or any of a number of other moneys from the IMF. These dollars and pounds become part of the country's official reserves, and they can be sold on the foreign

exchange market to further support the desired exchange rate.
The sources of these funds that the IMF lends to its members are
IMF *quotas*, which are essentially membership fees that every country pays when it joins the IMF. Quotas vary from country to country
according to formulas, and their size is also subject to negotiation
between the IMF and the country concerned. Large and developed
countries are charged large quotas; small and less-developed countries, small quotas. Until 1978, every country, large or small, was
obliged to pay one-fourth of its quota in gold and three-fourths in its
own domestic money. Since 1978, countries are obligated to pay in
acceptable foreign currencies instead of gold. The result is that the
IMF as an institution is a very large owner of gold—and also of bank
deposits (or other acceptable assets), which are held in the IMF's
name in every country with membership.

IMF-owned dollar deposits, pound deposits, and so on are the
source of loans to central banks who need to borrow official reserves.
The terms *lending* and *borrowing* are, however, technically inaccurate. A country borrows dollars from the IMF by *purchasing* them
with its own domestic money. The IMF adds the domestic money
temporarily to its quota holdings. Then the loan is repaid in the future
(with interest and servicing fees) when the country *repurchases* its
own domestic money (with dollars or other acceptable currency) from
the IMF.

A country often finds these purchase/repurchase arrangements
valuable, because they allow it to transform a limited amount of its
own money into official reserves when necessary. A country can purchase official reserves worth one-fourth of its quota virtually automatically, since those purchases are backed in a sense by that country's
transfer of gold to the IMF. Such purchases are referred to as purchases within the *gold tranche (reserve tranche)*. Purchases of official reserves within the *first, second, third,* and *fourth credit
tranches*—purchases that exceed one-fourth, one-half, three-fourths,
or all of the quota, respectively—are subject to increasing degrees of
IMF scrutiny and may sometimes be turned down. The IMF insists on
making its loans *conditional* (the principle of *conditionality*) on
countries' planning and carrying out a satisfactory program of policy
changes designed to eliminate a deficit in a way that does least harm
to their trading partners. Because permission to make such credit-
tranche purchases is conditional, most countries count only one-
fourth of their quota as official reserves per se. The rest is often
referred to as *reserve credit*.

Credit-tranche loans (purchases) from the IMF are frequently
approved but are carried out in installments sometime after the approval. (Occasionally loans are approved yet never carried out.) Such
approvals with installment provision of the funds are known as
stand-by arrangements. Stand-by arrangements are widely pub-

licized and are usually viewed as an IMF vote of confidence in the present exchange rate and policies of the government concerned. Thus they often succeed in reducing misinformed speculative pressure on a country's money. And they often make commercial banks more willing to grant loans to national governments for purposes of rebuilding official reserves—a practice discussed at greater length in Chapter 7.

The IMF also makes special loans. The *Compensatory Financing Facility* and the *Buffer Stock Facility* are both special loan arrangements available to countries that produce primary products (minerals, raw materials, and some foodstuffs). Temporary revenue losses caused by the marked variability of primary-product prices can be offset by IMF loans under these facilities. The temporary *Oil Facility* of the mid 1970s provided special loans of a similar nature to countries whose balances of payments had been most severely affected by the drastic change in the world price of oil. The *Extended Facility* provides longer-term loans to countries whose balance-of-payments problems are due to social and structural characteristics that cannot be altered quickly.

Besides being the basis for loans, IMF quotas have two other functions. First, they determine voting power in IMF deliberations. Beyond a small number of votes that every member receives, votes are literally bought with larger quotas. Thus, while large developed countries pay the highest membership fees to join the IMF, they are compensated by receiving the greatest voting power. (And they are also able to borrow the most.) Voting power in the IMF as of mid-1978 is recorded in Table 2B.1. It is notable that developed countries hold almost two-thirds of the votes, and that the United States and the European Community each hold more than 20 percent. Because some IMF decisions require 70 percent of the votes, and some require 85 percent, the United States and the European Community both have some degree of veto power.

The last important function of IMF quotas is to determine the distribution of the one type of official reserves that the IMF creates— *Special Drawing Rights*, or *SDRs*. These are discussed below. IMF members receive rights to SDRs in proportion to their quotas. Thus developed countries receive the bulk of SDRs, and this has caused considerable ongoing discontent on the part of less-developed countries.

The entire size and structure of IMF quotas must be reviewed by the IMF at least every five years. Typically these quota reviews have increased quotas by differential amounts for all members. In 1978 the oil-producer nations' quotas (and their voting power) were increased dramatically from roughly 5 percent of total quotas to 9 percent, and the IMF committed itself not to reduce the voting power of the remaining less-developed countries.

TABLE 2B.1. *Voting Power within the IMF,
June 30, 1978*

Country or Group	Percentage of total IMF votes
United States	20.0
European Community[a]	25.6
Japan	4.0
Canada	3.3
Other developed countries[b]	5.8
OPEC oil-producing countries[c]	8.8
All other countries	32.5

[a] Belgium, Britain, Denmark, France, Germany, Ireland, Italy, Luxembourg, Netherlands.
[b] Australia, Austria, Finland, Iceland, New Zealand, Norway, Sweden.
[c] OPEC stands for Organization of Petroleum Exporting Countries.
Source: International Monetary Fund, *Annual Report 1978*, pp. 142–144.

THE IMF AS A CREATOR OF OFFICIAL RESERVES: SDRs AND GOLD

The IMF is also an international central bank insofar as it oversees the creation and distribution of a unique official-reserve asset, Special Drawing Rights (SDRs). Putting it simply, SDRs are no more than entries in a set of accounts that the IMF created in the early 1970s on behalf of its members. They are thus quite literally official reserves created out of thin air. Central banks that own SDR accounts (very much like official-reserve checking accounts) did not purchase them in any way and deposited nothing with the IMF to acquire their ownership. But they did agree among themselves that each central bank would surrender its own or other moneys to a second central bank that wanted to transfer SDRs to the first. In this case, the IMF would add the transferred SDRs to the first central bank's account, and withdraw them from the second's—all by a few strokes of the pen.

That agreement alone gave the SDR value as official reserves. And it reveals why they are sometimes referred to as *fiat* official reserves—official reserves by decree, or agreement, of central banks. Central banks also decreed at first that SDRs would be exchangeable for money at the same rate as 1/35 ounce of gold. Thus (35) SDRs would be "as good as (an ounce of) gold"—not because gold backed them in any way, but because central banks agreed to take them as if they were gold. As one economist commented at the time, official reserves, like money, derive their value from being accepted by a large group of *takers*, not backers. After all, what has ever backed the value of gold itself? For good reason, SDRs were initially called *paper gold*.

Central-bank abuse of such a mechanism is not impossible. Thus safeguards were built into the system from the beginning. Countries that transfer SDRs to others are charged interest on their transfers. Countries that are willing to add SDRs to their accounts earn interest on their additions (the same interest the users paid). No country can use more than 85 (initially 70) percent of its SDR account, except temporarily. And no country is obligated to accept additions to its SDR account after it reaches triple its original size. In addition, 85 percent of the IMF's votes were required to create the initial SDR deposits, and 85 percent will be required as new SDRs are created in the future. Any member country can refuse to participate, and it will receive no SDRs (eight countries did not initially; only one still refuses).

A total of $9.3 billion of SDR accounts were created in 1970, 1971, and 1972, and the IMF agreed to create a slightly greater amount in 1979, 1980, and 1981. Even though SDRs have been dwarfed by massive additions of dollars to official reserves during the 1970s, they have served well the purposes for which they were created. They have been freely transferred and accepted among central banks. They have become a unit in which the IMF as well as some private agents value transactions and set prices (international air fares are set in SDRs, although they may be quoted in money equivalents). Some countries peg their money to the SDR. And the IMF is committed to making them the foundation asset of a new international monetary system.

Their original purpose was to serve as an internationally controlled substitute for gold, as described in the text. But gold's role in the international monetary system has been undercut by the U.S. declaration of dollar-gold inconvertibility and by an IMF commitment to bring about its complete demise. Besides eliminating gold's use in any IMF transaction (Chapter 7), and reducing the IMF's own stock of gold (see below), IMF members agreed to sever the relation between the SDR and gold in mid-1974. Since then the IMF has decreed the value of the SDR to be equal to a basket of fixed units of sixteen of the world's leading moneys. The SDR is now a *currency composite*; it is no longer paper gold.

There was no strong sentiment during the mid-1970s for additional creation of SDRs. But strong support among less-developed countries (LDCs) grew for the so-called *link proposal*: if and when new SDRs were created, they should be distributed disproportionately in favor of LDCs, not according to IMF quotas. The proposal would "link" solutions to the twin problems of insufficient international control over official-reserve creation and insufficient prosperity in LDCs to allow them to hold adequate official reserves. Proponents argued that the link proposal provided a costless way of providing financial aid to developing countries (since SDRs are created from nothing) without political strings. Opponents feared that the link proposal would undermine confidence in the SDR—and confidence is, of course, all its value rests on. It is not clear, however, exactly how confidence would be undermined. If LDCs used their SDRs, developed countries would end up holding them just as if they had initially received them new and directly from the IMF. If LDCs didn't use their SDRs, and continued to hold them, then their responsible action would seem to *add* confidence to the SDR. Other fears about global inflationary impacts from "spending" of SDRs seem comparably hard to defend—global price pressure from any tendency for LDCs to use SDRs more than developed countries do could be offset by creating fewer of them.

The second creation of SDRs in 1979, 1980, and 1981 was not linked to development assistance any more than the first. The IMF has, however, already established the philosophical precedent for the link proposal in its gold arrangements of the late 1970s. The IMF returned (*restituted*) one-sixth of its gold stock directly to member countries and auctioned off another one-sixth on the world gold market for purposes of providing official-reserve support only to less-developed countries. While the gold *restitution* was carried out proportional to IMF quotas, the open-market gold sales created official reserves and official-reserve loans for LDCs only. Some of the currency proceeds from these gold sales were added directly to the official reserves of the poorest LDCs. Most were channeled into the IMF *Trust Fund,* which provides supplementary official-reserve loans on favorable (concessional) terms to a long list of eligible LDCs.

LDC advocacy of the link proposal, demands for a greater voice in IMF decision-making, and recommendations for differentially greater access to IMF loans are all important aspects of the proposed *New International Economic Order,* discussed in Chapter 14.

Supplement 2C
The Balance-of-Payments Accounts and Alternative Measures of "Balance"

A country's *balance-of-payments accounts* are a set of tables that attempt to record the size of transactions between residents of that country and the rest of the world during a particular time. The accounts themselves are a collection of numbers. From them emerge several measures of the *balance of payments,* each of which is a single summary number.

THE BALANCE-OF-PAYMENTS ACCOUNTS

The balance-of-payments accounts are the quantitative equivalent to Chapter 1's stylized schema of international exchange, Schema 1.3. The accounts are made up of two parts that mirror the schema, the *current account* and the *capital account*, as well as a third part, the *official-reserves account*.

The *current account* attempts to record private[1] residents' exports and imports of

C: commodities, and
S: services

at various levels of detail.

The *capital account* attempts to record private residents' exports and imports of

A: assets

at various levels of detail. (On the terminology of the capital account, see Supplement 1B.)

The information that the balance-of-payments accounts provide illustrates their usefulness and shows why all countries compile them. The commodity-trade part of the U.S. accounts, for example, records items of such importance to U.S. consumers as exports of foodstuffs and imports of petroleum. The service-trade part of the U.S. accounts records items such as the value of international tourism trade (important information for U.S. airlines) and the value of earnings on U.S. financial investment in foreign countries (important information for the U.S. multinational corporations discussed in Chapter 13).[2] The asset-trade part of the accounts records items such as loans from U.S. banks to foreign residents and foreign purchases of U.S. corporate stock from U.S. stockholders. The former is viewed as the import of an asset into the United States—a foreign IOU, to be exact. The latter is viewed as the export of the ownership of a U.S. asset. Asset trade also includes many operations of multinational corporations, encompass-

---

[1] *Private* transactions in the balance-of-payments accounts include almost all transactions except those undertaken by central banks. More pointedly, they include many government exports and imports that are undertaken by agencies other than the central bank, such as foreign aid and purchases of foreign weapons by the military.

[2] Earnings on U.S. financial investment in foreign countries are viewed by the balance-of-payments accountant as a good measure of the current services being provided by U.S. "capital"—U.S. financial resources that had been loaned to foreign residents in the past. The earnings hence are treated as a current *services* export from the United States to foreign countries. (When the capital itself moved in the past, it was treated as a *capital* export. See the discussion of terminology in Supplement 1B for clarification.)

ing international mergers, takeovers, liquidations, expropriations, and the more mundane expansion and contraction of foreign affiliates.

The third part of the balance-of-payments accounts, the *official-reserves account*, records purchases and sales of official reserves by a country's central bank. For the United States—and less prominently for Britain, France, and Germany, all of whose money forms a part of the official reserves of other countries (see Chapter 2, footnote 4)—this account also records purchases and sales of dollars, pounds, francs, and marks by the central banks of other countries.

The balance-of-payments accounts are kept according to a practice known as *double-entry bookkeeping*. This practice recognizes that every economic transaction has two sides. For example, many demands for goods in a monetary economy are simultaneously supplies of money (which is itself a good). Other demands for goods, when the purchase is financed by credit, are simultaneously supplies of IOUs. Many supplies of goods are simultaneously demands for money, and so on.

Since the supplies of and demands for money that are counterparts to international demand (importing) and international supply (exporting) determine foreign exchange rates and intervention, it makes sense to keep track of both sides of every transaction. As a requirement of double-entry bookkeeping, when Boeing exports an aircraft to British Airways, the U.S. balance-of-payments accountant records not only the commodity export but also an asset import: Boeing imports the ownership of pounds from British Airways, as represented by its receipt of British Airways' pound check.

Because double-entry bookkeeping can be confusing when first encountered, it is helpful to outline a set of balance-of-payments accounts in personal terms before discussing the U.S. accounts. Your economic life as an individual is one of continual interaction with "foreign" institutions, made up of all other individuals, corporations, and governments. As such, a set of balance-of-payments accounts can be defined for you personally that are wholly analogous to those defined for a country. The absence of any equivalent to foreign exchange transactions is irrelevant. (Balance-of-payments accounts exist between two countries even in those rare cases where they use the same money.)

Suppose that your week included the following events:

(a) Work, for which you received your weekly paycheck of $200 from your employer.
(b) The sale of a case of homemade wine to your brother for $15, on credit—he said he would pay you next week.
(c) The receipt of $5 as interest from your savings account.
(d) The payment of your $50 weekly rent.
(e) The payment of your $40 weekly grocery bill.

TABLE 2C.1. *Your Personal Balance-of-Payments Accounts in Detail*

		Dollar value of your personal exports		*Dollar value of your personal imports*	
Current account	Commodities	Wine	15(b)	Groceries	40(e)
	Services	Labor services	200(a)	Rental services	50(d)
		Services of your "capital"	5(c)		
Capital account	Assets	Money[a]	50(d)	Money[a]	200(a)
		Money[a]	40(e)	Money[a]	5(c)
		Money[a]	65(f)	Money[a]	300(g)
		Savings account[b]	300(g)	Brother's IOU	15(b)
				GM stock	65(f)

[a] You "export money" from either your checking account or your pocket when you pay for a purchase. You "import money" into either your checking account or your pocket when someone pays you.

[b] You export the ownership of your savings account because you give it up. You give it up to obtain money. As the balance-of-payments accountant would see it, you sell your savings account to buy money.

(f) The purchase of one share of General Motors stock for $65.

(g) The withdrawal of $300 from your savings account.

Your personal balance-of-payments accounts for the week could be represented as in Table 2C.1. A moment's inspection reveals that they reflect double-entry bookkeeping.

When transactions of the same type are consolidated, your accounts can be made to look less cluttered. Furthermore, it is fruitful to suggest that your savings account is really your "personal official reserves," much like the official reserves held by a country. In withdrawing $300, you have "drawn down" your official reserves. And, like countries that do this, you can be said to have experienced a $300 balance-of-payments deficit last week. Consolidating your accounts and pursuing this analogy leads to the revised set of personal accounts in Table 2C.2.

With these examples in mind, stylized U.S. balance-of-payments accounts can be constructed for a hypothetical week that includes the following events:

(a) International Business Machines licenses a foreign computer company to use a patented process and is paid $200 million in return.

(b) Grain exporters ship $15 million worth of wheat to the Soviet Union, which will pay for the wheat in three months' time.

TABLE 2C.2. *Your Personal Balance-of-Payments Accounts Consolidated*

		Dollar value of your personal exports		Dollar value of your personal imports	
Current account	Commodities	Wine	15	Groceries	40
	Services	Labor services	200	Rental services	50
		Services of your "capital"	5		
Capital account	Assets	Money	155	Money	505
				Brother's IOU	15
				GM stock	65
Official reserves account		Savings account[a]	300		

[a] Had you gained official reserves, rather than losing them, such a gain would have been recorded in the right-hand column as an import.

(c) Texaco remits $5 million to its American shareholders as earnings on its foreign business.

(d) The U.S. government pays the Philippine government $50 million for the use of naval and air-force bases.

(e) Sony's U.S. distributor picks up $40 million worth of television sets at the San Francisco customs house and simultaneously sends Sony of Japan a $40 million check.

(f) First National City Bank acquires controlling interest in a small foreign bureau of exchange for $65 million, paid immediately to the present foreign owners.

(g) The U.S. Treasury auctions off $750 million worth of the U.S. gold stock, of which $300 million worth is purchased by foreign buyers.

The U.S. balance-of-payments accounts for this week are displayed in Table 2C.3. Three differences from Table 2C.2 are notable: (1) the language is different, reflecting the language actually used in the U.S. balance-of-payments accounts; (2) exports are entered with positive signs, or as *credits* in the language of the accountant, whereas imports are entered with negative signs, or as *debits*; (3) the capital account is divided into trade in short-term assets and trade in long-term assets.[3] Historically, this division has been made to segregate

[3] Long-term assets are technically defined as assets that have indefinite lives, such as property and common stocks, plus assets that come due (mature) in more than one year, such as most bonds and many time deposits. Short-term assets are technically defined as assets that can be redeemed on demand, such as the demand-deposit component of money, plus assets that come due (mature) in less than one year.

TABLE 2C.3. *Hypothetical U.S. Balance-of-Payments Accounts for a Week*

		Value ($ millions) of U.S. exports (credits, +)		Value ($ millions) of U.S. imports (debits, −)	
Current account	Commodities	Merchandise	15	Merchandise	−40
	Services	Fees and royalties	200	Direct defense	−50
		Income on U.S. direct investments abroad	5	expenditures	
Capital account	Long-term assets			U.S. direct investments abroad	−65
	Short-term assets	Change in claims reported by U.S. banks	155	Change in claims reported by U.S. banks	−505
				Change in claims reported by U.S. nonbanking concerns	−15
Official reserves account		Gold	300		

asset trade that seemed most likely to be speculative (see Chapter 1 and Supplement 1A) from all other asset trade.

ALTERNATIVE MEASURES OF "BALANCE"

Many economists believe that the balance-of-payments accounts should attempt no more than Table 2C.3. In practice, however, every country tries to provide interpretation and analysis, not only by dividing the accounts into subaccounts, as illustrated, but also by the process of *striking a balance* within the accounts, or drawing *a line* through the accounts. This process is a natural extension of organizing the accounts into subaccounts. *Striking a balance* is defined as adding up exports and imports within some selected set of subaccounts and then subtracting the latter from the former. The *line* is the boundary between the selected accounts and omitted accounts: accounts *above the line* are included; those *below the line* are excluded.

For example, one summary number often used worldwide is "the" balance of payments discussed in the text of this chapter, described more precisely as the balance of payments on *official settlements basis* or *official reserve transactions basis*. It is calculated by striking a balance for the current and capital accounts taken together, where the line separates them from the official reserves account. Although the U.S. government has stopped calculating this balance in its periodic balance-of-payments reports (Chapter 2, footnote 18), it is nevertheless calculated by others. The U.S. balance of payments for the week in Table 2C.3 is

in *deficit* by $300 million,

that is, it was −$300 million.

The purpose of this balance is to approximate foreign-exchange-market intervention by central banks. That is, the recorded balance of payments is a proxy for excessive private supply or demand in the foreign exchange market at current exchange rates. But it will be recalled from the text that under managed floating, excessive supply and demand were hard to define, and the foreign-exchange-market intervention of central banks was more voluntary than it had been when parities were being formally defended. Furthermore, the U.S. balance of payments never corresponded very closely, if at all, to *U.S.* government action in the foreign exchange market. Under managed floating, therefore, the interpretative and analytical value of this measure of balance-of-payments surpluses and deficits has been diminished. Yet it still gives a good impression of what countries have decided to do with official reserve stocks during the period in question.

Another balance that is frequently struck (although again, not by the U.S.) is the balance of payments on current account and long-term capital, colloquially known as the *basic balance*. In this case the line is drawn so that trade in short-term assets joins trade in official reserves below the line. The U.S. basic balance for the hypothetical example of Table 2C.3 is

in *surplus* by $65 million,

that is, it was +$65 million,

since the value of exports above the line ($220 million) exceeds the value of imports above the line ($155 million) by exactly that amount.

The purpose of the basic balance is to isolate transactions that are thought to be normal, fundamental, stable, and nonspeculative. This balance might be considered to be a proxy for the difference between the *normal* supply and *normal* demand in Figure 1.3 of Chapter 1. The basic balance would then approximate excessive *normal* supply or demand, while the balance of payments would approximate excessive *total* supply or demand. In principle, the basic balance washes out short-term speculative trade in assets that supposedly masks more fundamental factors in the balance of payments on official settlements basis. In practice, the basic balance was always a dubious proxy for this fundamental balance. Much speculation actually is accomplished through trade in commodities, services, and long-term assets (recall, for example, the discussion on pp. 15–17 of how Boeing speculated). The problems of interpreting this summary measure of balance are even more pronounced under managed floating.

The *balance on current account* is struck by drawing the line just below the current account. In Table 2C.3 the United States has a

current-account *surplus* of $130 million

for the week illustrated.

The current-account balance is useful because it comes closer than the others to measuring the net contribution of exports and imports to gross national product.[4] Gross national product includes the value of commodity-service exports, because we obviously do produce what we ship abroad. Hence exports of *current* commodities and services (X) must be added to consumption (C), investment (I), and government spending (G) to arrive at gross national product. Furthermore, since consumption, investment, and government spending, as defined in the national-income-and-product accounts, all *include* current imports of commodities and services[5]—which we obviously did not produce—they must be subtracted from $C + I + G + X$ to arrive at gross national product.

Finally, the *balance of trade,* or *merchandise trade balance* (or simply *trade balance*), is equal to the difference between commodity exports and commodity imports. In Table 2C.3 U.S. commodity trade is

in *deficit* by $25 million.

The trade balance is more prominent than it deserves from an economic perspective. On the one hand, it is more closely linked than the current-account balance to the net effect of international trade on domestic employment: much trade in services does not generate employment (for example, income on foreign investments). On the other hand, it is not clear that unemployment is ever *caused* by the existence of a trade deficit, or that it gets any worse if deficits of the same size persist year after year (see Chapter 5). Nor is it clear that unemployment can best be remedied by restrictive domestic policies toward imports or by export stimulation (we discuss this in Chapter 9). Nor is

---

[4] The U.S. balance-of-payments accounts include one balance that is closer (although it is not exactly "net exports of goods and services" in the gross national product). It is the *balance on goods and services,* and it differs from the current-account balance chiefly by excluding certain charitable services, such as foreign aid and private contributions to international welfare agencies, relegating them to below the line.

[5] In the national-income-and-product accounts, *consumption* includes spending by consumers on imported commodities and services; *investment* includes spending by corporations on imported equipment and on imports of commodities to be added to corporate inventories; and *government spending* includes a limited number of commodities and services that government purchasing agents themselves buy from foreign producers.

it clear that countries should necessarily seek "improved international competitive positions," which is the euphemism often substituted for larger trade surpluses.

The preceding discussion suggests that nearly all single-number summary measures derived from a country's balance-of-payments accounts are flawed. Some are inadequate proxies for the concept they attempt to measure. Others, such as the trade balance, are flawed even in their purpose. In light of the frequency with which economic policies are attacked or defended on the grounds of what they do to this or that international balance, this conclusion is worth reinforcing in future chapters.

Chapter 3

Why Nations Care About Exchange Rates and the Balance of Payments

One of the most confusing features of international finance, besides its terminology, is the infrequency with which "why" questions are answered. It is usually taken to be self-evident that balance-of-payments deficits are problems, that large stocks of official reserves are good, and that depreciation of one's money on the foreign exchange market is humiliating. Whether all this really *is* self-evident is doubtful. When attempts are made to explain why, they often beg the question. For example:

Q: Why are balance-of-payments deficits a problem?

A: Because they cause a country to lose official reserves.

Q: All right, but I don't feel fully informed. Why are official-reserve losses a problem?

A: Because official reserves are socially useful.

Q: In what ways?

A: Well, for one thing, they allow governments to intervene in the foreign exchange market.

Q: Why is that so important?

A: Because foreign-exchange-market intervention usually stabilizes exchange rates.

Q: That sounds desirable. But on second thought, an exchange rate is just a particular kind of price, right? And we don't expect the government to stabilize every price in the economic system, do we?

A: But the exchange rate is a much more important price than most others.

Q: How so? And even if you could show me, would you have made your case for *stabilizing* important prices? Maybe the more important a price is, the more benefits come from letting it vary. Economists regularly preach the merits of allowing supply and demand to rule, even though that leads to price variation. Why make exceptions for important markets like the foreign exchange market?

This chapter will answer such questions less familiarly, but more fundamentally, than the hypothetical respondent does. Because the most probing questions are those toward the end of the string, we begin with them.

Why Exchange Rates Matter— How Much—And to Whom

Economists differ deeply on many of the issues raised in this chapter, yet almost all agree that exchange rates are important prices, not only for international economic conditions but even on the domestic economic scene. Ultimately, it is the pervasive *domestic* consequences of depreciation and appreciation of a country's money in the foreign exchange market that make governments care about their exchange rates.

Depreciation and appreciation have domestic effects that are more far-reaching and dramatic than those of almost any other single price change, even in the price of such crucial commodities as oil or such crucial assets as government bonds. This holds even for relatively "closed" economies like the United States, which are not as dependent on international goods markets as are "open" economies like Britain, Canada, and Japan. That is, even in the United States, changes in the foreign-money value of the dollar have fundamental domestic consequences, although they are sometimes subtle and indirect.

To demonstrate the local, day-to-day importance of exchange-rate change, it is useful to catalog some domestic effects of, say, a depreciation of the U.S. dollar in the foreign exchange market. A somewhat overlapping list of categories includes the effects of exchange-rate change on (1) production, prices, and profits; (2) the cost of living; (3) wages, incomes, and employment; and (4) wealth and indebtedness. It will become apparent that dollar depreciation creates many domestic gainers and many domestic losers and that the gains and losses can be large. It will also become apparent that most of the domestic effects of exchange-rate change are symmetric. Americans who gain from dollar depreciation lose from dollar appreciation; those who lose from depreciation gain from appreciation.

PRODUCTION, PRICES, AND PROFITS

When the price of the dollar declines in the foreign exchange market, U.S. producers of *tradeable* commodities and services unambiguously gain. Tradeables are made up of two types: (1) exportables—

commodities and services for which U.S. producers serve foreign as well as U.S. customers; and (2) importables, or import substitutes— commodities and services for which U.S. producers face competition from imported varieties of the same good. In practice, the distinction between exportables and importables is not always clear. Boeing not only exports a large proportion of its aircraft production to foreign buyers but also faces some import competition from British short-range commercial jetliners and from French airbuses.

From any perspective, however, Boeing gains from dollar depreciation because it produces tradeables. From an exportable perspective, when dollars fall in value relative to British pounds, the pound check that British Airways sends to Boeing as payment for 747s can be sold by Boeing on the foreign exchange market for *more* dollars than previously. Dollar depreciation means that pounds become more valuable in terms of dollars. Thus the dollar value of Boeing revenues and profits should rise when the dollar depreciates, even if Boeing's aircraft sales remain constant.

But the British are no fools. Why should they offer the same number of pounds to Boeing for a 747 after the dollar value of a pound has risen? That would be equivalent to passing up some potential savings for themselves. British Airways could probably still obtain the same number of 747s from Boeing for fewer pounds, because they know that Boeing will find each pound more valuable in terms of the dollars it can purchase on the foreign exchange market. Thus a bargain will be struck. British Airways will bid less pounds per 747 than it used to, but Boeing's profits will still rise because those pounds have become more valuable.

The story will not likely end there. When British Airways is able to buy each 747 for fewer pounds, it may be tempted to buy more 747s than it had planned to before dollar depreciation. Because aircraft cost less, British Airways may raise its desired fleet size. Or British Airways may cancel orders for French airbuses (whose pound prices are unchanged) to buy cheaper 747s. Through such inducements, Boeing's aircraft sales should rise slightly as a result of dollar depreciation. That, too, increases Boeing's profits.

Finally, regardless of what happens to sales, Boeing will make greater dollar profits on every aircraft sold to a foreign buyer than it does on domestic sales.[1] This will tempt Boeing to do either (or both) of two things. It will not pass up the opportunity to make an export sale at the expense of a U.S. sale, and it will feel justified in raising the

[1] In a limiting extreme case this is not true. If Boeing had no significant market power or bargaining power compared to British Airways, British Airways and competition might force it to accept the same dollar price as before the dollar depreciated. Then profits per aircraft would be unaffected. Boeing's profit per aircraft exported might also differ to begin with from its profit per aircraft sold to U.S. buyers. Dollar depreciation would cause any positive difference to become larger and any negative difference to become smaller.

dollar price of aircraft sold to *U.S.* customers, since it is now earning more dollars on every export sale. Both indirectly and directly, therefore, dollar depreciation leads to higher prices for domestic U.S. purchasers of Boeing aircraft.

This last point is worth stressing because it is frequently misunderstood. To think that exchange rates affect only the export part of Boeing's business is comforting but incorrect. Dollar depreciation tends to raise domestic U.S. aircraft prices, too, and to cut back on domestic aircraft sales (or at least to increase the time it takes Boeing to produce and deliver an aircraft ordered by a domestic airline). U.S. airlines may not link Boeing's higher prices and larger order backlogs to dollar depreciation, but they should. An example closer to home relates to food prices in the United States in the early 1970s. A significant part of food-price inflation in the U.S. was due to dollar depreciation. Higher *domestic* food prices cannot be divorced from the greater dollar rewards that dollar depreciation generated for U.S. food producers in their export business.

To return to Boeing, the effects of dollar depreciation will be qualitatively the same even if aircraft exports are paid for in the alternative way outlined in Chapter 1—even if British Airways is forced to pay Boeing in dollars. Boeing's profits, production, and prices will all be pressed higher.[2]

On the import-substitute side, Boeing gains from dollar depreciation in similar ways and for similar reasons. When dollars fall in value relative to pounds, potential U.S. importers of British aircraft that compete with Boeing's will think twice. They may be faced with giving up more dollars to buy the same number of pounds on the foreign exchange market in order to pay for their imports. And if not, say because they pay British aircraft producers in dollars, then they will certainly be forced to give them more dollars directly—British producers would be foolish to accept the same number of cheapened dollars per aircraft as they used to. After thinking twice, some potential U.S. importers will be discouraged and will turn to Boeing. When they do, Boeing's sales will rise, as will profits. So will aircraft prices, if Boeing uses the increased U.S. demand as a justification for charging more per aircraft.

As this example shows, dollar depreciation is virtually certain to

---

[2] Suppose that, as a matter of corporate policy, Boeing refused to accept pound checks from British Airways in payment and required that British Airways obtain dollars in the foreign exchange market to finance its aircraft purchases from Boeing. British Airways would then stand to gain handsomely from dollar depreciation, because it could buy the needed dollars more cheaply in terms of pounds. But Boeing would be foolish to pass up the opportunity to extract some share of British Airways' windfall. It could extract a share handily by raising the dollar price of every aircraft sold to British Airways. Boeing's profits would rise on its export sales; British Airways would still be left with some savings and might be tempted to purchase more Boeing aircraft; and Boeing would have a justification for raising prices on sales of aircraft to U.S. buyers. All these consequences parallel those in the text.

raise the sales and profits of U.S. producers of import substitutes and possibly their prices as well.[3] To take another example, American gin producers would gain as dollar depreciation raised the price of imported Beefeater's. So would American rum producers if the higher average price of gin (including any justified by U.S. gin producers because of booming business) induced people to switch from traditional martinis to those made with rum. The point is that the class of products called *importables* should be as broad as the class of all products that substitute for imports. Producers of close substitutes for imports will gain more in general from dollar depreciation than producers of distant substitutes, but all gain to some extent.

Unlike U.S. producers of tradeables, who gain from dollar depreciation, U.S. producers of *nontradeables* tend to lose. Nontradeables are commodities and services that are produced solely for the domestic market and that face no competition from imports. In practice, of course, almost no commodity or service is a pure nontradeable. Many come close: construction, education, wholesaling and retailing, domestic transportation, government, and much of the household service industry (cleaners, repair shops, and so on).

Nontradeables producers lose from dollar depreciation principally because of its effect on their costs of doing business, not because it has any significant effect on the demand facing them, although an important exception will be mentioned.

Take Delta Airlines, for example—a U.S. airline with largely domestic routes.[4] When the dollar depreciates and when prices of aircraft, gin, and rum rise as a result, Delta's operating and equipment outlays increase. It now costs more to stock the bar on every Delta flight, and it costs Delta more to buy aircraft. Yet Delta's output of air transportation services may be little affected by dollar depreciation—they are largely nontradeable. As a result, Delta's profits will fall. Its input costs have risen in the face of stable demand for its output. The airline may be forced to cut back marginally profitable service, and production will decline. Delta will tend to lose from dollar depreciation, as will all producers whose output is less tradeable than their inputs.[5]

---

[3] Prices could remain the same if the import-substitute industry had substantial excess capacity. They might even fall in such industries if the increased business allowed fixed costs to be spread over a larger volume, or if the industry were subject to gains from large-scale production (increasing returns to scale).

[4] Delta, of course, does sell its services to some foreign residents traveling in the United States and hence could be considered to be producing an exportable. It could also be considered to be producing an import substitute, since it competes with Air Canada and European carriers on several runs in selling its services to Americans. But we will consider it to be producing a nontradeable.

[5] This point is very similar to that raised in the discussion of *effective protection* in footnote 37 to Chapter 14: U.S. producers may lose from U.S. barriers to trade if they raise the cost of inputs more than they shield output from foreign competition.

The important exception occurs when there is substantial excess capacity and unemployment all through the economy. Under these conditions, dollar depreciation will cause much less temptation for tradeables producers such as Boeing to raise price. They need all the business they can get, and they will not be as prone to risk sacrificing volume gains by asking for a higher price. Nontradeables producers such as Delta will then find their input costs raised very little as a result of dollar depreciation. And they may find their business picking up, because increased demands facing tradeables producers set in motion a demand-induced expansion of the entire economy (pp. 166–172). On balance, therefore, it is possible that even U.S. nontradeables producers gain from depreciation of the dollar. The greater the overall slack in the U.S. economy, the more likely this gain is, and the larger it will be when it does occur.

There is no doubt, however, about the depreciation-induced gains to tradeables producers. The gains may change character as general economic health does, but they occur regardless. When the economy is slack, tradeables profits increase primarily because volume does. When the economy is tight, they increase primarily because prices do.

THE COST OF LIVING

The effect of dollar depreciation on the U.S. cost of living is a direct consequence of its effect on prices. Because dollar depreciation causes the price of tradeables to rise, dollar depreciation raises the U.S. cost of living; and the closer the U.S. economy is to full employment and high capacity utilization, the more dramatic is the rise in the U.S. cost of living that depreciation brings about. On the consumption side alone, every American is a loser from dollar depreciation (excepting, of course, those who do not consume tradeables, who are extremely scarce).

The quantitative importance of this conclusion is frequently minimized by those who misunderstand the effects of dollar depreciation on domestic prices. Their incorrect argument goes like this:

> Trade—imports if we talk about consumption—makes up only about 10 percent of U.S. economic activity. (We are a relatively "closed" economy.) Thus even a massive dollar depreciation, say of 20 percent, affects prices in only 10 percent of the economy. At the very most, it could raise the U.S. cost of living by 2 percent (0.20 times 0.10)—a small amount.

What this argument neglects is that dollar depreciation raises prices of tradeable goods generally,[6] not just those tradeables that actually move internationally. The rise in the price of tradeables in turn influences the price of nontradeables such as Delta's airfare, because many tradeables are production inputs. Furthermore, these

---

[6] Keep in mind the exception raised in footnote 3.

tendencies apply as much in the United States as they do in any other country. Even though domestically produced textiles, shoes, drugs, appliances, automobiles, and other consumer products satisfy ten or eleven times more of the U.S. market than imports, their prices do not remain constant when the dollar depreciates. They rise, too, for reasons made clear in the discussion of aircraft and gin. If a domestic import substitute is not quite identical to the import itself (imperfect substitutes), its price will not rise as much as import prices. But it *will* rise. In the extreme, some domestic textiles, shoes, and so on are physically and qualitatively identical to imports of the same commodity. Dollar depreciation will force up all these domestic textile and shoe prices by exactly the same amount as import prices. With enough such "perfect substitutes," the impact of dollar depreciation on the cost of living would be dramatic.

To cast further light on this issue, Table 3.1 compares the United States to other, more open economies. "Openness" and "closedness" are frequently measured by the *average propensity to import* (the proportion of income devoted to import purchases) recorded in the lefthand column. Although by this measure the United States is a very closed economy, it differs little from the other countries in the proportion of its economic activity that is devoted to tradeables. Since this latter measure is crucial in assessing the cost-of-living effects of depreciation, these effects should not be expected to be minimal just because the United States has a lower average propensity to import than other economies. From the table, the impact of a 20 percent depreciation of the dollar on the U.S. cost of living probably lies between 2 percent (0.20×0.10) and 6 percent (0.20×0.31), depending on just how substitutable U.S. import substitutes really are and also on how much U.S. exportable prices rise. Both of these figures are extremes, but the latter is made less improbable by its neglect of any induced rise in nontradeables prices and of any induced *wage-price spirals* from a dollar depreciation.

WAGES, INCOMES, AND EMPLOYMENT

Ascribing gains and losses from dollar depreciation to "producers" and "consumers" does not reveal the individual identity of gainers and losers. Almost every American is simultaneously a producer (often of labor services) and a consumer. Table 3.2 summarizes the likely pattern of immediate gainers and losers, taking into account both the producing and consuming roles of individuals.[7]

[7] The longer-run gainers and losers from dollar depreciation may be somewhat different than Table 3.2 suggests. In the long run, dollar depreciation may force a number of resources of all kinds, including labor, to move from the nontradeables to the tradeables sector. As Chapter 13 suggests, those resources and labor best suited for ("used most intensively in") production of tradeables may be better off than they were before dollar depreciation—even if they originally worked in the nontradeables sector.

TABLE 3.1. *Two Measures of an Economy's* "*Openness*"

Country	Average propensity to import[a]	Share of tradeables in economic activity[b]
United States	0.10	0.31
Japan	0.11	0.44
Germany	0.24	0.46
Canada	0.26	0.28
Britain	0.33	0.31
Belgium	0.53	0.34
Netherlands	0.55	0.34
Uruguay	0.17	0.37
Nigeria	0.18	0.64
Thailand	0.28	0.51

[a] (Imports ÷ Gross Domestic Product). *Source:* International Monetary Fund, *International Financial Statistics*, various issues, October–December 1975. Data are for 1974 for all countries except Japan and Nigeria, which are for 1973.
[b] (Gross Domestic Product generated in tradeables ÷ Gross Domestic Product). *Source:* United Nations, *Monthly Bulletin of Statistics*, various issues, Table 64. Tradeables are defined in the table as agriculture, hunting, forestry, and fishing; mining and quarrying; and manufacturing. Nontradeables are defined in the table as electricity, gas, and water; construction; wholesale and retail trade; restaurants and hotels; transport, storage, and communications; and "others" (finance, insurance, real estate, and business services; community, social, and personal services; producers of government services).

The effects of exchange-rate change depend more on where Americans earn their income than where they spend it, because spending patterns differ little across our society. Thus the immediate U.S. gainers from dollar depreciation tend to be shareholders, management, and labor in tradeables industries. Dollar depreciation raises profits for Boeing and for General Motors, leading to larger dividends for shareholders and bonuses for managers. Labor unions in the aircraft and auto industries should be able successfully to demand higher wages by pointing to higher profits and sales, and the higher sales themselves will lead to an expansion of employment opportunities in these industries, encompassing fewer layoffs and more overtime possibilities.[8]

[8] See pp. 170–172.

TABLE 3.2. *Immediate Individual Gainers and Losers from Dollar Depreciation*

	Americans as consumers: Primary use of income is spending on	
Americans as producers: Primary source of income is earnings from	*Tradeables*	*Nontradeables*
Tradeables	Probably gain[a]	Gain[b]
Nontradeables	Lose[c]	Probably lose[d]

[a] For example, an autoworker who spends little on services (a do-it-yourself expert).
[b] For example, a farmer who spends much of his income buying adjoining farmland and improving the structures on it.
[c] For example, a lawyer who spends sizable amounts on luxury automobiles and jet-setting.
[d] For example, a civil servant who has taken a leave of absence to get a master's degree.

By contrast, shareholders, management, and labor in U.S. non-tradeables industries tend to lose from dollar depreciation: profits tend to shrink and volume tends to fall off. If, however, there is substantial slack in the overall economy, then Table 3.2 will be misleading; almost all Americans will benefit from the depreciation-induced stimulus to the sagging economy. But the relative impacts will remain— Delta workers will still gain less from dollar depreciation than Boeing workers. The usual existence of at least some excess capacity and unemployment in the U.S. economy also suggests that any absolute losses to Delta workers will be smaller than the gains to Boeing workers.

WEALTH AND INDEBTEDNESS

The effects of dollar depreciation are not limited to current U.S. incomes, spending, and costs of living. Wealth and balance-sheet consequences of exchange-rate change are also important, even though they are not as close to the average American's wallet. Banks have been forced into insolvency because of these consequences;[9] some multinational corporations have made tremendous windfall gains because of them.

[9] See footnote 5 to Supplement 1A.

The primary impact of dollar depreciation on U.S. wealth and indebtedness is simple.[10] American individuals and corporations who own assets valued in foreign money experience *capital gains*—increases in the dollar value of these assets. For example, Americans who have Swiss-franc bank accounts are gainers from dollar depreciation, because their Swiss francs are worth more dollars after dollar depreciation than before. Americans who have gone into debt in foreign money experience *capital losses*. For example, American gin wholesalers who have accepted a shipment of Beefeater's on credit, and thus have a pound-denominated debt to Beefeater's, lose from dollar depreciation. The pounds they must buy to pay off their debt cost more dollars after dollar depreciation than before.

SUMMARY

Almost all economists agree that these are the domestic distributional consequences of dollar depreciation in the United States. Almost all agree that the domestic consequences of dollar appreciation are the opposite. A *rise* in the foreign-exchange-market value of the dollar causes U.S. tradeables producers such as Boeing to lose. Profits fall off, sales may decline, and prices may fall—or at least not rise as fast as otherwise. American nontradeables producers such as Delta may gain if dollar appreciation sufficiently lowers their costs of doing business. If not, say because domestic tradeables prices are "sticky downward," then even Delta will lose, too, because dollar appreciation causes a contraction in the level of overall U.S. economic activity. The slump will spill over from tradeables to nontradeables. Dislocation, shutdowns, layoffs, and falling profits will pervade the economy. The immediate domestic effects of appreciation can also be translated into individual terms as in Table 3.2. Boeing shareholders, management, and labor almost surely lose from dollar appreciation. The same groups at Delta usually lose less and often may gain from dollar appreciation. The more overheated (inflationary) the U.S. economy is when appreciation takes place, the more likely these gains are to Delta employees and owners.

Economists differ, however, in their beliefs about the size of domestic gains and losses from exchange-rate change. And even economists who agree that the gains and losses are large often disagree on the implication of that belief for government policy: it does not follow logically that when price shocks generate large gains and losses, those price shocks should be avoided by government price-stabilization policy.

[10] There are a great many secondary effects that are too complicated to cover in this book.

The Case for and against Exchange-Rate Stabilization

Economists who favor floating exchange-rate systems minimize the special nature of exchange rates. They oppose government intervention and stabilization in the foreign exchange market because they oppose it in most markets. Price variation serves a purpose, even in the foreign exchange market, signaling buyers and sellers to alter behavior until the market is "cleared." Exchange-rate variability may create gains and losses, but so does variability in any price. Exchange-rate variability may create more pronounced and pervasive domestic gains and losses than other prices, but that does not by itself create a case for stabilization. Variability means ups and downs. The x percent of a country's population who lose from today's depreciation will gain from future appreciation. Over time, they will not be losers, nor will the remaining $(100 - x)$ percent be gainers.

Proponents of exchange-rate stabilization—including most governments, businessmen, and bankers, in addition to many economists—tend to dismiss these views as logically correct but too simple to describe real-world institutions. Any of a number of descriptive economic regularities establish the case for stabilizing exchange rates in their minds. Among them are the following:

1. Exchange-rate variability causes injury and dislocation more severe and far-reaching than that caused by variability in any other price. Frequently the current losses are so great that losers cannot hold out for the prospect of future gains. Furthermore, responding to exchange-rate change is more costly than responding to any other price change. Appreciation will force people and equipment out of the tradeables sector into temporary unemployment until they can be retooled or retrained and rehired for the nontradeables sector. Then depreciation will force them back again into temporary unemployment and ultimate rehiring for the tradeables sector. All price changes cause such tendencies, with potential social (as well as individual) losses, owing to temporary idleness and constant shifting back and forth.[11] But few price changes create dislocation and injury severe enough to justify government price-stabilization machinery. Exchange-rate changes do.

2. Exchange-rate variability can conceivably cause domestic inflation because the gains and losses from a change in exchange rates are not trivial and are widespread. The reasons pertain partly to economics and partly to social dynamics. Organized labor, for example, tends to bargain on the basis of equity. When exchange-rate changes benefit certain industries and the labor employed there, these industries become the yardstick for all others in wage bargaining. Everyone feels

---

[11] Chapter 10 gives a detailed discussion of social costs of dislocation and adjustment similar to those being mentioned here.

that he or she deserves what the most fortunate unions in the economy receive. But higher wage demands in loser industries cannot be met out of larger profits. They can be satisfied only if prices are raised. Thus depreciation that raises tradeables prices because of demand pressures may also raise nontradeables prices from imitative wage demands.[12] Appreciation can be inflationary for similar reasons: losers emulate the wage demands of gainers. This outcome is less probable only because gains from appreciation are uncertain and tend to be smaller when they do occur. Furthermore, the culprit here is not necessarily labor's rapacity. Similar effects could follow from emulative pricing policies by producers or emulative demands by shareholders for "equitable" dividends.

In order for exchange-rate variability to have this inflationary impact, the domestic government must be a silent partner in ratifying the demands of losers for equity with gainers. The government must avoid combating the inflationary impulse with contractionary monetary policy and other tools. Governments do frequently avoid such combat because anti-inflation policy frustrates the losers' attempts to catch up (not that they do anyway) and reduces the government's popular support. Even authoritarian governments need some popular support, and they tend to some extent to underwrite the inflation.

Because of the importance of the government's response in determining inflationary impacts, this argument for exchange-rate stabilization is sometimes summarized in the words: Floating exchange rates undermine a government's "financial discipline." The coincident occurrence of less stable exchange rates and higher world inflation in the 1970s is consistent with this view, but it is hardly conclusive evidence. As Chapter 6 will show, world inflation is one reason why a country may choose to adopt floating exchange rates. Causal links may therefore run both ways.

3. Exchange-rate variability is an extra dimension of uncertainty facing businesses engaged in international trade and financial investment. The same extra uncertainty indirectly confronts the laborers who work in tradeables industries.[13] Groups engaged in international exchange have to face all the familiar uncertainties faced by everybody—unreliable suppliers, unpredictable business conditions, changing tastes, natural disasters—plus those associated with exchange-rate change, which is clearly capable of altering wages, prices, and profits. If exchange rates were free to vary, therefore, more uncertainty would be associated with international trade and invest-

[12] This view is known as the *Scandinavian model* of the inflationary impact of depreciation because it was first popularized there. Note that depreciation tends to raise nontradeables prices anyway, since the prices of tradeable inputs rise.

[13] Because the forward foreign exchange markets described in Supplement 1A do not exist for every future period in the real world, they can only partially insure against exchange-rate uncertainty.

ment than with other kinds of economic activity, and less international economic activity would be undertaken than if uncertainty were equalized. The implied payoff to exchange-rate stabilization is to reduce this extra uncertainty and to place international commerce on the same footing as strictly domestic commerce. This goal is worthwhile because international exchange is socially beneficial. It should not be discouraged without some good reason.

4. Exchange-rate variability wastes resources. If exchange rates could be stabilized for long periods, all of the following resources could be freed to produce other goods and services: foreign exchange officers of banks and corporations; journalists and civil servants who report on the state of the foreign exchange market; international economists who write textbooks on the topic; and the office space, typewriters, and the like that cooperate with labor to produce these services. These resources could be freed because differences between national moneys would lose significance if the public ever came to have genuine confidence in one enduring set of exchange rates. Then people would cease to care what kind of money they used or received, and the whole purpose of the foreign exchange market would vanish. The difference between dollars and pounds would be identical to the difference between dollars and quarters in the United States. Very few Americans see any monetary difference between four quarters and one dollar, although the physical differences are real enough. As a result, Americans are almost indifferent between keeping accounts and savings in dollars and keeping them in quarters, or between using either for transactions. The same could be true for different national moneys under rigidly fixed exchange rates.

The argument is correct but idyllic. It is correct because the foreign exchange market is really a *barter* market, a market where one good (dollars) is exchanged directly for another good (pounds) and where there is no supermedium of exchange. Barter markets are inefficient—resource-wasting—by comparison with monetary markets. If they could be eliminated by rigidly stable exchange rates, resources would be saved.

Yet the argument is idyllic because rigidly fixed exchange rates severely constrain monetary independence. Governments recognize that the exchange rate can be a policy tool, similar to and frequently as powerful as domestic monetary policy (see Chapter 5). Hence, even as they seek exchange-rate stability, governments shun plans that would limit their monetary independence—including their ability to alter exchange rates on occasion and to make the quarter supply grow faster than the dollar supply when desired. Note that there is no logical inconsistency in these government preferences. Exchange-rate variability is like war. Nations try to avoid it; if it comes, it comes as a necessary evil; yet no nation will voluntarily give up its right to resort to it.

Proponents argue, nonetheless, that this argument for exchange-rate stabilization is valid all along the continuum of exchange-rate variability. They argue that the less stable exchange rates are, the more resources have to be devoted to essentially unproductive foreign-exchange-market activity. To make their case airtight, these moderate proponents recognize that practical exchange-rate stabilization does have its own resource cost—all the labor and resources that central banks devote to their intervention in the foreign exchange market. But they assume that this public-resource cost of exchange-rate stabilization pales in comparison to the private-resource cost of exchange-rate variability.

5. Exchange rates have a politically symbolic role. Appreciation of the dollar on the foreign exchange market is viewed as a signal of U.S. soundness and strength. Depreciation of the dollar is viewed as an American humiliation. While absolutely no economic, or even logical, support can be found for these sociopolitical prejudices, their role in motivating governments to seek stable exchange rates cannot be dismissed. Governments fear the political consequences of international humiliation. Indeed, democratic governments have frequently lost power after major depreciations. Some, however, have lost power after major appreciations. This suggests that the economic impacts outllned earlier may weigh more heavily than the sociopolitical ones.

SUMMARY AND REFLECTIONS

The controversy over whether exchange rates should be more flexible, or less so, rages on and on. Very few combatants lean toward the extremes—cleanly floating or rigidly fixed exchange rates forever. Those who favor intermediate and realistic positions often fail to make clear their definitions of such key terms as stability, variability, and uncertainty. Proponents of managed floating, for example, are generally willing to tolerate variability that is defined as frequent, but small, changes in exchange rates. Proponents of adjustable-peg exchange-rate systems prefer variability that is defined as infrequent, albeit sometimes large, changes in exchange rates. Both sides defend their system as being characterized by greater "stability" and less "uncertainty." It is a difficult issue to resolve. Are large, infrequent changes in a price necessarily better than small, frequent changes? Table 3.3 shows three reasonable and familiar definitions of variability (stability) for which they are not better, and one equally reasonable and familiar definition for which they are.

Another way to make the same observation is to note that exchange-rate variability of some sort is practically inevitable. Thus, arguments that exchange-rate variability causes (1) dislocation, (2) inflation, (3) uncertainty, (4) resource costs, and (5) political problems do *not* suffice to establish the case for exchange-rate stabilization along traditional lines. What must be added is hard empirical evidence that these social costs are smallest when governments inter-

TABLE 3.3. *"Variability" and "Stability" of Exchange Rates under More and Less Flexibility*

End of year	More flexibility (managed floating)	Less flexibility (adjustable peg)
	Hypothetical dollar price of a pound	
1963	2.80	2.80
1964	2.70	2.80
1965	2.60	2.80
1966	2.50	2.80
1967	2.40	2.40

Definition of variability (stability)	Measure of variability (stability)	
Number of changes	4	1
Average annual change	.100	.100
Absolute deviation[a]	.120	.128
Standard deviation[b]	.141	.160

[a] The average absolute difference of an observation from the mean of the five—sometimes used as a measure of statistical variability or risk.

[b] The square root of the variance, or the square root of the sum of squared differences of each observation from the mean of the five divided by five—often used as a statistical measure of variability or risk.

vene in the foreign exchange market directly, control foreign-exchange-market transactions administratively (when necessary), and allow major exchange-rate movements only occasionally.

Such hard empirical evidence exists for certain times and places. As an extreme example, on the day that President John F. Kennedy was shot, actions taken by central banks almost certainly stabilized exchange rates (by any definition) and avoided social costs.[14] Less dramatic examples abound. But it would seem foolish to attempt to establish a universal and timeless case for a particular kind of exchange-rate stabilization. Countries differ in the degree to which exchange-rate variability produces the social costs outlined above and in their tolerance for the same amount of dislocation, inflation, uncer-

[14] A highly readable account of these actions can be found in the *New York Times*, November 16, 1975, Section 3, p. 1, excerpted from Charles A. Coombs, *The Arena of International Finance* (New York: Wiley, 1976).

tainty, and so on. Countries also change over time, as do the economic conditions that control the size of these social costs. It should not be surprising, then, if the most desirable type and amount of exchange-rate stabilization differed across countries and over time. It would seem to be a fool's enterprise to argue the universal and timeless case for any given exchange-rate system.

The Balance of Payments as a National Problem

THE TRADE-OFF BETWEEN THE BALANCE OF PAYMENTS AND EXCHANGE-RATE STABILITY

The inevitable consequences of government action to stabilize exchange rates are balance-of-payments deficits and surpluses. In fact, the previous chapter stressed the one-to-one correspondence between the most familiar measure of a country's balance of payments and its own central bank's intervention in the foreign exchange market. Although the United States is historically a special case, it, too, shares in this correspondence. Attempts by governments to avoid depreciation inevitably generate balance-of-payments deficits; attempts to avoid appreciation inevitably generate surpluses.[15]

Yet balance-of-payments surpluses and deficits can themselves be national problems. Thus countries often find themselves in a quandary. Solving the problem of exchange-rate variability creates the balance-of-payments problem. Efforts to attain a perceived good introduce an otherwise nonexistent bad. A policy trade-off similar to that between unemployment and inflation confronts international economic policymakers: the more stable the exchange-rate system they choose, the more likely are balance-of-payments problems, and the more severe they are when they exist.

In illustrating the problematic nature of the balance of payments, it is useful to start with an unfamiliar question. When are balance-of-payments surpluses a problem? Considering the connotations that the word *surplus* has and the way in which politicians and the media point with pride to surpluses when they occur, it is surprising that the answer is *not* "Never!" On the contrary, balance-of-payments surpluses sometimes are so large that a government chooses to escape from them by weakening its commitment to stable exchange rates and

---

[15] The only important exception to this generalization is for the many countries that practice exchange control (see Supplement 2A). By administratively controlling access to the foreign exchange market, governments can hide the fact that balance-of-payments surpluses or deficits exist. They simply do not show up in the balance-of-payments accounts (see Supplement 2C). It is more than semantics to insist that such surpluses and deficits *do* really exist, but have been suppressed.

allowing its money to appreciate faster on the foreign exchange market. Germany, Japan, the Netherlands, and Switzerland voluntarily did just this during the 1970s because their surpluses were too large.

The first aspect of the balance-of-payments-surplus problem was introduced in Chapter 2: surpluses may be inflationary stimuli in the domestic economy. Of course, inflationary stimuli may sometimes not be problematic, as when the economy is in a general slump. But the potential importance of this link between surpluses and inflation should not be minimized; it will be discussed in detail in Chapter 5.

The second aspect of the balance-of-payments surplus problem is equally fundamental but more subtle. Whether exchange rates are pegged or subject to managed floating, a British balance-of-payments surplus implies[16] that the British central bank is holding down the dollar price of pounds by selling pounds and buying dollars, which are then added to British official reserves. A British balance-of-payments surplus also implies by definition that the "private" part of the British economy—everyone except the British central bank (which, in the parlance of international finance, is the "official" part of the economy)—is selling more commodities, services, and assets to the rest of the world than it is buying from the rest of the world. This may sound desirable, but selling implies giving up real goods, and buying implies getting real goods. A British balance-of-payments surplus therefore implies that most of Britain is giving up more than it is getting, producing more real goods for export than it consumes through imports. Surpluses no longer sound so desirable. From the perspective of private Britain alone, they represent outright gifts of real goods to foreigners.

The private perspective, however, is too narrow. To assess the true desirability of the British surplus, we need to bring the British central bank into the picture. The central bank is gaining official reserves, which belong in a real sense to the entire British population.[17] Thus a balance-of-payments surplus is not an outright gift to foreigners; it, too, is an international exchange—of real goods for additional official reserves. A British surplus measures exactly the value of the commodities, services, or assets that Britain gives up in order to gain ownership of additional dollars, gold, or other official-reserve assets.

Of what usefulness are extra official reserves to British society? Why should Britain choose to give up goods that yield clear material

---

[16] See Chapter 2 for a review of the details that follow. Britain is chosen as an example to preserve continuity. In reality, however, Britain's balance-of-payments problems do differ slightly from those of other countries because small amounts of pounds are held as official reserves by countries with long-standing ties to Britian. However, the British balance-of-payments problem still is more similar to those of other countries than to that of the United States. The dramatic impact of the dollar's official-reserve role on the U.S. balance-of-payments problem is discussed in the next section.

[17] The exchange of British pounds that corresponds to these private and official transactions simply mirrors them; it can be ignored.

benefits for more dollars, gold, and the like, whose benefits appear to be many steps removed from everyday life? These questions are crucial because if no satisfactory answers could be given, British balance-of-payments surpluses would always be a problem for Britain itself. Average Britishers would be hurt, not helped—unless, of course, they had a burning desire to be charitable to foreigners.

THE SOCIAL VALUE OF OFFICIAL RESERVES

Official reserves have national economic value that is, in fact, linked to everyday prosperity. The national value of official reserves has four overlapping aspects: (1) sufficient official reserves insure a country against excessive depreciation; (2) sufficient official reserves insure a country against disruption caused by unforeseen events, such as crop failures, civil strife, or war; (3) official reserves are a measure of a country's international creditworthiness in the eyes of private and governmental lenders; and (4) official reserves are a national financial investment in assets that do earn returns for the nation and for its citizens. Official reserves are, in a nutshell, a kind of "national insurance." This is evident in aspects 1 and 2, but it also characterizes aspects 3 and 4. Just as individuals are able to borrow from banks against life insurance policies that they own, governments are able to borrow from international credit sources against official reserves that they own. Just as an individual's life insurance is a kind of financial investment, often paying interest on accumulated premiums, countries also earn interest (or reap capital gains) on their official-reserve holdings.

The national insurance nature of official reserves is crucial to an understanding of balance-of-payments problems. The insurance that buffer stocks of official reserves provide against currency depreciation (aspect 1) has already been discussed, but official reserves also insure against unforeseen disaster (aspect 2). They are to a nation exactly what a cash nest egg is to an individual. Like the nest egg, they can be used for unexpected expenditures, such as the dramatically higher expenditures for oil that the Organization of Petroleum Exporting Countries (OPEC) forced on oil-consuming countries in the mid-1970s. Or, like the nest egg, they can be used to maintain purchasing power when an unexpected income shortfall occurs. Portugal's official reserves dropped dramatically in 1975 because civil and political unrest discouraged tourism and brought some production to a standstill. Both events reduced Portuguese income and exports, but the use of official reserves to finance Portuguese purchases kept imports and the standard of living from falling as dramatically as income.

These examples illustrate a peculiar usefulness of official reserves: they insure that a country can run a balance-of-payments deficit when necessary. What may seem peculiar is the implication that balance-of-payments deficits are sometimes socially desirable. All the connotations of the word "deficit" suggest the opposite. Deficits are, however, often good, just as surpluses are often bad, as will be shown.

Countries faced with dramatically higher oil bills or with civil strife may choose not to sell official-reserve stocks of national insurance, however. Instead, they may choose to "borrow against" official reserves, using them as security or collateral for the loan (aspect 3). In 1974, for example, the Italian government borrowed $2 billion from the German central bank and backed up its creditworthiness by pledging a portion of its official-reserve gold stock as security for the loan. Developing-country governments also borrow against official reserves as a matter of course. The loan applications that these countries make to intergovernmental aid institutions such as the World Bank and to large private commercial banks[18] are more likely to be approved if their official-reserve position is strong.

It may seem puzzling that countries do not simply sell official reserves, but borrow against them. Individuals do the same, however, and for similiar reasons. It is often more convenient and less costly to remortgage a house than to sell it and buy a cheaper one. And lenders are sometimes satisfied with collateral that does not quite match the value of the loan. Similarly, Italy finds it more convenient and less costly to pledge gold than to sell it, and developing countries often find that they can obtain international loans that are many times the value of their official reserves.

Finally, official reserves have potential social value as a national financial investment (aspect 4). The British central bank's time deposits in U.S. banks earn interest, as do the U.S. Treasury bills and bonds that it owns. The interest earnings are treated as income to the central bank and are usually passed along to the British Treasury (Exchequer), where they substitute for tax revenues in financing British government spending. Thus, though indirect, British interest earnings on official reserves find their way into the pockets of British residents. Were it not for these interest earnings, British taxes would have to rise to maintain the same level of government spending.[19] Even the gold component of British official reserves should be seen as a national financial investment, albeit a speculative one. Britain earns no predictable return on gold but can benefit from capital gains

---

[18] Governments of many countries were prompted by the oil crisis of the 1970s to become borrowers from private commercial banks, especially from large *Euro-banks*. These multinational corporate financial institutions accept deposits and make loans in more than one country's money. They are sometimes economically larger and financially sounder than the governments themselves. See Chapter 7 for more detail. Note also that the World Bank, whose full name is the International Bank for Reconstruction and Development, is not the same as the IMF. The World Bank's purpose is to borrow money from governments and private lenders worldwide and to channel it into development projects, generally in less-developed countries.

[19] The British government could issue additional government debt instead of raising taxes.

as a result of increases in its world price. Britain can also experience capital losses on its gold, of course, as it can on its dollar holdings, too, when the dollar depreciates.

BALANCE-OF-PAYMENTS SURPLUSES AND OFFICIAL-RESERVE ADEQUACY

To summarize, official reserves are useful to Britain because they have many of the security and investment characteristics of national insurance.[20] Thus balance-of-payments surpluses *may* be beneficial to Britain. By adding to official reserves, they add to national insurance. In other ways they may not be beneficial. Adding to official reserves is not costless: Britain must give up more real goods to foreigners than it receives from them. Thus Britain must spend less than it earns— must constrain its national consumption, in a broad sense, relative to its national production. Whether additional official reserves are worth this cost depends on how adequately Britain is insured in the first place. It is possible for Britain to be overinsured—in the same way, for example, as a poor, unmarried, orphaned college student who has been fast-talked into a $100,000 life insurance policy is overinsured. Adding more insurance in such circumstances would be foolish. The monthly premium payments already leave little of the student's income for consumption of other real goods, including tuition. Similarly, for Britain to run continual balance-of-payments surpluses when it already had enough official reserves would be foolish. It would be an unwarranted constraint on the British public's desire to consume real goods (other than official-reserve insurance).

Japan is the best recent example of a country whose balance-of-payments surplus created problems for these reasons. Table 3.4 records Japanese stocks of official reserves from 1967 through 1978. The mammoth jump in Japan's reserves during the early 1970s prompted the Japanese government in 1973 to ease many restrictions. Several commodity import barriers were removed; Japanese tourists were allowed to globe-trot freely; and Japanese investors availed themselves of newfound opportunities to purchase sizable foreign assets (including many Hawaiian golf courses and hotels). That the Japanese succeeded in reducing their balance-of-payments *surplus* problem is reflected in 1973's pronounced fall in official reserves. Japan acted similarly in the late 1970s after once again experiencing a significant jump in official reserves in 1977 and 1978.

In practice, assessing whether a country has enough official re-

[20] A large literature in international finance concerns itself with a nation's (and the world's) demand for reserves and optimal stock of reserves. *Demand* and *optimality* are usually defined with respect to some or all of the four aspects of reserves.

TABLE 3.4. *Dollar Value of*
Japan's Stock of Official Reserves

End of year	Japan's official reserves (value in $ billions)
1967	2.0
1968	2.9
1969	3.7
1970	4.8
1971	15.4
1972	18.4
1973	12.2
1974	13.5
1975	12.8
1976	16.6
1977	23.3
1978	33.5

Source: International Monetary Fund, *International Financial Statistics*, various issues, Table on Total Reserves, valued when necessary by end-of-year dollar value of SDRs.

serves is a difficult task for any government. The investment aspect of official reserves only complicates the problem. The greater the prospective rate of return on official reserves, including both interest and capital gains, the more desirable they are as a national investment, regardless of their insurance value. Thus the greater the prospective return on official reserves, the less likely it is that any given balance-of-payments surplus will be a problem.

These criteria differ from those of early and modern *mercantilists*. The mercantilists of the sixteenth and seventeenth centuries were economic philosophers who believed that balance-of-payments surpluses were always desirable: they allowed a nation to build up its gold stock. Gold measured a nation's wealth as well as signaling its prestige and power. Modern mercantilists hold similiar views. They see balance-of-payments surpluses as a sign of financial virtue and national competitiveness with foreigners. Deficits, by contrast, signal financial profligacy and the loss of "our competitive edge." Neither early nor modern mercantilists accept even the potential existence of a balance-of-payments surplus problem. Both favor policies that stimulate "our" exports and help out "our" producers of import substitutes. Mercantilists insist on these policies even though, when pressed to their extremes, they lead a nation to give up more than it obtains in international exchange. National economic welfare is properly measured by what a country receives, not by what it surrenders. Mercantilists neither perceive nor admit that, after a point, the social value of additional official reserves is negative, and balance-of-payments surpluses become inimical to economic welfare. Unfortunately, the language used in international finance retains many mercantilist vestiges. Exports are referred to as "positive" items in the balance of payments, imports as "negative" items. Increased surpluses and reduced deficits are spoken of as "improvements" or "favorable changes" in the balance of payments. Headlines then trumpet the "good news on the balance-of-payments front." All such sweeping characterizations must be viewed with great caution. There is no economic support for mercantilist positions. Balance-of-payments surpluses are sometimes boons and sometimes banes.

BALANCE-OF-PAYMENTS DEFICITS AS PROBLEMS

The problematic nature of balance-of-payments deficits is entirely symmetrical. Contrary to popular belief, deficits are not always problems. But they may be.

First, balance-of-payments deficits may be contractionary stimuli in the domestic economy: they may indirectly increase unemployment and promote an economic slump. Of course, contractionary stimuli are sometimes welcome, as when the economy is overheated (inflationary).

Second, a British balance-of-payments deficit implies that Britain is losing official reserves—even under managed floating. A deficit signals that the British central bank is propping up the dollar price of pounds by selling dollars from official reserves on the foreign exchange market and buying pounds. It also signals that everyone in Britain except the central bank is buying more commodities, services, and assets from foreigners than they sell to them; in other words, except for the central bank, the British are obtaining real goods of a greater value than those they give up in exports—which might seem advantageous. When we focus on the role of the central bank, however, we can recognize the balance-of-payments deficit for what it really is: a particular kind of international exchange in which Britain swaps official reserves for commodities, services, and assets. The deficit measures simultaneously the value of the official reserves that Britain surrenders and the value of the goods that it receives in return. A deficit is not a gift from foreigners; it costs reserves.

Because a country's official reserves have tangible economic value, broadly summarized before as national insurance value, the swap of reserves for goods that a deficit represents may not be in society's best interest. Then a balance-of-payments deficit is a problem. Most governments do see deficits in this way, since they view estimates of reserve adequacy with great skepticism and tend conservatively to feel underinsured. They feel it is in society's best interest to have a few more official reserves, even if that means a few less goods. Since the way to build up official reserves is to run a surplus, deficits are to be eliminated if possible.

Deficits are often described as instances where a country "lives beyond its means." This characterization is not quite accurate and has unwarranted connotations. It is more appropriate to say that a country "lives off its wealth (or capital)" when it has a deficit. Individuals do the same after they retire, drawing down personal wealth that they had built up in pension funds and savings. But since countries never retire, the analogy is not perfect. Given their indefinite lifespan, there are reasons why most countries should build up official reserves to a desirable level, welcoming balance-of-payments deficits only when for some reason, fewer reserves are desired.

THE ADEQUACY OF GLOBAL OFFICIAL RESERVES

Are there enough official reserve assets in the world to satisfy every country's desire for a certain amount of national insurance? The supply of new gold for official reserves has always been constrained by the technological barriers and economic incentives facing gold producers. The supply of new dollars to official reserves has usually been constrained by the size of the U.S. balance-of-payments deficit. For a long time, in fact, the supply of new dollars to official reserves was measured precisely by the size of the U.S. deficit.[21] During the 1950s the U.S. balance-of-payments deficit was generally acknowledged to be too small to satisfy the world's demand for additional official reserves, a problem that was described as *dollar shortage*. During the 1960s, the tide turned, and the problem became increasingly one of *dollar glut*. It is now generally agreed that creating the right amount of official reserves for the world is an international problem, not an American one, and that it should be solved under the auspices of the IMF. Actually, a small but symbolically significant portion of world official reserves has already been created by international agreement. These are the *Special Drawing Rights* (SDRs) discussed in Supplement 2B.

The "right" amount of official reserves is itself variable over time. Among the many economic variables that affect the perceived need of governments to hold reserves, the size of available *reserve credit* is extremely important. Many countries are able to borrow official reserves over short periods to supplement their *owned* reserves. The IMF itself is a major lender of official reserves to its members, making

---

[21] Since the advent of the *Euro-dollar market*, the U.S. deficit has represented only one source for the supply of new dollars to official reserves. See p. 216.

available to them deposits of foreign exchange that other countries pay the IMF upon joining (see the discussion of IMF *quotas* in Supplement 2B). Central banks lend each other official reserves temporarily by trading (swapping) their own money for the money of the cooperating central bank. Central banks sometimes even borrow foreign exchange from private commercial banks to bolster their official reserves (see Chapter 7).

Instead of focusing on whether there are enough official reserves in the world, attention is sometimes directed toward their rate of return. The higher it is, the more desirable official reserves are as national financial investments, and the larger national and world demands are to hold official reserves instead of living off them by running balance-of-payments deficits. One way for the United States to have relieved the dollar glut of the 1960s was to raise interest rates paid on dollar assets owned by the British central bank and others. This was actually attempted. Special, nonmarketable, high-interest U.S. government bonds were created for central banks alone to hold (*Roosa bonds*, named after former Under Secretary of the Treasury Robert V. Roosa). In a similar manner, a world shortage of official reserves can be eased by lowering rates of return on them.

Rates of return on official reserves also affect the likelihood and severity of balance-of-payments deficit problems. A country with a given stock of official reserves will find that a balance-of-payments deficit is more of a problem at high rates than at low. The official reserves that it loses will be more attractive as a national financial investment.

The U.S. Balance of Payments as a U.S. Problem

Balance-of-payments problems for the United States are in some ways the same as those for every country, but fundamental differences arise. To highlight these differences, it is useful first to present and defend an arresting, but ultimately misleading, proposition about the U.S. balance-of-payments problem. The proposition has elements of truth and is useful for illustrating the asymmetrical role of the United States and the dollar in the international monetary system.

ILLUSTRATIVE PROPOSITION ABOUT
THE U.S. BALANCE OF PAYMENTS

The illustrative proposition may be stated as follows: Balance-of-payments deficits are never a problem for the United States. Balance-of-payments surpluses always are. The larger the U.S. balance-of-payments deficit, the better off the United States is, taken as a whole.

DEFENSE OF THE PROPOSITION
BY AN AMERICAN EXTREMIST

Balance-of-payments deficits are never a problem for the United States because most of the world's existing and new official reserves are dollars and dollar assets. This makes the dollar the most important *reserve currency* in the world. The advantage of this role is that our central bank (the Federal Reserve System) can choose to remain completely passive in the foreign exchange market, never intervening. It need not hold official reserves as other countries do. It doesn't even have to hold gold—the U.S. commitment to back the dollar with gold was withdrawn partially in 1968 and totally in 1971 (see Chapter 2). Yet the United States can still experience balance-of-payments deficits. They are the counterpart of foreign surpluses and are financed by foreign central banks' voluntary additions of dollars to their official reserve stocks.

As a consequence, our balance-of-payments deficits are beneficial, not problematic. Unlike other countries, we do not have to surrender any official reserves to be able to import more than we export—to be able to get more internationally than we give up. We don't have to "cash in national insurance" when we run a balance-of-payments deficit. We don't have to "live off our wealth." Of course, our balance-of-payments deficits are nevertheless a kind of international exchange. We do give up ownership of certain bank deposits and U.S. government bonds to foreign central banks in return for real goods. But what we give up is socially costless! There is no significant national resource cost and no national sacrifice in creating bank deposits and U.S. government bonds for foreign central banks to hold! These assets don't even leave the country. Contrary to the impression often given in the media, U.S. balance-of-payments deficits do not mean that "dollars are flowing abroad," lost forever to Americans. The dollar assets that foreign central banks obtain stay right here and are available for use by American institutions and individuals. Commercial-bank deposits owned by foreign central banks can be loaned out to Americans in the same way as those owned by anyone. United States government bonds owned by foreign central banks are loans to the U.S. government that finance the provision of government services to Americans in the same way that all bonds do. The cost of big government would be a lot higher to the average American if the United States didn't have a balance-of-payments deficit. Foreign central banks wouldn't then be lending money to the U.S. government by buying bonds.

Therefore the United States gains from its balance-of-payments deficit. In return for something that costs us nothing, we are able to absorb more real commodities, services, and assets from foreigners than we supply to them. The value of the real goods that we get for nothing is precisely the size of our deficit. Our deficits, unlike any other country's, are gifts from abroad.

In essence, we are the world's friendly insurance salesman. United States deficits—foreign surpluses—are no more than the rest of the world's purchases of official-reserve national insurance from us. Furthermore, our insurance business is immensely profitable. Annual U.S. revenues from sales of official reserves to the rest of the world are measured exactly by the U.S. balance-of-payments deficit. Annual costs are next to zero. Our profit rate is almost infinite. We have a near-monopoly position in the insurance industry because the dollar is so predominant in official reserves.

For similar reasons, U.S. balance-of-payments surpluses should be avoided. Our balance-of-payments surplus is the rest of the world's balance-of-payments deficit with us. They finance it by drawing down their official reserves—cashing in their U.S. bank deposits and selling their U.S. government bonds back to Americans. We receive back the ownership of bank deposits and government bonds that cost us nothing to give up in the first place. Hence they are worth nothing to us now. By contrast, we give up to foreigners commodities, services, and assets that do have real value to us, because we export more than we import. We give up something but receive nothing. Balance-of-payments surpluses are always foolish for the United States precisely because balance-of-payments deficits are always good.

CRITIQUE OF THE EXTREMIST'S DEFENSE

It is true that the dollar's unique position as a *reserve currency* allows the United States to be completely passive in the foreign exchange market. It is also true that if the United States chose to be passive, it would not need to hold official reserves for purposes of stabilizing exchange rates. It is also true that if the United States chose to be passive, its balance-of-payments deficits would be financed by foreign central banks' adding to their dollar reserves. It is also true that these dollars usually do not leave the United States, and the United States might well gain from its deficit in some of the ways outlined by the extremist.

But one important question is left unanswered by the extremist. Why should the United States choose to be passive in the foreign exchange market? The United States might well gain even more from intervention, in support of the actions undertaken by foreign central banks, than it would from remaining passive. Exchange rates would more likely be stabilized with cooperative U.S. intervention than without. Whatever case there is for stable exchange rates applies qualitatively to the United States as much as to any other country. If the United States does gain more from helping to stabilize the value of the dollar than from being passive, the extremist position is undermined. The United States then has a reason for holding official reserves of foreign money: to stabilize exchange rates just as other countries do.

Ever since 1961 the United States has held small amounts of Belgian francs, Canadian dollars, German Deutsche marks, and a number of other foreign moneys in official reserves. They were used to intervene occasionally in the foreign exchange market during the 1960s and much more frequently during the 1970s. More importantly, the United States, in cooperation with foreign central banks, has devised a significant network of emergency sources for borrowing official reserves: the *reciprocal currency arrangements,* or the *swap agreements,* described in Supplement 3A.

The extremist argument is also weakened by any other aspect of official reserves that might lead to a U.S. demand for them. While exchange-rate stabilization seems to be the most persuasive reason for the United States to hold official reserves, precautionary motives may have some importance. As long as the dollar maintains its dominant reserve-currency role, U.S. balance-of-payments deficits due to unforeseen disasters can be financed by foreign central banks' absorbing more dollars. The dollar may not always be dominant, and U.S. buffer stocks of gold and foreign money serve as insurance against this eventuality.

Furthermore, cooperation among central banks is sometimes made difficult by disagreement over the exact values of exchange rates to be stabilized. Such disagreement grew into open conflict during the depression-ridden 1930s, when countries jockeyed for depreciation because of its domestic expansionary effects (see Chapter 5). Official-reserve stocks insure that the United States can "vote" on the value of the dollar in such circumstances by foreign-exchange-market intervention, or at least by threatening it.

Any motive for holding official reserves is also a motive for changing official reserves as circumstances change. Once the United States is given such a motive, U.S. balance-of-payments surpluses conceivably become desirable in certain circumstances and deficits undesirable—most obviously, whenever the United States wants to add to its own official reserves.[22]

---

[22] To be exact, the United States does not have to run a balance-of-payments surplus to acquire official reserves, nor does any other country whose money is used as a reserve currency. In any given period, if the dollars that foreign central banks add to their reserves exceed in value the foreign money assets that the Federal Reserve System adds to its own reserves, then the U.S. balance of payments will still be in deficit. Thus it is conceivable that the United States could build up its reserves despite a balance-of-payments deficit. Also when the United States engages in active policy to build up or draw down its own official reserves, identification of the British balance of payments with the change in British reserves is no longer valid. This identification was made in Figure 2.7, for example. In fact, area *ABJK* represents the dollar value of the sum of two elements: British official-reserve losses and American official-reserve gains. If the Federal Reserve System chose to purchase all *AB* pounds for official reserves, Britain could lose none of her own official reserves, even though she would have a deficit of £*AB*.

Indeed, until the 1970s, under the adjustable-peg exchange-rate system, the United States was obligated by its commitment to the IMF to be concerned about its official-reserve gold stock. It was not a matter of choice. U.S. gold stocks backed the dollar's gold value. For as long as the United States observed this commitment, U.S. balance-of-payments deficits were problems to the extent that they led indirectly to a drain on the U.S. gold stock. The extremist is correct, however, that after the United States unilaterally abandoned this commitment in 1971, there was no longer any link, indirect or direct, between U.S. deficits and the U.S. gold stock.

The extremist is also correct that it is virtually costless for the United States to create official reserves for the rest of the world to hold. However, it is not necessarily costless for the United States to pay interest on those same official reserves, a detail that the extremist conveniently omits. Interest payments on U.S. government debt owned by foreign central banks are an element of U.S. government spending. If these interest payments are financed by taxes that the U.S. government levies on the general public, the United States as a whole (including the government) is unable to purchase as many real goods as it could without such interest payments. There is a cost to the U.S. balance-of-payments deficit—it adds to the interest burden that the United States must bear to reward foreign holders of dollar reserves.[23]

In this light, we see the United States less as an insurance salesman for the world and more as a borrower from it. The dollars that foreign central banks hold as official reserves are American IOUs. By "borrowing" from foreign central banks, the United States is able to spend more than it earns—that is, to run a balance-of-payments deficit. This is not necessarily bad. Corporations regularly spend more than they earn by borrowing through corporate stock and bond issues. They use the proceeds of their borrowing for investment (expansion), and they gain to the extent that the return on their investment exceeds the cost of their borrowing. For similar reasons, the U.S. balance-of-payments deficit may not have been bad. Most U.S. deficits from World War II to the 1970s can be identified with private U.S. financial investment abroad, as Table 3.5 shows. Furthermore, much of this investment was expansion by U.S. multinational corporations (see Chapter 13) into foreign markets. All available data suggest that U.S. multinational corporations earned returns on their foreign investments that far exceeded the interest paid by the United States to foreign central banks. Thus a case could be made that the United

[23] The extremist might well point out the illusory nature of this cost, however, if the interest payments themselves can be financed by sales of *additional* U.S. government bonds to foreign central banks. Then the interest payments themselves contribute to the U.S. balance-of-payments deficit and can be financed costlessly from an American point of view, because foreign central banks continue to be willing to accept more official-reserve dollars— even as interest payments on the dollars they already own!

TABLE 3.5. *Average Annual Components of the U.S. Balance of Payments, 1951–1978 (Billions of Dollars)*

	Private exports minus imports of commodities[a]	Private exports minus imports of services[b]	Private exports minus imports of assets[c]	U.S. balance of payments[d]
1951–54	2.4	−0.3	−2.5	−0.4
1955–58	4.3	−0.7	−3.9	−0.3
1959–62	4.0	−0.3	−5.6	−1.9
1963–66	5.2	1.5	−7.8	−1.1
1967–70	1.8	1.5	−5.5	−2.2
1971–74	−3.6	4.7	−14.5	−13.4
1975–78	−16.4	17.5	−25.8	−24.7

[a] Equal to the merchandise trade balance (see Supplement 2C). *Source:* U. S. Department of Commerce, *Survey of Current Business* 53 (June 1973), and other issues.
[b] Equal to the balance on goods and services minus the merchandise trade balance (see Supplement 2C). *Source:* See note a.
[c] Equal to the balance on official-reserve-transaction basis minus the balance on goods and services (see Supplement 2C). *Source:* See notes a and d.
[d] Equal to the sum of the first three columns. Equal also to the balance of payments on official-reserve-transaction basis (see Supplement 2C). *Source:* For 1960–78, same as in note a. For 1951–59, a proxy for the official reserve transactions balance was calculated. The proxy was the sum of two elements: (i) the change in U.S. official reserve assets, net, and (ii) the negative of the change in liabilities of the United States to monetary authorities and other official agencies. *Source:* For (i), U.S. Department of Commerce, *Survey of Current Business* 53 (June 1973): 54, line 46; for (ii), International Monetary Fund, *International Financial Statistics*, various issues from 1961 and 1962, table entitled "Reconciliation of Foreign Exchange Assets and Liabilities."

States as a whole benefited from its balance-of-payments deficits. On the other hand, this perspective also suggests a criterion for evaluating U.S. balance-of-payments deficits: they are bad when the rate of return on them falls short of the interest rates paid on official-reserve dollars held by foreign central banks. Here, again, the extremist position is undermined: U.S. balance-of-payments deficits can cause problems.

In the 1970s, U.S. deficits were prominent in commodity trade. Whether they were a U.S. problem depends on whether the extra consumption goods, raw materials, and productive equipment that the United States acquired through its trade deficit justified the interest cost of the borrowing necessary to finance them. The question is exactly the same as that for an individual who wonders whether it is worth borrowing to purchase consumption goods such as autos, appliances, or vacations, or "investment goods" such as tools, books, and an education.

EVALUATION OF THE ARGUMENTS

Many aspects of the extremist position are valid, but the strong conclusion is not. Balance-of-payments deficits can sometimes be a problem for the United States, and balance-of-payments surpluses can sometimes be welcome. Many aspects of the balance of payments that are problematic for other countries are equally so for the United States. Some special reserve-currency reasons that do not apply to other countries can make the balance of payments a problem to the United States.

Nevertheless, the importance of the dollar's special role should not be minimized. It seems fair to say that, in general, U.S. balance-of-payments deficits will be larger, and more welcome, than deficits for any other country. United States balance-of-payments surpluses, similarly, will be smaller, and less welcome, than surpluses for any other country. Moreover, as long as the dollar remains the key component of additions to world official reserves, U.S. balance-of-payments deficits will be a normal, and frequently innocuous, state of affairs. As the world grows physically and economically, world demand for official-reserve insurance probably grows too. In principle, this growing demand can be satisfied exactly by recurring U.S. balance-of-payments deficits of the proper size. Neither the resulting U.S. deficits nor the corresponding surpluses in the rest of the world are in any way problematical.

Finally, the existence and nature of the U.S. balance-of-payments problem is controversial. Supplement 3B outlines the controversy in more detail, discusses the view that U.S. deficits victimize the rest of the world in a neo-imperialist way, and identifies the alternative perspectives with prominent themes in recent international finance: *benign neglect*, *seigniorage*, and *international financial intermediation*.

Summary

Why does the U.S. government care so much about the foreign-exchange-market price (value) of the dollar? One reason is that the exchange-rate price of the dollar is almost as consequential as the quantity of dollars in existence. Governments care about exchange rates for much the same reasons they care about money stocks. They plan exchange-rate and balance-of-payments policies for much the same reasons that they plan monetary policy.

To be precise, dollar depreciation raises prices, production, profits, wages, and employment in tradeables industries—which make up roughly one-third of U.S. economic activity—and perhaps also in the whole economy if tradeables expansion absorbs involuntarily idle resources. Otherwise, those whose incomes are dependent on the nontradeables sector are losers from dollar depreciation. It also unambiguously raises the cost of living for everyone. Dollar appreciation has the opposite effects.

In order to avoid the less welcome of these consequences, people favor government stabilization of exchange rates. Exchange-rate variation may cause internal dislocation, inflationary pressure, and economically costly shifts of resources back and forth among sectors. The uncertainty it entails may also discourage international exchange. Yet all feasible methods by which governments stabilize exchange rates still allow periodic variation, and there is no obvious reason to expect dislocation, inflation, and uncertainty to be smaller in an adjustable-peg system with infrequent, large revaluations and devaluations than in a managed float with frequent, small appreciations and depreciations.

Conventional exchange-rate stabilization, however, saddles a government with other potential problems. It requires nations to accept balance-of-payments surpluses and deficits. The surpluses sometimes required to stabilize exchange rates may be both inflationary and an undesired drag on the nation's ability to acquire goods for consumption and investment. The deficits sometimes required may be both recessionary and an undesirable drain on a nation's official reserves—which have insurance, nest-egg, collateral, and investment value to its citizens.

The United States has historically borne fewer of the costs of exchange-rate stabilization than other countries. The special reserve-currency role of the dollar has absolved the U.S. government of responsibility for intervening in the foreign exchange market. This has meant in practice that balance-of-payments deficits for the United States are less problematical than those for every other country in the world. They are not typically recessionary, nor do they necessarily lead to any loss in U.S. official reserves (as long as their size remains moderate). It is even more significant that they have traditionally allowed the United States to consume more than it produces—to receive more tangible commodities, services, and property from foreigners than it gives up.

Key Terms

tradeables;
  nontradeables
average propensity
  to import
mercantilists
dollar shortage;
  dollar glut

Roosa bonds
reserve credit
IMF quotas
reserve currency

Key Concepts and Review

How exchange rates affect prices, profits, production, employment, and income distribution.

Fixed versus floating exchange rates.

National benefits from adequate official reserves.

Surpluses, deficits, and exchange-rate change as means of altering official-reserve stocks.

The trade-off between the goals of exchange-rate stability and ideal official-reserve stocks.

The unique character of the U.S. balance of payments.

Supplement 3A
Reciprocal Currency Arrangements (Swap Agreements)

Although since 1961 the United States has chosen to hold official reserves other than gold, its perceived need for them has been moderated considerably by the network of *swaps* among major central banks. The swap agreements, known formally as *reciprocal currency arrangements*, are emergency sources of official reserves for central banks that participate.

Swaps are in some ways similar to the IMF's *stand-by arrangements* discussed in Supplement 2B, but they are permanent lines of *reserve credit*. For example, the *swap line* between the Federal Reserve System and the Bank of England (Britain's central bank) is a permanent agreement to exchange up to $3 billion for roughly £1.5 billion at a moment's notice from either party. Its purpose is to allow the United States to counter a speculation-induced depreciation of the dollar without touching its official-reserve stocks. Instead, it could "draw" on its swap line with Britain, and the Bank of England would immediately credit the Federal Reserve System with up to £1.5 billion in deposits at the Bank. These deposits would then be sold by the Federal Reserve System to buy dollars on the foreign exchange market in order to keep the dollar's value up.

The distinction between official reserves and swaps is a subtle one. Once the United States draws on its swap line with Britain, it appears to own up to £1.5 billion of additional reserves. But it does not really own them. It has just borrowed them for a short time. As a rule the United States is obliged to repay its swap drawing within several months. (Swaps are renewable, and the United States recently took eight years to repay one with Switzerland.) For its part of the bargain, the Federal Reserve System credits the Bank of England with up to $3 billion of deposits at the Fed until the swap is repaid. The term *swap* is therefore appropriate—the two central banks swap deposit accounts.

If the United States sells some of the pounds it draws to support the value of the dollar, it must repurchase them to pay back its swap in the future. When the support succeeds and confidence in the foreign-exchange-market value of the dollar is restored, the United States is able to buy pounds on the foreign exchange market at a later date without taking any loss on its purchases and sales. When the support fails, the dollar depreciates still further before the swap is repaid. The United States is forced to buy more expensive pounds than it sold in order to repay the swap. The Federal Reserve System must then grin and bear a capital loss in the same way as any central bank that tries unsuccessfully to stabilize exchange rates (see p. 43).

Swap agreements exist on a bilateral basis among European, Middle Eastern, and Southeast Asian central banks. The United States is not always directly involved. The system has grown dramatically since its inception in the 1960s. As Table 3A.1 reveals, the size of the reciprocal currency arrangements to which the United States is a party is actually larger than its official reserve holdings and far, far larger than the foreign money component of those holdings (although $36 million worth is atypically low—the average balance in the 1970s was more usually several hundred million dollars worth).

The swap network is an ingenious way for all countries to economize on their need for fully owned official reserves. It is also a striking example of the level of cooperation that exists among major central banks in the international monetary system. Amid all the

TABLE 3A.1. *U.S. Official Reserves and Reciprocal Currency (Swap) Arrangements: November 1978 (Millions of Dollars)*

Official reserves by type of asset	
Gold[a]	11,655
Special Drawing Rights (SDRs)	3,097
IMF Reserve Tranche	4,147
Foreign money	36
Total	18,935

Maximum size of swap possible with various central banks	
Austria	250
Belgium	1,000
Britain	3,000
Canada	2,000
Denmark	250
France	2,000
Germany	6,000
Italy	3,000
Japan	5,000
Mexico	360
Netherlands	500
Norway	250
Sweden	300
Switzerland	4,000
Other[b]	1,850
Total	29,760

[a] Valued at $42.22 per ounce.
[b] Includes swap agreements for other European moneys and with the Bank for International Settlements.
Source: Official reserve data from U.S. Treasury Department, *Treasury Bulletin*, November 1978, Table IFS-1; reciprocal currency arrangement data from Federal Reserve Bank of Chicago, *International Letter* 382 (November 10, 1978).

recent foreign-exchange-market crises, this cooperation provides grounds for considerable optimism that international monetary relations will not soon degenerate into nationalistic conflict as they did during the 1930s (see p. 197).

Supplement 3B
Alternative Views on the Historical U.S.
Balance-of-Payments Problem

The proposition that the U.S. balance-of-payments deficit is not really a U.S. problem has attracted an assortment of unlikely bedfellows. They include some conservative Republican politicians, who used this view to justify a policy of so-called *benign neglect* toward the U.S. balance of payments in the early 1970s; some French economists and journalists, who see the asymmetry between the United States and other countries as an undeserved American advantage; and some radical opponents of a new American imperialism, who see U.S. deficits as an especially sinister problem for surplus countries. These groups agree on many aspects of the perspective outlined in the text. They disagree most importantly on whether or not the United States benefits from its deficit at the expense of the rest of the world.

Argument on this subject frequently proceeds by way of analogy, and the analogies appealed to in the text are not the most familiar. More familiar, first, is an analogy often drawn between the United States and the seignior or master of a feudal manor. The seignior was able to extract *seigniorage gains* from his vassals by forcing them to use in all transactions money that he personally created at little cost—for example, pieces of paper with his signature. To obtain money, the vassals had to sell real goods to the seignior. The seigniorage gains could be measured by the difference between the seignior's valuation of the goods and the costs he incurred to create the money. Indeed, if it were possible for a group of individuals to replace the U.S. Treasury as the sole producer of U.S. currency, they, too, would be able to extract huge seigniorage gains. The Treasury itself extracts these gains, of course, but in the name of the country as a whole.

By analogy, the United States is the creator of the largest component of "international money"—official reserves. The rest of the world obtains this international money by selling real goods to the United States. Both sides of the transaction could be measured by the U.S. balance-of-payments deficit. The United States gains because the social value of the goods it receives outweighs the resource costs of creating international money, which are near zero.

Comparing the United States to a seignior is somewhat like comparing it to an insurance salesman, as done in the text. Comparing the

United States to a corporation that borrows and invests (pp. 112–113) has a counterpart in the *international financial intermediation* perspective, which compares the United States to a financial intermediary such as a commercial bank. All commercial banks "borrow" from their depositors by accepting their money, and lend it in turn to others who put it to use. Banks mediate or "intermediate" between depositors, who want a safe, liquid way to save, and borrowers, who want loans of predictable terms and lifespan so that they can invest. Intermediation is profitable because banks charge for their services: interest rates on loans exceed those on deposits.

By analogy, the United States during the 1950s and 1960s was like a bank when it ran a balance-of-payments deficit. It accepted deposits from foreign central banks, who viewed them as safe and liquid forms of national saving. And it loaned the official-reserve deposits to private U.S. investors, who used them among other things to buy foreign assets and to expand foreign operations of U.S. multinational corporations. United States "intermediation" through its balance-of-payments deficit was profitable to the extent that it paid less to depositors (foreign central banks) than it earned on foreign investments.

The French especially have always embraced this perspective on the U.S. deficit. In their view, it is no coincidence that the boom in U.S. multinational operations in France and elsewhere occurred simultaneously with the boom in official-reserve dollar stocks. They view the historical U.S. deficit as the opportunity for American corporations to gain control of foreign economies—in exchange for official-reserve dollars that have less fundamental value than the real assets for which they were swapped. Of course, such exchanges were in some measure voluntary. Central banks of surplus countries could always have avoided growth in their official reserves, with its allegedly concomitant U.S. corporate penetration, by allowing their money to appreciate. But the French point out that this course of action would have meant accepting the evils of variable exchange rates, outlined earlier. Forced to choose between two evils, almost all countries chose ongoing U.S. balance-of-payments deficits as the lesser.

The French position implies that U.S. balance-of-payments deficits victimize other countries. Thus U.S. deficits may not be a U.S. problem, but they are certainly problems for everyone else. Those who accuse the U.S. of *neo-imperialism* through the foreign expansion of U.S. multinationals also subscribe to this position.

Indeed, other countries can be victimized when U.S. balance-of-payments deficits and foreign surpluses become excessively large, as they did in the early 1970s and again in 1977–1978. Foreign central banks are then prompted to abandon their foreign-exchange-market intervention because their official reserves are already excessive or because they fear the inflationary consequences of extraordinary surpluses. The result is that the dollar depreciates dramatically, and foreign central banks voluntarily but reluctantly accept capital losses on their official-reserve dollars. Such dollars will no longer buy as much foreign currency as previously, nor therefore as many real goods. Such dollars may not even buy as many *U.S.* goods as previously, because dollar depreciation often creates upward pressure on U.S. goods prices (see pp. 86–94 and 166–172).

On the other hand, it is by no means clear that *moderate* U.S. balance-of-payments deficits injure other countries, even when they are beneficial to the United States. Referring back to one of the analogies, the depositors at a commercial bank are not necessarily victimized by earning less interest on their deposits than the bank charges on its loans. As a rule, both the bank and its depositors gain from the financial exchanges that are made. Similarly, U.S. balance-of-payments deficits may be simultaneously and mutually beneficial to the United States and to countries that absorb the excessive foreign-exchange-market supply of dollars into official reserves.

To assess foreign gains or losses from a U.S. deficit, it is too simple to compare interest rates earned by foreign central banks on official reserves to earnings made by American multinational corporations. Even if it is true that historical U.S. deficits were a grand international exchange of dollars for corporations (they had to be an exchange of dollars for something, but more recently the something has been commodities or services), such a comparison is misleading for two reasons. First, interest rates earned on official reserves probably understate their true national value to countries that own them. The interest rate measures only the national investment value of reserves (aspect 4 from the text), not their stabilization, precaution, or collateral values (aspects 1, 2, and 3 from the text). Second, earnings of the subsidiaries and affiliates of U.S. multinationals probably overstate what native foreign corporations could earn on similar investments. As Chapter 13 will demonstrate, a portion of the foreign profits of U.S. multinationals represents payment for expertise or technology that is unique to the U.S. corporation. Native foreign corporations could not have had access to that same technology or expertise unless they bought it from the U.S. corporation. Therefore their profitability would be lower in the same enterprise; they incur higher costs either from doing without the unique technology and expertise or from paying for it. The upshot of these two biases is that foreign countries may well gain from U.S. balance-of-payments deficits, even if it means giving up ownership of real assets for paper ones. The official reserves they gain through running balance-of-payments surpluses may well be worth the real-goods cost.

Indeed, the principal conclusion of this chapter is that official reserves provide services of real, tangible value to countries that own them. There is, then, a presumption that the analysis of Part II of this book applies to trade in official reserves. In the absence of evidence to the contrary, at least some international trade in official reserves is nationally and mutually beneficial, to the United States as exporter of reserves and to foreign countries as importers of reserves. Phrased more traditionally, this conclusion is that over the long haul, at least some U.S. deficits and foreign surpluses should be simultaneously welcomed by all countries.

Chapter 4

Effects of Domestic Economic Activity on Exchange Rates and the Balance of Payments

We have not yet probed very deeply into the source of exchange-rate variability and balance-of-payments problems. It is clear from Chapter 1 that the immediate source is some change in normal and speculative international trade or financial investment. Yet such changes are not haphazard. Other economic variables cause them. Changes in these other, more basic economic variables are the fundamental cause of shifts in foreign-exchange-market supply and demand.

The most important fundamental variables that determine exchange rates and the balance of payments are familiar from macroeconomics: gross national product (GNP), interest rates, and inflation. These variables also affect employment, growth, and income distribution, to all of which societies attach considerable importance. Macroeconomic policies such as monetary and fiscal policy are proximately justified as tools to control GNP, interest rates, and inflation and are ultimately justified as means for reaching national goals for employment, growth, income distribution, exchange rates, and the balance of payments. The last two elements belong in the list because of their significance for national economic welfare, discussed in Chapter 3. Controlling exchange rates and the balance of payments by policy, however, is not easy. The problem of how to do so is known as the *balance-of-payments adjustment problem.*

This chapter focuses on the ways in which changes in gross national product, interest rates, and inflation influence exchange rates and the balance of payments. It also describes how governments use monetary, fiscal, and international policies to offset any such influences that they find undesirable.

Effects of Recession and Expansion

Recession and *expansion* usually refer to changes in the level of "real" economic activity—the physical production of commodities and services. When national production slackens, so that unemployment and excess capacity increase, an economy is said to be in a slump, downturn, or recession. When it rises, so that unemployment and excess capacity decrease, an economy is said to be in a boom, upswing, or expansion. The most familiar measure of real economic activity is *real gross national product*, the value of all commodities and services that a country produces for final use, valued in some unchanging benchmark prices. Real GNP can also be defined as a kind of national income—wages, salaries, dividends, interest, and rents that are earned by domestic residents in producing commodities and services.

Defining recession and expansion as ups and downs in national income is the key to outlining their exchange-rate and balance-of-payments effects. Individual and national demands for almost all commodities and services are income sensitive. Demand curves *shift* when income changes. For normal commodities and services, higher incomes lead to a demand for more at every price. Income is therefore characterized as a *demand-shift variable*—a variable that lies unseen behind every demand curve and that shifts the location of the curve whenever its own value changes.

Income-sensitive demand characterizes imported commodities and services as much as any others. The implication is that increased individual and national incomes shift individual and national demand curves for normal imports out and up: more imports are demanded at every price.

This has a clear impact on the foreign exchange market. As Chapters 1 and 2 (especially Figures 1.2 and 2.7) imply, larger imports usually require larger foreign-exchange-market purchases of foreign money and corresponding sales of domestic money. For example, larger British imports require larger supplies of pounds on the foreign exchange market in order to buy the dollars desired by the U.S. exporter. When British incomes rise, the value of daily British imports demanded at every exchange rate will rise too. Therefore the daily supply of pounds at every exchange rate will rise. British income (real GNP) turns out to be a fundamental shift variable underlying the supply-of-pounds curve in the foreign exchange market.

The bottom half of Figure 4.1 illustrates this graphically. Because British imports are income sensitive, and because they require a foreign-exchange-market supply of pounds, the entire supply-of-pounds curve shifts in a southeasterly direction as real British GNP

FIGURE 4.1. *Effects of Recession and Expansion of Real GNP on the Foreign Exchange Market*

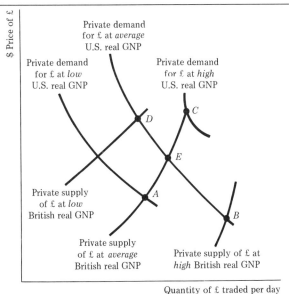

rises.[1] The higher real British GNP is, the larger will be the foreign-exchange-market supply of pounds at every exchange rate.

The top half of Figure 4.1 illustrates the symmetric relationship between U.S. economic activity and the demand for pounds. The U.S. demand for imports from Britain is responsive to individual and national income in the same way as are U.S. demands for all commodities and services, wherever produced. Because imports from Britain generally require a foreign-exchange-market purchase of pounds (and sale of dollars), U.S. income (real GNP) turns out to be a fundamental shift variable underlying the demand-for-pounds curve in the foreign exchange market.

[1] The shift is certain if no other shift variables change when real British GNP rises. Among other shift variables, however, are prices and interest rates, as we will see below. It may not be realistic to talk about holding them constant as real British income rises. That criticism, however, has no analytical significance. It simply posits that the income-induced shift described in the text may be reinforced or counteracted by price-and-interest-rate-induced shifts that occur in reality because GNP, prices, and interest rates usually vary together. The criticism does not posit that the income-induced shift is logically incorrect.

Effects of Recession and Expansion   125

Figure 4.1 suggests an important influence that recession and expansion have on exchange rates and the balance of payments. Under floating exchange rates, a British recession that is unmatched in the rest of the world leads to appreciation of the pound. Equilibrium in the foreign exchange market moves from a point such as E to a point such as D. As Britain recovers from such a recession, however—that is, as British real GNP rises back toward its average—the pound depreciates. Equilibrium in the foreign exchange market moves from a point such as D back toward E. The pound depreciates also if the British economy enters a period of above-average expansion of real GNP that is not matched elsewhere in the world. Equilibrium in the foreign exchange market moves toward a point such as B.

Because exchange-rate variability has undesirable features, the British government may intervene in the foreign exchange market to dampen the GNP-induced exchange-rate variation. To dampen pound appreciation during recession, the government must sell pounds and buy official reserves, thereby creating a British balance-of-payments surplus. To dampen pound depreciation during expansion, the government must buy pounds with official reserves, thereby creating a British balance-of-payments deficit. Indeed, under a pegged exchange rate system the British are obligated to eliminate almost all the exchange-rate variation in exactly this way. Under pegged rates, then, British recession drives the British balance of payments toward surplus, and British boom drives it toward deficit. In reality, depending on other factors, recession may simply shrink an existing balance-of-payments deficit, and expansion may shrink an existing surplus, but the direction of the effect is the same.

The effects of recession and expansion on the balance of payments under pegged exchange rates can sometimes be a severe constraint upon macroeconomic policy that is designed to pull an economy out of a slump. If a country's official reserves are too low, and if expansion of economic activity would create balance-of-payments deficits that would deplete reserves still further, the country is in a quandary. Unemployment and excess capacity of considerable duration may be the price paid for insufficient official reserves. Of course, devaluation would alleviate the official-reserves problem immediately (and the slump as well, as Chapter 5 demonstrates) but would carry its own price: the abandonment of stable exchange rates. Therefore an unpleasant choice must be made among perceived evils: economic slack, insufficient national insurance, and variable exchange rates. Britain found herself in just such a position during the mid-1960s, opting for slack initially and devaluation eventually (in 1967). Quandaries such as this are discussed at greater length in the next section and toward the end of this chapter.

Under managed floating, the impact of ups and downs in real GNP is usually twofold. Recession brings about some appreciation and some tendency toward surplus. Expansion brings about some depreciation and some tendency toward deficit. This is as true for the United States as for Britain. In Figure 4.1, U.S. recession that is not mirrored elsewhere moves foreign-exchange-market equilibrium toward point A—an appreciation of the dollar (depreciation of the pound). United States expansion that is not mirrored elsewhere moves foreign-exchange-market equilibrium toward point C—a depreciation of the dollar.

Realistically, however, real GNP fluctuations frequently coincide and are mirrored worldwide. (Chapter 6 outlines some of the reasons why.) There may then be very little effect on exchange rates, since foreign-exchange-market demands and supplies rise and fall together. Pronounced procyclical effects will occur on the volume of trade and foreign-exchange-market transactions, however.

Realistically, too, recession and expansion of real GNP are frequently accompanied by changes in other fundamental variables. Upswings in the economy often feature rising prices and interest rates. Downturns often feature prices that rise less rapidly than normal or that even fall together with interest rates and real GNP. Let us look now at the impact of these additional variables on exchange rates and the balance of payments.

Effects of Financial Conditions

Financial conditions are the availability and cost of credit, and they are usually reflected in interest rates. Interest rates are high when credit is "tight" and low when it is "easy." Their foreign-exchange-market impact derives from the fact that individual and national demands to hold particular assets are interest-rate responsive. If Beefeater begins to offer higher-than-average interest rates on its corporate bonds, investors will probably buy more Beefeater bonds for their "portfolio"—a list of the identities and amounts of their investment assets. To do so, they will sell off other bonds that pay below-average interest rates.

On the international monetary scene, many individuals and institutions hold both foreign and domestic assets for investment purposes. When British interest rates rise relative to U.S. interest rates (and nothing else changes), British assets become relatively more attractive. International investors will tend to buy these more attractive British assets and to sell off U.S. assets. Indeed, this is precisely the activity known as *interest arbitrage*, discussed in Supplement 1A.

Such portfolio adjustments have a clear impact on the foreign exchange market. International investors who sell off their Boeing corporate bonds to Americans and buy newly attractive Beefeater corporate bonds from current British owners (or from Beefeater itself) will have to make a foreign-exchange-market transaction. Dollars will be received from the sale of Boeing bonds; pounds must be given up to buy Beefeater bonds. The result is a *temporarily* increased demand for pounds (supply of dollars) on the foreign exchange market that was not motivated by any change in exchange rates. That is, when British interest rates rise, the demand for pounds rises at every exchange rate. British interest rates turn out to be fundamental shift variables underlying the demand-for-pounds curve in the foreign exchange market.

Temporarily is an important modifier. The outward and upward shift in the demand-for-pounds curve may not be permanent, even if British interest rates remain permanently higher than U.S. interest rates. Once international investors have reorganized their portfolios to reflect the new pattern of interest rates, there will be no incentive for them to buy still more Beefeater bonds or to sell still more Boeing bonds unless British interest rates jump even higher. After the initial portfolio reorganization, there will be no corresponding extra demand for pounds on the foreign exchange market. The demand for pounds will drop back close to where it was normally, despite the continued existence of relatively more attractive British interest rates.

In a growing world, the foreign-exchange-market demand for pounds will not drop back fully, however. New international investors are continually entering the scene, and established international investors are continually expanding the size of their portfolios. Every week new decisions have to be made on the most desirable asset in which to hold new savings—that is, additions to total wealth. If British interest rates continue to remain at their new higher level, Beefeater bonds will attract a larger proportion of these new portfolio investments than otherwise, and there will be a corresponding *permanent* increase in the demand for pounds on the foreign exchange market because new dollar savings must be converted into pounds first in order to purchase Beefeater bonds.

The top half of Figure 4.2 illustrates graphically these impacts of higher British interest rates on the demand curve for pounds. When British interest rates rise, the demand curve for pounds first shifts dramatically up and out, as investors stack existing portfolios toward the more attractive British assets. But after this adjustment has taken place, the only source of permanently higher demand for pounds is the tendency of investors to shift a larger proportion of *additions to* existing portfolios into British assets. Reflecting the temporary and permanent nature of these shifts, the first is often described as the (once-and-for-all) *stock* effect of a change in British interest rates, and the second as the (ongoing) *flow* effect.

The bottom half of Figure 4.2 illustrates the effects of higher U.S. interest rates on the foreign exchange market. They are entirely symmetric. Higher U.S. interest rates make it more attractive for international investors to hold U.S. assets, leading to attempts to increase their share both in existing portfolios and in increments to them. Such

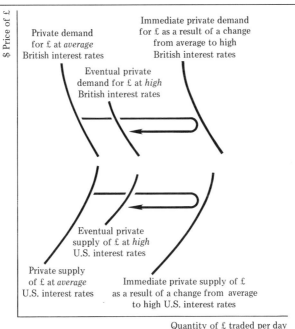

Quantity of £ traded per day

attempts often involve the sale of British assets for pounds and the conversion of the pounds into dollars to pay off the current U.S. asset owners. Such conversions represent additional foreign-exchange-market supplies of pounds at every exchange rate. Hence they lead to a dramatic immediate shift in the supply-of-pounds curve and to an eventual moderation of the shift, as indicated.

Figure 4.2 implies the impact of financial conditions on exchange rates and the balance of payments. Roughly speaking, tighter credit and higher interest rates in Britain cause the pound to appreciate; easier credit and lower interest rates cause it to depreciate. The initial short-run change in exchange rates may be dramatically larger than the ultimate change, a condition sometimes described as *overshooting*. If Britain chooses to avoid such exchange-rate variability by intervening in the foreign exchange market, then tighter credit and higher interest rates cause British balance-of-payments surpluses; easier credit and lower interest rates cause balance-of-payments deficits. These surpluses and deficits will also be larger in the short run than in the long run. More precisely stated, tighter credit causes either more dramatic appreciation and more dramatic balance-of-payments surpluses, or else less severe depreciation and less severe balance-of-payments deficits. Looser credit creates either less dramatic appreciation and surpluses, or else more severe depreciation and deficits. These conclusions also characterize the United States.[2]

It should now be clear why excessively large depreciation and balance-of-payments deficits sometimes reflect a government's lack of financial discipline. It should also be clear why it is usually true that a country's money strengthens on the foreign exchange market after its government announces some new plan of financial austerity and tight credit.

The fact that interest rates and real GNP often vary together makes it difficult to predict the qualitative impact of real-world business fluctuations on exchange rates and the balance of payments. Recession is frequently accompanied by progressively looser credit; expansion, by progressively tighter credit. That the net impact of the two is qualitatively indeterminate can be seen in Figure 4.3. British expansion that is accompanied by tighter credit causes both supply and demand to shift out in the foreign exchange market. The pound might appreciate or depreciate, depending on the relative strength of the shifts. The balance of payments might tend toward either surplus or deficit. All that can be said is that the chances of pound appreciation and a tendency toward surplus are greater in the short run than in the long. The reason is that the shift in the demand-for-pounds curve induced by tight financial conditions is most pronounced in the short run.

Figure 4.3 also casts light on a heated controversy in international economics. Assuming that exchange rates are stabilized, do balance-of-payments problems constrain a country's economic growth? Until recently, most economists answered yes. They had in mind the impact of real GNP on the balance of payments: the faster a country grew, the more rapidly real GNP increased, the more the country imported, and the larger its balance-of-payments deficit became. At some point, the ongoing deficit would cause official-reserve national insurance to fall to a crisis level, and rapid growth would have to be foregone for a while in order to rebuild reserves.

[2] Note that the mechanism of interest arbitrage, described in Supplement 1A, assures some parallel rise in all countries' interest rates when one is altered. Thus it may not be realistic to talk about holding U.S. interest rates constant as British interest rates rise. Again, however, that conclusion has no analytical significance. It does not imply that the shifts described in Figure 4.2 are logically wrong; it implies only that they tend to happen together. In fact the analysis of interest arbitrage can demonstrate that the size of the impact (exogenous) change in one interest rate generally exceeds the size of the induced change in the other. So the qualitative conclusions that follow from Figure 4.2 remain intact.

FIGURE 4.3. *Indeterminate Effects of Simultaneous British Expansion and Tighter Credit on Exchange Rates and the Balance of Payments*

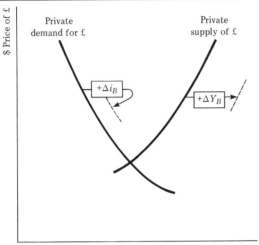

Key:
For +, read "a positive."
For Δ, read "change in."
For Y_B, read "British real GNP."
For i_B, read "British interest rates."

These beliefs about economic growth and the balance of payments never squared very well with the experience of some countries. During the period after World War II, some of the fastest-growing economies were those with large, ongoing balance-of-payments surpluses, notably Germany and Japan. Some of the slowest-growing economies were those with large, chronic balance-of-payments deficits, notably the United States and Britain.

Furthermore, the traditional beliefs ignored financial conditions altogether. Recently many economists have reversed this neglect and, when asked whether balance-of-payments problems constrain economic growth, have tended to answer: "No; faster economic growth leads to balance-of-payments surpluses, not deficits, and this is consistent with the evidence we see around us."[3] Consistent though it is, this answer is no more deserving of universal and timeless application

[3] This answer and the reasoning that supports it have come to be known as the *monetary approach* to the impact of growth on the balance of payments.

than the earlier yes. It is clear from Figure 4.3 and the accompanying discussion that a country *could* potentially grow at almost any rate without incurring balance-of-payments deficits. All it has to do is maintain tight enough financial conditions. If a country has control over its financial conditions, it can make sure that any real-GNP-induced shift in the supply curve in Figure 4.3 is dominated by a tight-credit-induced shift in the demand curve. Most countries have at least partial control over their financial conditions. It is just in order to achieve such control that almost every country retains its own money and monetary policy rather than using another country's money as medium of exchange, store of value, and unit of account.

In the real world, however, policymakers' financial control is often severely limited by political, institutional, and technical considerations as well as by the simple desire to attain goals other than growth and a particular balance of payments. For example, interest rates often cannot be driven through ceilings prescribed by usury laws (that prescribe maximum "fair" interest rates), nor will any sane U.S. politician drive them so high that citizens cannot afford the interest payments on home mortgages. Given these limitations, many countries are realistically in the position where balance-of-payments problems do indeed constrain their growth.

If financial control were not limited too severely, then Britain's quandary of the 1960s, described in the preceding section, would be no quandary after all. Britain could pull itself out of a slump without having to worry about increasing its balance-of-payments deficit, as long as it did so by a policy that did not require financial ease. On the contrary, it should keep credit tight to avoid balance-of-payments problems. We discuss this strategy further in the last section of this chapter.

Effects of Inflation

The third fundamental shift parameter underlying supply and demand in the foreign exchange market is the general level of domestic-money prices. It enters importantly into the *competitiveness* of a country's commodities and services in world markets. The higher the domestic-money prices of tradeables are, the less attractive a country's exports and import substitutes are to potential buyers. Increases in domestic rates of inflation that are unmatched elsewhere in the world generally lead to declines in the volume of a country's exports and increases in its imports.[4] As Figure 1.2 suggests, such

[4] That inflationary impulses originating in one country are often transmitted to others cannot be denied. This is discussed at length in Chapter 6. But the assertion has no analytical significance for the argument in the text. See footnotes 1 and 2.

changes will affect *both* the supply and demand curves in the foreign exchange market.

For example, an increase in British domestic prices (or an increase in the British rate of inflation) discourages all potential buyers of British commodities and services, both in the United States and in Britain. Americans will find Beefeater gin more expensive than it used to be relative to U.S. gin (and rum). They will buy fewer bottles and will probably (an important word, as we shall see) spend less on it. British exports will fall. British Airways will find British-made Concordes, Tridents, and BAC-111s more expensive relative to Boeing aircraft and may be tempted to switch purchases to the more competitive U.S. aircraft producer. If they do so, British imports will rise.

British exports generally require someone to make foreign-exchange-market purchases of pounds. Since exports fall in value (probably), the demand for pounds will be reduced at every exchange rate when British prices rise. The higher prices will cause the demand curve for pounds to shift toward the origin. British imports, on the other hand, generally require someone to supply pounds on the foreign exchange market in order to obtain the dollars to pay off, say, Boeing. Since imports rise, the supply of pounds will be increased at every exchange rate when British prices rise. The higher prices will cause the supply curve of pounds to shift out in a southeasterly direction.

These shifts are illustrated in Figure 4.4. Granted the assumptions just discussed, the inevitable consequence of higher British prices is pound depreciation, a tendency toward British balance-of-payments deficit (a larger deficit or a smaller surplus), or both. Indeed, countries such as Argentina, Brazil, and Chile, which have had triple-digit domestic inflation at certain times in their history, have often found it impossible to maintain any exchange-rate stability. Week-by-week depreciations of their money in the foreign exchange market have been foregone conclusions.

Figure 4.4 complicates the indeterminacy associated with the effects of growth on exchange rates and the balance of payments (Figure 4.3). The rate of inflation does tend to rise during expansion and fall during recession. Thus it would seem that the ebb and flow of British inflation during economic ups and downs reinforces the tendency of increased real GNP to shift the supply curve in Figure 4.3 and counteracts the tendency of increased interest rates to shift the demand curve. But inflation and financial conditions are hardly independent of each other. Sufficiently tight credit and financial conditions could dampen the domestic rate of inflation so much that it falls below inflation elsewhere in the world, therefore reinforcing the demand-curve shift and offsetting that of the supply curve. That scenario is consistent with German experience since World War II.

Figure 4.4 and the discussion rest on one crucial assumption: that higher British prices lead the United States to spend *less* on British exports. While this may be probable, it is not at all certain. Suppose

FIGURE 4.4. *Probable Effects of Higher British Prices on the Foreign Exchange Market*

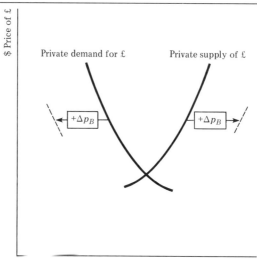

Key:
For +, read "a positive."
For Δ, read "change in."
For P_B, read "British prices."

that Americans insist on three martinis at lunch and before dinner, finding other mixed drinks unpalatable. Suppose also that American tastes are such that "there is no martini like a Beefeater martini." Given these preferences, U.S. demand for Beefeater gin may be relatively unresponsive to its price, so that when British prices rise by *x* percent, the number of bottles of Beefeater bought by Americans falls by *less* than *x* percent. Then U.S. *spending* on Beefeater will actually rise as British prices rise. The following hypothetical demand pattern illustrates this phenomenon:

British pound price of a pint of Beefeater	Millions of pints bought yearly by Americans	Yearly American spending on Beefeater (£ millions)
2	40	80
3	35	105
4	30	120

FIGURE 4.5. *Possible Effects of Higher British Prices on the Foreign Exchange Market*

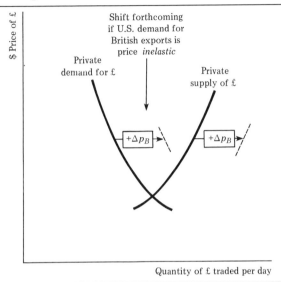

The impact of such unresponsive gin demand on the analysis is dramatic: now as British prices rise, the United States spends more on British exports. Quantities exported fall, but the pound value of exports rises. As a result, at any particular exchange rate, Americans require more pounds at high British prices than at low—to pay off Beefeater. The foreign-exchange-market demand curve for pounds shifts out and up, not down and in, when British prices rise.

This unusual phenomenon, illustrated in Figure 4.5, is due to what economists call *price-inelastic demand* for commodities—demand so unresponsive to price that spending rises when price rises, and falls when price falls. Among the many examples of price-inelastic commodity demand are consumers' demand for food, millionaires' demand for luxury automobiles, and general demands for energy. (As a matter of fact, a far more realistic example than Beefeater of a British exportable that is likely to face price-inelastic demand is British North Sea oil.) However, for the foreign-exchange-market demand curve for pounds to shift up and out with higher British prices, world demand for *all* British export products—Beefeater, oil, and so on—must on average be price inelastic.[5] Since this seems unlikely, especially in the

---

[5] Note that two different kinds of demand are being discussed here: commodity demand and the foreign-exchange-market demand for money. Supplement 4A clarifies this still further.

long run, we label Figure 4.4 the "probable" effects of British inflation on the foreign exchange market, and Figure 4.5 only the "possible effects."

The most important implication of price-inelastic U.S. demand for British exports in Figure 4.5 is that the effect of higher British prices on exchange rates and the balance of payments becomes ambiguous. Higher British prices cause foreign-exchange-market supply and demand both to shift in the same direction. This could cause the pound to appreciate and the British balance of payments to move toward *surplus* (smaller deficits or larger surpluses), but this outcome is even more improbable than the simple existence of price-inelastic U.S. demand for British exports. Commodity demands would have to be *so* price inelastic on average that the shift in the foreign exchange market's demand curve dominated the shift in its supply curve.

Apparently a few countries' exports really do face price-inelastic world commodity demand on average. United States commodity exports, for example, are mostly foodstuffs and high-technology machinery that face little competition from foreign producers.[6] For the exports of one set of countries, the oil-exporting countries, demand was so price inelastic that dramatic domestic price hikes produced balance-of-payments surpluses. From 1970 to 1975 the price of oil and oil products increased by several hundred percent, owing primarily to actions undertaken by the Organization of Petroleum Exporting Countries (OPEC) (see pp. 260–263). Table 4.1 shows the result: an impressive *growth* in OPEC's official reserves as a result of huge balance-of-payments *surpluses*. Such surpluses would be inexplicable except for price-inelastic world demand for imported oil. Had oil-exporting countries faced elastic commodity demand during the early 1970s, their attempt to raise the price of their products would have impoverished them. Not only would world demand for oil have declined in quantity terms, but world spending on oil would have declined too. Oil-exporting countries would have faced mammoth balance-of-payments deficits, as Figure 4.4 suggests, not surpluses.

Prices and inflation in the United States are equally fundamental shift variables underlying supply and demand in the foreign exchange market. An increase in the dollar price of tradeables in the United States, if unmatched elsewhere in the world, will tend to make American producers of aircraft and liquor less competitive relative to foreign producers whose prices have not risen. Decreased U.S. competitiveness will tend to reduce the number of aircraft exported from the United States and to increase the amount of gin imported. United States spending on imported Beefeater is sure to rise, and therefore

---

[6] One implication is that neither Boeing, IBM (International Business Machines), nor U.S. farmers complain seriously about how U.S. domestic inflation causes them to lose competitiveness to foreign producers. On the contrary, they welcome the opportunity to raise prices on certain items that they export.

Chapter 4: Effects of Domestic Economic Activity

TABLE 4.1. *Approximate Effects of Increased Oil Prices on the Balance of Payments and Official Reserves of Oil-Exporting Countries*

	Average Saudi Arabian export price of oil during year[a]	Official reserves of oil-exporting countries at end of year[b]	Approximate balance-of payments surplus of oil-exporting countries[c]
1970	1.80	5.2	n.a.[d]
1971	2.19	8.4	3.2
1972	2.46	10.9	2.5
1973	3.29	14.5	3.6
1974	11.58	47.0	32.5
1975	12.73	56.5	9.5
1976	13.67	65.2	8.7
1977	14.72	75.5	10.3

[a] Average wholesale price of a barrel of 34–34.9 grade oil in dollars, f.o.b. Ras Tanura, Saudi Arabia — an approximate benchmark price for all crude oil.
[b] Billions of dollars worth.
[c] Billions of dollars; approximate because it is calculated as the year-to-year change in column 2.
[d] Not available.
Source: International Monetary Fund, *International Financial Statistics*, July 1977 and July 1978. SDR value of official reserves converted to dollar value by end-of-period dollar values of the SDR, from the 1978 issue.

the foreign-exchange-market demand for pounds will be higher at every exchange rate, given the increased U.S. dollar prices. The demand curve for pounds must shift out and up.

But the shift in the foreign-exchange-market supply curve of pounds as a result of higher U.S. prices is ambiguous. If British demand for Boeing aircraft is price elastic, they will buy fewer aircraft and spend less on what they do buy. In this case, fewer pounds will be supplied on the foreign exchange market at every exchange rate because fewer dollars will have to be purchased to pay Boeing. The supply curve of pounds will shift in a northwesterly direction. But if British demand for Boeing aircraft is price inelastic, they will buy fewer aircraft but spend more on them. More pounds will have to be supplied on the foreign exchange market because the dollar value of the aircraft purchased is larger than at lower U.S. prices. The supply curve of pounds will shift in a southeasterly direction.

Furthermore, for reasons made clear in Supplement 4A, another consequence of price-inelastic British demand for U.S. exports is that the supply curve of pounds has a *negative* slope.

The results of higher U.S. prices under both price-elastic commodity demand and price-inelastic commodity demand are illustrated in Figure 4.6.

Fundamental Influences Summarized

Real economic activity, financial conditions, and inflation are the most fundamental variables that influence exchange rates and the balance of payments. Table 4.2 summarizes all these influences as if they were independent of each other. In reality they are rarely independent. Analysis is still possible when they are not, however, as illustrated below for policy-induced packages of shocks to real GNP, interest rates, and price. None of the shocks in the package is independent; all have a common origin—a particular policy decision. Their influence on exchange rates and the balance of payments is simply the sum of the influences they would have had if they really were independent.

FIGURE 4.6. *Effects of Higher U.S. Prices on the Foreign Exchange Market*

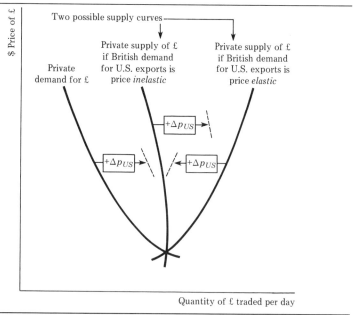

TABLE 4.2. *Effects of Changes in Real GNP (Y), Interest Rates (i), and Prices (p) on Exchange Rates and/or the Balance of Payments*

Change in fundamental variable (shock)	Floating exchange rates		Pegged or stabilized exchange rates			
	Pound . . .	*Dollar . . .*	*If Britain has a deficit, it becomes . . .*	*. . . and corresponding U.S. surplus becomes . . .*	*If Britain has a surplus, it becomes . . .*	*. . . and corresponding U.S. deficit becomes . . .*
$+\Delta Y_B$	depreciates	appreciates	larger	larger	smaller	smaller
$+\Delta Y_{US}$	appreciates	depreciates	smaller	smaller	larger	larger
$+\Delta i_B$	appreciates	depreciates	smaller	smaller	larger	larger
$+\Delta i_{US}$	depreciates	appreciates	larger	larger	smaller	smaller
$+\Delta p_B$	depreciates[a] ?[b]	appreciates[a] ?[b]	larger[a] ?[b]	larger[a] ?[b]	smaller[a] ?[b]	smaller[a] ?[b]
$+\Delta p_{US}$	appreciates[c] ?[d]	depreciates[c] ?[d]	smaller[c] ?[d]	smaller[c] ?[d]	larger[c] ?[d]	larger[c] ?[d]

[a] If U.S. demand for British exports is price elastic.
[b] If U.S. demand for British exports is price inelastic.
[c] If British demand for U.S. exports is price elastic.
[d] If British demand for U.S. exports is price inelastic.

Other Influences

Other variables besides GNP, interest rates, and prices shift supply and demand in the foreign exchange market. At times they may even be more significant causes of exchange-rate and balance-of-payments movement than the so-called fundamental variables. For example, revised expectations of future exchange-rate movements often shift foreign-exchange-market supply and demand dramatically, as outlined in Chapter 1 (see Figure 1.3). So do changes in other kinds of expectations—even expectations of future real GNP, interest rates, and inflation! So do changes in tastes (for example, for small foreign automobiles) and saving behavior (a rise in saving may increase asset imports). So do strikes in tradeables industries (such as the U.S. steel industry) and in the industries on which international trade depends (maritime industries, including dockworkers). So does anticipation of such strikes. The list of shift variables is almost endless, but it does not yet include government policy, to which we now turn.

Balance-of-Payments Adjustment by Monetary, Fiscal, and International Policies

Governments often find undesirable the foreign-exchange-market effects of alterations in the shift variables just described. They place governments in any of a number of quandaries, such as the one of choosing among the evils of economic slack, excessive loss of official reserves, or exchange-rate variability. At such times it is useful for governments to have policy instruments that themselves shift supply and demand in the foreign exchange market. Monetary and fiscal policy do so indirectly by their effects on real GNP, interest rates, and inflation. Various international economic policies do so directly.

MONETARY POLICY

Monetary policy can be defined as the attempt by a country's central bank to tighten or ease domestic credit conditions. It often involves conscious efforts to make the stock of domestic money grow less rapidly than usual (and sometimes even shrink) or to grow more rapidly than usual. The former is described as *contractionary* monetary policy, which usually leads to tighter credit, and the latter as *expansionary* monetary policy, which usually leads to easier credit.

In the notation of Figures 4.3 through 4.6, monetary policy has the following package of impacts on domestic economic activity:

Contractionary monetary policy leads to	Expansionary monetary policy leads to

$$\left\{ \begin{array}{l} -\Delta Y \\ +\Delta i \\ -\Delta p \end{array} \right\} \qquad\qquad \left\{ \begin{array}{l} +\Delta Y \\ -\Delta i \\ +\Delta p \end{array} \right\}$$

where $-\Delta Y$ and $-\Delta p$ may represent simply slower-than-normal growth in real GNP and domestic prices rather than an absolute fall in both.

Monetary policy has these effects in several ways. One depends on the fact that much spending in the economy requires prior borrowing. Consumers cannot purchase newly built homes and new cars when credit is not available. By contrast, they will make such purchases sooner and more readily when loans are easily come by and when interest costs are low. Much business spending on new plants, new equipment, and additional inventory is also financed by credit. If the central bank contracts the stock of money in existence, credit becomes tight, interest rates rise ($+\Delta i$), and some of this credit-sensitive spending by consumers and business is cut off. The so-called reduction in aggregate demand for homes, automobiles, machinery, and so on causes real GNP to grow more slowly or fall ($-\Delta Y$) and causes domestic inflation to moderate ($-\Delta p$). The opposite effects occur when the central bank expands the stock of domestic money. Another channel of monetary policy's influence is more direct. When the money stock is reduced, a part of the society must end up holding less money than previously. People probably view such reductions as a decline in wealth and consequently feel more insecure and prone to save. These feelings generally translate into reduced aggregate demand for all goods, causing reinforced slackening in real GNP and inflation. When the money stock is increased, the opposite happens.

Because of its package of consequences, monetary policy has a clear impact on the foreign exchange market as long as commodity demands are price elastic. Contractionary British monetary policy causes both supply and demand in the foreign exchange market to shift in such a way that the pound appreciates or the British balance of payments tends toward surplus.[7] This is illustrated in Figure 4.7. By contrast, expansionary British monetary policy causes the pound to depreciate or the British balance of payments to tend toward deficit.

Partly because of its unambiguous impact, monetary policy is often used to attain and defend goals for exchange rates and the balance of payments. Contractionary monetary policy in particular is often used

---

[7] When commodity demands are price inelastic, this conclusion is not necessarily correct, although it may be.

FIGURE 4.7. *Effect of Contractionary British Monetary Policy on the Foreign Exchange Market*

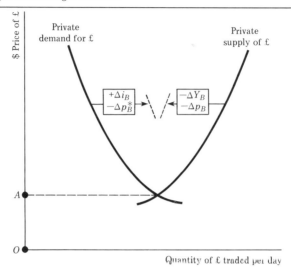

Key:
For + and −, read "a positive" and "a negative" respectively.
For Δ, read "change in."
For Y_B, i_B, and P_B, read "British real GNP," "British interest rates," and "British prices" respectively.
Effects of the shifts depicted:
  Under floating exchange rates; the dollar price of pounds rises above *OA*.
  Under an exchange rate pegged at *OA*; an excessive demand for pounds develops at *OA*, a British balance-of-payments surplus.
  Under managed floating; both some pound appreciation and some British balance-of-payments surplus may result.

---

* If the U.S. demand for British exports is price elastic.

as a weapon to deter depreciation and to reduce the size of a country's balance-of-payments deficit. But using monetary policy in this way often has a price: it creates domestic economic slack—increased unemployment and idle machinery and plants. There is a trade-off between foreign-exchange-market goals and domestic prosperity. That is where fiscal and other policies come in. They can often be used to neutralize the "price" imposed on the domestic economy by monetary policy that is aimed solely at the foreign exchange market. They can solve the trade-off problem. Mixing several policies turns out to be better than relying only on one to attain social goals. The problem of determining the best mix, the one that brings the economy closest to satisfying all goals, is known as the *optimal-policy-mix problem*. To illustrate it, it is helpful to outline the foreign-exchange-market impact of fiscal policy.

FISCAL POLICY

Fiscal policy can be defined as the attempt by a government to change total domestic spending (aggregate demand) by altering taxes or government spending. Contractionary fiscal policy requires either increased taxes or reduced government spending. Expansionary fiscal policy requires either reduced taxes or increased government spending. Usually fiscal policy has the following package of effects on domestic economic activity:

Contractionary   Expansionary
fiscal policy   fiscal policy
leads to   leads to

$$\left\{ \begin{array}{c} -\Delta Y \\ -\Delta i \\ -\Delta p \end{array} \right\} \qquad \left\{ \begin{array}{c} +\Delta Y \\ +\Delta i \\ +\Delta p \end{array} \right\}$$

These packages differ qualitatively from those associated with monetary policy.

The channels whereby fiscal policy has its effects on real GNP and domestic prices are fairly direct. Contractionary fiscal policy either reduces the income available to private individuals to spend by raising their taxes, or it reduces government purchases of goods and services. Both reduced private purchasing power and reduced government purchases contract aggregate demand, weakening private incentives to produce and undermining any temptation to private producers to raise price. Expansionary fiscal policy has the opposite effects.

Fiscal policy also has interest-rate impacts, which are less direct. Expansionary fiscal policy usually pushes the government's budget toward budget deficit.[8] The government's budget deficit is the extent to which tax revenues fall short of government spending. (Budget deficits should be differentiated from balance-of-payments deficits.) Expansionary fiscal policy causes an existing budget deficit to grow larger. This requires the government to increase the borrowing that it does from the general public whenever its income is less than its spending. The government borrows by selling new government bonds to the general public—new IOUs or new additions to the national debt. Generally the more bonds it must sell, the higher the interest rate it must offer to make the bonds appealing to additional investors.

---

[8] There is a special case in which this is not true. Expansionary fiscal policy of the so-called *balanced-budget* variety increases taxes and government spending equally. That this can be expansionary is shown in most macroeconomics textbooks. But it has no effect on the government's budget.

FIGURE 4.8. *Ambiguous Effect of Expansionary British Fiscal Policy on the Foreign Exchange Market*

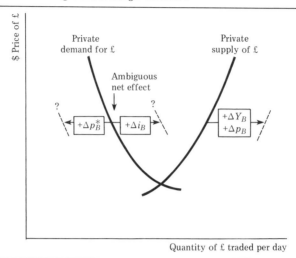

* If the U.S. demand for British exports is price elastic.

Thus expansionary fiscal policy usually raises interest rates because it leads to larger budget deficits requiring larger government bond sales to the general public. Contractionary fiscal policy, by contrast, usually reduces interest rates.

The foreign-exchange-market consequences of fiscal policy are ambiguous, as Figure 4.8 illustrates. British fiscal policy has predictable effects on exchange rates and the balance of payments only if something is known about the comparative strengths of the offsetting curve shifts. That is one reason why fiscal policy is infrequently employed on its own to attain or defend foreign-exchange-market goals.[9]

POLICY MIXES

When combined (mixed) with monetary policy, fiscal policy can have a significant role in avoiding the quandaries created by conflicting goals. It can be used to skirt policy trade-offs such as that sketched before, where contractionary monetary policy could achieve a foreign-

[9] In fact, for reasons that differ somewhat from those in the text, it is often recommended that fiscal policy be "assigned" solely to solving internal employment-inflation problems and that monetary policy be "assigned" solely to solving exchange-rate and balance-of-payments problems. This recommendation, called the *assignment rule*, is an example of the policy mixes described below.

exchange-market goal only at the expense of increased domestic economic slack.

A simple example of an optimal policy mix will demonstrate this conclusion. Suppose that Britain wants to eliminate its balance-of-payments deficit, yet keep exchange rates, real GNP, employment, and inflation where they are. In principle, Britain could devise a mix of contractionary monetary policy and expansionary fiscal policy that would do just this. It would be neutral in its effects on aggregate demand and therefore in its effects on real GNP and prices, yet it would be reinforcing in its interest-rate effects. In other words, the intensity of monetary contraction and fiscal expansion could be gauged so that their opposing effects on real GNP and prices just canceled, while their parallel effects on interest rates were mutually supportive. Schematically:

Some particular contractionary monetary policy

Some particular expansionary fiscal policy

$$
\begin{Bmatrix} -\Delta Y \\ +\Delta i \\ -\Delta p \end{Bmatrix} \quad + \quad \begin{Bmatrix} +\Delta Y \\ +\Delta i \\ +\Delta p \end{Bmatrix} \quad = \quad \begin{Bmatrix} 0 \\ +\Delta i \\ 0 \end{Bmatrix}
$$

The foreign-exchange-market impact of such a policy mix is clear in Figure 4.2. It is exactly as desired: the British balance-of-payments deficit will shrink without any adverse employment-inflation effects.

In practice, optimal policy mixes are difficult to implement. They require a precise calculation of the economic effects of policy, in order to assure exactly offsetting GNP-price effects. They require either that policies be initiated at the same time and take hold at the same rate of speed, or else that policies be subject to continuous, flexible monitoring and "fine-tuning" in order to assure the desired results. For the specific policies discussed, they require a degree of coordination between the monetary and fiscal authority that is rare, especially in countries such as the United States, where the former is a nonpolitical, independent central bank and the latter is a politically sensitive legislature.

Nevertheless, the principle underlying optimal policy mixes is valid. And other policies that have significant foreign-exchange-market consequences often can be mixed with either monetary or fiscal policy to achieve multiple goals.

INTERNATIONAL ECONOMIC POLICIES

The most important of these other policies have direct effects on the foreign exchange market or on the international trade and financial investment that lie immediately behind foreign-exchange-market supply and demand. For this reason they can be described as international economic policies. They include:

EXCHANGE CONTROL AND MULTIPLE-EXCHANGE-RATE SYSTEMS. These policies administratively appropriate the foreign-exchange-market supply of foreign money and ration the potential demand for it. (See Supplement 2A.)

TAXES, SUBSIDIES, AND QUANTITATIVE RESTRICTIONS ON COMMODITY TRADE. These policies (see Chapter 9) are used to encourage and discourage international commodity trade. Changes in British export incentives shift the demand-for-pounds curve. Changes in British import incentives shift the supply-of-pounds curve. Usually changes in commodity-trade policies that are motivated by foreign-exchange-market conditions are temporary, chiefly because well-developed and accepted routes for retaliation are open to countries injured by another's trade policies (see p. 352). Among the more popular temporary trade policies are *import surcharges*, additional taxes placed on top of existing import taxes (tariffs); *import quotas*, ceilings on the quantity of imports permissible in a given period; and *import deposit schemes*, requirements that importers prepay a portion of their import bill to the government, which then sits on the money for several months before returning it (often without interest) and before permitting the import actually to take place. These particular commodity-trade policies are employed temporarily by countries with balance-of-payments-deficit problems.[10] More rarely, countries with balance-of-payments surplus problems loosen import restrictions. Japan did this in the early 1970s, and Germany in the mid-1960s.

RESTRICTIONS ON TRADE IN SERVICES. These policies have the same effects on the foreign exchange market as commodity-trade restrictions. For example, a great many countries limit the amount of domestic money that touring residents can take abroad. British restrictions of this kind effectively limit the foreign-exchange-market supply of pounds that pay for overseas tourist services imported by British residents. Many countries also limit the ability of resident foreign corporations to repatriate earnings, which is considered a service transaction (see footnote 2, Supplement 2C). Such restrictions are tightened by countries that wish to ward off depreciation and deficit and are loosened by those that fear appreciation and surplus.

TAXES AND RESTRICTIONS ON TRADE IN ASSETS. The most pervasive of all international economic policies are those that influence and

[10] Britain, Canada, Denmark, France, and the United States have employed import surcharges in the recent past. Britain, Italy and many less-developed countries have devised import deposit schemes. And most countries have adopted temporary import quotas at some time that were justified on balance-of-payments grounds.

control international financial investment. A few examples are (1) taxes such as the U.S. Interest Equalization Tax (1963–1974), which placed an extra tax on the interest earned by U.S. buyers of foreign bonds, and which effectively dried up U.S. purchases of foreign bonds altogether; (2) legal quotas or ceilings on commercial-bank loans to foreigners, except to finance exports, such as existed in the United States from 1965 to 1974; (3) negative interest rates (penalty rates) forced on foreign depositors in Swiss and Dutch commercial banks periodically during the 1970s to discourage such deposits. The U.S. policies in this brief list were oriented toward reducing U.S. balance-of-payments deficits and the threat of depreciation. The Swiss and Dutch policies were oriented toward reducing their balance-of-payments surpluses and checking appreciation.

Summary and a Look Ahead

Exchange rates and the balance of payments reflect domestic economic conditions in all countries that engage in international exchange. Their day-to-day and year-to-year flux is not arbitrary, although it may be very hard to predict. It is explained typically by different rates of real growth from country to country, different philosophies toward financial markets and credit conditions, different rates of domestic inflation, alterations in tastes, and ever-changing expectations of the future course of these fundamental variables.

No one would care about the objective causes of exchange-rate variability, nor therefore about the balance of payments, were it not for their important economic role sketched in Chapter 3. Given reason to care, governments are naturally concerned about the fundamental variables that can unfavorably affect the foreign exchange market. Apart from tastes and expectations, all these fundamental variables are susceptible to policy influence. One might think that a government could by policy manipulate growth, credit, and inflation to attain any exchange rate and balance-of-payments position it found desirable. This belief is misleadingly simple. Governments are not indifferent to domestic growth, credit, and inflation either, for obvious social, economic, and political reasons. Conflicts often develop among multiple goals, and some goals must be sacrificed or traded off against others. For example, governments that find it politically advantageous to foster rapid economic growth and easy credit are usually forced to put up with dramatic short-run losses in official reserves and with recurrent depreciation.

In principle, with enough policy instruments, governments could attain all goals by mixing all policies. But instruments such as monetary policy, fiscal policy, and exchange control are always uncertain in their quantitative effects, usually have limited flexibility, and often are ineffective for political and technical reasons. Which goals shall be pursued most attentively, then, and which shall be sacrificed? Governments must choose their medicine.

The quandary is awkward and the choice complex partly because of *feedback*. This feature of international economic activity has been ignored in Chapter 4 but is taken up in Chapters 5 and 6. Chapter 4 described the way in which real GNP, interest rates, and inflation affect the foreign exchange market. Those same foreign-exchange-market effects *feed back* on real GNP, interest rates, and inflation. For example, changes in exchange rates themselves alter growth and financial conditions. The direction of causation can be reversed, and in the real world, causation almost always runs both ways.[11]

In a similar vein, the mere existence of a balance-of-payments surplus or deficit implies stimuli that tend to alter real GNP, interest rates, and inflation. The most important stimuli come from the potential effect of the balance of payments on the domestic money stock. This particular feedback does not always exist, though. Strong central banks attempt to short-circuit it, as will be shown in the next chapter. This short-circuiting, however, is subject to technical problems and may be ineffective in small countries or in those without strong central banks. The result is a strong tendency for the balance of payments to cause changes in domestic economic activity.

Finally, there are important feedbacks between economic activity in one country and economic activity in others. Chapter 4 has analyzed the foreign-exchange-market impacts of growth, credit, and inflation in either the United States or Britain. In fact, one country's unusual growth, financial shocks, and inflationary flux generally cause changes in the rest of the world's growth, credit, and inflation. The international transmission of problems and prosperity is analyzed in Chapter 6.

Key Terms

recession; expansion
demand-shift variable
easy and tight credit
overshooting
price-elastic; price-inelastic
demand

contractionary and expansionary
policies
(optimal) policy mixes; the assignment rule
import surcharges, quotas, deposit schemes

Key Concepts and Review

Immediate versus fundamental reasons why exchange rates and the balance of payments vary.

[11] Some of the ways in which exchange rates cause changes in domestic economic activity were implicit in Chapter 3.

How domestic economic variables affect international economic variables independently: GNP, interest rates, prices.

How packages of domestic economic variables affect international economic variables interdependently: monetary and fiscal policies.

Trade-offs between domestic and international goals.

Feedback (reciprocal causation) among domestic variables and international variables.

Supplement 4A
Effects of Price-Inelastic Commodity Demand
on Slopes in the Foreign Exchange Market

The text outlines in detail the effects of commodity demand elasticity on inflation-induced *shifts* in foreign-exchange-market supply and demand. But commodity demand elasticity also affects the *slopes* of these curves. When U.S. demand for British exports is price inelastic on average, the supply curve of pounds in the foreign exchange market is negatively sloped. Similarly, we will show that when British demand for U.S. exports is price inelastic on average, the supply curve of *dollars* in an alternative depiction of the very same foreign exchange market is negatively sloped.[1]

The easiest way to draw these conclusions is through a hypothetical example. The example we shall use, summarized in Table 4A.1, relies on the assumption that every international exchange of goods requires a foreign-exchange-market transaction. The pound price of a pint of gin is held constant at £2, and the dollar price of a Boeing 747 is held constant at $40 million. These constancy assumptions are required if we want to examine the slope of a single supply curve. Otherwise, if domestic prices were allowed to vary, the example would produce a set of points on many different supply curves, as the text above shows (see Figures 4.4, 4.5, and 4.6). Finally, it is assumed that both the U.S. demand for Beefeater gin and the British demand for Boeing 747s are price inelastic.

The information contained in Table 4A.1 is summarized graphically in Figures 4A.1 and 4A.2. Several things are notable about Figures 4A.1 and 4A.2. First, both supply curves have unusual negative slopes. The negative slope of the supply-of-pounds curve in Figure 4A.1 is due solely to British price inelasticity of demand for Boeing 747s. Boeing may be willing, as in Chapter 1, to accept pound checks from British Airways in payment for the aircraft that it exports, but it will usually convert these pound checks immediately into dollars at its own commercial bank: it will supply them to the foreign exchange market. Boeing's total pound supply over the course of a year will vary directly with two things: (1) the number of pounds it takes to acquire $40 million, the dollar amount that Boeing insists upon ultimately receiving in order to agree to export one 747; and (2) the number of

---

[1] The numerical example below will implicitly demonstrate how the supply curve of pounds in one representation of the foreign exchange market illustrates the same behavior as the demand curve for dollars in the alternative representation. Similarly, the demand curve for pounds reflects the supply curve of dollars. This is not surprising in light of Chapter 1's characterization of the foreign exchange market as a market where one country's money is "bartered" for another's. In a barter market, the supply of one good and the demand for another *is* the same thing.

747s that it exports. Rises in both of these variables increase Boeing's annual supply of pounds to the foreign exchange market.

As the dollar price of the pound falls, variable 1 rises because pounds are worth less, and Boeing therefore insists on receiving more pounds per plane from British Airways to assure a revenue of $40 million; and variable 2 falls because the pound price of 747s faced by British Airways rises, choking off British demand for 747s. (The pound price of a 747 is its constant dollar price multiplied by the pound value of a dollar.) The rise in variable 1 and the fall in variable 2 are offsetting. One raises Boeing's yearly supply of pounds; one lowers it. It is entirely possible for the rise in the first to outweigh the fall in the second, especially when the second response is weak. The consequence is the strange supply of pounds illustrated: a supply that rises with falling prices.

A little experimentation will establish that the rise in variable 1 (number of pounds needed to acquire $40 million) always outweighs the fall in variable 2 (number of 747s exported) when British demand for 747s is price inelastic—when quantity demanded responds so little to price changes that spending varies positively with prices. A good way to begin such experimentation is to investigate perfect price inelasticity of demand, in which quantity demanded does not respond at all to price. Then there is no fall in variable 2, only a rise in variable 1. In that case, both variable 1 and the supply of pounds will rise by the same proportion that the dollar price of pounds falls. A 10 percent depreciation of the pound will increase the supply of pounds 10 percent.[2]

The negative slope of the supply-of-dollars curve in Figure 4A.2 is due solely to the U.S. price inelasticity of demand for Beefeater. The explanation is completely parallel to that above and is left to the student.

A second curious aspect of Figures 4A.1 and 4A.2 is that there are two equilibria—two points at which supply equals demand. One of these turns out to be *stable:* the one at the exchange rate $4 per pound. By stability, economists mean that any price other than $4/£, but close to it, sets in motion the forces of supply and demand that lead the price to *move* toward $4/£. Prices such as $3.90/£ don't persist because of the pressure of excessive demand against supply. Prices such as $4.10/£ don't persist because of the pressure of excessive supply against demand. Slight divergences from the equilibrium price $4/£ cannot last. It is a stable equilibrium price. By contrast, $2 is an *unstable* equilibrium price. If the market were to happen upon that price by chance, both suppliers and demanders would be fully satisfied, and the market would be "at rest" (meaning "in equilibrium"). But if the market were

[2] In fact, as long as commodity-demand curves never have positive slopes (as they do for "Giffen goods"), the supply curve has its most negative slope in this case —one consistent with a supply elasticity of −1.

TABLE 4A.1. *Hypothetical Example of Price-Inelastic Commodity Demand and Its Foreign-Exchange-Market Effects*[a]

Data Relating to Beefeater Trade

Exchange rates		Commodity prices		Commodity demand	Foreign exchange market	
Dollar price of a pound	Pound price of a dollar	British pound price of a pint of Beefeater	U.S. dollar price of a pint of Beefeater	Millions of pints bought yearly by Americans	Supply of $ — Dollar value of Beefeater shipped from Britain to U.S. yearly (millions)	Demand for £ — Pound value of Beefeater shipped from Britain to U.S. yearly (millions)
2	0.50	2	4	40	160	80
3	0.33	2	6	35	210	70
4	0.25	2	8	30	240	60

Data Relating to Boeing Trade

Exchange rates		Commodity prices		Commodity demand	Foreign exchange market	
					Supply of £	Demand for $
Dollar price of a pound	Pound price of a dollar	U.S. dollar price of a 747 (millions)	British pound price of a 747 (millions)	747s bought yearly by the British	Pound value of 747s shipped from U.S. to Britain yearly (millions)	Dollar value of 747s shipped from U.S. to Britain yearly (millions)
2	0.50	40	20	4	80	160
3	0.33	40	13.33	5	66.67	200
4	0.25	40	10	6	60	240

[a] Chapter 1 and 2, especially Figures 1.2, 2.7, and 2.8, may be useful in reviewing the correspondences in the two right-hand columns of this table.

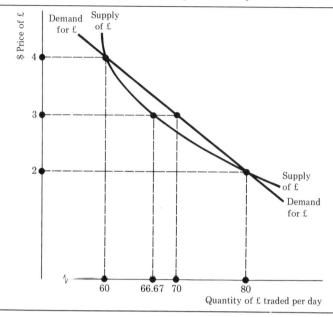

to experiment with any price slightly above $2/£, the forces of supply and demand would drive the price all the way up to $4/£, not back down to $2/£. And if the market were to experiment with any price slightly below $2/£, the forces of supply and demand would drive the price down to some other equilibrium point, not back up to $2/£. It is this "hilltop' characteristic of the equilibrium at $2/£ that leads us to call it unstable: a ball might remain stationary at the very peak of a hill, but not slightly below; on the north side, it would roll to the north foot; on the south, to the south foot, and so on.

Instability and volatility of this kind may be more than theoretical curiosities. Many practical analysts of the foreign exchange market believe that they exist at certain times and for certain kinds of exchange-rate changes. Price-inelastic commodity demands cannot be ruled out as a fact of life, especially in the short run after a major change in commodity prices. Demanders take time to respond to any alteration in price, being constrained by existing contracts and long-standing business relationships and wary of the impermanence of any price change. In the instant after a price change, probably *all* demands for *all* commodities are price inelastic. Thus if responses to price change are slow enough, and if they pervade enough demands for imported commodities, then in the analysis of the short-run effect

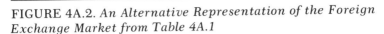

FIGURE 4A.2. *An Alternative Representation of the Foreign Exchange Market from Table 4A.1*

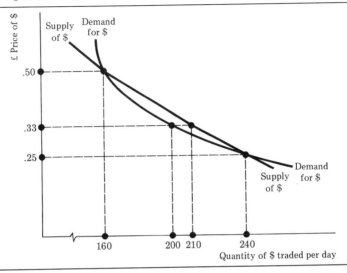

of an exchange-rate change Figures 4A.1 and 4A.2 may be relevant, strange though they seem.

To illustrate this relevance, Figure 4A.1 implies an unusual but empirically observed pattern of adjustment for the balance of payments when the exchange rate changes. At $3/£, Britain has a balance-of-payments surplus. If the British government were to devalue and depreciate the pound to $2/£, the British surplus would disappear. If it were to devalue the pound below $2, a balance-of-payments *deficit* would emerge. Yet this runs completely counter to intuition and to analysis based on the usual diagram. Pound devaluation and depreciation should cure a British deficit, not cause one. Britain's surplus at $3/£ should have been enlarged by devaluation, not erased.

Yet if commodity demands are sufficiently price inelastic in the short run, British devaluation and depreciation will initially work opposite to intuition. Only as time goes on, as demanders begin to adjust their purchases to reflect fully the new price regime, will enough commodity demands become price elastic to restore a positively sloped supply-of-pounds curve in the foreign exchange market (or a negatively sloped one that is more vertical than the demand curve). Then pound devaluation will begin to have its expected effects: British deficits will shrink, or else British surpluses will grow.

Many of the major exchange-rate changes of the 1960s and 1970s

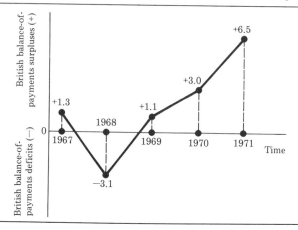

FIGURE 4A.3. *The British Balance of Payments before and after the November 1967 Devaluation of the Pound (Billions of Dollars)*

Source: International Monetary Fund, *Balance of Payments Yearbook* 24.

have produced balance-of-payments consequences consistent with negatively sloped short-run supply. For example, Britain's balance-of-payments position before and after the 14.3 percent devaluation of the pound in November 1967 is recorded in Figure 4A.3. Connecting the points in the diagram produces a line that very roughly resembles the letter *J.* Because of this, the unusual response to exchange-rate changes sketched above has come to be known as *J-curve adjustment* of the balance of payments. J-curve adjustment is a direct consequence of a short-run supply curve like that illustrated in Figure 4A.1, one that rotates clockwise over time toward a more normally sloped supply curve.

J-curve adjustment has many implications. It implies counterintuitive changes in a surplus country's balance of payments when it first revalues. The surplus becomes temporarily larger, as Germany's did after several of its revaluations. It also implies that countries contemplating major devaluations should carry them out before official reserves become too low: the largest rate of loss of official reserves may take place immediately after the devaluation, not immediately before it.

Finally, it must be said that J-curve adjustment and negative foreign-exchange-market supply response are theoretical constructs, not necessarily facts. They are consistent with the facts for many countries, but not for others, and as such remain an interesting possibility.

Chapter 5

Effects of the Balance of Payments and Exchange Rates on Domestic Economic Activity

Some people are surprised that seemingly exotic variables such as the balance of payments and exchange rates have important *domestic* effects. Others are not surprised because the beliefs are widespread, for example, that balance-of-payments deficits cause people to lose jobs and that depreciations make things more expensive. But people who hold such beliefs are often hard pressed to explain why.

This chapter illuminates these matters. We will examine the impacts of both the balance of payments and a change in exchange rates on domestic employment, growth, inflation, wealth, and general economic well-being. Many of these domestic impacts are quite powerful, even in countries as large and self-sufficient as the United States. Thus the international economics of this chapter is not only for the internationally minded.

Effect of the Balance of Payments on Money Stocks, Real GNP, Interest Rates, and Domestic Prices

In Chapter 4 real GNP, interest rates, and domestic prices were shown to be the fundamental determinants of a nation's balance of payments under pegged exchange rates. In this chapter causal relations run in the opposite direction. We shall see that balance-of-payments positions sometimes feed back on the domestic conditions that brought them about. In fact, sometimes the course of domestic economic prosperity will be almost dictated by the state of the balance of payments.

157

THE BALANCE OF PAYMENTS AND THE MONEY STOCK

The cornerstone for these conclusions is a crucial potential link between a nation's balance of payments and the stock of its domestic money in existence. There is a natural tendency for balance-of-payments deficits to bring about contraction in the domestic money stock and for surpluses to bring about expansion. Monetary contraction and expansion in turn affect employment, inflation, and credit conditions. There may, therefore, be conflict between explicit monetary policy and the money-stock consequences of the balance of payments. The attempt by central banks to override these consequences is called *sterilization* or *neutralization* of the money-stock effects of the balance of payments.

To explain these matters more fully, some review from Chapter 2 is helpful. Balance-of-payments surpluses and deficits arise because governments intervene in the foreign exchange market in order to stabilize exchange rates. When market forces bring about undesirable depreciation of the pound on the foreign exchange market, Britain's central bank often chooses to "support the pound." It does so by using official reserves to buy pounds from private sellers. The central bank's demand for pounds keeps the pound's foreign-exchange market value higher than it would be otherwise, but the central bank's simultaneous supply of, say, dollars reduces the British official-reserve stock. By definition, a British balance-of-payments deficit exists. Similarly, when market forces bring about undesirable pound appreciation, the British central bank often "restrains the pound." It actually sells pounds in the foreign exchange market to eager private buyers. In return, the central bank accepts dollars, which are added to the British official-reserve stock. By definition, a British balance-of-payments surplus exists.

Exchange-rate stabilization along these lines must affect the British money stock as long as the British central bank takes no offsetting sterilization action. To understand this fully, we need another definition. Britain, like almost every country in the world, defines its money stock[1] as the sum of (1) the stock of currency in private circulation—British pound notes and coins held by individuals, corporations, and institutions (including parts of the government itself); and (2) the stock of privately held demand deposits (checking accounts) in the commercial banking system—legal claims on com-

---

[1] A more conventional term for *British money stock* is *British money supply*. Using the more conventional term may create so-called stock-flow confusion. The British money supply—the *stock supply* of pounds in existence, is not the same creature as the supply of pounds on the foreign exchange market—the *flow supply* of pounds in a given period of time that holders want to convert to dollars. In fact, the discussion will identify when a flow supply of pounds on the foreign exchange market changes the stock supply and when it does not.

Chapter 5: Effects of the Balance of Payments and Exchange Rates

mercial banks that entitle individuals, corporations, and institutions to obtain currency on demand.[2] The key word in this definition is *private*. Among other things, private holdings *exclude* (1) the central bank's own stock of currency; (2) its own legal claims on commercial banks (such as the debts they occasionally incur by borrowing from the central bank); and (3) all other assets owned by the central bank, no matter how moneylike they are.[3] The upshot is that when the British central bank buys pounds from private sellers in the foreign exchange market, the purchased pounds disappear from private circulation; they cease to exist as a part of the British money stock. When the British central bank sells pounds to private buyers in the foreign exchange market, the sale is an injection of new pounds into private circulation; "privately owned" pounds rise. British balance-of-payments deficits, foreign-exchange-market purchases of pounds by the British central bank, and shrinkage in the British money stock are all different sides of the same coin. So are balance-of-payments surpluses, foreign-exchange-market sales of pounds by the central bank, and expansion of the money stock.

EXAMPLE. Assume for simplicity that on a particular day the only desired foreign-exchange-market transaction at the ruling exchange rate arises from Boeing's desire to convert a £5 million check from British Airways into dollars. By definition, Boeing is supplying pounds on the foreign exchange market—offering them for sale. If some private institution, say Boeing's own commercial bank, had been willing to accept the pounds and give up dollars, there would have been *another* desired foreign-exchange-market transaction: a matching demand for pounds. No change in the exchange rate would have taken place, and there would also have been no change in the British money stock—the stock of pounds in existence in private hands. Pounds that were originally owned by British Airways would have changed hands first to Boeing, then to Boeing's commercial bank.

But we have assumed that no one is willing to accept Boeing's pounds at the ruling exchange rate, even Boeing's own commercial bank. Downward pressure on the value of the pound will develop. A

---

[2] Some subtleties to defining the money stock are ignored here because they are not important for our purposes. Broader definitions of the money stock also are sometimes recommended as preferable. All definitions include items 1 and 2.

[3] The definition is not arbitrary. Data on a nation's money stock are collected because the size of the money stock, relative to the economy's immediate needs for it to facilitate transactions or to "store value" for the future, is believed by economists to affect both inflation rates and real economic activity. By statute, central banks neither engage in current market transactions for economic motives nor save for the future by holding money or other assets. Their own cash requirements are minuscule and irrelevant. What really matter are the money assets that they allow to be placed in the hands of economic agents who do transact and invest for normal economic reasons.

supply exists but no demand. Demand will be forthcoming only when the pound becomes cheaper. Assume also that the British central bank does not want the pound to depreciate. It will commit itself to buy the £5 million Boeing offers by announcing to brokers its willingness to use official-reserve dollars and buy all pounds for sale at the ruling exchange rate. At the end of the day the effects of this action will have been (1) no change in the exchange rate; (2) a British balance-of-payments deficit for the day equal to £5 million; and (3) a reduction in the British money stock of £5 million.

The last effect is clarified in the following accounting. At the beginning of the day British Airways, a "private" corporation (even though publicly owned and a part of the government), owned a £5 million claim on (or deposit at) its commercial bank. This deposit was by definition a part of the stock of pounds in existence. At the end of the day the British central bank owns that same £5 million claim on British Airways' commercial bank. It is no longer (by definition) a part of the British money stock.[4]

An example of how British balance-of-payments surpluses tend to bring about expansion in the British money stock can be similarly constructed.

THE ATTRACTIVENESS OF STERILIZATION (NEUTRALIZATION)

Modern central banks do not usually welcome the impacts of the balance of payments on the money stock. In stabilizing exchange rates by intervening in the foreign exchange market, they introduce a potential for the balance of payments to dictate monetary policy. Narrowly domestic goals, say for larger real GNP and lower interest rates, may require easy monetary policy. These goals will be frustrated if the central bank is confronted with a balance-of-payments deficit that reduces the money stock. The deficit's undesired impact on GNP and interest rates is illustrated in the top half of Schema 5.1.

Historically, concerns about such conflicts were not always compelling. Under the gold standard (see Supplement 2A) of the early twentieth century, for example, national goals for full employment and

---

[4] The British money stock could shrink even more than £5 million in the ensuing few days. In Britain's *fractional reserve* commercial banking system, British Airways' commercial bank will have lost a full £5 million of its own *bank reserves*. (Such commercial bank reserves should be distinguished from official reserves of Britain's central bank.) It may be required by law to replenish them, which may force it to call in some of its loans to private borrowers and to channel the proceeds to its own deposits at the British central bank. The result is that even more pounds will cease to exist—those owned by unlucky borrowers from the commercial bank whose loans have been terminated. This multiple shrinkage of the British money stock is described by economists as *multiple credit contraction*.

SCHEMA 5.1. *Effect of the Balance of Payments on Domestic Economic Activity When Central Banks Do Not Sterilize*

| Balance-of-payments deficits | $\longrightarrow$ | Contraction of the domestic money stock in existence | $\longrightarrow$ | $\begin{Bmatrix} -\Delta Y \\ +\Delta i \\ -\Delta p \end{Bmatrix}$ |
| Balance-of-payments surpluses | $\longrightarrow$ | Expansion of the domestic money stock in existence | $\longrightarrow$ | $\begin{Bmatrix} +\Delta Y \\ -\Delta i \\ +\Delta p \end{Bmatrix}$ |

Key:
For $\rightarrow$, read "leads to" or "causes."
For $+$ and $-$, read "a positive" and "a negative" respectively.
For Δ, read "change in."
For Y, read "real GNP."
For i, read "interest rates."
For p, read "prices."

stable prices were poorly articulated or nonexistent. Central banks themselves were weak or nonexistent. Market forces and downward price flexibility made both unemployment and inflation less enduring and less frequently severe. Therefore balance-of-payments surpluses and deficits were allowed to have the domestic macroeconomic consequences illustrated in Schema 5.1.

But modern central banks are often given statutory responsibility for promoting full employment, smoothly functioning financial markets, and stable prices. A necessary tool in carrying out these statutory directives is sterilization. It is simply defined as the short-circuiting of the link between the balance of payments and the money stock. Successful sterilization therefore short-circuits also the link between the balance of payments and domestic economic activity.

STERILIZATION IN PRINCIPLE

In operation, sterilization amounts to consciously returning domestic money to circulation when it is withdrawn through a balance-of-payments deficit, and consciously withdrawing new money from circulation when it is created through a balance-of-payments surplus. In principle, sterilization can be carried out by any of the familiar tools of monetary policy:

1. Sterilization by *open-market operations*. A central bank that is financing a balance-of-payments deficit will simultaneously purchase government bonds from the public. It thereby places new money into

Money Stocks, Real GNP, Interest Rates, and Domestic Prices   161

circulation to replace what the deficit withdrew. In fact, the central bank will plan to purchase government bonds worth exactly the same value as the official reserves that it had to sell to support the exchange rate. Open-market bond purchases balance foreign-exchange-market official-reserve sales. A central bank that is financing a balance-of-payments surplus, by contrast, will simultaneously sell bonds to the public. It thereby withdraws the money added to circulation when it bought official reserves on the foreign exchange market.

2. Sterilization by changes in commercial-bank *reserve requirements*. Commercial banks are usually required by law to hold reserves of currency and deposits at the central bank. These enable it to meet all withdrawal requests from depositors. By loosening reserve requirements, central banks free up reserves which commercial banks can then loan out to private borrowers, expanding the amount of money in private circulation. In principle, this loosening could compensate for the tendency of a balance-of-payments deficit to reduce the money stock. Tightening reserve requirements, by contrast, would contract the money stock and could be used to absorb extra money created by balance-of-payments surpluses.

3. Sterilization by *discount-rate* operations. Central banks can influence the money stock by raising and lowering the discount rate—the interest rate paid by commercial banks that borrow from the central bank to meet reserve requirements.

Sterilization is also possible through less familiar tools of explicit monetary policy, including banking regulations and the moral authority of the central bank to sway commercial banks' behavior. European central banks have even sterilized balance-of-payments surpluses occasionally by selling official reserves temporarily to their own commercial banks! Arrangements are simultaneously made to buy back the official reserves in the future at a rate attractive enough to make the commercial banks willing. In the interim, private European commercial banks have their potential loan money tied up holding the central bank's official reserves. This temporarily contracts European money stocks. Such arrangements also make European balance-of-payments surpluses shrink deceptively, since the central bank's official reserves appear to decline. These operations are known as *forward swaps* (not to be confused with the swaps of Supplement 3A).

STERILIZATION IN PRACTICE

Sterilization is rarely complete or perfect; monetary control is simply too imprecise an art. For example, many of the world's central banks cannot rely on open market operations to the degree that the Federal Reserve System does in the United States. Some cannot rely on them at all. Bond markets in these countries are insufficiently broad and deep to allow the central bank to trade without destabilizing interest rates and private borrowing and lending. Moreover, the ability of central banks in some countries to engage in open market operations is constrained by their responsibility for keeping the interest cost of government borrowing low. Furthermore, central banks that are not usually constrained in these ways may be so constrained when balance-of-payments surpluses or deficits are too large. During periods of foreign-exchange-market speculation, for example, the huge open market operations needed to sterilize huge surpluses or deficits may be institutionally impossible to arrange. Finally, frequent and flexible alterations in reserve requirements and discount rates are usually undesirable. They would make private commercial banking highly unpredictable and would require frequent and massive rearrangements of bank assets.

In sum, despite attempts by modern central banks to sterilize, the balance of payments tends in many cases to affect domestic economic activity just as illustrated in Schema 5.1.

CONSEQUENCES OF UNDERSTERILIZATION

Many countries that are wedded to stable exchange rates are unable to sterilize perfectly. Smaller European countries are in this position, as are groups of less-developed countries that peg their money to the U.S. dollar, British pound, or French franc (see Table 2.4). This has four important consequences.

1. Monetary policy has reduced power and predictability in such countries. If Britain wishes to contract the money stock to combat domestic inflation, the monetary contraction will create a balance-of-payments surplus that did not exist previously (see Figure 4.7). Unless it is fully sterilized, the surplus will tend to undo what the monetary authorities intended. When only half of it can be sterilized, the initial British monetary contraction must be much larger. A more severe problem is unpredictability. When the British monetary authorities are unsure of how much of the surplus they can successfully sterilize, they are equally unsure of the ultimate outcome of their monetary policy on inflation.

2. Monetary events in these countries depend on monetary policy in others. For example, unusually rapid expansion of the U.S. money stock, such as took place during the Vietnam War build-up of the late 1960s, will tend to spill over into unusually rapid expansion of the British money stock, too. United States monetary expansion will cause any U.S. balance-of-payments deficit to enlarge, along with the corresponding British balance-of-payments surplus. Since British surpluses are imperfectly sterilized, larger surpluses will lead to larger rates of growth in the British money stock. A part of world monetary expansion will be determined by U.S. monetary policy.[5]

---

[5] This conclusion has led one international economist, Charles P. Kindleberger, to recommend somewhat facetiously that foreign central bankers be given a vote in the committee of the Federal Reserve System that is responsible for U.S. monetary policy!

Monetary authorities outside the U.S. will have limited independence. The so-called *monetary approach* to explaining the worldwide inflation of the early 1970s emphasizes precisely this monetary interdependence. It is discussed in greater detail on pp. 188–190.

3. Balance-of-payments surpluses and deficits in such countries sow the seeds of their own destruction. That is, they tend to eradicate themselves. Surpluses lead to monetary expansion, which leads to increased GNP, lower interest rates, and more rapid inflation, which lead in turn to smaller surpluses, which lead to additional (yet smaller) monetary expansion, which leads to even smaller surpluses, and so on. Deficits are similarly transitory. These automatic self-elimination properties are implied by Schema 5.1 and Figure 4.7 taken together. In reality, of course, surpluses and deficits may not disappear, because reality is characterized by recurrent shocks of the kind described in Chapter 4. These may accelerate or frustrate the tendencies outlined before. Successful sterilization itself frustrates these tendencies, but does so for the sake of achieving other goals.

4. Popular intuition that balance-of-payments deficits lead to increased unemployment is correct for such countries. So is the somewhat less popular intuition to the effect that balance-of-payments surpluses are inflationary.

These four consequences of understerilization also hold, although with somewhat less force, for countries whose foreign exchange markets are characterized by managed floating. Central banks will allow the foreign-exchange-market value of their money to vary but attempt to dampen both excessively sharp appreciation and depreciation. In the former case, they must add to official reserves and experience a surplus. In the latter case, they must lose official reserves and experience a deficit. The fact that such surpluses and deficits are largely voluntary is irrelevant; central banks will attempt to sterilize their monetary impacts when they conflict with domestic goals. If the banks fail, then even the voluntary surpluses and deficits alter domestic money stocks and lead to the familiar consequences.

THE U.S. BALANCE OF PAYMENTS, STERILIZATION, AND DOMESTIC ECONOMIC ACTIVITY

Its special role in the international monetary system makes the case of the United States somewhat different. Sterilization is a less relevant issue in determining the impact of the U.S. balance of payments on U.S. economic activity. Before 1961 the Federal Reserve System never intervened in the foreign exchange market. It did so only rarely in the 1960s and less frequently and dramatically than other central banks during the 1970s. As a result, U.S. balance-of-payments deficits largely reflect foreign central banks' acquisition of official-reserve dollars, not Federal Reserve System sales of U.S.-

owned official reserves. United States surpluses largely reflect reduction in world stocks of official-reserve dollars, not additions to U.S. stocks of official reserves.

Whenever the Federal Reserve Stystem is passive in the foreign exchange market, no predictable link exists between the U.S. balance of payments and the U.S. money stock. Hence no predictable link exists between the U.S. balance of payments and U.S. economic activity. United States deficits do not cause dollars to disappear from private circulation (or to "flow abroad").[6] Nor do U.S. surpluses pump up the financial resources available to the U.S. public by causing "dollar reflow." United States deficits *do* cause dollars to change ownership—from U.S. gin importers to the British central bank—but they do not thereby become unavailable to potential American borrowers.

Only on those rare occasions when the Fed itself buys and sells dollars in exchange for official reserves is the link created between the U.S. balance of payments and the U.S. money stock. Then there is the same natural tendency for the money stock to change as in other countries. But the tendency materializes only when the Fed sterilizes imperfectly.[7] In practice, unlike many other central banks, the Fed appears to be successful at sterilizing perfectly.

This special U.S. situation has three important implications: (1) U.S. monetary policy is more powerful, predictable, and independent than that of most other countries; (2) U.S. monetary events are less subject to the influence of foreign monetary policy than are monetary events in other countries; and (3) U.S. balance-of-payments surpluses and deficits only rarely have any very direct impacts on U.S. GNP, growth, employment, interest rates, and inflation. Thus the intuition that U.S. balance-of-payments deficits increase U.S. unemployment is generally wrong. So are suspicions that U.S. balance-of-payments surpluses are inflationary.

On the other hand, something very close to popular intuition is true for all countries including the United States. *Getting rid* of a balance-of-payments deficit by depreciation will generally reduce any involuntary unemployment that exists. To be precise, involuntary unemployment is larger in the presence of a deficit than it would be if the deficit were erased by depreciation. In that weak, opportunity-cost sense, the existence of a U.S. deficit might be argued to aggravate

[6] See pp. 108–110. There are several exceptions to these generalizations. For example, if the British central bank deposits its dollar acquisitions in a U.S. Federal Reserve Bank, then the Fed itself winds up inheriting the gin importers' check on a U.S. commercial bank. If the Fed did nothing else, the U.S. money stock would fall, but the Fed can and does offset (sterilize) these impacts as well as those from its own initiatives in the foreign exchange market.

[7] Then U.S. deficits cause dollars to "flow back to the Fed"—not "abroad," and surpluses cause "dollar reflow from the Fed"—not from "abroad."

U.S. unemployment. Similarly, the existence of a U.S. surplus might be argued weakly to aggravate inflation (compared to what inflation would be if dollar appreciation were somehow negotiated or allowed to take place). But these matters really deal with the effects of exchange-rate changes, which are discussed in the next section.

Effects of Exchange-Rate Changes on Real GNP, Interest Rates, and Domestic Prices

In Chapter 4 we saw that real GNP, interest rates, and domestic prices are fundamental determinants of a nation's exchange rate under clean floating. But linkages run in the opposite direction, too, because exchange rates are rarely allowed to float cleanly. Indeed, as the adjustable-peg exchange-rate system and managed floating imply, governments usually have the will and the power to choose an exchange rate other than that dictated by the private market. Exchange rates can be viewed in part, therefore, as an instrument of government policy. Obviously they affect the rate of official-reserve growth, but they also powerfully affect real GNP, interest rates, and prices. Causal forces run both ways between domestic economic activity and exchange rates. Shocks to one cause response in the others, which then feeds back upon the first. It is not surprising that forecasting international economic events is an inexact science. It is often impossible in a world of two-way causation to sort out the true sources of observed fluctuations in exchange rates and domestic economic activity.

EXCHANGE-RATE CHANGES AND AGGREGATE DEMAND

The influence of exchange rates on demand facing all producers of commodities and services in a nation—so-called *aggregate demand*—is fairly certain. From the U.S. perspective, dollar depreciation increases aggregate demand facing U.S. producers; dollar appreciation reduces it. From the aggregate-demand consequences alone, depreciation has effects very much like expansionary fiscal policy; appreciation, very much like contractionary fiscal policy. As a result, conscious and strategical depreciation is a tempting weapon for governments wanting to draw their economies out of business slumps. Similarly, governments sometimes allow appreciation as a counter-inflationary device.

The seeds for these conclusions were planted in Chapter 3. There we saw that dollar depreciation generally raises the sales and profits of U.S. tradeables producers (such as Boeing), because it expands the demand for their products. By contrast, dollar depreciation generally has no immediate impact on demand facing U.S. producers of non-tradeables (such as Delta Airlines).

TABLE 5.1. *Immediate Impacts of Dollar Depreciation on Demand Facing U.S. Producers*

	U.S. demand for . . .	British demand for . . .	Total demand facing U.S. producers
U.S. tradeables			
U.S.-produced aircraft	(1) encouraged	+ (2) encouraged	= encouraged
			+
U.S.-produced rum and gin	(3) encouraged	+ (4) encouraged	= encouraged
			+
U.S. nontradeables			
U.S. domestic airline services	(5) not directly or significantly affected	+ (6) (zero by the definition of nontradeables)	= not directly or significantly affected
			=
U.S. output as a whole			Aggregate demand encouraged

These conclusions are summarized in boxes 1 through 6 of Table 5.1.

Boxes 1 and 3: When the dollar depreciates, its value declines in terms of foreign money. Every dollar will buy less foreign money than it used to. When the price of foreign money goes up, so do the prices of all foreign goods in the eyes of Americans. The reason is that when Americans purchase British aircraft or Beefeater gin, pounds must usually be bought in the foreign exchange market in order to complete the transaction.[8] A rise in the price of pounds therefore has the same impact on American prices of British goods as does a rise in the price of the goods themselves. But prices of U.S.-made aircraft and gin (or rum) will not change immediately or by as much. Many U.S. buyers will therefore shift their purchases from British goods to U.S. goods. Demand facing U.S. producers of tradeables will rise.

Boxes 2 and 4: Prices of U.S.-made goods may not change immediately or significantly in the eyes of Americans, but they certainly do in the eyes of the British. For the British to purchase Boeing 747s or American gin (or rum), they must usually buy dollars in the foreign exchange market in order to complete the transaction.[9] But dollars become cheaper in terms of pounds as a result of dollar depreciation and therefore so do all American goods that dollars buy. Many British purchasers will shift their purchases from British goods to American goods. Demand facing U.S. producers of tradeables will rise for these reasons too.

Boxes 5 and 6: By definition, the British do not buy U.S. nontradeables, and Americans have nowhere else to turn to buy them. Therefore dollar depreciation has no short-run influence on demands for these goods.

The immediate impact of dollar depreciation on aggregate demand is the sum of these six effects. Dollar depreciation clearly increases aggregate demand facing U.S. producers and is therefore expansionary. Table 5.2 shows that the immediate impact in Britain is exactly the opposite. Dollar depreciation deflates aggregate demand facing British producers. That is not surprising, because a dollar depreciation is a pound appreciation, too.[10]

---

[8] Note that it does not matter to the conclusion whether the Americans must buy the pounds with their dollars, or whether the British exporters are willing to accept dollars and buy the pounds themselves in the foreign exchange market. In the former case the price of transacting, from the U.S. buyers' perspective, rises directly. In the latter case it rises indirectly: British exporters are unlikely to be willing to go on accepting the same number of dollars per product exported as before, because they are now worth less. They will probably demand more dollars from U.S. buyers, and the price facing the buyers will rise in that way.

[9] Again, as in footnote 8, it does not matter who actually buys the dollars.

[10] These conclusions ignore the question of demand-price elasticity that occupied much of Chapter 4. In fact, however, demand-price elasticity could be important here. If British demands for U.S. exports were sufficiently price inelastic (boxes 2 and 4 of Table 5.1), then U.S. exporters might actually *lose* revenue from dollar depreciation, even though real British demand (quantity terms) for their product was encouraged. If U.S. demands for imports from Britain (Table 5.2) were also sufficiently price inelastic, then even though U.S. buyers were discouraged from buying British goods in quantity terms, they might nevertheless spend *more* of their income on them and leave less to be spent on U.S. goods. Both this and the loss in U.S. export revenue could drain purchasing power away from U.S. producers and potentially lead to a reduction in aggregate demand facing them, not an increase.

TABLE 5.2. *Immediate Impacts of Dollar Depreciation on Demand Facing British Producers*

	British demand for . . .		U.S. demand for . . .		Total demand facing British producers
British tradeables					
British-produced aircraft	discouraged	+	discouraged	=	discouraged
					+
British-produced gin	discouraged	+	discouraged	=	discouraged
British nontradeables					+
British domestic airline services	not directly or significantly affected	+	(zero by the definition of nontradeables)	=	not directly or significantly affected
					=
British output as a whole					Aggregate demand discouraged

The effects of dollar depreciation on aggregate demand are expressed in many different ways. It is sometimes said that dollar depreciation taxes U.S. imports and subsidizes U.S. exports. This is an apt characterization. It illustrates the similarity between an exchange-rate change and a combination of import tariffs and export subsidies (see Chapter 9). It also makes clear why exchange-rate changes can substitute for fiscal policy: they are implicit, rather than explicit, changes in taxes and spending. Another familiar way of describing

SCHEMA 5.2. *Aggregate-Demand (Fiscal) Effects of Exchange-Rate Changes on U.S. Domestic Economic Activity*

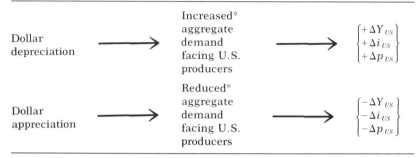

* Subject to the exception in footnote 10.

these consequences is to say that dollar depreciation enhances the *international competitive position* or *international competitiveness*, of U.S. producers; it lowers their prices (but not their profits) relative to those elsewhere in the world. Finally, dollar depreciation is also described as an *expenditure-switching* policy. It switches worldwide demand (expenditure) toward U.S. producers and away from competitors.

AGGREGATE DEMAND, REAL GNP, INTEREST RATES, AND DOMESTIC PRICES

When dollar depreciation stimulates aggregate demand facing U.S. producers, its impacts on domestic economic activity are familiar from standard macroeconomics and from the discussion of fiscal policy in Chapter 4. Schema 5.2 summarizes these relationships.

The way in which the consequences of dollar depreciation resolve into real growth $(+\Delta Y_{US})$ and domestic inflation $(+\Delta p_{US})$ depends chiefly on the state of the economy when the depreciation takes place. When there is substantial excess capacity and unemployment, most of the changes will be "real." A large pool of unemployed and underemployed laborers weakens the desire and ability of labor unions to obtain higher wages when aggregate demand expands. Working longer hours appears more lucrative than receiving more pay per hour. Substantial idle capacity in plant and equipment makes management reluctant to raise both wages and prices when aggregate demand increases because, again, increasing volume appears more profitable than receiving a higher price per unit sold.

Under these conditions, dollar depreciation sets in motion an aggregate-demand-induced expansion of the entire economy. Table

5.1 will characterize only the immediate impact of dollar depreciation. The multiplier process takes over from there. Increased demand for tradeables raises real GNP. Increased real GNP raises spending on tradeables and nontradeables alike. Increased additional spending will generate yet more real GNP, which will in turn be respent, and so on. Ultimately, the demand facing U.S. producers of nontradeables will be encouraged, too, contrary to the immediate impact of Table 5.1.

By contrast, the closer the U.S. economy is to full employment and optimal capacity utilization, the more likely dollar depreciation is to create U.S. inflation and little else. Tradeables producers will not be able to enlarge the resources at their command quickly to meet increased aggregate demand. They will be unable to bid resources away from nontradeables producers in the short run because of adjustment costs. Raising their price will therefore become their most desirable way of raising their profit, since volume cannot be expanded.[11]

Under these circumstances, dollar depreciation sets inflation in motion throughout the economy, not only in the tradeables sector. A kind of "price multiplier process" takes over. Increased prices of tradeables raise the cost of producing nontradeables (if tradeables are inputs), tempting nontradeables producers to raise their prices too. These feed back on the tradeables sector by raising its costs, and prices rise throughout the economy. Wages also are likely to rise. Labor unions attempt to offset increased costs of living by demanding higher wages and attempt to capture a share of the increased profits induced by higher prices. A *wage-price spiral* is set in motion like the price-price spiral. Both spirals can conceivably lead to a rise in domestic prices of exactly the same magnitude as the dollar depreciation. In this case the dollar depreciation ultimately fails because the encouragement given to demands for U.S. tradeables will be vitiated by higher U.S. prices. For these reasons precisely, depreciation is not recommended for any country that is close to full employment, unless it is accompanied by explicitly contractionary monetary or fiscal policy. In the terminology of international economics, at full employment, *expenditure-switching* policies in order to succeed must be accompanied by *expenditure-reducing* policies.

The aggregate-demand effect of dollar depreciation also makes credit tight ($+\Delta i_{US}$). Some of the increased aggregate demand is for autos, appliances, and other consumer durables. Some is demand by businesses for new plant, equipment, and inventory. Many such demands require the buyer to borrow in order to spend, and the direct

---

[11] These points can be made quite simply with reference to the *Phillips curve*. A relation very much like it can be plotted between the rate of domestic price inflation and the rate of unemployment (or excess capacity). The aggregate-demand effects of exchange-rate changes move countries along such a curve.

pressure of increased borrowing on available funds raises the cost of borrowing—the interest rate.[12]

In sum, depreciation is "fiscally" expansionary, "fiscally" inflationary, or both. (In the next section we dismiss one other alleged influence of depreciation on interest rates, one that would tend to lower them.)

AN ALLEGED DIRECT INFLUENCE OF EXCHANGE-RATE CHANGES ON INTEREST RATES, COSTS OF BORROWING, AND RATES OF RETURN

It is sometimes believed that aggregate demand for assets can be treated in a way parallel to that discussed in the preceding section. To illustrate, after the dollar depreciations of the early 1970s, there were forecasts that this would buoy the U.S. stock market. The belief was that U.S. stocks—ownership claims on U.S. corporations—were now cheaper for foreigners to buy and that therefore investors would shift their demand toward them.[13]

If this belief had been well founded, its implications would have extended beyond the U.S. stock market. It would have meant that U.S. corporations could float new stock issues more easily, instead of borrowing in financial markets. There would therefore have been less pressure to borrow after dollar depreciation than before, and U.S. interest rates might have come down. In fact, the same line of reasoning suggests that foreigners would have found U.S. bonds—and all other U.S. IOUs—cheaper after dollar depreciation than before and would have been more willing to purchase them. And therefore the interest paid by U.S. borrowers would not have had to be as high to attract a foreign lender. U.S. interest rates again would have fallen from dollar depreciation.

[12] In the macroeconomist's *IS-LM* analysis, the aggregate-demand effects of dollar depreciation are captured by an outward shift in the IS curve (except for the exceptional case discussed in footnote 10). From this effect alone, interest rates tend to rise. Increased real GNP and domestic prices both increase the aggregate stock demand for money: a larger number and higher value of transactions must be financed. If there is no compensating increase in the stock supply of money, then interest rates will rise toward the point where the aggregate stock demand for money is discouraged enough by high interest rates to leave the economy satisfied after all with the existing stock. One way in which this can happen is through individuals' attempting to sell off bonds in order to rebuild their personal money stock. Taken as an aggregate group, they must be unsuccessful in increasing the aggregate money stock. But they will succeed in driving down bond prices and raising interest rates.

[13] For example, "Let me turn briefly to the probable effects of the Smithsonian Agreement [see Chapter 7]. . . . The lower price of dollars abroad will . . . tend to stimulate foreign investment in the U.S." Arthur F. Burns, Chairman, Board of Governors of the Federal Reserve System, in testimony before the United States Senate Committee on Banking, Housing, and Urban Affairs, February 24, 1972, reproduced in the *Federal Reserve Bulletin* 58 (March 1972): 272.

Chapter 5: Effects of the Balance of Payments and Exchange Rates

But such beliefs are not generally well founded. The reasoning on which they are based is fallacious. Changes in the demand for U.S. assets as a result of dollar depreciation cannot be examined in the same way as changes in the demand for U.S. commodities and services.

The reasoning ignores the fact that the most important determinants of international financial investment are actual and expected rates of return and rates of interest, not prices of stocks or bonds. An average annual rate of return on one share of Delta Airlines stock, for example, is defined (apart from capital gains or losses) as

$$\frac{\text{Delta's annual dollar dividends per share}}{\text{average dollar price of one share of Delta stock}}$$

It is true, as claimed, that dollar depreciation immediately lowers the foreign-currency equivalent of the price in the denominator, but it is also true that dollar depreciation immediately lowers the foreign currency value of the dividend in the numerator by the same percentage! Depreciation thus has no immediate impact on rates of return on U.S. assets.[14] It is impossible to predict unambiguously whether or not foreign investors will be attracted to U.S. assets after dollar depreciation.

In sum, contrary to expressed opinion, exchange-rate changes probably have no strong direct influences on rates of return or on interest rates. The indirect influences, through aggregate demand for goods, remain.

A DIRECT INFLUENCE OF EXCHANGE-RATE CHANGES ON PRICES

One very important impact of exchange rates on price stands independent of their effect on aggregate demand. Regardless of what happens to aggregate demand in the United States, dollar depreciation causes import prices to rise. Appreciation causes them to fall. To be more precise, there is no getting around the fact that dollar depreciation raises the U.S. price of imported Beefeater and British aircraft. It is true even when there is so much unemployment and excess capacity that dollar depreciation has no impact at all on U.S. domestic prices (the prices of the things Americans produce). It is also true even if the aggregate demand response to dollar depreciation is zero.

In a nutshell, dollar depreciation unambiguously raises the average price of what Americans buy—the U.S. cost of living (see pp.

[14] One can make a better case that foreign investors will be attracted to Boeing stock, since Boeing's future profits and dividends will rise as a result of dollar depreciation. But they will also be discouraged from buying stock in U.S. Beefeater distributorships and other businesses that rely heavily on imports. The question of which force outweighs the other is an empirical one.

90–91). It does so directly and also indirectly via inflated aggregate demand. The certainty of this conclusion is what underlies the comparatively new *monetary approach* to the impact of exchange-rate changes on domestic economic activity.

EXCHANGE-RATE CHANGES AND REAL NATIONAL WEALTH: THE MONETARY APPROACH

Exchange-rates changes affect real national wealth principally because they affect the cost of living. From the perspective of the United States, the most likely impacts are that (1) dollar depreciation reduces real national wealth by raising the cost of living, and (2) dollar appreciation raises real national wealth by reducing the cost of living.

Some definitions are helpful. *National wealth* means the value of all the land and resources owned by American residents and the U.S. government, including what they own abroad. It includes U.S.-owned financial assets that are debts of foreigners (such as a British Treasury bill or a Beefeater bond). It does not include financial assets that are debts of one American, yet owned by another, because the first American's debt nullifies the second American's asset when we add up aggregate U.S wealth. Finally, it includes U.S. currency (notes and coins) and the official reserves of gold and foreign exchange owned by the Federal Reserve System.

Real national wealth means the quantity of real goods and services that could be purchased with national wealth. If prices of purchased goods and services rise, and the value of national wealth rises less, then real national wealth must decline. Fewer goods and services can be obtained.

Dollar depreciation is likely to do exactly that. The cost of living is sure to rise. Likely to rise are the values of those elements of national wealth, such as land and resources, that usually keep step with domestic inflation. But at least one prominent element of national wealth does not rise in value with domestic inflation: currency itself. In fact, its real value falls, which is just another way of saying that inflation forces everyone to give up more money for the same quantity of goods.

The monetary approach to exchange-rate changes focuses on those elements of national wealth whose real value falls with depreciation and rises with appreciation.[15] Since currency is the most prominent of

---

[15] Note that there are some elements of national wealth whose dollar value rises rigidly in step with dollar depreciation—for example, official reserves owned by the Federal Reserve System, and foreign land, resources, corporations, and financial assets (including foreign money) owned by U.S. residents. Thus it is not inevitable that total real U.S. wealth declines upon dollar depreciation. The outcome depends on how large this element of U.S. wealth is relative to currency and elements whose real value declines. It depends also on how much dollar depreciation pushes up the U.S. cost of living. Unfortunately, data are insufficient to allow us to make any firm judgment on these matters.

SCHEMA 5.3. *Real-Wealth (Monetary) Effects of Exchange-Rate Changes on U.S. Domestic Economic Activity*

Dollar depreciation	$\longrightarrow \ +\Delta p_{US}^{*} \longrightarrow$	Reduced** real U.S. national wealth	$\longrightarrow \left\{ \begin{array}{l} -\Delta Y_{US} \\ +\Delta i_{US} \\ -\Delta p_{US}^{*} \end{array} \right\}$
Dollar appreciation	$\longrightarrow \ -\Delta p_{US}^{*} \longrightarrow$	Increased** real U.S. national wealth	$\longrightarrow \left\{ \begin{array}{l} +\Delta Y_{US} \\ -\Delta i_{US} \\ +\Delta p_{US}^{*} \end{array} \right\}$

* In the top line, reduced real national wealth moderates the extent to which prices increase, but can never offset it. Otherwise real national wealth would have increased. In the bottom line, increased real national wealth moderates the extent to which prices fall (or moderates the extent to which inflation is reduced).

** Subject to the exception in footnote 15.

these, the immediate effects of dollar depreciation are very much like those of contractionary monetary policy. Dollar appreciation has immediate effects like those of expansionary monetary policy. These are illustrated in Schema 5.3.[16]

With one exception, the schema shows that the wealth impact of exchange-rate changes on domestic economic activity mirrors the impact of aggregate demand. The exception is real GNP. In principle, it is possible for the contractionary real-wealth influence of depreciation to dominate the expansionary "fiscal" influence. If it does, then a somewhat strange link between the exchange rate and employment will be implied. Depreciation will increase unemployment problems; appreciation will alleviate them.[17]

Whether this ever happens in practice is extremely difficult to determine. Governments often purposefully adopt contractionary policies after depreciation, and expansionary policies after appreciation, in order to offset the expected "fiscal" impacts on employment. Data on actual experience with depreciation and appreciation are usually not sufficiently rich or reliable to permit researchers to identify *why* real GNP and employment responded as they did—whether because of explicit government policy or because of natural fiscal and real-wealth effects. Casual observation is equally inconclusive. German unemployment problems do not seem to have been significantly worsened by recurrent appreciation of the Deutsche mark. British unemployment problems do not seem to have been significantly al-

[16] In the macroeconomist's *IS-LM* analysis, the real-wealth effects of dollar depreciation are captured in part by an upward shift in the LM curve (except for the exceptional case discussed in footnote 15). From this effect alone, real GNP falls, interest rates rise, and there is less upward pressure on domestic prices than there would otherwise be.

[17] The conclusion is certain for the exceptional case noted in footnote 10.

leviated by recurrent pound depreciation. But in other cases the fiscal impacts appear to dominate.

Summary and Synthesis

Both the balance of payments and policy-determined changes in exchange rates have consequences for domestic economic prosperity, and governments worry about both for this reason. Another reason (from Chapter 3) is that governments care what happens to national stocks of official reserves. Deficits reduce them; surpluses enlarge them. Deliberate exchange-rate changes are believed to alter those deficits and surpluses. In fact, exchange-rate changes are usually engineered or accepted primarily for their effect on the balance of payments and only secondarily, or not at all, for their effect on domestic economic activity.

The international and domestic impacts of changing exchange rates are closely related. If the "fiscal" impact of changing exchange rates is very strong, and is ignored, then domestic aggregate-demand fluctuation may ultimately counteract any intended international impact. A depreciation may be intended to create a balance-of-payments surplus and may temporarily do so. But the surplus will not last if the depreciation stimulates domestic real GNP or domestic inflation excessively. What the depreciation does directly to increase exports and reduce imports can be defeated by what increased real GNP and domestic inflation do in the opposite direction.

Similarly, if monetary authorities are unable to sterilize the money-stock consequences of the balance of payments, the domestic impact of changing exchange rates may again counteract the international impact. A depreciation may temporarily create a balance-of-payments surplus and may even enlarge the surplus by acting like contractionary monetary policy in its initial real-wealth effects, but the surplus will not last if unsterilized. It will lead to faster-than-normal growth in the domestic money stock. This will reexpand the economy and erase the surplus. Exchange-rate changes will have only transitory effects on the balance of payments.

Other examples could be given to show how the purpose of exchange-rate changes can be frustrated by domestic impacts. All examples will illustrate the same two fundamental points: (1) It may not be surprising that the money of certain countries depreciates continually with no enduring effect on their balance of payments. Many less-developed countries seem to be modern examples. Likewise, it may not be surprising that the German Deutsche mark and the Swiss franc experience continual appreciation with no enduring effect on the German and Swiss balance of payments. (2) Whether or not exchange-rate changes affect the balance of payments permanently depends crucially on assumptions about domestic fiscal and monetary policy. Exchange-rate changes for balance-of-payments reasons may work only to the extent that they are accompanied by conscious and appropriate alterations in fiscal and monetary behavior.

Key Terms

monetary approach
aggregate demand
international competitiveness

expenditure-switching,
expenditure-reducing policies

Key Concepts and Review

Monetary impacts of the balance of payments.
Subsequent impacts on employment, output, prices, and interest rates.
Sterilization (neutralization).
The United States as a special case again.
Similarities between exchange-rate changes and fiscal policy.
Linkages between exchange rates, the cost of living, and real national wealth.

Chapter 6

Effects of Domestic
Economic Activity in One Country
on Domestic Economic Activity
in Others

Chapters 4 and 5 showed how domestic growth, recession, and inflation alter exchange rates and the balance of payments, and how these alterations "feed back" on real GNP and domestic prices. The present chapter completes the causal links by illustrating how one country's growth, recession, and inflation are transferred to another country. This important and sometimes controversial phenomenon is known as the *international transmission of business fluctuations.*[1]

Importance and Prominence of International Transmission of Business Fluctuations

In Chapter 8 we shall see that international trade in commodities and services is unambiguously beneficial for every nation. The fact that every nation engages in at least some international trade confirms this observation. Yet the blessings provided by international trade are not unmixed. A disadvantage, for example, is that nations lose self-sufficiency and economic independence.

[1] This chapter will be concerned narrowly with the transmission of recession and expansion—negative and positive changes in real GNP (Y), and with the transmission of inflation and deflation—positive and negative changes in domestic price levels (p). We will for the most part ignore the international transmission of financial conditions—tighter and looser credit, as signaled by higher and lower interest rates (i). Our neglect does not imply that changes in national interest rates and credit conditions are bottled up in the country where they occur. On the contrary, the international transmission of such financial shocks is even closer to being perfect than the transmission of inflation, recession, and growth. But its transmission channels have already been described in Supplement 1A's discussion of interest arbitrage, and they are highlighted again on pp. 231–234.

178

An important aspect of the interdependence that trade brings about is that national economies tend to vary together, for better or for worse. Prosperity in some nations promotes prosperity in all. Ill health in some nations breeds ill health in all. Exports, imports, and the balance of payments are the channels through which this interdependence is felt. Thus international trade gives a society the opportunities to stimulate domestic production and employment when worldwide business expands and to dampen domestic inflation when worldwide inflation recedes. Among its social costs, however, are the inability to avoid the effects of worldwide recession and the necessity to share in accelerated worldwide inflation.

The degree to which business fluctuations are transmitted from country to country depends first and most importantly on the exchange-rate system, as we shall see. In general, the closer the system is to cleanly floating exchange rates, the weaker is the transmission. This is a fundamental reason why systems of pegged exchange rates have broken down in the past, and why systems of managed floating are sometimes subject to such chaotic pressures that central banks withdraw altogether from the foreign exchange market. When countries are "importing" severe recession or inflation from the rest of the world, they are tempted to sacrifice exchange-rate stability in order to *insulate* their economy from the world recession or inflation. Yet they cannot altogether escape the transmission. This fact is often not made clear. Several international links remain between rates of national growth, employment, and inflation even under cleanly floating exchange rates. Consistent with this are the data presented in Figures 6.1 and 6.2.

Figures 6.1 and 6.2 reveal striking similarities in Canadian and American experience with growth, recession, and inflation. With only two exceptions, whenever the U.S. economy grew faster or slower, so did the Canadian economy. With only two exceptions, whenever inflation rose or fell in the United States it did the same in Canada. Even the rates are similar. Business fluctuations were shared between the two countries under both pegged and floating exchange rates. But the parallelism is not quite so striking during the 1970s period of managed floating. The growth-inflation experiences are more divergent. Each economy appears to have been partially insulated from upswings and downturns in the other.

A second feature on which transmission depends is the integration of the world markets that international exchange establishes. In a "perfectly integrated" market, one and only one price rules (see the discussion of gold on pp. 67–68). The less significant the natural and governmental barriers to trade and international financial investment, the more "integrated" are national markets for any specific good. When integration is extreme, there are no national markets at all, only world markets. In this extreme, market slumps are universal, as are price pressures. The real world is, of course, not so extreme. Yet

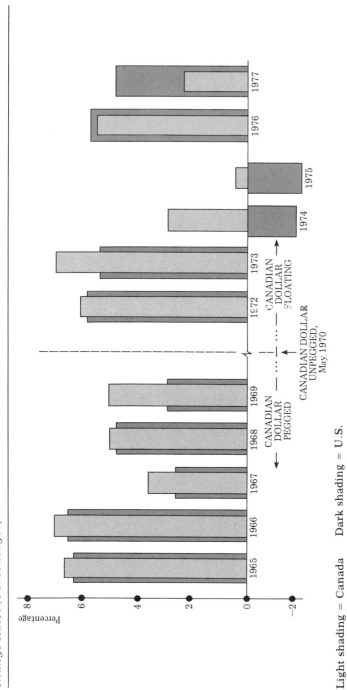

FIGURE 6.1. *Canadian and American Growth Rates of Annual Real GNP (Y)* under Pegged and Floating Exchange Rates (Percentages)*

Light shading = Canada   Dark shading = U.S.

* Gross national product in constant dollars.
Source: International Monetary Fund, *International Financial Statistics*, 1966–78; Organization for Economic Cooperation and Development, *Main Economic Indicators*, 1966–78.

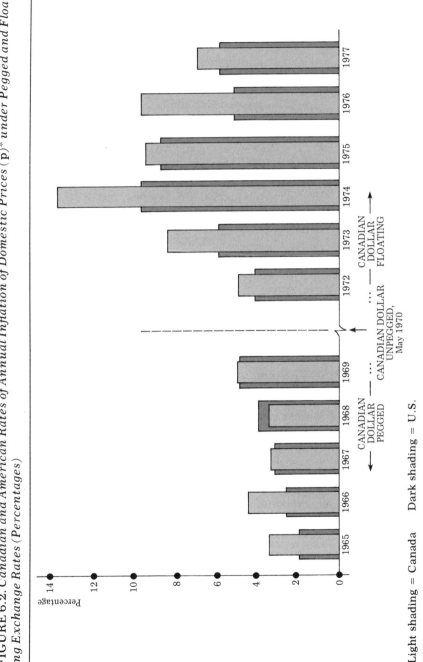

FIGURE 6.2. *Canadian and American Rates of Annual Inflation of Domestic Prices (p)* under Pegged and Floating Exchange Rates (Percentages)*

Light shading = Canada   Dark shading = U.S.

* Year-to-year percentage change in the implicit price deflator for gross national product.
Source: International Monetary Fund, *International Financial Statistics*, 1966–78; Organization for Economic Cooperation and Development, *Main Economic Indicators*, 1966–78.

it appears to be moving in that direction as government barriers to international trade are negotiated away (see Chapter 11), as technological advances reduce international transport and communications costs, and as Euro-banking draws national financial markets together (see pp. 231–234).

Third, we will see that transmission depends heavily on how trade-dependent a country is and how trade-dependent other countries are on it. For example, the United States is less dependent on exports and imports than is Canada, and Canada is extremely dependent on U.S. sellers for its imports and on U.S. buyers for its exports, as illustrated in Table 6.1. As a result, the United States is generally less affected by world growth, recession, and inflation than Canada, and Canada is more sensitive to U.S. upswings and downturns than to those anywhere else in the world.

TABLE 6.1. *Overall and Bilateral Trade Dependence of the United States and Canada, 1977*

	United States	Canada
Exports		
Total exports as a percentage of GNP	8.0	24.3
Bilateral[a] exports as a percentage of total exports	21.4	68.2
Imports		
Total imports as a percentage of GNP	9.5	24.3
Bilateral[a] imports as a percentage of total imports	19.5	67.5

[a] Bilateral exports in the column headed "United States" are exports from the United States to Canada; those in the column headed "Canada" are exports from Canada to the United States. A similar meaning is attached to bilateral imports.

Source: International Monetary Fund, *International Financial Statistics*, December 1978, and *Direction of Trade Annual, 1971–77.*

Chapter 6: Effects of Domestic Economic Activity on Others

International interdependence has importance not only for explaining domestic economic activity but for controlling it as well. Stable, intelligent macroeconomic policies in the largest countries in the world are necessary conditions for stable, prosperous economies in every country. If only one of the largest countries acts irresponsibly in its policy decisions, it tends to "visit its iniquities" upon every country. Undoubtedly, inflationary U.S. financing of the Vietnam War contributed to inflation in nearly every country during the early 1970s. Even if the largest countries simply disagree on responsible macroeconomic policy, the outcome in each tends to be frustrated by the policy choice of the other. United States efforts to choke back inflation in the mid-1970s both counteracted and were counteracted by the desires of Britain, Canada, and Italy to keep unemployment low. The modern emphasis on international cooperation and coordination in policymaking is a direct outgrowth of these observations and of the international transmission of business fluctuations.

Transmission under Pegged Exchange Rates and Managed Floating

Whenever governments intervene in the foreign exchange market to maintain stable exchange rates, business upswings and downturns tend to be shared worldwide. For this reason pegged exchange rates in particular are said to breed the *international synchronization of business cycles* observed in Figures 6.1 and 6.2.

When this synchronizing property of exchange-rate stabilization is spreading prosperity from country to country, all welcome it. When problems are being spread, there is a temptation to blame domestic recession and inflation on foreign influences, as implied by the terms *imported inflation* and *imported recession*.

Under pegged exchange rates and managed floating, domestic economic swings in one country flow to others through two familiar channels: (1) aggregate-demand channels, which result from interdependent aggregate demands; and (2) money-stock channels, which result from interdependent money stocks.

AGGREGATE-DEMAND CHANNELS OF TRANSMISSION

In no country in the world is the aggregate demand facing its producers independent of world events. This was apparent in Tables 5.1 and 5.2. Aggregate demand facing U.S. producers includes *British* demands for U.S. aircraft, gin, and rum; aggregate demand facing British producers includes *U.S.* demands for British goods.

The international interdependence of aggregate demands is also implicit in the familiar accounting identity for gross national product:

$$Y = C + I + G + X - M$$

where

Y = gross national product—aggregate demand facing domestic producers;

C = consumption—aggregate demand by domestic households for commodities and services that are consumed, including those which are imported;

I = investment—aggregate demand by domestic businesses and households for newly produced plant, equipment, and housing, including imports of such goods;

G = government spending—aggregate demand of the domestic government for goods, including imports;

X = exports—aggregate demand of all foreign households, businesses, and governments for domestic commodities and services;

M = imports—aggregate demand of domestic households, businesses, and governments for foreign commodities and services.[2]

Aggregate demand facing U.S. producers (Y_{US}) is the sum of demands from two sources: U.S. demand for U.S. goods ($C_{US} + I_{US} + G_{US} - M_{US}$) and foreign demand for U.S. goods (X_{US}). Similarly, aggregate demand facing British producers includes U.S. demand for British goods (M_{US}). Each country's GNP depends in part on the other's demand.

The result of this interdependence when exchange rates are stabilized is that every domestic boom or bust has repercussions abroad. Consider, for example, a U.S. recession, caused by declining consumer and business confidence together with a cautious government spending program. Consumption, investment, and government spending all simultaneously fall, illustrated on the left-hand side of Schema 6.1. As a result, real U.S. GNP falls, as do measures of real national income. When real GNP and incomes fall off, income-sensitive U.S. demand falls again for all goods, whether they are produced at home or not (see p. 124). So U.S. import demand for British aircraft and gin must slip too. But these are demands facing British producers! Their incomes and real GNP fall when U.S. imports do, and their own income-sensitive demand declines. That in turn

[2] Exports and imports in the gross national product identity refer to commodities and services only. They do not refer to assets, although earlier chapters have distinguished exports and imports of assets, too. Note that imports appear explicitly only once in the GNP identity, but they are really included twice—once as a part of $C + I + G$. Hence they are really not a part of Y at all. They are both added and subtracted on the right-hand side. This makes good sense, because imports generate no domestic production (Y). See also footnote 11.

SCHEMA 6.1. *Transmission of U.S. Recession to Britain under Pegged Exchange Rates: Aggregate-Demand Channels*

$$\left\{\begin{array}{l} -\Delta C_{US} \\ -\Delta I_{US} \\ -\Delta G_{US} \end{array}\right\} \longrightarrow -\Delta Y_{US} \longrightarrow -\Delta M_{US} = \begin{array}{l} \text{Reduced} \\ \text{U.S. demands} \\ \text{facing} \\ \text{British} \\ \text{producers} \end{array} \longrightarrow -\Delta Y_B$$

Key:
For →, read "leads to" or "causes."
For + and −, read "a positive" and "a negative" respectively.
For Δ, read "change in."
For definitions of C, I, G, X, and M, see text.

reduces British purchases of U.S. exports, further contracting U.S. real GNP and demand. So the recessionary stimuli are passed back and forth between the United States and Britain.

The same is true for a U.S. inflation, whether caused by overexuberant consumers, investors, and governments or by rising costs facing producers. If the U.S. economy has little unemployment or excess capacity, overexuberance will be translated into U.S. *demand-pull* inflation, and rising costs into *cost-push inflation*. Schema 6.2 illustrates their effects. Domestic U.S. inflation will discourage British and Americans alike from purchasing U.S. goods and will make British substitutes more attractive, as we saw in Chapter 4. United

SCHEMA 6.2. *Transmission of U.S. Inflation to Britain under Pegged Exchange Rates: Aggregate-Demand Channels*

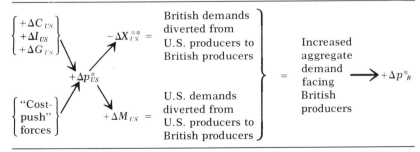

* Assuming that neither the United States nor Britain has substantial unemployment or excess capacity.
** If British demand for U.S. exports is price elastic; see Supplement 4A.

States exports to Britain will fall,[3] and U.S. imports from Britain will rise. British producers will enjoy new business, but if the British economy is similarly lacking in unemployed resources, such booming business can lead only to British demand-pull inflation. That may set in motion a cost-push inflation as well, as British wage-earners attempt to keep their standard of living from falling. Both of these inflationary trends divert demand back toward U.S. producers, who are thus faced with some secondary inflationary stimuli. These are reflected back to Britain, then back to the United States, and so on.

The importance of trade dependence for this transmission is implicit in Schemas 6.1 and 6.2. The more trade dependent the U.S. economy is, the more pronounced will be the impact of changes in Y_{US} and p_{US} on X_{US} and M_{US}. The larger these changes are, the more dramatically they will affect Y_B and p_B. Similarly, the more dependent the British are on the U.S. economy, the more prominent the international transmission. Changes in Y_B and p_B will be minuscule if X_{US} and M_{US} are very small compared to Y_B.[4]

MONEY-STOCK CHANNELS OF TRANSMISSION

The money-stock channels by which business fluctuations are transmitted internationally under exchange-rate stabilization spring from the impact of the balance of payments on the domestic money stock. On pp. 162–163, we saw how difficult it is for many countries to sterilize these effects. Regardless of attempts to do so, there remains at least some tendency for the domestic money stock to rise in a balance-of-payments-surplus country and to fall in a deficit country.

The result of understerilization is reinforcement of the tendency for business cycles to be synchronized. For example, it is likely that U.S. recession leads to a reduction in the U.S. balance-of-payments deficit.[5] The British surplus is simultaneously reduced, leading the British money stock to rise less rapidly than it would otherwise. Slackened monetary growth in Britain will be recessionary if Britain already has substantial excess capacity and unemployment. It will be anti-inflationary if the British economy is overheated. In similar fashion, U.S. inflation may well spread to Britain if it increases the U.S.

[3] Provided that demand for U.S. exports is price elastic, as discussed in Chapter 4.

[4] By this measure, the United States is less trade dependent than other countries (see Table 4.1). Thus the United States is less susceptible to transmission from abroad than other countries but is nevertheless an important transmitter.

[5] Chapter 4 demonstrates that this relation is not inevitable. If U.S. recession is accompanied by a sufficiently deep fall in interest rates, the U.S. balance-of-payments deficit may be enlarged, not shrunk (see Figure 4.3). In the long run, however, as the effect of lower interest rates on the balance of payments is dissipated, the relation assumed in the text becomes more and more likely.

SCHEMA 6.3. *Transmission of U.S. Business Fluctuations to Britain under Pegged Exchange Rates: Money-Stock Channels*

$\left\{\begin{array}{l}-\Delta Y_{US}\\-\Delta p_{US}\end{array}\right\}$ →	Reduced U.S. balance-of-payments deficit* =	Reduced British balance-of-payments surplus* →	Reduced rate of growth in British money stock** → $\left\{\begin{array}{l}-\Delta Y_{B}\\-\Delta p_{B}\end{array}\right\}$
$\left\{\begin{array}{l}+\Delta Y_{US}\\+\Delta p_{US}\end{array}\right\}$ →	Increased U.S. balance-of-payments deficit* =	Increased British balance-of-payments surplus* →	Increased rate of growth in British money stock** → $\left\{\begin{array}{l}+\Delta Y_{B}\\+\Delta p_{B}\end{array}\right\}$

* See footnotes 3 and 5.
** Understerilization is assumed.

balance-of-payments deficit (British surplus).[6] British monetary expansion will become more rapid than otherwise, and it will translate into British inflation if there is insufficient growth, unemployment, or excess capacity in the British economy.

These monetary channels of transmission are illustrated in Schema 6.3. Again the importance of trade dependence is implicit. The balance-of-payments effects of U.S. recession and inflation will probably be larger when the U.S. economy is more trade dependent, and the British balance of payments will be larger relative to the British money stock the more trade dependent Britain is. Any significant balance-of-payments surplus or deficit will then bring about dramatic changes in British monetary growth.

SOME OTHER TRANSMISSION CHANNELS

Growth, recession, inflation, and deflation are all transmitted internationally through more direct channels. For example, such transmission is facilitated by the structure of the *multinational corporation* (see Chapter 13). Much world business is carried on by these large corporations and their worldwide affiliates, so that national outputs as well as national investments in new plant and equipment are linked. When automobile sales slip in the United States, Ford Motor Company cuts back on its purchases of fully assembled autos from its Canadian subsidiary and of Pinto engines from its British subsidiary. Ford's layoffs in the United States are mirrored by its layoffs abroad. If the U.S. recession is not specific to autos but general, all U.S. multinational corporations will behave the same way. Furthermore, with

[6] This relation is not guaranteed either, as Figure 4.6 illustrates. But demands would have to be highly price inelastic to reverse it.

respect to investment itself, widespread U.S. recession reduces the profits accruing to U.S. parent corporations. They will have less to reinvest both at home and abroad. Plans for expansion of foreign affiliates will be curtailed—expansion that would have generated jobs and growth abroad. Business upturns spread internationally in similar fashion.

For inflation there is also a channel of transmission that is quite direct and independent of those described before. When U.S. prices rise under pegged exchange rates and managed floating, the British must pay more to buy U.S. goods. Even if the British government offsets the aggregate-demand effects of U.S. inflation by fiscal policy and sterilizes its money stock impacts through the balance of payments, inflation will still be "imported." Prices facing Britain as a buyer rise, even though British selling prices (domestic prices) might not initially. Inflation is inevitable in indexes of buyers' prices, like the *consumer price index,* or in indexes of unit materials costs facing British producers who import inputs.[7] Finally, it is extremely difficult in practice for the government to keep such direct imported inflation from eventually spilling over into domestic commodity prices and wage demands.

International transmission of inflation through direct price effects depends very clearly on trade dependence. Transmission of growth and recession through multinational corporate structure depends as well on foreign investment dependence. In Canadian economic activity, for example, foreign multinational corporations play an important, often dominant, role. United States multinationals are the most prominent of all. Because of such foreign-investment dependence, the Canadian economy tends to be particularly subject to the transmission mechanisms already described—and most of all to those that originate in the response of U.S. multinationals to U.S. economic activity.

RISING WORLD INFLATION IN THE LATE 1960s AND EARLY 1970s

All these channels have played important roles in recent experience. Figure 6.2 reflects the rise of worldwide inflation in the late 1960s and its dramatic jump in the mid-1970s. Several complementary explanations for the later phase exist, including hikes in oil prices by oil-producing countries (see pp. 99–101 and 257–262), unfavorable weather and consequent food shortages, simultaneously misguided macroeconomic policies in a number of major countries, and managed floating. But a single explanation of the early phase is

---

[7] This direct tendency for inflation to be transmitted internationally is comparable to the direct impact of an exchange-rate change on domestic prices, discussed on pp. 173–174.

compelling to many observers: the international transmission of accelerating U.S. inflation, caused primarily by the Vietnam War.

The foregoing is, of course, only a hypothesis. It does not claim to encompass all possible explanations for accelerating world inflation, but it is consistent with what occurred in the late 1960s and early 1970s and with what has been said above about imported (and exported) inflation.

Let us look more closely at the situation. Because of the particular unpopularity of the Vietnam War in the United States, the U.S. government was afraid to finance it in a noninflationary way. Raising taxes would have aroused even more antiwar sentiment. Cutting back the government's nonmilitary spending would have done the same. Therefore the government chose to finance the war through fiscal and monetary expansion. This had its own political cost: inflation. The inflation was both indirect and delayed. It came about because the U.S. economy was already close to full capacity and employment when U.S. involvement in Vietnam escalated in the mid-1960s.

United States exports, imports, and the balance of payments responded more or less as expected, as Table 6.2 illustrates. While both exports and imports of commodities grew in the late 1960s, imports grew nearly twice as fast as exports. United States export growth was retarded because foreign buyers turned to substitutes produced in their own countries. United States import growth was stimulated as U.S. buyers found foreign goods relatively cheaper and therefore more attractive. Both phenomena increased aggregate demand pressures

TABLE 6.2. *United States Trade and Balance-of-Payments Trends during Accelerating U.S. Inflation*

Years	Percentage rate of growth of commodity exports[a]	Percentage rate of growth of commodity imports[a]	Balance of payments ($ billions)[b]
1964, 1965	20.7	20.7	−2.8
1966, 1967	15.4	30.2	−3.2
1968, 1969	16.8	31.4	4.4
1970, 1971	20.9	23.9	−39.6

[a] Percentage rate of change in the sum of exports or imports for the two years over the same sum for the previous two years.

[b] The sum of the balance of payments on official reserve transaction basis (see Supplement 2C) for the two years.

Source: U.S. Department of Commerce, *Survey of Current Business* 54 (June 1974): 30, 34.

Pegged Exchange Rates and Managed Floating 189

on foreign economies, pushing them toward their own inflation. These pressures moderated around 1970 with the Nixon administration's anti-inflationary domestic policy. At the same time, however, the U.S. balance of payments plunged into deep deficits. The size of the deficit in 1970–1971—the last two years of the adjustable-peg exchange-rate system—was, from a historical perspective, astounding (see Table 3.5). To sterilize it entirely was impossible, and as a direct result foreign money stocks rose.

Table 6.2 suggests that the inflationary pressures of sympathetic monetary expansion followed and reinforced those of transmitted aggregate demand. Growth in world inflation in this period is consistent with both a *Keynesian approach* to world inflation and a *monetary approach*. The former might stress transmission channels through interdependent aggregate demands, the latter those through interdependent money stocks. There is no conflict between the different approaches to these events. Nor can transmission of historical U.S. inflation through any of the other potential channels be ruled out.

Transmission and Insulation under Cleanly Floating Exchange Rates

No effort was made in the preceding section to distinguish international transmission of business fluctuations under pegged exchange rates from that under managed floating. Yet there are reasons to believe that business cycles will be *less* synchronized under managed floating—and *least* synchronized under cleanly floating exchange rates. Increased variability of exchange rates blocks some of the transmission, but not all. And floating exchange rates themselves introduce some potential transmission channels that do not exist under rigidly pegged exchange rates.

Because it is likely on balance that variable exchange rates reduce imported recession and inflation, they are said to *insulate* a country from foreign economic problems. Insulation is sometimes invoked to defend the superiority of floating to pegged exchange rates. Yet the invocation is logically invalid. Floating exchange rates also insulate a country undesirably from foreign economic prosperity. Whether or not a country should prefer them to pegged exchange rates on these grounds depends on circumstances. In general, a country that is naturally less subject to economic ups and downs than the rest of the world—say because its macroeconomic policy tools are more powerful and predictable—should welcome the insulation property of floating exchange rates. By contrast, countries with extraordinarily volatile economies should welcome the restraining influence of the external world economy that comes from *non*insulation under pegged exchange rates or under heavily managed floating.[8]

INSULATION AND AGGREGATE-DEMAND CHANNELS

Cleanly floating exchange rates block some, and sometimes even all, of the aggregate-demand transmission channels. Britain will be partially insulated from U.S. recession if the pound depreciates as the U.S. economy slumps; it will be partially insulated from U.S. inflation if the pound appreciates. Both changes in exchange rates have effects on the aggregate demand facing British producers that offset the initial aggregate-demand effects of the U.S. recession or inflation.

These conclusions can be seen in Schema 6.4. Rows 1 and 2 illustrate transmission of U.S. recession (or deflation) to Britain under cleanly floating exchange rates. Row 1 condenses and reproduces the links described in Schemas 6.1 and 6.2. Row 2 illustrates the additional links that occur when exchange rates are allowed to vary. In fact, Schema 6.4 is appropriate for managed floating as well as for clean floating, but under managed floating the row 1 links will generally dominate the row 2 links.

Row 2 illustrates how the pressure of increased U.S. exports and reduced U.S. imports lowers the value of the British pound. (It reproduces several of the entries in Table 4.2.) More pounds will be supplied in order to increase British purchases of U.S. goods (X_{US}). Fewer pounds will be demanded because U.S. imports from Britain (M_{US}) fall. The pound depreciates, and depreciation is favorable to British aggregate demand, as the British analog to Schema 5.2 would imply. Thus British producers face countervailing influences from rows 1 and 2. The pegged-rate transmission coming from row 1 will be reduced by the variable-rate offset coming from row 2.

The same exercise carried out for rows 3 and 4 of the schema will illustrate how floating exchange rates weaken the transmission of U.S. growth and inflation to Britain.

Under an unlikely set of circumstances, there will be no transmission at all through aggregate-demand channels; insulation will be perfect. The unlikeliness of the circumstances weakens occasional recommendations that clean floating is a foolproof way to avoid all imported recession and inflation. The circumstances are (1) that none of the changes described directly affects exports or imports of financial assets and (2) that none of the changes described directly affects the aggregate demand of British residents (British $C + I + G$); or (3)

---

[8] One well-known economist has remarked caustically, "There is no virtue in having more independence if you are determined to use it to be more stupid than your neighbor" (Harry G. Johnson, "Inflation, Unemployment, and the Floating Rate," *Canadian Public Policy* 1:2 (Spring 1975): 179).

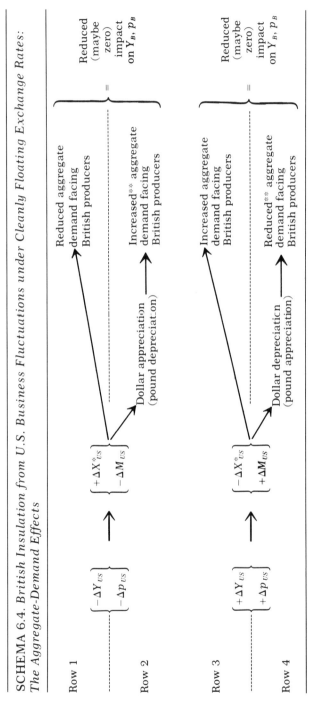

SCHEMA 6.4. *British Insulation from U.S. Business Fluctuations under Cleanly Floating Exchange Rates: The Aggregate-Demand Effects*

Row 1

$$\begin{Bmatrix} -\Delta Y_{US} \\ -\Delta p_{US} \end{Bmatrix} \rightarrow \begin{Bmatrix} +\Delta X^*_{US} \\ -\Delta M_{US} \end{Bmatrix}$$

Row 2

Dollar appreciation
(pound depreciation)

Reduced aggregate demand facing British producers

Increased** aggregate demand facing British producers

= Reduced (maybe zero) impact on Y_B, p_B

Row 3

$$\begin{Bmatrix} +\Delta Y_{US} \\ +\Delta p_{US} \end{Bmatrix} \rightarrow \begin{Bmatrix} -\Delta X^*_{US} \\ +\Delta M_{US} \end{Bmatrix}$$

Row 4

Dollar depreciation
(pound appreciation)

Increased aggregate demand facing British producers

Reduced** aggregate demand facing British producers

= Reduced (maybe zero) impact on Y_B, p_B

* If British demand for U.S. exports is price elastic. See Supplement 4A.
** Subject to the exception noted in footnote 10 of Chapter 5.

that whatever changes take place under circumstances 1 and 2 offset each other. To see how this prescription makes insulation perfect, it is helpful to recall that the balance of payments is always zero under cleanly floating exchange rates. Therefore exchange rates must always vary to make [9]

$$\begin{pmatrix} \text{Exports} - \text{Imports} \\ \text{of commodities} \\ \text{and services} \end{pmatrix} = (X - M) = \begin{pmatrix} \text{Imports} - \text{Exports} \\ \text{of assets} \end{pmatrix}$$

In light of this, when circumstance 1 holds, exchange rates must vary to keep $X - M$ constant. When circumstance 2 holds, nothing affects British $C + I + G$ either. Therefore nothing can affect British Y (which equals British $C + I + G + X - M$). Row 2 in Schema 6.4 will balance row 1 exactly, and row 4 will balance row 3. We shall see, however, several reasons why these circumstances are indeed unusual.

INSULATION AND MONEY-STOCK CHANNELS

Cleanly floating exchange rates do block the money-stock channels of transmission perfectly. The balance of payments is necessarily zero under cleanly floating exchange rates, because central banks refuse to buy and sell their own money in the foreign exchange market. Thus there are no tendencies for any country's balance of payments to alter its domestic money stock, and questions of sterilization are irrelevant. Insulation for these channels is perfect.

INSULATION AND OTHER CHANNELS

Cleanly floating exchange rates do block some of the direct transmission channels that exist under pegged exchange rates. For example, Ford Motor Company in the United States will be less ready to cut back orders of Pinto engines from Britain when a U.S. recession is accompanied by depreciation of the British pound. Pinto engines can then be bought more cheaply with dollars. As a result, without sacrificing profit, Ford can offer Pintos to Americans at lower prices in order to combat the auto slump. And its sustained purchases from Britain will help Britain avoid inheriting the U.S. recession. As another example, U.S. inflation coupled with pound appreciation may not directly raise the prices of goods that the British buy. United States inflation alone has this direct impact, but pound appreciation alone directly lowers the same British prices (see pp. 173–174).

Some direct channels remain open, however, even under cleanly floating rates. When recession is deep in the United States, and profits are low, the Ford Motor Corporation may be forced to curtail expan-

---

[9] See the first definition of the balance of payments on p. 48.

sion plans worldwide, regardless of the exchange-rate system. These real investment links are not necessarily blocked by floating rates.[10]

SOME UNIQUE TRANSMISSION CHANNELS UNDER FLOATING EXCHANGE RATES: NONINSULATION

Certain channels for the international transmission of business fluctuations exist only under floating exchange rates and not under pegged exchange rates. They differ in this way from aggregate-demand and real-investment channels, which exist in varying degrees under all exchange-rate systems.

One of these "floating channels" is the real-wealth impact of exchange-rate variability. Depreciation usually reduces a nation's real national wealth, and appreciation usually increases it (see pp. 174–176). This presumption alone, for example, causes transmission of U.S. recession to Britain under cleanly floating exchange rates, as illustrated in Schema 6.5. United States recession causes the pound to depreciate, raising the British cost of living and lowering real national wealth in Britain. British spending may be reduced as individuals save more to rebuild lost wealth. Because of the additional desire to save at every level of income, British real GNP will tend to fall. United States recession will be reflected in Britain because of (not despite) pound depreciation.

Of course, Schema 6.5's expenditure-reducing effects of pound depreciation may not outweigh the expenditure-switching effects illustrated in row 2 of Schema 6.4; on the contrary, the latter probably outweigh the former, but that does not affect two important conclusions from Schema 6.5. First, the real-wealth impacts of exchange-rate change fail to insulate at all. Second, on balance, with all impacts considered, the insulation provided by floating exchange rates is less than perfect.

Another transmission channel for recession and expansion under variable exchange rates rests on their implications for international financial investment. United States recession probably reduces the expected future profitability of aggregate investment in the United States and generally inspires a bleak outlook. Thus it is usually accompanied by hard times for investors in the U.S. stock market and by declining interest rates. If, as a result, investors decide to move into British stocks and bonds, purchasing pounds on the foreign exchange market in order to do so, then the pound's value will be higher than it would otherwise have been. The added value of the pound will discourage the purchase of British commodities and services through the familiar aggregate-demand (expenditure-switching) effects and encourage it through real-wealth effects. On

---

[10] Exchange-rate variability could, however, allow Ford to realize large speculative capital gains that would dominate the impact of U.S. recession on Ford's world profitability.

SCHEMA 6.5. *British Noninsulation from U.S. Recession under Cleanly Floating Exchange Rates: The Real-Wealth Effects*

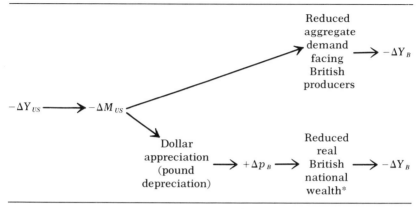

* Subject to the exception noted in footnote 15 of Chapter 5.

balance, aggregate demand facing British producers will probably be lower than it would have been otherwise. United States recession will be spread to Britain because under floating exchange rates *anything* that makes British assets more attractive to world investors also makes British commodities and services less attractive, since it keeps the pound more costly. These recessionary impulses could even dominate whatever insulation variable exchange rates do provide to Britain through the familiar aggregate-demand channels. Regardless, they certainly counteract the traditional insulation properties of floating exchange rates by causing the pound to depreciate less than it would otherwise. The upshot is again that, despite floating exchange rates, some U.S. recession is almost certainly transmitted to Britain.

These two examples of noninsulation illustrate why the two circumstances stated earlier as necessary for perfect insulation are unlikely. (1) Extraordinary growth or recession almost certainly affects exports and imports of assets. Probably inflation and exchange-rate changes do too. (2) Exchange-rate changes do alter the aggregate demand of British residents (British $C + I + G$) because they alter real national wealth in Britain.[11] Probably U.S. recession and inflation do,

[11] Another reason for predicting that exchange-rate changes affect $C + I + G$ is that C, I, and G all include imported commodities and services *by definition* (see footnote 2 above). Suppose that British C were made up of consumption of only two kinds of commodities—Beefeater gin and imported rum. Then pound depreciation would switch British consumers from rum to Beefeater. But it would leave C unchanged only if the British increased gin spending by exactly the same amount that they reduced rum spending. This seems unlikely. In fact, of course, British C is made up of consumption of many more than two commodities. Some of these, however, have no close domestically produced substitutes—such as tea. When the pound depreciates, the British reduce tea

too, because parts of real British wealth are investments in the U.S. stock market, U.S. property, and U.S. bonds.

Finally, with respect to inflation instead of recession, at least one potential transmission channel exists under variable exchange rates. It rests on the possibility discussed on pp. 95–96 that variable exchange rates are inherently inflationary because of their redistributive impact within an economy. United States inflation that is coupled with pound appreciation will create both gainers and losers in British society. The gains and losses will be less dramatic if the inflation and appreciation take place simultaneously, but they will always be there. If they are dramatic enough, then wage-price demands of the losers for equity with the gainers may be ratified by the government for political reasons. The result will be a British wage-price spiral despite variable exchange rates.

Competitive Depreciation (and Appreciation?)

It should now be clear why tremendous pressures are brought to bear on pegged exchange-rate systems during periods of worldwide recession or inflation. Every country believes it has problems enough of its own without importing those of other countries. There is a tendency to abandon the pegged exchange-rate system in favor of managed floating, which provides every country with at least some insulation from the woes of others.

But in practice, insulation is rarely perfect. Some recession or inflation is still passed back and forth. When either problem is severe, countries are often tempted to do more than just passively adopt floating exchange rates. During periods of world recession, every country is tempted to bring about *over*depreciation of its money. During periods of world inflation, some countries may be tempted to bring about *over*appreciation.[12]

COMPETITIVE DEPRECIATION

Conscious attempts by governments to overdepreciate are known as *competitive depreciations*. The rationale for them can be best shown in an example. By allowing the pound to depreciate on the

---

spending (at least a little) and probably do not increase spending by as much on any domestic substitute. Since this is true for all the imports in British C with no good domestic substitutes, it is virtually certain that British C falls when the pound depreciates. This conclusion is also implied by the likely impact of pound depreciation on real national wealth.

[12] To recall the language of Chapter 2, overdepreciating one's money is the process of bringing about its *undervaluation*. Overappreciating one's money is the process of bringing about its *overvaluation*.

foreign exchange market, Britain can insulate itself partially, but not totally, from U.S. recession. An effective way in which Britain might bring about total insulation, however, is by forcing the pound to depreciate even further than is dictated by the private market. If a little depreciation alleviates the disease of British recession, then a lot of depreciation should wipe it out. One blatant way of accomplishing this is for the British central bank to sell pounds on the foreign exchange market, not to stabilize the pound's value but to drive it down. Not only will these pound sales enhance British insulation through the familiar channels, but they will also create a British balance-of-payments surplus. The surplus will tend to make the British money stock rise and will dampen recessionary impulses still further. One of the most attractive features of this policy is the absence of economic constraints on it: the number of pounds that the British government can offer for sale on the foreign exchange market is virtually unlimited; the government creates pounds, and official reserves obviously will be rising.

There are, however, some serious international political constraints. In the real world, if Britain attempts to avoid U.S. recession in this way, then the pound depreciates not only relative to the dollar but relative to the franc, the Deutsche mark, and all other moneys as well. Their appreciation relative to the pound only makes their recessionary situation worse. In essence, what British overdepreciation does is to shift some British recession to other countries. Britain benefits from this policy at the expense of her neighbors. For this reason, conscious overdepreciation is often described as a *beggar-your-neighbor* policy. International tempers flare dramatically whenever a country is suspected of overdepreciation. It is, indeed, a kind of economic warfare.

Of course, the winners of wars don't always abhor them. When world recession is deep and enduring, every country is tempted to behave in the way just described for Britain. Each hopes to win in the sense of successfully lowering the value of its money on the foreign exchange market. Each competes to depreciate more than the other, which is why this practice is known as competitive depreciation. As a matter of arithmetic necessity, not every country can win. But if the losers simply try harder, a vicious vortex of depreciation upon depreciation can develop. Its result is that very few countries succeed in overdepreciating because everyone is trying to. Therefore very few countries insulate themselves fully from the world recession. International exchange becomes chaotic, and nationalistic recrimination abounds.

This scenario provides a fairly accurate description of the 1930s, when the entire world languished in depression. Almost every major country (including the United States) devalued its money relative to gold, and many did so more than once. (Their real purpose, of course, was to devalue relative to each other.) International exchange stagnated, and economic nationalism became even more prominent.

During the steep world recession of the mid-1970s, many voices were raised to point out the futility and damage of competitive depreciation. They apparently carried more weight than they did in the 1930s. Tension existed nonetheless. When the British pound fell rapidly through $2 in early 1976, disgruntled rumors circulated that the British central bank had actually abetted its decline by selling pounds secretly.[13] Although the British central bank hotly denied these rumors, it is not at all clear that the British were unhappy that the pound had slipped so far.

Attempts by countries to overdepreciate to avoid recession are not always blatant. Instead of openly having the British central bank sell pounds on the foreign exchange market, the British government might introduce measures to induce the private sector to sell more pounds (and to buy less). That is, the government might attempt to induce shifts in the supply and demand curves in the foreign exchange market to bring about greater pound depreciation than would have taken place otherwise. The most familiar ways of "depreciating through the back door," as it sometimes is described, are by manipulating the *international economic policies* described at the end of Chapter 4. Britain might attempt to insulate itself from U.S. recession by export subsidies, import surcharges and quotas, restrictions on financial investment abroad, administrative control over certain transactions, and prohibition of others. All such policies bring about greater depreciation and insulation than would otherwise take place, if no other country did the same. But all such policies deepen the recession facing other countries and tempt them to reciprocate (retaliate) in kind. The result may again be failure in all countries to avoid recession, despite their efforts. Indirect, like direct, beggar-your-neighbor policies are usually both inflammatory and fruitless.

COMPETITIVE APPRECIATION

In principle, a worldwide inflationary surge might bring about attempts to overappreciate—*competitive appreciations*. When the British move to floating exchange rates to avoid importing U.S. inflation, they nevertheless import some. Thus they may be tempted to drive the pound even higher than the foreign exchange market dictates. In principle, a blatant way to do so is for the British central bank to buy pounds—to seek pound appreciation aggressively and competitively. Competitive pound appreciation cannot, however, be as easily accomplished as competitive depreciation. Competitive appreciation is constrained by losses of official reserves. It will not be pursued too dramatically and cannot be pursued indefinitely because official reserves will sink too low. And the same constraint inhibits indirect

[13] *Wall Street Journal,* March 8, 1976, p. 7.

competitive appreciation "through the back door." British restrictions on exports and on foreign investment in Britain—and encouragement to imports and to British investment abroad—unfortunately drain official reserves. They may bring about the desired overappreciation of the pound if other countries do not follow suit. But they do so at some national cost to Britain: her loss of official reserves. In sum, competitive appreciation is a considerably less tempting policy than competitive depreciation.

Competitive appreciation impinges on other countries in exactly the same way as competitive depreciation. It, too, is a beggar-your-neighbor policy. If Britain were to overappreciate the pound as a response to U.S. inflation, the value of francs, Deutsche marks, and all other moneys would fall relative to the pound, aggravating other countries' inflation problems. Britain would have succeeded in insulating herself from world inflation at the expense of her neighbors.

It is difficult to point to any historical instance of competitive appreciation. United States inflation in the late 1960s and early 1970s was a fundamental cause of major appreciations relative to the dollar that took place in 1971 and 1973. But there is no evidence, or even rumor, that such appreciations were overappreciations. They were in fact delayed by foreign governments as long as possible. The world stock of official reserves continued to grow rapidly during the mid-1970s, which suggests that countries were not busy selling official reserves to buy their own currency, drive its prices excessively high, and insulate themselves from world inflation.

VARIABLE EXCHANGE RATES AS INSULATORS AGAIN

Competitive depreciation and appreciation illustrate a further failure of variable exchange rates to insulate. Variable exchange rates partially protect domestic jobs and the cost of living from foreign booms and busts, but they do not protect them from the efforts of foreign governments to influence exchange rates. Foreign central banks' sales and purchases of official reserves, in attempts to manage the float, have direct and sometimes dramatic effects on domestic unemployment and inflation. This is not true under pegged exchange rates. In fact, under variable exchange rates domestic unemployment and inflation are directly affected by shocks to international financial investment as well. Such shocks alter the exchange rate, and thereby alter exports and imports of commodities and services. This need not occur under pegged exchange rates. To put these matters another way: pegged exchange rates insulate domestic economic activity from certain shocks, variable exchange rates from others. Insulation under any exchange-rate system is unlikely to be perfect. Thus, in a world of international exchange, it is virtually impossible to divorce domestic prosperity and problems from foreign events.

Summary

International economic interdependence involves both good news and bad news. The good news is that the prosperity and sensible policy of one country are almost always enjoyed by others as well. The bad news is that recession and inflation in one country spill over to others for the same reasons. When governments peg their money by intervention, these spillovers are most pronounced; when they let it float freely, the spillovers are moderated.

There are many channels through which business swings in one country are transmitted elsewhere. One of the most important is aggregate demand. Aggregate demand *by* residents of one country is in part aggregate demand *for* imports produced by others. Shocks to one country's aggregate demand inevitably influence another's, and the influence is more pronounced the more trade dependent the nations are. A second important channel, when floats are managed and sterilization is incomplete, is through the balance of payments and the money stock. Higher (lower) incomes and prices in one country cause balance-of-payments surpluses (deficits) abroad, which expand (contract) foreign money stocks and cause higher (lower) incomes and prices there, too.

Floating exchange rates impede the flow in these channels by deflecting aggregate demand shocks back on their country of origin and by shrinking the size of surpluses and deficits. At the same time, however, they open up several unique tributary transmission channels. Even floating exchange rates do not usually insulate a nation perfectly from the macroeconomic virtues and vices of its neighbors.

In fact, managed floating tempts governments in some circumstances to a vice known as beggaring your neighbors. One government can effectively transfer its unemployment and slow growth to others (provided they don't retaliate) by consciously trying to undervalue (overdepreciate) its money in the foreign exchange market. The specific weapon available is aggressive government sales in the foreign exchange market of its own money, not to stabilize exchange rates but to *de*stabilize them. Beggaring your neighbors conceivably could also take the opposite form: exporting your inflation to them by consciously overvaluing your money.

Key Terms

international transmission and synchronization of business cycles

imported inflation and recession

Keynesian, monetary approaches

beggar-your-neighbor policy

Key Concepts and Review

Globally integrated markets.
Trade dependence of a nation.
Channels of transmission.
The insulation properties of floating exchange rates.
Competitive depreciation and appreciation.

Chapter 7

Reform and Structural Change in International Monetary Relations

After two decades of comparative stability, significant structural change in international monetary relations punctuated the 1970s. Through recurrent crises, the international financial regime evolved (many would say devolved) from a structured, internationally supervised system of pegged exchange rates into a loose, nationalistic system of managed floating. Gold's price skyrocketed, although gold itself entered a state of limbo after having been the foundation of the adjustable-peg exchange-rate system. The dollar maintained its special role as the chief official-reserve asset, but its luster grew tarnished. Stronger European currencies moved haltingly toward stable exchange rates among themselves and toward potential rivalry with the dollar as an official-reserve and intervention currency.

Institutional change followed the structural change. The International Monetary Fund (IMF) spent much of the mid-1970s trying to outline and initiate a new "system," only to be drawn into the awkward position of ratifying exchange arrangements that were practiced and put forward by homogeneous and prominent subgroups of IMF members, including the United States alone on some matters. European Community countries partially filled the institutional vacuum with agencies and periodic forums to administer their collective commitment to stable exchange rates among themselves. Large multinational commercial banks emerged as institutional substitutes for both the IMF and the United States, especially as depositories for official reserves and as sources of credit to supplement them.

Let us take a closer look now at this sequence of events.

A Broad International Monetary History, 1968 to the Late 1970s

As we have seen earlier in this book, U.S. balance-of-payments deficits grew erratically larger and more worrisome during the 1960s. Their growth was a product of many factors: the increased competitiveness and attractiveness of goods from and investments in a reconstructed Europe and Japan; the *devaluation bias* of the adjustable-peg exchange-rate system (p. 48); the expansionary macroeconomic policies of the Kennedy–Johnson administrations; and the inflationary financing of the Vietnam War. United States deficits became more worrisome because they increased the proportion of dollars to fixed-price, slowly growing gold in global official reserves. This aggravated concerns that the U.S. gold stock would be insufficient to back the dollar, becoming too small to guarantee unlimited conversion of dollars into gold at the officially assured gold price of the dollar (pp. 54–57).

The 1968 *two-tier gold market* (pp. 57–58) and the 1970–1972 creation of *Special Drawing Rights* (SDRs) (pp. 74–76) were the most important initial attempts to alleviate these problems. The first was designed to reduce losses of U.S. gold reserves by making the dollar "privately inconvertible." In practice, this amounted to allowing the dollar price of gold to float freely in transactions among sellers and buyers other than central banks and then sealing off all central-bank gold transactions in a segregated "official" market where the stable official gold value of the dollar (dollar price of gold) was maintained at its historical level. SDRs were designed to be official-reserve assets that were as "good as gold" in the sense that they shared all its characteristics. By supplementing world stocks of gold with something that was its equivalent, the designers of SDRs intended to diminish pressure on the United States by other central banks to convert unwanted official-reserve dollars into gold.

In retrospect, these innovative structural changes were too little and too late. The U.S. balance-of-payments deficit mushroomed in 1970–1971 (see Table 6.2), and foreign central banks were forced to buy prodigious and inflationary quantities of dollars in the foreign exchange market. The beginning of the end of the adjustable-peg exchange-rate system might be traced to the morning of May 5, 1971, when the German central bank found itself able to defend the mark/dollar parity only by purchasing dollars in the foreign exchange market at the rate of $1 billion per hour. At that rate, Germany alone was absorbing official-reserve dollars at almost double the rate that the United States was producing goods and services.[1] The Germans

---

[1] The German central bank absorbed $1 billion during the first hour's trading. At that rate, it would have accumulated $8 billion each eight-hour day,

promptly ceased intervention and allowed the mark to float upward more or less freely for the duration of 1971. The Dutch immediately followed suit, and Austria and Switzerland revalued.

At best, the implied depreciation of the dollar in May only moderated the growth of the U.S. balance-of-payments deficit. This led to an even more important set of actions on August 15, 1971. The Nixon administration, convinced that dramatic changes in both domestic and international economic programs were long overdue, announced unilaterally a New Economic Policy. The international parts of the package effectively administered the coup de grace to the adjustable-peg exchange-rate system. United States commitments to the IMF were voided, and the gold backing of the dollar collapsed, as the United States declared the dollar to be inconvertible into gold for everyone, central bank or not.[2] The rest of the world was instructed none too subtly to contemplate a new set of exchange-rate parities, which was taken as an invitation for all to float temporarily while exchange-rate negotiations began. To drive home the seriousness of U.S. intentions to seek a lower value for the dollar relative to most foreign moneys, the Nixon administration imposed a temporary 10 percent *import surcharge*, to be removed upon the establishment of mutually agreeable new parities.

International negotiations and generalized floating continued simultaneously until December 1971 when the Smithsonian Agreement was announced. The Agreement featured a major realignment of exchange-rate parities, with revaluations of almost every major money relative to the dollar and with especially large revaluations for the principal balance-of-payments-surplus countries, Germany and Japan.[3] Wider bands were established around the new parities in an attempt to permit central banks somewhat more breathing room in their foreign-exchange-market intervention. Central banks were obliged to maintain market exchange rates within $2\frac{1}{4}$ percent of the parity, instead of within 1 percent, as under the old system. For cosmetic and political reasons the official dollar price of gold was raised 8.6 percent, from $35 to $38 an ounce, which was equivalent to devaluing the dollar relative to gold by 8.6 percent. This enabled a large number of countries that had revalued their money relative to

---

$40 billion each five-day week, and $2080 billion each 52-week year. United States gross national product (GNP) in 1971 was $1063 billion.

[2] As the United States repeatedly stressed, the dollar was not made inconvertible in the same way as currencies subject to exchange control (Supplement 2A). Dollars could still be freely converted into goods or other moneys — but not into gold. What was more accurately made inconvertible, therefore, and consequently shut out of the system, was gold, not dollars.

[3] That is, Germany and Japan revalued the mark and the yen not only relative to the dollar but also by smaller percentages relative to other moneys.

the dollar by exactly 8.6 percent to claim (correctly, and with some disdain) that the value of their money, unlike the dollar, had remained stable relative to gold. Japan, Germany, and several other countries could even claim that the gold value of their money had increased. Furthermore, all could claim that the United States had been humiliated, illustrating again the curious cloak of pride and nationalism that envelops exchange rates. The United States removed the import surcharge and accepted the increased dollar price of gold as the concessions necessary to prompt agreement on new parities. But the United States refused to restore convertibility of the dollar into gold, which made the new official $38 gold price an economic irrelevancy.[4] Indeed, no official transactions in gold were ever made at that price.

President Nixon hailed the Smithsonian Agreement as the "greatest monetary agreement in history," but it lasted for just over a year. Even during that year, severe inflation in Britain and consequent official-reserve losses caused it to abandon defense of its Smithsonian parity and to begin managing the float of a depreciating pound. Canada also floated throughout the year.

Crises developed again in early 1973. A massive balance-of-payments surplus induced Switzerland to forego foreign-exchange-market intervention; a correspondingly massive deficit induced Italy to do the same. German and Japanese balance-of-payments surpluses had continued much larger and longer than originally expected at the new parities, and speculative purchases of marks and yen quickly aggravated the situation painfully for the intervening central banks. Central bankers met feverishly in Tokyo and Europe over a three-day weekend in February 1973 and agreed on yet another set of exchange-rate parities. These were implemented principally through yet another cosmetic 10 percent rise in the official dollar price of gold, with most other countries holding the gold value of their money constant. The result was a 10 percent devaluation of the dollar relative not only to gold but to most other moneys as well. Japan was also induced to float, and the yen rose in value against both the dollar and other moneys.

[4] Nor has the United States had any desire since 1971 to restore official *convertibility* of the dollar into gold. In U.S. thinking, restoration of the gold backing for the dollar would represent a throwback to an exchange-rate system that has outlived its feasibility (making gold, as Keynes once said, a "barbarous relic"). To back the dollar credibly would require a massive increase of several hundred percent in a new official price of gold. In U.S. thinking, such an increase would chiefly reward undeserving Russian and South African gold producers and French and Arab gold hoarders ("gold bugs"). It would once again surrender control over the size of the United States' own reserves (largely gold) to foreign dollar holders. And it would hamstring U.S. policy, insofar as the United States might have to more actively keep the size of any balance-of-payments deficit under control.

The new parities lasted all of two weeks. Massive intervention requirements in the same old direction prompted European central banks to close European foreign exchange markets. What emerged from meetings during the next two weeks was a decision for a number of European countries to float independently and for a small group of other European countries to float "jointly" by maintaining exchange rates among their own moneys at mutually agreed intra-European parities. This agreement was actually just a modification of steps taken by several European governments in 1972 to move toward a single, common European currency.

With a few exceptions, the exchange-rate arrangements that emerged in early 1973 have persisted. Britain, Canada, and Japan have experimented with informal and unilaterally chosen pegs, but otherwise they have continued to manage independent floats. France, Italy, and several other European countries have floated in and out of the European joint float, now known as the European Monetary System (EMS). Smaller countries, developed and developing, have been left to themselves to choose the exchange-rate system most accommodating to their needs. Some pegged, either to one currency or to several; some devalued and revalued frequently; some floated in a highly managed way; and a few floated more or less freely.

The magnitude of exchange-rate variation during this period has not been small. For example, from June 1977 to October 1978, the dollar depreciated by 51, 28, and 64 percent against the Japanese yen, German mark, and Swiss franc respectively, with most of the movement coming in the last few months. When, on November 1, the Carter administration borrowed massive amounts of yen, marks, and Swiss francs and announced its intention to bid up the dollar, its average prices rose 12–15 percent in a single month.

Large recent exchange-rate variation suggests that a revised pegged exchange-rate system would have been subject to recurrent crises and would have functioned no better than the Smithsonian Agreement. Fundamental reasons for the persistence of floating among major countries have been the global inflation of the early 1970s, overlapping with and followed by the global stagnation of the mid- and late 1970s. Most large nations have placed high priority on the insulation properties of floating exchange rates, sheltering them from importing even worse inflation and stagnation (see Chapter 6).

National preferences for managed floating were reinforced in the 1970s by the fourfold increase in the world price of oil brought about by the Organization of Petroleum Exporting Countries (OPEC) in 1973. Oil price hikes aggravated both inflation and recession (outside of the OPEC countries themselves). OPEC furthermore saddled oil importers with huge balance-of-payments deficits, which would probably have been even larger if the pegged exchange rates of the Smithsonian Agreement had somehow been maintained. As we will see, both these deficits and OPEC's corresponding surpluses have led to a number of concerns about the stability of the international financial system.

Many of the events discussed above are summarized briefly in Table 7.1. We turn in the next section to the one that is not, the Second Amendment of the IMF's Articles of Agreement.

International Monetary Reform

The phrase *international monetary reform* describes cooperative governmental efforts to "re-form" the international financial system. Yet the system largely re-formed itself, while waiting for official efforts to bear fruit. After the demise of the adjustable-peg exchange-rate system in 1973, governments independently chose exchange-rate systems that seemed most desirable to them on nationalistic grounds. Conflicts—such as the U.S. suspicion that Japan was deliberately holding down the value of the yen to stimulate Japanese employment in the late 1970s—were ironed out bilaterally between the governments concerned.

Two new sources of official reserves evolved. First, the two-tier gold market was abolished in 1973, and governments became free to sell their gold, if necessary at inflated private market prices. Official reserves were created in the sense that governments "realized" their historical capital gains on gold stocks. Second, governments began increasingly to borrow dollars from private commercial banks in order to supplement their official reserves.

Intergovernmental negotiations over the shape of international monetary reform proceeded throughout this time under the auspices of the IMF. At first they were aimed at restoring a workable system of pegged exchange rates. As events overtook them, they were aimed more at (1) codifying guidelines for responsible government management of a floating exchange rate, and (2) reducing the role of both gold and dollars as official reserves in favor of assets that were less capriciously priced and created.

Reform efforts culminated in the Second Amendment to the IMF's Articles of Agreement, which took effect in 1978.[5] The Amendment contained two important structural changes.

NATIONAL DISCRETION AND SURVEILLANCE

National governments were explicitly granted discretion to choose their own exchange-rate system. No longer were the rigid rules and procedures of the adjustable-peg exchange-rate system binding. Yet

[5] The First Amendment had established Special Drawing Rights (SDRs), as outlined in Supplement 2B.

TABLE 7.1. *Important Structural and Institutional Changes in Recent International Monetary Relations*

Dates	Description	Page reference
March 1968	Two-tier gold market created: dollar becomes inconvertible into gold for all except official holders; dollar price of gold in private segment of market allowed to float	57–58
July 1969	First Amendment of International Monetary Fund Articles of Agreement takes effect: $9.2 billion of Special Drawing Rights created and distributed as official reserves from 1970 through 1972; designed to be equivalent to and to supplement gold stocks	74–76
August 1971	Nixon administration New Economic Policy: dollar becomes inconvertible into gold for all holders; United States induces other countries to float as prelude to exchange-rate realignment; United States levies 10 percent import surcharge	204
August– December 1971	Generalized managed floating	
December 1971	Smithsonian Agreement: restoration of pegged exchange-rate system with substantial realignments of parities; wider band around parity instituted; dollar devalued relative to most moneys and gold; U.S. import surcharge removed	204–205
May 1972	First European steps toward common European currency: narrow margins agreement (snake in the tunnel) implemented	211–213
December 1971– January 1973	General pegged exchange rates for the last time during the 1970s: Canada floats independently throughout, Britain through part	205

even though governments had "freedom of choice" in exchange arrangements, they did not have "freedom of behavior." Obligations were spelled out. Governments were expected to intervene when necessary to keep foreign exchange markets "orderly" and to avoid domestic policies that would inhibit stability. Obligations were *symmetric*. Policies that generated large balance-of-payments surpluses and significant appreciation were as irresponsible as policies that

TABLE 7.1. *CONTINUED*

Dates	Description	Page reference
January–March 1973	Foreign-exchange-market crises: dollar devalued again relative to most moneys and gold; Italy, Japan, and Switzerland float independently; joint European float begins	205–206
November 1973	Two-tier gold market ends: central banks free to value and sell gold stocks at private world-gold-market price	207
October–December 1973	Organization of Petroleum Exporting Countries (OPEC) raises oil prices fourfold; institutes selective oil embargo	136–137; 206; 260–263
April 1978	Second Amendment of International Monetary Fund Articles of Agreement takes effect: ratifies national discretion in choice of exchange-rate system, subject to IMF surveillance; one-third of IMF gold sold or returned to members, and gold's role in IMF operations drastically curtailed	76; 207–211
November 1978	Massive intervention by the U.S. Treasury and Federal Reserve System to bid up the weak dollar in the foreign exchange market; financed by borrowing from Germany, Japan, Switzerland, and the IMF and by increased official sales of U.S. gold	206
March 1979	Further European steps toward common European currency; European Monetary System implemented	214

generated large deficits and depreciation.[6] Beggar-your-neighbor manipulation of exchange rates was explicitly prohibited.

The IMF was charged with *surveillance* of these obligations. It was empowered with rights to require "consultations" with countries that ignored them and to comment publicly on national behavior that was inconsistent with the Amendment's description of responsible behavior. Forced consultations and public commentary are more powerful weapons than they may appear. International bankers and brokers

---

[6] Thus an attempt was made to eliminate the *devaluation bias* of the adjustable-peg exchange-rate system, described on pp. 47–48, and to make strong-currency countries and weak-currency countries symmetrically responsible for stable exchange rates.

for international bond issues take very seriously a critical IMF judgment. "National credit ratings" suffer, and residents of a "wayward" country can find themselves seriously restricted in their access to the international financial resources that help to fund exports, imports, and domestic investment projects.

Surveillance is a vague and controversial concept. What it will lead to in practice is not yet clear. It gives the IMF great *potential* power over national governments, which may become actual power if defenders of strict surveillance succeed in solidifying it in rules. Some recommend that the IMF periodically calculate and declare *reference* exchange rates and then pressure countries to avoid actions that would allow their currencies to slip beyond a satisfactory margin of the reference rates.[7] Nationally sensitive opponents of this *reference rate proposal* find it smacks too much of international interference in domestic affairs, and it makes the IMF too similar to a world central bank. In their view, guidelines for surveillance should be *presumptive indicators* rather than rigid rules: guidelines should provide flexible criteria for presuming to identify irresponsible national action, not inflexible grounds for rooting it out. Extreme opponents of any guidelines at all exist too. They favor minimal surveillance and maximal national discretion, with the IMF providing only a forum for settlement of international monetary grievances.[8]

Only time will tell whether surveillance will really re-form the system. Optimists see the combination of surveillance and national discretion leading to regulated freedom. Pessimists worry that the outcome will be nationally based exchange-rate anarchy.

GOLD, SDRs, AND DOLLARS

The Second Amendment purported to shrink the role of gold in international monetary relations. Gold's uses as the IMF's unit of account and as backing for Special Drawing Rights, dollars, or any other money were proscribed. The IMF also prohibited itself from accepting gold in any normal transaction. Finally, the Second Amendment formalized the Fund's decision to dispose of one-third of its own holdings of gold.[9]

---

[7] An extreme version of this proposal favors *reserve indicator* rules for calculating reference rates. Reference rates and national obligations would be altered automatically if official reserves diverged quickly or greatly enough from an "ideal" level. The ideal level might be calculated by the IMF or else simply identified with the size of some recent stock of official reserves. Symmetric reserve indicator rules would force balance-of-payments-surplus countries to adjust as promptly and significantly as balance-of-payments-deficit countries.

[8] IMF surveillance over exchange-rate practices would then be very much like GATT (General Agreement on Tariffs and Trade) surveillance over international trade practices. See Supplement 11B.

[9] The IMF's gold holdings were acquired through assessment of membership fees, or IMF quotas, under the adjustable-peg exchange-rate system. One-quarter of the fee had to be paid in gold. See Supplement 2B.

In some measure, these reforms again simply ratified accomplished facts. Gold stocks had been a large but inactive part of global official reserves ever since the United States declared the dollar to be inconvertible into gold.

On the other hand, there has been an awkward disparity between the professed purpose of the reform and the practice of most central banks. Ingrained habits die hard, and gold has not disappeared from the official reserves of national governments. On the contrary, its official-reserve value and quantity have grown—through revaluation of existing stocks at private market prices, through purchases of gold in the open market by central banks, and through return (*restitution*) of half of the gold that the IMF disposed of directly to governments. Even periodic U.S. sales of its gold reserves at open auctions have been minuscule compared to the remaining U.S. gold stock.

The Second Amendment also purported to enhance the role of the IMF's own created reserve asset—Special Drawing Rights (SDRs), but the Amendment contained no practical steps for doing so. Nor did it contain any provisions for shrinking the role of the dollar in worldwide official reserves, although this matter had figured prominently in discussions leading up to the Amendment. United States obligations under the "reformed" exchange-rate arrangements seem to be the same as those for any other country. But no special attention was paid to the mammoth dollar balances currently in official reserves, nor to the ways in which arbitrary changes in them can disrupt foreign exchange markets as much as changes in U.S. policies. The United States has been unwilling to agree to any proposals for replacing these dollar balances, say with SDRs (proposals described variously by the words *asset substitution* or *asset settlement*).

Evolution may outdistance reform in creating a substitute for the dollar. Ongoing efforts by European countries to form a successful *currency bloc* by pegging exchange rates among their own moneys may ultimately succeed, producing a unified European currency that rivals the dollar as an official-reserve asset and a private store of value. But many barriers stand in the way of European monetary harmonization, and the experience of the 1970s is not encouraging.

The Move Toward a Common European Currency

Before the international monetary upheavals outlined in Table 7.1, many European governments were convinced that a move toward a single European money was desirable. The economic cost of exchange-rate variability among European Community moneys seemed especially striking. Each economy had a very large tradeables sector, because European Community membership required elimination of almost all barriers to trade with other members. Thus exchange-rate variation among members seemed likely to cause particularly severe dislocation and had uncertainty-enhancing, trade-reducing effects very much like those of the prohibited trade barriers, alternately intensifying and isolating foreign competition (see pp. 95–97). Furthermore, only occasionally during the 1950s and the 1960s had macroeconomic conditions been notably dissimilar among European Community countries, and macroeconomic policies were on the whole parallel. Thus, exchange-rate variability was not sought for its reputed insulation properties, and there existed an illusion of monetary independence, even under pegged exchange rates. Parallel monetary policies constrained the size of intra-European balance-of-payments deficits and surpluses and disguised the degree to which monetary events in one country depended on monetary policy in others (Chapter 5).

The move toward a common European currency was agreed to in 1970 and implemented in 1972 through a *narrow-margins agreement* among seven countries.[10] The narrow-margins agreement obligated each central bank to maintain an even narrower range of variation for intra-European exchange rates than the 4-1/2 percent Smithsonian band around their parity dollar price. If the Deutsche mark was sufficiently strong relative to the French franc, for example, central banks were required to take action *even when* both the mark and the franc were within the permissible band around their dollar parity. Either or both central banks would endeavor to sell marks in order to buy francs in the foreign exchange market, thus restoring the desired mark value of the franc.

Successful intervention along these lines indirectly kept changes in the dollar price of marks very close in size to changes in the dollar price of francs. A vision of the mark, franc, and other European currencies as tied together in a tight bundle that moved together over time within bands around their dollar parities led the narrow-margins agreement to be referred to picturesquely as the *snake in the tunnel*. The accuracy of the metaphor is reflected in Figure 7.1.

The original intention of the narrow-margins agreement was gradually to narrow the permissible variation in intra-European exchange rates to zero. That is, picturesquely, the snake was to become thinner and thinner, until it wasted away to nothing. At this point, exchange rates would be rigidly fixed, as they are between quarters and dollars (p. 97), and much of Europe would be in possession of essentially one common money.

The international monetary crises of the early 1970s undermined that intention. Britain left the snake after only two months to float; Italy after only nine months. Both remained outside the snake. France

[10] Belgium, France, Germany, Italy, Luxembourg, the Netherlands, and Britain (whose membership in the European Community was impending). The original seven were later joined by Denmark, Norway, and Sweden (although neither Norway nor Sweden became a European Community member).

FIGURE 7.1. The "Snake in the Tunnel" over a Hypothetical
13-Day Period

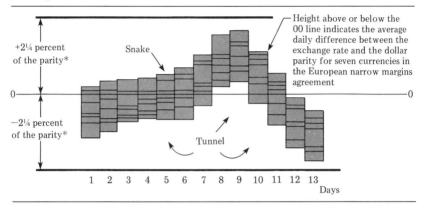

* The 2¼ percent indicates the maximum permissible deviation of exchange rates
from their dollar parity under the Smithsonian Agreement, December 1971 through
March 1973.

withdrew twice temporarily in order to float, and Denmark and Sweden once each. Intrasnake parities were altered by significant devaluations and revaluations once a year on average. The tunnel became
irrelevant after less than a year, as snake moneys were allowed to float
as a group against the dollar (the so-called *joint European float*).

Almost every failure of the snake to hold together was due to macroeconomic divergence and transmission. Britain's and Italy's monetary growth and inflation rates were persistently higher, and Germany's persistently lower, than the average for snake members.
Rather than "deflating" their economies in order to keep the pound
and the lira strong enough to remain in the snake, Britain and Italy
chose to depart. The remaining snake members concurred in order to
avoid inheriting "excessively" expansionary British and Italian monetary policy through massive balance-of-payments surpluses with their
former partners, and to dampen the direct inflationary transmission of
British and Italian demand pressure to their own economies. Germany,
on the other hand, because of deep-seated fears of inflation, chose
several times to revalue the mark within the snake. Its own massive
surpluses were highly expansionary, and eliminating them by conscious monetary or fiscal stimulus would be comparably inflationary.
The remaining snake members again concurred to avoid importing
"excessive" German caution when their own economies were afflicted
by unacceptable unemployment and undercapacity.

Despite these instances of failure, the move toward European monetary unification is not dead, nor therefore is the possibility that exclusive regional currency blocs, rather than the globally constituted but

unwieldy IMF, will increasingly determine the practical conduct of international monetary relations. European governments agreed in establishing the European Monetary System (EMS) in March 1979 to encourage recommitment of former snake members by allowing them temporarily wider-than-normal bands for permissible exchange-rate variation. Italy rejoined on these terms and France on normal terms. The groundwork for efficient cooperative intervention was laid in the establishment of a common official-reserve fund of dollars, gold, and national moneys on which each member could draw easily and predictably to defend snake parities.

The common official-reserve fund is very similar to what the IMF has historically provided for its own members out of the pool of financial resources made available by payment of IMF quotas (Supplement 2B).[11] To some extent, therefore, the common EMS pool may diminish the recourse of European nations to the IMF and short-circuit its surveillance (despite European protestations that their arrangements are fully compatible with the IMF's Articles). Furthermore, a successful, strong, unified set of European moneys could conceivably displace some dollars in the asset portfolios of central banks and private financial institutions. Europeans should welcome this possibility, and the United States should not, if the United States really has enjoyed advantages on balance from the special role of the dollar over the past thirty-five years. (Pp. 108–113 and Supplement 3A outline these advantages and some disadvantages as well.)

Commercial Banks as Lenders and Creators of Official Reserves

During the 1970s, another set of institutions began to compete with the United States as a creator, and with the IMF as a lender, of official-reserve assets: privately owned multinational commercial banks. Such banks are just particular sorts of multinational corporations, having geographically diffuse operations but geographically concentrated ownership (see Chapter 13). What enables these banks to compete with the United States and the IMF is that they are almost always *Euro-banks*, banks whose branches accept deposits and make loans in the currencies of many different nations, even though they

---

[11] Members of the EMS have agreed to pay into the common fund 20 percent of their official reserves of dollars and gold plus an equal amount of their own money. They are then able to "purchase" other European moneys up to the full amount of their *entire* contribution (and perhaps more) and to add them to their official reserves for intervention. "Purchases" are reversed by "repurchases" in exactly the same fashion as under IMF operations. These arrangements in essence transform the domestic-currency part of the "snake quota" into potential official reserves just as under IMF arrangements.

are located and chartered in only one. For example, a typical branch of Chase Manhattan in London, Zurich, or even Singapore is prepared to accept and lend dollars, pounds sterling, Deutsche marks, Swiss francs, and several other moneys *without* any necessary conversion of one to another through the foreign exchange market; so are the worldwide branches of Barclay's Bank (British-owned), Dresdner Bank (German-owned), and a number of other large multinational banks.

Euro-banking is discussed at greater length in Supplement 7A. Important here are two facts: (1) Many governments and central banks chose during the 1970s to hold large amounts of official-reserve dollars as *Euro-dollar deposits*—dollar deposits in commercial banks outside U.S. borders, beyond the oversight of the U.S. Federal Reserve System, and even relatively free of regulation by the countries that host them. (Britain cares a great deal more about the sterling loans and deposits of Barclay's British branches than about their Euro-dollar loans and deposits, because the sterling operations more directly affect domestic British prosperity.) (2) Many governments and central banks have found *Euro-currency loans* from private banks to be an excellent way of temporarily supplementing official reserves. This has been especially true of a select group of less-developed countries but also of Britain, Canada, and Italy. Borrowing official reserves and using them to support a weak currency in the foreign exchange market defers or avoids the bitter medicines of devaluation, depreciation, fiscal austerity, and monetary tightness; and borrowing from private commercial banks instead of from the IMF short-circuits the IMF's surveillance and the frequently painful conditions that it imposes before approving loans of official reserves (pp. 71–72).

EURO-BANKS AS DEPOSITORIES FOR GLOBAL OFFICIAL RESERVES

Euro-dollar deposits have become an increasingly attractive way of holding official reserves, as Table 7.2 reveals. One reason is the dramatic growth of Euro-banking itself, with its ability to offer higher interest rates on Euro-dollar deposits than are offered on comparable U.S. assets (due in turn to the economies of large-scale Euro-banking transactions, and to minimal regulation of Euro-banks, both discussed in Supplement 7A). Another reason is the anonymity and protection that Euro-dollar official reserves can provide but that holdings of U.S. government bonds or bank accounts cannot. The latter feature has been especially attractive to OPEC members, who fear retaliatory seizure of any official-reserve dollars held in the United States—for example, in the event of conflict over oil pricing or supply. The United States cannot easily discover the size of OPEC official-reserve holdings in nonresident commercial banks and would find it next to impossible to block OPEC withdrawals from such Euro-banks. Much of the

TABLE 7.2. *Source of Official-Reserve Dollars*

| End of year | Global stock of official-reserve dollars ($ billions) | | Percentage share of Euro-dollars in global official-reserve dollars |
	Held as claims on Euro-banks	Held as claims on U.S.-resident institutions	
1968	3.8	17.3	18
1969	4.9	16.0	23
1970	10.5	23.8	31
1971	11.3	50.6	18
1972	19.5	61.6	24
1973	25.5	66.8	28
1974	39.5	76.9	34
1975	45.1	80.7	36
1976	53.0	92.0	37
1977	70.5	126.1	36

Source: International Monetary Fund, *Annual Report* for 1975 (Table 15, p. 39), for 1976 (Table 15, p. 38), for 1977 (Table 14, p. 44), and for 1978 (Table 16, p. 53). Values converted from SDRs to dollars by year end exchange rates from International Monetary Fund, *International Financial Statistics*, July 1978, p. 7.

growth of Euro-dollar official-reserve deposits since 1973 may have been due to OPEC alone.

Official-reserve holdings of Euro-dollars are important for several reasons. First, while they do not reduce the special role of the dollar in the world's monetary system, they do reduce any advantages that U.S. residents derive from that role. As always, foreign countries can add dollars to official reserves only by running balance-of-payments surpluses. But their acquisition of Euro-dollars does not require the United States to run a balance-of-payments deficit. Since Euro-dollars are a liability of a foreign commercial bank, not of any U.S. resident, there is no necessary direct effect of the acquisition on the U.S. balance of payments.[12] United States deficits are thus not the only source whereby other nations can build up official-reserve national insurance (pp. 108–113). Nor are U.S. residents the world's only friendly insurance salesmen. Nor can U.S. deficits be either as large or as

---

[12] To be more exact, there is no effect on the U.S. official reserves account (p. 78), or on the U.S. balance of payments on official-settlements (official-reserve-transactions) basis (pp. 81–82), even though there are positive effects on the comparable account and balance of the rest of the world. This is the most important reason why summing comparably measured recorded balances of payments across nations does not result in a zero, contrary to what should definitionally be the case (pp. 51–52).

unproblematic in the presence of this competitive alternative source of official-reserve dollars.

Second, central-bank holdings of official reserves in commercial banks can magnify speculative pressure against exchange-rate targets that the central bank is attempting to defend. The central bank is thereby put in the awkward position of undermining itself. Suppose that because of speculative sales of dollars to purchase pounds, the pound is appreciating faster than the British central bank thinks desirable. To dampen that appreciation, the British central bank is obliged to intervene in the opposite direction—selling pounds and purchasing dollars, which are then added to official-reserve stocks. If the British central bank deposits its newly acquired official-reserve dollars in a commercial bank, at least some of them will be loaned out to speculators who *want* to borrow dollars in order to sell them on the foreign exchange market for pounds. The speculative sale forces the British central bank to acquire the "same" dollars again (although it doesn't identify them as such); to add them to its growing official-reserve account; to see them loaned out again; to reacquire them again; redeposit them again; and so on. The British central bank in essence provides loans to finance speculation against the pound it is pledged to defend! Commercial banks do what comes naturally, acting as intermediaries between the lender (the British central bank) and borrowers (speculators).

The circular nature of this problematic sequence has led to its characterization as the *Euro-dollar carousel*. Major industrial countries found it sufficiently destructive of their efforts to peg and manage exchange rates that in 1971 they renounced any further additions to their official-reserve stocks of Euro-dollars. They also committed themselves to a gradual reduction of Euro-dollars in their official reserves. A 1973 effort to impose similar commitments on all IMF members failed, however. And the data in Table 7.2 suggest that on the contrary, the potential for Euro-dollar carousels is increasing.

Since Euro-dollar carousels weaken a central bank's ability to influence exchange rates by intervention, they make less likely any widespread return to pegged exchange rates. They also hinder official management of floating exchange rates. It is ironic that central banks have undercut the chief usefulness of official reserves by their choice of one particular form in which to hold them.

COMMERCIAL BANKS AS SOURCES OF BORROWED OFFICIAL RESERVES

For as long as international commerce has existed, commercial banks have had some role in its financing. And for as long as public agencies have themselves engaged in or encouraged such commerce, commercial banks have often been creditors of governments. Furthermore, commercial banks have a long history of helping to finance specific governmental projects both at home and abroad—roads, canals, power plants, land reclamation, industrial parks, and others.

The 1970s brought two modifications of these traditions. Euro-banks in particular began to extend significant Euro-currency loans to governments for general "balance-of-payments support"—that is, for replenishment of depleted official reserves. While Britain, Canada, and Italy benefited from them, the loans were otherwise concentrated to an unprecedented degree on less-developed countries (LDCs).[13] These trends are at least partially[14] reflected in Table 7.3.

There are a number of reasons for the recent burgeoning of *sovereign debt*, as central-government indebtedness to commercial banks is sometimes called. The first is the increased availability of Euro-bank credit together with the increased needs for it created by OPEC's predatory oil pricing in 1973. A significant proportion of OPEC's dollar revenues from oil exports, so-called *petrodollars*, were deposited in Euro-banks[15] because of the attractive return/security features discussed above. Banks looking to lend out these new deposits also found a new and eager set of borrowers—governments of oil-importing countries whose official reserves had been made suddenly less adequate by the massive shift toward balance-of-payments deficit that OPEC forced upon them. By comparison, OPEC made far fewer petrodollars available for direct loans or for expanding the pool of reserves available to oil importers through the IMF's temporary *Oil Facility* (p. 73). Thus commercial banks became the chief inter-

---

[13] Commercial-bank loans for balance-of-payments support to Communist Eastern European countries also became increasingly prominent during the 1970s. They raise many of the same concerns as loans to LDCs.

[14] The figures in the table do not reveal how governments' share of total Euro-bank loans has increased in the 1970s. Furthermore, the figures on outstanding LDC debt in the table include debt for all purposes. It is impossible to determine how much of it was directly or indirectly for balance-of-payments support. Trying to make such distinctions quantitatively precise in the data is fruitless, since even loans to a country's private residents provide a kind of balance-of-payments support, and conserve official reserves, by shifting outward the supply curve of foreign exchange and increasing the foreign-exchange-market demand for domestic currency (see pp. 12–15 and Figure 1.2).

[15] The U.S. Department of the Treasury estimates that OPEC residents and governments channeled $41 billion into Euro-bank deposits during 1974, 1975, and 1976. If none of these dollars had been deposited in Euro-banks by previous holders, then that $41 billion would have represented roughly a 20 percent expansion of global Euro-bank deposit resources. In fact, some of it was no doubt withdrawn from Euro-bank deposits owned by oil importers in order to pay OPEC for oil. But chances are that there was nevertheless substantial net expansion in Euro-bank deposits because of OPEC investors' relatively stronger preference for large proportions of anonymous and secure Euro-bank deposits in their portfolio.

TABLE 7.3. *Government Indebtedness to Commercial Banks*

Instances of commercial bank loans for balance-of-payments support of developed countries

Country	Year	Size of loan ($ billions)
Italy	1976	1.8
Britain	1977	1.5
Canada	1977	1.5

Indebtedness of 84 less-developed country governments[a]

End of year	Owed to commercial banks ($ billions)	Owed to other institutions[b] ($ billions)	Percentage share of bank debt in total debt
1969	4.6	57.9	7.4
1970	5.8	65.3	8.2
1971	8.4	75.1	10.1
1972	11.7	84.9	12.1
1973	19.0	97.8	16.3
1974	28.5	119.2	19.3
1975	40.6	133.3	23.3

[a] Includes most OPEC members and more advanced Mediterranean countries such as Greece, Portugal, Spain, Turkey, and Yugoslavia.
[b] Includes government-to-government debt, debt to multilateral institutions, and "suppliers' credits," even though these last often consist of bank loans themselves.
Source: Federal Reserve Bank of Chicago, *International Letter*, nos. 302 (November 26, 1976); 311 (January 28, 1977); 351 (November 4, 1977); World Bank, *External Public Debt of Eighty-Four Developing Countries: Calendar Year 1975 (and 1976 estimates).*

mediary in channeling OPEC's newly acquired loanable funds into the hands of financially strained oil importers, a process known as *recycling petrodollars,* or simply *recycling.*

A closely related reason for the expansion of commercial-bank lending to newly needy governments was the ability of Euro-banks to offer lower interest rates on Euro-currency loans than could be secured from narrowly domestic banks or in national capital markets. (This was due to the natural economies of large-scale Euro-banking transactions, aided by the cooperative *syndication* of large Euro-currency loans through *consortia* of many Euro-banks, discussed in Supplement 7A).

Finally, less-developed debtor countries had few alternatives but to turn toward short-term, hard-terms Euro-bank loans, as supplies of concessionary *bilateral* and *multilateral foreign aid*[16] stagnated during the late 1960s and 1970s.[17] Ironically, the stagnation in foreign aid was itself partly due to the success of a group of former LDCs—the OPEC nations—at extracting wealth transfers by economic aggression rather than by special pleading. But the deeper roots of the stagnation lay in the increased opposition in both developed and less-developed countries to a "liberal" international economic order, of which foreign aid was a representative program. The grounds for this opposition are discussed in Chapter 14.

There are a number of reasons for concern about the widespread recourse of governments to private Euro-banks for balance-of-payments support. The IMF worries that borrowing governments can thereby avoid surveillance and thus act more aggressively and less responsibly than internationally mandated IMF guidelines allow. Borrowing governments, of course, often find this an advantage, since it precludes the IMF, and indirectly the rest of the world, from what they view as unwarranted meddling in their internal affairs. The IMF more narrowly frets at the institutional competition that private Euro-banks provide as alternative sources of borrowed official reserves. Commercial banks, by contrast, have frequently welcomed the IMF's presence, because its right to consultations with governments and its access to official data often enable it to make superior evaluations of a country's creditworthiness. Thus occasionally commercial bank loans to governments have been made conditional on the government's successfully obtaining an IMF loan as well, which encourages the satisfaction of IMF recommendations and enhances its surveillance. Conditional, interdependent loans of this sort are sometimes called *parallel financing.*

Less-developed countries themselves are hardly unanimous in their evaluation of sovereign debt. The reason is that very few have bene-

---

[16] Bilateral foreign aid describes direct government-to-government financial assistance, usually in the form of a loan from a developed-country government to an LDC government. Multilateral foreign aid describes financial assistance that is channeled through an international institution, such as the United Nations, the World Bank (International Bank for Reconstruction and Development), or a regional development bank (Inter-American Development Bank, Asian Development Bank, African Development Bank). To be precisely classified as aid rather than investment, however, loans must have some combination of "concessional" terms: an interest cost below the market rate, an atypically long time to repay (*maturity*), or a grace period before payment of interest or principal begins. Loans with these characteristics are described as *soft loans,* in contrast to both *hard loans* (on market terms) and *grants* (extremely concessional terms to the point of requiring no repayment).

[17] Official development assistance from seventeen of the wealthiest western countries declined from .52 percent of their collective gross national product in 1960, to .31 percent in 1970, to .27 percent in 1975. A further decline was projected to .21 percent by 1980. See John W. Sewell and the staff of the Overseas Development Council, *The United States and World Development Agenda 1977* (New York: Praeger, 1977), p. 231.

fited. Commercial-bank loans to LDC governments and public agencies have been highly concentrated on the most-developed LDCs. Brazil and Mexico alone accounted for roughly half in the late 1970s. Comparatively wealthy and populous OPEC members (Algeria, Iran, and Indonesia) have been important borrowers as well as periodic depositors. Middle- and lower-income LDCs have been left to rely on increasingly inadequate traditional sources of loans. From their point of view they are being inequitably denied credit opportunities that other nations arbitrarily enjoy. They identify the concentrated channeling of petrodollars into developed-country investments and into loans to a privileged group of LDC governments as the *recycling problem.*[18] From the point of view of private Euro-banks, however, poorer LDCs are also poorer credit risks than the more prosperous LDCs.[19] Highly competitive Euro-banking penalizes with insolvency banks that make loans based on "need" rather than on the strictest measures of financial quality and fiscal responsibility.

The most important concerns about sovereign debt to commercial banks, however, are those of the developed countries about the financial stability of world banking. The fear is that commercial-bank loans to governments for balance-of-payments or budgetary support are riskier than traditional loans, raising the likelihood of the collapse of several major Euro-banks. Such a collapse might have a "domino effect" throughout the Euro-banking system, since many Euro-banks hold their precautionary bank reserves as deposits in *other* Euro-banks. The failure of one could freeze reserve deposits of others, leading to a run on Euro-banks to withdraw deposits before the remaining Euro-banks exhausted their unfrozen reserves. Depositor panic would cause additional bank failures, and the failure cycle

---

[18] Occasionally the label *recycling problem* is applied to the alleged inequity between original recipients of petrodollar deposits/investments and those who have to borrow them. The supporting intuition is that borrowers have to pay (interest) to obtain the use of petrodollars, whereas the developed countries, in which most OPEC deposits/investments are made, receive them "free." The allegation is hard to justify, however, because the original recipients themselves must also pay for their receipt of petrodollars—in the form of interest on OPEC-owned Euro-bank deposits or government securities, and in the form of profits and capital gains on OPEC-owned property. If there is any inequity, it can be measured only by the difference between the "cost per petrodollar" that ultimate borrowers and original recipients pay. And even much of that can be justified as a necessary cost of financial intermediation.

[19] Parallel equity issues arise in domestic political economy. Is it "unfair" that the fiscally conservative, creditworthy rich can easily obtain bank credit, while the poor cannot? Should there be any such thing as a "right" to credit? Aren't financial institutions acting sensibly and responsibly toward their depositors by "redlining" urban ghettoes (refusing to extend mortgage loans for the purchase of property)? Wouldn't they be acting unfairly to them if they did not? Issues similar to these also underlie much of Part II of this book, especially LDC demands for a *new international economic order,* described in Chapter 14.

would begin again in a wider ring, assuming that there was no central-bank "lender of last resort" in the relatively unregulated Euro-banking system.

In fact there *are* little publicized lender-of-last-resort arrangements to preclude exactly these developments. Central banks of thirty major countries each agreed in 1974 to act as lender of last resort for all commercial banks within their geographical boundaries, whether foreign-owned or not, and whether conducting Euro-currency operations or not. But parent banks of foreign-owned branches would be required to reimburse any central bank that rescued a branch, and if they could not do so, then the reimbursement obligation would fall to the parent bank's central bank.[20]

Lender-of-last-resort arrangements for multinational commercial banks are not entirely reassuring, however. Rescue operations are frequently inflationary, as central banks are forced to purchase the assets of insolvent commercial banks just as they purchase bonds in the open market. Furthermore, there is an awkward tendency for central-bank rescue arrangements to make commercial banks more secure and hence somewhat more willing to undertake risky lending. This increases the likelihood of collapse that brought forth the rescue arrangements in the first place.

Given these arrangements, just how valid are the fears that Euro-bank loans have become riskier with the growth of sovereign debt? An answer depends on four considerations: loan quality, loan serviceability, loan maturity and deposit volatility, and LDC renunciation of debt.

LOAN QUALITY. Concern is sometimes voiced that the heavy representation of LDCs and governments-in-trouble as borrowers of Euro-currencies makes such loans intrinsically more risky. In response, Euro-banks point to the purposefully selective choice of creditworthy borrowing governments discussed above; to their historical record of

---

[20] Karin Lissakers, *International Debt, the Banks, and U.S. Foreign Policy*, A Staff Report prepared for the use of the Subcommittee on Foreign Economic Policy of the Committee on Foreign Relations of the United States Senate (Washington, D.C.: U.S. Government Printing Office, 1977), pp. 26–27. The lender-of-last-resort arrangements have been dubbed the *Basle Agreement*, after the Swiss city that is the home of the Bank for International Settlement (BIS), under whose auspices they were first worked out. The BIS is a regionally constituted "central bank's central bank." It was created in the 1930s by subscriptions of capital from its members—almost all European central banks, plus those of Japan, Canada, Australia, and South Africa—and now serves as a deposit institution and source of short-term credit for them. It also keeps account of financial transfers among member central banks and provides data collection, research output, and the forum for their monthly meetings (at which the U.S. Federal Reserve System is an observer). Although the BIS has the potential to be an institutional substitute for the IMF, its central-bank members have scrupulously avoided casting it in that role.

smaller losses on foreign loans than on domestic; and to the fact that the major bank failures of the mid-1970s (Franklin National in the United States, Herstatt in Germany) were most directly caused by speculative foreign-exchange-market losses, not by defaults on poor-quality loans.

LOAN SERVICEABILITY. Some commentators feel that more tra-ditional project-related loans have inherent security because they are "self-liquidating." At the very worst, commercial banks can foreclose on a project with some economic value. Sovereign debt seems to have no comparable security (collateral) because a bank can hardly seize the services that a government provides. Nor does what a government produces (such as statutes, statues, local defense forces, welfare sup-port) necessarily have marketable value, so that general-purpose loans are not predictably self-liquidating. What this concern neglects, however, is the sovereign power of every government to tax, whether directly or by inflationary monetary policy. Governments, unlike cor-porate borrowers, can assure a creditor that the money for servicing debt *can* be there, because it has the power in principle to appropriate it (or perhaps more accurately, to expropriate it) from its citizens.

LOAN MATURITY AND DEPOSIT VOLATILITY. Concerned critics worry that Euro-bank deposits are of considerably shorter maturity than Euro-bank loans. Particular banks therefore might find them-selves unable to call in enough loans to meet unexpectedly large deposit withdrawals at short notice. Commercial banks respond that deposit maturities have always been shorter than loan maturities ("the business of banking is to borrow short and lend long"); that banks adequately insure themselves against this kind of risk by hold-ing and varying secondary reserves of liquid assets; and that the increasing share of sovereign debt does not compromise their ability to look out for themselves (after all, no bank knowingly chooses to fail). The same response is given to occasional concerns that OPEC might deliberately disrupt Euro-banking for political reasons by massive movements of its volatile short-maturity deposits. Here the confident tone of the banker's response should fade slightly, because private Euro-bankers may be less likely than governments themselves to foresee a *politically* motivated undermining of international banking stability.

LDC RENUNCIATION OF DEBT. Growing Euro-bank claims on LDC governments are sometimes viewed with alarm because of radi-cal calls for a global *moratorium* on all LDC debt, in the name of a more equitable world distribution of wealth. (A moratorium is a post-ponement or forgiving of all debt.) Any negotiated compensation for Euro-banks and other creditors of LDCs would likely be inflationary on a global scale, as would central-bank attempts to save the banking system from global financial collapse in the absence of any compensation. This is probably the least valid of the concerns about sovereign debt, because this scenario is highly improbable. A debt moratorium has little support among most LDC governments, especially those with the largest Euro-bank loans. They understand that collective LDC renunciation of debt would dry up the future international transfer of financial resources for decades.[21] Some, for fear of scaring off creditors, are reluctant to countenance even milder calls for debt relief. It is true that many LDCs have experienced unforeseen difficulties in servicing debt obligations. But virtually all have *rescheduled* or *renegotiated* their debt, not renounced it. Rescheduling involves lengthening the time for repayment; renegotiation involves easing all the current terms of debt, but usually in return for larger payments in the future. Creditors are usually inconvenienced but not significantly injured by rescheduling and renegotiations, because temporary losses are offset by future gains, and because banks sometimes foresee the likelihood of renegotiation quite confidently, yet grant loans anyway (on appropriate terms).

Summary

The years since 1971 have been a time of institutional and operational flux in international monetary matters. The exchange-rate system for twenty-five years prior to 1971 had been centered on one institution (the IMF), one money (the dollar), one fundamental asset (gold), and one set of rules for government action that were common to almost all non-Communist nations (the adjustable-peg exchange-rate system). In the years since 1971 other institutions, reserve assets, and rules have become increasingly prominent: Euro-banks and the European monetary system; official reserves held as German-mark deposits, Euro-currency deposits, and Special Drawing Rights; managed floating according to national choice—including pegging (flexibly) to gold, dollars, marks, currency baskets, SDRs, and nothing at all.

Institutional and operational pluralization has certainly made the international monetary system more complex. Some commentators think it has become more unstable, too, as private and public institutions implicitly compete with each other to be sources and depositories for official reserves, as movement becomes more pronounced among the multiple types of official-reserve assets, and as national sovereignty and trial-and-error rule in exchange-rate systems. Instability is

---

[21] International movements of financial capital were minuscule throughout the 1930s, 1940s, and 1950s after widespread defaults at the beginning of the period and renunciations of debt after World War II.

only a possibility, however. Other commentators identify competition as a virtue—even among governmental institutions and reserve assets; they identify movement as arbitrage, and they are ready to believe that adaptable, nationally sensitive exchange-rate systems will have many of the desirable properties that consumer sovereignty induces. Time will determine whether the pessimists or the optimists were the more accurate forecasters.

Key Terms

Smithsonian Agreement
Second Amendment to the IMF's
  Articles of Agreement
surveillance
reference rates; presumptive
  indicators
asset substitution or settlement
narrow-margins agreement; joint
  European float

the snake; the snake in
  the tunnel
Euro-banks; Euro-currency deposits, loans, and carousels
sovereign debt
petrodollars; recycling
parallel financing
moratorium; rescheduling;
  renegotiation

Key Concepts and Review

The 1970s as a period of intermittent international monetary crises and reforms.

Institutional flexibility: the IMF, currency blocs, and private commercial banks.

Methods of official-reserve creation, lending, and depositing.

The stability of the international banking system.

Supplement 7A
Euro-Currency Banking

One of the most colorful, important, and misunderstood private institutions of international finance is the *Euro-currency bank*. Euro-currency banking has expanded rapidly since its advent in the late 1950s. With it have grown untraditional sources of credit and money creation as well as challenging problems for governmental administration of monetary and exchange-rate policy.

DEFINITION AND DESCRIPTION

Euro-currency banks are simply private commercial banks with a difference. The difference is that they accept deposits and make loans simultaneously in many moneys. This sets them apart from other commercial banks, even those with foreign exchange departments. Standard commercial banks never make loans in foreign money and will accept it only to convert it into (resell it for) "home" money. Euro-banks, by contrast, don't necessarily have a home money. Their loans and deposits in the money of their residence are often dwarfed by loans and deposits in other moneys, referred to as Euro-currencies—or more accurately as *external currencies* to distinguish them from home currency. Euro-currency banks qualify as the most completely international of institutions, devoid of nationalistically narrow geographical or currency preferences.

Yet it bears repeating that Euro-banks are simply private commercial banks. As such, they compete strongly with other commercial banks. The demand deposits and time deposits that Euro-banks accept are readily substitutable for deposits in any commercial bank. So are the loans that Euro-banks grant. There are, however, some differences. Compared to standard commercial-bank deposits, Euro-bank deposits are larger, pay higher interest, and are not usually protected by government deposit insurance. Compared to standard loans, Euro-bank loans have lower interest costs and are available only to a select group of enormous, highly creditworthy firms, institutions, and governments. Compared to standard banking, Euro-banking is subject to minimal government supervision. The reasons for these institutional differences are discussed in the sections that follow.

Virtually all Euro-banks have long-established traditional banking operations as well. Chase Manhattan and Barclay's (British) each have numerous branches that deal only in dollars or in pounds sterling. They concentrate these in the United States and Britain, of course, while their Euro-bank branches are scattered throughout Europe, Canada, the Caribbean, the Mideast, and Singapore. The far-flung locations of Chase Manhattan and Barclay's branches illustrate how misleading the prefix *Euro* is. Europe (especially London) is the historical center of activity, but Euro-banking's growth is most rapid in the comparatively unregulated, untaxed, secretive, and accommodating *offshore banking havens*—almost all of them small and less-developed countries. That is why Euro-banking is increasingly described as *offshore banking* or *external-currency banking*.

From 70 to 75 percent of all Euro-banking has been carried out in U.S. dollars. *Euro-dollars* describe dollar deposits in or loans from banks not resident in the United States and therefore not regulated by the U.S. Federal Reserve System. Euro-dollar banks thus include foreign branches of Chase Manhattan, Citibank, and a number of other "U.S." banks. Euro-currencies also include prominently *Euro-sterling, Euro-marks,* and *Euro-francs* (Swiss francs),[1] as well as others. The whole Euro-currency banking system is frequently called the Euro-currency *market;* its parts are referred to as the Euro-dollar market, and so on. This terminology is unfortunate, because we don't usually talk about "trade" taking place in a "market" for bank deposits and loans. The words thus obscure what Euro-currency banking really is: a multinational, multicurrency system of financial intermediation between lenders (depositors) and borrowers (loan applicants).

WHY EURO-CURRENCY BANKING?

Euro-currency banking is alleged to have its historical roots in the conflict between communist and capitalist blocs. Even during the cold war of the 1950s, substantial international trade was carried out between Western and Eastern European countries, most of it financed in U.S. dollars. Almost all Western European currencies at that time were subject to strict post-World War II *exchange control* (see Supplement 2A), and Eastern European currencies have always been similarly *inconvertible* (p. 65). Eastern European governments thus periodically earned U.S. dollars in the course of trade with the West. Yet they feared the potential expropriation or freezing of these dollars if they held them in U.S. banks. An ingenious solution was to hold their earnings as dollar deposits at, say, one of Barclay's British branches. In the very simplest of worlds Barclay's branch would simply redeposit the dollars it received into its own account at some U.S. bank, withdrawing them as needed in order to meet any withdrawal demands by the Eastern European government itself. The ultimate ownership of the dollar balances was consequently hidden from both the U.S. government and the U.S. banking system. From the U.S.

[1] The terms Euro-currency, Euro-dollar, Euro-sterling, and the like all refer to bank deposits or bank loans. They should be distinguished from the term *Euro-bond,* which describes a financial asset issued directly by a borrower and offered initially through bond *underwriters* to potential bondholders (lenders) in several different countries. The *Euro-bond market* describes the institutional setting in which such multinationally marketed bonds are bought and sold.

point of view, dollar deposits that were once owned by, say, a German buyer of Eastern European exports, had become owned by a British branch of Barclay's.

The example illustrates how Euro-dollars can come into existence without any necessary direct impact on the U.S. banking system—or on the U.S. money stock, credit available to U.S. borrowers, or the U.S. balance of payments. The U.S. banking system as a whole is completely unaffected when the ownership of a particular bank deposit passes from a German to a Britisher, as is the U.S. balance of payments. Yet Euro-dollars have nevertheless been created, in the form of a dollar deposit at Barclay's British branch that was never there before. Contrary to popular opinion, these new Euro-dollars are not a "drain on the U.S. banking system," nor do they "overhang the foreign exchange market, threatening to drive the dollar down." Nor are they physically or legally very different from any dollar deposit at any commercial bank. They are clearly not U.S. bills and coins sitting in Barclay's vault, and they are obviously not "printed up" by Barclay's. They do not stem from a "flood of unwanted dollars," caused by excessive U.S. spending. Nor are they directly caused by the U.S. balance-of-payments deficit. Finally, it seems distinctly inappropriate to characterize them as "rootless" or "homeless" dollars

It is unfortunate that the foregoing denials are necessary. Popular journalistic reporting on Euro-currencies is inexcusably uninformed; consequently it is alarmist—for reasons that have no better basis than our instinctive fear of the unknown. There are some good reasons for concern over trends in Euro-banking, but they lend no weight to the bad ones.

If Communist asset preference had been its only historical stimulus, then Euro-currency banking would be no more than a minuscule curio. Instead, Euro-banking has grown from virtually nothing in the 1950s to the point where its dollar pool of deposit and credit availability is roughly one-sixth that provided by competitive U.S. resident financial institutions.[2] Three additional factors explain this remarkable growth: natural competitive advantages, banking law and regulation, and U.S. balance-of-payments policies.

[2] Euro-banks offer demand (*call*) deposits and time deposits that compete not only with U.S. commercial-bank deposits but also with those offered by savings and loan associations, mutual savings banks, and credit unions in the United States. The size of all such U.S.-institution deposits at the end of June 1977 was $1,364 billion ($M_5$), roughly six times larger than the estimated $230 billion of Euro-dollar claims of Euro-banks on the same date. And Euro-dollar banking was growing faster. Sources: Board of Governors of the Federal Reserve System, *Federal Reserve Bulletin* 64 (January 1978): A-14; International Monetary Fund, *IMF Survey*, November 21, 1977, p. 357, and February 16, 1976, p. 53. The last two sources provided, respectively, a size for Euro-currency claims ($317 billion) and a dollar share of such claims (73 percent).

NATURAL COMPETITIVE ADVANTAGES. Euro-currency banks enjoy several competitive advantages over strictly domestic banks. The most important is associated with the size of their average transaction. Euro-banks have traditionally maintained multimillion-dollar minimums for Euro-currency deposits and loans. The labor and resources required to process a single large deposit and loan are not significantly different from those required to process a single small one, yet the revenues, measured by the difference between interest earnings on the loan and interest payments on the deposit, are vastly larger for the larger transaction. Profits are comparably larger, too. Banks that deal only in large transactions, therefore, can afford to "shade" profits by offering higher interest rates to depositors and charging lower interest rates on loans.[3] They cultivate a natural price advantage in competing with other banks for both deposits and loans. Banking laws and regulation reinforce this natural competitive advantage by frequently forbidding strictly domestic commercial banks from excluding depositors or borrowers simply because their transactions are small. As explained below, Euro-banks are not usually subject to the same constraints.

Euro-currency banks also have a competitive edge over strictly domestic banks in part of their loan business. European corporations wanting to borrow dollars, for example, often find it difficult to obtain "prime borrower" status and favorable interest rates from U.S. banks. They are less well known in the United States and sometimes smaller than the bank's prime U.S. customers. Barclay's Euro-bank branches, however, can attract their loan business by being more willing to offer favorable terms, since they can often assess the creditworthiness of European corporations more readily than U.S. banks.

---

[3] The persistence of a hierarchy, or of *tiers* (ranks), among Euro-banks is explained most readily by this phenomenon. The largest few Euro-banks in the top tier are those with the smallest *spreads* (differences) between interest rates on loans and deposits. They can afford to pay more to depositors and charge less to borrowers because their reputation and historical place allow them to insist on mammoth minimum transactions. Second- and third-tier Euro-banks are often themselves important depositors at top-tier Euro-banks, and borrowers from them. They also cooperate (collaborate) with the top-tier banks and with each other in the *syndication* (collective negotiation) of Euro-currency loans and in Euro-bank *consortia*. A *consortium* is a cooperative (collusive) arrangement among Euro-banks to be primarily responsible for each other's business interests either in particular regions or in particular functions where each participating bank has had notable comparative success. It is a perfect example of "trade" among banks based on the *rule of comparative advantage* discussed in Chapter 8. The hierarchy of Euro-bank tiers became prominent in the mid-1970s when the earliest OPEC deposits of petrodollars were concentrated almost exclusively in top-tier Euro-banks, causing nervousness among them and tremendous competitive pressure against lower-tier Euro-banks.

Banking Law and Regulation. Euro-currency banking is subject to little or no regulation by central banks (for reasons to be discussed). An unintended result is to encourage Euro-banking at the expense of other kinds of financial intermediation. Euro-banks, for example, are not generally required by law to hold precautionary reserves of cash or deposits at the central bank. They do *voluntarily* hold precautionary bank reserves, of course, but they may be smaller than required reserves, and, unlike cash and central-bank deposits, they are usually held in interest-earning forms—short-maturity deposits at other banks and highly liquid securities. That Euro-banks earn income even on their precautionary reserves enhances their competitive edge.

Even more encouraging to the growth of Euro-currency banking is its exclusion from statutory interest-rate ceilings on deposits and loans.[4] Since many governments prohibit interest payments altogether on demand deposits (such as checking accounts) and on very short-maturity time deposits, Euro-banks have been able to compete away the largest of such deposits by offering any interest at all. And in periods of tight credit, when interest-rate ceilings bind on almost all maturities of bank deposits, and when credit may otherwise dry up, Euro-banks are able to continue to service borrowers at interest rates that would be illegal in a regulated setting.

U.S. Balance-of-Payments Policies. During the late 1960s and early 1970s, the United States, in attempting to shrink its balance-of-payments deficit, also encouraged Euro-currency banking. One program restricted U.S.-resident banks from lending to foreigners. Another limited the amount of U.S. financing that U.S. multinational corporations could enlist to expand their overseas investments.[5] The result was to redirect frustrated foreign borrowers of dollars and U.S. multinationals toward alternative sources. European branches of U.S. banks and other Euro-dollar banks were happy to oblige.[6]

---

[4] In the United States, maximum interest rates on bank deposits are established by the Federal Reserve System's *Regulation Q*. Maximum interest rates on bank loans in the United States are frequently imposed by state governments under anti-usury laws.

[5] The first was called the Voluntary Foreign Credit Restraint (VFCR) Program, the second the Foreign Direct Investment (FDI) Program. Both existed, with many modifications, from 1965 until 1974. The U.S. Interest Equalization Tax (IET), described on p. 147, probably provided similar (but milder) encouragement to expansion of Euro-banking. Its most dramatic stimulus, however, was to the Euro-bond market described in footnote 1 to this supplement.

[6] It is tempting and intuitively attractive to claim that U.S. balance-of-payments deficits themselves were a direct encouragement to the expansion of Euro-currency banking. But the image of "dollars flowing out of the United States and into Euro-banks" is false. United States deficits encouraged Euro-banking only indirectly—through U.S. policies adopted to shrink the deficit, or through the natural tendency for some of the official-reserve dollars purchased by foreign central banks in supporting the value of the deficit-weakened dollar to find their way into Euro-dollar deposits (see the text of this chapter).

THE IMPORTANCE OF EURO-CURRENCY BANKING

Euro-currency banking has created an unprecedented worldwide network of financial intermediation among large lenders and large borrowers in which national identities of lenders and borrowers matter little. As such, it has provided on a global scale the same substantial benefits that a well-functioning competitive banking system provides to a community or nation. This was dramatically illustrated in the aftermath of OPEC's oil price hikes of 1973. OPEC almost surely gained more than it would have in the absence of highly liquid, highly unregulated, and high-paying Euro-bank deposits for petrodollars. And oil-importing countries faced less severe hardship than they would have in the absence of massive and quickly arranged Euro-bank loans, which allowed them to adjust more gradually and carefully to higher energy prices. Euro-banks served as speedy and efficient channels for conveying the new accumulations of petrodollar wealth from oil producers back to oil consumers—for a price, of course, equal to the cost of borrowing.

But the benefits from Euro-currency banking are not necessarily unmixed, as we have seen in the text:

1. Placements of official reserves in Euro-currency deposits can make government stabilization of exchange rates more difficult.

2. OPEC's Euro-currency deposits and oil importers' Euro-currency indebtedness both pose at least some threat to the stability of international and domestic banking systems.

3. Both deposits and loans of official reserves in the form of Euro-currencies can circumvent the internationally sanctioned surveillance of the International Monetary Fund.

This supplement has suggested at least one additional concern about Euro-currency banking:

4. Euro-currency banking can interfere with government's ability to control the availability of credit. In the examples given above, Barclay's will probably lend out at least a part of the Eastern European country's dollar deposit. The dollar credit created will not be subject to either British or U.S. regulation and may even be unnoted by the regulators. Yet it will finance spending or investment in the same way as any other dollar credit.[7] In fact, because very short-

---

[7] Furthermore, it may "multiply," in the same way that an infusion of bank reserves is multiplied into a larger amount of bank credit in a fractional-reserve commercial-banking system. Suppose that the Eastern European deposit is $100 million, of which Barclay's holds back $10 million as precautionary reserves against withdrawal and lends out $90 million. Suppose that borrowers of the $90 million pay $60 million to institutions that hold deposits in U.S. commercial banks and $30 million to institutions that hold Euro-dollar deposits. Barclay's and other Euro-banks will see this $30 million as an influx of new deposits and lend out, say, $25 million of it, holding back $5 million as precautionary reserves (a higher reserve ratio than $10 million out of $100 million, perhaps because the maturity of the new $30 million of deposits is

maturity Euro-dollar deposits are essentially the same as demand deposits, Euro-currency banking may inhibit monetary policy—the government's attempt to control the (real) stock of money outstanding.[8]

Euro-banking also causes concern because it helps to *integrate* national financial markets. That is, it helps to "de-segregate" or denationalize them, linking them in the extreme into global financial markets where only one set of interest rates rules worldwide. The reasons for such globally parallel interest rates are obvious in a single currency. Interest rates on dollar deposits and loans at Chase Manhattan in London or Singapore will almost never differ from those at Chase Manhattan in New York because many large depositors and borrowers can freely choose the most attractive branch with which to deal. But even between currencies, only rarely will interest rates on bank deposits and loans differ by more than the expected change in the exchange rate. A London branch of Chase Manhattan will typically set its dollar and pound interest rates, and the spot and forward exchange rates it quotes, so that depositors cannot profit risklessly at the bank's expense from *covered interest arbitrage* within its own walls—movements from pound deposits to dollar deposits and back, as described on pp. 25–28.[9] The *interest parity conditions* hold nearly perfectly within Euro-currency banking, tying together interest rates on pound and dollar loans as well as deposits. Furthermore, because bank deposits and loans substitute (though less than perfectly) for bonds, short-term corporate IOUs, and other securities, *all* interest rates will be tied together to some degree across national boundaries by Euro-currency banking and will be tied to exchange

---

shorter). The $90 million of original "Euro-credit" creation would have been "multiplied" into $115 million (90 + 25) of ultimate Euro-credit creation. If the $25 million of loans is in turn used in such a way that $4 million is redeposited in Euro-banks, then the original $100 million Euro-dollar deposit will have been multiplied into $134 million (100 + 30 + 4) of ultimate Euro-dollar deposits. Students should be able to carry the example arbitrarily further, depending on their choice of assumptions. It is worth noting, however, that multiple credit creation in the Euro-currency banking system is not as deterministically predictable as in domestic banking, since no analogs exist to relatively stable required-reserve and currency-to-demand-deposit ratios. It is also instructive to show that there is no necessary or uniform impact of any of the transactions above on credit creation in the U.S. banking system.

[8] The concern is not unique to Euro-currency banking. It applies also to any comparatively unregulated financial intermediary. In the United States, such intermediaries include commercial banks that are not members of the Federal Reserve System, savings and loan associations, mutual savings banks, credit unions, pension funds, and insurance companies.

[9] See, for detail, Richard J. Herring and Richard C. Marston, "The Forward Market and Interest Rates in the Eurocurrency and National Money Markets," in *Eurocurrencies and National Financial Policies*, ed. D. Logue, J. H. Makin, and C. Stem (Washington: American Enterprise Institute, 1975).

rates as well by interest arbitrage.[10] The ties will be tighter, the more substitutable alternative financial assets are and the more perfectly Euro-banking integrates commercial banking worldwide.

Internationally integrated financial markets and globally parallel interest rates in turn lead to three additional concerns related to Euro-banking.

5. By integrating world financial markets, Euro-banking weakens government's ability to influence interest rates. For example, at a given set of exchange rates, British government attempts to keep British interest rates high in the face of lower U.S. interest rates are undermined by worldwide shifts of lenders toward high-yield pound-denominated assets, and of borrowers toward low-cost dollar loans. Both shifts cause downward pressure on British interest rates and quantitatively diminish the success of the government's interest-rate support. Variable exchange rates complicate the example slightly because they permit some degree of independent interest-rate policy, but interest-rate independence is nevertheless weaker with Euro-banking than without.

6. By integrating world financial markets, Euro-banking increases the transmission of financial shocks from one country to another. In the example above, to the extent that the British government succeeds even slightly in supporting British interest rates, U.S. interest rates will be higher than otherwise. That is, British financial policy will be transmitted to the United States. So will other financial shocks. Inflation-related tendencies in a given country for the wealthy to hold larger amounts of their wealth in land, gold, and art collections raise interest rates on financial assets not only in that country but globally.

---

[10] The new *asset approach* to exchange rates, discussed in more advanced treatments of international economics, makes much of the parallel between the way in which interest arbitrage integrates financial markets worldwide and the way in which gold arbitrage integrated gold markets worldwide under the gold standard, as described in Supplement 2A. Just as private gold arbitrage determined and maintained foreign exchange rates then, so will private interest arbitrage in highly integrated world financial markets today. But national asset prices and interest rates, unlike national gold prices under the gold standard, are not fixed. They vary in response to changing supplies of and demands for money, bonds, and other financial securities. Therefore exchange rates *must also vary* in a parallel way, not being fixed as under the gold standard. Government attempts to alter or stabilize exchange rates will invariably be swamped by massive and infinitely profitable interest arbitrage. The asset approach thus blames increased global integration of financial markets almost entirely for the collapse of the adjustable-peg exchange-rate system. Furthermore, the asset approach explains current day-to-day variation in exchange rates almost solely by day-to-day variation in supply/demand conditions in markets for financial assets. Changes in real economic activity, inflation rates, commodity exports and imports, and trade balances have *no* impact on exchange rates, contrary to much of what has appeared in earlier chapters of this book, except indirectly through their influence on asset prices and interest rates.

Bank failure in one country causes depositors worldwide to move temporarily into safer assets, increasing global deposit rates and the spread between them and loan rates. These international financial links are, of course, strongest under invariant exchange rates. Yet variable exchange rates do not eliminate them (perfect insulation, as described in Chapter 6); they simply weaken them.

7. Euro-currency banking makes foreign-exchange-market speculation easier and less costly. Within the same four walls of any Euro-bank, a well-established customer can find a source for loans denominated in moneys the customer expects to depreciate in the future; deposits denominated in moneys the customer expects to appreciate in the future; and foreign-exchange-market conversion of the borrowed money into the deposited money. Successfully speculating bank customers will earn both interest and a speculative gain on their deposit, offsetting all or part of the interest cost of their loan by being able to buy and repay the borrowed money in the future at a cheaper price than had been generally expected.

WHY DON'T GOVERNMENTS REGULATE EURO-BANKING?

The undermining of government control over credit, money, interest rates, and exchange rates is welcomed by conservative economists who feel that governments have abused this control. But government representatives themselves rarely share those feelings. Thus it may seem strange that governments do not regulate Euro-banking more than they do.

One historically important reason for nonregulation has been the predominant concern of every government for its own domestic problems. From a British point of view, Euro-mark banking in London seems only indirectly related to British prosperity. And while Euro-sterling banking in Germany seems much more likely to affect the British economy, as an alternative source of sterling credit, its regulation is necessarily the province of the German authorities. They in turn are lukewarm to regulating it, because it seems only indirectly related to German prosperity.

Nationalism reinforced by political pressure from banking interests is a second reason why governments are unwilling to regulate Euro-currency banking tightly. Such banking has become extremely profitable, despite its highly competitive nature.[11] (Even competitively

[11] For example, earnings from international business exceeded earnings from domestic business for six of the largest U.S. commercial banks in 1976. Chase Manhattan and Citicorp derived 78 percent and 72 percent of their earnings from international business, although only a portion of these were earnings from Euro-currency banking. See Karin Lissakers, *International Debt, the Banks, and U.S. Foreign Policy* (Washington, D.C. U.S. Government Printing Office, 1977), p. 10.

"normal" profits, coupled with high volume, can be large.) The British fear that imposing interest-rate ceilings, reserve and reporting requirements, and other restrictions on British Euro-currency banking would lead to large national losses, since much British Euro-banking would be forced by competitive pressure to close down or to flee elsewhere. The Germans fear the same.

Even proposed cooperative regulation of Euro-banking by the central banks of Europe, Canada, Japan, and the United States might not be feasible and could lead to large collective losses. Large-scale commercial banking is one of the most footloose (mobile) of industries, requiring little more than good telephone and teletype connections and a few managers. As global communications technology has improved, particularly to facilitate electronic transfers of funds, and as some moves have been made among major countries toward cooperative regulation, Euro-banks have been increasingly attracted to banking havens in the Bahamas, the Cayman Islands, the Netherlands Antilles, Panama, Singapore, and Bahrain. Governments of these small, less-developed countries have actively encouraged the movement by assuring banks of no regulation or reporting requirements and of considerable tax advantages. Their national gains are the banking-center profits that the developed countries fear losing. The havens themselves have only slight natural incentives to regulate Euro-banking, because they possess only limited monetary independence and control in the first place.

Part II

International Trade

The economics called *international trade* is concerned with the causes of and benefits from nation-to-nation exchanges of commodities, services, resources, technology, and even corporations and people themselves. These phenomena sometimes arouse strong feelings, which are not always supported by economic reasoning. On one hand, many Americans feel comfortable purchasing Japanese automobiles, Korean television sets, Argentinian computer parts, German buses, Taiwanese toys, Italian shoes, Brazilian coffee, and the services of migrant Mexican farm labor. On the other hand, some Americans decry what they see as the "loss of U.S. technological leadership" that "unfortunately" led to the purchases early on the list. Still other Americans feel that temporarily resident Mexican farm workers cause American migrant farm workers to lose their jobs. Many Americans cannot unreservedly endorse purchases of foreign sugar, meat, dairy products, steel, or clothing, because they may be "unfair" to hard-pressed American producers of such items, and because they also may lead Americans to lose jobs. A few Americans find it frankly unpatriotic to buy anything from foreign producers, but especially goods such as Cuban cigars, Communist Chinese mushrooms, and vacations in the Soviet Union.

Likewise, most Americans are comfortable selling farm equipment and trucks to Canada; corn, chicken, and soybeans to Europe; fertilizer and pharmaceuticals to less-developed countries, and computers and commercial aircraft to the entire world. But there are varying degrees of opposition to sales of Alaskan oil to Japan, oil-drilling equipment to the Organization of Petroleum Exporting Countries (OPEC), partially assembled television sets to Mexico, wheat to the Soviet Union, weapons to dictatorial governments, and technological expertise to any foreign country.

The first chapters of Part II explain why many of these foreign

237

purchases and sales *are* materially beneficial for a nation and describe the occasional circumstances in which they are not. International trade will be said to be materially beneficial for a nation when it permits the population as a whole to acquire more goods for the same effort than would have been possible without trade.

Yet trade may improve national economic welfare by making the rich much richer and the poor slightly poorer; or by eliminating the urban jobs of relatively unskilled female garment workers; or by mushrooming the profits of multinational corporations at the expense of their employees' wages; or by forcing most U.S. steel producers out of business. In these cases, even though international trade improves the command of the whole nation over goods, it may do so in a way that most people find undesirable or unfair. International trade always causes certain groups and individuals to lose and others to gain.

Should the government step in and manage or regulate trade when the undeserving gain and the innocent lose? Should it do so even if the measured gains of the former are much greater than the measured losses of the latter? The question is loaded and is more difficult to answer than it appears. Addressing it occupies much of Part II.

The fact is that almost all governments manage international trade more attentively than they manage internal domestic trade. Their constituents do not allow them to be passive about the types, amounts, and locations of foreign sales and purchases that natural economic behavior creates. Instead, all governments try to influence the natural trade that arises from international differences in resources, technology, skills, tastes, size, and market power (the subject of Chapter 12). They subsidize and encourage some trade (such as sales of sophisticated manufactures to foreigners, and purchases of foreign-owned corporations from them). They tax and discourage other trade (such as sales of strategic weaponry to foreign enemies, and purchases of food and manufactures that are competitive with domestically produced substitutes). And all governments reserve the right to retaliate with trade policy against foreign trade policies that cause domestic injury.

In fact, it is all but inevitable that "their" government management of trade injures some of "our" citizenry. National trade policies almost always involve discrimination against foreign producers or consumers and in favor of domestic producers or consumers (Chapter 9). This feature is what turns intergovernmental negotiations over trade policy (Chapter 11) into complicated, drawn-out, sometimes acrimonious exercises in which each country jockeys to extract maximum concessions from others with minimum surrender of its own.

Chapters 8 through 11 describe government management of international trade and evaluate its advisability. Chapters 12 and 13 describe the powerful economic forces that would bring trade about even in the absence of government policy—trade not only in commodities but also in resources, property, productive information, people (migration), and even whole corporations (multinational corporations).

Migration, multinationals, and international exchanges of property and technology all cause unique reactions and raise new questions. Who gains and loses in the United States from illegal immigration of low-skill workers from Mexico? from legal immigration of doctors, scientists, and engineers from less-developed countries (the "brain drain")? from investment and operations abroad by American multinational corporations? from foreign purchases of U.S. farmland and of plants to produce U.S.-made Volkswagens and Sony TV sets? from foreign "takeovers" of U.S. firms? Should the U.S. government do anything about any of these phenomena?

The whole question of how much (if anything) governments should do to shape the natural market and institutional forces that underlie international exchange comes up again in the last chapter. Governments of less developed countries increasingly answer "more." They perceive a way of reclaiming politically what they believe they lose through international economic weaknesses: weakness toward oligopsonistic purchasers of their primary products; weakness toward established European, Japanese, and North American producers of manufactures; weakness toward oligopolistic multinational corporations with unique ownership claims on advanced technology; and weakness in negotiating trade policy with developed countries under the conventions of the General Agreement on Tariffs and Trade (the GATT, described in Chapter 11). Less-developed countries seek a new, much more highly politicized way of "ordering" international commerce (Chapter 14), and they look hopefully to the example of OPEC success as a model.

The economics of *international trade* has a traditionally stronger normative element than the economics of *international finance*. More effort is devoted in Part II to assessing the advisability of government trade policy than in Part I to evaluating government exchange-rate policy. Prescription is as prominent in Part II as description; discussions of what should be are as frequent as discussions of what is. Such consideration of better and best policies will quickly become confusing unless the reader keeps in mind the crucial question, "Better or best for whom?" What is economically preferable for a nation as a whole is not always economically preferable for groups or individuals within it. And what is economically good for one nation can be economically bad for others. Furthermore, value judgments are inextricably tied to normative, prescriptive economics. Those underlying Part II of this book will become clear as the chapters proceed.

Chapter 8

Why We Trade:
The Strong Case for
Some International Trade

The Case for Trade

Nearly every country has an extremist fringe who consider international exchange unpatriotic at best and treasonous at worst ("No truck nor trade with foreigners"). In the United States, even the more moderate majority may feel uneasy about purchasing imported automobiles or selling wheat to the Soviet Union. (Couldn't we have provided jobs for Americans by buying domestic automobiles? Couldn't we have held down the price of wheat for American consumers by prohibiting wheat exports?) Underlying these fears and objections is the suspicion that international trade may not be beneficial—at least not to "us."

When concern about the merits of international trade is voiced in such a sweeping way, it can muster very little economic support. One of the most robust of all economic propositions is that some international trade is better than none at all. Thoroughgoing national self-sufficiency may be a virtue in some ways, but any country that attempts it pays a huge economic price.

These and other important observations are engagingly illustrated by James C. Ingram in a fable of trade and technology:

> During the middle decades of the twentieth century, an adventurous entrepreneur bought a thousand acres of the Great Dismal Swamp in coastal North Carolina. After draining the land and building a road and rail spur, the mysterious entrepreneur, Mr. X, built a 12-ft. electrified fence around his entire property, posted guards at the gates, and allowed no one to enter except his own trusted employees. He advertised for workers, offering $3 per hour, and hired 5000 workers, all sworn to secrecy.

Mr. X announced that he had made several scientific discoveries and inventions which enabled him to transform coal, wheat, tobacco, petroleum, machinery, and other products into a variety of finished products, including textiles, cameras, watches, chemicals, and TV sets. Within a few months, vast quantities of materials were pouring into Mr. X's guarded compound from all parts of the country, and a flood of low-price industrial and consumer goods began to pour *out* of Mr. X's gates and into the nation's markets, where housewives and industrialists eagerly bought them at prices 20 to 30% below the competition. Mr. X's company, Consolidated Alchemy, Inc., (CAI) reported large profits, and was soon listed on the New York Stock Exchange where it became the growth stock of the century—a favorite of institutional investors.

Meantime, the nation hailed Mr. X as a genius and benefactor of mankind, a man whose inventions greatly increased the productivity of labor and improved the standard of living of the masses. He was favorably compared to Eli Whitney and Thomas Edison.

It is true that grumbles were heard in some quarters. Several manufacturers of TV sets tried to prevent their dealers from stocking or servicing CAI sets; textile manufacturers tried to persuade Congress to establish production quotas for each firm based on average output in the previous 50 years; a labor union picketed stores carrying CAI merchandise; and three New England legislatures passed laws requiring that stores display "Buy New England" posters. None of these activities had much effect, however. Buyers could not resist the low CAI prices, and many communities were prospering because of their rapidly increasing sales to Consolidated Alchemy. The Houses of Congress resounded with speeches calling upon the people to accept the necessity for economic adjustment and urging the benefits of technical change.

As for coastal North Carolina, it was booming as never before. Schools, houses, and roads were constructed; the Great Dismal Swamp was drained and used for truck gardens, its extraordinarily fertile land was selling for $3000 per acre; employment expanded, and average wages rose to $4 per hour.

Then, one Sunday morning, a small boy, vacationing with his family at a nearby seaside resort, tried out his new skin-diving equipment, penetrated Mr. X's underwater screen, and observed that Consolidated Alchemy's "factories" were nothing but warehouses and that its "secret technical process" was nothing but trade. Mr. X was, in fact, a hoax; his firm was nothing but a giant import-export business. He bought vast quantities of materials from United States producers, loaded them under cover of night onto a fleet of ships, and carried them off to foreign markets where he exchanged them for the variety of goods that he sold throughout the United States at such low prices.

When the boy told what he had seen, a wire service picked up the story, and within 24 hours Mr. X was denounced as a fraud, his operation was shut down, his thousands of high-paid workers were thrown out of work, and his company was bankrupt. Several congressmen declared that the American standard of living had been protected from a serious threat of competition from cheap foreign labor, and urged higher appropriations for research in industrial technology.[1]

The fable suggests the following conclusions:

1. From an economic standpoint, every country should and will choose to engage in international trade voluntarily, and because of self-interest. The case for international trade is based on greed, not altruism. Economists argue that the United States will engage in at least some international trade because it makes *us* better off, not because it makes the world better off (although it does that, too). Thus the belief that international trade is beneficial is much more firmly founded than the belief that, say, United Nations membership is beneficial. The latter is based partially on the view that we should be good world citizens. The former requires only that we look out for ourselves.

2. The gains that the United States realizes from some international trade do not come at the expense of other countries. A parallel fable exists for every country that engages in international exchange. International trade is not a "zero-sum game," in which the gains to some players are balanced by the losses to others. In fact, one way to dramatize the case for trade is to demonstrate how it allows every country to get something for nothing. The same national effort will provide more material goods and services with trade than without, or else the same basket of goods and services with less effort.

3. International trade is qualitatively very much like ordinary production. Production is the activity of transforming certain goods and services called *inputs* into physically different goods and services, called *outputs*. Trade is the activity of transforming certain goods and services called *exports* into physically different goods and services called *imports*. In general, there are no firmer grounds for attacking international trade as a "bad" than for attacking production as a bad.

4. The kind of "production" that international trade represents is more *efficient* than conventional production. That is, for the United States, a ton of coal and a bushel of wheat can be transformed into more textiles and TV sets through international trade than could be produced by diverting the coal and wheat resources in the United

[1] James C. Ingram, *International Economic Problems*, 2nd ed. Copyright © 1966, 1970 by John Wiley and Sons, Inc. Reprinted by permission of John Wiley and Sons, Inc.

States to producing textiles and TVs here. International trade actually increases the productivity of a country's resources in much the same way that a technological advance does. That again illustrates the something-for-nothing character of the gains from trade.

5. International trade among countries is qualitatively identical to day-to-day exchanges among individuals. Farmers export what they grow and import the goods and services that other members of a society produce. Teachers export what they know and import, among other things, the farmer's production. International exchange is beneficial to a country for precisely the same reasons as day-to-day exchanges are beneficial to individuals. Thus persons who argue that it is better for a country not to trade at all internationally are generally inconsistent unless in their personal lives they prefer to be self-sufficient hermits.[2]

There is a superficial "proof" of all these conclusions. It is to note that:

> Obviously, certain countries produce some things more cheaply than we do, such as textiles, and we produce some things more cheaply than they, such as aircraft. Therefore both exports and imports are beneficial. Exports provide jobs and income to U.S. labor and resource-owners; imports reduce the U.S. cost of living because they are priced lower than their U.S. equivalents.

While these observations are true, they do not prove that trade is beneficial to the United States, any more than the superpatriot's fears that exports raise U.S. prices and imports displace U.S. workers "prove" the case false. In fact, the descriptive observations appealed to by each opposing camp are usually simultaneously true. Somewhat crudely, exports generate employment and upward pressure on prices; imports take away employment but hold down prices. Thus we must go beyond these superficial statements to prove that some international trade is preferable to none.

To prove the case for trade conclusively, we must demonstrate its

---

[2] The language is strong because the national case for preferring some international trade to none is very strong. As we shall see in Chapters 9 and 10, the cases for "free," unrestricted, competitive trade and for "freer" trade are not nearly so strong. Then our choice of language must be tempered. Furthermore, this chapter does not claim that the more international trade a country engages in, the better off it will be. As Chapter 9 demonstrates, allowing international trade to increase above a certain level could be harmful to a country. In reality, it is unlikely that any country approaches this level of trade. But the conclusion does suggest caution in assessing the wisdom of national export stimulation policies, such as loans to promote exports that the U.S. Export-Import Bank arranges and oversees, and such as tax concessions that the United States provides to domestic corporations whose business is almost exclusively foreign (domestic international sales corporations, discussed in Chapter 11).

something-for-nothing character in terms of real, physical, tangible goods and services. We must demonstrate either that international trade can increase a country's consumption of real goods and services without any increase in its use of resources, or that international trade can "free up" resources for voluntary leisure, yet still allow a country to consume the same goods and services as it did without trade. In a nutshell, we must demonstrate that international trade lets a country get more and give up less.

These propositions would not be hard to demonstrate in a make-believe world where every country produced at least one good more productively than other countries. That is, the real, tangible gains from international trade would be obvious if Japan required less labor and resources than the United States for every television or shirt that it produced, while the United States required less labor and resources than Japan for every bushel of wheat or Boeing 747 that it produced. Both Japan and the United States would gain from specializing in producing the goods in which their resources were the most productive, and exporting any surplus of production over domestic consumption to the other country. Extra output would be available for the same input, or alternatively, extra leisure could be taken by Japanese and Americans alike, while still maintaining their standard of living.

But the real world is not like this. Some countries are more productive than others across the board in virtually everything they produce. For decades after World War II the United States had a pronounced technological advantage over the rest of the world, producing nearly every manufactured product and many agricultural goods with less labor and resources than any other country. Intuition suggests that international trade was not very beneficial for the United States during this period, if at all. What possible gain could there be in buying imported goods from a foreign seller who produced them *less* productively than we did? Remarkably and paradoxically, intuition is wrong in this case. International trade was beneficial for the United States then just as it is now, and the size of those benefits has not been changed in any predictable way by the recent narrowing of the technological gap between the United States and the rest of the world. In fact, technological gaps have nothing directly to do with the benefits from international trade. The United States could be many, many times more productive than the rest of the world at producing all goods, yet still benefit by international trade (while the rest of the world did too).

This point is worth stressing, since U.S. business, labor, and government spokesmen abound who decry the nation's "loss of technological leadership" and by implication its loss of ability to "compete" with the rest of the world: when the U.S. loses its technological edge entirely, "we won't have anything left to sell that the world wants to buy! We'll be broke, producing nothing for export. And obviously we'll be unable to gain from trade."[3] It is reassuring that such nightmares have little economic foundation, and no relevance to the conclusion that international trade is beneficial to the United States. As we will show, even if America lost its technological leadership altogether, the rest of the world would *still* find it in their own economic self-interest to buy American goods, and possibly even the same ones they had always bought. It will simply never come about that the United States has nothing left to sell that the world wants to buy. Loss of technological leadership provides no grounds for questioning the wisdom of engaging in international trade, nor for suspecting that its benefits are declining.

This paradox is characteristic also of individual economic exchange. It pays for me to cooperate with you in the economic system, rather than isolating myself, even if I am superior to you in every dimension. It is useful to demonstrate this before applying the same reasoning to countries engaged in international exchange.

Benefits from Trade in the Office

Suppose you and I work in the same office. I happen to be more able than you at both typing and at filing letters—the two things our jobs entail. Consequently I earn more than you do. But we share equally in one complaint: the boss is a taskmaster. Every day, the typing and filing assignments that he gives us occupy the entire eight hours that we are at work. There is no time for lunch, no time for a coffee break. We are both fed up. As we ponder our plight, it strikes me that there is a way out. If we cooperate on the sly, instead of working in isolation on the boss's assignments, we can each have a coffee break! I won't be exploiting you, since we both get coffee breaks; and even though you do everything more slowly than I, it will be in my interest to let you do some of my work.

To be exact, suppose Table 8.1 describes our abilities. I type 90 words per minute; you, only 60. I file two letters per minute; you, only one. I am absolutely more productive. Suppose Table 8.2 describes the boss's work assignments for us. He knows how productive we are and, being hardnosed, he assigns us work that will fully occupy our day, as the following considerations show:

[3] "As we have seen, technological advantage no longer remains at home, nor does capital. Our . . . margin of safety has been reduced and is fast disappearing . . . . If present trends continue, we will become a net importer of the very group of commodities where, according to theory, we should always have a competitive edge" (Stanley H. Ruttenberg and Associates, *Needed: A Constructive Foreign Trade Policy* (Washington, D.C.: Industrial Union Department, AFL-CIO, 1971), p. 100).

TABLE 8.1. *Productivity in the Office*

	Typing	*Letter filing*
I	90 words per minute	2 letters per minute
You	60 words per minute	1 letter per minute

18,000 words of typing takes me 200 minutes (18,000/90 = 200);
560 letters to file takes me 280 minutes (560/2 = 280);
so my whole eight-hour day is taken up by work (200 minutes + 280 minutes = 8 hours);
18,000 words of typing takes you 300 minutes (18,000/60 = 300);
180 letters to file takes you 180 minutes (180/1 = 180);
so your whole day is taken up by work, too (300 minutes + 180 minutes = 8 hours).

The idea that occurs to me is to *swap* jobs in such a way that we can both have a coffee break. I propose to you that you specialize in typing; I in turn will specialize in filing. Of course, we won't inform the boss. In particular:

let me do all the filing, yours as well as mine. Thus I will file the 560 letters assigned to me, and the 180 assigned to you, for a grand total of 740. This will take me 370 minutes (740/2 = 370);
in return for this, you will do 9900 words of my typing, as well as your own. I will do the rest. This will take you 465 minutes (27,900/60 = 465);
the typing that remains for me is 8100 words. This will take me 90 minutes (8100/90 = 90);
therefore, I will end up working only 460 minutes of my day (370 + 90), not 480.

The work the boss gives us obviously gets done, just as it used to. Yet you save fifteen minutes of your day for coffee or lunch by cooperating with me, and I save twenty minutes of my day by co-operating with you—even though I have a "technological advantage" over you in everything. Cooperation (trade) pays off even if each of us is completely selfish, even if we dislike each other intensely. We produce the same office output with less input. We generate something (a coffee break) for nothing (what have we sacrificed?).

Now, we need not take the time freed by my proposal to have coffee. Instead, we might each go in to the boss and request an extra fifteen or twenty minutes of work. The boss will naturally be impressed, and he will probably figure that we had become more skillful or more committed to our work—more productive than Table 8.1 indicates. The boss

TABLE 8.2. *Daily Work Assignments in the Office*

	Typing	Letter filing
I	18,000 words	560 letters
You	18,000 words	180 letters

is, of course, wrong. We appear to have made a technological leap, but secretly we have only traded work assignments. Regardless, if the boss obliges and gives us extra work, we will naturally be in a more favorable position to ask for a promotion or a raise. In a somewhat different fashion, we will have generated something (more output of typing and filing) for nothing (we still work only eight hours, the same as before trade).[4]

For this particular proposal, the benefits from trade in the office are quite measurable: thirty-five minutes of time. In fact, I could have made an infinite number of other proposals, all of which would have produced benefits, as long as they followed one simple rule: the *rule of comparative advantage.* This rule can be stated in two ungrammatical but revealing ways:

specialize in producing what you're "most best" at; or
specialize in producing what you're "least worst" at.

In the office, I am best at everything, and you are worst at everything. In the language of international trade, I have an *absolute advantage* over you in everything that we do. You have an *absolute disadvantage* in everything. Yet trade will be beneficial to each of us as long as I specialize in what I'm "most best" at—the activity where my absolute advantage is most pronounced. Since I am twice as productive as you are in filing, but only one-and-a-half times more productive in typing, my absolute advantage is most pronounced in filing. In the language of international trade, even though I have an absolute advantage in both filing and typing, I am said to have a *comparative advantage* in filing, because my absolute advantage there is greatest *compared* to my absolute advantage in other activities. Trade will also be beneficial to you, as long as you specialize in the activity where your absolute disadvantage is least pronounced (where you are "least worst"). You

---

[4] Of course, if the boss himself thought about this in the same way that we did, he would see that his work assignments were foolish. He himself should have assigned you only typing and assigned me all the rest of the day's assignments. That way he could have increased the output of his staff without increasing their productivity, taking the credit himself. His option in no way voids the key insight, which is that there are benefits from specialization and exchange that must accrue to someone.

will have a *comparative advantage* in typing, even though you have an absolute disadvantage in both typing and filing.

Just as long as a country specializes and trades according to the rule of comparative advantage, some international trade will be preferable to none. Were the United States consistently more productive than the rest of the world, it would still pay the United States to specialize in producing goods where its productivity edge was greatest. It should then export these goods to other countries for goods in which the U.S. productivity edge was smallest, even though Americans did produce them absolutely more productively. Similarly, were the rest of the world's nations underdeveloped and technologically backward, it would still be in their interest to specialize in producing goods where they were least unproductive. They should then export these goods to the United States in exchange for goods in which they had a comparative disadvantage. International trade that violates the rule of comparative advantage is always harmful to at least some countries and possibly to all.

In practice, the recommendation to specialize goes against the grain for many individuals and countries. In the office example, you may feel that typing all day is drudgery and that if you were obliged to give up the boss's small filing assignment, both the quality of your typing and your happiness on the job would suffer. Similarly, in the real world, many countries resist specializing in such a way that they are "hewers of wood, and drawers of water" (for example, Canada), or in such a way that they are left with no industrial base whatsoever, because they import all their industrial products (the less-developed countries). These objections, however, can be alleviated by engaging in *less* trade than otherwise. In the office, you might keep some, or even most, of your filing to do. In world trade, Canada and less-developed countries inevitably try to subsidize and protect an industrial sector. Nevertheless, it will still be in your interest for me to do at least *some* of your filing, and for Canada and the less-developed countries to export at least *some* "wood," "water," and simple manufactures in order to import more complex industrial products. Thus the conclusion that

$$\left(\begin{matrix} \text{some international} \\ \text{trade along the} \\ \text{lines of comparative} \\ \text{advantage} \end{matrix} \right) \quad \begin{matrix} \text{is} \\ \text{better} \\ \text{than} \end{matrix} \quad \left(\text{none} \right)$$

is not undermined by countries' aversion to specialization and preference for industrialization.[5]

---

[5] What may be undermined is the conclusion that unrestricted international trade is desirable for a country. This and other arguments for trade restrictions are discussed in the next chapter.

FIGURE 8.1. *A Hypothetical U.S. Production Possibilities Curve*

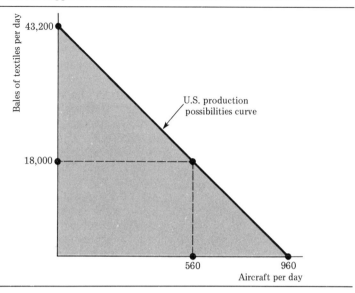

Benefits from Some International Trade

The benefits from some international trade can be illustrated more generally in a diagram that is used frequently in later chapters and that has many attractive features. First, it allows us to measure the tangible, real gains from international trade. Second, it demonstrates dramatically their something-for-nothing character, and finally it introduces the variable that determines how the overall gains from international trade are distributed among individual countries—the *terms of trade*. The diagram depicts a country's *production possibilities curve*, the set of maximum outputs that the country can produce, given its resources and decision to work. That is, the U.S. production possibilities curve gives the menu of maximum output combinations that could be produced by shifting available resources from industry to industry. If the United States could produce only two goods, say textiles and aircraft, the U.S. production possibility curve might look like the negatively sloped line in Figure 8.1.[6] The curve

---

[6] In general, there are a number of economic reasons why a country's production possibilities curve is not a straight line. These are treated as they arise, on pp. 255, 322, and 404–405. They do not affect the conclusions of this chapter.

suggests that by devoting all of its labor, machines, land and other resources to the textile industry, the United States could produce at most 43,200 bales per day. By devoting all these productive resources to the aircraft industry, the United States could produce at most 960 aircraft per day. If the United States chose to produce 18,000 bales of textiles per day, the largest number of aircraft it could produce with the resources left over would be 560.[7]

Of course, the United States could choose to produce 18,000 bales of textiles and less than 560 aircraft. But that would suggest that some resources who wanted to work would not be needed. Thus, output combinations given by points below the production possibilities curve (shaded) may imply involuntary unemployment as well as underutilization of machines, land, or other resources. There seems to be no reason why any country would ever choose such output combinations below its production possibilities curve, unless the desire for leisure increased on the part of labor or other resource owners.[8] These characterizations explain the negative slope of the production possibilities curve—more of one good can be produced only by reducing the production of other goods so as to make available the needed resources for the first.

Nor would a country generally seem able to consume output combinations outside (northeast of) its production possibilities curve, since that would seem to require more resources than the country voluntarily has available. Indeed, what seems to be true *is* true in the absence of international trade: a country is constrained to consume output combinations on its production possibilities curve, combinations that represent both production possibilities and consumption possibilities. The exact consumption point chosen depends on underlying demand conditions (tastes, income distribution, and so on). Precisely how it does so is not important for the moment (see pp. 401–407) because trade opens up national consumption opportunities in a similar way for any and all patterns of demand.

In particular, countries that engage in international trade are *not* constrained to consume along their production possibilities curve; what seems to be true simply is not. Every country through trade is able to consume outputs described by points that lie *outside* (northeast of) its production possibilities curve. And these consumption

---

[7] Note that the numbers chosen match the example of trade in the office. In that example, production possibilities curves could have been defined for you and for me as well, given that we were willing to work eight hours every day. Along the axes of the diagram, we would measure words typed per minute instead of bales of textiles produced per day, and letters filed instead of aircraft. But the numbers would remain the same.

[8] Then the country would just be producing within its *old* production possibilities curve. A *new* production possibilities curve would have to be defined for the higher level of leisure in the country, one that would lie uniformly within the old.

FIGURE 8.2. *Benefits from Some Trade: The Same Outputs for Fewer Inputs*

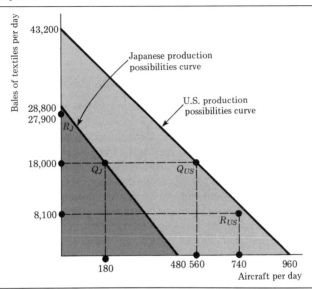

points are clearly better than any that lie on the production possibilities curve, since they imply that the country can consume more of every good. The production possibilities curve will still be relevant, since countries must still produce along it. But the something-for-nothing character of trade relates to *consumption* possibilities: without using any additional resources or inputs in production, a country can command a larger consumption bundle of all goods with international trade than without. It does so by specializing in the production of goods where it has comparative advantage, producing more of them than it consumes (national production will not equal national consumption in a world of international trade),[9] and exporting the excess supply abroad. In return, the country receives imports of goods in which it has a comparative disadvantage, consuming them even though it did not produce them.

These conclusions are illustrated in Figures 8.2 and 8.3. The U.S. production possibilities curve has been reproduced there, as has another for the rest of the world, which we will simplify by identifying

[9] To be precise, for any country engaged in international trade:

$$\begin{pmatrix} \text{National} \\ \text{production} \\ \text{of any good} \end{pmatrix} = \begin{pmatrix} \text{National} \\ \text{consumption} \\ \text{of it} \end{pmatrix} + \begin{pmatrix} \text{Exports of it} \\ \text{to foreign} \\ \text{consumers} \end{pmatrix} - \begin{pmatrix} \text{Imports of it} \\ \text{from foreign} \\ \text{producers} \end{pmatrix}.$$

See pp. 183–184 and 275–277.

FIGURE 8.3. *Benefits from Some Trade: More Outputs for the Same Inputs*

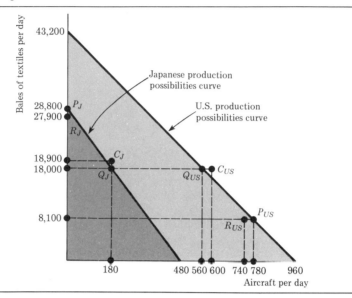

as Japan.[10] We cannot determine from the diagram which, if either, country has an absolute advantage in producing textiles or aircraft (the United States may be simply larger than Japan, and not more productive). But comparative advantage can be determined from the relative slopes of the production possibilities curves. If all the resources in the United States were allocated to aircraft production, twice as many could be produced as in Japan under the same allocation. But if all resources in the United States were devoted to textile production, only one and a half times as many textiles could be produced as in Japan. Therefore the United States has comparative advantage in producing aircraft, and Japan in producing textiles.[11] The rule of comparative advantage suggests that trade is beneficial to both

[10] As in Part I, it is expositionally easier to deal with a two-country world. Most conclusions from this admittedly unrealistic world can be shown to be valid anyway in a multicountry world. Those that cannot will be flagged.

[11] The diagram suggests a polar case in which comparative advantage cannot be defined (as did the numerical trade-in-the-office example): when the slopes of the two production possibilities curves are equal. For this unlikely case, and for it alone, we can show that a country should be indifferent to whether or not to engage in international trade. The benefits are zero (and so are the losses). Thus a technically accurate statement of the key proposition of this chapter is: some international trade is usually better than, and always as good as, no trade.

countries if the United States specializes in producing aircraft and exports them to Japan in return for Japan's specialty, textiles.

This conclusion can be illustrated in Figure 8.2. Suppose that without international trade, demand conditions in the United States would lead to production and consumption at point Q_{US}: 18,000 bales of textiles and 560 aircraft per day. Suppose that without trade, demand conditions in Japan would lead to production and consumption at point Q_J: 18,000 bales of textiles and 180 aircraft per day. Suppose further that the United States proposes to Japan the opening of international trade on the following basis:

the United States will produce all the aircraft that both countries consumed without trade, a total of 740 aircraft per day (560 for the United States, 180 for Japan);

in return, Japan will produce 9900 bales of textiles per day that the United States used to produce for itself without trade; in addition, of course, Japan will continue to produce 18,000 bales of textiles per day for itself, for a grand total of 27,900 bales per day;

the United States will continue to produce the remaining 8100 bales of textiles per day that, along with the 9900 that Japan produces *for* the United States, will bring its total daily consumption to 18,000;

the United States will export 180 aircraft to Japan every day, and will import 9900 bales of textiles; Japan will export those same textiles and import those same aircraft;

both countries will therefore continue to consume at points Q_{US} and Q_J, respectively.

The remarkable thing about this proposal is that Japan does not need all its resources to produce 27,900 bales of textiles per day. Nor does the United States need all its resources to produce 740 aircraft and 8100 bales of textiles per day. The points in Figure 8.2 that indicate this production mix in each country—R_{US} and R_J—both lie *inside* their respective production possibilities curves. Thus both the United States and Japan have extra resources that were needed without trade but are no longer needed with trade. Yet consumption would remain the same in each country as it always was. International trade would be beneficial in the same way as a technological innovation, enabling each country to obtain the same goods to consume with fewer resources—the same output for less input.

Of course, this is not an unmixed blessing if the countries want to put the resources freed by international trade to work. The resources are then technically unemployed.[12] But a minor alteration in the pro-

---

[12] This explains why labor and resource owners who are displaced by international trade oppose it as vehemently as they do a displacing technological innovation. But there is a puzzle here. If *everyone* in Japan and the United States consumed exactly the same commodities with trade as without—and they could, since consumption remains at Q—why would anyone object to

posal to trade, as illustrated in Figure 8.3, would skirt this problem:

Let Japan use the resources freed by trade to produce an extra 900 bales of textiles (28,800 – 27,900) for itself to consume. Then Japanese consumption of textiles could be 900 bales larger than it would have been without trade, and its consumption of aircraft will be the same. It will consume at point C_J, a point that is obviously better than Q_J and that lies *outside* its production possibilities curve. It will produce at point P_J, and its resources will be fully employed, as they wish to be.

Let the United States use the resources freed by trade to produce an extra 40 aircraft (780 – 740) for itself to consume. Then U.S. consumption of aircraft could be 40 larger than it would have been without trade, and its consumption of textiles will be the same. It will consume at point C_{US}, a point that is obviously better than Q_{US} and that lies *outside* its production possibilities curve. It will produce at point P_{US}, and its resources will be fully employed, as they wish to be.

The remarkable thing about this modified proposal is that with trade, both countries can consume at points that were impossible without trade, because they lay beyond the production possibilities curve. International trade creates something for nothing: more goods for all to consume, without any increase in the effort or resources devoted to producing those goods. The gains from trade are, furthermore, quite measurable and tangible. Japan gains 900 bales of textiles every day, and the United States gains 40 aircraft, compared to what was possible without trade. The same number of jobs exist in each country with trade as without, and the standard of living is higher. [13]

There is nothing special about the detail of either proposal for international trade. An infinite number of other proposals can be made, differing only in the terms that they lay down. What all proposals have in common, as long as they follow the rule of comparative advantage, is that they allow both countries simultaneously to consume more of every good available for the same effort. That is, they

---

working less, or perhaps not working at all? No one would have been hurt in terms of consumption, and the opportunity to get the same goods with less work and more leisure should please all. In practice, what precludes this blissful outcome is the fact that not everyone does share equally in the gains from international trade. Some persons cannot maintain the same consumption with trade as without, although they could if the trade gains of others were taxed to support them. These income-distributional consequences of trade are examined in detail in Chapters 9 and 10.

[13] However, the problem of how to move *toward* trade without temporarily costing labor some of its jobs and displacing other resources is difficult and frequently impossible to solve in practice, as Chapter 10 shows.

Chapter 8: The Strong Case for Some International Trade

allow consumption at points northeast of Q, the country's most desirable consumption point without trade.

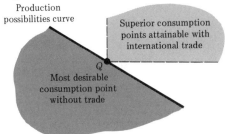

Neither is there anything special about the assumptions underlying the Japanese and American production possibilities curves. For example, if either country fears specialization, it might well be true that the more specialized they became, the less productive their effort. Lack of variety in the types of work available may cause worker alienation, boredom, and depression and may also reduce incentives for investment and education. The result would be a production possibilities curve that was "bowed in" at its ends. (Additional reasons for this conventional shape of the production possibilities curve are discussed on pp. 322 and 404–405.) But international trade would still be beneficial.

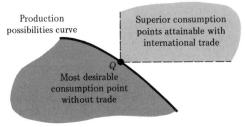

Or, by contrast, both textiles and aircraft might be subject to *economies of large-scale production*—the property of being produced at a cheaper unit cost in large batches than in small (pp. 398–399). If such scale economies were dramatic enough, the production possibilities curve could be "bowed out" at its ends. Specialization would promote large-batch production. But again international trade would still be beneficial.

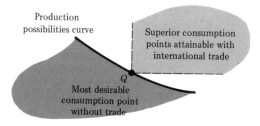

The Terms of Trade

One of the most important differentiating characteristics of the infinity of mutually beneficial proposals for trade is the *terms of trade*. Their importance is to determine the size of one country's gains from international trade relative to another's. The overall benefits from international trade—for example, the 900 bales of textiles and 40 aircraft mentioned earlier—can be viewed as a pie, which is to be divided among all trading countries. The terms of trade control how the pie is cut. Within limits, the terms of trade have nothing to do with the conclusion that every country gets a piece of pie (the conclusion that some trade is beneficial). But they do determine the size of each country's slice. Thus their primary impact is on the *distribution* of the gains from trade, not on their *existence*.

Each country's terms of trade can be defined conceptually as the quantity of imports that it receives for every unit of exports that it gives up—the rate at which imports flow in divided by the rate at which exports flow out. For example, Japan's terms of trade in Figures 8.2 and 8.3 are $(180)/(28{,}800 - 18{,}900)$, which simplifies to 1/55. Japan receives 1/55 of an aircraft for every bale of textiles that it gives up; Japan gives up 55 bales of textiles for every one aircraft that it gets. When phrased in these ways, the significance of Japan's terms of trade for its economic welfare becomes clear. Given the choice, Japan would much rather receive 1/50, or 1/20, or even 1/2 of an aircraft for every bale of textiles that it gives up. These would be progressively more *favorable* terms of trade for Japan, because it naturally prefers to get more for what it gives up. By contrast, Japan would hate to see its terms of trade deteriorate,[14] say from 1/55 to 1/100. That would imply that the country was obliged to export 100 bales of textiles for every aircraft that it imported. The United States, on the other hand, would be pleased to see a deterioration in Japan's terms of trade, because that would imply an improvement in its own—from 55/1 to 100/1.

Figure 8.4 shows why Japan prefers the terms of trade 1/50 to the terms of trade 1/55. Japan could then receive 198 aircraft from the United States instead of only 180, even though it might export the same 9900 bales of textiles $[9900 \times (1/50) = 198]$. Such an improvement in Japan's terms of trade would increase its gains from trade from 900 bales of textiles (the difference between consumption points C_J and Q_J) to 900 bales of textiles *and* 18 aircraft (the difference between consumption points D_J and Q_J). The United States, on the other hand, would find that the corresponding deterioration in its terms of trade from 55/1 to 50/1 has shrunk its gains from trade. Some

---

[14] Technically, increases in the terms of trade are always described as favorable changes or improvements, and decreases are described as unfavorable changes or deteriorations.

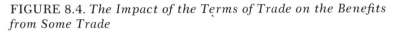

FIGURE 8.4. *The Impact of the Terms of Trade on the Benefits from Some Trade*

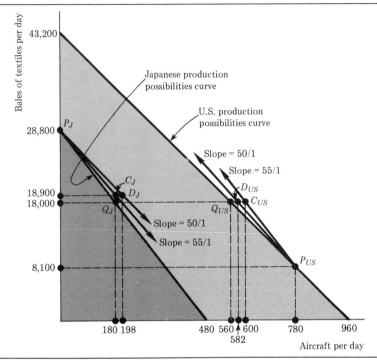

trade would still be beneficial to the United States but less so. The United States would be obliged to give up 198 aircraft, instead of only 180, in order to get 9900 bales of textiles. Its gains from trade would shrink from 40 aircraft (the difference between consumption points C_{US} and Q_{US}) to only 22 aircraft (the difference between consumption points D_{US} and Q_{US}).[15]

In fact, if the United States' terms of trade deteriorated enough, say to 45/1, it might cease trading. At least, the United States should be indifferent to trading at 45/1, because that is exactly the slope of its production possibilities curve. Why transform aircraft into textiles through international trade when it can be done at the same rate through conventional production? (Giving up production of 1 aircraft in the United States allows production of 45 bales of textiles with the

[15] In the example of typing-filing trade between you and me, the terms of trade determine the relative length of our coffee breaks. If my terms of trade deteriorated (because yours improved) from 55 to 50 words of typing for every letter filed, my coffee break would shrink from 20 to 10 minutes, and yours would rise from 15 to 30 minutes.

freed resources.) In this limiting case, an alteration in the terms of trade would erase the benefits from trade. In practice, it is unlikely to occur. If the United States stops trading, Japan loses its gains from trade, too, even though its terms of trade might have improved. Thus, in practice, countries welcome only limited improvements in the terms of trade—limited by the necessity to leave *some* gains for the rest of the world, at least enough to preclude even the threat of a cessation of trade. In the diagrams, the range of all terms of trade that allow both the United States and Japan to gain from trade runs from 45/1 (the slope of the U.S. production possibilities curve) to 60/1 (the slope of the Japanese production possibilities curve).

The importance of a nation's terms of trade can be illustrated in a more down-to-earth way. They are completely comparable to your own "*personal* terms of trade," defined with respect to the world outside of you—all other persons and institutions with whom you have day-to-day economic contact. Your personal terms of trade are precisely what economists call *real wages:* the average number of goods you buy in, say, a week (food, shelter, education, and recreation that you "import") divided by the average number of goods you sell (most people "export" around forty hours of labor services per week). It is obvious that most persons prefer higher real wages to lower.[16] On similar grounds, the United States collectively, and all Americans individually, should prefer more favorable U.S. terms of trade to less.[17]

The terms of trade facing a nation, however, are not solely under its control any more than your own real wages are solely under your personal control. Global patterns of demand and the market power of individual domestic and foreign producers shape the rate at which

[16] This statement is extreme. In some circumstances individuals might prefer low real wages to high. For one example, employers may be able to guarantee individuals more work at low real wages than at high—so much more that real *incomes* are higher at lower real wages. If the extra real income is worth more in the individuals' minds than the leisure foregone, they will prefer lower real wages. By analogy, a nation may sometimes prefer less favorable terms of trade to more, if national employment and capacity utilization can be made sufficiently greater thereby. As a second personal example, individuals may sometimes be willing to accept low real wages in the present if somehow they are linked to compensatory high real wages in the future. Mechanics' apprentices, graduate-student teaching assistants, and medical interns and residents all illustrate such preferences. The value of the training they are acquiring is reflected in future real wages and makes them willing to accept a low present wage (along with lots of training). By analogy, a nation may sometimes prefer less favorable present terms of trade to more, if the result is sufficiently favorable future terms of trade. Successful *predatory dumping* by U.S. exporters in foreign markets, discussed in Chapter 9, is an illustration of such a preference.

[17] We will support the conclusion in Chapter 9 by demonstrating how the U.S. government itself lays claim to these terms-of-trade gains. Thus in a very real way they are collective. They either finance the provision of additional government services or generate lower U.S. taxes, both of which benefit individual Americans, and neither of which would exist under free trade.

Chapter 8: The Strong Case for Some International Trade

FIGURE 8.5. *Japan's "Trade Triangle"*

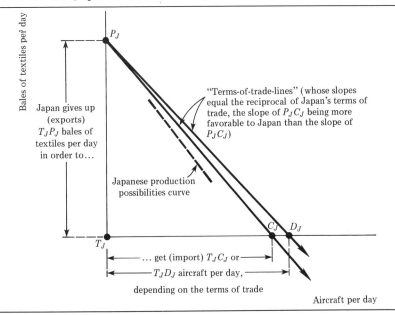

goods are exchanged internationally for each other. National political decisions also are important, as we shall see for the case of oil.

The mutual influence of demand forces, supply forces, and the terms of trade on each other is revealed in technical aspects of Figure 8.4. International economists often speak of "terms-of-trade lines" linking production points Q and consumption points C (or D). The name is appropriate because the slope of the line joining production (supply) and consumption (demand) points does indeed define the terms of trade. Economists also speak of "trading along" the terms-of-trade line from P to C (or D). This language is also appropriate because the sides of the right triangle for which the line PC (PD) is the hypotenuse measure quantity exported and quantity imported. Japan's "trade triangle," and what it illustrates, are depicted in Figure 8.5.[18]

[18] In our two-country world, the United States trades along the terms-of-trade lines $P_{US}C_{US}$ or $P_{US}D_{US}$, whose slopes are necessarily the same as those of Japan's terms-of-trade lines. The U.S. trade triangle is therefore congruent to Japan's—of identical shape and size—because the sides of the U.S. trade triangle represent (a) the quantity of U.S. exports, which must be the quantity of Japanese imports, and (b) the quantity of U.S. imports, which must be the quantity of Japanese exports. This jargon can be useful as a kind of shorthand in future chapters, especially 10 and 12. But in using technical jargon we should not forget that a country's terms of trade are of considerable practical importance in the day-to-day life of its residents.

Practical Importance of the Terms of Trade: World Oil Prices

The real-world importance of changes in the terms of trade was illustrated dramatically in late 1973 by the international organization of oil-producing countries known as OPEC (Organization of Petroleum Exporting Countries). OPEC nearly quadrupled the price of the oil they exported. By so doing, in essence, they demanded from the rest of the world four times as many imported goods for every exported barrel of oil as they formerly received. OPEC's quadrupling of the price of oil was in fact a successful effort to improve their terms of trade. The fact that the rest of the world grudgingly accepted the oil-induced deterioration in their own terms of trade, without ceasing to trade with OPEC, simply indicates that, in the eyes of oil-consuming countries, some international trade with OPEC is still preferable to none. Of course, for them, it is less beneficial than it was previously, and for OPEC, much more beneficial. But this just reflects the conclusion that a change in the terms of trade alters the pieces of the international-trade pie but does not usually affect their existence.

As the example suggests, the terms of trade can be related to prices of goods traded as well as to quantities. It is actually more conventional and preferable to define the terms of trade as the ratio of a country's export prices to its import prices. This definition is preferable because it separates the effects of changing terms of trade from those of a changing balance of trade.[19] Changes in national economic welfare take place from changes in relative prices alone—pure terms-of-trade effects—even if they have no impact on the trade balance.[20]

In the case of OPEC's quadrupling of oil prices, the impact of the

[19] The balance of trade is the difference between the value of commodity exports and the value of commodity imports (pp. 83–84). When the terms of trade are defined as quantity imported ÷ quantity exported, they may improve or deteriorate both because relative prices of exports and imports change and because trade balances change. The effects of the latter changes on national economic welfare are studied at length in Chapter 3 and in the context of OPEC policies.

[20] In fact, if trade is always balanced, the two alternative measures of a country's terms of trade are identical. If trade is balanced, then by definition

$$\left(\begin{array}{c}\text{price of}\\\text{exports}\end{array}\right) \times \left(\begin{array}{c}\text{quantity of}\\\text{exports}\end{array}\right) = \left(\begin{array}{c}\text{price of}\\\text{imports}\end{array}\right) \times \left(\begin{array}{c}\text{quantity of}\\\text{imports}\end{array}\right)$$

so that

$$\frac{\left(\begin{array}{c}\text{price of}\\\text{exports}\end{array}\right)}{\left(\begin{array}{c}\text{price of}\\\text{imports}\end{array}\right)} = \frac{\left(\begin{array}{c}\text{quantity of}\\\text{imports}\end{array}\right)}{\left(\begin{array}{c}\text{quantity of}\\\text{exports}\end{array}\right)}$$

and a country's terms of trade can be measured either way.

Chapter 8: The Strong Case for Some International Trade

pure terms-of-trade effect alone on the welfare of the average American and foreigner was striking. Between 1973 and 1974 the U.S. terms of trade deteriorated roughly 20 percent,[21] owing almost entirely to increased prices of imported oil. Thus if the United States had exported the same quantity of goods in 1974 as in 1973, and if its trade had remained balanced, it would have had to settle for 20 percent fewer imports in quantity terms. America's "real national consumption" of imports would have declined 20 percent. And since imports in 1974 made up almost 10 percent of all the goods America "consumed," its total national consumption in 1974 would have declined 2 percent (0.20 × 0.10) because of its terms-of-trade deterioration.[22]

It is inflammatory, but completely appropriate, to view this 2 percent decline in real national consumption as equivalent to a transfer of 2 percent of the real income of every American to foreign residents in 1974—and for as long after that as the U.S. terms of trade remained at their depressed level. Yet on the other hand it can hardly be described as an unwilling collective transfer, since the United States failed to retaliate against OPEC and continued to trade at the new, less favorable terms of trade. One can indeed defend the U.S. willingness to do so on the grounds that the alternatives—retaliation or an embargo on trade with OPEC—were economically and politically less desirable than accepting the deterioration.

That the terms of trade are important to the man on the street is even more dramatic in the case of OPEC members such as Saudi Arabia. Since nearly all of Saudi Arabia's aggregate national production is oil, and since nearly all is exported, the quadrupling of oil prices improved Saudi Arabia's terms of trade by close to 300 percent. It is again appropriate to view this improvement as equivalent to a 300 percent increase in Saudi Arabia's national consumption—a huge windfall that could in principle (although not in practice) be doled out in equal shares to every Saudi. Saudi Arabia's improved standard of living is simply the opposite side of the coin from the decline in the standard of living in oil-consuming countries. A change in the terms of trade is simply a transfer of some countries' gains from international trade to other countries.[23]

Recent changes in the terms of trade represent something of a

[21] The International Monetary Fund's *International Financial Statistics* reports that U.S. export prices rose 28 percent in this period while U.S. import prices rose 48 percent.

[22] Consumption is being used here in a broader way than is usual from the national income and product accounts. It denotes "goods available to a society," including goods used for conventional consumption, investment, and the provision of government services. As such, it corresponds exactly to point C_{US} in Figures 8.3 and 8.4 and also to gross national product less exports plus imports. See footnote 9 above and pp. 183–184.

[23] Changing only the terms of trade, unlike changing the volume of trade, is a "zero-sum game": the consumption possibilities that one country gains are lost by others.

TABLE 8.3. *Rough Percentage Changes in the Terms of Trade between the United States and Saudi Arabia*

	Percentage changes over four-year period			
	Saudi Arabian export price of oil[a]	*Index of general U.S. export prices*	*Saudi Arabian terms of trade with U.S.*	*U.S. terms of trade with Saudi Arabia*
1950–1954	+13	+13	0	0
1954–1958	+8	+7	+1	−1
1958–1962	−14	0	−14	+14
1962–1966	0	+7	−7	+7
1966–1970	0	+13	−13	+13
1970–1974	+644	+59	+585	−585

[a] Export price of 34–34.9 grade oil in dollars, f.o.b. Ras Tanura, Saudi Arabia.
Source: International Monetary Fund, *International Financial Statistics*, various issues.

reversal in trends, or so many economists believe. Before OPEC's success in improving its terms of trade, there was a widespread belief in the *secular deterioration hypothesis* regarding the terms of trade of less-developed countries (LDCs), including OPEC. The hypothesis was that, over long periods, LDC terms of trade inevitably tend to decline and those of the industrialized world tend to improve. Recent happenings seem to have refuted the inevitability of the process, and the empirical evidence supporting it was always weak. But because it has profoundly affected the international economic policies of less-developed countries over the past twenty years, it is discussed further in Supplement 8A. Indeed, OPEC justified its quadrupling of oil prices partially on the grounds that its terms of trade had deteriorated in the past. This is qualitatively true. But the magnitude of the deterioration fell far short of 300 percent, as Table 8.3 suggests. Table 8.3 is, of course, only an approximation of the true movement of the terms of trade of all OPEC countries with the rest of the world. The data do not exist to make the latter calculation. It is unlikely, though, that the true movement differs significantly from that recorded in Table 8.3.

In a growing world, the effects of changes in the terms of trade on national economic welfare may be swamped by growth. Since the overall benefits from international trade generally grow as well, changes in the terms of trade may have no effect on any country's absolute prosperity. That is, no country need lose. The benefits from international trade will simply grow more slowly than average for countries whose terms of trade are deteriorating. International trade will still be beneficial for every country compared to isolation, and perhaps even more and more so over time.

But when the world economy is growing slowly, or when changes in the terms of trade are as large as those generated by OPEC's oil policy, then the terms of trade are no longer of only secondary interest. Many countries will consciously attempt to improve their terms of trade, and most will attempt to counter any deterioration. There are two principal mechanisms for doing this: (1) cooperation or collusion in the production and marketing of exports; (2) restriction of trade, either imports or exports, by government taxation policy.

Cooperation or collusion is one way of enhancing the market power of a country's export producers. It brings them closer to a monopoly position in their foreign markets. If cooperating producers do act like a monopolist, they will presumably restrict exports and raise export prices, both of which improve the country's terms of trade.[24] In some cases the proposed cooperation or collusion is strictly internal and relates to corporations. This is illustrated by the exemptions that American exporters enjoy from antitrust legislation, at least in their international business. In other cases the proposed cooperation or collusion is international and relates to governments. This is true for OPEC as well as for governments that have attempted to imitate OPEC's success by establishing *international cartels* in commodities that they export (see Chapter 14). International cartels are cooperative or collusive organizations of producers or governments in order to maximize their market power as producers and sellers. The beginnings of such intergovernment cooperation to improve terms of trade exist among producers of iron ore, tin, copper, phosphate, coffee, and bauxite (the raw ore that is converted into aluminum).

The fact that erecting barriers to trade can also improve a country's terms of trade is curious; barriers would seem to reduce the benefits from international trade. Can improvements in a country's terms of trade outweigh losses of the direct benefits? From the perspective of an individual country's welfare the answer is always, "Yes, in principle, if the barriers to trade are not too high." But in the real world, as we shall see in the next chapter, only rarely can this conclusion provide practical justification for a country to restrict trade.

Summary

International trade benefits an economy for many reasons. Having some is materially better than having none although more and more is not necessarily better and better.

[24] In a market characterized by monopoly production, output is smaller and its price higher than if the market were competitive.

This is one of the least assailable of all economic propositions. It is as true as the commonplace observation that people gain from selling to and buying from each other. And it is true for exactly the same reasons.

Impossible as it sounds, trade enables every country to get more and give up less. It can increase every country's overall consumption of real goods and services without increasing its use of resources, or it can free resources for voluntary leisure while still allowing a country as a whole to consume the same goods and services as it did without trade.

International trade performs this magic because it is completely analogous to superior technology: it allows inputs to be transformed into outputs more productively than would be possible without trade—only exports are the inputs into creating physically different outputs called imports. Just as superior technology allows a country to get more for less, or something for nothing, so does trade. Nations thus choose to trade internationally out of self-interest, not altruism. The added material benefits obtained thereby are not due to the exploitation of other countries; all can gain simultaneously, just as they can from superior technology.

Trading partners do not gain equally, however. Which of them gain most from international trade is largely determined by the terms of trade—the price of exports relative to the price of imports. The more favorable (larger) this ratio is for a nation, the more it is able to import for any given quantity of exports (without encountering trade-balance problems). And every nation wants to get as much as it can for what it gives up, just as individuals and unions do in negotiations over wages and salaries. National desires for more favorable terms of trade are held in check, however, by economic forces. Some benefits must be left for trading partners, or else no beneficial trade at all will take place. And market pressures, among both competitive foreign suppliers of a nation's imports and competitive foreign demanders of its exports, may make it impossible for the nation to alter its terms of trade significantly. Market power, by contrast, makes manipulation of the terms of trade entirely possible, redistributing the benefits from international trade toward those with the power. This lesson was reconfirmed dramatically by OPEC oil-pricing policy in the 1970s.

For trade to deliver any benefits at all, exports must be concentrated in goods for which a nation's productivity lead over other nations is most pronounced, or in goods for which its productivity lag is least pronounced. Imports must be concentrated symmetrically on goods where productivity leads are least pronounced or lags most pronounced. Trade is then said to take place according to the rule of comparative advantage. There are perfectly natural economic reasons why it not only should, but generally *does*, do so. These reasons are discussed in Chapter 12.

Key Terms

absolute, comparative advantage
terms of trade (lines)
production possibilities curve
consumption possibilities

trade triangle
Organization of Petroleum
    Exporting Countries (OPEC)
secular deterioration hypothesis

Key Concepts and Review

The something-for-nothing similarity of international trade and technological progress.

The "rule" of comparative advantage and the gains from specialization.

How consumption possibilities can exceed production possibilities (stated verbally and graphically).

The economic importance of the terms of trade.

OPEC and the terms of trade.

Supplement 8A
Less-Developed Countries and
Secularly Deteriorating Terms of Trade

Other things remaining equal, no country welcomes a deterioration in its terms of trade. A country that faces long and steady deterioration (that is, secular deterioration) is particularly disadvantaged. Its real, tangible benefits from international trade will grow more slowly than if its terms of trade had been stable over time—and they may even shrink.

During the 1950s and 1960s it was widely believed that less-developed countries (LDCs) were in precisely this position, facing continually less favorable terms of trade. Since LDCs were also the poorest countries, the implications were distributionally disquieting. It implied that rich countries were getting richer from international trade faster than poor countries and were appropriating a larger and larger share of the world's benefits from international exchange.

The hypothesis that LDCs' terms of trade deteriorated over the long run was based on two casual observations and some supporting arguments. The first casual observation was that LDCs tended to have comparative advantage in producing primary products—minerals, raw materials, basic foodstuffs—and comparative disadvantage in producing manufactures. The second casual observation was that there seemed to be some tendency even within a country for the price of primary products to fall relative to the price of manufactures over time. Granting a few exceptions, these observations suggested that by and large, LDCs' terms of trade would deteriorate.

The first economic regularity that weakly supports these observations is *Engel's law*, which suggests that the larger a family's income, the smaller the proportion of that income spent on food and other necessities. By analogy, the larger per capita income is, worldwide, the smaller the proportion of that income spent on food—and supposedly on other primary products. Thus, as the world standard of living rose, world demand facing producers of manufactures would grow faster than world demand facing producers of primary products. The pressure of unequally rapid demand growth on (implicitly) equally rapid supply growth would lead to a secular decline in the price of primary products relative to manufactures.

This argument rests on a dubious progression of analogies. Further, unequally rapid demand growth has come to seem less likely than unequally rapid *supply* growth. A great deal of current economic concern focuses on the pressures of growing populations and economies on finite land and resources. Primary product production may be physically limited in a rather rigid way—or at least more limited than the production of manufactures. If so, then the long-run pressures of supply relative to demand should suggest secular *improvement* in the terms of trade of LDCs.

A second argument for the secular deterioration hypothesis relates to an institutional regularity: market structure in primary-product markets seems to be more competitive than it is in manufactures markets (oil, aluminum, textile, and shoe markets are obvious exceptions). Furthermore, prices are frequently inflexible downward in noncompetitive markets. Producers prefer to adjust output than to adjust price, if they have the power to do so. If these beliefs are correct, then one might expect divergence in the price of primary products from the price of manufactures over the business cycle. During upswings, prices of all goods would rise in response to the pressure of booming demand. But during downswings, only the price of primary products would fall in response to slack demand. The price of primary products would therefore decline relative to the price of manufactures over the course of every business cycle.

A third argument is closely related to the second. Because of the pressures of competitive market structure, it is sometimes believed that the benefits from technological progress in producing primary products must be passed on to consumers in the form of lower prices. By contrast, because of the noncompetitive structure of much manufacturing, organized labor and owners of capital can often transform the productivity gains from technological progress into higher wages and profits, while holding the price line for consumers. Thus if technological progress takes place at roughly the same rate everywhere, primary-product prices decline over time relative to manufactures prices, and the terms of trade of primary-product producers deteriorate.

Almost all the reasoning supporting the secular deterioration hypothesis can be empirically verified or rejected, as can the basic hypothesis itself. The hypothesis has been examined empirically many times, with about as many claims for rejection as for verification. The conflicting conclusions are not surprising, since many arbitrary choices must be made: What countries should be included among LDCs? What commodities should be included among primary products? What year begins the "long run" and what year ends it? (Obviously, the hypothesis could be "proved" by selecting a "peak" year to begin and a "trough" year to end—or "disproved" by doing the opposite.)

In light of these and other empirical problems, as well as the vagueness of the analytical reasoning itself, most economists conclude that the jury is still out on the secular deterioration hypothesis.

Chapter 9

Why We Trade:
The Not-So-Strong Case for
Free Trade

Many people accept the conclusion of the previous chapter without being able to prove it: it makes sense that some international trade is better than none. If trade were outlawed, a country would be sealing itself off from profitable export markets and from imports that it does not produce itself (in the United States, for example, coffee, natural rubber, Mercedes automobiles).

But should foreign exporters be accorded the *same* access to domestic markets that domestic producers have? Should foreign importers be entitled to the *same* bidding opportunities to buy domestic goods as domestic consumers have? Most people hesitate. Foreign automakers could drive American Motors out of business. Russian wheat buyers could cause U.S. wheat shortages. Neither of these possibilities seems fair to fellow citizens. It seems more reasonable that Americans should have first crack at American markets, whether on the selling side or the buying side. Reasonable as this position may appear, however, it raises awkward questions that relate to prejudice and chauvinism. Why is it "unfair" if foreign automakers drive American Motors out of existence, but "normal business flux" if General Motors does? Why is it "unfair" if a Russian beats me to the last loaf of bread on the shelf (in effect), but "one of those breaks" if my neighbor does?

All these issues relate to the central question examined in this chapter. Is free trade preferable to managed trade from the standpoint of any particular country? *Free trade* is the somewhat seductive term given to trade without discrimination against foreign producers and consumers. It means treating them in every way as if they were domestic producers and consumers. *International trade management*, by contrast, describes official government discrimination in favor of domestic producers and consumers—the maintenance of trade policies that place foreigners at a disadvantage relative to domestic residents. Such trade barriers take many forms, and we will examine the most common—import taxes—in this chapter. Others are described in Supplement 9A and in Chapter 11.

The pros and cons of free trade can also be examined from the perspective of competition. Free trade describes the opportunity for foreign producers and consumers to compete on equal terms with domestic producers and consumers. It implies that the forces of supply and demand are allowed to operate on a global basis and that they are unencumbered by government regulation. In fact, to the extent that competition among buyers and sellers is desirable as a general rule, free trade is preferable to managed trade from a global perspective, but that doesn't necessarily imply that it is preferable for every country. Just as what is good for General Motors is not the same as what is good for the United States, what is good for the United States is not the same as what is good for the world. In fact, no country in the world practices free trade. On the other hand, no country restricts international trade so much that it is self-reliant. That would be foolish, as Chapter 8 demonstrates: some international trade is always preferable to none. We shall see whether there is a similar rationale for every country's revealed preference for managed trade over free trade.

From the competitive perspective, international trade restrictions are simply barriers to international competition. When their existence is questioned by those who wonder why any exception to competitive principles should be made for foreign competitors, they are usually defended by reference to their domestic economic consequences. Quantitative limits on shoe imports are defended as protecting impoverished New England towns; tariffs on sugar imports are defended as preserving American agriculture.

Whether these defenses are valid economic justifications for trade restrictions is an open question in normative or welfare economics. By contrast, identifying the consequences of trade restrictions is a settled question in positive or descriptive economics. (See the discussion of the two types of economics in the opening of Part II.) In this chapter we will answer these questions in the following order: First, what do international trade restrictions do? Second, is what they do good or bad for the nation?

Economic Consequences of Tariffs and Free International Trade

TARIFFS: DEFINITION AND EXAMPLE

Tariffs on imports are the dominant worldwide trade barrier, although since World War II their dominance has been slipping. An import tariff is simply a tax, in its effect very much like an excise or a sales tax. It is unlike them, however, in that it is discriminatory, not general. It is levied on a commodity that is produced abroad and sold domestically but not on a similar commodity that is produced at home.

To describe tariffs more exactly, it is useful to outline how they are assessed. All commodities coming into the United States—including those in your suitcase when you return from traveling abroad—must "clear U.S. Customs." The U.S. Bureau of Customs or Customs Service is a branch of the U.S. Treasury Department, and *clearing* customs means obtaining permission from the Service to bring commodities into the United States. If there is a U.S. tariff on a particular item, however, such permission is not automatic. It is conditional on payment of the tax—often right on the spot to the customs agent.

For example, suppose that the United States has a tariff on imported textiles of $20 per bale,[1] and that a representative of Sears, Roebuck goes to the Customs House on the dock in San Francisco to pick up 150 bales of Japanese textiles. He must write a check for $3000 to the U.S. government before he can load the textiles onto his trucks. If Sears refuses to pay the $3000, the customs agent refuses to release the textiles. They will sit in storage at the Customs House until they can be auctioned off to some other American who *is* prepared to pay the tariff. Thus, to a buyer like Sears, the $3000 represents an extra cost of imported textiles *additional* to what is paid to the Japanese textile producer.

Note that Sears would not have paid any tax on virtually the same textiles if they had been bought from a U.S. textile mill. Sears could have sent its trucks directly to the mill, and no government sanction or clearance would have been required. Sears would have written only one check, payable to the U.S. producer. By contrast, Sears had to write two checks to buy the Japanese textiles, one to the Japanese producer and one to the U.S. government.

Notice now that U.S. and Japanese textile producers do not receive the same revenue for their sale, even when they supply identical goods and services. For example, suppose that the textiles in question are made precisely to specifications regarding material, quality, and so on, and that the services provided by the producers, like warranties, delivery times, and assurance of future supply, are closely compara-

[1] This is an example of a *specific* tariff, one defined as "$20 per *unit* (quantity) imported." The other prominent kind of tariff, called an *ad valorem* tariff, is defined, for example, as "20 percent of the *value* imported." For a commodity whose price per unit was $50, a $20 specific tariff would be equivalent to a 40 percent ad valorem tariff, and a 20 percent ad valorem tariff would be equivalent to a $10 specific tariff. One of the important differences between specific and ad valorem tariffs is that the former lose significance as inflation raises prices generally, while the latter maintain their potency. However, specific tariffs are often easier to apply, since quantity (weight, volume, number) can be more precisely measured than value (value when? where? in whose eyes?). The United States has both specific and ad valorem tariffs but is moving to replace the former with equivalent values of the latter.

TABLE 9.1. *Revenues and Spending under a U.S. Import Tariff If Japanese Textile Producers Stay Competitive with U.S. Textile Producers*

		U.S. revenues		Japanese revenues
	Price per bale paid by Sears	*Paid by Sears to U.S. textile producers*	*Paid by Sears to the U.S. government*	*Paid by Sears to Japanese textile producers*
Purchases of Japanese textiles	$100	0	$20	$80
Purchases of U.S. textiles	$100	$100	0	0

ble. Then Sears and other buyers will not be interested in *both* Japanese and U.S. textiles unless their cost is the same. If the cost of textiles from the U.S. producer is $100 per bale, then no one will purchase Japanese textiles unless their price is $80 per bale[2] or less, because the full cost to Sears (or anyone) of buying a bale of Japanese textiles will be $80 *plus* the $20 tariff, or $100 per bale, the same price as the U.S. producer charges. The upshot is that Japanese producers can compete with American producers only if they are willing to accept $20 less revenue on every bale—an amount equal exactly to the tariff. And willingness to do so may not be sufficient. Japanese costs of textile production may be greater than $80 per bale. If so, then Japanese producers must choose between two evils—compete at a loss or withdraw from the U.S. textile market. In the long run, they must withdraw in order to survive.

The key aspects of this example are summarized in Table 9.1 and will be referred to again. Briefly, import tariffs always discriminate in favor of domestic producers and against foreign producers. American import tariffs make sales of foreign goods to the U.S. market less profitable for foreign producers, and they reduce or eliminate U.S. imports that would otherwise occur without the tariff.

Import tariffs have other consequences as well. These consequences are most easily illustrated in three supply-demand diagrams that describe world textile markets under free and managed trade:

---

[2] Japanese producers will probably quote a price per bale of textiles in terms of their own money—yen. But this will not affect the example in any way. Every yen price per bale implies a particular dollar price per bale when it is multiplied by the appropriate foreign exchange rate (see Chapter 1): the dollar value of yen.

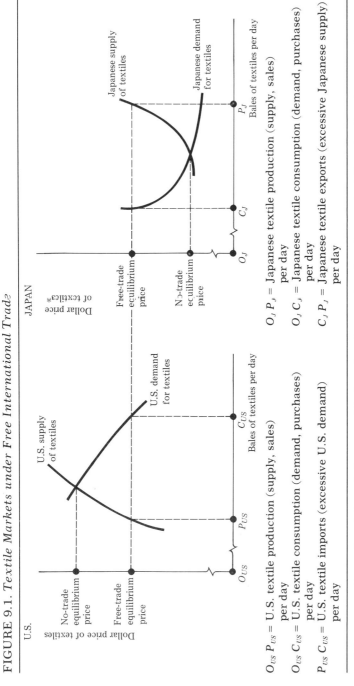

FIGURE 9.1. Textile Markets under Free International Trade

U.S.

Dollar price of textiles

No-trade equilibrium price

Free-trade equilibrium price

U.S. supply of textiles

U.S. demand for textiles

O_{US}

P_{US}

C_{US}

Bales of textiles per day

JAPAN

Dollar price of textiles*

Japanese supply of textiles

Japanese demand for textiles

Free-trade equilibrium price

No-trade equilibrium price

O_J

C_J

P_J

Bales of textiles per day

$O_{US} P_{US}$ = U.S. textile production (supply, sales) per day

$O_{US} C_{US}$ = U.S. textile consumption (demand, purchases) per day

$P_{US} C_{US}$ = U.S. textile imports (excessive U.S. demand) per day

$O_J P_J$ = Japanese textile production (supply, sales) per day

$O_J C_J$ = Japanese textile consumption (demand, purchases) per day

$C_J P_J$ = Japanese textile exports (excessive Japanese supply) per day

* Japanese textile supply and demand almost certainly depend on the yen price of textiles, not the dollar price. But given an exchange rate, defined as the dollar value of one yen, every yen price can be converted to a dollar price. See footnotes 2 and 5.

Figures 9.1, 9.2, and 9.3. These diagrams describe approximately the same economic regularities as the production-consumption possibilities diagrams of the preceding chapter (Figures 8.1 through 8.3) although in different detail.[3] Japan's comparative advantage in textile production is mirrored in Figure 9.1[4] by the fact that without international trade, the equilibrium price of Japanese textiles would be lower than the equilibrium price of U.S. textiles.[5]

FREE INTERNATIONAL TRADE— A DIAGRAMMATIC TREATMENT

For free international trade, Figure 9.1 illustrates a surprising conclusion: *equilibrium* is *not* determined by the intersection of either the Japanese or the American supply and demand curves. The broad reason for this unusual property is that the textile market is bigger than any nation, once international trade exists. Textile-market boundaries envelop national boundaries. More exactly, with international trade, the geographical area that is subject to the forces of

[3] The detail is different because money prices are explicit in the supply-demand diagram but implicit in the production and consumption possibilities diagrams of Chapter 8. There only the *relative* money price of textiles to aircraft appeared—the terms of trade. The supply-demand diagram of the textiles market, moreover, is an approximation. It ignores what is going on in the aircraft market. In reality, changes in tastes, technology, and market structure that relate to aircraft do have indirect impacts on the textile market; they all shift textile (as well as aircraft) supply and demand curves. These indirect impacts are often quantitatively small, which is why many economists neglect them when they employ supply-demand diagrams. Because they are neglected, this approach is usually described as *partial-equilibrium* analysis (*partial* denoting incomplete), whereas the approach of Chapters 8 and 10 is described as *general-equilibrium* analysis (*general* denoting comprehensive). The upward slope of the partial-equilibrium supply curves of this chapter suggests a general-equilibrium production possiblities curve that is "bowed in" toward the origin at its ends. Such a curve is more likely to describe reality than a straight line for reasons outlined on p. 255, footnotes 2 and 8 in Chapter 10, and pp. 404–405. More advanced textbooks in international economics discuss partial- and general-equilibrium approaches in greater detail.

[4] However, the real and tangible gains from some international trade according to the rule of comparative advantage cannot be illustrated well in Figure 9.1. For reasons outlined in Chapter 8 they could correctly be illustrated by outward shifts in all demand curves—expansion of consumption possibilities given the same production possibilities (supply capacity). But ignoring these shifts does not qualitatively change the conclusions of the present chapter.

[5] In order to make the left and right sides of Figure 9.1 comparable, textile prices in both countries have been recorded in a common money. Dollars have been chosen, even though yen could have been, and even though the Japanese textile producer is probably concerned about yen prices, as mentioned in footnote 2. Therefore, another reason that these diagrams are approximate (partial-equilibrium) is that potential changes in the dollar price of yen are ignored. (They would shift both the Japanese supply curve and the Japanese demand curve in Figure 9.1 if they were taken into account.)

textile supply and demand expands. These forces do not bring about the equality of U.S. supply (production by U.S. residents) and U.S. demand (consumption by U.S. residents). Even when U.S. demand for textiles exceeds the U.S. supply of textiles, as it does at the free-trade equilibrium price in Figure 9.1, it will not drive up the U.S. price as long as Japanese textile producers are willing to satisfy the excessive U.S. demand at that price. Similarly, the excessive Japanese supply of textiles that exists at the free-trade equilibrium price in Figure 9.1 — greater production of textiles by Japanese residents than they themselves want to consume — will not drive down textile prices, because U.S. buyers are willing to accept the excessive Japanese supply at the existing price.

In fact, what makes Figure 9.1's free-trade equilibrium price a legitimate equilibrium price is that the Japanese excessive supply of textiles is just exactly balanced by the U.S. excessive demand for them: the length of $C_J P_J$ just equals the length of $P_{US} C_{US}$ at the equilibrium price. The forces of supply and demand under free international trade tend to bring about the equality of *world* (Japanese plus American) textile supply and *world* textile demand at a single price. The reader can check this out in Figure 9.1 by actually measuring: the sum of the distances $O_J P_J$ and $O_{US} P_{US}$ (world supply) does equal the sum of the distances $O_J C_J$ and $O_{US} C_{US}$ (world demand). At prices higher than the equilibrium price, world supply would exceed world demand. At prices lower, world demand would exceed world supply. Neither situation could persist long if the forces of supply and demand worked. Frustrated sellers in the former instance would tend to shade their prices to get rid of their unwanted inventory. Unsatisfied buyers in the latter instance would reluctantly express willingness to pay higher prices in order to "get the goods." Price would converge to the equilibrium price.

As illustrated in Figure 9.1, free international trade in textiles establishes a single *world* textile price. This conclusion needs emphasis, since it is the distinguishing characteristic of free as opposed to managed trade (as Figure 9.3 shows). Indeed, under perfectly free international trade every commodity market would be a world market, completely swamping the significance of any national border for determining commodity prices. Trade restrictions restore the potential for commodity prices to differ from nation to nation.

Yet the preceding paragraph and Figure 9.1 are too extreme to be a description of free international trade in the real world. In practice, free textile trade only tends to establish one world price for textiles. There remain several important natural and inevitable reasons why Japanese textile prices would differ from U.S. textile prices despite free international trade. One is the cost of shipping textiles from Japan to the United States. This cost often significantly exceeds internal transportation and delivery costs. Thus U.S. textile prices could be higher than Japanese textile prices, yet not so much higher that Sears would find it profitable to buy Japanese textiles and pay the international transport cost, nor so much higher that Japanese textile producers themselves would be willing to pay the transport costs in order to break into the more lucrative U.S. market.[6] A second reason why U.S. and Japanese textile prices would still differ under free trade is that, in reality, U.S. and Japanese textiles are almost never qualitatively identical products, nor are the warranty, delivery, or reliability services provided by Japanese and American textile producers usually the same. Qualitative differences like these often make buyers willing to pay a premium for the superior product, despite free international trade.[7]

Ultimately, however, as we shall see, whether free trade actually equates prices worldwide or only tends to is irrelevant here. Regardless of the answer, government restrictions on free international trade cause commodity prices to diverge from nation to nation more than they otherwise would and have other predictable and important consequences.

The implications of Figure 9.1 are worth reviewing in different words, both because they are initially somewhat confusing and because the impact of international trade restrictions is analyzed below in a similar framework. With international trade, U.S. textile production and U.S. textile consumption are not identical.[8] In fact, U.S. production falls short of U.S. consumption by the quantity of textiles imported. Imports are measured exactly by $P_{US} \, C_{US}$, as indicated at the bottom of Figure 9.1. America's textile imports could also be measured by $C_J \, P_J$, because its imports from the world (Japan) are identically their exports to America. $C_J \, P_J$ represents their textile exports

[6] It is likely that the growing importance of multinational corporations in international trade (see Chapter 13) has made international shipping costs a less significant reason why prices would differ among countries despite free trade. For products with high value relative to their shipping costs, like machinery and sophisticated electronic equipment, it is profitable for a multinational corporation to quote a single worldwide "delivered" price, where the delivery points are major ports in most countries. This saves considerable internal accounting costs, and it parallels exactly the common retail pricing of many goods throughout the United States, whether located near to or far from the actual production site. On the other hand, even in the U.S. market there is no common sticker price for automobiles, because the differing internal transport costs are assessed proportionately to the buyer's distance from the production point.

[7] In Supplement 9A, trade restriction by a U.S. export tax is analyzed in the world aircraft market, where the Japanese are assumed to be unable to produce any aircraft comparable to U.S. aircraft. The interested reader can apply this analysis straightforwardly to a world textile market where Japanese and U.S. textiles are not qualitatively comparable either.

[8] This point was introduced briefly in Chapter 8 in the discussion of Figures 8.2 and 8.3 and in footnote 9. The mix of products produced by each country under international trade, as given by the production points R and P, was not the same as the mix of products each consumed, as given by the consumption points Q and C.

FIGURE 9.2. *An Alternative Language for the World Textile Market*

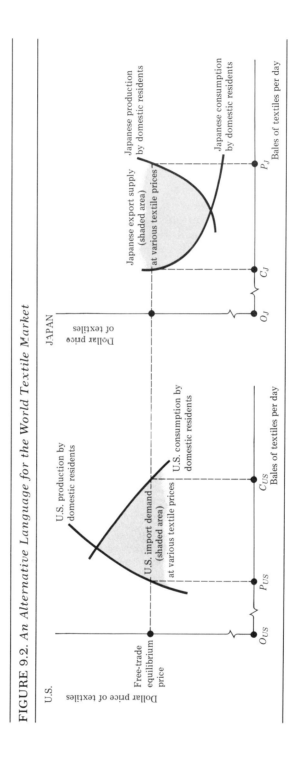

because it indicates the amount by which Japanese textile production exceeds Japanese textile consumption. This alternative language for the same phenomena is summarized in Figure 9.2.

This production/consumption/trade accounting is true of *any* international trade, whether free or restricted. What is not, and is true only of perfect free trade, is that a single world price of textiles is established by the forces of supply and demand. In Figure 9.2, at any price below the equilibrium price the U.S. demand for imported textiles would exceed the quantity that Japan wished to export. The pressure of U.S. import demand (excessive demand) on Japanese export supply (excessive supply) would drive the world price up toward its equilibrium. Similarly, at any price above the equilibrium price the Japanese supply of textiles for export would exceed U.S. import needs, and its pressure would push prices back toward equilibrium.

TARIFF-RESTRICTED INTERNATIONAL TRADE: A DIAGRAMMATIC TREATMENT

A U.S. tariff of $20 per bale on textile imports can dramatically change this picture of the world textile market. A tariff is a tax, and the essence of any tax is the wedge it drives between the price paid by a buyer and the price received by a seller in any transaction. This wedge characterizes even income taxes, where the income you and I receive from work is less than our employer pays for our labor services. Every buyer must "pay" any tax; no seller receives it.[9] In an economic system with taxes there is no such thing as "the" price of any product: there are always two.

Since tariffs are taxes, the same is true for them. Buyers of imports face a price that includes the tax; foreign sellers receive a payment that does not. The government of the importing country pockets the difference. We saw all this in the example summarized in Table 9.1. Sears paid $100 per bale for imported textiles, but Japanese textile producers received only $80 per bale. The U.S. government, through its Customs Service, collected the $20 difference.

The existence of two prices as a result of government taxation is especially important in the case of a tariff. The domain of the two prices coincides with national boundaries: each reigns in a different country. The higher, tariff-inclusive price of textiles applies throughout the U.S. textile market, and the lower, tariff-exclusive textile price applies throughout the Japanese textile market. Not only Sears but

---

[9] This applies strictly only to the direct effects of the tax. When both the buyer and seller are citizens of the same country, both have an implicit claim on the government's tax revenue, and both may benefit from any resulting government expenditure. Thus buyers may not really "pay" all the tax, and sellers may after all receive some of it indirectly. These observations are important below because the buyer and seller are citizens (or residents) of different countries.

FIGURE 9.3. *Textile Markets under Free International Trade and with a $20 U.S. Import Tariff*

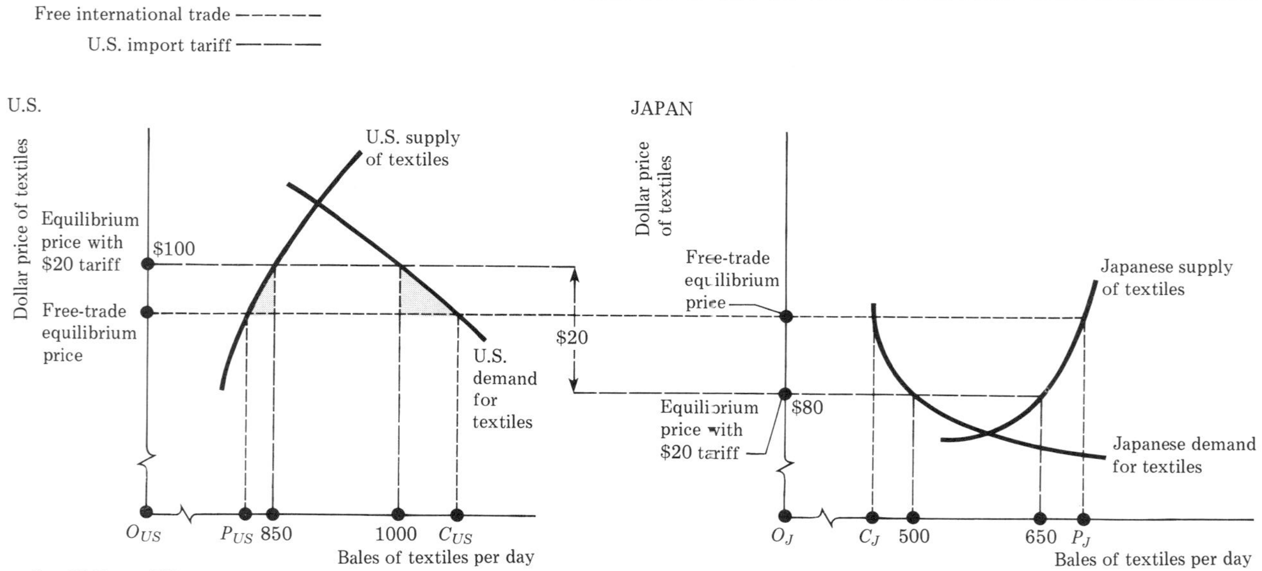

Free international trade ‑ ‑ ‑ ‑ ‑
U.S. import tariff ————

Under the U.S. tariff:
850 = U.S. textile production per day
1000 = U.S. textile consumption per day
150 = U.S. textile imports per day

Under the U.S. tariff:
650 = Japanese textile production per day
500 = Japanese textile consumption per day
150 = Japanese textile exports per day

every U.S. buyer acts as if $100 per bale were "the" price of textiles, and for them it is, even when they buy textiles from U.S. producers. No U.S. textile producers will charge $80, $90, or $99 per bale if they know they can get $100. U.S. textile producers plan production, investment, and payrolls under the belief that $100 per bale is "the" price of textiles. So there turns out to be only one U.S. price of textiles after all—unless someone attempts to smuggle in Japanese textiles without paying the tariff. Smuggling generates a set of *black-market* prices that are probably below $100 per bale.[10]

In Japan there is also only one price, but it is $20 lower than the U.S. price: $80. The forces of supply and demand in Japan assure this. If Japanese textile producers could receive more than $80 per bale locally, they would stop exporting to the United States. To the extent that exports to the United States continue, Japanese producers and consumers both act as if $80 per bale were "the" Japanese price of textiles—and it is, if there is no smuggling, no transportation cost, and qualitative identity between Japanese and U.S. textiles.

In Figure 9.3 the consequences of the two national textile prices induced by the U.S. tariff are illustrated and compared to textile markets under free international trade. International trade in textiles under a $20 U.S. import tariff brings about an equilibrium in which (1) U.S. import demand matches Japanese export supply, just as it did under free trade, but in which (2) the U.S. price is $20 higher than the Japanese price, instead of their being equal as under free trade. In other words, equilibrium in this situation describes *two* prices, which differ by the tariff, and at which excessive U.S. demand for textiles is just balanced by excessive Japanese supply. (Thus world textile supply still matches world textile demand.) No matter how they are phrased, these equilibrium requirements are satisfied in Figure 9.3 at prices of $100 and $80 per bale on a day when the United States wants to import and Japan wants to export only 150 bales of textiles—a mutually agreeable order.

What makes this situation an equilibrium? Couldn't prices differ by more or less than $20? Couldn't they be higher or lower than ($100, $80)? The answers are, respectively, the forces of supply and demand, no, and no. No other set of prices than ($100, $80) can endure, given the configurations of supply and demand. By comparison, the combi-

---

[10] Black-market prices are those that rule on goods obtained or sold illegally. The black-market price of smuggled Japanese textiles in the United States would lie below $100 if possession, use, or resale of smuggled goods were a U.S. crime. Then buyers would have to be compensated—by a price below $100—for the risk they bore in purchasing "hot" merchandise. The smuggler's profits would be the difference between the black-market price and $80, the price charged by the Japanese exporter. Smuggling is in fact a prominent activity in countries with particularly burdensome restrictions on international trade or with underdeveloped systems of law enforcement. Burdensome restrictions make for higher expected profitability of smuggling; lax law enforcement lowers its riskiness.

nation ($100, $90) would generate larger quantities of textiles that Japan wants to export (supply) but would leave U.S. import demand unchanged. The pressure of larger Japanese export supply on constant U.S. import demand would quickly bring the $90 price down toward $80. (And how could the Japanese have marketed their textiles at $100 per bale in the United States when a $20 tariff was levied on top of a $90 price?) Nor is a combination like ($110, $90) any better, although its prices do differ by $20. United States import demand will be even smaller at $110 per bale than at $100 per bale, and Japanese export supply will be larger, once again pressing prices down. Similar imbalances in world supply and demand can be seen to exist for every combination other than ($100, $80).

Most of the consequences of a U.S. import tariff are now clear in Figure 9.3. By comparison with a free-trade situation:

1. United States textile prices are higher, although not by the full amount of the tariff.
2. United States textile production is higher. Under free trade, it is $O_{US}P_{US}$ bales per day; with the tariff, 850.
3. United States textile consumption is lower. Under free trade, it is $O_{US}C_{US}$ bales per day; with the tariff, 1000.
4. United States textile imports are lower. Under free trade, imports are $P_{US}C_{US}$ bales per day; with the tariff, 150.

In addition, although it is not immediately obvious from Figure 9.3:

5. The U.S. terms of trade are more favorable.

In Japan, most of the differences between its economy under free trade and under trade restricted by a U.S. tariff are exactly the opposite in character. Textile prices, production, and exports are lower with the U.S. tariff; consumption is higher; and the terms of trade are less favorable to Japan.

These five consequences of tariffs are the foundation for almost all the arguments used to defend government management of international trade, as we shall see. Except for the terms-of-trade consequences, they can be explained verbally almost as easily as diagrammatically. That is, they appeal to our intuition about the effect of import tariffs. Since an import tariff is a discriminatory tax on the output of foreign producers, it is no surprise that the U.S. demand for imported textiles is smaller with the tax than without—they are what is taxed. And it is no surprise that Japanese producers find it more difficult to compete in U.S. markets and as a result have smaller market penetration. They are diverted thereby to compete more intensively in their own market, thus lowering Japanese textile prices and expanding textile consumption there.

United States textile producers are the beneficiaries of the business that is diverted from imports because of the tariff. Many enjoy larger sales and may therefore raise their prices. Unless the U.S. textile industry is perfectly competitive, every firm's profits are higher too.

The combination of higher prices, better potential business, and larger profits stimulates expansion; investment and employment are greater than they would have been under free trade. Or in the case of an industry that for some reason faces an increasingly bleak future (textiles in the United States are a perfect example), import tariffs check the decline that would otherwise take place under free trade. It is primarily for this last reason that tariffs and all import barriers are referred to as *protectionist* policies. They shield domestic producers from foreign competitors, protecting them from misfortune that would otherwise take place.

But while *protection* via import tariffs may ease misfortune for the U.S. textile industry, it does so by transferring the misfortune to consumers and to other producers. American consumers of textiles are worse off with textile tariffs than they would be under free trade. Sears must charge consumers more for the Japanese textiles it buys, because Sears must pay the tariff as well as the Japanese textile price. Consumers even pay higher textile prices if they (or Sears) purchase from domestic producers, as Figure 9.3 illustrates. Some consumers are sufficiently deterred by these higher prices that they purchase fewer textiles altogether: consumption is lower with import tariffs than under free trade. Nobody in the role of consumer gains from import restrictions.

American producers of goods other than textiles lose from textile tariffs as well. Aircraft producers pay more for upholstery, hospitals pay more for uniforms, and homebuilders pay more for carpeting. Their costs of production are higher. If they nevertheless hold the price of their products constant, profits are smaller than under free trade. If they pass along their higher costs to the consumer through higher prices, their sales are lower, and profits are smaller anyway.[11] Furthermore, if labor and credit markets are "tight" (little unemployment and reluctant lenders), a larger protected textile industry may imply higher wages and interest rates, both of which are again costs of production to nontextile producers.[12]

How accurate is this collection of consequences as a description of the real-world difference between free and restricted trade? Generally, it is very accurate. None of these consequences of import tariffs depends qualitatively on the assumptions that transport costs are zero or that Japanese and American textiles are identical, and few depend on

[11] The observation that tariff protection for textile producers may actually expose other producers to higher costs, rather than protecting them, is the key point underlying the concept of *effective protection*, discussed in footnote 32 of Chapter 14.

[12] This entire paragraph illustrates nicely why Figure 9.3 is described in footnotes 3, 4, and 5 as approximate or partial-equilibrium analysis. In the figure, the impact of the textiles tariff on the costs facing aircraft producers is unseen and ignored. Were it to be taken into account, the supply curve for aircraft under a textiles tariff would lie above that under free trade, owing to the higher costs.

perfectly competitive market forces (see footnote 1 to Supplement 9A). First, in the real world, transport costs make Japanese and American textile prices diverge even under free trade.[13] Adding import tariffs on top of transport costs makes them diverge even more, so that restricted trade still differs from free trade in every one of the five dimensions listed before. If we grant, further, that Japanese textiles do differ importantly in character from American textiles, qualitative analysis of the consequences of trade restrictions is unaffected. The more pronounced the differences in the products, however, the smaller will be the quantitative consequences. Finally, even the existence of multinational textile corporations (and there are not that many) who are simultaneously U.S. suppliers and Japanese suppliers alters few of the conclusions. The analysis becomes somewhat more complicated, and it is no longer clear that the forces of supply and demand work in such an obvious way. But it is inevitable that the presence of a U.S. tariff makes Japanese affiliates that produce textiles for the U.S. market less profitable and makes U.S. affiliates with solely domestic business more profitable. In fact, for Canada, Australia, and many less-developed countries, an important and often attractive sixth consequence to add to the list above is the incentive tariffs give for multinational corporations from abroad to set up shop.

Free versus Government-Managed Trade

The previous sections describe the economic consequences of an existing tariff. Those to come wrestle with the difficult question of whether these consequences are "good" or "bad" from a national point of view. Supplement 9A gives a similar treatment of export taxes. The link between identifying the consequences (a *positive* exercise) and evaluating them (a *normative* exercise) consists fundamentally of identifying whose oxen trade restrictions gore and whose pockets they line. The rest of the chapter deals with these gains and losses from interference with free trade.

Is free trade economically better for the nation as a whole than government-managed trade, in the same way that some trade is better than no trade (Chapter 8)? The question is complicated and controversial. Every nation's government answers no, while most economists answer yes. Regrettably, politicians often don't understand the economic costs of all government management, and economists don't

---

[13] In fact, if the transport costs associated with U.S. textile imports from Japan were $20 per bale, Figure 9.3 would be a perfectly adequate illustration of the real-world textile market with transport costs but without tariffs (free trade). And with the exception of the terms-of-trade effects, the economic consequences of a tariff and of higher transport costs would be the same.

appreciate the subtleties and distortions that justify government trade policy.

Regrettably, also, protagonists in the controversy often ignore the fact that government trade policy makes some people better off and some people worse off. One hears arguments such as: "The nation's better off with fewer imports because the union movement is better off," or "The nation's better off with free trade because profits are higher." Such arguments are simple-minded, propagandistic, and misleading because they involve a fallacy of composition. What is good for me is not necessarily good for the nation as a whole, nor is what is good for the nation necessarily good for the world as a whole (see the last few pages of this chapter). It is necessary in evaluating national-welfare arguments for and against free trade to weigh the gainers' gains against the losers' losses. Although this weighing is extremely difficult, we can in many situations conclude that the gains to those made better off from trade policy are "greater" or "more important" than other people's losses. In those situations, society is better off than under free trade.[14] Most of the arguments for trade restrictions rely on some subjective weighting of the economic welfare of some individuals against that of others.

The most significant argument *against* trade restrictions and in favor of free trade does not rely on any such weighting. It is that government management of trade interferes with the valuable role that prices play in making the most desirable (optimal) economic decisions. We will turn to it before we turn to the arguments in favor of government management.

GOVERNMENT TRADE POLICY, MARKET PRICES, AND THE PRICE SYSTEM

Almost all the reasons why nations prefer government-managed trade to free trade rest on their market-price impact. What is sought, however, is usually not a different market price in itself but rather its

[14] The vague wording here reflects how difficult (and perhaps impossible) the calculation really is. How can greatness or importance be measured? Who does the measuring? Policymakers? Voters through the ballot box? Chapter 10 discusses these awkward questions in considerably more detail. Note also that the difficulty is not limited to international economics. Virtually all economic changes create gains and losses—growth, technological advance, environmental control, resource conservation, and so on. If there is no way to judge whether trade restrictions are socially good or bad, because individual gains and losses cannot be lumped together in any acceptable fashion, then there is no way to judge whether *any* economic change is socially good or bad. Growth, technological advance, environmental control, and resource conservation may sound socially beneficial, but proving it in all circumstances is impossible. A more affirmative conclusion is that if we do feel competent as individuals to make judgments on the social worth of these other policies, we should also feel competent to do so with respect to government management of trade.

consequent impact on production, consumption, and trade, as is apparent from Figure 9.3. That is, governments influence market prices in order to alter production, consumption, and trade—presumably (but not necessarily) in the "national interest." Alterations in market prices are generally the means to another end.[15]

But altering market prices by trade restrictions has subtle economic costs. While politicians say that restrictions "influence" prices, economists usually say that they "distort" prices and place economic "burdens" on a society. In this section we will focus on these distortions and burdens. In subsequent sections we shall see that governments may be willing to accept the economic burden of price distortions if they bring about other consequences that are perceived to be socially beneficial.

Trade restrictions alter the channels through which prices work to assure consumers of maximum economic satisfaction and to signal producers to supply those goods that are most highly valued. Prices have this role even in socialist economies as long as the socialist planners are seeking the greatest possible economic well-being of their nation.[16] Thus, *price-distortion* losses that trade restrictions impose are not limited to market-oriented, private-enterprise, capitalist economies.

---

[15] About the only occasion when certain trade restrictions are justified on their market-price effects alone is when they are invoked temporarily as an anti-inflationary measure. In this case, export restrictions have the desired consequences, implying lower market prices for exportable commodities (see Supplement 9A). Import restrictions cannot be defended on these grounds; they tend to raise market prices. In fact, in order to bring about lower prices in the early 1970s, the United States moved *toward* free trade by abandoning import restrictions on oil and meat. The United States also restricted trade on the export side during the same period by temporarily limiting exports of lumber, soybeans, and steel scrap. Domestic lumber, soybean, and steel prices were made temporarily lower than they would have been otherwise, but they bounced back when the export controls were removed. So did oil and meat prices when import restrictions were restored. And export control and import liberalization affect only the present level of price, not necessarily its future rate of inflation. To have permanent price-level effects, they must be adopted permanently. To affect the rate of inflation, they must be invoked again and again (and that process has natural limits—where imports are unrestricted and exports are prohibited).

[16] In such economies, administrators of the production system ask questions such as, How valuable would it be to society to devote more resources to heavy industry and less to agriculture? Their social valuation of both resources and alternative types of output is really a system of "pricing them out." But because such prices exist only in the planners' calculations and are never seen by producers or consumers in any "market," they are known as *shadow prices*— implicit prices behind the scene. It is a remarkable conclusion of the branch of economics known as comparative economic systems that when the socialist administrators do their calculations without error, their shadow prices exactly match the prices that hypothetical competitive markets would establish.

One way to illustrate price-distortion losses is to recall Chapter 8's discussion of the benefits from some international trade. International trade allows every country to expand its menu of consumption possibilities beyond its menu of production possibilities. The best way of converting exports into importable products is to exchange them through international trade. Greater quantities of importables are obtained in that way than by breaking exports up into their component resources and using those resources at home to produce the importables. Economists describe international trade therefore as a more *efficient* way than domestic production for a country to get importable products: more of them can be obtained for the same resources. All international trade restrictions discourage this efficient activity. They figuratively shrink the consumption possibilities available to a nation, moving it back toward its economically inferior existence in the absence of trade. There is less to go around for everyone than under free trade.

But this description obscures the role of price distortions. It is through the price mechanism that all this happens. United States tariffs, for example, discourage the purchase of imports. Consequently, as Figure 9.3 shows, they lead to higher U.S. textile prices (and profits). This encourages additional U.S. production of textiles, in which the United States is comparatively disadvantaged. This in turn draws resources away from U.S. producers of aircraft, raises their costs, and reduces their profitability, thereby discouraging U.S. production of aircraft. The result will be that more U.S. resources are devoted to textiles production and less to aircraft production than under free trade.

The production bias that U.S. tariffs create through their price effects obviously defies the rule of comparative advantage. Too many textiles, and too few aircraft, are produced. Economists describe this technically as *misallocation* of resources. Without trade restrictions and other price distortions, resource owners would have directed (allocated) their resources to where they were most valuable. For example, suppose that by accident too few aircraft were being produced to satisfy society's demands, and too many textiles. The pressures of market demand (or the revised calculations of the socialist planner) would normally raise aircraft prices and profits and reduce textile prices and profits. Resources would be stimulated to move from textiles into aircraft—including labor, who would share both the suffering generated by low textile prices and profits and the windfall generated by high aircraft prices and profits. The movement would continue until "just enough" textiles and aircraft were produced to satisfy society's demands. "Just enough" is defined by stable prices having the property that extra resources directed to aircraft production are neither more nor less valuable than if they were directed to textiles production.

United States trade restrictions alter these ideal prices as a result of taxation, not social demands.[17] The distorted prices create and perpetuate a situation in which some U.S. textile resources would really be more valuable to U.S. aircraft producers but cannot be bid away. The bidding power of the textiles industry will have been enhanced by the extra gains (price and profits) that textile tariffs bring.

The ultimate effect of misallocating resources through trade restriction may be smaller national consumption possibilities—less for everyone. Not only is consumption smaller, it is misdirected as well. Too many aircraft will be consumed and too few textiles. Without tariffs and other price distortions, consumers would have directed their spending so that their last dollar's worth of textiles bought and their last dollar's worth of aircraft (services) bought yielded the same satisfaction. Otherwise they could have made themselves happier by buying more of the good yielding more satisfaction with the dollars saved from buying less of the other. United States tariffs, however, raise textile prices for reasons that have nothing to do with consumer preferences.[18] As a result, consumers can buy fewer textiles for a dollar at the distorted prices and more aircraft (services). A "distorted dollar's worth" of textiles will yield less satisfaction than under free trade and aircraft, more. Therefore, fewer textiles will be purchased and more aircraft. Yet the consumer satisfaction yielded by these distorted-price purchases must be less than that yielded under free trade—or consumers would have made the distorted-price purchases in the first place![19]

This conclusion is carefully hedged. In practice, too much can be made of the way in which government management of trade misallocates resources and misdirects consumer preferences. The fact is that almost *all* taxes are distortionary in the sense defined, not just tariffs

---

[17] Potential awkwardness occurs in the reasoning here, especially in a democratic society. If people vote to be taxed by trade restrictions, either directly or through their elected representatives, are they not expressing a kind of social demand that may have little to do with narrow economic well-being? For example, they may be voting to become self-sufficient, simply because self-sufficiency breeds security. And security is psychologically valuable, even at some economic cost (the cost of traditional "misallocation").

[18] Do they really have nothing to do with consumer preferences? See the preceding footnote.

[19] It is even possible under some circumstances to calculate dollar estimates of these price-distortion or efficiency losses from trade restrictions. The estimates represent the amount of income a country sacrifices due to resource misallocation and consumer misdirection. The calculation has to do with measurement of concepts known in economics as *producers'* and *consumers' surplus*. Estimates include the small shaded triangles of Figure 9.3 (as well as some of the government's revenue from the trade restrictions). The measurements can be made, however, only under very restrictive assumptions. And when they have been made in practice, they usually reveal very small trade-restriction losses. For the United States, most estimates are well under 1 percent of gross national product.

and export taxes (Supplement 9A). If we agree with the familiar aphorism, "In this world, nothing is certain but death and taxes," reducing taxes on international trade will probably require raising them elsewhere. One distortion is replaced by another, and it is not clear that the second misallocates and misdirects any less severely than the first.

Even without such pessimism about the inevitability of taxes, the practical case for free trade on price-distortion grounds is not airtight. Suppose that import tariffs could be removed without altering any other taxes. Real-world free-trade prices would still not correspond to the ideal prices generated in competitive markets nor to the shadow prices employed by the socialist planner. The reason is the existence of other distortions, such as government regulations, monopoly, and economic *externalities*.[20] These may well have distorted oppositely to trade restrictions. In the United States, for example, the net impact of all price distortions taken together (including trade restrictions) may be to misallocate resources toward aircraft and misdirect consumption toward textiles. By comparison, free trade would be even worse. Aircraft production, already too large, would be even larger; too-small textile production would become smaller. Aircraft consumption, already too small, would become even smaller; too-large textile consumption would become larger. In this situation, even though restricted trade entailed more price distortions than free trade, it would actually feature smaller price-distortion costs. Everyone would gain, not lose, from trade restrictions. The example illustrates a fundamental implication of the economist's *Theory of the Second Best*: in the presence of many price distortions, there is no guarantee that removing any one makes a society better off; it may actually lead to an inferior allocation of resources and consumption.[21]

We shall encounter another, more positive implication of the Theory of the Second Best later on. What the theory undermines here is not the conceptual existence of efficiency losses from government management of international trade but the absolute certainty that they will exist for every country and at every time in the real world.

[20] *Externalities* are a type of economic gain or loss. They arise in cases where one economic agent's unencumbered actions in a market cause benefits or costs (externalities) to someone else that cannot themselves be priced in any market (they are *external* to the market mechanism). Important examples of external costs are air and water pollution caused by production processes or by consumption of automobile services. Examples of external benefits are pollination services provided by honey producers to apple growers, and your consumption of sweeter air when everyone around you consumes soap.

[21] This implication applies also to nonprice barriers to international trade, which are discussed in more depth in Chapter 11. Quantitative restrictions (such as *quotas*) on imports and exports also distort prices. But in the presence of other distortions, removing them might distort prices even further from the ideal norm.

GOVERNMENT TRADE POLICY TO STIMULATE
PRODUCTION OR EMPLOYMENT

Price-distortion losses notwithstanding, government preferences for managing trade are probably based more often on production-employment consequences than on anything else. Import barriers in particular are justified because some (or all) production and employment is larger than under free trade. Similarly justified are export promotion and subsidization policies—government management of international trade to encourage *more* exports than would occur under free trade, thereby discriminating in favor of domestic exporters and against their foreign competitors (see Chapter 11).

Five important production-employment arguments for import restriction and export promotion relate to selected industries. A sixth relates to production and employment nationwide, and a seventh relates to production and employment in a particular region. We will devote considerably more space to the first than to the other six, not because it is more important but because it can be used to introduce recurring and important considerations.

THE NATIONAL SECURITY ARGUMENT AGAINST FREE TRADE. Free international trade is often considered harmful to a country when it implies the nonexistence or insufficient size of an industry deemed vital to national security. National defense industries are the obvious candidates. Many countries are so comparatively disadvantaged in the production of armaments that, under free trade, their entire military defense would be supplied through imports. That in itself provides no ground for restricting free trade as long as imports continue; the nation can maintain its defenses most efficiently through imports at the chosen level. But future armaments imports cannot always be assured. Conflict or war with the armaments supplier is always possible, and for most countries international transportation channels are more easily severed by an adversary than internal transportation channels. In such dire circumstances, international trade in armaments would still yield private profits and national benefits, but it might be rendered almost impossible. The survival of an independent nation therefore might depend on the existence of domestic national defense industries.

Such domestic national defense industries will necessarily waste resources for a nation during peacetime (after all, its security needs could be supplied more cheaply—using fewer resources—from abroad). The tangible economic benefit from the existence of these industries may never actually materialize; conflict and war may be avoided. What is important is their intangible economic benefit: their insurance value. Even inefficient national defense industries are in essence a national insurance policy against the possibility of being left defenseless. National insurance, just like personal insurance, has economic value even if you never have to collect on it. The peacetime economic costs of a domestic national defense industry are properly viewed as premium payments.

National security considerations are often applied much more broadly. United States policies to reduce dependence on imported oil are designed to diminish vulnerability to OPEC's aggressive use of economic market power, in the same way that reducing dependence on imported armaments reduces vulnerability to military aggression. In many countries, even agriculture falls under the umbrella of national security. There is national reluctance to rely exclusively (or even largely) on imports of food because of the especially severe consequences of disruption in normal supply channels. Indeed, some OPEC nations cultivate their own immensely inefficient and socially costly agricultural sectors. These can be economically justified as national insurance in light of the occasional recommendation in oil-consuming countries that "if they cut off our oil, we ought to cut off their food." Of course, national security justifications are often pushed to unlikely extremes by self-serving lobbyists: reduced U.S. dependence on imported clothespins was once sanctioned on national security grounds!

Restrictions on imports is one way simultaneously to reduce foreign dependence and to insure larger domestic production of such commodities than would have existed under free trade. Higher market prices and industry profits are the catalyst in the process. Consumers and producers of other commodities are implicitly taxed in order to encourage the favored producers of national security goods to increase production. The economic losses of the losers are judged to be "worth it" to obtain the goal.

Export promotion and subsidization accomplish the same purpose in countries with comparative advantage in commodities vital to national security. United States export subsidies on some agricultural products and special French government promotion of armaments exports can both be defended on these grounds.

But are these sensible defenses for a nation's preferring government-managed to free trade? Not always. To take an extreme example, I can defend burning down my house as *one* reliable way to get the spiders out of the bedroom. But my defense is stupid because there are clearly less costly ways to accomplish my (wife's) goal. In fact, anyone who accepted my defense—destroying my house was beneficial because the spiders are gone—would be as foolish as I. So it is with the national security argument against free trade. It is acceptable as a reason for trade restrictions *only* in the absence of less costly policies that obtain the same goal. When less costly policies exist, it is foolish and illegitimate to appeal to national security to oppose free trade.

To clarify these points, we need to be more precise about the national security problem under free trade. The problem is that too little national security insurance—armaments, oil, food—is available from domestic producers, and by implication, there are too many other goods. The problem is thus the free-trade allocation of resources to production; there is no particular problem with consumption. Yet restricting trade alters both production and consumption decisions, and one of its economic costs (among others) is its misdirection of consumers through distorted prices. The original misallocation (too few national security goods produced) may well be redressed, but at the expense of misdirection of consumer preferences (too little oil and food will be consumed). It cannot even be said in general whether the initial production misallocation was worse or better for the nation than the ultimate consumption misdirection. One problem replaces another. The cure may actually be worse than the disease!

Intuitively, a better policy than government management of trade in this example is one that minimizes the consumption misdirection. Such a policy exists in principle. It is simply for the government to subsidize production of national security goods and to finance the subsidy by taxing the production of other goods. The subsidy-tax policy works directly on production allocation. Its consumption effects are indirect and incidental; given the political desire to encourage production, they do not constitute misdirection. And although the policy appears to have nothing directly to do with foreign trade, it does in fact induce less dependence on imports by encouraging and allowing domestic producers to compete more intensely with foreign suppliers. The national security goal is satisfied—without one of the economic costs imposed by trade restrictions.

This intuitive conclusion is supported powerfully by another implication of the economist's Theory of the Second Best: when the costs of administering all policies are the same, those that solve economic problems most directly impose the smallest economic cost on society. These direct policies can be called *first-best* policies, although economists frequently restrict this term to policies that impose no economic cost on society, such as *lump-sum* or *head* taxes. Policies that impose higher economic costs are *second best*, *third best*, and so on. As applied to the problem of national security, production subsidies and taxes are a first-best solution. At best, import restriction and export subsidization are second best.

Real-world problems are never this simple. They are made more complex, for example, by the fact that government policy has other goals. Yet the rule of choosing the most directly applicable policies can still be used. As an example, agricultural import restriction and export promotion might be defended as an ideal solution to the twin problems of agricultural national security and collective national obesity (assuming some legitimate social reason existed for discouraging people's private right to be heavy). These interferences with free trade induce larger production and smaller consumption of food, as desired by assumption.

Another practical consideration is that otherwise first-best policies may be more costly than others to administer. When administrative costs are factored into the calculation, these policies may end up second or third best. Nor are economically first-best policies always politically tractable. United States production subsidies to national defense producers, financed by production taxes on other industries, would probably be attacked in Congress as a gross and militaristic inequity. Import restrictions and export subsidies that achieved the same results (and others) more discreetly might well be sanctioned without uproar. On joint political-economic grounds, they may therefore be preferable policies.

It must be granted that the problems of determining first-best policies usually make a careful calculation impossible. Precise information is required on price distortions, terms-of-trade effects (discussed later in this chapter), and the resource costs of administering government policies. In flagrant cases, nevertheless, we can make judgments. For example, the United States as a whole would almost certainly be economically better off in abandoning its quantitative limitations on imports of cheese and dairy products and replacing them with an expanded program of production subsidies to dairy farms that would leave them equally protected. The administrative machinery to do so already exists, and the costs of not doing so are spread dramatically to almost all Americans because of the importance of dairy products in most consumer budgets.

Finally, even if the costs of alternative policies are impossible to calculate in practice, there is a presumption that the most direct policies are the best. Usually (but not always) the presumption will be right. Therefore, in the absence of hard evidence, national security arguments should be presumed to provide no grounds for opposing free trade. Trade barriers are not the most direct policies for altering production. The burden of proof to the contrary rests properly on protectionists. In its absence, free trade should win by default.

THE INFANT-INDUSTRY AND ANTIDUMPING ARGUMENTS AGAINST FREE TRADE. Free international trade is also considered harmful if it allows foreign producers to perpetuate monopoly power in supplying imports—if it prevents the establishment of a domestic industry that would survive under more competitive world market conditions. Or, to reverse the emphasis, government management of trade may be preferable to free trade if it circumscribes foreign monopoly power.

Two instances are frequently discussed. One involves a country where growth, technology, and development have made just profitable the establishment of an entirely new domestic industry—for example, a commercial aircraft industry in Japan. Such an *infant industry* might represent a long-term threat to U.S. aircraft producers, who had been supplying the Japanese market exclusively. If these U.S. producers are competitive, their power to act is limited by the market, and they must grin and bear the threat. If they are monopolistic, they may be able to keep the Japanese infant industry from being born or else kill it quickly by undercutting it in price or service. Because of start-up costs, barriers to entry, and the need initially to operate on a small scale (even though economies of large-scale production might be available in the future), an infant is particularly vulnerable (unprofitable) in its early years. It cannot open up and close down operations immediately or costlessly. These weaknesses might allow U.S. aircraft suppliers to reestablish their monopoly supply and price with impunity after driving the Japanese infant out of business. To keep this from happening, the Japanese government might offer protection to its commercial aircraft industry during infancy through import restriction. Later, as start-up costs are covered and scale of operation expands, the protection can be withdrawn because the former infant is able to stand on its own feet.

Infancy apart, foreign producers are sometimes able to drive an otherwise viable domestic competitor out of business through an activity known as *dumping*. Dumping with this goal in mind is known as *predatory dumping*, usually with the implication that the foreign producers exploit their monopoly power once they have driven domestic competitors out of business.

Dumping itself is defined as a producer's practice of selling the same product abroad more cheaply than at home. In predatory dumping, foreign producers are willing to accept lower current profits (or even losses) in order to reap larger future profits after extinguishing domestic competitors. Not all dumping is motivated by such economic aggression. *Sporadic dumping* describes a situation in which unexpectedly large supplies, usually of agricultural products, are sold on world markets below home prices. Its purpose is not to establish any monopoly position, but to prevent the adverse effects of low current home prices on future supplies. Sporadic dumping provides some revenue to producers; spoilage would provide none. *Persistent dumping* describes a situation in which producers regularly have more market power (less severe competition) in home markets than abroad. Thus they always act more like monopolists at home and more like competitors abroad, with persistent and predictable price differentials in favor of their customers abroad. The motivation for persistent dumping is to try to remain in business, not to establish a monopoly position by driving competitors out of business.[22]

All dumping requires economically segregated markets, unlike those pictured in Figures 8.1 through 8.3, where Japanese and Ameri-

---

[22] The classic textbook example of a persistent dumper is a producer who has some market power both at home and abroad and who faces demand at home that is less price responsive (or elastic) than abroad. The theory of *price discrimination* demonstrates how this producer maximizes profits by always charging a lower price where the demand is most price responsive—by persistent dumping.

can prices either are identical or differ only by taxes. Without segregated markets, dumping would be economically impossible. Everyone could reap profits from buying the product where it was cheap and quickly reselling it where it was expensive.[23] Demand pressure would raise the low price, supply pressure would lower the high price, and equality (equilibrium) would eventually be reattained.

In the real world of international trade, transportation costs, exclusive marketing arrangements, and trade barriers themselves all segregate markets geographically. Dumping appears to be a familiar phenomenon. United States chemical producers appear to dump their products in European markets, and some European automakers appear to dump their passenger cars in the U.S. market. Other examples include U.S. agricultural surpluses and Japanese radios, televisions, and stereos.

It is very difficult to say in practice what kind of dumping these examples represent. To do so requires being able to read producers' minds. Lacking a means for distinguishing motivations, most governments consider all dumping to be *unfair competition*—at least when practiced by foreign producers. The international convention that oversees national trade policies, the General Agreement on Tariffs and Trade (the GATT; see Supplement 11B) sanctions import tariffs to combat dumping when it injures domestic producers. These are known as *antidumping duties*.[24] Like all import restrictions, they protect domestic producers, raising their sales, revenues, and profits.

From the perspective of domestic producers, of course, all dumping appears to be "unfair." It reduces their sales, revenues, and profits. Predatory dumping reduces them to zero. But domestic producers rarely admit publicly that *all* competition has such effects and therefore can be equally "unfair." No individual producer benefits from having competitors. He would be better off without them (he would be a monopolist), and if he can bring this about by indicting some competition in the public mind as "unfair," so much the better.

From the perspective of domestic consumers, only predatory dumping is undesirable (unfair). Persistent and sporadic dumping make them better off than otherwise, and antidumping duties to protect domestic producers only introduce a misdirection in consumer preferences, discouraging consumers by taxes from consuming inexpensive dumped goods.

Consideration of the consumer's perspective highlights several familiar points. Persistent and sporadic dumping may be problems for

---

[23] Economists call this riskless activity *arbitrage*. See Supplements 1A and 2A for other illustrations that apply, respectively, to financial assets and gold, instead of to commodities.

[24] Another kind of "unfair competition" that has economic consequences very much like dumping is explicit governmental subsidization of exports. The GATT in this case also sanctions special import tariffs on the offending country's goods, known as *countervailing duties*. See footnote 2 to Chapter 11.

domestic producers but not necessarily for the nation as a whole. Why should producer losses be deemed more important than consumer gains? And antidumping duties are not necessarily the best policy to solve even the predatory dumping problem, nor are protective import restrictions necessarily the best policy to solve the infant-industry problem. Both problems are concerned with the allocation of resources to production: under free trade, too few resources would be devoted to the infant industry and to the victims of predatory dumping. Neither problem involves consumer preferences directly. Yet import restrictions alter both production and consumption. Consumers are prevented from consuming as many infant-industry and dumped products as they would under free trade, and they are unambiguously less satisfied by their consumption.

It is not clear therefore that infant-industry protection and anti-dumping duties make a nation better off than it would be under free trade, even though they do successfully solve the two implied resource-allocation problems. What might make the nation even better off when predatory foreign producers threaten to establish a monopolistic domestic market position is free trade plus an effective *antitrust* (antimonopoly) policy, applied to all suppliers in domestic markets. This policy solves the infant-industry and dumping problems directly. In most developed countries its administrative costs are low, since antitrust machinery already exists. And it is certainly politically feasible. In countries that have no effective antitrust policies, a better solution might be to subsidize production by infants and potential victims of predatory dumping out of taxes levied on other production (but not consumption). This policy should be politically feasible, too: subsidizing producers who are victimized by "unfair foreign competition" has the ring of propriety, unlike subsidizing defense contractors and munitions makers for national security reasons.

In sum, infant industries and predatory dumping provide no sensible arguments against free trade unless more direct policies can be shown to be either administratively more costly (by a large enough amount) or else, in practical terms, infeasible.

THE GROWTH-TECHNOLOGY ARGUMENT AGAINST FREE TRADE. Free international trade is sometimes opposed if it concentrates a nation's resources in supposedly low-growth, low-technology industries. Usually these include traditional agriculture and most mining, services, and elementary fabrication and processing of raw materials. Government barriers to both imports and exports are favored in such countries because they encourage production in supposedly high-growth, high-technology industries—mechanized, cash-crop agriculture and manufacturing. Whatever economic losses trade restrictions impose by violating the rule of comparative advantage are assumed to be offset eventually by the nation's more rapid economic growth, as

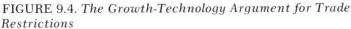

FIGURE 9.4. *The Growth-Technology Argument for Trade Restrictions*

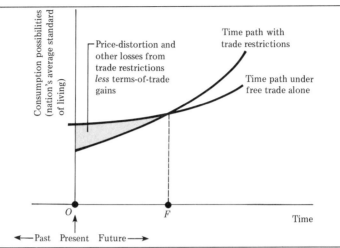

illustrated in Figure 9.4.[25] When a nation already has comparative advantage in high-growth, high-technology industries, the same considerations are often used to justify governmental export promotion.

The argument usually rests vaguely on the presence of positive externalities (see footnote 20) in manufacturing and sophisticated production. For example, manufacturing is thought to be more valuable to a nation than free markets (and free trade) simply because it generates a nonmarketable infrastructure that serves other producers and consumers as well as itself: transportation and communications networks and so on. Manufacturing is also thought to provide workers more efficiently than other industry with skills that are then transferable to other industry: operation of equipment, financial management, inventory control, personnel administration. Manufacturing, more than any other industry, is also believed to provide technological innovation with external benefits to the entire society. Furthermore, it is thought that manufacturing profits are plowed back into investment and expansion more typically than profits in less sophisticated

[25] Figure 9.4 does not establish any airtight case for a nation to prefer restricted trade to free trade. One reason not mentioned in the text is that the time interval from *O* to *F* may be exceptionally long. If it were, say, 100 years, the nation's present generation would prefer restricted to free trade only if their psychic gains from contemplating more prosperous grandchildren and future generations compensated them for the real, lifelong economic losses that they would have to suffer.

industries. All industries share together, however, in the prosperity that manufacturing investment and expansion generate. Finally, manufacturing occasionally may even generate psychic benefits for the nation as a whole, as in the case of less-developed countries that must have a steel mill for reasons of national prestige, or in the case of Canadians, who are willing to pay collectively to avoid the discomfort of being "hewers of wood and drawers of water" for the rest of the world.

These special external benefits are only sketched here because their existence is controversial and is not well documented empirically. A countercase can even be made that manufacturing creates external costs and lower growth: assembly-line techniques alienate workers, sour them on working anywhere, reduce their productivity permanently, and so on. If this contrary view is right, from a national perspective free markets and free trade may generate "too much" manufacturing: manufacturers are not sufficiently discouraged from their activity by these costs because they do not feel all of them directly. Some are external.

Whether and how the controversy is resolved is irrelevant to the case against free trade. That case rests on the encouragement of high-growth, high-technology production, whatever industry it may be found in, and discouragement of other production. International trade barriers can indeed create these incentives through their price-profit consequences. But do trade barriers accomplish this in the best way? Not necessarily. Trade barriers may be administratively costly and may misdirect consumer preferences. These consequences are undesirable by-products of solving the resource-allocation problem by trade restrictions. They may even "cost" more than solving the resource allocation problem is worth. For many countries, therefore, direct policies to stimulate growth and technological advance will dominate trade restrictions. This dominance is illustrated in Figure 9.5. These direct policies might involve production subsidies for manufacturing financed by taxes on less sophisticated industry. Or they might involve even more precisely targeted stimuli such as investment tax credits and long-lived patent rights for technological innovation. There is no reason to alter consumption. Nor is there any economic support here for government management of international trade, unless the most direct policies can be shown to be infeasible or sufficiently more costly to administer than trade restrictions.

THE DIVERSIFICATION ARGUMENT AGAINST FREE TRADE. The diversification case against free trade is closely related to the growth-technology case, and it shares some of the national security concerns about free trade. Free trade encourages specialization of production on products where a nation has comparative advantage. Yet many governments fear production specialization both for psychological reasons (pp. 248 and 255) and economic reasons:

FIGURE 9.5. *How Trade Restrictions May Be Second-Best Policies for Stimulating Growth and Technology*

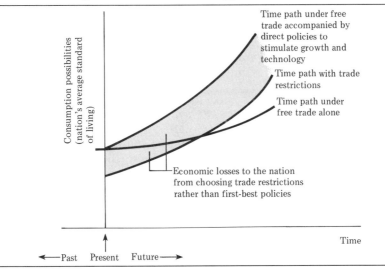

1. Specialization for some countries (especially less-developed countries; pp. 483–485) precludes production of allegedly high-growth, high-technology manufactures and processed foodstuffs.
2. Specialization for some countries necessarily implies producing primary products, whose terms of trade are alleged to decline continually over time (Supplement 8A), condemning such countries to enjoy smaller and smaller shares of the global gains from international trade.
3. Specialization of production for all countries may make for more unstable swings in their overall employment, inflation, exchange rates, and balances of payments. The overall economy mirrors faithfully the ups and downs of the few commodities on which production is concentrated. Diversification, by contrast, gives a country some assurance that hard times for producers of certain commodities will be counterbalanced by prosperity for producers of others. Thus the volatility of overall economic activity in a diversified economy will be milder than that of individual product markets.

The unreasonableness of arguing against free trade on these grounds alone should now be familiar. Specialization/diversification problems are production problems most directly solved by production taxes and subsidies along with other government incentives for resource allocation. Free trade coupled with such policies avoids the wasteful misdirection of consumer preferences caused by government management of trade and allows the nation to enjoy greater material prosperity from international trade. Only when government production-mix policy is sufficiently less feasible or sufficiently more costly to administer than trade policy is a government well advised on the grounds of national economic welfare to turn to the latter.

THE UNEMPLOYMENT AND REGIONAL-HARDSHIP ARGUMENTS AGAINST FREE TRADE. Closely aligned with arguments for trade restrictions based on their production effects are those based on their employment effects. If free trade could be shown to leave more of a nation's people involuntarily unemployed than otherwise, it might be opposed on the grounds that full employment is a collective national goal. (It is a national goal because some among us are willing to bear some economic burden to finance the operation of government unemployment agencies and other services that help others among us to find a job.)

There is a widespread belief that "international trade costs American workers their jobs." By implication, government import restrictions and export promotion can be defended on the grounds that they will promote employment. The beliefs are based on the fact that tariffs and export promotion discriminate in favor of domestic producers.

Yet there is a fallacy of composition in the argument. Even though there are more jobs in U.S. textile mills with import tariffs than under free trade, there is not necessarily more national employment. Nor is there necessarily more national employment if, owing to official U.S. government promotion of aircraft exports, more labor is devoted to producing aircraft. We have seen earlier that tariffs and export promotion draw resources away from domestic retailers, hospitals, home builders, and airlines and imply higher costs and possibly smaller production and employment in these industries. Their employment losses conceivably may be as large as the employment gains in textiles and in the aircraft industry. This becomes more likely as the economy operates closer to full employment and maximum utilization of resources. Under the latter conditions, national employment could easily be larger rather than smaller under free trade.

This possibility is arresting because it seems to defy common sense. The key to reconciliation is an important distinction that underlies all of Chapter 10. Common sense is based (correctly) on what a *change* in trade policy will do to national unemployment *temporarily*. The present chapter focuses, by contrast, on what the *existence* of trade restrictions implies for *permanent* national unemployment. Unilateral movements toward free trade, such as reductions in tariffs and export subsidies, almost certainly create more layoffs than new jobs in the short run, but in the long run, after people have adjusted to the new resource allocation, permanent unemployment could be either greater or smaller. This distinction is not meant to minimize short-run unemployment problems (see Chapter 10), but it should undercut any sweeping theoretical support for the proposition that the national unemployment problem is less severe with managed trade than under free trade. This proposition does find empirical support in many countries at different times, but it is not a logical inevitability.

In practice, free trade is sometimes accompanied by permanently higher unemployment when a country is characterized by *regional immobility* of resources. Regional resource immobility describes the unwillingness of workers and other resource owners to relocate outside their familiar surroundings, even if they are laid off or if their pay is far inferior where they are. Such people are not economically irrational. They simply assign a larger subjective value to security, certainty, and familiarity than to the other goods that extra income could buy.

Occasionally, production of import substitutes will be concentrated in such a region and will account for a large share of total regional production and employment. The former concentration of U.S. textile and shoe production in New England, together with the region's continued dependence on these industries, is a good case in point. If the United States were to adopt free trade in textiles and shoes, it is virtually certain that New England's excess capacity and unemployment would be permanently higher. This could well imply permanently higher national slack as well. Regional resource immobility would keep resources from leaving even in the long run. And New England factory towns would be even more depressed economically than at present.

In this instance, a case can be made that a nation should prefer restricted trade to free trade. Not only might national unemployment be more severe under free trade, but its severity would be regionally concentrated. The regional hardship implied by free trade frustrates a democratic government's commitment to equitable treatment for all citizens—a commitment that presumably reflects a social demand for "fair play" that cannot be expressed through the market.

But once again, the case against free trade made on these grounds is unreasonable and unacceptable when superior policies exist. In most modern developed countries, the national unemployment argument for trade restrictions is invalid because unemployment is dealt with directly by a wide range of policies and institutions, including monetary and fiscal policy, employment incentives, public job programs, and employment offices. Relying on these means for dealing with national unemployment problems, while simultaneously choosing free trade, is almost certainly less costly to the nation than the perpetuation of trade restrictions. Both consumer misdirection and misallocation of resources are thereby avoided.

Historically, however, effective policies for dealing with national unemployment have not always been available or administratively cheap. Because of their absence during the worldwide Great Depression of the 1930s, the case for trade restrictions on national employment grounds was slightly stronger then than it is today, but the case still is hardly strong in an absolute sense. When all countries are suffering severe unemployment problems simultaneously, discriminatory trade barriers imposed for national employment purposes practically guarantee foreign *retaliation*. Retaliation is usually "in kind." It consists, for example, of Japan's maintaining international trade barriers comparable to those of the United States, which tend to neutralize any favorable U.S. employment effects that U.S. trade barriers have. When Japanese retaliation is factored in, U.S. unemployment may be no smaller with trade barriers than under free trade. Although it is attractive in theory, therefore, government management of trade for employment purposes may not work at all in practice, even in a second-best way. Nevertheless, severe trade barriers justified on these grounds were adopted by almost all nations during the 1930s; they were described as a kind of *beggar-your-neighbor* policy.[26]

The regional-hardship case for government management of trade is less assailable than the national-employment case, because effective and inexpensive first-best policies for avoiding regional depression and promoting regional development are generally lacking. Efforts by the U.S. government to alleviate economic hardship in New England and Appalachia, and by the British government to promote Scottish economic development, have been costly and have enjoyed only limited success. Under these circumstances, well-defined trade restrictions, such as those that the United States imposes on textiles and shoes, may be the best available policies for alleviating regional hardship after all.

GOVERNMENT TRADE POLICY
TO DISCOURAGE CONSUMPTION

International trade restrictions are occasionally defended as a way

---

[26] Other beggar-your-neighbor policies are described in Chapter 6. Nations were not irrational during the 1930s; they were simply uncooperative, viewing themselves in competition with other nations for limited available world jobs. From their own narrowly nationalistic standpoint, their own employment would be higher if they adopted trade restrictions, regardless of what the rest of the world did. If the rest of the world avoided trade restrictions, the first country would gain at their expense. If the rest of the world adopted trade restrictions, the first country would avoid having them gain at its expense (as would have happened if it had refrained from trade restrictions). Trade restrictions were rational for each country individually, but not optimal. All could have done better (experienced higher employment) by agreeing cooperatively to refrain from trade restrictions. That individual national rationality can cause collective world irrationality (suboptimality) is an example of a classic problem in *game theory* known as the *prisoner's dilemma*.

of discouraging certain "socially undesirable" types of consumption. The best example is the exorbitantly high tariffs levied on imported luxury goods in many poor countries. The economic philosophy underlying these tariffs is that "the nation" (as represented by the government in power) would be better served if its rich citizenry saved more and consumed fewer luxuries. The extra saving could presumably be channeled into domestic investment and thereby into more rapid growth and a more desirable average standard of living. From the nation's point of view, free-market consumption of color televisions, automobiles, and other consumer durables is too high, and free-market savings are too low because individual savings have external benefits to the nation as a whole.

Import tariffs on luxury goods will successfully discourage consumption by generating higher market prices. But tariffs also have some unfortunate and unwanted by-products—chiefly that resources are misallocated toward producing luxury goods and away from producing other things. Color televisions and automobiles may not be precisely the luxuries produced. But lavish estates and domestic resorts are good substitutes that require less technical skill to produce. Saving by the rich may well be increased by import restrictions, but at the expense of production of necessities. It is not clear whether the nation is better off with too many luxury goods being consumed or with too many being produced. Import restrictions solve one problem and create another.

By now the argument should be familiar. Import tariffs are a second-best policy for discouraging consumption of luxuries. Better, if it is feasible and not more costly to administer, is a direct tax on consumption of luxuries. Undesirable by-products of import tariffs are avoided, and the same reduction in luxuries consumption can be achieved. Arguments defending import tariffs because of their desirable consumption effects are unreasonable. Free trade coupled with a luxuries consumption tax is better for this purpose than restricted trade.

GOVERNMENT TRADE POLICY TO IMPROVE THE BALANCE OF PAYMENTS

Import restriction and export promotion are sometimes defended on the ground that a nation's balance of payments is made more favorable than it would be under free trade. The prediction is generally valid unless other countries retaliate: when commodity imports are discouraged, and exports encouraged, the difference between exports and imports of all goods—the balance of payments—is made more positive. But the defense is not generally valid. Exchange rates dominate trade restrictions as a socially less costly way to alter the balance of payments. Balance-of-payments considerations do not justify trade restrictions any more than spiders in the bedroom justify burning down the house.

What makes trade restrictions a second-best balance-of-payments policy in practice is their nonuniformity. The tariffs we observe differ dramatically from product to product. On finished consumer goods they are often very high; on semimanufactured industrial inputs they are usually very low or nonexistent (see pp. 483–485). Export promotion also differs greatly across products. The result of nonuniformity is price distortions. Resources will tend to be misallocated toward those industries where import protection and export promotion are most pronounced. Consumers will be induced to overconsume products where import protection and export promotion are least pronounced. Unless there is some other valid national reason for these price distortions, they should be reckoned as undesirable side-effects of achieving a more favorable balance of payments through government management of trade. And there is no reason why a nation needs to put up with them. An altered exchange rate can have identical effects on the balance of payments without any of these side-effects.[27]

GOVERNMENT TRADE POLICY TO IMPROVE THE TERMS OF TRADE

Government management of international trade is sometimes defended as a useful way to improve a nation's terms of trade.[28] To illustrate how a U.S. tariff might do so, an implication of the textiles example must be highlighted: the "market" price of imported textiles *in* the United States is not the same as the "national" price of imported textiles *to* the United States. Up to this point, the only U.S. textile prices we have discussed have been market prices, those faced by individual U.S. producers and consumers: $100 per bale under a $20 tariff. But the United States as a nation does not really pay $100 for every bale of Japanese textiles; it pays only $80, exactly what the Japanese exporter charges. The other $20 that Sears and American consumers must hand over in the market is a payment to the U.S. government and thus indirectly a transfer back to themselves and to other Americans. Sears and American consumers are not really

[27] The discussion implicitly suggests that a uniform x percent tariff on all imports, whose revenues are used to finance a uniform x percent subsidy to all exports, would have the same consequences as an x percent devaluation of domestic currency (including impacts on the allocation of resources and direction of consumer preferences). Readers who have completed Part I of this book will want to evaluate this suggestion. Questions to consider are whether the alternative policies affect international trade in assets (financial claims) differently, and whether or not the value of commodity exports equals the value of commodity imports.

[28] Terms-of-trade improvement is less predictable when the government manages its trade through nontax policies such as import quotas and quantitative export restriction. For the reasons why, see pp. 378–379.

FIGURE 9.6. *The Burden of a $20 U.S. Import Tariff on Textiles*

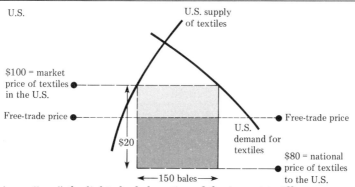

U.S.

U.S. supply of textiles

$100 = market price of textiles in the U.S.

Free-trade price

$20

Free-trade price

U.S. demand for textiles

$80 = national price of textiles to the U.S.

←—150 bales—→

Americans "pay" the light-shaded portion of the import tariff.
Japanese "pay" the dark-shaded portion of the import tariff.
The United States government collects both shaded areas ($3000).

paying $100 for imported textiles; they are paying $80 for textiles and $20 for their own government's services. This is evident in Table 9.1 and Figure 9.3.

The textile tariff in the United States does cause the market price of textiles to be higher than it would be under free trade, but Americans *collectively* pocket the tax that makes the textile price they face *individually* higher. The price of imported textiles to the nation as a whole is lower with an import tariff than under free trade. Privately, textile imports come more dearly; collectively, they come more cheaply. The U.S. terms of trade are more favorable because imports to the nation are less expensive.

This initially arresting conclusion can be buttressed in three ways. First, it accords with more informed intuition. With a U.S. tariff, the U.S. demand for Japanese textiles is discouraged. Japanese textile producers are faced with reduced demand and a smaller market, and will compete harder for the limited U.S. business. They will lower their price and improve their product and service.[29] The United States as a whole is the beneficiary.

Second, the conclusion can be supported graphically. Figure 9.6 is a modification of part of the U.S. side of Figure 9.3. The entire area of the shaded rectangle represents the revenue of the U.S. government from its import tariff — $3000 ($20 per bale times 150 bales). In a very real way the Japanese themselves pay a portion of these U.S. government taxes—the darkly shaded lower portion of the rectangle. They bear a part of the U.S. tax burden by being (reluctantly) willing to

[29] For a potential exception to this rule, consider the analog to footnote 2 of Supplement 9A.

accept a lower price for their textiles than they would under free trade. The pressures of supply and demand force them into this position. Only the remainder of the rectangle—the lightly shaded upper portion—is really paid by Americans to their government. That is just another way of concluding, as Figure 9.6 shows, that the U.S. market prices with a $20 tariff are not $20 higher than under free trade: they are less than $20 higher. Americans do not bear the full burden of their own import tariff, although they do claim all the revenues, so that the country as a whole benefits.

Third, the conclusion of the graphics can be summarized in a short equational statement:

$$
\begin{pmatrix}
\text{National} \\
\text{price of} \\
\text{imported} \\
\text{textiles} \\
\text{to the} \\
\text{United States}
\end{pmatrix}
=
\begin{pmatrix}
\text{Market} \\
\text{price of} \\
\text{imported} \\
\text{textiles} \\
\text{in the} \\
\text{United States}
\end{pmatrix}
-
\begin{pmatrix}
\text{United States} \\
\text{tariff} \\
\text{on} \\
\text{imported} \\
\text{textiles}
\end{pmatrix}
$$

Under free trade the equation would still hold, only the U.S. tariff would be zero; the United States would not discriminate against foreign producers. Market price would be lower and equal to national price, which would be higher.

In sum, U.S. import tariffs improve the U.S. terms of trade by reducing the nation's import prices. They create revenue for the U.S. government, and therefore for all Americans, by indirectly taxing foreigners.

Curiously, export taxes do the same thing, only by raising the nation's export prices. This is demonstrated in Supplement 9A.

The conclusion that a nation's terms of trade are more favorable under its own trade taxes than if it practiced free trade is not as strange as it may at first seem. In fact, it is a perfect illustration of the benefits to be derived from *market power*. The market power of a *monopolist* (a sole seller) is his ability to raise the price at which he sells by restricting supply. Similarly, a nation's monopolistic market power is its ability to raise its export prices by restricting supply through export taxation (see Supplement 9A). The market power of a *monopsonist* (a sole buyer) is his ability to lower the price at which he buys by restricting demand. Similarly, a nation's monopsonistic market power is its ability to lower the import prices it faces by restricting demand through import taxation.[30]

---

[30] In fact, just as there exists an *optimal* output and price combination for the monopolist, where his profits are maximized, there also exists an *optimal export tax* for a nation, where its consumption possibilities are maximized. Just as it does not profit the monopolist to restrict his output and raise his price beyond the optimal combination, neither does it benefit a country to raise its export taxes and improve its terms of trade beyond the optimal tax. The same holds with respect to import tariffs. There is an *optimal tariff* (defined for a given export tax), beyond which higher tariffs reduce a nation's consumption

These analogies help to make clear, however, why one should be wary of attaching too much practical significance to the terms-of-trade gain from a country's own trade restrictions. Very few real nations can be said to have significant market power as either sellers or buyers. As exceptions, South Africa dominates the world gold market as a seller, and Saudi Arabia, the world oil market. The United States weighs heavily as a buyer in world markets for a number of mineral products. Most other nations face competitive world markets for their exports and dominant world markets for the goods they import, which swamp their own small purchases. In practice, then, their government policy can have only imperceptible impacts on their terms of trade. Import tariffs, for example, will have only insignificant effects on world prices, since the nation's purchases are just a drop in the world's bucket.

These statements are usually summarized in international economics by the rule that *"small countries* cannot generally affect their own terms of trade." In market power most countries are "small." They are like perfect competitors in their export markets and like atomistic buyers in their import markets.[31]

A second aspect of trade restrictions that reduces the practical importance of their terms-of-trade benefits is that they also are beggar-your-neighbor policies: their benefits come at the expense of other countries. Japan's terms of trade are less favorable under U.S. tariffs and export taxes than under free trade. And if Japan suspects that U.S. trade restrictions are designed to improve American economic welfare by reducing Japanese, it will probably retaliate, thereby neutralizing any favorable terms-of-trade effects that U.S. barriers have. Once again, trade barriers for these purposes are alluring in theory, yet usually unsuccessful in practice.

Exceptions occur, of course. More favorable terms of trade, a major goal of OPEC's boost in oil prices (Chapter 8), were accomplished essentially through a gargantuan increase in export taxes.[32] OPEC collectively was hardly a "small country" in the world oil market, and the potential retaliation by oil-consuming countries that might have

---

possibilities, even though they continue to improve its terms of trade. More advanced textbooks in international economics illustrate the precise calculation of these optimal taxes.

[31] Figure 9.3 will illustrate these "small-country" conclusions if one country's supply and demand curves are shifted far to the right horizontally. That country will become large compared to the other. For the other (small) country, national prices and the terms of trade under tariffs and export taxes will differ very little from those under free trade. And in Figure 9.6, the large country will "pay" very little of the small country's trade taxes; most of their burden will be borne internally. For small countries, also, the optimal tariffs and export taxes described in the preceding footnote will be near zero.

[32] So it was also in the case of explicit taxes levied on the export of bauxite by Jamaica and other major producers during the mid-1970s. (Bauxite is the raw ore from which aluminum is made.)

discouraged further OPEC restrictiveness was never forthcoming.

It is curious that the $2-per-barrel tariff on imported oil that President Gerald Ford imposed and removed (under pressure) during 1975–1976 was an act of U.S. retaliation against OPEC. To judge from critical journalistic and congressional commentary at the time, the tariff made no sense. It seemed simply to aggravate and extend the economic losses that OPEC had already forced upon U.S. society, and that was indeed true with respect to higher market prices of oil products in the United States and their consequences. But the critical commentary gave insufficient emphasis to the crucial difference between an OPEC export tax and a U.S. import tariff. In the former case OPEC collects all the revenue and Americans are taxed to help pay it. In the latter the United States collects all the revenue and OPEC is taxed to help pay it. The effective national price of imported oil to the United States was *lower* with the temporary $2 tariff, not higher. And the U.S. terms of trade were made temporarily more favorable by the retaliation, yielding dollar benefits to the average American.[33]

Another instance in which the terms of trade play an important practical role in trade policy is discussed further in Chapter 14. Less-developed countries (LDCs) as a group have recently negotiated preferential treatment for exports of their products to developed countries. Preferential treatment consists of concessionary developed-country import tariffs that are lower for LDC suppliers than for other world suppliers. Less-developed countries welcome such discrimination in their favor partly because of the extra volume of business that their producers enjoy. But an equally important justification is that their collective LDC terms of trade are more favorable in the absence of import restrictions in the developed world. Preferential treatment is a form of development aid, therefore, that rests on the terms-of-trade impact of trade barriers.

GOVERNMENT TRADE POLICY FOR OTHER PURPOSES

THE REVENUE ARGUMENT AGAINST FREE TRADE. In many countries, import tariffs (and export taxes) are the primary source of government revenue. Free trade is inferior to restricted trade because the government's tax base would vanish and government services would have to be curtailed.

A glib retort to this defense comes readily. Are taxes on international trade the most direct way of raising government revenue? If not, the problem would be better solved by adopting free trade and the first-best tax collection method. There would be no valid revenue argument for trade restrictions; their undesirable consequences for resource allocation and consumer preferences could be avoided.

---

[33] OPEC's oil prices did not actually decrease during the tenure of the U.S. tariff. But a good case can be made that the removal of the U.S. tariff accelerated and aggravated their subsequent increases.

For many countries this retort is inappropriate. Taxes on international trade are so much cheaper to collect than direct taxes that they turn out to be justified on national welfare grounds. This is true, for example, in many less-developed countries whose internal systems of transportation, communication, law enforcement, and data collection are primitive. Effective collection of income taxes or sales taxes would be prohibitively costly. By comparison, collection of taxes on international trade is simple and effective. The border must be patrolled in any event, a Bureau of Customs would exist even if conventional taxes were collected, and most internationally traded goods enter or exit through only a few major ports or terminals. Therefore, only a few Customs Houses are necessary, staffed by people who serve simultaneously as customs officers and tax collectors, and surveillance forces need not be spread nationwide.

THE BARGAINING ARGUMENT AGAINST UNILATERAL FREE TRADE. If we could conclude that a nation would be economically better off by abandoning government management of trade, that conclusion would not necessarily support a case for it to adopt free trade unilaterally (by itself). Take the United States as an example. Even better than unilateral free trade might be a situation in which both the United States *and* other nations abandoned discrimination and adopted free trade together (multilaterally). There may be no hope that this will occur if the United States unilaterally abandons its own trade restrictions, but if the United States uses the prospect of its own lower restrictions to coax lower restrictions from the rest of the world, then current trade restrictions are justified economically. Presently high restrictions serve as a bargaining device for bringing about lower future restrictions on a multilateral basis. Given the realities of international negotiations on trade policy (see Chapter 11), they are probably even a first-best bargaining device. By comparison, unilateral free trade is better in the present but worse in the future.

This argument is analogous to the political case against unilateral disarmament. Once the United States has disarmed, it has no means of pressuring other nations to do so. They may even be less motivated, because good fortune has already satisfied one of the purposes of their own disarmament—namely, U.S. disarmament.

While both of these arguments are correct in principle, in practice they often result in only minor reductions in trade barriers or armaments. Each side jealously guards its bargaining power for future rounds. Thus the bargaining power of trade restrictions provides no airtight case for maintaining them. Markedly lower trade barriers that are brought about unilaterally may imply greater national welfare than minisculely lower trade barriers brought about multilaterally. Nor is the bargaining power of trade restrictions an acceptable ground for increasing barriers. Opponents are sure either to retaliate and neutralize the temporary bargaining advantage or to demand a return to the status quo before bargaining begins in earnest. As an example, it is unlikely that the U.S. imposition of a 10 percent import surcharge (extra tax) during the autumn of 1971 increased its bargaining power in bringing about exchange-rate alterations (see p. 204). An agreement to remove an arbitrarily imposed restriction is not seen by an opponent as a concession.

INCOME-DISTRIBUTIONAL ARGUMENTS AGAINST FREE TRADE. Free trade is sometimes opposed on national welfare grounds because certain socioeconomic groups will be worse off than under restricted trade. What legitimately makes this a *national* concern is a collective social commitment to the welfare of particular socioeconomic groups, such as the retired, the handicapped, and the poor.

As an example, restricted trade might be defended on these grounds if free trade could be shown to make the nation's rich richer and its poor poorer. Yet in principle such a defense is unreasonable. More direct means of altering income distribution exist: progressive taxation, the welfare system, and so on. If these devices could be employed without excessively large administrative costs, both rich and poor would be better off under free trade after all—free trade accompanied by redistribution to restore the previous income shares.

In practice, altering income-distributional policies is often politically inflammatory, and the administrative and economic costs of doing so can run high (see the last half of Chapter 10). In these circumstances, retaining trade restrictions, even with the welfare losses they create through price distortions, may be justified as a second-best but feasible way of avoiding socially unwelcome losses to particular groups and individuals.

LOOSELY REASONED ARGUMENTS FOR GOVERNMENT MANAGEMENT OF INTERNATIONAL TRADE

A number of arguments against free trade have substantial propagandistic appeal but very little economic content. We will examine two of the most frequently encountered.

THE "CHEAP FOREIGN LABOR" ARGUMENT AGAINST FREE TRADE. Free trade is sometimes opposed—for example, by organized labor in the United States—on the grounds that it allows unlimited access to the U.S. market for products produced by oppressed or low-wage foreign labor. Such competition is claimed to be "unfair" to domestic labor for a number of reasons. Foreign labor, especially in less-developed countries, may not be organized and may not benefit from union- or government-mandated labor law and safety standards. Thus foreign laborers may include underage children, may be forced to work twelve-hour days, may be demeaned by their employer, and may lose their own self-respect. If the products of such labor are sold freely in the U.S. market, competition indirectly pressures U.S. labor to sink to the same low standards—to retrogress to the sweatshops and other intolerable conditions (by today's standards) of the industrial revolution.

As a description of foreign labor conditions and their competitive impact on U.S. labor, this portrait has some validity. But as an explanation of why the United States as a whole would be economically better off under restricted trade, it is generally invalid. Competition in labor markets from "cheap foreign labor" is only as "unfair" as competition in product markets from foreign producers who persistently dump. Few individuals like to compete with others. All personal competition seems unfair. That this textbook has to compete with others is "unfair" to me: my royalties are lower. But that is not unfair to you. In fact, you gain. And the cheap-foreign-labor argument against free trade has the same weakness. Competitive domestic labor loses, but the rest of us gain more. There is nothing unique about the benefits from this kind of international trade. Unless as a nation we have some social commitment to the particular people competing with cheap foreign labor (are they extraordinarily poor, disadvantaged, or the like?), there are no economic grounds for opposing free trade. Even then, the grounds may be second-best.

Many people, however, see in this argument a moral aspect that dominates materialistic economic considerations. They believe it is simply not right to buy products from nations that allow intolerable social conditions. Moral reasoning along these lines supports world boycotts of Rhodesian chrome as well as U.S. boycotts of California lettuce not picked by the United Farm Workers. It cannot be dismissed summarily, but the economics of moral boycotts is awkward. First, there is a clear economic cost to those who take the moral stand (and is it moral to deprive ourselves?). More importantly, by discriminating against foreign producers, trade restrictions and boycotts also inflict losses on the very people who are oppressed: those who work for them. There are first-best ways to encourage morality, too, and restricting trade is probably not among them.

THE "TRADING WITH THE ENEMY" ARGUMENT AGAINST FREE TRADE. Free trade with an avowed enemy is often opposed on similar grounds. The United States, for example, still prohibits trade with some communist countries. Exports are illegal; imports are confiscated by U.S. Customs. The idea behind these prohibitions is that we do other countries a favor when we engage in international trade with them: we provide them either with our goods or with our markets. Since enemies by their very nature do not welcome such generosity, why should we extend it? And why extend one's enemies any favors anyway?

Where this argument misleads economically is in implying that international trade is solely a matter of generosity. On the contrary, as Chapter 8 illustrates, we do *ourselves* a favor, too, when we engage in international trade. There is no way of generally predicting whether the pain we inflict on our enemy by restricting trade is worth the pain we inflict on ourselves. (When is cutting off my nose worth spiting my face?) In circumstances involving national security, it will be worth it: prohibiting exports of up-to-date weaponry to enemies makes good economic and common sense. But in other circumstances, it will not be worth it: prohibiting U.S. wig makers from using hair of communist Chinese origin had doubtful economic and strategic value (yes, such a prohibition once existed).

Summary and a Look Ahead

Argument and counterargument in the last half of this chapter may have left the student's head swimming. Just where does the chapter stand on free trade? In one place it says that the practical case for free trade is not airtight; in another, that free trade can be presumed best until proven otherwise. But these two assertions are not really contradictory, and they do summarize the stand of this chapter.

But *stand* is too strong a word, connoting a principle rejected only by the self-serving and weak-willed. Free trade is not such a principle. The case for free trade is like situation ethics. What is appropriate under one set of circumstances is not necessarily appropriate under another. There is no universal, timeless answer to the question, Is free trade better than restricted trade? Unfortunately, protagonists in the controversy often imply that there is.

An important lesson from this chapter is that international trade restrictions are a way of achieving many national goals, but not always the *best* feasible way. When other policies can achieve these goals better, government-managed trade is then wasteful: it wastes time, effort, goods, and services. The nation would be better off to choose the best feasible policies and to allow free trade. The point may seem obvious, but this chapter has revealed how alluring the arguments for trade restrictions are that are based on doing something "good," something in the national interest. Trade restrictions *can* do this—they have predictable effects on domestic prices, production, and consumption, and also on exports, imports, and the terms of trade—but often they do not do it *best*. Good intentions coupled with costly trade policies can cause more ills than they cure. Free trade can be presumptively preferred until someone demonstrates infeasibilities, economic costs, or wastefulness of the alternative policies that are often superior to government trade management. Then government management of trade may be in the economic interest of the nation as a whole—but only then.

Evaluating free trade for a nation, or for that matter evaluating more restricted trade, is a complex task. Among the considerations are the effects of government management of trade on (1) the nation's terms of trade; (2) the nation's income distribution, and whether adverse impacts can be offset when they are socially undesirable; (3) the nation's allocation of resources, and whether and how much efficiency is promoted or retarded; (4) the nation's consumption possibilities, the degree to which consumer preferences are frustrated, and whether the frustration is imposed in pursuit of some social purpose that could be achieved by a better policy; (5) foreign nations, whether adverse impacts will prompt retaliation, and if so what the effects will be on the domestic terms of trade, income distribution, resource allocation, and consumption. Also (6) the administrative costs of trade restrictions and auxiliary or alternative policies must be taken into consideration, as must (7) their political feasibility.

It is no wonder that periodic international negotiations over trade policy themselves require remarkable resource commitments. The considerations above merely ask: Would our nation like freer trade, once we got there, better than the status quo? But at the heart of international trade negotiations lies a second question: Shall we go? The questions are different because movement itself "costs." Adjustment to a new situation uses resources that could have been producing something else. Dislocated resources are wasted resources. As Chapter 10 stresses, it is entirely possible for a country to answer the first question yes and the second, regretfully, no.

This chapter has examined the first question only: whether or not the state of the nation under free international trade is economically better than under trade that is influenced by government policy. Chapter 8 was also concerned with comparative states of the nation—whether or not complete insular self-sufficiency was better for the nation than engaging in international trade (whether free or restricted). In brief, the answers were that some international trade is almost certainly better than none but that the type generated by free trade is not necessarily best. An unfortunate aspect of even well-informed commentary on the free-trade controversy is that these two answers are seldom differentiated. Knowledgeable economists often defend *free* trade publicly and in textbooks with arguments appropriate to the demonstration that *some* trade is nationally beneficial. Since their answer does not apply to the question asked, their advice is often rejected as irrelevant by policymakers and participants in international trade.

A closing reminder: in these chapters and throughout this book, "better," "worse," and "best" always refer to *economic* welfare, which is only a part of what we mean familiarly by welfare or happiness; this choice of referent reflects the universal importance of material considerations in overall welfare. And *welfare* is always defined with respect either to the nation or to groups within it: the world perspective is almost never taken. These choices reflect the real nationalistic bias of all governments and the real egocentric inclination of most individuals. Had we taken a world perspective, the welfare economics of this chapter would be meaningless, or simply wrong. As one illustration, a world terms of trade or balance of payments cannot be defined. As another, one nation's textile tariffs generate higher national textile production but lower world textile production. Similarly, one nation's export promotion of aircraft generates higher world aircraft consumption but lower (or the same) national aircraft consumption. Trade restrictions that alter a nation's income distribution in one direction often alter the rest of the world's income distribution oppositely. Ultimately, the implication of adopting a world perspective is that the case for free trade in preference to government management of trade becomes very strong indeed.

Key Terms

tariffs
protection(ist)
first-best, second-best policies
infant industry
dumping: predatory, sporadic, persistent

unfair competition: antidumping duties, countervailing duties, "cheap foreign labor"
diversification
retaliation
beggar-your-neighbor policy

Key Concepts and Review

Government trade policy as economic discrimination and a barrier to competition.

The effects of trade and tariffs on prices, production, consumption, imports (exports), tax revenues, and the terms of trade (graphical and verbal analysis).

How free trade tends to establish a common world price.

Price-distortion losses, misallocation, misdirection, efficiency, and externalities.

Applications and implications of the Theory of the Second Best.

Fourteen (and more) arguments for government intervention in international trade: acceptable, conditionally acceptable, unacceptable.

Market price versus national price, monopoly/monopsony power, and optimal taxes.

Supplement 9A
Economic Consequences of Export Taxes

This supplement examines the economics of export taxes in the same way that import taxes (tariffs) were examined in the text. The analytical apparatus is readily applicable also to examinations of governmental export promotion and subsidization (mentioned above, and outlined in greater detail in Chapter 11).

Taxes on exports at first seem indefensible (popular and political wisdom being that exports should be encouraged) and therefore irrelevant. For Americans this feeling is strengthened by the absence of any U.S. export taxes; they are in fact unconstitutional (Article 1, Section 9, Clause 5). But from time to time even the United States has restricted exports by other means (for example, by temporary quantitative limitations on wheat, soybeans, and lumber exports during the 1970s) that generated virtually the same economic consequences as an export tax. The constitutional prohibition is thus subtly skirted. And other countries rely heavily on export taxes for a number of reasons. One of these, applicable to many less-developed countries, is that export taxes provide an administratively cheap way of collecting government revenue. (They can thus be justified in the same way as import tariffs for the same purpose.) A second justification—that export taxes imply more favorable terms of trade for a country that levies them—is in fact the chief basis for OPEC's quadrupling of its oil prices. That OPEC's oil-pricing policy was essentially an export tax we can see by defining export taxes more precisely.

An export tax is a discriminatory tax levied against foreign buyers and, therefore, in favor of domestic buyers. That residents of OPEC countries were not generally victimized by higher oil prices is illustrated by the huge disparity between gasoline-pump prices there and elsewhere. Export taxes are levied in exactly the same way as import tariffs. Exporters of commodities bearing export taxes must clear customs and pay the tax while doing so or else be subject to legal sanctions. Oil companies operating in OPEC countries must, in essence, write a check to OPEC governments to obtain permission to remove oil for export. The companies pass part of these taxes on to oil consumers, who implicitly pay the companies not only for the oil but also for OPEC export taxes.

Export taxes, like import tariffs, drive a wedge between the price paid by a buyer and the price received by a seller in any transaction. The ultimate buyer of OPEC oil faces a price that includes OPEC's taxes; the oil company that sells the oil ultimately receives a payment that does not. OPEC governments pocket the difference. The result is the simultaneous existence of two prices. The high tax-inclusive price of oil prevails throughout the world outside OPEC; the low tax-exclusive price prevails in OPEC countries.

FIGURE 9A.1. *Aircraft Markets under Free International Trade and with a $5000 U.S. Export Tax*

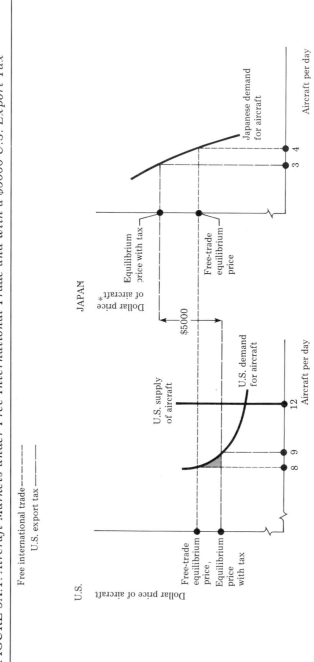

Free international trade — — —
U.S. export tax ————

* Japanese aircraft demand almost certainly depends on the yen price of aircraft, not the dollar price. But see the note to Figure 9.1 in the text.

The consequences of an export tax are illustrated in Figure 9A.1, which is similar to Figure 9.3 in the text. With one important exception, the two figures are mirror images of the consequences of import tariffs. Instead of dealing with OPEC oil taxes, Figure 9A.1 describes a hypothetical U.S. export tax of $5000 per aircraft. In addition, Figure 9A.1 describes a situation in which U.S. aircraft are unique: Japan cannot produce a competitive product, perhaps because it simply does not have the requisite technology (see Chapter 12). Finally, the U.S. aircraft supply curve in Figure 9A.1 shows no responsiveness to price, as it might not if the United States aircraft industry were not highly competitive. These special features are incorporated into Figure 9A.1 to reinforce an important point: predictions made in this chapter about the consequences of restricted trade for production and consumption are quite robust. Most of them continue to hold even in the presence of product differentiation (production of unique commodities in each country) and uncompetitive market structure.[1]

Given the $5000 U.S. export tax, international trade brings about an equilibrium in which (1) Japanese import demand for aircraft—in this case their total demand—matches the U.S. export supply, and in which (2) the average U.S. price of an aircraft is $5000 lower than the average Japanese price. The equilibrium in this case is assured by the forces of price-responsive demand alone (supply is fixed). By comparison with the free-trade situation:

1. United States aircraft prices are lower, although not by the full amount of the export tax.
2. United States aircraft production is the same (12 aircraft per day), but would have been lower given any normal price responsiveness of supply.
3. United States aircraft consumption is higher. Under free trade it is eight aircraft; with the export tax, nine.
4. United States aircraft exports to Japan are lower. Free-trade exports are four aircraft per day; restricted-trade exports are three.

Export taxes and other export restrictions have opposite effects to import taxes and restrictions, as the list above and Figure 9A.1 indicate. Barriers to the export of aircraft in the United States make aircraft producers worse off than they would be under free trade. But domestic consumers and producers of all other goods are likely to be better off, unless the economy is operating well below full capacity. Aircraft producers are worse off because the foreign part of their business is taxed or impeded. In Figure 9A.1 aircraft sales are not any

[1] For a challenging exercise, the student might assume, alternatively to the vertical supply curve, that the U.S. aircraft producer is a profit-maximizing monopolist. Export taxes can (but will not necessarily) have the familiar consequences, even in this case. When they do, Figure 9A.1 can then be a useful simplification of the world oil market. Replace "U.S." with "OPEC," "Japan" with "non-OPEC countries," and "aircraft" with "oil."

lower, but aircraft prices, and therefore profits, are. Aircraft producers reduce prices as they attempt to substitute new domestic business for lost foreign business.[2] To the extent that this happens, U.S. consumers of aircraft services (airline passengers), and U.S. industries that use aircraft or aircraft services in their day-to-day business are economically better off than under free trade. Their consumption will be stimulated. Other U.S. industries will also be better off regardless of what happens to aircraft prices if the smaller size of the aircraft industry reduces any tightness of labor or credit markets.

Therein lies an occasional defense of export barriers. They can in principle alleviate inflation and domestic shortages, but they do so only temporarily, unless they are applied with increasing severity (and export barriers can become no more severe than prohibition, called an *export embargo*). Furthermore, they almost invariably invite foreign retaliation and hence fail in practice to alleviate inflation and shortages. Even when they succeed, they are often unreasonable, inferior, second-best policies to more direct ways of solving the inflation and shortage problems.

When there is little inflation, substantial unemployment, and excess capacity in an economy, however, barriers to export sales may cause the aircraft industry to contract, contrary to the vertical supply behavior depicted in Figure 9A.1. The additional layoffs and idling of plants and equipment might subsequently cause contraction of aggregate economic activity. And this could counteract the normally favorable impacts of export barriers on consumers of aircraft services and other industries.

Finally, although it is not immediately obvious from Figure 9A.1, a fifth and rather strange consequence may be added to the list:

5. The U.S. terms of trade are more favorable with the export tax than under free trade. Both U.S. import tariffs and U.S. export taxes alter the U.S. terms of trade in the same direction, but they have opposite effects on prices, production, consumption, and trade.

To illustrate the terms-of-trade consequences of an export tax, it is helpful to return to the $5000 U.S. export tax on aircraft illustrated in Figure 9A.1. The market price received by private U.S. aircraft producers is lower as a result. But collective U.S. national receipts per aircraft exported are not lower. These receipts include not only the aircraft producer's revenue, but also the revenue that the U.S. government earns on every aircraft exported. In the presence of the U.S. export tax, national revenue from exporting exceeds market revenue from exporting. Americans *collectively* pocket the tax that causes aircraft income they earn *individually* to be lower.

[2] On the other hand, there is a chance that reduced business will lead aircraft producers to charge higher prices, especially if the aircraft industry is subject to gains from large-scale production (increasing returns to scale). This could be illustrated in Figure 9A.1 by a negatively sloped supply curve.

FIGURE 9A.2. *The Burden of a $5000 U.S. Export Tax on Aircraft*

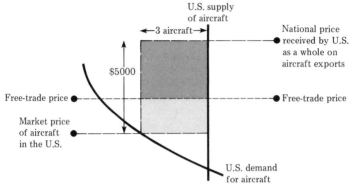

Americans "pay" the light-shaded portion of the export tax.
Japanese "pay" the dark-shaded portion of the export tax.
The United States government collects both shaded areas ($15,000).

United States export taxes improve the U.S. terms of trade because they raise foreign market prices. The pressures of supply and demand force foreign buyers to bid a higher price for U.S. aircraft than under free trade. To close the sale, not only must they pay the U.S. producer for the basic aircraft, but they must in part reimburse the producer for paying the U.S. export tax. Once again, Americans and Japanese share the burden of the U.S. tax. Their shares are illustrated by the light and dark rectangles in Figure 9A.2, which is analogous to Figure 9.6 in the text. The phenomenon is also summarized in the following equation:

$$\begin{pmatrix} \text{National} \\ \text{price of} \\ \text{aircraft} \\ \text{exported} \\ \text{from the} \\ \text{United States} \end{pmatrix} = \begin{pmatrix} \text{Market} \\ \text{price of} \\ \text{exported} \\ \text{aircraft} \\ \text{in the} \\ \text{United States} \end{pmatrix} + \begin{pmatrix} \text{United States} \\ \text{tax on} \\ \text{exported} \\ \text{aircraft} \end{pmatrix}$$

Under free trade, market price would be higher and equal to national price, which would be lower.

In sum, hypothetical U.S. export taxes improve the nation's terms of trade by raising its export prices. They also create revenue for the U.S. government, and therefore for all Americans, by indirectly taxing foreigners.

Chapter 10

Why We Trade:
The Ambiguous Case for
Freer Trade

It should not be surprising sometimes to find simultaneous political consensus on both of the following propositions. (1) Our nation would enjoy a higher average standard of living if we were engaging in less government management of international trade. (2) It is nevertheless not in the national interest to tamper with our existing trade policy. What appear to be contradictory positions are in fact fully consistent. The first is a position evaluating *states of being*. The second is a position evaluating *movement* between them. Real decisions on whether or not to change international trade policy require both evaluations. So do many other economic decisions.

On the hottest, muggiest weekend of the summer, for example, most families agree that it would be nicer to be high in the mountains relaxing on the porch of a lakeside cabin than to be sweltering at home running weekend errands. But that doesn't imply that they agree to go. Going imposes costs that may far outweigh the pleasure they derive from the lakeside cabin. Going requires fighting traffic on the hottest weekend of the year, a burden that falls especially harshly on the driver. It also requires time to pack and unpack, a burden that falls especially on whoever is responsible. So it is not at all strange that being at the cabin is better than being at home, but going to the cabin is worse than staying at home.

Chapter 9 was concerned with being—specifically, how to value national economic welfare under free trade and under government-managed trade.[1] This chapter is concerned with moving—specifically, how to value costs of *trade liberalization*. Trade liberalization is movement toward the state of freer trade and away from government management.

[1] Chapter 9 (as well as Chapter 8) was an exercise that economists describe as *comparative statics*—that is, comparing states. *Statics* unfortunately connotes dormancy or moribundity. A more accurate word would be "state-ics."

Trade liberalization imposes two important costs of movement on a society. The first—*dislocation cost*—is the goods sacrificed from any temporary unemployment of labor and other resources that trade liberalization causes. Such unemployment can stem from the rigidity of many prices and contracts over short periods of time. The second—*adjustment cost*—is the goods sacrificed to retrain labor, retool machines, refurbish factories, and relocate all inputs that trade liberalization causes to move from industry to industry. This cost stems from the need to divert some resources from productive activity to adapting the inputs being transferred. Taken together, dislocation and adjustment costs can in some circumstances outweigh the benefits from trade liberalization that have been stressed in previous chapters.

A third potential cost of trade liberalization involves the income distribution. It arises from the markedly uneven pattern of temporary gains and losses that sometimes results from movements toward freer trade. Some persons in a society experience substantially reduced incomes and other distress, but whether this is a *national* problem, and therefore whether there is a real distributional cost to trade liberalization, is debatable. It matters first who is injured, as we saw on p. 283, and second how much other people gain from the same changes that impose the burdens on some. It is not always clear how to compare the gains of one segment of society with the losses of another.

Notice that evaluating the national economic costs of movement has a much broader application than just to international trade liberalization. Such costs are imposed on society and individuals by virtually every kind of economic shock and flux, including technological advancement, population growth, wartime resource mobilization, and even movements *away* from trade liberalization (toward protectionism).

Wage-Price Rigidities and Dislocation from Trade Liberalization

DOWNWARD INFLEXIBILITY OF PRICES AND SHORT-RUN DISPLACEMENT

Dislocation describes both the temporary additions to national unemployment that trade liberalization can cause and the temporary idling of productive plant and equipment. Dislocation is always due to the fact that many wages and prices are downwardly rigid over short periods—in the short run.

Short-run downward inflexibility of prices in the economy is well documented. Producers are reluctant to lower prices in the face of reduced volume or increased competition; many of their costs (wages, rents, interest) are contractually determined and cannot be similarly reduced. Their reluctance is understandable. Cutting price in such circumstances, while trying to maintain production, cuts directly into profits. Producers in competitive markets must cut price anyway, despite their reluctance, or else lose all business. But producers with market power can often translate their reluctance temporarily into rigid prices. They will maintain profits better by cutting production instead of prices. The inability to cut wages, rents, and interest rates leads producers instead to cut employment, office space, and borrowing. Workers are laid off, assembly lines are idled, and whole plants are shut down. Labor, land, and machines all become involuntarily unemployed.

Unemployed labor and underutilized plant and equipment are made temporarily unproductive. The national economic cost of their temporary nonproductivity is measured by the value of the goods that could have been produced, but were not. (And there are also subjective and psychic costs to the unemployed that might unfavorably affect their future productivity.)

The same reason that has idled workers, plant, and equipment keeps them that way: wages and prices are not immediately flexible downward. If they were, then laid-off workers, for example, could become immediately reemployed by simply bidding down wages until employers elsewhere found it profitable to rehire them. In fact, their initial employer might never have fired them in the first place if they had been willing and able to accept a sufficient cut in pay. But when wages are contractually determined, this is impossible.

Over longer periods, many temporarily rigid prices and wages become flexible. Contracts must be renewed. Producers pass along some of the burden of bad business to their own employees and suppliers through harder bargaining in labor negotiations, lease renewals, and loan applications. Their success at doing so makes them more willing to lower their own prices, or else to raise them less readily than others do (profits don't suffer as much). Unemployed labor exerts indirect downward pressure on contract-renewal wage demands. Those already employed recognize that widespread unemployment makes them less likely to find another job if their wage demands lead to more layoffs. Generally poor demand for rental property and loans makes landlords and lenders willing to bargain on rates. And substantial overcapacity makes stockholders eventually willing to forego dividends.

Nevertheless, even short-run rigidity of wages and prices is relevant to trade liberalization. In its presence, moving toward freer trade can sometimes (not always) cause extra unemployment and excess capacity. The goods foregone as a result must all be reckoned as short-run national economic costs of trade liberalization. As a useful shorthand below, we will describe these extra costs as *dislocation costs*.

FIGURE 10.1. *The Impact of Extreme Downward Wage-Price Rigidity on Production Conditions*

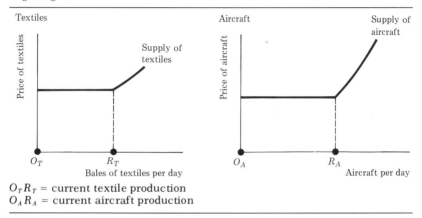

$O_T R_T$ = current textile production
$O_A R_A$ = current aircraft production

SHORT-RUN SUPPLY AND PRODUCTION POSSIBILITIES CURVES

Dislocation costs can be fatal to the economic-welfare case for trade liberalization. They can provide an economic justification for a nation's retention of its barriers to international trade, even when freer trade would *be* better for it in the long run. The long-run benefits are not worth the short-run costs.[2]

One way in which these conclusions can be illustrated is by tracing the impact of dislocation costs on the curves that we have employed in the previous two chapters. Figure 10.1 illustrates U.S. supply curves for the most extreme downward rigidity of prices imaginable. It depicts a situation in which all prices are contractually determined and no price (or wage) can ever fall. Supply curves are horizontal to the left of the point indicating current production. Declines in the demand for textiles and aircraft below $O_T R_T$ and $O_A R_A$ would call forth no compensating declines in price on the part of suppliers.

In practice, downward rigidity of wages and prices is never that pronounced even in the very short run. Some prices can always be bargained down (for example, those of certain farm products, raw materials, and loans). And all prices become less and less rigid as time passes. The less extreme implications for supply curves—and production possibilities curves, too—are illustrated in Figure 10.2. The sup-

---

[2] Downward rigidity of wages and prices is in fact a price distortion, similar to the others discussed in Chapter 9. And this section is just an extended illustration of one of the implications of the Theory of the Second Best, discussed in Chapter 9: removing one price distortion (trade restrictions) while maintaining another (price rigidity) is not necessarily nationally beneficial.

FIGURE 10.2. *The Impact of Moderate Downward Wage-Price Rigidity on Production Conditions*

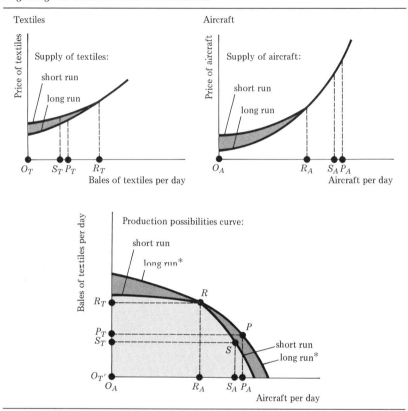

* See footnote 3.

ply curves illustrate how inward shifts in demand generate smaller impacts on price in the short run than in the long run, reflecting producers' inability to alter their costs and unwillingness to alter their asking price. They also illustrate corresponding larger impacts on output in the short run than in the long. The production possibilities curves reflect this same thing.[3] Shaded gaps between the short- and long-run curves reflect the costs of temporary unemployment and unused productive capacity that can accompany any move from pro-

---

[3] The long-run production possibilities curve is slightly bowed in at the ends for reasons that are discussed on pp. 255, 404–405, and in footnote 8 below. Most of these reasons also underlie the assumed positive slope of long-run supply curves. None of the results of this chapter is altered qualitatively by the degree of curvature of the long-run production possibilities curve.

duction point R to P. The textiles industry must contract. Contraction with wage-price rigidities leads to layoffs and shutdowns. If the expanding aircraft industry cannot *immediately* absorb the dislocated resources, the result will be temporarily unproductive labor and resources. The goods thereby foregone are measured exactly by the shaded gaps.

The lesson of Figure 10.2 is simple. With short-run wage-price rigidity, moving from R to P usually imposes dislocation costs on an economy. Because of unemployed resources, it must spend time temporarily at production points such as S inside the long-run production possibilities curve.

Short-run dislocation costs can exist even in the presence of permanent unemployment and unutilized capacity. Forcing the textile industry to contract will cause additional layoffs and shutdowns unless the aircraft industry is expanding rapidly. The ranks of the unemployed will be temporarily swelled, so that even more goods are sacrificed. Thus dislocation costs still exist even if R and P are themselves within the long-run production possibilities curve. But the costs may be smaller than under conditions of generally full employment, because wages and prices may be less inflexible.

SHORT-RUN DISLOCATION COSTS AND THE
GAINS FROM TRADE LIBERALIZATION

The short-run production possibilities curve can be employed to show how short-run dislocation costs of trade liberalization may sometimes dominate its long-run benefits.

Figure 10.3, an enlarged portion of Figure 8.4, can be used to illustrate the long-run benefits. Point R represents the U.S. textiles-aircraft production point under government-managed trade. Point D represents the corresponding U.S. consumption point.[4] The United States consumes more textiles than it produces (by an amount equal to its imports, TD) and produces more aircraft than it consumes (by an amount equal to its exports, TR). The triangle DTR is thus the U.S. trade triangle (see p. 259) under government-managed trade. Similarly, points P and C represent U.S. production and consumption points under more liberalized trade (because of, say, lower tariffs on imported textiles). By contrast, at point Q, trade barriers are so heavy that no trade takes place, and U.S. production and consumption points are identically Q. Figure 10.3 also reflects some information from Chapter 9: production, consumption, exports, imports, and the terms of trade are all altered by changes in trade restrictions in the

---

[4] It differs in its location slightly from D_{US} in Figure 8.4, which was a possible or potential consumption point. D in Figure 10.3 is assumed to be the actual consumption point chosen (from among all the potential ones) by U.S. buyers on the basis of their tastes, income distribution, and other factors (see pp. 250, 258–259).

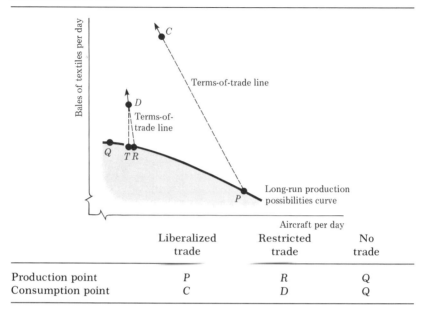

FIGURE 10.3. *Production and Consumption under Restricted and Liberalized Trade*

	Liberalized trade	Restricted trade	No trade
Production point	P	R	Q
Consumption point	C	D	Q

directions predicted there. Most important for this chapter is the observation that increased tariffs misallocate resources toward producing textiles in the United States and away from producing aircraft (and other nonimportables). Trade liberalization reverses this misallocation.

Figure 10.3 has been drawn to represent a situation in which the United States would *be* better off with freer trade. Point C is a superior consumption point to D because it allows more of both textiles and aircraft to be consumed. But that doesn't necessarily imply that the United States should *move* toward more liberalized trade. By lowering its tariffs and liberalizing trade, the United States will promote resource reallocation toward aircraft and away from textiles[5] and will

---

[5] Recall that export promotion and subsidization was also an aspect of government trade management in Chapter 9. It misallocates production resources in the opposite direction—toward exportables and away from import-substitutes. Hence trade liberalization that encompassed removal of both tariffs and export promotion could have any or no effect on resource allocation. Since tariffs and import restrictions usually dominate export promotion in practice, however, the direction of resource reallocation suggested in the text is most likely. And most of the points raised in this chapter apply anyway, regardless of the direction in which resources are shifted when countries move toward freer trade.

FIGURE 10.4. *A Possible Production Adjustment Path from U.S. Trade Liberalization: $RS_1 S_2 P$*

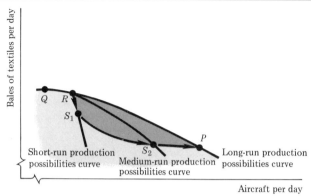

S_1 = production point one unit of time after trade liberalization
S_2 = production point two units of time after trade liberalization

eventually reach production point P and consumption point C. To reach them, however, it may have to travel through production points S_1 and S_2 illustrated in Figure 10.4. S_1 lies on a short-run production possibilities curve that reflects the dislocation costs outlined in previous sections. S_2 lies on a "medium-run" production possibilities curve that accounts for the gradual decline in dislocation costs over time as the aircraft industry absorbs unemployed resources and as wages and prices become less rigidly linked to their initial values. Other short-run production points lie all along the production adjustment path $RS_1 S_2 P$.

Trade liberalization that generates a production adjustment path such as $RS_1 S_2 P$ is problematical. The problem is that dislocation costs are so high that national consumption can actually decline temporarily. Consumption points can fall below point D in the very short run, as illustrated in Figure 10.5. $DE_1 E_2 C$ is a possible consumption adjustment path that corresponds to $RS_1 S_2 P$ under extremely rapid terms-of-trade adjustment.[6] All points along it that are southwest of D are inferior to it: they allow less consumption of both textiles and aircraft.

Figure 10.5 implies that in order to make itself better off in the distant future by liberalizing international trade, the United States has to make itself worse off in the near future. Contrary to polemics on both sides of the issue, there is no simple way to determine whether

[6] $DE_1 E_2 C$ is drawn on the assumption that the terms of trade decline immediately on trade liberalization. Consumption paths other than $DE_1 E_2 C$ would be consistent with gradual deterioration of the terms of trade or with slow adjustment of demand decisions to a new set of prices.

FIGURE 10.5. *The Consumption Adjustment Path from U.S. Trade Liberalization in Figure 10.4.: DE₁ E₂ C*

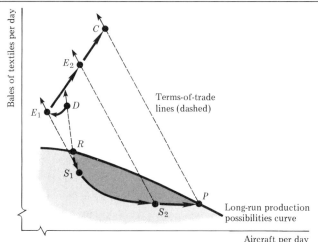

(S_1, E_1) = (production, consumption) point one unit of time after trade liberalization

(S_2, E_2) = (production, consumption) point two units of time after trade liberalization

the permanent (but distant) benefits of liberalized trade are worth the temporary (but immediate) dislocation burden. Indefinite maintenance of the status quo at consumption point D may be superior to liberalizing trade, or it may be inferior. In order to decide, we must make some judgment on quantitative magnitudes. Are the national gains from being in a state of liberalized trade large or small? Are the dislocation costs heavy or light? Do they decline quickly, or do they endure? Should future gains and losses be discounted?

In practice, these questions are impossible to answer with quantitative precision. Yet they are crucial for legislators and policymakers, who determine government trade policy. A graphic way to pose them is illustrated in Figure 10.6 (which recalls Figures 9.4 and 9.5). Is standard-of-living C a significant improvement over D? Is standard-of-living E_1 a comparatively small deterioration from D? Is there only a short period of dislocation during which the country is worse off having liberalized trade (is one-and-a-half time periods small)? For each question, if the answer is yes, the eventual gains from removing trade barriers will be large relative to the transitional losses. Maintaining existing international trade barriers would more likely be an economically harmful policy for the nation as a whole.

FIGURE 10.6. *Another View of the Consumption Adjustment Path from Figures 10.4 and 10.5*

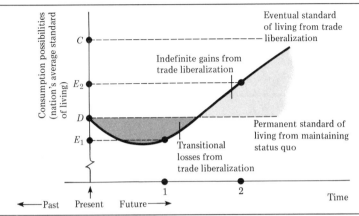

If *time preference* did not exist, then Figures 10.5 and 10.6 would be easy to assess, and the trade-liberalization questions would be easy to answer. The eventual gains from trade liberalization last indefinitely and must therefore eventually dominate short-run dislocation costs. (The lightly shaded area in Figure 10.6 must be larger than the darkly shaded area when all future time is considered.) But time preference almost certainly exists. It describes the natural tendency for everyone to prefer receiving a dollar today to receiving a dollar tomorrow. That is, people *discount* future gains and losses compared to present gains and losses.[7] If the gains from trade liberalization are concentrated on great-grandchildren and generations beyond, but the costs are concentrated now, present generations will almost certainly reject it. And they will be economically justified as long as the hypothetical votes of future generations are agreed to carry less weight than those of living generations. Whether such discounting is morally justified is a difficult question (which economists usually skirt). It touches a large number of important issues besides the liberalization of international trade, including environmental policy, population control, and the exhaustion of finite natural resources.

Evaluating the case for trade liberalization is not always this difficult. In particular, precise knowledge about discounting of the future and the length of the dislocation period will be unnecessary if the terms of trade change gradually and if dislocation is mild. Mild dislocation describes minor temporary displacement of workers, machines, and land as a result of movement toward freer trade. Such

---

[7] The percentage rate at which they reduce the subjective value of future gains (or cost of losses) is sometimes called a *discount rate.*

Wage-Price Rigidities and Dislocation from Trade Liberalization 327

FIGURE 10.7. *Production and Consumption Paths under Mild*
Dislocation

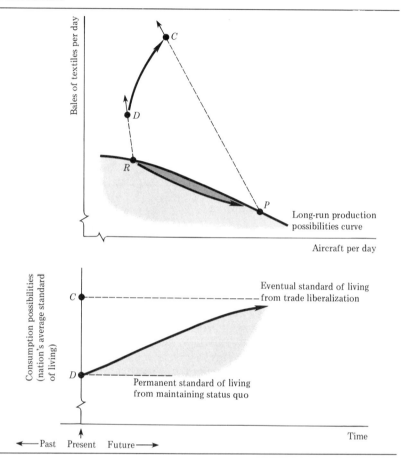

a case is illustrated in Figure 10.7. Dislocation costs there are never large enough to outweigh the benefits from liberalizing international trade, even in the very short run. From the standpoint of the economy as a whole, neither long-lived dislocation nor a pronounced preference for the present can alter the conclusion that trade liberalization is in the national economic interest.

Costs of movement toward freer trade are made smaller by a number of characteristics. We will illustrate below how governments design trade liberalization in the real world specifically to minimize dislocation: the process is gradualist, multilateral, and reversible. Dislocation is reduced naturally by broadly trained, flexible, mobile labor and by versatile, adaptable, movable machines, buildings, and other resources. Dislocation is also reduced by pressures in other industries to expand; resources may actually be hired away from a potentially contracting industry before they are laid off.

Most important, however, in minimizing dislocation costs from trade liberalization is operation of an economy at close to overall full employment. Dislocation in one industry is then likely to be offset by expansion in other industries. In fact, since almost all governments have commitments to full employment, extreme proponents of freer trade often refuse to accept dislocation costs as an objection to their position under any circumstances. Even government failure to honor its commitment does not phase them. Their retort is, "Why tar international trade liberalization with a brush that should be swiping at faulty full-employment policy?" Their position recalls the Theory of the Second Best. Dislocation will never take place if trade liberalization is combined with a direct, efficient, and effective first-best policy for maintaining full employment.

As we saw in Chapter 9, however, full-employment policies are not always effective, especially in the short run. Temporary unemployment may be more accurately called permanent, and so dislocation costs should not be glibly dismissed. Furthermore, even if national measures of full employment (for example, 96 percent of the labor force) are maintained, the identity of those who remain unemployed (4 percent) will not be the same. They will probably be represented in greater numbers than before by those who were dislocated from the U.S. textiles industry and from import-substitute industries in general. Their personal problems are not fully solved by the government's policy toward the economy as a whole. On balance, they are still losers from trade liberalization. Whether this makes their personal problem a national problem is a difficult question in economic philosophy (should the government compensate losers?). It occupies the last part of this chapter. If the answer is yes, then national dislocation costs from trade liberalization still exist, even when nationwide full employment is maintained.

Industry-Specific Resources and Adjustment to Trade Liberalization

Another important national economic cost of trade liberalization is the cost of transferring resources from one industry to another. These adjustment costs are important not only in their own right but also because they aggravate any dislocation that occurs, tending to make it less mild and more enduring.

Even if resources could be moved quickly without dislocation from industry to industry, they cannot usually be moved costlessly. The most important reason is the *industry-specific* character of many resources. Both labor skills and resource productivity are in some measure specific to an industry. They have been built up by practice and experience and cannot be transferred to another industry. For example, a teacher's exam-grading skills would have little usefulness if he or she were to become a corporate executive. Nor does the fertilization history of farmland matter much to the developer of an industrial park. More importantly, a worker's initial productivity in a new job—say, the teacher's as a corporate executive—will be lower than his or her eventual productivity. Certain skills that are helpful can only be acquired through experience in the job, an example of what economists (and everyone else) call *learning by doing*. Other corporate executive's skills will have to be taught directly. Similarly, both land and machines will be temporarily less productive if they must be modified in specific ways to shift them from one industry to another.

Furthermore, other resources may be diverted from what they otherwise could have produced in order to retrain the worker and modify machines and land. In the short run, both they and the transferred resources produce fewer final goods. Finally, geographic shifts may be required to move resources from one industry to another, so that other resources must be temporarily devoted to transportation and reorganization, not to ongoing provision of goods.

The implication of industry-specific resources for trade liberalization (tariff removal) is that moving resources from import-substitute industries to others requires time, temporary sacrifices of productivity, and temporary diversion of other resources into retraining, retooling, refurbishing, and relocating those that are moved. Productivity losses forced by adjustment mirror those forced by dislocation. And the consequent goods that the society forgoes must be similarly counted as a short-run cost of trade liberalization (or of any resource reallocation). We will describe these temporary reallocation costs as *adjustment costs*.

Adjustment problems stemming from industry-specific resources have both indirect and direct effects on trade liberalization. Indirectly they lengthen dislocation when it occurs, thereby raising short-run dislocation costs. Corporations will be reluctant to hire laid-off college professors until they have acquired some business-specific skills (say, by obtaining an M.B.A.). Expanding industries may let former farmland lie unused until it is made suitable for development.

But adjustment also has direct costs as well, even in the absence of dislocation. These can be analyzed with production and consumption adjustment paths such as those illustrating mild dislocation in Figure 10.7.[8] The darkly shaded areas represent goods sacrificed either to dislocation or to adjustment. Resources that have just moved from textiles to aircraft are temporarily less productive, as are the veteran aircraft resources who are diverted from normal production to train, modify, and move those transferred. These direct impacts of adjustment costs diminish any nation's gains from trade liberalization.[9]

Finally, it should be noted that adjustment costs of trade liberalization exist even when there is a large pool of permanently unemployed resources to draw on, although the costs are smaller. Industries still find it more difficult and costly to expand output in the short run than in the long run. Laid-off workers who are recalled require some time to return to full productivity, and both time and resources must be devoted to restarting machines that have been shut down and reopening plants that have been closed.

[8] It is a useful exercise to show that temporarily industry-specific resources imply short-run supply curves that contrast with those illustrated in Figures 10.1 and 10.2. Extreme specificity implies vertical (not horizontal) supply curves: the skills and productivity of resources in one industry are totally worthless to the other. Moderate specificity implies short-run supply curves that are steeper to the right of production points R_T and R_A (not flatter to the left of them). Expansion beyond current output is more expensive and difficult in the short run than in the long run, reflecting the adjustment costs of adding new resources from other industries. It is also useful to show that industry-specific resources imply short-run production possibilities curves that are indistinguishable from those implied by downward wage-price rigidity—even though the supply curves differ. (In fact, resources that are permanently industry specific, even in the long run, are one reason why production possibilities curves are usually drawn with an outward bow.)

[9] More advanced treatments of international economics prove that the direct impacts of adjustment can never completely eliminate the gains from trade liberalization, as can the sharp dislocation costs illustrated in Figures 10.5 and 10.6. A partial explanation for this difference starts from the observation that wage-price rigidities distort prices and price signals (see Chapter 9), whereas industry-specific resources do not. Dislocated resources are sealed off involuntarily from voting on wages and prices in the market (I am not allowed to keep my job by accepting a lower wage). The result of involuntary unemployment can be inimical to all (witness economic depression). Adjustment, by contrast, involves no involuntary action. If the costs of transferring resources from textiles to aircraft production are so high that they outweigh the gains from doing so, then no one will do it. Textile workers will not be forced to accept training that is worth less than it costs. And aircraft producers will have no interest in retraining textile labor or retooling textile machines. Unless the discounted gains of moving along a production path such as RS_1S_2P in Figure 10.5 outweigh the short-run costs, there will be no voluntary incentive to do so, and the economy will remain producing at R, despite trade liberalization. National economic welfare would increase, even though the economy remained producing at R, to the extent that eliminating the misdirection in consumer preferences dominated the terms-of-trade deterioration.

Adjustment, Dislocation, and Gradual, Multilateral, and Reversible Trade Liberalization

Both adjustment and dislocation help to explain three important characteristics of trade liberalization:

1. It is gradual. Trade barriers are usually removed only in small increments over time, and not all at once.
2. It is multilateral. It is usually carried out simultaneously by several countries through international negotiations.
3. It is reversible. All countries reserve the right to slow down or to abandon trade liberalization, if the adjustment or dislocation that it generates is too severe.

GRADUALISM

Gradualism in trade liberalization has two prominent features. First, it is piecemeal. None of the recurrent negotiations on trade barriers (see Chapter 11) has ever attempted to plan the total removal of all government trade policy. Indeed, enabling legislation in the United States usually prohibits international negotiators from bargaining the total removal of any U.S. trade barrier unless it is insignificant already. Second, it is phased. All modern international agreements to liberalize trade have been implemented through bit-by-bit reductions in trade barriers. For example, when the Benelux countries, France, Germany, and Italy formed the European Community (Common Market) in 1958, they agreed to remove almost all trade barriers among themselves. But the reductions took place in stages, as illustrated in Table 10.1. Full removal was achieved finally in 1968.

Dislocation costs provide an explanation and defense of gradualism in international trade liberalization. Sufficiently gradual liberalization can guarantee the mild adjustment paths of Figure 10.7 and avoid the dilemma of sharp dislocation—the necessity to sacrifice in the present to gain in the future. Also avoided, therefore, is the uncertain evaluation of whether trade liberalization is in the national interest. The same ultimate reduction in trade barriers can be clearly beneficial to a nation if carried out gradually, but possibly harmful if carried out abruptly.

These conclusions are illustrated in Figure 10.8. Both the g (gradual) paths and the a (abrupt) paths lead ultimately to the same state of freer trade. Yet the gradual paths never require any absolute standard-of-living sacrifice during the adjustment period. If time preference is prominent and if adjustment is long (suppose that the subscripted number 2 denotes two decades), current generations are almost sure to value area I much more highly than area II (which is discounted severely). Area I represents the relative benefits of gradualness over abruptness.

TABLE 10.1. *Gradual Removal of Tariffs on Industrial Goods among the Original Six Members of the European Community*[a]

Year	Proportion of each 1958 tariff remaining at end of year
1959	0.90
1960	0.80
1961	0.70
1962	0.50
1963	0.40
1964	0.40
1965	0.30
1966	0.20
1967	0.15
1968	0.00[b]

[a] Industrial tariffs of the newest three members, Britain, Ireland, and Denmark, were removed gradually over the five years from 1973 to 1978.

[b] Complete removal took place in July of 1968. Several times during the process of removal, reductions were accelerated. (Why?) Complete removal had been originally planned for January of 1970.

Source: European Economic Community Commission, *First General Report on the Activities of the Communities*, 1967, p. 34.

Area II, conversely, represents the hypothetical benefits of abruptness over gradualness. In principle, such benefits might exist because abrupt liberalization takes less time than gradual, as Figure 10.8 reflects. The number subscripts on production and consumption points suggest that abrupt liberalization takes at most only three-fourths as long as gradual liberalization.

Dislocation is the principal explanation of both the relative pattern and relative speed of gradual and abrupt adjustment. When reductions in trade barriers are phased in incrementally, dislocation need not take place at all. United States textile producers may be able to avoid layoffs and the idling of productive plant and equipment by simply not replacing workers who retire or quit voluntarily, or machines and plants that depreciate to the point where they have no productive value.

On the other hand, when foreign competition is allowed to increase only slightly and gradually over time, textile producers may be lulled into passivity. In the short run, they may refuse to make the hard decisions to contract through attrition. They may also be discouraged from contracting gradually by the hope that foreign competition will decline in the future, either because of a reversal of trade liberaliza-

FIGURE 10.8. *Production and Consumption Paths under Gradual and Abrupt Trade Liberalization*

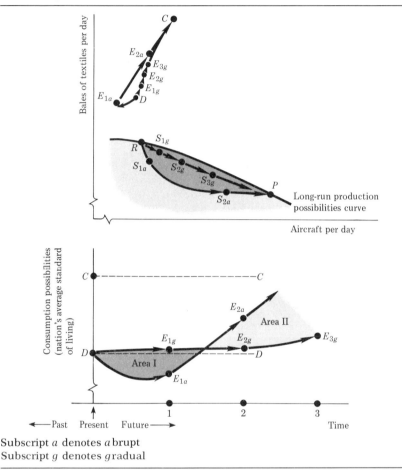

Subscript a denotes $a$brupt
Subscript g denotes $g$radual

tion or because of unforeseen events. Eventually they may be forced into the same contraction and dislocation that immediate and abrupt liberalization would have generated.

Figure 10.8 illustrates this by providing no necessarily conclusive grounds for a nation to prefer periodic, phased trade liberalization. If time preference were weak, and the subscripted number 2 denoted only two years, not two decades, current generations might conceivably value area II more highly than area I. The earlier arrival of the full benefits from freer trade could more than compensate a nation for its transitory losses when standards of living sank initially below D.

Similar caution must be applied in evaluating the case for gradualism based on adjustment costs. Gradualism might appear appealing because it spreads direct adjustment costs into the heavily discounted future. Future adjustment is perceived to cost less because of time preference. In essence, the costs of retraining, retooling, refurbishing, and relocating are shared by future generations. This seems equitable, since they also share in the permanent gains from trade liberalization. One flaw in the argument, however, is that gradualism also defers the benefits from trade liberalization. Furthermore, because gradual adjustment is leisurely, it may also be less efficient (it may require more resources per worker retrained, for example); adjustment incentives are less pronounced. For either reason, earlier and more rapid receipt of the rewards from trade liberalization may be worth more than the leisurely bearing of its adjustment burden.

The hypothetical economic superiority of abrupt trade liberalization clearly conflicts with the revealed preference of modern governments for gradualism. The conflict may suggest that time preference and the speed and efficiency of adjustment do make gradualist approaches generally superior in reality.[10] But conclusive evaluations depend on circumstances. There is no sweeping answer to the question of whether sharp, short pangs are preferable to dull, enduring pains.

MULTILATERALISM

Almost all modern trade liberalization is carried out cooperatively. Only rarely do nations act unilaterally: Germany reduced trade barriers unilaterally in the 1950s; the United States unilaterally removed its long-standing quotas on imported oil during the early 1970s; some developing countries have unilaterally liberalized as a part of general economic and structural reform. Dislocation and adjustment costs provide an important reason for these regularities.

Under multilateral trade liberalization, resource reallocation signals are strong. Adjustment consequently is rapid and efficient, and dislocation short-lived. To illustrate why, consider a likely case in which the United States reduces discrimination against Japanese textile producers at the same time as the Japanese reduce discrimination against U.S. aircraft producers. The first action discourages U.S. textile production at the same time as the second encourages U.S. aircraft production. American aircraft producers have a direct and

[10] It may also suggest irrationality on the part of governments, concern for special interests rather than the entire nation's economic well-being, or political and social considerations that override the economist's calculus, such as the need to be reelected in the short run.

unmistakable incentive to hire and train new labor, to draw in other resources necessary for expansion, and to do so quickly and efficiently so as to capture the new Japanese market demand that trade liberalization has generated. At least some of the labor and resources absorbed into aircraft expansion will come directly from the contracting textiles industry. Other labor and resources will be drawn out of involuntary unemployment, in some cases caused directly by dislocation in the textiles industry.

By contrast, a unilateral liberalization through reduced U.S. import barriers might not be as beneficial as the multilateral. In the short run, its resource reallocation signals are considerably weaker. The stimulus for the U.S. textiles industry to contract will be at least as strong, but the stimulus for the U.S. aircraft industry to expand will be much more indirect. It will arise principally from lower wages and other costs brought about by hard times in the textiles industry. These occur as dislocated textiles workers seek employment in the aircraft industry, as do even the labor, management, and creditors who continue to be employed in the textiles industry. They will be motivated to explore opportunities in aircraft because of the bleak outlook for textiles wages and profits. The initiative for their movement rests almost solely on their shoulders. The aircraft industry responds to their overtures, possibly employing and retraining the most mobile and adaptable, but doing little more.

As a result, adjustment will likely be slower and more haphazard, and dislocation more pronounced and more enduring, under unilateral than under (even equivalently beneficial) multilateral trade liberalization. Only effective, immediately responsive government full-employment policy would shrink the costs of unilateral trade liberalization toward those of multilateral. The case for moving toward freer trade cooperatively is clear.[11]

[11] A second, indirect reason for multilateral trade liberalization relates to the terms of trade. Unilateral liberalization causes them to deteriorate. Multilateral liberalization weakens (and perhaps erases) the terms-of-trade penalty of unilateral liberalization. This in turn reduces dislocation and adjustment costs. A rigorous demonstration is implicit in Figure 10.5. Temporary declines in the nation's standard of living below point D are less likely if the U.S. terms of trade remain approximately equal to the slope of DR. They remain so when liberalization is multilateral, but they deteriorate when it is not (as illustrated by the flatter slopes of S_1E_1, S_2E_2, and PC in Figure 10.5).

Still another reason for multilateral trade liberalization is that it can usually provide more of a good thing than unilateral. Having the United States and Japan reduce barriers simultaneously often means in practice having more liberalization overall than could have been attained unilaterally, and therefore having higher national consumption possibilities: more favorable C's in Figures 10.5 through 10.8. The bargaining argument against free trade in Chapter 9 outlines one reason why. In the imagery of this chapter, multilateral trade liberalization provides a more significant prize (state of being) than unilateral, and thus may make active participation (movement) more worthwhile.

FIGURE 10.9. *Consumption Paths When Safeguard or Escape Clauses Are Invoked*

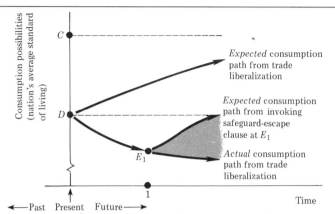

Shaded area represents expected benefits from invoking safeguard or escape clause.

REVERSIBILITY

Dislocation costs are a primary reason for the tentative and reversible character of all voluntary movements toward freer trade.

Reversibility of trade liberalization is captured in legal *safeguard clauses* and *escape clauses,* on which all countries insist. Both allow a nation to restore trade barriers that were previously reduced in multilateral negotiations if substantial unforeseen dislocation occurs — a process referred to as "seeking relief" from trade liberalization. Restoring trade barriers that were previously bargained away does not, of course, please a nation's trading partners. Compensation is generally expected. Such compensation usually entails either reducing some other trade barrier (chosen for its presumably lower or nonexistent dislocation costs) or allowing the injured trading partners to retaliate (which could cause dislocation in domestic export industries). Recourse to safeguard and escape clauses depends on resource-allocation considerations, too. Governments are more prone to invoke them when dislocation takes place in industries where governments feel that too little production is taking place anyway.

Unforeseen dislocation costs do establish a case for reversibility. If a nation expects mild dislocation and adjustment from moving toward freer trade but is confronted with severe dislocation and adjustment instead, it may be preferable for that country to cut its losses and return to its former trade policy. Such an instance is illustrated in Figure 10.9.

Evaluating the desirability of invoking safeguard or escape clauses is as difficult as evaluating trade liberalization in the first place. Withdrawing from agreed trade liberalization midway through the adjustment period has the potential for imposing new dislocation and adjustment costs. Resources are signaled to move out of textiles into aircraft and then they are called back again. Some of the same resources might be dislocated and adjusted twice in the process—once from textiles and once from aircraft. Governments that were unable to foresee the severity of dislocation and adjustment from moving toward freer trade may be equally unable to foresee its severity from moving back again. Uncertainty is especially prevalent when foreign countries retaliate. And finally, seeking safeguard or escape-clause relief should always be compared to possible alternatives. Direct policies to deal with dislocation may dominate reversibility on first-best, second-best grounds. Thus the case for making trade liberalization reversible, while valid under certain circumstances, is awkward at best.

Distribution, Compensation, and National Welfare

THE PROBLEM OF IDENTIFYING "NATIONAL" ECONOMIC WELFARE

Besides complicating the national-welfare evaluation of trade liberalization, short-run adjustment and dislocation highlight a fundamental definitional problem that has been only hinted at.[12] How can "national" economic welfare be measured? Indeed, how can it even be conceived in principle? Does an assertion like "Freer trade would be good for the nation" have any more operational content than slogans such as "Power to the people" or "We need government that serves the national interest, not special lobbies"?

Adjustment and dislocation highlight these problems because they generate a well-identified set of dramatic losers from trade liberalization. These losers lose real income and consumption possibilities from the need to change jobs as well as from temporary unemployment. In light of the fact that moving toward freer trade doesn't make everyone in a society better off, how can anyone conclude unambiguously that trade liberalization is nationally beneficial—even when the gainers gain much more than the losers lose? Is a large gain always more significant than a little loss, even when the gainer is a wealthy landlord and the loser is his elderly, widowed, incapacitated tenant?

Until now, we have implicitly said yes. In fact, all welfare analysis

---

[12] For example, see pp. 283, 299, and 308.

that is based on national aggregates—for example, national consumption points like *C*, *D*, and *E* in this chapter's diagrams—implicitly says yes, too. Extreme materialists will not find this approach at all dubious. They are willing to assert that human satisfaction can be accurately measured by quantities of goods consumed. A transfer of goods from one person to another makes the second happier to the same degree that it displeases the first. Most people reject this crass theory of human happiness. But even they would be able to accept the welfare economics of this and preceding chapters if every trade policy that increased a society's claim on goods and services were accompanied by a change in its income-distribution policy that compensated all losers. Everyone would then be made better off—as is indeed possible, since the society's collective claim on goods and services rises.

In the absence of *compensation* for losers, any reference to national economic welfare is tenuous and a matter of opinion. Adjustment and dislocation provide a graphic illustration. Suppose that trade liberalization increased consumption possibilities for 99 out of every 100 persons by 2 percent. For the hundredth person, however, it led to temporary dislocation that reduced consumption possibilities to zero (or to the basket of goods that unemployment compensation will buy). In the aggregate, as a lump, the society's average standard of living would rise even in the very short run.[13] Adjustment would be of the mild variety depicted in Figure 10.7. Previously we claimed that such trade liberalization was unambiguously beneficial for the nation. But is it so unambiguous? A small minority of society is made desperately worse off; a large majority is made somewhat better off. In rejecting extreme materialism, we must accept the possibility that the moderately increased satisfaction of the many is insignificant compared to the dramatic unhappiness of the few.[14] The uneven distributional impact of such trade liberalization may violate many people's sense of equity. It is reasonable to insist that policies undertaken in the name of the whole society should not burden any one part of it excessively. In a nutshell, that is the philosophical case for compensa-

[13] This statement might not be true when those dislocated had standards of living that were well above average. If, by contrast, their standards of living were average, then society's average standard of living would rise by almost 1 percent. (If the average standard of living were 100 to start with, the new standard of living under liberalized trade would start at 100.98—(0.99 × 102) + (0.01 × 0)—in the very short run.)

[14] Early economists believed that satisfaction was measurable (*cardinal utility*) and that the additions to satisfaction provided by an extra unit of consumption declined as consumption increased (diminishing marginal utility of income or consumption). That is, they believed that the rich are more careless with their money than the poor. These assumptions could easily imply that the additional satisfaction (utility) that trade liberalization provides to the 99 winners is outweighed by the lost satisfaction (utility) imposed on the loser.

tion.[15] Compensation is the most direct solution to the distributional costs imposed by any change in national policy.

Compensation in this example requires taxing away some of the gains from the 99 percent and redistributing them to the 1 percent, in order to make everyone in the society better off. Since the gains to the gainers are quantitatively larger than the losses to the losers, the goal is technically feasible. The vote for liberalized trade with compensation should consequently be unanimous. And trade liberalization could be said unambiguously to be in the national interest.

TRADE ADJUSTMENT ASSISTANCE

In many developed countries, formal compensation does exist for the short-term losers from trade liberalization. It is known as *trade adjustment assistance*. Such compensation usually provides both dislocation and adjustment aid. Among adjustment aspects of the compensation are worker retraining programs, payment of moving costs associated with shifting to a new job, and subsidized technical advice to firms that are forced by trade liberalization to contract. All these actions reduce the extent to which the resource owners themselves "unfairly" bear the adjustment costs of retraining and retooling. The burden of dislocation is similarly diffused by income-support programs for displaced workers (similar and, in some countries, additional to unemployment compensation) and by low-interest loans to firms whose owners have suffered losses as utilization of their plant and equipment fell off. Trade adjustment assistance programs are usually financed out of general government revenues. The gainers from trade liberalization are, of course, among those taxed to compensate the losers. United States trade adjustment assistance programs are described in greater detail in Supplement 10A.

At first thought, trade adjustment assistance might seem to seal our now familiar approach to trade liberalization. The steps seem straightforward. (1) Determine whether freer trade would *be* a preferable state for the nation. If so, then (2) determine whether the benefits from being in the state of freer trade outweigh the dislocation and adjustment costs of *getting* there. If so, then (3) eliminate any distributional costs by implementing an adjustment assistance program that spreads transitory dislocation and adjustment costs equitably across society. The outcome would seem to be improved individual welfare for everyone and thus for the society as a whole.

It is unfortunate that the problem cannot be resolved so simply.

---

[15] The philosophical case rests also on the belief that policies undertaken in the name of the whole society should have widespread and not concentrated benefits. Trade liberalization would not seem to be in any acceptably defined national interest if it quadrupled the consumption possibilities of 1 percent of the population and reduced those of the remainder by 2 percent—unless compensation were provided.

Trade adjustment assistance does not satisfy all the compensation needs that arise from trade liberalization. Furthermore, because of implementation problems, it has done little historically to equalize the burden of short-run dislocation and adjustment. Finally, a philosophical case can be made *against* trade adjustment assistance and other types of compensation. All of these points resurrect the awkward problem of defining and measuring national economic welfare. The practical failings of trade adjustment assistance are discussed in Supplement 10A. Its coverage and philosophical underpinnings are discussed in the next two sections.

TRADE ADJUSTMENT ASSISTANCE AS INSUFFICIENT COMPENSATION

Trade adjustment assistance represents compensation only during the short-run adjustment period to freer trade. Ignored are a set of permanent, long-run losers from freer trade. Textile producers in the United States, for example, are not only temporarily but permanently worse off from trade liberalization (pp. 280–281). Or with regional resource immobility, citizens in certain regions may also be perpetual losers from freer trade (p. 299). Or the rich may be permanently better off and the poor worse off, or vice versa. Or as shown in Chapter 13, owners of property and resources may ultimately gain from trade liberalization at the expense of labor, or they may lose. It is inescapable that trade liberalization without compensation causes pervasive gains and losses in the long run as well as the short.

One inference that might be drawn from these observations is that both permanent and temporary losers from trade liberalization should be compensated. Trade adjustment assistance is insufficient; what is also needed is "trade compensation assistance." Only then can a society be sure that there are no losers from trade liberalization and, consequently, no national distributional costs.

In fact, for both philosophical and practical reasons, no country attempts to compensate *all* losers from trade liberalization. As a result, the question of defining national economic welfare returns. How is the United States to resolve whether free trade in textiles is in the national interest? Poor, immobile, New England textile workers may be permanently deprived of a large fraction of their accustomed standard of living even if they remain employed. Rich, mobile, textile firm owners may lose less by shifting their investments to the American South or to Taiwan. Other Americans may collectively gain several times as much as these losses from lower market prices for clothes, rugs, drapes, towels, bedding, and upholstery. How can different people's gains and losses be compared to arrive at some statement about the national economic welfare? It is not clear that a numerical majority should determine the national interest, nor that the dollars constituting gains and losses should either.

While national politicians (and sometimes even economists) solve such problems to their own satisfaction in practice, there can be no objective guidelines for doing so. One source becomes apparent for the notorious disagreement among equally intelligent men on whether trade liberalization is socially desirable or disastrous. Some weigh severe losses for the few more heavily in national welfare than others. Some, feeling that poor New England textile workers are already victims of an ungenerous society, will recommend foregoing large gains to avoid victimizing them further. Others disagree, feeling that poor New England textile workers have largely victimized themselves by their unwillingness to move when all the signals prompted them to. (Trade liberalization is rarely a surprise.) No such thing as a correct position can be found on these matters of opinion, interpretation, and subjective judgment. When distributional costs from trade liberalization exist, they exist in hearts and minds, not on paper.

TRADE ADJUSTMENT ASSISTANCE AS EXCESSIVE COMPENSATION

Distributional concerns may appear to be compelling. But compensation is controversial. A case can be made that attention to compensation and attempts to define national economic welfare are irrelevant. In this view, the absence of compensation should not affect the approach to trade liberalization taken in this chapter or the previous two. At least four arguments can be marshaled in support. Each will be presented positively, with the task of developing criticism and counterargument left largely to the reader.

THE POTENTIAL COMPENSATION ARGUMENT. In any society where citizens have access to the government,[16] it is acceptable to make judgments about national welfare even when only the *potential* for compensation exists. Compensation need not be carried out in every circumstance.

This argument views government as responsive to competitive pressures from its citizenry. If removing U.S. trade barriers to textile imports really does cause textile workers such grievous harm that it should outweigh all the gains to others in the society, these workers will be willing to go to great lengths to convince the government. The intensity of their lobbying compared to that of the gainers will enable governments to weigh gains versus losses. When loser lobbying is relatively heavy, trade liberalization may be abandoned. When loser lobbying is only moderate, some special relief may be found to compensate them. When loser lobbying is relatively light, compensation

---

[16] Democratic government obviously features access in principle. But so do kingdoms where the king entertains petitions, communist governments where anyone may join the communist party, and dictatorships where there are representative counsels of advisors.

is probably not worth its administrative cost. Trade liberalization should be recommended in any event, and the lobbyists should be turned loose.

Advocates of this position view the government essentially as a marketplace, with citizens bidding against each other for its favors. The more subjectively valuable a favor is to a group of citizens, the higher the price they are willing to pay for it by devoting resources formally and informally to lobbying and political pressure. If textile workers do not succeed in extracting compensation for their losses from trade liberalization, those are simply the breaks of the marketplace.[17]

Rigid, automatic compensation schemes are undesirable in such a view because they will usually be either too generous (when demands for compensation are weak) or too niggardly (when the case for compensation is particularly well taken). Maintaining only the potential for compensation through normal government operations is desirable because it allows flexible compensation. (Potential compensation does not necessarily imply no compensation.)

THE RESOURCE-COST ARGUMENT. Thoroughgoing compensation is a Pandora's Box that imposes substantial unforeseen resource costs on a society. The problem with advocating compensation for the losers from trade liberalization is that logically one must then advocate it for the losers from every government action. All such losers are victimized by an action that supposedly is taken by representatives of the whole society.[18] There seem to be no grounds for excluding any loser. Firms that are forced by government environmental standards to cease polluting should be compensated for their clean-up costs. Millionaires who presently pay no taxes should be compensated when the government closes their loopholes. If the protest is raised that such firms and individuals were profiting unfairly at the expense of others in the society, why shouldn't the same indictment be made of textile workers and producers who profited from trade barriers? (See the historical inequity argument below.)

The prospect of thoroughgoing, economywide compensation for the losses imposed by any government action is frightening. Everyone has been hurt at one time or another by government action. To determine the approximate value of that injury is a horrendous exercise, requiring extensive investigation and, in many cases, litigation. Investigation and litigation require resources (economists and lawyers,

---

[17] This is approximately the view taken by a small group of economists who have devised a so-called economic theory of democracy. One objection to it is that the wealthy have more votes than the poor, because "voting" is carried out in large part by lobbying. The objection is not shared, of course, by people who feel that their superior wealth reflects their superior effort.

[18] Such losers differ from those who suffer from actions taken individually in the private market—bankrupt firms and their workers, unsuccessful prospectors and gamblers, and the like.

especially). These resources are devoted to transferring goods from citizen to citizen, not to producing them. While some resource-transfer resources are necessary and are socially beneficial to any society organized around codified law, thoroughgoing compensation would inevitably lead to too many. The result would be a decline in real national resource productivity, as suing-for-injury drew more and more resources, and a shrinkage of the production and consumption possibilities available to society as a whole.

THE INCENTIVE-COST ARGUMENT. Thoroughgoing compensation is undesirable because it dampens individual incentives to do what is ultimately in society's interest. It is important in this view that no one should be compensated for short-run adjustment or dislocation costs. Thus this argument is focused particularly against trade adjustment assistance.

Suppose that the losses imposed by trade liberalization on textile workers and producers were fully compensated. Little monetary incentive would remain for them ever to explore opportunities in other industries; they would have nothing to lose from staying where they were. Adjustment to the freer-trade allocation of resources would take longer with compensation than without. If slower (lower) adjustment paths with compensation were sketched into Figures 10.6, 10.7, and 10.8, the area between the two paths would represent a real cost to society: the incentive cost of compensation. For many countries, this cost might be large enough to dominate the assumed social benefit of compensation, and for some it might even make trade liberalization disadvantageous. Instead of facilitating freer trade, compensation might actually frustrate it.

In other words, thoroughgoing compensation dampens the private incentive to obtain socially useful information. It reduces the private reward for predicting accurately when trade liberalization will take place, what it will do to business, and how to plan production-employment decisions appropriately in advance. Reduced incentives to acquire such information have the same impact on national welfare as reduced productivity: they decrease it.

THE HISTORICAL INEQUITY ARGUMENT. Compensation for any permanent, long-run losses from trade liberalization is undeserved on equity grounds. Trade liberalization is not inequitable; it just reverses historical inequity. (Trade adjustment assistance still stands as an acceptable policy, however.)

In this view, the status quo is not accepted as a norm. No trade policy has existed from the beginning of time; each was implemented by the government at some point in the past. Textile workers and producers have probably been the permanent, long-run beneficiaries of U.S. barriers to imported textiles for as long as such barriers have existed. Their permanent gains have come at the expense of other individuals—consumers and producers of other goods. It would be unfair to compensate textile workers and producers for the losses they sustain from the removal of textile import barriers, yet not to have compensated everyone else who lost through history because of their imposition. Textile workers and producers don't "lose" from trade liberalization (except for short-run adjustment and dislocation); rather they "forego unfair advantage."

Even from the perspective of the present generation of textile resource owners, compensation beyond trade adjustment assistance is undeserved. They bear an *opportunity loss* compared to the standards of living that they could have realized had restricted trade been perpetuated. But they are burdened with no absolute loss. They simply forego a gain that would have been simultaneously someone else's misfortune.

Summary

Dislocation, adjustment, and redistribution—these are the prominent features of movement toward freer trade in the real world. All weaken the case for international trade by providing grounds for opposing liberalization. Dislocation and adjustment together provide the firmest; distribution, the most controversial.

Dislocation describes the temporary extra unemployment of labor and extra underutilization of other inputs that declining demand brings about in the face of wage-price rigidity. Its social cost is the value of the output sacrificed from the involuntary unproductivity of resources, discounted over the duration of the sacrifice. The sacrifice will diminish eventually, as wages and prices achieve some flexibility and as expanding demand in other sectors absorbs those displaced. Multilateral trade liberalization causes domestic production of importables to decline and causes exportables sectors to expand even when phased gradually over time. Short-run dislocation costs shrink the indefinite gains from freer trade discussed in Chapters 8 and 9 and could even outweigh them in discounted value. In that sense dislocation weakens the case for freer trade.

Adjustment does so as well. It describes either the temporarily lower productivity of displaced labor and inputs that must be conditioned to new tasks (in exportables sectors instead of importables sectors) or the temporary diversion of other labor and inputs from production tasks to retraining, retooling, refurbishing, and relocating those needing such services.

Income-distributional considerations may also weaken the case for freer trade when losers are uncompensated. Their losses can conceivably undermine a population's sense of equity, so that it is willing to forego trade-related gains in order to avoid penalizing the undeserving. Of course, a better solution might be to keep the trade-related gains and adopt a direct, first-best, income-redistribution policy for compensating losers from socially mandated action. That is precisely what U.S. trade adjustment assistance is in practice. But whether a compensation policy really is desirable is, from both economic and philosophical perspectives, a more subtle and complex issue than it first appears. At least four arguments can be marshaled against it, which appeal to politics and history as well as to economics.

But the reader should be wary. Weakening the case for trade liberalization does *not* simultaneously strengthen the case for additional government management of international trade. That, too, is movement and involves its own dislocation, adjustment, and distribution costs. The features examined in this chapter enhance the benefits of the status quo. They provide no particular insights into choosing between alternative movements toward more managed international trade or less.

Finally, if the world were perfect, there would be no need for this chapter. If wages and prices were perfectly flexible, both up and down, if resources were instantaneously and perfectly adaptable and movable, and if people were genuinely benevolent and devoid of envy, then there would be no dislocation, adjustment, or distribution costs to speak of. Nor would there be any need to distinguish a short run from a long run. And real trade liberalization would be a comparatively bland exercise, unlike the uneasy mix of conflict and cooperation that is described in the next chapter.

Key Terms

comparative statics
wage-price rigidity
industry-specific resources
time preference, discounting,
   and discount rates

safeguard clauses, escape
   clauses
trade adjustment assistance

Key Concepts and Review

Causes and costs of dislocation and adjustment.
Production possibilities curves and supply curves in the short and long run.
Graphical analysis of production, consumption, and standard-of-living adjustment paths from trade liberalization.
Gradual, multilateral, reversible adjustment versus abrupt, unilateral, irreversible adjustment.
Compensation, income distribution, and the problem of defining "national" economic welfare.
The case for and against compensation.

Supplement 10A
United States Trade Adjustment Assistance

Before 1962 there was no trade adjustment assistance in the United States. The philosophical objections to loser compensation, summarized at the end of the chapter, weighed heavily on congressional opinion.

Prodded by organized labor, Congress introduced cautious and carefully circumscribed trade adjustment assistance as part of the Trade Expansion Act of 1962. The dislocation provisions of this legislation were

— for labor: up to one year of income support at 65 percent of normal income (more generous than standard unemployment compensation) and up to a year and a half of support for workers who were over sixty (note the distributional goal) or being retrained;
— for firms: special tax privileges that enabled them to increase after-tax profits.

The adjustment provisions were

— for labor affected (or threatened) by trade liberalization: various training, counseling, and job-placement programs; and relocation allowances covering family moving expenses to a new job elsewhere;
— for firms affected (or threatened) by trade liberalization: low-interest loans or loan guarantees for modernization or retooling of plant and equipment and for acquisition of working capital (inventories of raw material and finished goods); free technical consultation on adapting to change and on sales outlooks and forecasts.

In practice, trade adjustment assistance under this legislation was at first nonexistent. The support of organized labor for the U.S. program quickly dried up as seven years went by without a single approval of any adjustment assistance case. (Six cases were turned down.) Adjustment assistance, in the eyes of most labor spokespersons, was a cruel hoax.[1]

What created this unusual dormancy of a government welfare program was a combination of stringent criteria for eligibility and strict interpretation of the criteria by the officials responsible for ruling on each case. To be approved for adjustment assistance benefits, labor and management had to prove not only that they had been injured by U.S. trade liberalization but that it had been the *major* cause of their

---

[1] During the mid-1960s, trade adjustment assistance was made available separately to U.S. autoworkers as part of the Canadian-American Auto Agreement (a limited form of trade liberalization described in Chapter 11). This program was drawn on more heavily than the general one, but it lapsed in mid-1968.

injury. *Injury* described both adjustment and dislocation burdens. And *major* was initially interpreted to mean "single most important." That conservative interpretation made adjustment assistance approval almost impossible: labor and management are continually buffeted by a myriad of other important shocks in addition to trade liberalization.

Furthermore, the process of applying for adjustment assistance was a bureaucratic nightmare. It not only diverted the services of company and union officials but also required lawyers and took considerable time. Each case had to be determined within roughly eight months, but other lags and delays could sometimes make it more than two years before the first adjustment assistance payments were made—if the case was approved.[2] Many firms and labor groups were unwilling to apply because even approval would have been unprofitable. For them, adjustment assistance might just as well not have been available. (Opponents of compensation, of course, are not surprised at these bureaucratic delays and red tape, especially those who stress the resource costs of compensation—the resource-cost argument in the chapter.)

A shift in personnel toward less strict interpretations revived U.S. adjustment assistance in the early 1970s. Both applications and approvals jumped. Legislative revision of the adjustment assistance program under the U.S. Trade Act of 1974 had an even more dramatic effect, as revealed in Table 10A.1. Outlays for adjustment assistance to labor in the last nine months of 1975 were four times as great as in the previous twelve and a half years! They have continued since then at a comparably high level.

By far the most important statutory changes leading to the mushrooming of adjustment assistance in 1975 related to eligibility.[3] First, adjustment assistance was made potentially available to firms and labor injured by imports for *any* reason, whether because of trade liberalization or not. And second, imports needed only to contribute importantly to the injury, not be its major cause.

While the second change is laudable in the spirit of compensation, the first represents a subtle and important imposition of additional

---

[2] One study of dislocated New England shoe workers reported an *average* delay of 19.4 months between layoff and receipt of the first adjustment assistance check! See James E. McCarthy, "Adjustment to Import Competition," *New England Economic Review*, July/August 1975, p. 8.

[3] Other statutory changes that made adjustment assistance more attractive included raising labor's income support to 70 percent of normal income and requiring that labor cases be determined in two, not eight, months, by the Secretary of Labor rather than by the slow-moving, quasi-judicial International Trade Commission. A Trade Monitoring ("early warning") System attempted to cut bureaucratic delay by forecasting future cases of adjustment and dislocation, so that adjustment assistance proceedings could be set in motion more readily on the basis of *threatened* injury. Finally, adjustment assistance for communities, as well as for firms and labor, became available for the first time.

TABLE 10A.1. *The Early History of U.S. Adjustment Assistance*

	Adjustment assistance for labor					Firm adjustment assistance		
	Cases approved	Cases denied	Number of workers in cases approved	Number of workers in cases denied	Dollar outlays (millions)	Cases approved	Cases denied	Dollar outlays (millions)
Under the Trade Expansion Act of 1962								
1962–1972[a]	56	80	23,519	27,632	n.a.	6	15	n.a.
1972–1975[b]	54	91	30,380	39,799	n.a.	22	n.a.	n.a.
Total	110	171	53,899	67,431	$75.6	28	n.a.	$45.3
Under the Trade Act of 1974								
1975[c]	123	112	51,261	56,887	≈ $300.0	13	1	n.a.

[a] October 1962, when the Trade Expansion Act took effect, through February 1972.
[b] March 1972 through March 1975, when the Trade Expansion Act was superseded by the Trade Act of 1974.
[c] The nine months from April to December.
n.a. = not available.
Sources: U.S. House of Representatives, Hearings Before the Subcommittee on Foreign Economic Policy of the Committee on Foreign Affairs, Ninety-second Congress, Second Session, April 24–26, May 9–11, 17, 1972, entitled *Trade Adjustment Assistance* (Washington, 1972), p. 49; and President of the United States, *Twentieth Annual Report on the Trade Agreements Program—1975*, pp. 47–50.

barriers to trade under the guise of adjustment assistance. As the text of Chapter 10 makes clear, compensation can be defended on the grounds that socially mandated government policy should not impose excessive burdens on any citizen. But compensation for market-determined injury is quite another matter; its defense is weaker. To take an extreme example, should the United States compensate domestic producers who are lazy or slow to adopt technological advances, thereby losing competitiveness to foreigners? If so, why? "Compensation" for such market-determined injury *is* possible under the new adjustment assistance program, but it should not properly be called compensation or even trade adjustment assistance. It is protectionism: the creation of restrictions that discriminate in favor of domestic producers and against foreign producers. It may ultimately be justifiable, but not on adjustment assistance grounds.

Since modern U.S. adjustment assistance has protectionist aspects, the existence of countervailing foreign programs is not unexpected. Both the French and British governments are committed to aiding industries that suffer pronounced structural dislocation and adjustment problems from any source, including the market. They and many other governments are also committed to the viability and development of particular sectors (national airlines), particular regions (depressed areas), and particular labor-force skills (science and engineering). In light of these facts, protectionist changes in U.S. adjustment assistance should perhaps be seen as defensive, equalizing policies, rather than as economic aggression.

Chapter 11

Trade Policy and Liberalization in Practice

The reality of international trade policy is a good deal less abstract than the discussion in Chapters 8 through 10. In some ways, it is remarkably colorful. Every government tries to outdo others in devising trade policy that is flexible and reliable, yet hard for foreigners to detect. Policymakers' imagination is matched only by the ingenuity of traders in circumventing the consequent discrimination, and by the persistence of foreign governments in uncovering and denouncing their trading partners' "nefarious barriers" as "grossly unfair and damaging to global economic harmony."

Ironically, none of this hyperbole and jockeying for advantage inhibits governments from negotiating periodically to reduce their own trade barriers—just so long as other countries reduce theirs "equally." But then the game is reoriented to the extraction of maximum advantage from other governments with minimum concessions from one's own. Negotiators search their own country's trade policies high and low for barriers with "water in them"—trade restrictions that are already so discriminatory that reducing them has almost no consequences of any kind. If found, negotiators magnanimously offer to reduce them, hoping for nontrivial, reciprocating liberalization by other countries. Furthermore, when serious reductions in trade barriers *are* offered, great care is taken to assure that one's "adversaries" are equally serious. If not, they are accused of bargaining in bad faith and undermining world progress. Acrimony is always present, as each country tries to cast itself in the role of virtuous free and fair trader and to vilify others for their unscrupulous practices. To a casual observer, it is amazing that such confrontations do usually result in cooperative movements toward freer trade.

Yet underlying the colorful convolutions of trade liberalization in the real world are the calculations and evaluations of the last three chapters. Thus this chapter will fill two roles. It will outline the detail of practical trade policy and it will recall many of the lessons that apply abstractly to all international trade policy. As such, it extends, expands, and summarizes Chapters 8 through 10.

Nontariff Barriers to Imports

Although tariffs have historically been the most prominent method of restricting imports, they are not the only way, nor is their prominence growing. Tariffs are being gradually reduced through the multilateral trade liberalization described below. Countries that have recently increased their protectionism have often resorted to means other than tariffs. Indeed, from a narrowly nationalistic perspective, these *nontariff barriers* to imports, or NTBs, have a number of advantages over tariffs.

TYPES OF NONTARIFF BARRIERS

Nontariff barriers are usually of four types: import quotas, government procurement policy, customs valuation, and bureaucratic barriers.

QUOTAS. *Import quotas* are quantitative restrictions on imports. Instead of taxing the sales of foreign producers, they limit them to no more than x units per time period. The strictest kind of import quota is an import *embargo*—an absolute prohibition of imports. For example, the U.S. import quota on Cuban cigars is zero—they are embargoed. Usually units are defined physically, as in the case of U.S. import quotas on dairy products (no more than 64 million pounds per year of cheddar cheese), or on crude petroleum during the 1960s (no more than 12.2 percent of domestic production). Occasionally, they are defined in terms of value. The earliest limitations on steel imported into the United States established a maximum dollar value of steel imports per year.

These early quotas on U.S. steel imports were notable for another reason. They were *voluntary export quotas*—quotas imposed by some European producers on their own exports to the United States. "Voluntary" signifies that they were established through a gentlemen's agreement between the U.S. government and foreign governments and producers. Such agreements spared the United States from the foreign retaliation that would have been incited by import quotas that were formally written into a statute. They allowed foreign producers more flexibility and opportunity for profit (see Supplement 11A) than strict U.S. import quotas would. The United States has negotiated similar "voluntary" (threat and aggressive bargaining play important roles) export quotas with several Far Eastern nations on their textile shipments to the United States and with Japan on color television sets. Many recent voluntary export quotas are being described as *orderly marketing agreements* (OMAs).[1]

Finally, *tariff-quotas* are a combination of tariffs and quotas. During the late 1970s, for example, U.S. honey imports up to 30 million pounds per year were assessed a penny-a-pound tariff; once that quota had been imported, there was a supplementary tariff of 30 percent on the value of any additional imports of honey. (It paid to ship your honey to America early in the year!)

GOVERNMENT PROCUREMENT POLICY. Statutory guidelines for purchases of goods and services by the government are usually quite protectionist. The governments of almost all developed countries discriminate against foreign producers in provisioning their agencies, armed forces, airlines, and nationalized enterprises. In some cases, residency is required to bid on contracts supplying branches of the government. A number of state governments in the United States embargo purchases of imported office supplies and motor vehicles for state use.[2] Since government purchases loom large in aggregate demand, protectionist procurement policies are highly significant NTBs.

Discriminatory government purchasing is not always mandated by statute but may nevertheless be standard operating procedure. Government purchasing agents often simply ignore foreign suppliers. Foreign dissemination of information on bidding for government contracts may be discouraged or prohibited.

In the United States, rigid discriminatory price differentials guide federal purchasing agents. They must purchase from U.S. defense contractors, from U.S. small businesses, and from any U.S. firm as long as their prices do not exceed comparable import prices by more than 50, 12, and 6 percent, respectively.

CUSTOMS VALUATION. Statutes express tariffs most frequently as a percentage of the value of imports. Such *ad valorem* tariffs (see footnote 1, Chapter 9) sometimes allow a country to enjoy higher real tariffs without higher tariff rates—protectionism through the back door. The key is to find a way to raise the assessed value of imports for customs purposes.

The most infamous example of such *customs-valuation barriers* to

---

[1] *Voluntary import quotas* are export quotas arranged by gentlemen's agreement. During 1974, when lumber shortages were prominent in parts of the United States, the United States persuaded Japan "voluntarily" to limit its lumber imports. Similarly, in 1975 when U.S. wheat prices began climbing rapidly, Poland agreed to "voluntarily" limit its U.S. wheat purchases.

[2] In some cases, *imports* even refers to products produced in other states. The state of Wisconsin's automobile fleet is disproportionately composed of American Motors products—from Kenosha and Racine, Wisconsin, not Detroit, Michigan!

imports in the United States is the American Selling Price (ASP) system of valuing imports of certain chemicals, gloves, and footwear. A 25 percent tariff on almost any other U.S. import implies that 25 percent of its value on board ship in the foreign port must be paid to U.S. Customs. A 25 percent tariff on ASP goods, however, implies that 25 percent of the value of comparable U.S. substitutes must be paid to U.S. Customs. This amount is considerably larger than the standard customs valuation. Comparable U.S. substitutes will clearly be more costly than the same goods in the foreign port, not only because of international transport costs but also because the tariff itself establishes a higher market price in the United States than abroad.[3]

Other countries are also guilty of customs-valuation protectionism. Most countries except the United States and Canada assess ad valorem tariffs on the *landed* domestic value of all imports—that is, on their value including international transport costs.[4] Thus a 25 percent foreign tariff is usually more taxing than an apparently similar 25 percent U.S. tariff.[5]

ADMINISTRATIVE RED TAPE, INDIRECT PROTECTION, AND NUISANCE REQUIREMENTS. Though harder to specify, the bureaucratic barriers involved in exporting are perhaps more important than any

---

[3] For example, the ad valorem tariff rate (with conventional valuation) that is implied by the textile example of Chapter 9 and Figure 9.3 is 25 percent ($20/$80). If the U.S. government shifted suddenly to ASP valuation, applying the same 25 percent rate, Sears' tariff payments to U.S. Customs would rise immediately from $20 per bale to $25 per bale (25 percent of $100 = $25)—and then even a little more. (Why?) The result of shifting to ASP valuation would be significantly increased textile import barriers.

[4] The technical description of value on board ship in the foreign port is *f.o.b. value* (f.o.b. stands for "free on board"). Landed domestic value is technically described as *c.i.f. value* (c.i.f. stands for "cost of insurance and freight").

[5] Customs-valuation practices are rarely changed. Thus although they clearly contribute to the *state* of government-managed trade, they are rarely manipulated as part of a *movement* toward either liberalization or protection. Another nontariff barrier that tends to be static is *border-tax adjustment*. By international (GATT—see Supplement 11B) convention, imports can be assessed for any domestic sales taxes (in addition to tariffs) when they enter a country. Europe relies heavily on taxes that are similar to sales taxes for general revenue, and these taxes are therefore levied on U.S. exports at the European customs house. By contrast, the United States relies heavily on income taxes for general revenue. They cannot (by convention) be charged to U.S. imports from Europe. Furthermore, the same convention allows Europe to spare its exporters from its sales tax on their exports but does not allow the United States to rebate income taxes to its exporters. Thus, in a sense, U.S. exporters get taxed twice (income taxes to the United States, sales taxes to Europe) and European exporters not at all. Naturally this historical disparity has always rankled the United States, its effect being comparable to that of a combination of extra European tariffs and export subsidies. In its defense, it is sometimes argued that sales taxes are reflected fully in product prices, whereas income taxes are not (being reflected instead in the incomes of resource owners). But this belief is extreme and dubious.

other NTBs to trade. Foreign vending licenses and credit status must often be obtained; foreign business practices must be learned; foreign lawyers must be hired; the metric system may have to be mastered, and so on.

All these are natural barriers to doing business in a foreign country. Yet similarly harassing administrative barriers exist that effectively discriminate against foreign producers. Many such barriers are designed to do exactly that; others do so incidentally. For example, Kennedy Airport noise regulations for a long time kept New Yorkers from importing Concorde flights. Italy requires safety inspections of certain imported machinery at the border before it is shipped on to its Italian buyer. Italian import inspectors are said to be so overworked that imported machinery often sits interminably in the customs house. The resulting delivery delays give a nontrivial competitive advantage to Italian producers. "Clearing customs" in any country can be a frustrating, costly, and time-consuming process. The expense of doing so discourages foreign exporters and forces those who persist to charge higher prices.

Protection is sometimes indirectly provided by requirements that do not seem to discriminate on the surface. United States stamp-of-origin requirements discriminated against Japanese exports in the 1950s when "Made in Japan" on a baseball glove was taken (by the author's friends, at least) to be a sure sign of inferior quality.[6] Many European countries tax automobiles proportionally to their weight or engine size. This effectively discriminates against U.S. exports because U.S. autos tend on average to be heavier and more powerful than their European counterparts. Italy even has a higher tax rate on larger engine displacement cars. Finally, health and safety standards, packaging and labeling guidelines, and mixing and milling requirements are often nondiscriminatory in principle but protectionist in practice.

THE ECONOMIC CONSEQUENCES OF NTBs

The economic impact of nontariff import barriers is qualitatively very similar to that of tariffs. The only important difference arises with respect to the terms of trade. Supplement 11A illustrates how nontariff barriers, unlike tariffs, do not guarantee more favorable terms of trade for the country that levies them.

Otherwise NTBs, like tariffs, imply higher domestic market prices and production, and lower domestic consumption and imports. In the example of Chapter 9 (Figure 9.3), the U.S. government could have achieved the same domestic impact from an import quota of 150 textile bales per day as it did from a $20-per-bale tariff. Both generate

---

[6] An apocryphal story has it that a city in Japan was named Usa so as to neatly skirt this barrier by stamping "Made in USA" on all the goods it shipped to the United States.

lower U.S. demand for Japanese textiles and shrink Japanese producers' business volume. Both divert the Japanese producers' attention toward competing more intensely in the Japanese home market, and divert U.S. buyers of textiles toward U.S. producers. The former diversion lowers Japanese textile market prices; the latter diversion raises U.S. textile market prices. United States consumption of textiles from all sources is smaller because of the higher U.S. market price, and U.S. production of textiles is larger for the same reason. United States textile imports—the difference between U.S. consumption and production—are necessarily smaller.

In making such broad forecasts, it matters very little that the tariff diverts by altering price while the quota diverts by altering availability. Prices and demand are affected the same, whether directly or indirectly.

SOME SUBTLE DIFFERENCES BETWEEN TARIFFS AND NTBs

Although tariffs and NTBs are similar in impact, they differ in some subtle ways.

CERTAINTY. NTBs such as import quotas have more certain consequences than tariffs. The effects of a tariff cannot be accurately predicted without knowledge of domestic and foreign supply/demand conditions. Governments can be sure, though, of the quantitative effect of most import quotas on imports.

Yet it would be wrong to overemphasize this virtue. Most of Chapter 9's arguments for trade restrictions rested on their effects on domestic prices, production, consumption, and income distribution. The quantitative size of these effects can be predicted no more accurately for import quotas than for import tariffs. Even the quantitative effect of import quotas on imports is uncertain when the quotas (quantities) are designed to improve the balance of payments by reducing the *value* of imports. Finally, many other NTBs besides quotas are as uncertain in their effects as tariffs—government procurement and customs valuation in particular.

ADMINISTRATIVE ADAPTABILITY, FEASIBILITY, AND COST. NTBs such as preferential government purchasing and administrative red tape are more flexible than tariffs and other trade barriers. They are not formally spelled out in statutes. Thus they can be adapted to changing circumstances quickly and easily—to provide either more liberalization or more protection, as conditions dictate. All that need to be altered are the operating instructions confronting government purchasing agents or customs officials.

Furthermore, administrative costs are lower if NTBs represent simple administrative procedures such as ignoring foreign bids or processing import paperwork at a snail's pace. Such NTBs will also be more desirable to the extent that they reduce purposeless domestic political furor and foreign retaliation. Both are avoided because the existence of vague nonstatutory discrimination against foreign producers is almost impossible to prove.

On the other hand, one person's flexibility may be another one's whim. Vaguely specified import restrictions often become subject to arbitrary interpretation, inhibiting both domestic and foreign residents from accurately predicting the future and planning accordingly. Nor is there always virtue in minimizing political costs. Who can distinguish purposeless from purposeful political furor? Foreign retaliation may sometimes be welcome if it inhibits trade barriers that serve narrow private interests at the expense of the rest of the nation.

Finally, the argument for any NTB on administrative-cost grounds is weakened considerably by the fact that most generate no government revenue. They do generate an analogous kind of windfall revenue that can sometimes accrue totally to domestic residents. In this case, the nation as a whole does not really lose the government revenue that equivalent tariffs would have produced. More typically, however, foreign producers lay claim to a share of this windfall revenue from NTBs, whereas the domestic government seizes it all under tariffs. Supplement 11A examines these matters in greater detail.

RIGIDITY. NTBs are usually more rigid than tariffs. Tariffs still allow some room for growth, technical advance, and changes in tastes. If foreign producers of textiles grow more rapidly, or produce more efficiently, or begin to market more appealing products, U.S. residents can still share in these benefits because imports will rise despite tariffs. U.S. consumers will benefit, and although U.S. producers may not benefit initially, some credible competitive threat is necessary if U.S. industry is to continue growing, producing efficiently, and discerning the tastes of American consumers.

Import quotas, on the other hand, take the pressure off American industry. Their usually rigid constraint on import quantities means that the same amount is imported regardless of foreign growth, technological advance, or changes in tastes. United States consumers share less, if any, of these benefits, and U.S. producers have less pronounced incentives to keep on their toes. (That is one reason why producers prefer import quotas to tariffs.)

MARKET STRUCTURE AND POWER. Rigid NTBs can be counted on to weaken the international forces of supply and demand and to enhance the private market power of both domestic and foreign producers. Quotas also choke off beneficial increases in foreign competitiveness. Tariffs, by contrast, often enhance price competitiveness among foreign producers, none of whom want to lose their U.S. market share. Tariffs retain the incentive for foreign producers to engage in cost-reducing innovation and price cutting. And U.S. producers correspondingly feel more foreign competitive pressure under import tariffs than under import quotas. Quotas represent insurmountable barriers to entry or expansion in the U.S. market; tariffs can be overcome. To the extent, then, that NTBs are accompanied by less residual competition than equivalent tariffs, U.S. market prices may be higher, production and consumption lower, and monopolistic distortions more pronounced.

Finally, Supplement 11A shows that private market power determines the international distribution of the NTB windfall gains that are the analog to government tariff revenue. Such gains undesirably raise the reward to both foreign and domestic producers from establishing monopoly positions. Tariffs do not alter such rewards, and private market power should therefore be less pronounced.

Export Promotion and Subsidization Schemes

Most countries discriminate not only against imports but in favor of exports. They promote and subsidize exports on the same grounds on which they restrict imports—national defense, technological growth, employment, balance of payments, and so on.[7] Though the national-economic-welfare argument is often shaky, export promotion is nevertheless quite common, and the illegality of explicit export subsidization (by international convention under the GATT)[8] has not deterred countries from subsidizing through the back door. Export promotion is a growing phenomenon, unlike import restriction. Only recently have some developed countries begun to express concern about the "export subsidization race" and "ruinous" competition among governments to promote their exports.

FORMS OF INDIRECT EXPORT SUBSIDIZATION

Indirect export subsidization usually takes three forms: government-subsidized export financing, tax inducements for export firms, and export promotional and informational devices.

GOVERNMENT-SUBSIDIZED EXPORT FINANCING. Many purchases must be financed by credit. Exports are no exception. For some exports, the credit period is very short—the difference between the

---

[7] A few tax or restrict exports, for reasons discussed in Supplement 9A.

[8] GATT rules consider export subsidization to be a type of "unfair competition" and allow retaliation against countries that explicitly practice it. Accepted retaliation takes the form of *countervailing duties*—special tariffs levied by the importing country on subsidized products from abroad. One can question the economic merit of countervailing duties, however, for the same reasons that one can question the merit of antidumping duties (Chapter 9).

seller's billing date and the receipt of the buyer's check. For other exports (such as ships and aircraft), the credit period is very long, and the cost of credit becomes a very large proportion of the final export price (as it does when one purchases a house or a car). Thus an effective way for a government to promote these exports, without subsidizing them directly, is to subsidize the financing that is a necessary part of their production and sale. Let export producers borrow at below-market interest rates to encourage them to buy the materials necessary to produce the export, and let foreign buyers borrow at below-market interest rates to encourage them as well.

In the United States a government agency known as the *Export-Import Bank* (or *Eximbank*) does exactly this. During the mid 1930s, it was endowed by the U.S. Treasury with cash that it has since loaned and reloaned to foreign buyers of U.S. exports, and that it has used to aid U.S. exporters. Since the interest rate that Eximbank charges on its loans is well below the market interest rate, it pays smaller yearly dividends to the U.S. Treasury—and hence to U.S. taxpayers—than it would otherwise. In this sense U.S. taxpayers are taxed to provide the subsidy necessary to promote U.S. exports.[9]

Almost every other developed country has a similar government export-financing bank. These and Eximbank do more than just subsidize the cost of export credit. They also guarantee export-related loans made by private commercial banks against loss due to default, exchange-rate changes, and political instability. Such guarantees make private credit more available to exporters and their customers, and thus also subsidize exports indirectly.

Export-financing subsidies are not trivial. They are even more significant outside of the United States. Table 11.1 records interest-rate costs of borrowing to finance the exports of a number of major countries in 1974. If U.S. market rates of interest are used as a very rough guide for the market rates of the entire world, the table shows that government subsidies reduce export-related borrowing costs by at least one-fifth (for the United States) and perhaps by almost one-half (for France).

TAX INDUCEMENTS FOR EXPORT FIRMS. Most countries discriminate in favor of their exporters by providing them with tax loopholes linked to their export performance. Some countries do not tax the export-generated profits of their companies at all. European countries rebate some taxes to exporters that producers for the domestic market must pay.[10] The purpose of these loopholes is to stimulate exports.

[9] Its name makes the bank sound more even-handed than it is. "Export-Import" suggests that the bank subsidizes U.S. imports as well. Such is not the case. It finances *foreign* imports from the United States, which are precisely and identically U.S. exports. Cynical U.S. importers should be forgiven for believing that the general public is being cleverly misled.

[10] See footnote 5 on border-tax adjustments.

TABLE 11.1. *Export-Financing Subsidies,*
August 1974

Country	Effective rate[a] of interest charged to exports	Hypothetical interest-rate subsidy[b]
France	6.8	5.9
Italy	7.0	5.7
Britain	7.0	5.7
Japan	7.6	5.1
West Germany	8.5	4.2
United States	8.7–10.7	2.0–4.0

[a] Rates are percentage annual rates.
[b] Calculated for illustrative purposes under the assumption that unsubsidized commercial bank loans worldwide were being made at the U.S. rate on such loans in August 1974, namely 12.7 percent.
Source: International Economic Report of the President (Washington, D.C.: U.S. Government Printing Office, March 1975), p. 80.

Either after-tax profits will be higher in export industries, thus attracting more resources and leading to increased export supply, or existing exporters will be more willing to shade their prices, leading to increased world demand for their products.

In the United States, firms that export sufficiently heavily can qualify as *Domestic International Sales Corporations* (DISCs). This allows them to shield half of their export-related profits from any tax at all.[11] United States firms that export sufficiently heavily in the western hemisphere can also qualify as *Western Hemisphere Trade Corporations* (WHTCs), which reduces their corporate income taxes by 14 percent.

EXPORT PROMOTIONAL AND INFORMATIONAL DEVICES. The governments of almost every developed country provide special encouragement to domestic exporters by furnishing them with free information and counseling on foreign markets. The U.S. and Japanese governments also encourage potential foreign buyers through a network of permanent trade centers in major foreign cities. (There are fifteen

[11] Technically, the U.S. Treasury just "defers" half of the taxes on the companies' export profits above a historically determined base amount. Thus the Treasury reserves the right (some day) to collect. But the DISC program also makes it clear that deferral may last indefinitely.

TABLE 11.2. *Export Promotional Subsidies, 1973*

Country	Government spending for export marketing and information services per $1000 of exports
Exports of Agricultural Goods	
Israel	$22.67
South Africa	14.42
Australia	9.59
Canada	8.12
Netherlands	3.86
United States	1.36
France	.94
Exports of Manufactured Goods	
Britain	3.53
Italy	2.44
Japan	1.35
France	1.31
Canada	1.19
United States	.83
West Germany	.62

Source: International Economic Report of the President (Washington, D.C.: U.S. Government Printing Office, March 1975), p. 82.

U.S. centers.) These centers are staffed by government personnel who specialize in planning how American or Japanese firms can penetrate foreign markets. Most governments also stage and finance temporary trade fairs, at which their exports are exhibited and advertised.

In the United States, the Department of Commerce regularly publishes a veritable flood of material explaining the virtues of exporting. It also assists U.S. firms in making foreign bids and helps them to line up advertising and financing that promote their foreign sales. It even sponsors therapy—"export awareness seminars"—and bestows export awards and commendations on particularly successful exporters ("Dallas company wins 'E' award," trumpets one Commerce press release).

The dollars for these promotional programs come ultimately from general tax revenues. The society at large is taxed to subsidize exports, and the expense is not small. Table 11.2 records the magnitude of indirect export subsidization from country to country in 1973. Even in the United States, which discriminates less than most in favor of exports, the tax on citizens for promotional services alone (to say nothing of subsidized financing or tax incentives) is roughly $2 per taxpayer per year.

EXPORT PROMOTION, Ntbs, AND TARIFFS

In most aspects, export promotion is qualitatively similar in its domestic impact to import restriction. Domestic market prices of favored exports are higher, as is domestic production. Domestic consumption is lower. Export promotion and subsidization devices also share some of the subtleties of NTBs. Many are administratively determined and easily adaptable to changing conditions. Many are so indirect in their impact that foreigners find it difficult to prove discrimination that justifies retaliation. And many reduce competitiveness and encourage market power. Most prominently in the United States, the Webb-Pomerene Act of 1918 allows U.S. firms to collaborate and collude for purposes of exporting in ways that would normally be illegal under U.S. antitrust law. Most other countries similarly exempt export activities from domestic antimonopoly law in order to favor exporters.[12]

Export subsidization differs from import restriction, however, in its effect on the terms of trade. It is presumed that import restrictions usually improve the terms of trade (see Supplement 11A) but export promotion usually worsens them. Subsidizing exports drives a wedge between market price and national price. Private exporters receive more than the nation as a whole for their exports. They receive both revenue from the foreign buyer and favors from their own government. Only the former is part of *national* revenue from exporting. The favors are transfers from one citizen to another.

Multilateral Trade Liberalization in Practice

We have seen that international trade policies are highly diverse and complex. Similarly, decisions to liberalize trade are far richer descriptively than the narrow national calculation of gain and loss on which we concentrated in Chapter 10. In practice, the most significant modern movements toward freer trade have been curious blends of conflict and cooperation. They have always involved more than two countries, have been marked as much by political games-

[12] That these exemptions do discriminate in favor of exporters is clear. Whether they stimulate exports is another question. On one hand, they place domestic firms in a stronger competitive position relative to foreign firms, perhaps expanding their foreign market share. But on the other hand, larger scope for collusive behavior could lead to higher export prices and smaller exports, as the theory of monopoly suggests.

manship as by economic evaluation, and havé sometimes shown little regard for the basic lessons from Chapters 8 through 10.

RECIPROCITY

Nowhere are these characteristics better illustrated than in the guiding principle of all modern multilateral trade liberalization: *reciprocity*. Reciprocity—sometimes called mutual advantage—is the principle of quid pro quo, the idea that I should never be expected to do you any favors unless you fully return them. Almost every nation makes reciprocity a condition for participation in trade liberalization, and a sensible justification can be offered on grounds of "fairness."

But a simplistic appeal to fairness (or equity) ignores the basic lesson of the previous chapters: lowering trade barriers is often in the national economic interest, even when other countries do not reciprocate. In this case trade liberalization is smart, not unselfish; justifiable on the grounds of greed, not generosity; a mark of business acumen, not altruism. Many economists believe that is almost always the case.

Why, then, are governments so obsessed with reciprocity? Why is a reduction in national trade restrictions always described as a concession, implying that the nation is sacrificing something to benefit others? Why not describe it as an aggression, implying that the nation benefits itself at the expense of others? Ludicrous as this sounds, it is no more inaccurate a description than the term *concession*. Many, and perhaps most, movements toward freer trade benefit every nation, whether reciprocity is practiced or not.

Nevertheless, at least two potentially sound defenses of reciprocity can be made. Both mix politics and economics. First, reciprocity forces trade liberalization to be multilateral and cooperative. Each nation's promise of lower trade barriers is conditional on another's— the bargaining argument for unilaterally maintaining trade barriers (Chapter 9) is formalized in the principle of reciprocity. Multilateral liberalization in turn makes dislocation and adjustment costs less prominent (Chapter 10). As a result, trade liberalization is more beneficial with reciprocity than without—as long as insistence on reciprocity does not make movement toward freer trade less frequent. If it does, then the case for reciprocity is not closed.

Second, if reciprocity is practiced, the ability of special interest groups to thwart the national economic interest by pressuring the government may be offset by the formation of equally self-concerned special interest groups that benefit from foreign concessions: for every textiles lobbyist against U.S. trade liberalization, there is an aircraft lobbyist for it. Thus reciprocity may make liberalization more politically feasible.

Reciprocity is an established part of multilateral trade liberalization, but each government defines it subjectively. It is not a statutory principle. In fact, it is hardly mentioned (and not well defined) in the General Agreement on Tariffs and Trade (GATT), the covenant that circumscribes the conduct of international trade policy (Supplement 11B).

GATT ROUNDS OF TRADE LIBERALIZATION

Much significant trade liberalization has taken place under the principles outlined by the GATT. Roughly 85 countries have signed the GATT and agree to abide by its provisions. One of these calls for periodic negotiations to bring about worldwide reductions in trade barriers. Since World War II, seven of these *rounds* of trade liberalization or MTNs (multilateral trade negotiations) have taken place. Although they are sponsored under the GATT, MTNs always include many nations that have not signed the agreement, yet still want to have some influence on the negotiations.

MTN rounds are complex and lengthy. (The *Tokyo round* of the 1970s took roughly six years to complete.) They usually begin with meetings of the high-level government officials responsible for international trade policy, at which national aspirations and broad bargaining positions are revealed. The real work begins afterward— periodic meetings of lower-level officials on government negotiating teams. At these meetings, proposals and counterproposals are formulated, position papers are discussed, reciprocally balancing concessions are hammered out, deals are arranged. Negotiations are not unlike any other adversary confrontation, from union-management relations to old-fashioned horse trading. Arguments erupt over matters of principle. Unfair treatment is alleged. The opponent's good faith in bargaining is rarely acknowledged. Threats are always implicit and sometimes quite conspicuous. Toward the end, high-level officials meet again to resolve remaining issues. When a trade-liberalization package is finally worked out, it may still have to be sent back to national legislatures for ratification (as is true for the United States).

Bargaining of this sort is unwieldy at best. It would be impossibly so if each of, say, 100 governments had to bargain separately with the other 99, striking reciprocity with each: 4950 different bargains would have to be struck—and perhaps restruck if any one pair of proposed concessions destroyed the reciprocity balance of another. The most important of all GATT principles is designed in part to skirt this hopeless jungle of bilateral bargaining. It is the *Most-Favored Nation* (MFN) *Principle,* or the rule of "MFN treatment."

THE MOST-FAVORED NATION (MFN) PRINCIPLE

The MFN principle states that no country should discriminate *among* different foreign nations in its trade policy. Most trade barriers discriminate against foreign nations by their very nature, but as long as such discrimination is even-handed, it is in accord with the MFN principle. As we shall see below, there are many exceptions to the MFN principle and many violations of it in practice.

MFN treatment practiced by the United States would imply, for example: (1) the same tariff on all imported textiles, no matter what country supplies them; (2) an overall quota defined for total textile imports, rather than country-specific quotas for textiles from each foreign producing nation; (3) customs-valuation practices that were uniform across all the source countries for imports.

The pure MFN principle also implies that a country's trade liberalization cannot be applied unevenly—to a select group of "most favored" nations alone. Trade concessions extended to one must be extended to all. Otherwise it would be impossible to claim equal degrees of discrimination for the trade barriers that remain. The most-favored-nation principle implies that "most-favored" nations should not exist: everyone should be favored equally.

It can now be seen how the MFN principle skirts the hopeless jungle of bilateral bargaining. No country would ever propose 99 different packages of trade concessions to 99 trading partners. It would instead propose the single concession that would apply to all of them individually and collectively. Then reciprocity is generally easier to secure. Instead of requiring equally valuable concessions from each of its 99 trading partners, a nation would be content with an equally valuable *sum* of concessions from the 99 as a group.

If it could be enforced by persuasive sanctions, the MFN principle would also reduce the potential for economic warfare. Strong nations with power over a small group of weak ones would not be able to prey on them (to improve the terms of trade, for example) by imposing especially heavy (discriminatory) restrictions applicable only to trade with the weak. Instead, nations would have to take on the rest of the world or else back off and keep the economic peace. Similarly, in multilateral trade negotiations, MFN treatment rules out the strategy of "divide and conquer"—the strategy of approaching countries with weaker bargaining positions one by one and extracting the maximum possible concession from each as the price of its reciprocity.[13] The same concessions must be offered to all. Weak countries are also strongly motivated to resist arm-twisting by any single opponent because an extra concession to one means an extra concession to all.

The language in the preceding paragraph highlights the nationalistic conflict that is latent even in a cooperative international endeavor such as multilateral trade liberalization. This conflict explains why there are in fact no persuasive sanctions to enforce MFN treatment.

Although most nations hold broadly to the MFN principle, every nation wants to reserve its own right to hold back or withdraw MFN treatment. The United States, for example, has withheld MFN treat-

---

[13] "Divide and conquer" strategy for a country's trade liberalization is analogous to price-discrimination strategy for a monopolist's sales-price decisions.

ment from most of the communist world.[14] Furthermore, the United States has sometimes claimed that its MFN treatment holds only *conditionally*. In this view, MFN treatment can be withheld from any nation that does not reciprocate economically. Most other nations disagree that the MFN principle should be conditional on bilateral reciprocity. But almost all agree on other exceptions. The GATT itself permits nonuniform discriminatory trade barriers against countries that either dump or subsidize their exports.[15] It also permits geographically limited liberalization, as long as it is complete (culminating in free trade) and comprehensive (applicable to almost all goods). Such complete, comprehensive liberalization establishes the regional free-trade areas and common markets discussed in the next section. Finally, most countries sanction geographically limited liberalization toward less-developed countries alone. This exception to the MFN principle, described as a *Generalized System of Preferences* (GSP), is defended as a desirable kind of foreign aid from rich nations to poor. Of course, because trade liberalization usually benefits the initiating countries as well, GSPs are hardly charity. They are discussed further in Chapter 14.

ACROSS-THE-BOARD BARGAINING

MFN treatment keeps multilateral trade negotiations from getting bogged down in thousands of bilateral bargains between participating countries. Across-the-board bargaining keeps them from becoming mired in thousands of individual product-by-product cases. This practice is comparatively new, having first been tried in the 1960s during the *Kennedy round* of MTNs. Before that, the bureaucratic costs of trade liberalization were dramatically higher. Every single trade barrier protecting every single product could conceivably be treated as a unique case, and reciprocity was sometimes even expected on a product-by-product basis. Across-the-board bargaining cuts through the mass of detail that characterized this *item-by-item approach*. It groups products into several broad categories of manufactures and agricultural goods.

Identical reductions in trade barriers are then negotiated across the board—the same cut for each product in a category. Countries can exempt certain products from across-the-board reductions by placing them on an *exceptions list*. The burden of proof is therefore on those who want to treat products uniquely rather than on those who want to

[14] Exceptions are Hungary, Poland, Romania, and Yugoslavia—to which the United States does accord MFN treatment. A major U.S. political issue in the mid-1970s was whether to extend MFN treatment to the Soviet Union. The Nixon Administration was in favor, as part of its policy of detente. The Congress was opposed—unless the Soviet Union made it easier for Soviet Jews to leave the country voluntarily.

[15] See footnote 8 above and Chapter 9.

treat them collectively. Exceptions lists themselves are bargainable —a lengthy U.S. list is sure to incur the displeasure of other countries and will cost some concessions that the United States otherwise would have received.

In sum, both the MFN principle and across-the-board bargaining make multilateral trade liberalization more efficient, lowering one of its most important resource costs (time and effort spent negotiating). Both loosen the strict application of reciprocity, establishing a kind of clearing house for trade concessions. Concessions made need not match concessions received on either a country-by-country basis or an industry-by-industry basis. Reciprocity is nevertheless achieved as long as the sum of concessions made matches the sum of those received—from all countries in all industries. The knotty problem of defining the value of concessions is left up to the subjective judgment of the negotiators.

Geographically Limited Trade Liberalization

THE EUROPEAN COMMUNITY

Although the most recent worldwide trade liberalization has taken place under the GATT, the single most dramatic instance has been the formation of the *European Community* (EC). The EC is a multidimensional economic alliance of nine European countries. The most important of these dimensions is completely free trade among its members. Belgium, France, West Germany, Italy, Luxembourg, and the Netherlands were charter members in 1957. In 1973 Britain, Denmark, and Ireland joined the original six. The EC is colloquially known as the (European) Common Market.

The European Community may be the most striking single illustration of the benefits of freer trade. During and since the period in which barriers to internal trade were removed among the original six members (1958–1968—see Table 10.1), they have prospered as never before. Average standards of living have risen steeply, as the expanded consumption possibilities available from freer trade suggest. Resource misallocation appears to have been alleviated, as European firms and countries have narrowed the range of products produced, specializing on longer production runs of unique products. These have been exported to EC partners in return for other narrow product lines (specialization and exchange from Chapter 8). Production also appears to have become more economically rational and more oriented toward growth. (It would therefore be hard to defend the EC's former internal trade barriers using the growth-technology argument of Chapter 9.) Dislocation and adjustment costs have almost surely not been large enough to outweigh the benefits from liberalization. The

British public even ratified their EC participation in a national referendum that was held during the depths of their short-run adjustment period (1975), when the transitory costs of movement toward freer trade were probably most pronounced. Unfavorable effects of EC formation on permanent rates of national unemployment have been impossible to discern. And effects on permanent rates of regional unemployment have been eased by joint regional development policies, joint regional adjustment assistance, and the removal of barriers to resource movements from one member country to another.[16]

These last features illustrate how the European Community is much more than just a free-trade area. The Europeans who guided its founding had visions of political union, in which economic union represented just one step. Little has come from these political visions, except for the formation of certain political bodies that, despite their names (Council of Ministers, European Parliament, Court of Justice), concern themselves largely with economic matters. But economic union has encompassed many other dimensions besides free internal trade. It has included joint planning of policies toward coal, steel, and agricultural production; joint research on atomic energy; and the beginnings of joint policies toward taxation, transportation, social-welfare programs, competitive market structure, the environment, and monetary policy.[17]

Free internal trade is nevertheless the foundation of the EC. Although the EC's economic success could conceivably be explained by other factors (for example, thoroughgoing modernization of plant and equipment after World War II, or the influx of American multinational corporations during the 1960s), most economic observers are persuaded of the importance of free trade.

It is perhaps not surprising that free trade within the EC has been so successful. More distant historical precedent exists. The United States itself is a vast free-trade area among the fifty states. It was not so in the early years of its existence. Many barriers to trade among the original thirteen states existed under the Articles of Confederation and were imposed by state governments for much the same reasons

[16] The only argument against free trade that appears to have some application to the EC is the balance-of-payments argument. The formation of the EC may have made balance-of-payments problems more difficult for some of its members. Almost every EC country in the 1970s was forced at one time or another to adopt barriers to trade and resource movements that violated the spirit, if not necessarily the letter, of the EC agreements.

[17] Symptomatic of the diversity of joint economic actions undertaken by the EC is that there is no one true European Community. Rather, there are three legally constituted communities: the European Economic Community (EEC), the European Coal and Steel Community (ECSC), and the European Atomic Energy Community (Euratom). But they share the same institutions and are always collectively called the European Community or Communities.

that national governments impose trade restrictions today. Furthermore, every current state is a free-trade area among its counties, and every county among its townships, and so on. The point is that any benefits from free international trade are the same as those from unencumbered economic exchange in general.

Benefits from freer trade are not inevitable, as Chapters 9 and 10 demonstrated. For many reasons (almost all falling under the familiar rubric of the Theory of the Second Best), the formation of the European Community *could* have been harmful to each of its members. None of the members of the EC removed all of its barriers to international trade. Liberalization was limited by geography—it applied only to trade carried on among themselves. As we saw in Chapter 9, removing some trade barriers (distortions) while retaining others in no way guarantees an improvement in national economic welfare. Supplement 11C illustrates this unfortunate possibility again, in a simple case of what economists call *trade diversion*.

Furthermore, the formation and expansion of the EC involved protectionism as well as trade liberalization. In addition to establishing free trade internally, the members of the EC harmonized their trade barriers toward the rest of the world. A *common external tariff* was determined by averaging the tariffs of the original six members.[18] Thus the Netherlands, which had had comparatively low universal barriers to trade before EC membership, had to raise tariffs on trade with non-EC countries while removing them on trade with the EC. And when Britain joined in 1973, it was obliged to abandon its very liberal policy toward all agricultural imports in order to harmonize with the complicated protection that the EC maintains for its agricul-

---

[18] The terminology that has sprung up around regional trade liberalization is worth noting. *Economic integration* describes the process of liberalizing trade among a select group of countries—and maybe doing more. Five progressively complex kinds of economic integration are usually distinguished. Establishing a *free-trade area* implies a complete movement toward free trade among the members and nothing else. The external tariff for an entire free-trade area tends to be the smallest external tariff of any member, since imported goods can enter there with the smallest duty and be transshipped to other members of the free trade area without further taxation. By contrast, a *customs union* is a free-trade area with common or harmonized external trade barriers. These could conceivably be higher than any average of the original barriers of its members. In this case, it might be inaccurate to describe the formation as a movement toward freer trade. A *common market* is a customs union that additionally abolishes barriers to movements of labor and corporate investment within the geographical limits of membership. An *economic union* is a common market that additionally harmonizes some of the fiscal policies of its members, such as systems of taxation and social-welfare programs. A *monetary union* is an economic union that additionally harmonizes the monetary policies of its members. In this classification, the EC is certainly an economic union and is taking hesitant steps toward becoming a monetary union (see Chapter 7).

ture.[19] Since that time, the cost of food has been rising predictably and dramatically in Britain.

On balance, it seems extremely hard to claim that the protectionist aspects of EC formation have outweighed the trade-liberalizing aspects. Indeed, the EC has reduced trade barriers in ways other than through formal membership. Almost completely free trade was implemented in the late 1970s between the EC and Austria, Switzerland, and the Scandinavian countries. Varying degrees of free trade have been planned or established between the EC and "associated" countries: Greece (which will join the EC in 1981), Spain and Portugal (which have applied for membership), Turkey (which contemplates application), and a large number of Mediterranean, African, Caribbean, and Pacific countries (including, but not limited to, former colonies and dependencies). Associates can exempt certain industries from free trade on infant-industry grounds, so trade is not fully free. Nor do associates take part in any other aspect of the EC—they do not adhere to common external trade barriers, free resource movements, or joint policies on industrial development, taxation, and so on.[20] Since none of these arrangements involves raising any country's trade barriers, it is fairly certain that most of them have represented international trade liberalization.

The proliferation of EC affiliations has sparked controversy between the United States and the EC. The United States argues that even if these affiliations can accurately be described as trade liberalization, Americans have nevertheless been their chief victims. The demand for U.S. exports in EC-affiliated countries falls when their trade barriers on EC goods vanish but those on U.S. goods remain. Another result is deterioration in the U.S. terms of trade. The United States therefore brands the EC's free-trade associations and arrangements as *preferential agreements* or *reverse preferences* and claims that they are incompatible with the Most-Favored-Nation principle. The EC responds that the GATT has always accepted complete, comprehensive, but geographically limited liberalization as a legitimate

[19] The European Community's Common Agricultural Policy (CAP) is highly protectionist and is a principal source of U.S. irritation with the EC. (In general, the United States has provided little opposition, and even positive encouragement, in the EC's early years.) The United States is the natural source of many of the grains and meat products whose import the EC restricts and is particularly opposed to a prominent barrier known as *variable levies*. Such levies are "flexible" tariffs that are periodically altered to raise the price of imported agricultural goods to the target price selected by EC agricultural planners. *Flexible* is the EC's word. *Arbitrary* is how the United States describes them. A famous instance of U.S. retaliation against these variable levies took place during the "Chicken War" of 1962–1963. When the EC's variable levies cut significantly into U.S. exports of frozen broiler chickens, the United States responded by raising tariffs on a number of EC export products.

[20] The EC and its associates can thus be said (almost accurately) to have formed a free-trade area (see footnote 18).

exception to the MFN principle. The United States retorts that the EC's preferential agreements are neither complete nor comprehensive, making exceptions for infant industries and failing to set clearly defined timetables for the eventual attainment of full free trade. If the United States is right, it is entitled either to compensation from the EC or to retaliation against the EC under GATT procedures (see Supplement 11B). But an equally desirable strategy, and one that is probably preferable from a world perspective, would be to establish similar preferential arrangements for free trade between the United States and the EC's affiliates.

LIMITED LIBERALIZATION BY THE UNITED STATES

The United States itself is hardly guiltless in engineering preferential trading agreements and in undermining the MFN principle. Like the EC, the United States has maintained reverse preferences with some of its former colonies and dependencies (for example, the Philippines).[21] And the Canadian-American Auto Agreement of 1965 was a blatant violation of GATT insistence on Most-Favored-Nation treatment.

The Canadian-American Auto Agreement is an example of trade liberalization that is limited not only geographically but also industrially and institutionally. It established free trade between the United States and Canada in automotive products alone — and only as long as Ford, Chrysler, General Motors, or American Motors carried out that trade. Corporate and individual consumers continued to be subject to tariffs if they wanted to import an auto or parts from the other country. The Agreement was not extended to any other country or to any other products. As such, it could hardly be described as a comprehensive movement toward freer trade, which would have made it consistent with MFN treatment under the GATT. Finally, its benefits were distributed disproportionately toward producers. Automakers gained from it directly because they were able to specialize Canadian production on lines of autos in which Canada had comparative advantage (typically small, standardized, long-production-run cars) and to specialize American production on the remainder, where it had comparative advantage. The auto output from specialized production was exchanged across the border (exported and imported) to accord with

---

[21] The United States argues that its reverse preferences, unlike the EC's, predate the GATT. Since the GATT includes a "grandfather clause" that exempts such preexisting discrimination from its provisions and prohibitions, U.S. preferential trading agreements are indeed justified on a fine legal point. But they clearly violate the spirit, if not the letter, of the GATT. The United States is therefore guilty of some hypocrisy in the reverse-preferences controversy. In this aspect, however, the United States is hardly unique. In confrontations over international trade policy, the United States appears to import about as much hypocrisy as it exports.

demand patterns in the two countries. Auto producers earned higher profits for the same sales because auto production was allocated more efficiently (rationally) than under previous trade barriers. Auto consumers gained, too, but only indirectly through trickle-down influences. Higher profits and less costly production were passed along to them in part in the form of lower prices as automakers competed among themselves for larger market shares. But auto consumers would have gained much more if the opportunity to engage in free trade had been extended to them, too.

It is unclear whether the Canadian-American Auto Agreement was a movement toward freer trade. It did discriminate implicitly against European and Japanese automakers. Their Canadian market shrank, because U.S. autos could be imported duty (tariff) free by Canadian subsidiaries of U.S. automakers and could therefore be marketed to Canadians at lower, more competitive market prices. Their U.S. market shrank for the same reason (many small Chevrolets, Fords, and Dodges that are sold in the United States are produced in Canada). This implicit discrimination against certain trading partners and in favor of others is precisely what the MFN principle outlaws in the name of harmonious international economic relations.

It should be clear from the illustrations above that trade liberalization beneficial to a group of countries will not necessarily be universally applauded. This is one instance in which our two-country examples lead us astray. Moving toward freer trade has effects on income distribution not only within a country but also among countries. Just as some individuals lose from particular kinds of trade liberalization, so can entire nations. That brings us back to what we have already seen in Chapter 9—government management of trade *is* sometimes in the national interest.

OTHER EXAMPLES OF REGIONAL TRADE LIBERALIZATION

A number of less dramatic examples of regional trade liberalization exist. Free trade is maintained among the members of both the European Free Trade Association (EFTA)[22] and the Latin American Free Trade Association (LAFTA), although each member country is free to erect its own unique barriers to trade with nonmembers. Geographically limited trade liberalization also exists among Central American countries and Middle Eastern countries, formerly existed in East Africa, and has been proposed for many other regional groupings.

[22] Current members of the EFTA are Austria, Iceland, Norway, Portugal, Sweden, and Switzerland. Before joining the EC, Britain, Denmark, and Ireland were also members. The EFTA was created in 1959 in hopes of imitating the EC's predicted economic success. Britain in particular was concerned about having made an economically unwise decision not to become a charter member of the EC in 1957.

THE CASE FOR REGIONAL LIBERALIZATION

Regional trade liberalization is potentially beneficial for the same reasons that any trade liberalization is, as summarized in previous chapters. Furthermore, if the region also erects common external trade barriers, its larger size and unified trade policy will usually carry more bargaining weight in multilateral rounds of trade liberalization under the GATT. Enhanced bargaining power provides obvious benefits to the members of a regional trade area. And it may even provide more widespread benefits if it hastens the progress of multilateral trade negotiations. An example is the dramatically liberalizing Kennedy round of GATT negotiations in the mid-1960s. Some commentators believe that it was hastened by U.S. apprehension that a powerful European Community would be a formidable future bargaining opponent; it may even have been hastened by the EC as well, anxious to assert its new united bargaining power.

Summary and Perspective

This chapter began by illustrating the diversity of discriminatory barriers against imports and in favor of exports. Most of these did not relate to prices in any clear and formal way, as tariffs and subsidies do. Indeed some of the vaguer, less rigid trade barriers do not relate clearly and formally to any measurable variable.

The implication for practical trade liberalization is fundamental. It is difficult enough to negotiate mutually advantageous reductions of well-identified trade barriers. When barriers can hardly be defined, it is almost impossible.

Multilateral trade liberalization has understandably attacked the easier problem first. And its success over the past thirty years has been remarkable. Yet that success has aggravated the problem of dealing with nontariff import barriers and export discrimination. As tariffs have been progressively reduced, nontariff barriers have become increasingly significant obstacles to trade. Some countries have compensated for reduced tariffs by imposing less obvious trade restrictions or by negotiating "voluntary" restrictions with trading partners.

One way to ease negotiations on troublesome issues is to negotiate with fewer participants. For this reason, it may be that smaller-scale, regionally restricted trade liberalization will gradually begin to dominate far-flung multilateral liberalization under the GATT. And if the geographical limits of regional liberalization expand as they have for the EC, then worldwide movement toward freer trade may not be slowed. It may simply change character. Freer trade may become universal by first becoming regional.

Key Terms

nontariff barriers (NTBs) to imports
import quotas, voluntary export quotas, tariff quotas
customs-valuation barriers (American Selling Price (ASP), border tax adjustments)
Export-Import Bank (Eximbank)
Domestic International Sales Corporations (DISCs), Western Hemisphere Trade Corporations (WHTCs).
Webb-Pomerene Act
General Agreement on Tariffs and Trade (GATT)
Multilateral trade negotiations (MTNs)

Kennedy round, Tokyo round
across-the-board bargaining, item-by-item approach, exceptions list
European Community (Common Market)
trade diversion
common external tariff
economic integration: free-trade area, customs union, common market, economic union, monetary union
preferential agreements, reverse preferences
Canadian-American Auto Agreement

Key Concepts and Review

Similarities and differences in the consequences of tariffs, nontariff barriers, and export-promotion schemes.

The economic rationale for reciprocity and Most-Favored-Nation (MFN) treatment.

The European Community as an illustration of the gains from (regional) trade liberalization.

Supplement 11A
The Ambiguous Impact of Nontariff Barriers
on the Terms of Trade

Import tariffs, nontariff barriers to imports (NTBs), and export promotion all have qualitatively similar effects on a country's domestic economy—except with respect to its terms of trade. United States tariffs almost certainly make the U.S. terms of trade more favorable, but U.S. NTBs do so only under special circumstances.[1]

From the perspective of national economic welfare, then, tariffs may be preferable to NTBs and export promotion that have equivalent production-consumption effects for a reason not outlined in the text of this chapter: their terms-of-trade effects are more predictably favorable.

To illustrate this conclusion, consider a U.S. import quota that had the same restrictive effect as the $20-per-bale tariff from Chapter 9—that is, a quantitative ceiling on U.S. textile imports of 150 bales a day shown in Figure 9.3. Since the U.S. government is thereby restricting the freedom of Sears and other Americans to buy textiles from Japan, the U.S. demand facing Japanese textile producers will fall, as will the price they receive. But U.S. market price will rise, because U.S. textile demand is diverted toward U.S. producers, whose sales are not limited. The difference between the lower Japanese textile price and the higher U.S. textile price is pure profit to anyone who is fortunate enough to be able to trade within the quota.[2] Such lucky traders can take advantage of the wedge that NTBs (as well as tariffs) drive between Japanese and U.S. textile prices. They "buy cheap and sell dear."

Most important quota systems are implemented through *import licenses*. The U.S. government, in our example, might license 150 U.S. importers to import one bale of textiles apiece per day. Textile imports by anyone else would be prohibited. Therefore another way of putting the previously stated conclusion about pure profits is to say: anyone lucky enough to receive a free license to import textiles to the United States has the chance to reap a windfall gain, equal to the difference between the U.S. and Japanese price of one bale of textiles.

In our example, the windfall gains available from the U.S. import quota will be exactly equal to the tariff revenue that is illustrated in Figure 9.5. For this reason, windfall gains are sometimes described as *quota revenue*.

The impact of the U.S. import quota on the U.S. terms of trade depends on only one thing—the distribution of the quota revenue. If

[1] Export promotion makes them deteriorate, except in special circumstances. See pp. 360–362.

[2] This whole discussion assumes that the quota is greater than zero—that is, that no outright embargo has been placed on imports.

Americans receive it all, then import quotas improve the U.S. terms of trade as much as import tariffs do. But if foreign residents receive some of the quota revenue, then import quotas improve the U.S. terms of trade less favorably than tariffs, and perhaps not at all. In fact, if foreign residents are able to appropriate all the windfall gains, then the U.S. terms of trade are unambiguously made less favorable than under free trade. All these conclusions stem directly from the distinction drawn on pp. 302–304 between market price and national price. National price was lower than market price under a U.S. tariff because the U.S. government collected all the tariff revenue. Part of U.S. market price under the tariff represented a transfer of money among U.S. residents, not a payment to Japanese textile producers. If the equivalent quota revenue in our example does not accrue to the U.S. government, nor to any American resident, then the market price of textiles *in* the United States will be equivalent to the national price of textiles *to* the United States. This implies that U.S. import quotas cause not only a higher market price of textiles but a higher national price as well, and consequently less favorable terms of trade. Foreigners will collect the implicit windfall revenue from U.S. quota restrictions.

Two circumstances determine the identity and nationality of the lucky recipients of the quota revenue. The first is the way in which import licenses are distributed, and specifically whether they are sold by the government or distributed free. The second is the market power (monopolistic or monopsonistic power) of private textile traders in the United States and Japan.

To illustrate the importance of these circumstances, consider an extreme case. Suppose that the U.S. government sells its 150 textile import licenses at a public auction (through the submission of sealed bids). Many textile traders bid, all of them highly competitive with each other. In this case, the U.S. government receives the entire quota revenue, the U.S. national price of imported textiles falls, and the U.S. terms of trade improve.

To see why, consider the ideal bidding strategy. Each trader recognizes that the maximum value of a license to import one bale of textiles is the difference between the U.S. and Japanese price—$20 from Figure 9.5. This amount would in fact be all profit if licenses could be obtained from the government for free. However, a low bid for an import license in the government's auction will be topped by other traders. Smart traders will submit bids that assure them some profit, yet stand a good chance of succeeding. More and more competition among bidders will force the profit margins on successful bids lower and lower. In the extreme, the only bids that succeed will be those that cut profits to the bone—successful bids will just shade $20. In this case, the U.S. government would collect nearly $20 of revenue on every bale of textiles imported under the quota. This is almost exactly what it would have collected from a $20 import tariff.

But import quota systems are rarely implemented by auctioning off licenses. More typically, the government distributes import licenses without charge to existing importers and rations them among competing individuals or corporations proportionally to their share of total imports (in some prior base year, as a rule). In this case, as long as competition among traders is still quite intense, the recipients of the licenses reap the windfall quota revenue. In the case of U.S. quotas, these recipients are U.S. residents. Therefore, from the point of view of the United States as a whole, the quota revenue still accrues to "the country"; the national price of imported textiles still falls; and the U.S. terms of trade still improve. Here, the only difference between a tariff and a quota is the type of interpersonal transfer it generates among U.S. residents. The source of the transfer in both cases is U.S. consumers, who are taxed explicitly or implicitly through higher market prices of U.S. textiles. But the recipients of the transfer differ. Under the tariff, the recipients are those who generally benefit from government expenditures. Under the quota, the recipients are the lucky importers of textiles who received licenses.

Like import-license auctions, perfect market competition among private traders is also rare. Its absence has two implications. First, if the government does auction off import licenses, there is no assurance that it will collect all the quota revenue. Noncompetitive bidders may perceive their interdependence and collude formally or informally to retain more than the minimal quota-revenue profit for themselves.

Second, if foreign suppliers are not competitive, but instead have natural market power or cooperative arrangements, then *they* may be able to lay claim to a great part of the quota revenue, leaving little for U.S. license holders, and none for the U.S. government. For example, suppose that the United States imposes quantitative import quotas on oil and oil products and distributes import licenses without charge to U.S. oil companies that have imported in the past. A monopolistic foreign supplier or collusive group of them, such as the Organization of Petroleum Exporting Countries (OPEC), will attempt to play off competitive U.S. importers (license holders) against each other. OPEC will say in essence to each U.S. holder of an import license:

> You may have a license from your government to buy oil from us, but you're crazy if you think we'll sell it to you at the price we charge to other buyers. We know that the U.S. market price of the oil you will receive is higher because of the quota. Therefore if you want to use your import license to buy oil from us (and we're just about the only seller), then you're going to have to pay us close to what *your* market price is, not ours. Otherwise there won't be any sale and your license will be worthless. Take it or leave it.

To the extent that this strategy succeeds, U.S. holders of free import licenses gain little from their privileged position. It only makes them more vulnerable to OPEC demands and entitles them to no more than being pressured into paying OPEC higher prices for imported oil than they would have under free trade. In brief, the availability of windfall gains to competitive holders of free U.S. import licenses only tempts monopolistic foreign suppliers to extract them by threat.

In this case, the quota revenue represents a transfer from U.S. consumers, who pay higher market prices for oil, to OPEC suppliers—not to other Americans. Therefore, the effect of a U.S. import quota is to raise both market and national prices of imported oil and to make the U.S. terms of trade less favorable.

Of course, if U.S. importers (license holders) have private market power (as do U.S. oil companies), then these tendencies are weakened. The distribution of quota revenue between U.S. and foreign residents becomes the outcome of complex bargaining, bluffs, and threats. In such a case, import quotas can affect the U.S. terms of trade in a variety of ways, depending on the comparative market power and bargaining prowess of the antagonists. By contrast, a tariff on oil imports almost always improves the U.S. terms of trade *despite* any market power of U.S. and foreign traders.

Indeterminacy also characterizes the way that NTBs other than import quotas affect the terms of trade. The "voluntary" export quotas that the United States has negotiated with trading partners are likely to produce even less favorable terms of trade than U.S. import quotas. By "forcing" foreign governments to restrict their exports voluntarily, the United States is essentially giving them the chance to issue export licenses to their own residents. When private market power is slight and traders are competitive, the quota revenue is guaranteed to accrue to foreign residents, and the U.S. terms of trade deteriorate. By contrast, an equivalent U.S. import quota would have reserved the quota revenue for U.S. residents and assured an improvement in the U.S. terms of trade.

Voluntary export quotas do, however, avoid the retaliation sparked by U.S. import quotas, retaliation that worsens the U.S. terms of trade. Furthermore, voluntary export quotas do *not* always worsen these terms. Sufficiently strong market power among private U.S. importers (monopsonistic power) could lead them to extract most of the quota revenue from competitive private foreign suppliers (in a similar fashion to OPEC's extraction of U.S. import quota revenue).

Other NTBs affect the terms of trade even more ambiguously because no explicit licensing implements their discrimination against foreign suppliers. All, however, drive wedges between foreign and domestic prices, creating the opportunity for windfall gains. Again, unless private foreign suppliers have greater dominating relative market power, these gains tend to accrue primarily to domestic residents. If they do not accrue *entirely* to domestic residents, however, a tariff that yields comparable production-consumption consequences will yield more favorable terms of trade.

Supplement 11B
The General Agreement on Tariffs and Trade (GATT)

The General Agreement on Tariffs and Trade (GATT) is the most important international organization that oversees international commodity trade and trade barriers. Yet that simple statement contains a technical inaccuracy that highlights the strange history and influence of the GATT. Strictly speaking, the GATT is not an organization at all. It is just a written document—an international code of acceptable and unacceptable international trade practices and of reciprocal rights and obligations of trading countries. Indeed, in its infancy during the late 1940s, there was no GATT bureaucracy. Since that time, a GATT Secretariat has developed, supported financially by countries that subscribe to the GATT, and the Agreement is supervised by a Council of Representatives.

The GATT has become an international organization by historical accident. During international reconstruction after World War II, a different organization was envisioned to be the sister to the International Monetary Fund (the IMF—see Supplement 2B). It was to be known as the International Trade Organization (ITO) and was to oversee international commodity trade in the same way that the IMF oversees international financial relations. But its complicated, protectionist characteristics met with so much opposition in the U.S. Congress that the broad proposal died worldwide.

The portion of the ITO plan most amenable to the United States survived, however. This document was the GATT, to which a number of countries voluntarily subscribed. Organizational and procedural trappings evolved slowly.

The GATT puts forth three broad goals for international trade. Each reflects U.S. economic philosophy and practice because of the country's dominant economic position after World War II. The three goals can be summarized as efficiency, equity, and harmony. Three principles of international trade were embodied in the GATT to implement the three goals: (1) maximum feasible scope for the market (for the forces of international supply and demand), (2) Most-Favored-Nation treatment, as discussed in the text, and (3) negotiation and consultation, which implied periodic meetings to liberalize trade and the right to challenge nations that deliberalized it.

Principles 1 and 3 together have made the GATT a potent force, almost a moral injunction, behind the dramatic trade liberalization that has characterized the past thirty years. Not only have import tariffs been strikingly lowered at the recurrent GATT rounds of multilateral trade negotiations, but in the early years many quantitative restrictions and other nontariff barriers to trade either disappeared or were replaced with tariffs. Checks on such nontariff barriers and disapproval of quantitative restrictions such as quotas are a prominent feature of the GATT and are designed to advance principle 1. (As we saw in the text, tariffs interfere less with competitive forces than do other trade restrictions.) It is notable that even replacement of nontariff barriers with equivalent tariffs is viewed as an important source of trade liberalization under the GATT. This fact illustrates another of the GATT's hallmark features—pragmatism. The Agreement, recognizing that thoroughgoing free trade is an impossible dream, is content to settle for any change that enlarges and enhances the influence of international market forces.

The principle of consultation (part of principle 3) has turned out to be much more important historically than its brief treatment in the written Agreement would suggest. All countries that contract to the GATT are bound (by their word of honor) to maintain the status quo with respect to their trade barriers. In fact, each contracting party (country) is expected to submit the documents outlining its own tariff legislation, which then become a part of the GATT itself. These submissions are called tariff *bindings* because a country is bound to observe them. If it does not and raises a tariff, other contracting countries to the GATT have the right to consult the violator. Consultation is really a kind of negotiation leading to conflict resolution. It is frequently invoked. When consultation succeeds, violators agree to compensate for the injury they have caused, usually by an equivalent reduction of some other tariff. When consultation fails, the GATT permits injured countries to retaliate equivalently against the violators. (For an example of GATT-sanctioned retaliation when consultation failed, see the brief account of the "Chicken War" in footnote 19 of the text.)

Whether consultation succeeds or fails, its historical prominence under the GATT has made it a remarkably beneficial principle. Negotiation replaces economic warfare. Adjudication and arbitration replace acrimony and aggression. Unfortunately, though, only a few countries bind all their tariffs into the GATT. And there is no similar system of bindings for nontariff barriers. Furthermore, formal sanctions for countries that do not respect the principle of consultation are nonexistent. But the system has nevertheless worked extraordinarily well.

Roughly 85 countries subscribe to the GATT, and another 20 apply it provisionally to their own trade policy. Among the 105 supporters of the Agreement are communist countries such as Czechoslovakia, Poland, and Yugoslavia, and also many less-developed countries. Yet the GATT's organizational features are far less structured than those of the International Monetary Fund. Votes are rarely taken on any matter. Instead, varying viewpoints on issues are summarized informally, and a consensus is drawn up by a working party. Joint decisions are almost never made, except to amend the GATT itself. Amendments concerning the Most-Favored-Nation principle and the system of bindings must be approved unanimously; others by a two-thirds majority. Strangely enough, the essentially nonexistent machinery for action has rarely hobbled the organization. This is a tribute to its flexibility and the willingness of most major adherents to abide by their word.

The future of the GATT is cloudy, however. The dramatic reductions in tariffs since World War II have made its preoccupation with them an anachronism. The recently increased use by many countries of quotas, export promotion, embargoes, discriminatory regional trade policy, and other nontariff barriers have challenged GATT's explicit opposition to them. The socialistic less-developed countries that form a larger and larger part of GATT membership have especially chafed at the GATT's bias toward competition and market solutions. Their pressure has successfully brought about a major exception to Most-Favored-Nation treatment—the Generalized System of Preferences (GSPs). (These matters are described at length in Chapter 14.)

Supplement 11C
Trade Diversion: An Example

Along with all the national economic benefits of geographically limited trade liberalization are some potential costs. One that has attracted substantial attention from economists stems from *trade diversion*. In principle, the cost of trade diversion could be so high that regional trade liberalization would be nationally harmful. In practice, this has probably rarely occurred, but several instances in which trade diversion has been very prominent will be cited.

Trade diversion occurs when, while selectively liberalizing trade, a country replaces a low-cost import supplier with a high-cost import supplier. So described, it sounds nonsensical. Why would any country choose to do that? It may happen because unless the country's economy is centrally planned and directed, private suppliers and demanders actually make the decision, and they face market prices that are distorted by the uneven trade barriers. The low-cost import may in fact have the higher market price. These market prices reflect neither true prices to the nation nor national prices (see pp. 302–304). Actually, choosing a high-cost supplier over a low-cost supplier is exactly what is implied by protectionism (in which "our own" high-cost producers are chosen over low-cost foreign ones). In this sense, a kind of trade diversion occurs every time a country raises barriers to trade.

TABLE 11C.1. Trade Diversion from Japanese Liberalization with Europe But Not with the United States (Millions of Dollars; $5 Million-per-Aircraft Tariff)

Price paid per aircraft by Japanese buyers	Components of price			Japanese prices	
	Paid to U.S. aircraft producers	Paid to European aircraft producers	Paid to Japanese government[a]	Market price	National price
Before limited liberalization					
For U.S. aircraft: 45	40	—	5	45	40
For European aircraft: 47	—	42	5	47	42
After limited liberalization					
For U.S. aircraft: 44	39[b]	—	5	44	39
For European aircraft: 43	—	43[b]	0	43	43

[a] The Japanese government observes Most-Favored-Nation (MFN) treatment before, but not after, its limited liberalization.
[b] Why might U.S. aircraft producers lower their price? Why might European aircraft producers raise theirs?

Trade diversion as a result of regional trade liberalization is a perfect illustration of the potential losses predicted by the Theory of the Second Best (Chapter 9). This theory suggests that if price distortions are only selectively removed, national economic welfare will not necessarily increase. A little liberalization—whether in size, timing, commodity coverage, or geographical scope—may be worse than none!

An example will serve to illustrate trade diversion as second-best economics. Suppose that our stylized country of Japan (from Chapter 9) negotiates membership in the European Community and removes its import barriers to EC products, while keeping them on U.S. products. It is entirely possible that the situation outlined in Table 11C.1 will result. The removal of the $5 million Japanese tariff on European aircraft will make them cheaper than U.S. aircraft to Japanese airlines and other private buyers. Their market price will fall when the original, MFN-consistent tariff is removed. But the comparable $5 million tariff on U.S. aircraft is maintained. Their market price is affected only indirectly by limited Japanese trade liberalization. (And students should consider why the example suggests any indirect effects at all, and the reason for their direction.)

In this example, the increased market competitiveness of European aircraft results in trade diversion. Private Japanese buyers will substitute European aircraft for U.S. aircraft. Yet the United States remains the low-cost producer—U.S. producers charge $39 or $40 million per aircraft, while European producers charge $42 or $43 million. Private Japanese buyers are nevertheless diverted from U.S. aircraft by their higher market price, which differs from their cost by precisely the $5 million Japanese tariff. The tariff has made market price artificially higher than cost. It is only slightly inflammatory to say that private Japanese aircraft buyers are "deceived" by the distorted market prices—they cannot see true costs clearly.

Therein lies the national economic cost of trade diversion. The remaining Japanese tariff is a part of the market price of aircraft *in* Japan, but not of the national price of aircraft *to* Japan (see pp. 302–304). By moving to free trade with Europe, Japan actually accepts a higher national price of imported aircraft (last column of the table)—the price per aircraft rises from $40 million to $43 million. The extra $3 million paid for every imported aircraft is part of the cost of trade diversion.

However, the benefits gained from liberalizing trade with Europe may outweigh trade-diversion losses. Otherwise it seems unlikely that Japan would ever choose to become a member of a regional free trade area with Europe. But trade-diversion losses do reduce these benefits and can be seen as a kind of membership fee.

If Europe and Japan had gone further than regional free trade, and had established a common external tariff on U.S. aircraft that was larger than $5 million, trade diversion losses would have been even greater. These additional losses, however, would have been due to protectionism, not liberalization.

Although Table 11C.1 is only hypothetical, trade diversion should not be dismissed as an irrelevant abstraction. European Community members such as Britain and Belgium pay a huge trade-diversion fee for membership with respect to their agricultural imports. If they were permitted to apply the same barriers to agricultural imports from EC partners that they presently apply to nonmembers, then the United States and former British Commonwealth countries would almost certainly become their dominant suppliers. Although the market price of food would be increased, the national cost of food to Britain and Belgium would be reduced. Similarly, the Western Canadian provinces pay a high membership fee for being part of the free-trade area of Canada. If they were to apply the same tariffs to imported industrial goods from Quebec and Ontario as they now apply to comparable U.S. imports, then low-cost U.S. suppliers would almost certainly replace high-cost Eastern Canadian suppliers. Although their market price would certainly rise, the real cost of industrial goods to the Canadian West would fall. The extra tariffs paid by Western Canadian residents would be transferred among themselves through their governments. Supporters of an independent British Columbia or an independent bloc of prairie provinces seem to dimly sense this advantage. This illustrates once again that the differences between international trade, interregional trade, and even interpersonal trade are very slight.

Chapter 12

Explaining International Trade Patterns

The last four chapters might mislead one into thinking that international trade is solely a government concern. But governments usually influence only the quantity and terms of trade.[1] Trade is fundamen-

[1] Two important ways in which international trade can be an extension of diplomacy, however, occur through *state trading* and *imperialism*. *State trading* is defined as international trade that is organized and implemented between governments, rather than between private corporations and individuals. Virtually all trading among socialist and communist countries falls under this heading. World trade in armaments and nuclear materials is also essentially state trading, even when carried out among market economies (because of government control). In explaining such trade, it is foolish to assert the dominance of economic over political explanations. *Imperialism* is a political-economic explanation of trade patterns that is stressed by Marxist and radical economists. Although definitions of imperialism vary widely, most emphasize the attempt by economically powerful "capitalist" (market-oriented) nations to impose "dependence" on unwilling but weaker nations. Dependence is fostered by promoting a trade pattern in which imperialist nations increase markets for their manufactures through exports to their subservient dependencies and in return import both raw materials and ownership claims on the physical wealth (land, corporations) of the dependency. Both increased export markets and the opportunity for acquiring dependency wealth increase profit rates in the imperialist nations. This counteracts what Marx and many radical economists believe to be an inevitable tendency for capitalism to overinvest, compete away all profits, and ultimately crumble. The political aspect of trade in this theory of imperialism stems from the cooperation of capitalist (formerly colonialist) governments in organizing and legally enforcing the desired trade pattern. Capitalist governments do so because their political support depends not on the "will of the people" (although see pp. 338–345 and footnote 4 below) but rather on the wealth of the owners of capital, who support them in acquiring and maintaining office. Radical and Marxist economists sometimes distinguish modern imperialism, organized on the initiative of multinational corporations with the support of governments, from colonial imperialism, organized on the initiative of governments with the support of home corporations that had not yet become multinationals.

tally explained not by diplomacy but by quite natural economic differences among countries, firms, and goods. These differences have to do with climate, history, location, and technology and would exist even in the absence of an active government role in the economy.

Nor are the determinants of international trade particularly exotic or mysterious; they are in fact quite common. The same natural differences that lead people to buy and sell within boundaries lead them to do so across boundaries.

This chapter describes the natural economic differences that induce international trade. Because its goal is to describe rather than to evaluate, the tone will differ from that of previous chapters. Whether a particular pattern of trade is "good" or "bad" for the economic welfare of a nation will here concern us only briefly. Why a particular pattern of trade happens to emerge among nations will concern us. The latter is a concern of positive economics; the former, of normative economics (see the opening of Part II). But the reasons for caring about describing the positive sources for trade are normative, as the next section shows.

Reasons for Caring About the Determinants of International Trade Patterns

There is more than just casual academic curiosity in the question of who exports which goods to whom. Most countries covet comparative advantage in goods that are believed to have special economic or strategic value: goods that feature stable export earnings and a monopolistic position in the world market; high-technology, growth-promoting manufactures; armaments. Many countries feel victimized by comparative advantage in goods with special costs: goods that face cyclically erratic foreign demands or secularly deteriorating terms of trade (Supplement 8A); goods for which productivity growth seems chronically low; goods whose production pollutes the environment and endangers the health of workers. Nor are countries indifferent to the number and identity of their trading partners. Most prefer a diversified set of politically stable suppliers and customers in order to avoid uncertainty. They also seek to avoid overreliance on only a few large trading partners, since that weakens their bargaining position and their capacity to resist monopoly and monopsony power (as well as political and military power).

Given these preferences, it can be seen why current trade patterns, illustrated in Schema 12.1, concern small, less-developed countries (LDCs) greatly but are generally agreeable to large developed countries. Except for crude petroleum and several minerals whose markets have been effectively monopolized, small LDCs produce few of the most coveted export commodities and import almost all. Their exports

SCHEMA 12.1. *The Commodity Composition and Direction of World Trade, 1974**

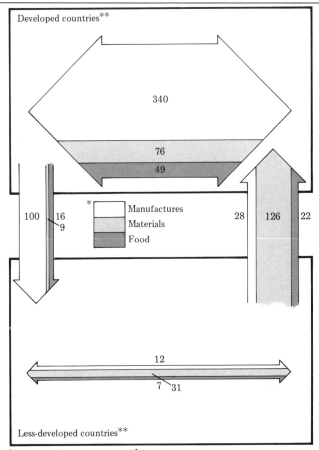

Horizontal arrows: intragroup trade.
Vertical arrows: intergroup trade.

* The thickness of the arrows and their shaded parts represent the size of international trade (exports) measured in millions of U.S. dollars. *No shading:* trade in manufactures (chemicals, machinery, and transportation equipment—Standard International Trade Classification (SITC) 5–8); *light shading:* trade in mineral fuels and crude materials (SITC 2–4); *dark shading:* trade in food, beverages, and tobacco (SITC 0–1). The general character of the schema will differ imperceptibly for more recent years than 1974, although the arrows will grow thicker, as international trade has grown.

** Developed countries are taken to include developed market economies, the Soviet Union, and centrally planned economies in Europe. Less-developed countries are taken to include developing market economies, centrally planned economies in Asia, and the Organization of Petroleum Exporting Countries (OPEC).

Source: United Nations, Department of Economic and Social Affairs, Statistical Office, *Monthly Bulletin of Statistics* 30 (August 1976).

are concentrated instead in primary products, whose production may entail undesirable social and economic consequences and whose prices are frequently set in highly volatile and competitive markets. Advanced industrial countries, by contrast, enjoy the supposedly ideal commodity composition of trade. The dramatically unequal width of the arrows illustrates that LDCs as a group are much more trade dependent on developed countries than they are on each other. The geographical concentration of trade for any particular LDC is even more pronounced and is often a holdover from the ties of colonial times. Failing to have numerous and diverse trading partners subjects LDCs to more uncertainty than developed countries. Failing to match the economic size and power of developed countries weakens the bargaining position of LDCs.[2] Developed countries as a group have much more diverse and less volatile trading patterns.

Practical-minded corporations and labor unions also care about the direction and commodity composition of trade. The economic influences discussed here and in Chapter 13 caused the Ford Motor Company to export Pinto engines from Britain to the United States when the car was first introduced. Changes in these influences caused Ford to abandon that trade pattern. Multinational corporations such as Ford or Unilever, which produce in many countries, monitor carefully the determinants of international trade patterns. Their monitoring leads to decisions on the ideal mix of commodities that each of their far-flung affiliated corporations produces and where new production operations can be profitably begun. Labor unions (such as those in the AFL-CIO) often find the resulting changes in trade patterns adverse. They lobby hard for policies that alter the volume, direction, and commodity makeup of trade favorably to wage earners.

Some reasons for trying to identify why any country exports certain goods and imports others are purely informational. Long-range planning by governments, corporations, and individuals is greatly facilitated by knowledge of the sources of comparative advantage. Uncertainty is reduced and future action is shaped more intelligently, for example, if it can be accurately forecast that above-average population growth in poorer countries will make marginal wheat growing more profitable in the near future. Foreseeing the consequences of the same demographic trend can greatly ease adjustment and dislocation if, for example, it is inevitable that textile production in New England will become completely unprofitable.

We shall see the reasoning underlying these forecasts below. We will also explain some forecasts that do not accord so well with intuition—for example, how rapid loss of U.S. technological leadership in consumer electronic equipment might possibly leave TV, radio, and stereo imports unaffected if the United States were losing technological leadership rapidly in every industry. Finally, we shall

[2] The trade patterns illustrated in Schema 12.1 are quite consistent with predictions from the theory of imperialism, described in the previous footnote.

Chapter 12: Explaining International Trade Patterns

see that describing the determinants of trade in commodities gives us the first clues toward explaining international labor migration, trade in resources, and movements by multinational corporations.

Simple and Fundamental Explanations of International Trade Patterns

Just as in the examination of the national benefits from trade, explanations of its direction and commodity composition come in many levels of sophistication. The simplest and least informative level appeals to prices and availability. Each good moves from countries in which it is cheap and available to those in which it is dear and unavailable. The forces of supply and demand assure this pattern. Without international trade, prices would differ dramatically from country to country, and some goods would be completely unavailable in some places. But given the opportunity to trade, demanders in every country would import goods that were cheaper abroad, and suppliers would export goods that were more expensive abroad. Profits would be made on both kinds of transaction, and price differentials would be dampened.

Of course, this simple explanation just begs the next question. What is it that causes supply, demand, prices, and availability to differ from country to country? Among the multitude of answers, three stand out as fundamental determinants of the pattern of trade: intercountry differences in (1) resource endowments, (2) technology, and (3) tastes.

Differential Resource Endowments as a Determinant of the Pattern of International Trade

Countries differ from each other in their resource endowments. This simple fact provides the first important reason why prices and availability vary among them. The United States is blessed with unusually abundant fertile land; West African countries are not. Coastal countries have 200-mile claims on rich ocean wealth off their shorelines; landlocked countries do not. Canada is mineral rich; most European countries are mineral poor. The population of the developed world is highly educated and skilled; that of the poorest countries is just ascending from widespread illiteracy. National stocks of productive plant and equipment are notably higher in industrial countries than elsewhere.

Resource inequalities lead in some cases to a predictable commodity composition and direction of trade. Because tin is available at a low price owing to the abundance of the ores from which it is extracted, Bolivia is a major tin exporter. Bolivia also imports fish. Otherwise, because the country is landlocked (ocean scarce), fish would be prohibitively expensive. In Iceland, fish are available, cheap, and exported, and tin is scarce, expensive, and imported, for precisely the opposite reasons.

Two important characteristics of every explanation of international trade patterns should be made clear. First, what really matters is countries' *relative* position. Bolivia is rich in tin ore and poor in ocean resources *relative* to Iceland. If, by contrast, each country had lots of both tin ore and ocean resources (or if each had only a little of both), then there would be insufficient information to draw any conclusions about their respective comparative advantages. Second, it is the *ratio* of prices that really matters for trade (except over short periods)—the price of tin relative to the price of fish. When the ratio of the price of a pound of tin to an ounce of fish in Bolivia is 45 to 1 and when in Iceland it is 60 to 1, the same opportunities for profitable trade exist as were discussed in Chapter 8 (see Figures 8.3 and 8.4 especially). Bolivians can get more than 45 ounces of fish for every pound of tin that they choose to export rather than sell at home. Icelanders can get more than 1/60 of a pound of tin for every ounce of fish that they choose to export rather than sell at home.[3]

The influence of differential resource endowments on the pattern of trade is not always so transparent, as a more general and conventional rendering of the influence will illustrate. Economists frequently find it useful to group resources into categories described as *labor* and *capital*. In its broadest sense, capital includes all productive resources except the primitive work capacity of the population, which is defined as labor. A pure laborer, by this definition, is unschooled and unskilled. Education and skills, while normally embodied in people, are not labor but "human capital."[4] Capital also includes arable land, mineral deposits, and productive machinery, equipment, and buildings.

---

[3] Over short periods, the pattern of trade can sometimes be influenced by absolute prices as well as price ratios. Even if fish and tin were the only two commodities that Bolivia and Iceland traded, the absolute prices of both could be lower in one country than in the other. Then the pattern of trade would be one-directional—both tin and fish would be exported by the low-price country and imported by the high-price country. But not for long. As Chapter 5 shows, the resulting export/import imbalance would tend to cause generalized inflation in the low-price country and generalized recession in the high-price country. This would make prices converge continuously until once again the absolute price of tin became lower in Bolivia, the absolute price of fish became lower in Iceland, and trade became two-directional. Transitory one-directional trade flows would be even quicker to vanish under floating exchange rates, as Chapters 4 and 5 show. Appreciation/depreciation would almost instantaneously erase the export/import imbalance, eliminate the tendency for both prices to be lower in one country, and restore a two-directional trade pattern.

[4] By this definition, almost everyone in the United States is in some measure a capitalist, even people with the lowest of skills. The observation would not surprise foreign commentators, who note that U.S. labor unions are among the least radical in the world and that the average American's standard of living is among the highest.

SCHEMA 12.2. *The Influence of Differential Resource Endowments on Trade Patterns*

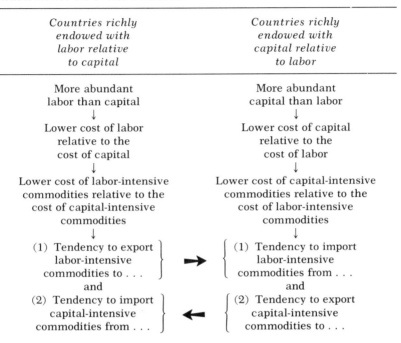

Countries richly
endowed with
labor relative
to capital

Countries richly
endowed with
capital relative
to labor

More abundant
labor than capital
↓
Lower cost of labor
relative to the
cost of capital
↓
Lower cost of labor-intensive
commodities relative to the
cost of capital-intensive
commodities
↓

More abundant
capital than labor
↓
Lower cost of capital
relative to the
cost of labor
↓
Lower cost of capital-intensive
commodities relative to the
cost of labor-intensive
commodities
↓

(1) Tendency to export
labor-intensive
commodities to . . .
and
(2) Tendency to import
capital-intensive
commodities from . . .

(1) Tendency to import
labor-intensive
commodities from . . .
and
(2) Tendency to export
capital-intensive
commodities to . . .

Key: For ↓, read "leads to" or "causes." Thick arrows represent direction of trade.
Labor-intensive commodities are those requiring more labor relative to capital in their production processes than *capital-intensive* commodities—which require more capital relative to labor.

Countries that are labor abundant and capital scarce by world standards can be expected to export those goods that require large amounts of labor relative to capital in their production process—simple manufactures such as textiles, clothing, shoes, leather products, furniture, and toys, and also agricultural products such as rice and fruits that are not amenable to automated planting and picking. All such goods are said to be produced *labor intensively*—in ways that require relatively much labor. These same countries can be expected to import other goods from their capital-abundant, labor-scarce trading partners—sophisticated manufactures, processed chemicals and mineral products, and capital-intensive agricultural commodities such as grains and meat. The chain of reasoning underlying this explanation of trade patterns appears in Schema 12.2.

Schema 12.2 depends on two additional assumptions that were only implicit in the Bolivia-Iceland example. One is that where resources are abundant by world standards, they will be relatively cheap; where scarce, they will be relatively expensive. The second is that goods differ uniformly and predictably in their suitability to labor-intensive or capital-intensive production techniques.

The first assumption seems reasonable on supply/demand grounds, but need not always be true. Abundant endowments (supplies) of capital in the United States may not be enough to give it lower capital costs than the rest of the world. United States consumption (demand) is also probably more concentrated on capital-intensive goods than is world consumption. The United States devotes a larger share of its expenditure (by world standards) to consumer durables, defense and aerospace equipment, drugs, grains, meat, and energy—all of which require substantial capital in production. Because demand for these commodities is relatively higher, the implied (derived) demand for the services of capital will also be relatively higher, and so capital may not cost less than elsewhere in the world despite its abundance. As we will see, international differences in consumption preferences (tastes) are themselves an explanation of trade patterns and can either offset trade patterns based on resource endowments or sometimes reinforce them (Bolivia is not only rich in tin ore, but probably spends proportionally less on tin than industrial countries).

This example raises an important general point. Each of the fundamental determinants discussed in this chapter helps in explaining a country's comparative advantage, but no single determinant can explain trade patterns by itself. Each in isolation explains partially; when examined with other determinants, each can either support or counteract the others. A comprehensive explanation of comparative advantage must appeal to many sources.[5]

---

[5] The fact that one determinant of comparative advantage can neutralize another does not make either one logically incorrect. It suggests that reliance on one to the exclusion of others is likely to give at best only a partially accurate explanation. It also suggests that examining one determinant without holding the others constant is likely to give misleading results. Indeed, the very first empirical attempt to explain the U.S. pattern of trade by resource endowments alone failed. Wassily Leontief, the Nobel-prize-winning economist, discovered to his surprise in a famous 1953 paper that U.S. exports seemed to embody more labor and less capital than U.S. imports. The finding subsequently became known as the *Leontief Paradox*. Similar "paradoxes" were reported in sporadic attempts to explain the trade patterns of Canada, India, Japan, and other countries by resource endowments alone. But there are no paradoxes *from* these empirical studies. Indeed, the principal paradox is *about* them— namely, that their findings were considered paradoxical in the first place. Since resource endowments are only one of several fundamental determinants of trade patterns, no one should have expected it to be sufficient as an explanation by itself. Economists who have recently examined the impact of resource endowments *together with* other fundamental determinants of trade patterns have only infrequently encountered paradoxical results.

Part of the second assumption is also dubious. Goods do differ from each other in their production processes[6] (tin mining requires no fishing boats, and fishing requires no tin ore). But it is not at all certain that goods can be unambiguously and uniformly ranked by the capital/labor intensity of their production processes.[7]

Despite these caveats, the resource-endowment explanation of trade patterns has long enjoyed a position of preeminence among international-trade economists. It is the only fundamental determinant of trade patterns to have been elevated to summary in a theorem! The *Heckscher-Ohlin Theorem* is named for the two economists who first emphasized trade's dependence on resource endowments:

> Heckscher-Ohlin Theorem: *Every country tends to export those goods that use its relatively abundant resources relatively intensively, and tends to import those goods that use its relatively scarce resources relatively intensively.*

Differential Technology as a Determinant of the Pattern of International Trade

Countries also differ markedly in their technology—the range of alternative processes available for producing each good. There are at least four reasons for such differences:

1. Slow, inadequate international flows of information (for example, the persistence of some primitive agricultural methods).
2. Purposeful secrecy to maintain a privileged market position (for

---

[6] This has important implications for the diagrammatic representation of resource-endowments trade in Figure 12.2.

[7] In Japan, for example, it is virtually certain that steel production is more capital-intensive than vegetable farming (which is frequently carried out by painstaking cultivation of small garden plots). In the United States, this is not at all certain. United States steel producers are believed to have traditionally lagged behind Japanese steel producers in adopting the most up-to-date mechanized techniques, and U.S. vegetable farming involves significant mechanization and vast tracts of cropland in the Southwest. In light of these observations, it seems dubious to claim that steel is everywhere produced more capital intensively than vegetables, or vice versa—it all depends on circumstances. The technical economic description of such indeterminacy is that the commodities are subject to *factor-intensity reversals*—reversal of their resource intensities compared to each other. In the presence of factor-intensity reversals, resource endowments are again insufficient to predict the pattern of trade. It is nonsense to predict that the United States will export its capital-intensive good (vegetables) to Japan in return for Japan's labor-intensive good (vegetables). The pattern of trade cannot be determined without knowledge of production conditions (factor intensities) as well as resource endowments.

example, an industrial secret such as the recipe for Coca-Cola syrup).

3. Government-sanctioned exclusive positions in the use of a new production technique or product design (for example, patents and trademarks).

4. Limits on the economic size of a country's markets, firms, plants, or production runs (large-scale production technology differs from small-scale production technology for a great many goods).

Multiple reasons for international differences in technology generate multiple explanations of trade patterns. Two explanations that figure prominently in practice are based on (a) differential *technological gaps* and *product life cycles* (reasons 1, 2, and 3), and (b) differential access to economies of large-scale production (reason 4).

TRADE PATTERNS BASED ON DIFFERENTIAL TECHNOLOGICAL GAPS AND PRODUCT LIFE CYCLES

The modern world is in technological flux. Private corporations, laboratories, think tanks, universities, and governments are continually engaged in research and development oriented toward more satisfying products and less costly production methods. Familiar and spectacular results include the assembly line, prefabricated structures, synthetic fabrics, transistors, pocket electronic calculators, supersonic commercial aircraft, guided missiles, nuclear power generation, miracle drugs, miracle fertilizers, miracle rice, and the necessary support systems to maintain life in outer space.

Even though *product* and *process innovation* proceeds continually, its importance (speed) varies from good to good. In addition, its benefits are not always diffused rapidly worldwide. Technological change in transportation equipment, communication systems, and data-processing machinery is currently very rapid. But such change in the production of shoes, steel, and toys is comparatively slow. Techniques for producing the former are known or available in only a few countries. Production techniques for the latter are well established, easily copied, and similar throughout the world.

Unevenness in technical change and diffusion provides an important explanation of comparative advantage. The development of synthetic fabrics over the past eighty years—nylon, rayon, polyester, acetate—provides an excellent illustration. First, these developments were concentrated on textile products and resulted in cheaper or better fabrics. Similarly dramatic innovations in nontextiles were not simultaneous. Second, synthetics were initially introduced in the countries that developed them, principally Britain, France, Germany, and the United States. Proliferation of the innovations to other countries was slow. Imitating technological breakthroughs is a time-consuming process, and many of the synthetics were legally protected by patents.[8]

Disparities among countries were the natural result. British, French, German, and American prices of textiles became lower than they would have been without the innovations, while (in the short run) very little happened to textile prices in other countries, or to nontextile prices anywhere. Prices and price ratios diverged. The price of textiles relative to nontextiles fell in the four innovating countries and it became profitable for them to export textile products to the rest of the world in return for nontextiles.

The resulting trade pattern was an example of *technological-gap* trade. It arose because of the uneven change in production methods, which created a gap between countries. To illustrate the importance of the unevenness of the change, suppose that Britain or any of the other countries had made a sweeping, all-encompassing technological breakthrough that reduced the production costs of *all* their goods proportionally. Neither comparative advantage nor trade patterns would have been affected, as we saw on pp. 244–245 and 248.[9] Nor would they have been affected if the technology required for manufacturing nylon, rayon, acetate, and polyester could have been spread instantaneously to all countries. It is unevenness in technological advance, not merely its existence, that alters the direction and commodity composition of international trade.

Trade patterns based on any particular technological gap are usually transitory. As time passes, the particular innovation spreads to other countries. Even before patents expire, patent holders in innovating countries often license their use by producers in other countries (for a fee—see Chapter 13). After a patent expires, producers throughout the world imitate the superior production methods or product of their innovating competition.

Figure 12.1 is a stylized illustration of how production and trade unfold after an innovation. It illustrates several points. First, comparative advantage is obviously not unchangeable. A country might

---

[8] Patents are governmentally sanctioned licenses granted to an innovator to retain exclusive use of a new production process or exclusive production rights for a new product for a limited period (seventeen years in the United States and many developed countries). Intergovernmental conventions and treaties create a fairly comprehensive worldwide system of exclusive rights that makes infringement on a foreign patent a crime. The economist's usual defense of monopolistic patents is that they are the reward necessary to encourage innovation. Whether they are the economically most desirable encouragement, however, is a controversial issue (see Chapter 14).

[9] In Figures 8.4 and 12.2 through 12.5 any such *even*, across-the-board technological breakthrough will shift one country's production possibilities curve outward from the origin without changing its slope at any given production mix. Comparative advantage, as defined below and in Chapter 8, therefore does not change.

FIGURE 12.1. *Trade Based on Differential Technological Gaps or Product Life Cycles*

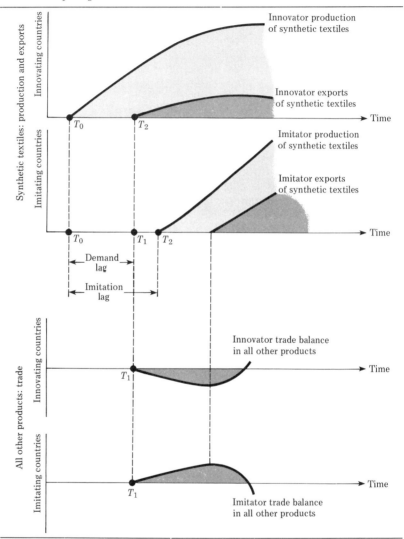

well proceed from being a textile importer on balance, to being a textile exporter, to being once again a textile importer.

Second, natural textile products may be among those other products imported in exchange for synthetic textile products. (Trade in such other products is illustrated in the bottom of the diagram.) Note that any country could be simultaneously an exporter and importer of the aggregate called textiles. Almost all trade data reveal this phenomenon, known as *two-way trade* or (less exactly) *intraindustry trade*. This is one of the consequences of defining a commodity too imprecisely. Avoiding it, however, hardly seems to justify going to the opposite extreme—for example, by denying any commonality between computerized electric typewriters (which the United States exports) and nonelectric portable typewriters (which the United States imports).

A third point is implicit in Figure 12.1: comparative advantage and trade patterns are not always attributable to differences in relative prices. Availability is often the immediate determining factor. Countries import synthetic textile products from innovating countries during the period from T_1 to T_2 not because they are cheaper but because they are unavailable elsewhere.

Fourth, in addition to the time taken to procure patents and the difficulty of prying loose industrial secrets, the lag between an innovation and its worldwide diffusion (the *imitation lag*) is often due to demand considerations. These are featured prominently in the *product-life-cycle* perspective.

The product life cycle describes the distinctive stages of economic life that many goods pass through. For example, when first produced, innovations such as nylon, rayon, acetate, and polyester are considered completely new products, rather than the same products (fabrics) produced by an innovative production process. Such "new" products face uncertain markets and require many adjustments to fill the needs of buyers. Early trousers made out of synthetic material frequently lost their shape; early wash and wear shirts required some ironing but were very heat sensitive; and early synthetic fishing line got terribly tangled. In order to correct such deficiencies, innovating producers tend to market new products to their own domestic customers, whose habits and reactions they know better than those of export customers. Producers can thus interpret the need for design alterations more readily and can perfect the new product more rapidly. Innovations in production processes are also initiated at home, where producers are better acquainted with the habits and reactions of production workers, foremen, and supervisors than they are abroad.

The usual result of such home-based experimentation is that for a short time after innovation (T_0 to T_1) no foreign marketing, production, or trade takes place. Only after a product or process reaches a "mature" stage in its life does marketing and production spread abroad (patents and licensing permitting). When a product finally reaches the stage of "standardization," where both specifications of demanders and ideal production methods are well known and available worldwide, its international trade is usually better explained by other determinants of trade patterns.

Figure 12.1 may give the false impression that trade patterns are only sporadically and occasionally influenced by differential technological gaps and product life cycles. On the contrary, this influence does not necessarily diminish as any single innovation is widely imitated or when any particular product becomes standardized. Other technological changes will be taking place in other products and will be spreading worldwide with varying rapidity. These changes will influence trade patterns, perhaps very differently from previous and future innovations but no less predictably.

TRADE PATTERNS BASED ON DIFFERENTIAL ACCESS
TO ECONOMIES OF LARGE-SCALE PRODUCTION

Some goods, such as buses, commercial aircraft, sophisticated weaponry, and specialized machine tools, are produced primarily in a few countries. Countries that import them frequently produce none at all. An important explanation of this geographical concentration of production and export concerns "economies" of large-scale production. *Scale economies* describe the lower per-unit production costs that larger producers enjoy. They are often associated with goods that, even for the production of only one unit, require large start-up, developmental, and other *fixed costs*. If these costs are large relative to those needed to produce units beyond the first (*variable costs*), average production costs may decline significantly as the scale of production rises. Economies of large-scale production are also present if production is characterized by *increasing returns to scale*, a technological property whereby applying more of all inputs at a particular rate leads output to expand at an even faster rate.

Because large-scale production of, say, commercial aircraft, is less costly and more productive than small-scale production, countries whose aircraft producers face large market demands will have a competitive advantage in that aircraft prices will be lower there than elsewhere. Other prices, however, will not be significantly influenced by the scale of aircraft production. Thus, because the ratio of aircraft prices to other prices will be low in these countries, the familiar opportunities for profitable exports and imports will exist.

In which countries will aircraft producers face large market demands? One traditional answer has been countries with large internal markets—the economically large countries.[10] Underlying this answer

[10] There are theoretical problems with the answer. Economies of large-scale production are usually thought to accrue to plants that enjoy long production runs or to firms that are able to spread fixed costs over a large number of activities. Scale economies do not conventionally accrue to *industries*. Having economically large countries with large internal markets guarantees large industries in the absence of trade, but in no way guarantees large firms or long production runs, compared to smaller countries. Smaller countries' industries may simply have fewer firms—but firms of the same size, with plants of the

is reasoning that is frequently linked to technological gaps. Large countries such as the United States, whose producers pioneer in developing commercial aircraft, have not only temporary but also permanent export potential. Innovative aircraft are marketed and produced first for U.S. markets (including the U.S. armed services), and economies of large-scale production are realized even before exporting begins. Because U.S. producers are already producing on a larger scale and at lower cost, small countries such as Britain and France, whose producers have also pioneered in developing commercial aircraft, face an insuperable barrier to entering export competition on more than a temporary, technological-gap basis. The Comet, Viscount, and Caravelle, all British or French commercial aircraft of the past thirty years, had at least the potential for temporary world export domination based on technological advantage. None established a dominant export position—in part because of the clear scale advantages of slightly later-blooming U.S. competitors.

Although large internal markets are helpful in promoting export specialization on goods characterized by scale economies, they are not necessary. Large export markets can substitute for large domestic markets and allow producers to realize these economies. Any historical accident, quirk of taste, or random shock that leads a small country to begin exporting goods suitable to large-scale production can also lead that country to establish permanent export dominance. Initial exports reduce costs of production, which make additional exports more competitive, which further reduce costs of production, and so on. Sufficiently dramatic economies of large-scale production fend off competitors in international trade for the same reasons that they act as a barrier to new firms in an established industry.

Among the small countries whose dominant export positions appear to be explained by scale economies are Belgium (standardized auto parts and other selected manufactured inputs), Denmark (furniture), Netherlands (electrical equipment), Poland (golf carts), Sweden (communications equipment), and Switzerland (pharmaceuticals). It is also widely believed that the formation of the European Common Market allowed a number of small European producers to realize scale economies through export to the broad European market.

Trade based on scale economies is frequently two-way. Different countries realize these economies in different variants of similar goods. The United States exports full-size cars and high-precision, environment-resistant bearings but imports small cars and standard bearings. Belgium exports white china but imports colored china.

_____

same size, with production runs of the same length, as those in the larger country. In order to make the unadorned answer theoretically acceptable, a presumption has to be established that large firms and plants are typically a consequence of large internal markets. The presumption is hard to defend as a generalization.

Japan (during the 1960s) exported small-screen television sets but imported large-screen sets.

This discussion illustrates again the interdependence and intermingling of the explanations of comparative advantage. Because predictable associations abound and because some influences may even cause others, it is hard to disentangle any one influence on trade patterns from another. Economies of large-scale production are often revealed in goods that are highly capital-intensive (especially in physical capital). Large-scale production is often believed to promote rapid technological change.[11] Abundance of human capital (education, skills) may promote technological advance.

With correspondences like these, it is often impossible to determine whether scale economies, resource endowments, or technological gaps explain a country's trade. Each one will be consistent with observed patterns.[12] The direction and commodity composition of world trade are subject to many influences.

Differential Demand as a Determinant of the Pattern of International Trade

Up to this point, differences among countries and commodities in supply conditions have been stressed, with only occasional nods toward preferences and demand. The latter two, however, provide some straightforward influences on trade. For example, although differential endowments of tropical climate are not irrelevant, demand readily explains why the United States imports more tourist services from Mexico and Caribbean islands than the latter import from the United States. Americans devote a larger share of spending to leisure-related activities like travel and exotic fishing trips than do residents of poorer countries. The relatively larger demand for related services will tend to make their relative price in the United States higher than elsewhere. This intercountry disparity in relative prices promotes international trade in a predictable direction: the United States will

[11] Large firms appear to devote more resources to research and development. Innovation also develops out of *learning by doing*, so that the longer a firm's cumulative production history, the more innovative it will be.

[12] The fact that the influences are interdependent and cannot realistically be disentangled does not make any single explanation of trade patterns logically incorrect. It is simply impossible to detect its importance, because its influences on trade are qualitatively identical to those of another explanation. When explanations are mutually reinforcing in every aspect, their separate individual significance cannot be inferred from observing world trade patterns. Or, to draw a useful comparison, it is only when symptoms differ in at least one respect that diseases can be differentiated. See footnote 5 for additional observations on the methodology of empirical international economics.

import leisure-related services, and the rest of the world will export them.

Other trade patterns that are influenced by international differences in demand include exports of productive equipment from developed countries (whose demand is more consumption oriented) to less-developed countries (whose demand is more investment oriented), and exports of minerals and fuels from less-developed countries to wealthier ones, whose consumption goods use more fuel. Some economists even predict that differing demands will affect the future trade pattern in environment-despoiling goods. Since environmental quality is still a luxury among less-developed countries, they predict that pollution-prone production will shift toward these countries and away from the developed world.

Demand also explains trade patterns more subtly through availability, not through relative prices. Many products that satisfy similar basic needs are nevertheless *differentiated* in the eyes of ultimate buyers. Exclusive trademarks, brand-name allegiance, and snob appeal are relevant to international trade as much as to domestic trade. A Rolls-Royce differs from a comparably equipped Cadillac, Sony television sets differ from Zenith, Schweppes mixers differ from Canada Dry, and there's no ham like a Polish ham. When close-to-identical products are this finely differentiated, trade patterns are influenced by the purchasers' insistence on variety alone without regard to relative prices. Rolls-Royces and Polish hams are available from Britain and Poland only. Americans who insist on them must import to satisfy their demand.

As some Britishers (perhaps U.S. expatriates) prefer Cadillacs, and some Poles prefer Oscar Mayer hams, two-way trade is again to be expected. Such trade seems to be especially substantial among developed market economies that have grown affluent enough to insist on variety for its own sake. International trade along these lines is fundamentally beneficial, not because it provides *more* goods, but because it provides different ones. Trade satisfies the demand for variety by supplying variations and brands of products that are unavailable at home.

Diagrammatic Illustrations of the Fundamental Determinants of International Trade Patterns

Although it is confining as an expository vehicle, the production-possibilities-curve diagram from Chapters 8 and 10 is frequently employed to illustrate the determinants of trade patterns. Differential resource endowments and technology create international differences in the shape of these curves. Differential demand creates differences in where each country chooses to produce on the curve. The diagram is confining, however, because it cannot convey either the way the

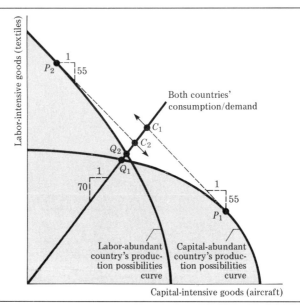

three fundamental determinants of trade patterns supplement each other, or their probable rich interdependence. Each is usually treated abstractly, as if the others did not exist. And the diagram's dimensions limit the discussion to only two groups of goods.

Figures 12.2 through 12.5 illustrate trade patterns that are based solely on one or another of the three fundamental determinants discussed in this chapter. Two extreme situations are always contrasted: complete absence of trade, where both production and consumption take place at points Q, and the presence of completely unencumbered, perfectly competitive free trade, where production takes place at points P and consumption at points C.[13]

Two general features of Figures 12.2 through 12.5 are notable. First, if trade were perfectly free and competitive, the ratio of market prices would be equalized from country to country. For example, at production points P in Figure 12.2, 55 units of the labor-intensive good

---

[13] Unencumbered free trade implies not only the absence of government trade barriers, but also the absence of transportation costs. The usual conditions that characterize trade lie between the extremes of free trade and no trade, and have already been illustrated in Chapters 9 and 10. Trade barriers and transport costs affect the direction and commodity composition of trade in ways described later in this chapter.

would be exchanged for 1 unit of the capital-intensive good in *both* countries. The ratio 55 to 1 is defined as their relative *opportunity cost*, measured by the slope of the production possibilities curve: the resources used to produce 55 units of textiles could be used equally profitably to produce one unit of aircraft. But it also represents the price ratio of the two goods, because each price reflects resource costs perfectly under market competition. (One product would really be "worth" 55 times the other.) Assuring the equality of relative market prices in the two countries, and implicitly underlying each diagram, are the forces of supply and demand outlined on pp. 273–277.[14]

Second, in order to simplify the exposition, demand preferences and tastes have been made very simple and rigid. The population of each country consumes commodities in fixed proportions, regardless of income or prices.[15] In Figure 12.2, they invariably consume 70 units of

[14] As implied by the discussion, the unencumbered forces of competitive supply and demand also assure that relative opportunity costs match the terms of trade from Chapter 8. That is, they assure that the slope of the production possibilities curve matches the slope of the terms-of-trade line (Figure 8.5), which can happen only if the terms-of-trade line is *tangent* to the production possibilities curve, as illustrated in Figures 12.2 through 12.5. Tangencies such as these were not encountered in Chapters 8 and 10 because few references were made to the extreme world of unencumbered free trade and competition. Nor is such reference necessary here. But it does serve as a convenient diagrammatical reference point. By way of contrast, the introduction of trade barriers or transport costs would cause the terms of trade to diverge from both relative market prices (pp. 302–304) and opportunity costs. And the introduction of any noncompetitive behavior would cause relative market prices to diverge from opportunity costs.

[15] Commodity demands in Figures 12.2 through 12.5 are thus perfectly price inelastic, unlike those in Chapter 9. More advanced treatments of international economics outline the determinants of trade patterns under the more flexible and conventional demand behavior illustrated in Chapter 9, and assumed elsewhere in this book. Some even propose *indifference-curve maps* for entire countries and superimpose these maps on Figures 12.2 through 12.5. These *community indifference curves* are generally drawn to be negatively sloped, nonintersecting, and "bowed out" from the origin at their ends. They are employed in a manner analogous to their use at the level of individual consumer decision making. With such curves, the no-trade production points Q are characterized by tangency between each country's production possibilities curve and one of its community indifference curves. Under unencumbered free trade, consumption points C are characterized by tangency between the terms-of-trade line (Figure 8.5) and a community indifference curve. Although this approach is more conventional than that adopted in this book, it is also diagrammatically more complex and adopts only slightly less extreme and restrictive assumptions. Advanced international economics demonstrates that community indifference-curve maps are *not* well-defined, nonintersecting, or appropriate indexes of "social utility," except under very restrictive assumptions—for example, when all individuals in a society have identical tastes, abilities, and endowments of capital. Otherwise, community indifference curves shift with any change in society's income distribution, intersect, and have no social-welfare meaning comparable to their interpretation for individual consumers.

the labor-intensive good for every unit of the capital-intensive good.[16] For this chapter, these extreme assumptions about demand are quite innocuous. Under more conventional demand assumptions, trade patterns will still be influenced as pictured in Figures 12.2 through 12.5.

Figure 12.2 illustrates a pattern of trade that is based on resource endowments alone. Neither technology nor tastes are assumed to differ between the two sets of countries. At the no-trade production points Q, and indeed at every production point between the Q's and the free-trade production points P, capital-intensive aircraft are relatively cheap in the capital-abundant countries and expensive in the labor-abundant ones. One aircraft costs less than 55 units of textiles in one place and more than 55 in the other. These relative-price differentials will make international trade profitable.

The relative-price differentials are in turn due to the different positions and slopes of the two production possibilities curves. Both curves are "bowed in" toward the origin at their ends. This curvature has a number of complementary explanations.[17] Here it results from a less rigid version of the industry-specific resources encountered in Chapter 10. Although labor and capital are useful to all production, capital is especially well suited to producing aircraft and labor to producing textiles. Consequently, producing more of one good and less of the other requires a sacrifice in output (relative to the situation where both resources are equally well suited for aircraft or textiles). Reducing production of textiles, for example, releases lots of labor and a little capital. But expanding production of aircraft requires only a little labor and a lot of capital. The resource amounts being released do not immediately match those being required. In the long run, when full employment is restored along the production possibilities curve, aircraft producers will have been induced by falling wages and rising capital costs to adopt techniques that make greater use of labor. Yet such techniques are not the ones best-suited for producing capital-intensive aircraft. Therefore, some aircraft output will have been sacrificed.[18]

The position of each production possibilities curve as well as its

[16] If all individuals in the population had such restrictive preferences, then their indifference-curve map (see the previous footnote) would be a set of right angles, all of whose vertices lie along a ray from the origin with a slope of 70 to 1. The two goods would then be considered *perfect complements* by every individual.

[17] In Chapter 8 it was seen to result from any reduced productivity of national resources due to lack of diversity in work experience and consequent alienation as nations became increasingly specialized. In footnote 8 to Chapter 10 it was seen to result from industry-specific resources.

[18] In the extreme, if labor were totally useless to aircraft producers and capital were totally useless to textile producers, then production possibilities space would degenerate into the interior of a rectangle. The production possibilities "curve" would then be the single point on the corner of the rectangle furthest from the origin. This is the outcome of completely industry-specific resources.

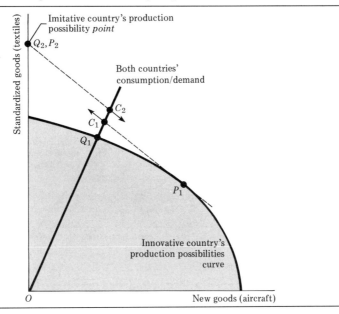

curvature is crucial to the resource-endowments explanation of trade patterns. Compared to the production possibilities curve of the labor-abundant country, that of the capital-abundant country appears to be squashed down toward the horizontal axis and bulging out to the right. That difference is precisely the consequence of differential re-source endowments. The greater the capital abundance and the labor scarcity in the capital-abundant country, the more dramatically it will be able to outproduce the rest of the world in aircraft, but the more drastically it can be outproduced in textiles.

Figure 12.3 illustrates pure technological-gap or product-life-cycle trade patterns based on innovations in aircraft production. Although demanders all over the world have acquired identical tastes for air travel, aircraft cannot yet be produced in technologically average imitative countries. In fact, their production possibilities space is one-dimensional—the line OQ_2— and their production possibilities "curve" is the single point Q_2. In this case, availability (not relative prices) dictates the pattern of trade. If aircraft technology diffuses throughout the world and aircraft themselves become standardized, then technological-gap trade disappears, relative prices reassert their role in explaining trade, and trade patterns become governed by other influences.

Figure 12.4 illustrates a pattern of trade that is based on the greater

FIGURE 12.4. *International Trade Patterns Based on Economies of Large-Scale Production*

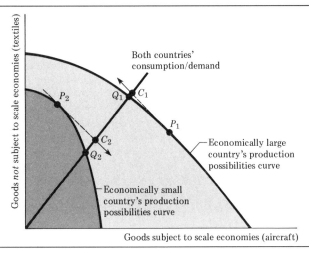

access that economically large countries may have to scale economies that characterize aircraft production. The economically large country has equiproportionally more of all resources than the economically small country. But the ratio of each country's labor endowment to its capital endowment is assumed to be the same. Thus there is no differential-resource-endowments basis for trade. Nor do tastes differ. Nevertheless, at the no-trade production points Q, and for any production point between the Q's and free-trade production at P, relative prices differ. Aircraft are relatively cheap in the large country. Textiles are relatively cheap in the small country.

Again for this case, the relative-price differentials are due to the differing curvatures of the two production possibilities curves. These are influenced by the potential for scale economies. The diagram reflects the belief that large internal markets encourage large firms, plants, and production runs, in which scale economies are normally assumed to be realized.[19] The production possibilities curves for both countries are flatter than they would be in the absence of scale economies, because the productivity of resources increases as more and more of them are devoted to aircraft. But since the small country's capacity for capturing scale economies is limited by its size, its pro-

[19] See footnote 10. If scale economies were large enough, they could cause the production possibilities curves to be "bowed out" at the ends away from the origin (for illustration see p. 255). But to do so, scale economies must dominate the forces that cause the production possibilities curves to be "bowed in" at the ends toward the origin, discussed above.

FIGURE 12.5. *International Trade Patterns Based on Differential Tastes*

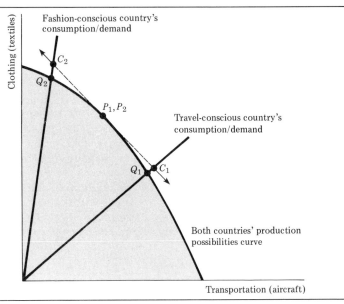

duction possibilities curve is not quite as flat as that in the large country.

Figure 12.5 illustrates a pattern of trade based on differential tastes alone. Countries are identical with respect to resource endowments, technology, and even economic size; thus their production possibilities curves coincide. They do however, differ in their demand mix. The demands of travel-conscious countries are much more rigidly oriented toward transportation than are the demands of fashion-conscious countries. Trade is warranted by the relative-price differentials that would exist in its absence. Aircraft would be comparatively cheap in fashion-conscious countries and would be exported to travel-conscious countries where they are comparatively expensive.[20]

---

[20] Note that if the production possibilities curves were straight lines, as they were in Chapter 8 or as they would be if one good were no more labor or capital intensive than the other, then differential demand would not influence trade patterns. Relative prices would be fixed by the slope of the production possibilities curve and identical between the countries. This is a particularly simple example of how one influence on trade patterns can counteract another (see footnotes 5 and 12). Other simple counteractions and complementarities among the fundamental determinants of trade patterns can be easily pursued in diagrams such as Figures 12.2 through 12.5.

Diagrammatic Illustrations of the Fundamental Determinants

Other Explanations of International Trade Patterns

Many other less important influences can supplement and moderate the fundamental explanations of trade patterns that have been sketched above.

One is the cost of international transport, including loading expenses and insurance, which affects the direction and volume of trade. Trade patterns are obviously related to geographical distance. Other influences being comparable, trade is greater among neighboring countries than among far-flung countries. Transport costs may occasionally affect the commodity composition of trade also: Alaska oil is exported to Japan; Oklahoma oil is not traded; New Englanders rely on imported oil (rather than Alaska or Oklahoma oil) almost exclusively. But usually the commodity composition of trade is better explained by other factors.

Although most government trade management influences the magnitude of a country's trade with various trading partners, it usually has little effect on the types of commodities traded. Pervasive government intervention in international trade, on the other hand, such as characterizes socialist and communist countries, can importantly shape the commodity composition of trade as well.[21]

Intercountry and interindustry differences in market structure also influence the commodity composition of international trade. If U.S. agriculture is unusually competitive by world standards while other industries are comparably oligopolistic, then the United States will have a comparative advantage in agriculture (other influences being comparable). Competition will lead to lower prices than those imposed under oligopolistic and monopolistic market structure, and a U.S. export position in agriculture would reflect this. In the rest of the world, comparatively oligopolistic agriculture would make manufactures cheap relative to food. The world's comparative advantage would lie with manufactures.

Multinational corporations with production operations in more than one country are an increasingly important force in international trade patterns. They frequently modify the three fundamental determinants of trade. They may, for example, undermine the importance of differential resource endowments. The existence of a British Ford Motor Company and a German General Motors (GM) even makes European resource endowments hard to define. Does "European capital" include the skills, education, and management expertise of U.S. personnel who are resident employees of Ford of Britain or GM of Germany? Does it include physical machinery leased to these Euro-

---

[21] So could imperialistic behavior on the part of governments in market economies. See the discussion of imperialism and state trading in footnote 1.

pean offspring of U.S. parent corporations? Does it include blueprints and operating instructions that are being used in Europe under license from U.S. parents? If European capital does include all these things, resource endowments in the United States and Europe differ much less than one might have thought, and their importance as a determinant of trade patterns diminishes.

On the other hand, although multinational corporations may short-circuit traditional commodity trade based on resource endowments, they introduce some untraditional trade along these lines. Through multinationals, the United States exports the services of education, technology, skilled management, and physical capital to Europe rather than the commodities that embody them. Direct European imports of scarce resources and technology through corporate channels substitute for imports of finished commodities. The general observation that international trade in resources and technology can substitute for international trade in commodities is discussed further in the next chapter.

Multinational corporations may also shorten and weaken trade patterns based on technological gaps and product life cycles. Close communication among their far-flung divisions speeds the international transmission of knowledge about process and product innovation. Corporate ties make international licensing of patented innovations administratively cheap and reduce the risk and uncertainty that hinder technology transfer between two unrelated firms (Chapter 13). Familiarity with worldwide market conditions, buyer preferences, and labor conditions reduces the tendency to produce and distribute new products experimentally in familiar home markets first.

Multinational corporations may expand the opportunities for trade based on economies of large-scale production. Only one or two divisions of a worldwide corporation may produce any particular component that is used by all other divisions. If the corporation insists on buying only from itself, large export markets for the component can be virtually guaranteed. This circumvents any need for large internal markets and enables even economically small countries to share comparative advantage based on economies of large-scale production. The best example of expanded scale-based trade through multinationals is probably the trade generated by the Canadian-American Auto Agreement (see Chapter 11).

Further, for better or worse, the burgeoning of multinational corporations has influenced world demand behavior. It has inevitably stimulated tastes for American and European products and life styles that never before existed, thus narrowing demand differences among nations. At the same time, it may have enhanced buyers' perceived need for variety as well as their ability to satisfy it.

Finally, as we shall see in the next chapter, the willingness of multinational corporations to plan on a world scale has helped governments to influence the location of world production and hence to affect international trade patterns.

Summary

The pattern of trade, not merely its existence, can be materially beneficial to a nation. Comparative advantage in certain goods is welcomed and in other goods, shunned. Some configurations of trading partners are more appealing than others.

Simply knowing the determinants of a nation's trade patterns is useful information, facilitating accurate forecasts and sensible policies.

There are many mutually reinforcing and offsetting influences on comparative advantage and trade patterns. Four are fundamental. Given other influences, a nation will tend to export those goods (1) that use its abundant (by world standards) productive resources intensively relative to other goods; (2) that are most advanced or least backward in their design/production methods relative to other goods, once again measuring by world standards; (3) whose least-cost scale of production best matches traditional operating sizes of the nation's supplier firms—goods most subject to scale economies for nations with the most typically large-scale production methods, goods less (or not at all) subject to scale economies for others; (4) that are in slight domestic demand compared to other goods (by world standards), or that satisfy foreign demands for unique (differentiated) domestic products. A nation will tend to import goods with the opposite characteristics.

For all situations short of completely free trade, each of these influences causes a nation to have lower prices (opportunity costs) of certain goods relative to others than exist elsewhere in the world. A nation will export and have comparative advantage in its relatively cheap goods, and import and have comparative disadvantage in its relatively expensive goods. Trade will be privately profitable for those who engage in it, and may well be nationally beneficial.

Key Terms

state trading, imperialism
labor, capital
endowments, intensity
Heckscher-Ohlin Theorem
Leontief Paradox
factor intensity reversals
(uneven) technological gaps,
    product life cycles

product, process innovation
two-way (intraindustry) trade
scale economies, increasing re-
    turns to scale
differentiated products
opportunity costs
community indifference curves

Key Concepts and Review

Why the pattern of trade (commodity composition and direction) matters.

Why *relative* (not absolute) national positions and price *ratios* (not price levels) ultimately explain it.

Graphical and verbal analysis of trade patterns and comparative advantage, based on relative: resource endowments, technology, tastes, transport costs, government policy, market structure, and prominence of multinational corporations.

Interdependence, intermingling, complementarity, and consistency of explanations of trade patterns and comparative advantage.

Chapter 13

International Movement of Corporations, Technology, and Productive Resources

History and habit among economists conspire to imply that international trade consists primarily of finished commodity outputs and scattered scarce raw materials. The facts are otherwise. Increasingly, international transactions involve semifinished parts and components, productive machinery, services of management and superior technology, and entrepreneurial control, vested in mammoth corporate enterprises that span national boundaries. What sets these international transactions apart from those already examined in Part II is that they all represent trade in inputs, not outputs. So does international migration, which has grown less dramatically.

This chapter focuses on international trade in inputs, the subject of some of the most heated controversies in international economics. Does illegal immigration into the United States cost American workers their jobs and constitute a national problem? Should American firms be allowed to sell superior technology to any foreign buyer who wants it? Is the tremendous technological gap between rich, developed countries and poor, less-developed ones fair or proper? Do American multinational corporations export American jobs? Do they pay their fair share of taxes? Are they agents for the maintenance of U.S. hegemony over the rest of the world? Will they swallow up national governments and labor unions?

Many of the questions above concern the distribution of income, either among groups within a nation, or among nations themselves. This is why input trade is controversial. It has readily apparent effects on both key elements of income—input prices (wages, salaries, profits, rents, and royalties) and employment (whether of labor, capital, or technology). Input trade also affects commodity prices, variety, and availability, but these effects are not so direct, nor so inflammatory.

Some Dimensions of U.S. Trade in Inputs

Table 13.1 reveals some of the dimensions of U.S. trade in inputs and labor services in 1975. Several things are notable. First, the United States is on balance an exporter of both physical capital (productive equipment) and the services of superior technology (patented innovations and trademark rights). In return, it is an importer of both people and any human capital that they bring (education, skills, expertise). The United States also imports scarce natural resources and materials (more than half of material imports are crude oil and petroleum products). As we will see below, none of these patterns is unexpected.

Although Table 13.1 omits any direct data on the proliferation of multinational corporations, their presence is indirectly reflected because they are the channels for much recorded trade in capital goods, material inputs, and technology. The special nature of such input trade within a corporate superstructure is discussed later in the chapter, when we examine the economic dimensions of multinational corporations in detail.

First, we turn to "pure" trade in inputs—international migration and resource/technology movements between unrelated (not linked by corporate kinship) sellers and buyers. Transactions of this sort, often spoken of as *arm's-length transactions*, include U.S. exports of construction machinery and lumber to foreign builders, and Lockheed's sale of production designs and engineering services to Japanese aerospace companies. We will find that many of the causes and consequences of international movements of people, equipment, and knowledge parallel the causes and consequences of international commodity trade.

"Pure" International Migration and Resource Movements

By world standards the United States is rich in land, productive skills, managerial expertise, and physical plant and equipment. Indeed, some of the U.S. endowment of productive capital is unavailable anywhere else in the world (for example, Boeing's 747 assembly facility in Seattle). By contrast, the world is relatively richly endowed with the services of low-skill labor.

Chapter 12 revealed how these intercountry differences in relative resource endowments could make capital relatively cheap in the United States and labor relatively expensive. United States exports of agricultural goods and sophisticated manufactures were stimulated by the availability and inexpensiveness of the land, skills, and machines that were used intensively in their manufacture. United

TABLE 13.1. *U.S. Trade in Inputs and Labor Services, 1975*

Individuals, services, or commodities	Exports	Percent of total exports of Services (S) or Commodities (C)	Imports	Percent of total imports of Services (S) or Commodities (C)
Labor, human capital, and knowledge:				
People	−34,000[a] (emigration)		386,000 (immigration)	
Technology and expertise[b]	4,285	10 (S)	433	1 (S)
Physical capital:				
Capital goods[c]	35,841	33 (C)	9,686	10 (C)
Material inputs:				
Raw and semifinished materials[c]	30,797	29 (C)	51,374	52 (C)

[a] Negative U.S. emigration comes about because of U.S. citizens who return to the United States from residence abroad. The figure in the table is a rough approximation, equal to the difference between net civilian immigration and gross immigration. *Source*: U.S. Department of Commerce, U.S. Bureau of the Census, *Statistical Abstract of the United States*, 1975 and 1976 editions, Tables 29 (1975), 26 (1976), and 162 (1976).
[b] Millions of dollars. Technology/expertise trade figures are fees and royalties from affiliated and unaffiliated foreigners. Total services trade is the difference between trade in goods and services and merchandise trade. *Source*: U.S. Department of Commerce, *Survey of Current Business* 57 (March 1977): p. 44, Table 1.
[c] Millions of dollars. Capital-goods trade excludes trade in automotive products. Materials trade is trade in industrial supplies and materials. Total commodity trade is total merchandise trade. *Source*: same as in note b, p. 47, Table 3.

SCHEMA 13.1. *Some Potential Causes and Consequences of International Resource Movements*

Inter-country differences in resource endowments	—*a**→	International resource movements	—*b*→	Reduction or elimination of inter-country differences in resource endowments	—*c*→	Reduction or elimination of international commodity trade that is caused by intercountry differences in resource endowments

Key: For →, read "leads to" or "causes."

* This movement occurs because, in the absence of technology gaps, labor would be better paid in labor-scarce countries than in labor-abundant countries, and capital owners would be better paid in capital-scarce countries than in capital-abundant countries. See the upper half of Schema 12.2.

States imports of simple, standardized manufactures were stimulated by the high cost of the low-skill American labor used intensively in their manufacture.

But why wouldn't the relative abundance of managers, skilled laborers, and machine owners in the United States cause them to move abroad, where their scarcity would gain them more handsome rewards? And why wouldn't the relative scarcity of low-skill labor in the United States generate massive immigration of the world's "tired, poor, and hungry"? Some of the answers are obvious: immobilizing differences in language, climate, and custom; strict governmental limitations on immigration, especially of the unskilled; transport costs that are greater for machines than for the goods they produce. Other answers are more subtle, such as the way in which technology gaps can upset any blithe predictions based on resource endowments (below and Supplement 13A).

The questions illustrate that intercountry differences in resource endowments *could* have resulted in international resource movements. This is illustrated very simply in Schema 13.1 by arrow *a*.

International resource movements could even have substituted for commodity trade. In the extremely unlikely absence of the barriers and immobilities facing international resource movements, the movements could eventually eliminate the endowment differences that caused them. This is illustrated in Schema 13.1 by arrow *b*. The United States would no longer be capital rich after its skilled labor and capital owners emigrated in search of higher incomes. Nor would it be labor poor after immigration. The movements would bring about adjustment toward an equilibrium in which neither wage rates nor returns to comparable kinds of capital would differ from country to country (more on this below). Furthermore, since differential resource endowments would be eliminated, so would any trade in commodities that was influenced by them, as illustrated by arrow c.

On reflection, the substitutability between migration/resource movements and commodity trade is not strange. Commodity outputs are really just combinations of their inputs. The same forces that prompt labor and capital services to move internationally in a rigid composite called a *commodity* cause them to move in unbundled form as well.

"Pure" International Technology Transfer

The United States has been a pioneer among twentieth-century nations in fostering technical change. Antibiotics and solid-state circuitry have improved the productivity of men and machines. Synthetic fabrics and electronic data processing equipment are innovative goods that were once universally unavailable and unknown.

Chapter 12 revealed how the unevenness of such technical change from country to country and from industry to industry made some products temporarily cheaper (or exclusively available) in innovating countries, which would then export them in return for standardized products.

But why not trade the technology itself? Developers of nylon, rayon, and acetate did in fact choose to trade not only their advanced products but also the patented techniques associated with making them. During the 1950s the United States effectively rebuilt the Japanese aircraft industry by selling it production plans, parts, and the temporary services of U.S. engineers, draftsmen, and managers who worked for U.S. aircraft companies. In return, the United States received royalties, license fees, and management service payments.

In order to trade technology—or more exactly the blueprints, machine tools, parts, and personnel in which it is usually embodied—sellers and buyers have to agree on terms and prices. That this is a serious obstacle is reflected in the small share of technology and expertise in overall U.S. trade (Table 13.1).

Agreement is difficult for several reasons, all of which lead to a situation in which the lowest price that innovators are willing to accept for their technology is still above the highest price that potential buyers are willing to bid. One reason is the difficulty of defining, translating, and quantifying many technological innovations. Innovations in the techniques of management, marketing, and labor relations are usually intangible and indistinguishable from the people who develop them. Innovations in production processes or product specifications are costly to describe (requiring, say, language or metric translation) and sometimes inextricably entwined with longstand-

SCHEMA 13.2. *Some Potential Causes and Consequences of International Technology Transfer*

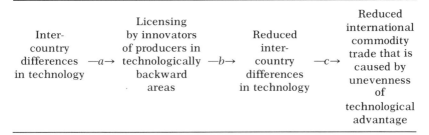

Inter-country differences in technology		Licensing by innovators of producers in technologically backward areas		Reduced inter-country differences in technology		Reduced international commodity trade that is caused by unevenness of technological advantage
	—a→		—b→		—c→	

ing standardized processes and products, so that their disembodied value is hard to assess. Furthermore, technological advance is sometimes no more than increased productivity that comes with experience. Under any of these circumstances, the buyers of technology are placed at an informational disadvantage relative to developers. Inferior information will usually lead the buyer to bid low in order to insure against a costly error.

A second reason for irreconcilable differences between the technology seller's asking price and the technology buyer's bid price is the temporary monopoly that innovators enjoy in the sale or use of their innovation and the implied guarantee of monopoly profits (Chapter 12). Innovators will usually have difficulty extracting the same profits in a sale to an exclusive buyer because the required purchase price would necessarily soak up all the monopoly profit and reduce the buyer's rate of return to a normal (competitive) level, at which point more secure and certain investments may dominate the technology purchase.

Finally, because the persistently superior technology in areas such as the United States, Canada, Europe, and Japan raises their standards of living, potential buyers of superior technology among poorer nations may be constrained by their poverty to bid less than sellers find acceptable (discussed later in this chapter).

Despite these difficulties, unevenness of technological progress among countries has sometimes led to technology trade as well as commodity trade, as illustrated by arrow *a* of Schema 13.2. Such trade evens out access to modern technology and shrinks technological gaps (arrow *b*). Commodity trade based on technological gaps also shrinks, because technology transfer substitutes for it (arrow *c*).[1]

---

[1] Just as technological-gap commodity trade is often two-way, so is the leasing of the technology itself. Within the same industry, the United States is often exporting some innovations and importing others through licensing.

Distributional Consequences of International Migration, Resource Movements, and Technology Transfer

The distributional consequences of international input trade are far more controversial than its substitutability for output trade. Two distributions are affected—that of each nation's income among groups within it, and that of world income among nations.

INCOME DISTRIBUTION WITHIN NATIONS

International migration and resource movements have a predictable effect on the slices of a nation's income pie that can be claimed by different groups of citizens. Immigration of low-skill labor from Mexico into the United States, for example, either takes jobs away from comparably skilled U.S. labor or holds down their wages from what they otherwise would have been. The reason is simply the market force of an extra supply of such labor resources. Job displacement is the most likely immediate effect of any bulge in immigration. Below-average raises for low-skill labor follow, owing to the pressure of displaced people on employers and unions for reemployment.[2] Finally, when temporary unemployment is eliminated by retirement, growth in the economy, relocation of the unemployed, or explicit government policy, then low-skill U.S. labor will find their wages permanently behind others, even though they may begin to rise as fast. Whether job displacement, substandard raises, or permanently lower relative wages are the cause, the inevitable consequence is reduced incomes for "native" low-skill labor—from what they would have been without the bulge in immigration.

The same predictions could be made about low-skill labor incomes in France, Germany, and Switzerland, all of which play host to large numbers of temporary migrant workers from Italy, Greece, Spain, and Turkey,[3] and about low-skill labor incomes in Middle Eastern oil countries, which have been depressed by an influx of Pakistani, Philippine, and Indonesian truck drivers, dock workers, and construction laborers.

---

[2] To recall Chapter 10, job displacement is certain if wages are temporarily or permanently inflexible downward. But over long enough periods almost all wages and prices are flexible.

[3] The number of these foreign "guest workers" has been greatly reduced from its peak in the early 1970s, before the worldwide economic slump. France and Germany discontinued the permits of many Greek, Spanish, and Turkish guest workers, and Switzerland did the same for all guest workers, in order to ease the burden of mid-1970s unemployment on "native" workers. Italians working in France and Germany were not affected, however, because labor migration within the European Community cannot be impeded by government policy, as one of the conditions of economic union (see footnote 18 to Chapter 11).

It should be clear why many U.S. labor unions oppose legalizing the status of illegally resident aliens. Union members already feel threatened by the "cheap foreign labor" that is embodied in commodity imports (see Chapter 9); the competitive threat to their security, living standards, promotion prospects, and work conditions is all the more palpable when the actual laborers are "imported."

But one group's loss may be another's gain.[4] One such group is the permanent migrants themselves. Once they locate jobs, low-skill legal immigrants to the United States will generally receive higher incomes than they had before they moved. As Americans-to-be, they will eventually have as much potential importance and weight as "natives." So will "low-skill Americans" have lost as a result of immigration from Mexico five years after the fact? Some will have lost, and some won't.

Others who gain from a bulge in such immigration are owners of the many firms manufacturing semiconductors and data-processing equipment in Texas who are able to hold down their labor costs and raise their profitability by hiring immigrant labor.[5] California vegetable and fruit growers gain for the same reason. To the extent that this also holds down the price of electronic equipment, vegetables, and fruit, heavy buyers of these goods gain, too. So do Americans who need housekeeping services in areas such as Washington, D.C., and Florida, which have large populations of low-skill immigrants.

At this point, one might subtract the losses from the gains and draw conclusions about the effect of immigration on "national" economic welfare. As we saw in Chapter 10, though, this raises a number of thorny issues, which are compounded in this chapter by the distinction between "native nationals" and "migrant nationals." Thus, even though the national-economic-welfare focus of Chapters 8 through 11 is already familiar, we touch on it indirectly in the sections on income distribution among nations.[6] Otherwise we adopt the perspective of subgroups within a nation, from which the most frequently encountered controversial issues arise.

[4] Note that the controversy over whether gainers should compensate losers arises here for international resource movements just as it did for international trade in Chapter 10.

[5] In certain circumstances, all "native" Americans might lose from immigration—for instance, if every immigrant remained unemployed, yet had to be supported by unemployment compensation or welfare payments that were transferred through the government from other Americans. Usually this would occur only for short periods, until wages became flexible enough to absorb the extra unemployed. But the problem cannot always be easily dismissed. Its potential seriousness grows when immigrants and their unemployment are concentrated geographically or when migration takes place primarily in a search for better welfare payments, rather than better jobs. Similar problems arise even for migration within the United States—for example, of American blacks and Puerto Ricans to Northern urban areas.

[6] See pp. 423–429 and 445–451. Supplement 13A, by contrast, is written principally from the perspective of national economic welfare.

TABLE 13.2. *Probable Income Gains and Losses*[a] *from International Migration and Resource Movements*

	Types of owner and resources		
	Immobile owners of labor	Immobile owners of capital	Owners of migrating (mobile)
	(low-skill laborers)	(high-skill laborers, white-collar workers, farmers, land-lords)	resources
Type of resource movement			
Immigration of labor	Lose	Gain	Gain
Emigration of labor	Gain	Lose	Gain
Imports of capital	Gain	Lose	Gain
Exports of capital	Lose	Gain	Gain

[a] Gains and losses are measured from what incomes would have been without any resource movement. Income losses for each group could be due either to unemployment of some labor or capital equipment or to reduced income for their owners.

These results are often generalized as follows. If countries differ from each other only in resource endowments and tastes, both the causes and consequences of international resource movements are straightforward. Resource owners always move their resources from countries where they are relatively abundant (or in slight demand) to countries where they are relatively scarce (or in great demand). Those who do so inevitably gain income, as illustrated in Table 13.2. Owners of abundant resources gain even when their own resources are not moved. Owners of scarce resources inevitably lose, because international resource movements make them less scarce.[7]

International diffusion of technology also alters the income shares of subgroups within a nation. When the United States provided technical aerospace assistance to Japan in the 1950s, it not only expanded Japanese aircraft production but increased incomes for Japanese

[7] Note that any person in a society may own both scarce and abundant resources. Few people are pure laborers or pure capitalists. See footnote 4 to Chapter 12.
More advanced treatments of international economics demonstrate some less transparent consequences of international migration and resource movement. For example, suppose that an influx of scarce labor to the United States has fairly small effects on relative commodity prices. In the long run, U.S. production of labor-intensive goods will expand (which makes sense). But production of capital-intensive goods will contract (which is strange, because the United States grows in absolute economic size from the labor migration). This tendency, known as the *Rybczynski effect*, is easy to demonstrate in an *Edgeworth-Bowley box diagram*.

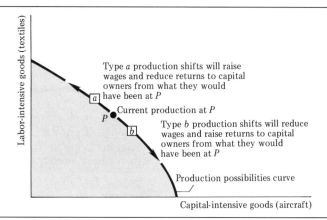

Type *a* production shifts will raise wages and reduce returns to capital owners from what they would have been at *P*

Current production at *P*

Type *b* production shifts will reduce wages and raise returns to capital owners from what they would have been at *P*

Production possibilities curve

Labor-intensive goods (textiles)

Capital-intensive goods (aircraft)

* The diagram assumes that commodities are uniquely labor intensive or capital intensive relative to each other. See footnote 7 to Chapter 12.

aeronautical and metallurgical engineers, toolmakers, and test pilots, all of whose skills (capital) were particularly well suited to aircraft production.

Furthermore, if such skilled craftsmen had to be lured away from other industries in Japan, then these industries could even be losers from the original technology transfer. As the availability of skilled craftsmen shrank and their cost rose, Japanese profitability outside the aircraft industry would slip. Some firms might close down, releasing more low-skill labor than could be absorbed at going wages by the expanding aircraft industry. Unemployment among the unskilled would rise, and increases in their wages and incomes would be held below the average in Japanese society. The income distribution would have shifted unfavorably to them.

In the United States, the same transfer of aerospace technology probably caused skilled labor to lose relative to unskilled labor. Had it not taken place, then the Japanese (for at least a time) would have had to buy aircraft abroad instead of learning to build them. Since the United States would have been the likely source of Japanese aircraft imports, U.S. production of aircraft would have been greater without the technology transfer. Therefore, U.S. engineers, toolmakers, and test pilots would have gained from prohibiting the transfer, although unskilled U.S. labor might have lost.

This reasoning should recall the explanation for curvature in national production possibilities curves, discussed on p. 404. These predictions are reflected more generally in Figure 13.1, which illustrates the effect of any production shift on the internal income distribution. When countries differ from each other only in relative resource endowments and tastes, these results are generalized as follows. Inward transfers of the technology specific to a capital-intensive industry tend to tilt the income distribution toward owners of capital and away from low-skill labor; outward transfers have the opposite effect.[8]

Figure 13.1 also illustrates how conventional commodity trade can affect the long-run income distribution just as significantly as immigration and technology transfer. Labor in labor-scarce countries suffers a permanent loss when larger commodity trade causes smaller production of labor-intensive textiles. Owners of capital are permanently aided by the corresponding encouragement to capital-intensive aircraft. These insights are summarized more generally in the *Stolper-Samuelson Theorem:*

> Stolper-Samuelson Theorem: *In the long run, reduced barriers to commodity trade improve the standard of living of those who own abundant resources and reduce the standard of living of those who own scarce resources.*[9]

In this setting, international commodity trade also tends to narrow intercountry differences in wage, profit, salary, and rental rates, just as do resource movements and technology transfer.[10]

Special settings and theorems aside, the forms taken by international transactions are malleable, adaptable, and substitutable for each other. If the U.S. government restricts imports of Mexican tomatoes in order to protect the livelihood of American migrant workers, more Mexican workers are thereby encouraged to cross the border illegally and work on U.S. farms. They then compete with American workers side-by-side instead of at a distance. The purpose of the commodity trade restriction is partially undermined by the extra migration it causes. When the U.S. government bars unlimited foreign fishing within 200 miles of the U.S. coast, in part to conserve the fish

---

[8] Similarly, inward transfers of technology that is specific to a labor-intensive industry tend to tilt the income distribution toward low-skill labor and away from owners of capital; outward transfers have the opposite effect. Although it is not illustrated in Figure 13.1, inward transfers of technology will also *shift* the production possibilities curve away from the origin, as well as causing the illustrated movement along it.

[9] To be exact, the theorem also requires that reduced trade barriers have little effect on the terms of trade, as more advanced textbooks in international economics show.

[10] More advanced textbooks in international economics show that there is even a set of conditions under which commodity trade would cause wage, profit, salary, and rental rates to be identical everywhere in the world. This state of affairs is known as *factor* (resource) *price equalization.* The conditions under which commodity trade causes factor price equalization are, however, extremely improbable.

population, it indirectly invites an explosion in U.S. fishing activity. Increased U.S. fleets fill much of the vacuum left by the foreigners, and U.S. fish exports boom. One of the purposes of the restriction on internationally mobile fishing resources is partially undermined by the extra commodity exports it causes.

NATIONAL ECONOMIC WELFARE AND THE INCOME DISTRIBUTION AMONG NATIONS

International trade in resources, technology, and even people is as predictably beneficial to nations as international trade in finished commodities. That is, nations would usually rather engage in some than none (Chapter 8), because national consumption possibilities (national economic welfare) are generally greater with trade in inputs than without. Yet such trade is hardly "free," as revealed by our discussion above of the natural and governmental barriers to international migration, resource movement, and technology transfer.

The most important consequences of these barriers are the striking income gaps among rich and poor nations. If technology were comparable worldwide and trade, migration, and all resource movements were completely free—not even impeded by the natural barriers of language, custom, race, religion, and the cost of moving—then there could be no rich nations and poor, no developed and less developed. Any inequality in living standards would quickly prompt movement that would erase it through competitive forces. Reality, however, is far different, as illustrated for a sample of countries in Table 13.3. The 1975 income per person in the richest country, the United States, is more than seventeen times as large as that in the poorest, Kenya. And Kenya is far from the poorest of all the world's countries.

Furthermore, these comparative income figures correspond very closely to comparative standards of living, which reflect average prices of goods purchased as well as income. Correspondence is close because a large number of commodity prices are influenced by world forces of supply and demand, which make them roughly comparable from nation to nation.[11] Even prices of highly localized nontraded goods such as haircuts, amusement park rides, and rent usually differ much less dramatically from country to country than the incomes in Table 13.3. This is evident from the comparative cost-of-living figures in Table 13.4. More or less comparable costs of living and dramatically different incomes per person translate jointly into dramatically different standards of living from nation to nation.

International inequality of income and living standards persists,

---

[11] The way in which world market forces tend to equate prices of traded goods from country to country was discussed on pp. 273–277. Average traded commodity prices cannot differ substantially from country to country except over short periods, as footnote 3 to Chapter 12 suggests.

TABLE 13.3. Income[a] per Person in Each Country
as a Percentage of U.S. Income per Person, 1975

Country	Income per person as percent of U.S. income per person
Kenya	5.7
India	6.9
Colombia	18.5
Hungary	52.7
Italy	46.7
Japan	66.9
Germany	75.5
United States	100.0

[a] Income is measured approximately, by Gross Domestic Product.
Source: World Bank updating of 1970 estimates by I. B. Kravis,
Z. Kennessey, A. W. Heston, and R. Summers, *A System of International Comparisons of Product and Purchasing Power* (Baltimore:
Johns Hopkins Press, 1975), in *World Bank Atlas: Population, Per
Capita Output, and Growth Rates* (Washington: International Bank
for Reconstruction and Development, 1977), p. 31.

and perhaps even grows, for the two fundamental reasons summarized in Schema 13.3. Thus far in this book, we have not made much of the mere existence of international gaps in technology (arrow a). In Chapter 8 we saw that some international trade was economically beneficial to every nation no matter how technically advanced or deprived it was. In Chapter 12 we saw that across-the-board differences between nations in technology had no influence on the pattern of trade and comparative advantage; technological gaps had to be uneven from industry to industry in order to explain trade. It is in explaining international income inequality that absolute technology gaps finally begin to matter.

National technological advantage is frequently general and pervasive. It is not always specific to a particular firm or industry, as has been implied by the examples of aerospace technology and synthetic textiles. The United States, Canada, Europe, and Japan enjoy general technological superiority over the rest of the world. They are able to produce the great majority of all goods more productively than any other country. That is, they produce one unit of most goods using less labor, fewer machines, and a smaller land area. For technologically sophisticated goods, the advantage is often infinitely large. Kenya, India, and Colombia could marshall all their resources and still fail to produce an Apollo moon capsule.

Thus, although technologically advanced countries apply the same national work effort as elsewhere, their effort results in greater quan-

TABLE 13.4. *Average Retail Prices in Each Country as a Percentage of U.S. Prices to Determine Salary Differentials of United Nations Officials*

Country	Prices as percent of U.S. prices	Date of comparison
Kenya	88	May 1975
India	75	April 1975
Colombia	65	January 1975
Hungary	n.a.[a]	
Italy	100	April 1975
Japan	111[b]	April 1975
Germany	130	April 1975
United States	100	

[a] n.a. = not available.
[b] Excludes differences in housing costs.
Source: United Nations, Department of Economic and Social Affairs, Statistical Office, *Monthly Bulletin of Statistics* 29 (August 1975), Special Table C. Copyright, United Nations 1975. Reproduced by permission.

tities of tangible, want-satisfying goods. Superior overall technology allows inputs to be transformed more economically into outputs. It enhances overall national productivity. In monetary terms, it blesses a nation with what at first appears to be impossible—higher wages, higher salaries, higher profits, higher rents, *and* roughly the same prices on average as exist elsewhere. The purchasing power and standard of living of the average American, German, Japanese, or Italian is necessarily higher than elsewhere.

Persistent capital abundance provides a second reason for international income inequality, as arrow *b* suggests. In one way or another, capital is always owned and controlled by people. The income that accrues to capital because of its productivity really accrues to skilled toolmakers, mechanics, engineers, electricians, doctors, shareholders, farmers, and landlords. Incomes per person are higher in the United States, Canada, Europe, and Japan because the average person's income includes both a return to raw labor effort and a return to capital ownership. In other words, everyone's low-skill labor is more productive when he or she has more education, training, productive machinery, land, and skilled associates to work with. Capital abundance raises people's productivity in the same way that superior technology does, enabling them to attain higher incomes and standards of living.

Across-the-board technology gaps cannot always be distinguished

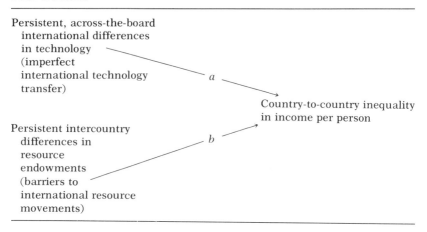

from international differences in resource endowments. Most technical expertise is embodied in someone or something. Skilled American managers, farmers, and craftsmen pass along their technical superiority to younger generations through agricultural, vocational, and business schools, apprenticeships, and on-the-job training. Other technical expertise is embodied in machines which make machines which make more machines—and so on. It follows that technologically advanced countries tend to be capital rich and that capital-poor countries are caught in a vicious circle that leaves them persistently deprived of modern technology. It is fruitless to transfer advanced, sophisticated blueprints and production plans to nations whose populations lack enough persons with the skill, education, and expertise to grasp what is being transferred. This suggested interdependence between resource endowments and technology can be illustrated in a stylized way by expanding Schema 13.3 to Schema 13.4.

To summarize, international income inequality depends on the persistent nature of international gaps in technology and barriers to resource movement. They persist because of exclusive patent privileges, the difficulty of identifying what technology really is, unfamiliar social customs and language, racial prejudice, religious intolerance, costs of moving, and government immigration policies. They persist also for another reason, which we shall now examine.

International income inequality itself impedes the transfer of technology and the elimination of capital scarcity. Again the circle is a vicious one, because causality also runs in the opposite direction. Nations that are poor in income per person are forced to spend most of their meager income on necessities such as food, clothing, health,

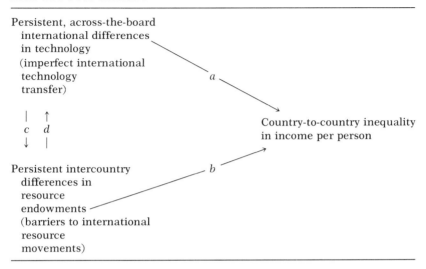

Persistent, across-the-board
  international differences
  in technology
  (imperfect international
  technology
  transfer)

| ↑
c d
↓ |

Country-to-country inequality
in income per person

Persistent intercountry
  differences in
  resource
  endowments
  (barriers to international
  resource
  movements)

a

b

housing, and defense. Failure to do so spells death. Little remains to spend on education, manpower training, productive machinery, resource development, and land reclamation. Capital endowments grow slowly in poor countries, if at all. Little is left to spend on research and development or on acquisition of superior technology through purchase or licensing. A poor nation's technological base grows slowly or not at all. Thus its technological lag behind rich nations may grow rapidly. Rich nations, by contrast, can use their wealth to create more wealth. They can comfortably invest in (purchase) additional capital and technology without depriving themselves. For clear economic reasons, therefore, success tends to breed success and failure to breed failure.[12]

The way international inequality of income feeds back on the factors that influence it is illustrated by arrows *e* and *f* in Schema 13.5, an even more elaborate expansion of Schema 13.3. Several things are notable. First, every factor in the schema is arguably a "cause" of every other factor. Second, this feature greatly complicates and in-

---

[12] Many less-developed countries claim exactly this—that technology gaps and international income inequality are growing, not shrinking. Their proposals to deal with this perceived problem are discussed in Chapter 14. Precisely the same mutual causation arises in analyses of income inequality among persons. Many of America's poor are poor because they are less innovative, less skilled, less educated, and less propertied than other Americans. But it is also true that they have less of these qualities and properties because they are poor.

SCHEMA 13.5. *An Even More Accurate Explanation for the Existence of Rich and Poor Nations*

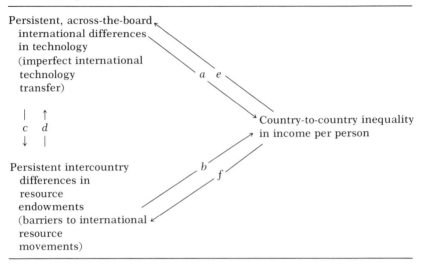

Persistent, across-the-board international differences in technology (imperfect international technology transfer)

a   e

c   d

Persistent intercountry differences in resource endowments (barriers to international resource movements)

b   f

Country-to-country inequality in income per person

flames discussions of whether the international distribution of income is "just" and whether the terms on which technology is transferred are "fair." Poor nations argue in the extreme that they are trapped by a self-perpetuating poverty and that rich nations remain so only by being happily rich in the first place. By this account, international differences in living standards are highly arbitrary, and the moral case for ungrudging economic benevolence of the rich toward the poor is compelling. Rich nations, by contrast, argue in the extreme that their wealth is due to historical frugality and diligence, which generated substantial capital formation and technological advance. By this account, their inheritance of capital and technology is a birthright, to be added to and passed on to future generations. Excessive charity toward poor nations would be squandering national wealth and undoing the work that previous generations sacrificed for. If poor nations want to follow, the historical example is there for them.

Both accounts have elements of truth, as Schema 13.5 illustrates. It is doubtful, however, where economic links are so highly interrelated, that any whole truth can be discerned. Therefore the differences in perspective will remain unresolved when we return to these issues in the next chapter.

The linkage illustrated by arrow *a* of Schemas 13.4 and 13.5 has additional importance in international economics. It causes international resource movements of an unusual kind, resource movements that do not take place according to the influence of relative resource abundance. Highly educated and skilled professionals in poorer nations may be induced to migrate to richer nations despite their scarcity in the former and abundance in the latter. The resulting *brain drain* is sometimes detrimental to the national economic welfare of poorer nations and, by aggravating technological gaps, will skew the international distribution of income even more dramatically against them. The brain drain and its problems are discussed in Supplement 13A.

Multinational Corporations: Description and Dimensions

Though much controversy surrounds "pure" input trade, it pales beside the passions aroused by multinational corporations. Multinational corporations are industrial giants with production operations and distribution networks that span many nations but with ownership and ultimate control usually concentrated in only one or two. Changes in the ownership and control position of multinationals are referred to as *foreign direct* (denoting control) *investment* (denoting ownership).

In order for a firm to become a multinational it must do one of two things. Either it must move personnel, resources, and know-how into a foreign country, while maintaining home-based control over their activities, or it must purchase enough ownership rights to personnel, resources, and know-how in existing foreign firms to gain operational control over them. The first course of action is often described as *green-field direct investment;* the second, as a foreign *takeover*. People, resources, and technology move internationally in the first case; only control over them changes hands in the second.

In this characterization lies much of the controversy surrounding multinationals. When resources, technology, and managerial control are tied together in a corporate package that moves internationally, economic power relationships are significantly altered. By contrast, "pure" and unpackaged movements of resources and technology alter international control relationships only slightly. When Japan *purchases* productive machinery and aerospace technology from the United States, there is little change in the capacity of Americans or their government to influence the Japanese economy. This is not the case when a U.S. multinational brings them directly.

Economic control and market power not only distinguish multinational corporations as a subject of controversy but are also their fundamental cause. Multinationals would exist only by accident in a world of perfect competition, where universally small economic agents enjoyed neither market power nor the ability to influence firms and households beyond their own.

Even the name multinational corporation is controversial. Less-developed countries and United Nations groups seem to find it too neutral. (They have the same complaint with *international corpora-*

TABLE 13.5. *Percentage of National Products* [a]
Accounted for by U.S. Multinational Corporations

	1966	1970
Developed countries	3	n.a.
Europe	3	2
Canada	14	13
Japan	1	1
Less-developed countries	5	n.a.
Brazil	3	3
Chile	9	2
Mexico	4	4
Venezuela	18	16
Iran	5	6
Libya	37	42
Liberia	21	16
India	1	1
Philippines	4	3

[a] (Gross product of foreign affiliates of U.S. companies) ÷ (Gross domestic product of host country) · 100. n.a. = not available.
Source: Ned G. Howenstine, "Gross Product of Foreign Affiliates of U.S. Companies," U.S. Department of Commerce, *Survey of Current Business* 57 (February 1977). Entries for 1970 were calculated by blowing up the 1970 sample data in Table 9 by the appropriate ratio of universe to sample for 1966, then deflating by 1970 gross domestic product from Table 5.

tion.) They prefer *transnational corporation*, perhaps because the prefix *trans* denotes not only "across" but also "beyond the scope of."

That such corporations are beyond the scope of national regulation is a frequently expressed fear. For economic reasons discussed in the next section, they are almost invariably large. Their size relative to that of national governments is often the subject of dramatic observations such as: "General Motors' annual world sales exceeds the gross national product of Switzerland."[13] Although true, this observation is misleading. It compares General Motors' gross sales to Switzerland's *value-added* (defined as gross sales *less* purchases of intermediate goods and raw materials). The multinational presence is more mean-

[13] By the same standard, Exxon is "larger" than Denmark, Ford dominates Austria, and ITT (International Telephone and Telegraph) surpasses the Chile with which it is notoriously connected. See Sheldon W. Stahl, "The Multinational Corporation: A Controversial Force," Federal Reserve Bank of Kansas City, *Monthly Review*, January 1976, p. 4, citing 1970 figures computed by Lester Brown, "The Interdependence of Nations" (New York: Foreign Policy Association), pp. 14–15. The statement also reflects Chile's devastating economic stagnation during the early and mid-1970s.

ingfully compared to the economic size of nations in Table 13.5. At first glance, the figures seem remarkably small. Only 3 percent of European production is accounted for by U.S. multinationals; even in Canada the figure is only 14 percent. Moreover, the proportions have not increased so dramatically between 1966 and 1970 as is implied by various colorful book titles: *The American Challenge, Sovereignty at Bay, Silent Surrender,* and *Global Reach.* In fact, for a large scattering of countries the share of U.S. multinationals in national production has declined.

Furthermore, concerns about control voiced by many countries are mollified by *joint venture* ownership arrangements, which usually give domestic partners substantial minority control and effective veto power. In fact, joint ventures are often forced on multinationals by countries that host them in order to weaken their control. Multinationals, of course, prefer their affiliated foreign corporations (called foreign *affiliates* or *subsidiaries*) to be *wholly owned.*

Joint ventures are still the exception and not the rule. And Table 13.5 is inadequate in several important respects. First, the figures are averages. They fail to reflect the much higher percentages that exist in some sectors. In Canada, for example, the percentages appropriate to mining, petroleum, and manufacturing run from 30 to 50. Second, affiliates of multinationals tend to be among the largest corporations in any given country. They may therefore wield economic influence far in excess of their share of national production. Third, the figures do not include non-American multinationals, among which European, Japanese, and Canadian corporations are very prominent. Royal Dutch/Shell (Shell Oil in the United States) is one example, being owned and controlled by British and Dutch interests. Unilever (Lever Brothers), Volkswagenwerk (Volkswagen), and Nestlé are others.

This catalog of foreign multinationals illustrates an important similarity between much commodity trade and resource movements through multinational corporations. Both are characterized by *two-way* or *intraindustry* exchange. Shell and British Petroleum produce and market petroleum products in the United States; Exxon does so in Britain. In the literature on multinationals this is usually referred to as *cross-penetration* of national markets. The last lines of Tables 13.6 and 13.7 summarize this process in the aggregate. Foreign penetration of U.S. markets is not nearly so large as U.S. penetration of foreign markets, but $30 billion can scarcely be described as trivial.

The tables reflect other features that characterize multinational corporations. Table 13.7 shows that cross-penetration among developed countries is much greater than between them and less-developed countries. Table 13.6 shows that multinational corporations operate in almost all sectors. (Only agriculture is notable in its lack of representation.) Finally, compared to foreign multinationals, U.S. multinationals are more highly concentrated in mining and manufacturing and less concentrated in services.

TABLE 13.6. *Industry Breakdown of Multinational Corporate Ownership, 1974*[a]

Industry	Percent of U.S. multi-nationals operating abroad in the industry	Percent of foreign multi-nationals operating in U.S. in the industry
Mining (and smelting)	5	2
Petroleum	25	24
Manufacturing	43	31
Transportation, communication, and public utilities	3	1
Wholesale and retail trade	10	17
Finance, insurance, and real estate	11	23
Other	4	1
Dollar value of 1974 ownership position[b] (millions)	118,819	26,512

[a] Later years of data are available, although on a different breakdown for foreign multinationals operating in the United States.
[b] "Ownership position" is the foreign direct investment position at year end.
Source: U.S. Department of Commerce, *Survey of Current Business* 56 (May 1976): p. 39, Table 2; 56 (August 1976): p. 48, Table 13.

In explaining the causes and consequences of multinationals, much is made of the sector in which they operate. A differentiation is often drawn between *extractive* multinationals (in mining and petroleum) and market-oriented multinationals (in manufacturing and services). Market-oriented multinationals are further divided into *horizontally* and *vertically integrated* groups. For extractive and vertically integrated multinationals, there is little resemblance among foreign affiliates and their *parent* corporation. Different affiliates specialize in different stages of production. *Upstream* affiliates explore, drill, and process products at an early stage in their fabrication. *Downstream* affiliates refine, finish, market, and service the products. Affiliates of horizontally integrated multinationals, by contrast, are usually all at the same level. Typically they mirror each other, producing broadly similar product lines either for export or for distribution to customers in their local markets.

Multinationals, especially the market-oriented group, grew explosively during the 1950s and 1960s. Their remarkable proliferation,

TABLE 13.7. *Area Breakdown of Multinational Corporate Ownership, 1976*

	Percent of U.S. multinationals operating abroad in the country	*Percent of foreign multinationals operating in U.S. from the country*
Developed countries	72[a]	89
Europe	40	66
Canada	24	19
Japan	3	3
Less-developed countries	23	11
Latin America	17	10
Middle East	0[b]	1
Dollar value of 1976 ownership position[c] (millions)	140,454[d]	30,182

[a] Includes Australia, New Zealand, and South Africa. Sum of U.S. multinational ownership percentages in developed and less-developed countries falls short of 100 by "international and unallocated" category.

[b] A recorded negative ownership position is treated as zero.

[c] "Ownership position" is the foreign direct investment position at year end.

[d] Negative Middle Eastern ownership position is ignored.

Source: U.S. Department of Commerce, *Survey of Current Business* 57 (August 1977): p. 45, Table 14.

documented in Table 13.8, underlies one last source of alarm about them.[14] Prophecies of the future influence of multinationals based on growth rates of the 1950s and 1960s suggest their impending absorption of all other institutions. Since governments and labor unions may both be among the fatalities, they have been the most vocal popularizers of the concern. But the growth of multinationals has leveled off, if not abated, in the mid-1970s, and public alarm has moderated similarly.

[14] Despite the explosion of the 1950s and 1960s, the multinational movement is not that recent, as the table reveals. Some corporations even had substantial controlled operations before 1900—among them, Colt Arms, General Electric, International Harvester, International Paper, National Cash Register, and Westinghouse.

TABLE 13.8. *Average Number of New Foreign Affiliates Formed Each Year by the 187 Largest*[a] *U.S. Multinational Corporations*

| Decade | Type of affiliate | |
	Market-oriented	Extractive
1920s	48	4
1930s	57	6
1940s[b]	58	3
1950s[c]	184	9
1960s[d]	453	11

[a] Based on *Fortune* magazine's list of the 500 largest U.S. industrial corporations that had foreign affiliates operating in six or more foreign countries in 1963 or 1964.

[b] Includes 1950.

[c] Excludes 1950.

[d] Based on average of data for 1960 through 1967 only.

Source: James W. Vaupel and Joan P. Curhan, *The Making of Multinational Enterprise* (Cambridge, Mass.: Harvard University Press, 1969), pp. 124, 126, 128. "Market-oriented" data are the sum of Vaupel's and Curhan's "manufacturing" and "sales" data. "Affiliates" are the corporations' "subsidiaries." Formation of the affiliate is identified with the year operations first began.

Causes of the International Movement of Multinational Corporations

If multinational corporations were no more than the sum of their parts, there would be little new to say in this section. We have already outlined the fundamental reasons why labor, skilled management, equipment, and productive know-how move internationally. If people, resources, and technology are bundled together and move beneath a corporate umbrella, what is there to add? What distinguishes Volkswagen's acquisition of U.S. automaking capacity from its sale of auto engines and technology to American Motors Corporation? Before the multinational boom of the 1950s and 1960s, economists tended to answer, nothing.

Perceptions changed as multinational investment and takeovers began to dominate "pure" movements of equipment, technology, and expertise. Economists observed that the ingredient making multinationals more than just an umbrella for resource movements was corporate market power. Corporate market power in turn was due to *oligopolistic advantage*, defined to be a firm's ability to extract profits that are greater than the perfectly competitive minimum (usually called *normal profits*). The desire to exploit profitable oligopolistic advantage is now believed to be the fundamental cause of the multi-national movement, a cause that underlies all others.

OLIGOPOLISTIC ADVANTAGE

Oligopoly is a market structure characterized by small numbers of firms, all of which are aware of their own ability to influence the market position of their rivals, and all of which act with due respect to the perceived plans and responses of those rivals. To preserve an oligopolistic market structure and the excess profits that are its reward, several things are helpful.

One is explicit or implicit agreement among existing oligopolists "not to rock the boat too hard" in their attempts to increase profits. Overly aggressive competitive action by one firm will drive down profits for others and for the industry in general. Ultimately such behavior may not serve even selfish purposes. If some firms are forced out of business or if the aggressive firm increases its market share too dramatically, government antitrust authorities may intervene, and all firms lose.

Movement abroad is now seen as a way in which aggressive and dominant firms in oligopolistic industries tried to expand profit opportunities rapidly without rocking the boat.[15] The interpretation is made credible by the failure of most antitrust statutes to regulate international activities of domestic firms as strictly as domestic activities.

But the boat may have been rocked anyway. In the picturesque language that is often applied to multinationals, foreign penetration by aggressive, advantaged firms seems to have led many others to "clamber aboard the bandwagon," fearing that otherwise they would be "left behind on the pier." Firms making such *defensive investments* may not always have found them initially profitable. But they nevertheless paid off if losses in the short run insured the affiliate's presence and profitability in the long run. The alternative might have been worse: ceding the market forever to aggressive oligopolistic rivals.

Another feature that preserves oligopolistic advantage and above-normal profits is barriers to the entry of new firms into an industry. Sometimes these *barriers to entry* rest on tactics as simple as early saturation of a market by existing firms. Inertia, habit, and product

---

[15] The *conglomerate movement* is often interpreted in the same way. *Conglomerates* are multidivisional corporations whose various divisions share no necessary similarity or linkage. The Hostess division of International Telephone and Telegraph, for example, produces Twinkies and other bakery products that have very little relation to the communications industry. Aggressive oligopolists are thought to have been able to expand without rocking the boat by taking over firms in less oligopolistic industries. Conglomerates enabled firms to diversify across industries; multinationals enabled them to diversify across nations.

differentiation that is reinforced by advertising then serve to preserve the market for the oligopolists and deter new firms (*new entrants*).

Some multinational penetration seems to have been influenced by just such preemptive saturation strategy. The nearly simultaneous entry of many American manufacturers into Europe when the Common Market was formed is the best example. These manufacturers and European rivals anticipated correctly the prosperous future growth of European markets. Had they not filled the vacuum, new entrants might have been enticed, whose entry would have weakened the oligopolistic market structure and lowered profits for the established firms.

TECHNOLOGY AS A BARRIER TO ENTRY

Frequently, however, barriers to entry rest on more than just inertia, habit, product differentiation, and advertising. Another important barrier is technological advantage, reserved for the exclusive use of innovating oligopolists by the patents and strict corporate secrecy discussed in Chapter 12. Technological advantage is often long-lived because existing oligopolists can afford to divert some of their above-normal profits toward research and development. Potential entrants, by contrast, cannot. They have yet to attain the profit base or credit-worthiness to finance innovation. Existing oligopolists thus benefit from a self-reinforcing circle: their above-normal profits endure because they innovate, and they can innovate because their profits endure.

SCALE ECONOMIES AS A BARRIER TO ENTRY

Another important barrier to entry for multinational corporations is economies of large-scale production, marketing, advertising, information gathering, research and development, and financing. Potential entrants usually must begin these activities on a small scale. Thus at first they will almost surely be uncompetitive with existing oligopolists, and they may not be able to carry or finance losses long enough to grow to a competitive size. Again a self-reinforcing circle protects existing oligopolists: their above-normal profits endure because their costs are low with large-scale production, yet their scale is large because they have endured long enough to grow.

Because of these last two barriers to entry, multinational corporations are not only oligopolistic but also generally the most technologically advanced and largest firms in the world's economies. Smaller, more competitive firms that produce homogeneous, undifferentiated products will find foreign production to be prohibitively unprofitable. Costly, natural obstacles stand in their way. New languages, customs, and marketing channels must be learned (all of which deter exporting as well). The firm must further master the intricacies of foreign labor relations, suppliers' channels, credit sources, judicial systems, and government bureaucracies. Large oligopolists that produce advanced differentiated products face the same obstacles, yet often have a sufficiently large profit cushion or access to loans to overcome them.

Such obstacles must be overcome at a fixed cost regardless of the level of output that a firm plans for its foreign affiliates. However, they need only be overcome once. Like all fixed costs, they intensify economies of large-scale operations on a global basis. Natural obstacles thus present an effective barrier to the entry of new multinational corporations and preserve global oligopolistic advantages for established multinationals. It is not surprising that General Motors and Ford have the largest and most widespread multinational operations of U.S. automakers, while Chrysler and American Motors have no foreign production at all (although Chrysler had a small foreign presence until the late 1970s).[16]

Smaller, more competitive firms can nevertheless have a foreign presence through exports or through licensing of superior technology to foreigners. Natural obstacles to these activities are lower than for full production abroad, which might be unprofitable. Large oligopolists such as Ford will usually find full multinational operations *more* profitable than exporting or licensing. They can spread the fixed cost of "going multinational" over a broad base, and by producing abroad, Ford can circumvent many foreign barriers to automotive imports that would reduce its profitability. Furthermore, Ford may realize certain tax advantages by doing so. And Ford is saved the awkward and sometimes intractable problem of packaging and pricing technology for sale outside the firm.

VERTICAL INTEGRATION AS A BARRIER TO ENTRY

Though broadly relevant, the discussion so far applies most readily to market-oriented, horizontally integrated multinationals. Extractive and vertically integrated operations feature one additional twist. Vertical integration and exclusive access to supplies of minerals, fuels, and raw materials are additional barriers to entry.

The nature of the barrier is clearest for extractive multinational investment. Deposits of petroleum, nickel, and high-grade bauxite and copper are highly concentrated geographically. A number of multinational corporations enjoy exclusive rights to these deposits through long-term leases and production arrangements with source countries. These corporations (for example, Exxon, Gulf, Mobil, and Texaco in the oil industry) benefit from significant advantages over

---

[16] One economist has concluded that the *only* discernible identifying characteristic of multinationals, compared to nonmultinationals within the same U.S. industry, is firm size. See Thomas Horst, "Firm and Industry Determinants of the Decision to Invest Abroad: An Empirical Study," *Review of Economics and Statistics* 54 (August 1972): 261.

firms that do not have such rights (independent oil companies in the United States). Most important among the advantages is the opportunity to extract oligopolistic profit at every stage of processing, which may make the vertically integrated multinational more profitable overall.[17]

The only channels open to potential entrants and to firms that are not as vertically integrated are imports and new exploration, but the high fixed costs of exploration imply substantial economies of scale, so that again the large, established, vertically integrated multinationals have a competitive advantage. Imports remain as the only supply source for smaller, younger firms that refine and process raw materials. Their suppliers often turn out to be the large rival multinationals themselves, which consequently extract some of their oligopolistic profits from the very firms competing with them at a later stage in the production process.

These considerations have recently stimulated vertical integration by U.S. multinationals even in market-oriented industries. Some of the resulting operations are aimed not only at foreign markets but at the U.S. home market. They have encouraged increased U.S. imports of clothing, automobiles, and electronic equipment for home and business use. Clothing is pieced together and sewn in Taiwanese or Hong Kong affiliates of U.S. apparel firms and then imported by the U.S. parent. Television receivers are partially assembled in Mexican affiliates of RCA, Sylvania, and Zenith and then shipped back to the United States for finishing. And American-brand computers, calculators, air conditioners, and scientific instruments all have components that were produced or processed in foreign affiliates of the American parent. The similarity of such transactions to extractive operations of multinationals extends even to occasional sales of components to nonmultinational competitors (Volkswagen's sale of engines to American Motors is one example, and Sears' purchase of

---

[17] It is worthwhile asking why resource-rich countries did not themselves capture the oligopolistic profits (or rents) that accrue to the few owners of scarce mineral deposits. They could have charged multinational corporations appropriately high royalties and fees for exclusive production privileges. Or they could have nationalized the resource industry. The answers vary historically, from ignorance and inferior bargaining position, to bribes of government officials, to the implied military force that underlay colonial imperialism. With the decline in colonial ties and international education gaps, resource-rich countries have increasingly laid claim to the oligopolistic profits earned from the sale of scarce resources. Bauxite-rich countries have dramatically increased the taxes on multinational aluminum companies that mine their deposits. Latin American countries have nationalized the operations of many extractive multinationals (petroleum operations in Peru, copper in Chile). And OPEC has done both to the multinational oil companies operating within its boundaries. Question: What are the economic advantages and disadvantages of capturing the oligopolistic profits through nationalization instead of fees and royalties?

television receivers from Japanese multinationals for marketing under the Sears label is another.)

RESOURCE ENDOWMENTS AGAIN

Vertically integrated, market-oriented multinationals illustrate nicely how important intercountry differences in resource endowments can be for international direct investment. After overcoming the fixed costs of unfamiliarity with global operations, multinationals become increasingly attentive to differences in production costs among all the national markets in which they operate. United States multinationals in these instances are indeed seeking areas of abundant low-skill labor, such as Mexico, Hong Kong, Korea, Singapore, and Taiwan, because its abundance there makes it relatively cheap. Multinationals export capital to the labor-abundant countries and import the labor-intensive, semiprocessed clothing and electronic components from affiliates back to the United States.

GOVERNMENT POLICY

Government policy also has a role in encouraging U.S. multinationals that aim at the U.S. market. The Mexican government facilitates their investment through its Border Industrial Development Program. Any affiliate of a multinational that produces entirely for export from Mexico and that employs Mexican labor within a twelve-mile wide border zone is rewarded with special privileges (including unimpeded and untaxed importation of machinery and raw materials). Taiwan, Korea, and many other less-developed countries also welcome export-oriented multinationals with tax breaks (such as temporary "holidays" from tax liability) and a host of other incentives.

Even the U.S. government indirectly encourages this sort of investment. It exempts from the U.S. tariff any portion of an import that was originally produced in the United States and then shipped abroad for further processing.[18] Furthermore, Mexico, Taiwan, and Korea are among the less-developed countries for which the United States has specially lowered its tariffs under the Generalized System of Preferences (discussed in Chapter 14).

More generally, government policy plays an important role in shaping the volume and type of all multinational investment. Some policy is negative. Japan has remained highly insular by rigidly regulating both foreign multinationals seeking Japanese production bases and Japanese firms wishing to become multinationals. Less-developed

---

[18] Labor unions in the United States have pushed to have tariffs levied on the *full* value of any import. To them, the so-called *offshore assembly* exemptions of U.S. tariff law (Items 806.30 and 807.00 of the Tariff Schedule of the United States) are anathema.

countries have effectively discouraged future foreign investment by expropriating the property of foreign investors or by nationalizing their operations without "fair" compensation.[19] Furthermore, some governments bar multinationals from politically sensitive activities, most commonly banking, transportation, journalism, broadcasting, and national defense.

By contrast, many governments find it in their interest to encourage multinationals. They can succeed because of the willingness of global corporations to plan on a global scale. The Bahamas and the Cayman Islands have become world centers for the production and export of banking services through absence of tight regulation, allowance for secrecy, and low or nonexistent corporate taxes (such countries are sometimes called *tax havens*). In similar ways, Panama and Liberia have attracted multinational shipping interests, and OPEC governments are currently succeeding in efforts to woo multinational producers and distributors of petrochemicals and other petroleum-based manufactures. Other countries jockey to attract high-technology multinational manufacturers by providing necessary infrastructure in industrial parks and by other special favors.[20]

The United States itself has long encouraged its own corporations to grow rapidly abroad by "deferring" all taxes on the reinvested earnings of foreign affiliates.[21] The *tax deferral* "loophole" has been defended occasionally on cosmopolitan grounds (U.S. multinationals are believed to be beneficial on the whole for countries where they operate—but so are American tourists, of course, and no one defers their taxes). But its unpopularity with U.S. labor unions is intense, and its current revenue cost to the U.S. Treasury is high.[22] The U.S.

[19] Compensation can almost never be "fair" from the perspective of the multinational. The nationalizing country will generally refuse to reward the multinational with all the future above-normal profits accruing to its oligopolistic advantage. The nationalizing country views such "excess" profits as undeserved exploitation, at least until it begins to collect some of them itself.

[20] Because policies to attract multinationals are very similar among countries, they often offset each other, and none succeeds. The problems that undermine these policies are the same as those encountered with respect to export subsidization races (Chapter 11) and beggar-your-neighbor policies (Chapter 6 and footnote 26 of Chapter 9).

[21] The statement in the text is not strictly accurate. United States taxes on affiliate earnings that are not returned (*repatriated*) to the United States are in fact deferred, in the sense that when the earnings *are* finally repatriated, U.S. taxes will be due. But in the meantime the foreign affiliate has an interest-free loan from the U.S. Treasury that can be reinvested, transferred to other affiliates, or paid out in dividends to stockholders abroad.

[22] Labor and others also object strongly to U.S. treaties that allow foreign taxes paid by foreign affiliates to be used dollar-for-dollar as a credit against taxes owed to the U.S. Treasury. These *tax credit arrangements* simply invite foreign governments to raise their taxes on corporate earnings up to U.S. levels. By doing so, they leave an affiliate's overall tax bill, and also its prosperity, unaltered. But they change the recipient of the tax payments—the foreign government gets all; the U.S. Treasury gets none. (Foreign governments are

government also encourages U.S. multinationals by insuring them against the risks of expropriation, war, and foreign exchange control through the government-chartered Overseas Private Investment Corporation (OPIC).

Finally, government trade barriers play an important role in stimulating movement by multinationals. Multinationals were attracted to produce within the European Common Market rather than to export to it in the face of the burdensome common external tariff that would have been levied on their export sales. Ireland has also been able to attract large numbers of multinationals by becoming a member of the Common Market—and because of low labor costs and beneficent government policy. Canada's high tariffs have traditionally been cited as a reason for the strong influence of multinational operations there "behind tariff walls."

To summarize, the pursuit of oligopolistic advantage is the fundamental cause of international transfers of ownership, control, resources, and technology through the multinational corporation. But oligopolistic advantage is supported and perpetuated by barriers to entry. These barriers are in turn attributable to international and interfirm differences in technology, scale economies, vertical integration, and the ability to differentiate products. The volume, location, and nature of multinational movement are further influenced by differential resource endowments and by government policy. So the fundamental determinants of comparative advantage and of "pure" resource and technology movements are not irrelevant in a world of multinationals, as some commentators declare. But their influence, while potent, is indirect.

Distributional Consequences of Multinational Corporations

How multinational corporations affect income and its distribution within and among nations is a question of considerable complexity and controversy. Answers depend on many considerations. Among the most important are whether multinational operations are extractive or market oriented, and if the latter, whether the orientation is toward external markets or home-country markets. Another important con-

---

said to be able to "draw dollars right out of the U.S. Treasury.") Of course, the United States can turn the same trick on U.S. affiliates of foreign multinationals, but their earnings are many times smaller (see Tables 13.6 and 13.7). Most proposals to reform the tax credit arrangements favor letting affiliates treat taxes paid to foreign governments as a deduction against their earnings, not as a credit against their U.S. tax liability.

sideration is whether multinationals take control of existing resources and technology in another country or whether they bring in their own.

INCOME DISTRIBUTION WITHIN NATIONS

Equipment, management, and expertise do frequently move from country to country along with multinational control. Lower-skill labor almost never does. Production workers, clerical staff, maintenance personnel, and the sales force are internationally immobile within the multinational corporation. They are also usually the most heavily unionized groups within any corporation. This observation alone explains much of the controversy and inflammatory rhetoric surrounding multinationals.

CONSEQUENCES IN HOME COUNTRIES WHEN RESOURCES MOVE. Affiliates of U.S. multinationals that produce for the U.S. market have raised a particularly strong outcry from U.S. labor unions. They brand them as *runaway plants*. In labor's view, when U.S. corporations construct plants and install equipment abroad, they are foregoing the opportunity to do the same thing at home and thus to provide extra jobs for unemployed U.S. labor in the short run. Runaway plants thus "export U.S. jobs." And in the long run, U.S. imports from runaway plants may well hold down U.S. wages and labor incomes from what they would otherwise have been. American corporations respond that the alternative is to allow others to invest abroad, thus making any U.S. facilities that might be built at home uncompetitive and causing U.S. labor ultimately to lose jobs, wages, and income anyway.

Furthermore, counterbalancing any losses to labor are clear gains to the shareholders of U.S. multinationals through higher profits; probable gains to skilled U.S. managers, consultants, engineers, supervisors, foremen, and experienced salespersons, whose services are in greater demand at home and abroad because the more competitive affiliate is likely to expand more than the parent contracts; and possible gains to U.S. consumers if multinationals pass on some of their higher profits in the form of lower prices (a profit-to-price link that labor unions deny is relevant to oligopolistic corporations).

In the case of multinational operations aimed at external markets, the distributional consequences are similarly complex. American unions usually claim similar injury when overseas GM and Ford affiliates produce autos for European consumers or when overseas IBM affiliates produce computer hardware and office equipment for European business. In labor's view, these products could have been assembled in the United States and then exported to the same European buyers. Had that been done, U.S. labor would never have lost the cooperative services of the equipment, management, and technology that Ford, GM, and IBM diverted to their European affiliates. The demand for low-skill U.S. labor would have been higher than otherwise. There would have been more jobs in the short run, and higher wages, larger incomes, and a bigger slice of the U.S. income "pie" in the long run.

Labor's position has an economic logic. But multinationals respond vehemently, and just as logically, that labor fails to account for several things, such as the favorable impact of Ford's, GM's, and IBM's foreign presence on their entire product line. The mere existence of foreign affiliates has advertising and security value. Ford in the United States is more likely to export trucks; GM in the United States is more likely to export Frigidaire appliances; and IBM in the United States is more likely to export computers—when European affiliates of these companies promote and service them. In addition, Ford, GM, and IBM all export more parts and equipment to their European affiliates than they would to nonrelated companies if the affiliates did not exist. Finally, multinationals doubt labor's presumption that they could have maintained their markets through exports. European import barriers and the probability that European oligopolists would have undercut their market had U.S. affiliates not been "on the spot" both suggest that the alternative to multinational investment was *no* foreign business for Ford, GM, and IBM. If this is the case, U.S. labor has nothing to gain from inhibiting this kind of multinational.

The business view also possesses economic logic. Resolving the business/labor conflict comes down to answering a difficult hypothetical question: what would U.S. exports have been with fewer or no foreign affiliates of U.S. corporations? Many self-serving attempts have been made to answer this question. Not surprisingly, both business and labor studies tend to support their respective positions in the controversy.

Extractive multinational operations provoke little controversy. The income-distributional consequences seem minor. Resources flow in two directions—U.S. equipment and expertise move abroad to mine and process crude oil, bauxite, and copper, and the processed natural resources move back to the United States. Low-skill labor loses the services of certain complementary resources but gains the services of others. Besides, if the United States had been forced to turn to its own limited oil, bauxite, and copper deposits, the scope for additional jobs and higher wages would have been limited. The only significant U.S. losers from extractive multinational activities seem to be small U.S. owners of stripper wells and low-grade bauxite and copper deposits.

CONSEQUENCES IN HOST COUNTRIES WHEN RESOURCES MOVE. In Europe and Canada the distributional effects of U.S. multinationals are symmetric and opposite to those in the United States. Operations of Ford, GM, and IBM affiliates have ambiguous broad effects on the European or Canadian income distribution. And it is hard to suggest any broadly defined groups in Canada who lose from the presence of U.S. oil and mining affiliates.

Some narrowly defined groups lose, however. Penetration of Europe and Canada by U.S. multinationals clearly dims the outlook for competitive European and Canadian firms. British Leyland and its employees would have been more prosperous without Ford of Britain; Volkswagen and its employees would be better off economically without GM's Opel; and Machines Bull (France) might have survived independently in computers had it not been for IBM and General Electric pressure.

Along with these losers are narrowly defined gainers: the labor employed by U.S. affiliates; the European management and skilled labor that they train; the engineers, scientists, and technicians who are exposed to U.S. technology; and the European suppliers, bankers, insurers, and advertisers whose prosperity is enhanced by dealing with large-scale, efficient affiliates of U.S. multinationals. Some of the gains to these groups are due to increased demands for their services and some to the intangible, nonmarketable skills that are acquired through exposure and learning-by-doing.

Benefits of this sort are often less significant and certain in less-developed host countries. Many multinationals find it more advantageous to import skilled labor and management than to train them in host countries. Multinationals also find it profitable to centralize research and development and to perform none in less-developed host countries. They often rely on imports for supplies and on multinational creditors, insurers, and advertisers for other services. Host-country "linkages" to multinational operations may be few and far between. *Enclaves* develop—segregated areas of multinational activity. Their isolation is often aggravated by regional concentration, government policy, and the lack of competitive forces in the labor market, and is usually most marked in extractive and component/assembly operations in which business is naturally oriented toward external markets. Host-country nationals who depend on the enclave almost invariably gain. But outside the enclave, real losses may occur. Multinationals "spirit away" the best domestic labor and management and "draw off" domestic financial resources. Potentially competitive domestic firms and indigenous entrepreneurial talent are discouraged or co-opted by the dominant enclave.

To alleviate these gains to the few and losses to the many that result from multinational enclaves, less-developed host-country governments often try by policy to assure favorable spillovers. Common methods are insistence on joint ventures with domestic firms and mandatory guidelines for employment of nationals, domestic research activity, and reliance on local suppliers.

PURE TAKEOVERS. Multinational investments do not always imply significant transfers of people, resources, or technology. When General Electric took over Machines Bull (computers) of France, and when Saudi Arabia reclaimed Aramco through nationalization from its American owners, the only real international movement was a shift in control. The internal income-distributional effects of these pure takeovers are small and subtle, in both home and host countries.[23]

NATIONAL ECONOMIC WELFARE AND THE INCOME DISTRIBUTION AMONG NATIONS

Do multinational corporations benefit host countries and reduce income inequality among nations? Promultinational propagandists answer with a resounding yes and proclaim a rosy gospel. In their view:

> Multinationals are the organizational salvation from a divided and mistrustful world. They provide global opportunities for management and skilled employees. They provide structures through which the most advanced technology can be applied anywhere in the world, without the uncertainties and imperfect information that plague its transfer between unrelated sellers and buyers. They provide equipment, space, and the organizational supervision whereby the world's jobless masses can be employed. They provide export markets for countries that could never develop them on their own. They provide bargaining power to hold down the price of imports that affiliates buy. They provide indirect access to international loans for countries whose credit ratings are shakier than their own.

Even if this were all true, it would not directly answer either the economic-welfare or the income-inequality question. First, multinationals provide none of these benefits either free or on concessional terms. Host countries must pay for them. Therefore the rich developed countries in which multinationals are based also gain. And if rich home countries gain proportionally more than poor host countries, then international income inequality is widened.

Consider the matter of payment. Unlike the providers of foreign aid,

[23] Some evidence suggests that takeovers of domestic firms by multinationals often occur when the domestic firm is being poorly managed or faces extinction. In these cases the takeover may preserve the jobs and income of labor that otherwise would have been laid off, and it may eliminate the jobs and income of the personnel responsible for poor performance. Takeovers can also alter the internal income distribution by heightening an industry's oligopolistic strength. To the extent that IBM, General Electric, and Machines Bull were more oligopolistic after GE's acquisition of Machines Bull, one would predict increased above-normal profitability for the American-owned "French" computer industry, all of which would come as an additional transfer of income from French computer buyers. Some commentators have even suggested that GE's acquisition of foreign affiliates enhances its U.S. market power. If so, then takeovers (and maybe other multinational movement) may increase the real incomes of people who depend on multinationals in the United States and reduce the real incomes of people in more competitive industries.

multinationals charge for the resources and technology they furnish. Host countries gain only the additional earnings that their own labor and resource owners are able to claim because of their increased productivity in cooperation with complementary multinational inputs. The multinational itself (and its home country therefore) may realize much greater gains, consisting of rents, royalties, salaries, and profits above what could be earned in any alternative opportunity. Of course, a host country will usually claim a share of the multinational's gains through taxation. But even though both gain (as is usual in most economic transactions), it is not presumed that a less-developed country that hosts multinationals will be able to gain enough to narrow the income gap between itself and the rest of the world.

There are indeed some reasons to surmise that whatever economic benefits multinationals have created worldwide are disproportionately distributed toward rich, developed countries. First, since most multi-national investments occur among developed countries (Table 13.7), the benefits may well accrue more to the rich than to the poor. Second, since most multinationals move in pursuit of the above-normal profits that their oligopolistic advantages allow, their proliferation may make the world economy more oligopolistic. Takeovers of domestic firms, for example, necessarily cut down on the number of firms in the world industry. International income inequality may be increased because oligopolistic profits are necessarily an income transfer from purchasers (rich and poor countries alike) to oligopolistic sellers (rich countries, for the most part).

A contrary point of view holds that multinationals may have made world markets more competitive, not less. They may have eliminated insulated domestic markets, where small national producers maintain monopolistic fiefdoms. In their place has come workable global competition among (an admittedly small number of) multinationals. There can be no presumption about what this replacement would do to the international distribution of income.

Sympathetic commentators on multinationals often choose to avoid any question about their influence on income distribution among nations. They view it as irrelevant, diverting attention from the generally favorable impact that they believe multinationals have in absolute terms. Why criticize a phenomenon that is beneficial to all, even if it is more beneficial to rich countries than to poor?[24] Furthermore, one cannot treat lightly the argument that the above-normal profits of oligopolistic multinationals are not really "excess profits" at all. They are the rewards of past research and development that created both innovation and oligopolistic advantage. Without those profits, research and development could not be financed, and technological

---

[24] There is a parallel observation on the case for international trade. Income might well be distributed more equally among completely self-sufficient nations than it is now, but it would also probably be lower everywhere.

advancement would slow worldwide, to the detriment of all. Seen from this perspective, increasing inequality of income between rich and poor nations is simply an innocuous side-effect of rapid income growth and economic advancement for rich and poor alike.

Other Consequences of Multinational Corporations

The influence of multinational corporations stretches far and wide. As organizations, they affect politics and social relations as well as economics. Within economics, their presence affects not only international trade and finance but also industrial organization, labor, public finance, development, and money and banking.[25] In this section we will touch lightly on some of these effects.

BALANCES OF PAYMENTS

Tremendous effort has been applied to discern the effect of multinational operations on various measures (Supplement 2C) of the balance of payments. Such effects clearly exist. Zenith exports machinery and components from the United States to its Mexican affiliates and imports partially assembled television receivers and parts. It extends loans to affiliates and may alter its ownership share in them. It returns interest on its affiliate loans and profits on its affiliate ownership to U.S. creditors and shareholders. All such transactions enter both the U.S. and Mexican balance-of-payments accounts, on opposite sides of their ledgers. Finally, both Zenith and its Mexican affiliates have international transactions with other affiliates and with completely unrelated parties. Accounting for these, it is possible that Zenith's operations cause positive changes in the balance of payments of both Mexico and the United States—but those positive changes must necessarily be some other countries' negative change.

Whatever conclusions are drawn about Zenith's effects on international payments, however, will not necessarily parallel those drawn for Exxon (an extractive multinational) or for General Motors (a foreign-market-oriented multinational). It is misguided to expect any sweeping answer to the question of what multinationals do to payments balance.

Concern over these consequences of multinationals should be further mitigated by the insights of Chapters 3, 5, 8, and 9. Not every positive change in a balance of payments is "favorable." Importing as

---

[25] Multinational banking was a late-blooming but quickly booming phenomenon of the late 1960s and early 1970s.

well as exporting enhances national economic welfare, and if, by a careful evaluation, the activities of some multinational are judged detrimental to the balance of payments, then restricting those activities is often an inferior policy to more direct macroeconomic and balance-of-payments policies.[26]

GOVERNMENT ECONOMIC POLICY

Do multinational corporations weaken the power of governments to influence their economy? Many commentators think so, and only a few (for example, the *Wall Street Journal*) mistrust government so much that they welcome the weakening.

A major concern is taxes. Multinationals are frequently the beneficiaries of treaties and standard tax practices that allow them to avoid significant taxation of their corporate earnings. Some illustrations have already been cited—foreign tax havens and holidays and U.S. tax deferral. *Transfer pricing* is another mechanism. Global tax payments can be reduced by lowering the price of transfers (exports) from affiliates in high-tax countries to other affiliates and raising the price of transfers in the opposite direction (imports). Such transfer pricing causes profits to shrink for affiliates in high-tax countries and to rise for affiliates in low-tax countries by exactly the same amount. Global after-tax profits, of course, rise. Multinational oil companies practiced tax-reducing transfer pricing prominently before OPEC's ascendancy, "taking" their profits in low-tax producing countries and claiming only marginal earnings, or even losses, on European and American refining and marketing.

Appropriate transfer pricing can also enable multinationals to avoid government barriers to international trade and international lending and borrowing. And they can disguise true profits in countries where the truth would arouse outcries from labor unions or from the government.

Fears also exist that multinationals skirt regional development policies of governments. They can shift activities to another country altogether, rather than to a region of the government's choosing. The evidence here is mixed, however. In Europe, U.S. multinationals

---

[26] The same observation applies even more practically to the distributional and employment consequences of multinationals. Labor unions may well be able to demonstrate that U.S. multinationals cause increased unemployment and an "adverse" shift in the U.S. income distribution, but this observation is not sufficient by itself to justify restriction or regulation of multinationals. Restriction or regulation may be dramatically more costly to economic prosperity than alternative, first-best policies (see Chapter 9) to alleviate unemployment and to redress income inequality. However, conceptually superior alternatives may be politically or economically infeasible. In any event, the choice of an ideal remedy is not as clear-cut as labor unions usually imply.

seem to have been more willing to operate in depressed areas than European firms.

Finally, if multinational affiliates are able to draw readily on one another for loans, then they may weaken a country's monetary policy. But this concern is relevant only to the few developed countries that do not simultaneously regulate international lending and borrowing.

GOVERNMENT INDEPENDENCE AND CONFLICT

More than any other consequence of multinationals, host countries are concerned about loss of independent governance. The concern has several aspects.

First, host-country citizens who depend on multinationals for their livelihood become inadvertent spokespersons for multinational interests. Despite Canadian uneasiness about the economic prominence of U.S. affiliates, little can be done to discourage those that are already there. The economic effects on Canadians make such discouragement politically undesirable. United States multinationals thus enjoy indirect political power in Canada that matches their economic power.

Second, multinationals may sometimes attempt to wield political power more directly, as illustrated in the 1970s by the sordid history of International Telephone and Telegraph's political intervention in Chile and by the magnitude of the bribes paid foreign government officials by U.S. multinationals.

Third, governments inevitably impose on each other's independence in the presence of multinationals. The Hickenlooper Amendment enables the U.S. government to cut off foreign assistance to any government that nationalizes a U.S. multinational's property without adequate compensation. Radical economists believe that protecting U.S. business interests was a main motivation for the prolonged U.S. interference in Southeast Asian government and also for U.S. government complicity in the ITT-Chile affair.

A less dramatic example is U.S. insistence on *extraterritorial* application of its export control and antitrust laws. The United States successfully barred Canadian affiliates of U.S. multinationals from selling to Cuba despite the Canadian government's approval of such sales. The extended embargo was not highhanded under U.S. law because a U.S. parent firm is legally accountable in U.S. courts for the actions of its foreign affiliates (despite their foreign incorporation). Because of this *extraterritoriality* the United States is able to prosecute Gulf Oil for allowing Gulf of Canada to take part in a worldwide uranium cartel that was organized with the blessing (and apparent encouragement) of the Canadian government during the mid-1970s. The United States is also able to prosecute American multinationals whose affiliates respect the Arab boycott on trade with Israel, although the boycott is strictly legal in the countries where the affiliates do business.

Multinationals and Alternative
Global Economic Futures

Apologists for multinationals are of two minds about their influence on government. They recognize the difficulties that multinationals cause for national economic policy and independence. Yet they argue that these difficulties may be welcome from a global point of view. For example, many of the government actions that multinationals undermine are expressions of economic nationalism—policies that beggar our neighbor in order to advance ourselves. No matter how well they are justified from a national perspective, such policies inevitably reduce the economic welfare of the world as a whole (the worldwide average of goods and services available per unit of effort). "Citizens of the world" therefore welcome what narrow nationalists fear.

The perspective of global economic welfare is not one that we have adopted in this book. Most of international economics springs directly from economic nationalism, as vested in separate national moneys, divergent national preferences for high employment and tolerance of inflation, and aggressive and retaliatory trade restrictions.

By contrast, owners and managers of multinational corporations frequently reject a nationalistic perspective.[27] They are increasingly citizens of the world, not out of altruism but because of their pursuit of worldwide profit (broadly defined), and they make no apologies for what appears to be crass materialism on a global scale. Instead they draw analogies. In their view, the growth of the multinational firm parallels the U.S. growth of the national firm during the 1800s. Only a few diehard critics doubt the benefits of the latter. Other nations look with envy at the large, prosperous, integrated American market. Out of such envy sprang the successful European Common Market, and even its success can be traced not to European governments but to firms that spanned its boundaries. By retreating from their economic nationalism, governments simply enabled the firms to make it work.

This vision of the past and present suggests a corresponding vision of the future. National governments will be forced by events to assume a diminished economic power, akin to that of state and local governments in the United States today. Yet the economic anarchy of laissez faire will not necessarily rule, nor do multinational apologists cherish it. Instead, they hold out the hope of economic cooperation among governments on a global scale, with benefits to all. While globally determined policy toward multinationals would have its costs

---

[27] It is significant, for example, that in the mid-1970s RCA was the one holdout from the U.S. television industry's successful petition for relief from TV imports. RCA is the most multinational of all U.S. TV manufacturers and probably saw little to be gained from shifting profits away from foreign affiliates and toward U.S. affiliates.

(for example, global antitrust), its benefits would be greater (for example, more freedom of international movement, provision for adequate compensation in the sale of property).

Finally, multinational visionaries (reluctantly) foresee the growth of globally organized labor unions as well. The internationalization of the labor movement would be likely in a world where both corporations and governments were globally organized. Global labor cooperation would parallel exactly the federation of U.S. labor unions during the 1900s, as they responded to the national scope of industry.

The prophecy cannot be dismissed as a wild dream. Both intergovernment cooperation and international exchanges of information among labor unions have increased markedly. Prestigious committees from the Organization for Economic Cooperation and Development (OECD) and from the United Nations are at work drafting worldwide codes of conduct for multinationals and the governments that deal with them. These codes may be the precursors of an intergovernmental body to supervise multinationals, similar to the International Monetary Fund (Supplement 2B) or to the General Agreement on Tariffs and Trade (Supplement 11B).

Yet the prophecy is unlikely to be approximated in the near future. Economic nationalism not only lives on but shows signs of increased vitality. Nations cast increasingly desperate glances toward beggar-your-neighbor policies, as less objectionable solutions to the problems of worldwide inflation and stagnation prove politically infeasible. Governments turn increasingly toward nationalization of weak domestic corporations and stricter regulation or sometimes expropriation of multinational affiliates. The future world economy may be the socialist model blown up to a global scale, not the U.S. model. Monolithic multinational corporations may be displaced by monolithic socialist enterprises with national bases and only very limited operations in other countries. International transactions may become increasingly dictated by administrative agreement and not by the market, as we shall see in the next chapter.

Whether economic nationalism shrinks, grows, or remains stable is not a question on which economists have special insight. Economic nationalism is largely the reflection of national, racial, and ethnic prejudice. It will go as they go. If it expires, or if it intensifies in a socialist direction, the international economics of the future will have to be substantially rewritten.

Summary

International trade involves not only the amalgams of inputs that we refer to as commodities or goods, but also the inputs themselves.

Real international migration and trade in technology, raw materials, semifinished products, and capital goods have a larger value (however measured) than trade in finished goods.

So-called "pure" international trade in inputs takes place largely in a familiar forum—a market between unrelated sellers and buyers, but a more significant part of input trade takes place instead between related affiliates of multinational corporations.

Migration and "pure" input trade are influenced by the same variables that affect output trade: relative resource endowments, technological advancement, and tastes (including tastes for a familiar language and culture and proximity to family). Input and output trade also have similar effects on income distribution within a nation. Domestic resource owners and workers lose about as much from imports of competitive resources and immigration of comparably skilled people as they lose from imports of goods embodying those same resources or skills. But barriers to input trade—especially to migration and technology transfer—are important causes of the pronounced income inequality across nations.

International income inequality itself influences input trade, so that identifying cause and effect, disease and cure, or credit and blame becomes exceedingly complex and controversial.

Multinational corporate trade in inputs is even more complex and controversial. Both its causes and its consequences vary, depending on how many people and resources (if any) actually move when multinationals trade ownership and control of inputs, and whether multinational activity is extractive or market-oriented and vertically or horizontally integrated.

Multinational corporate transactions are influenced not only by the familiar determinants of comparative advantage and pure input trade but also by the desire to extend, consolidate, and defend profitable positions of market power. Market power, oligopolistic advantage, and exploitation of barriers to entry (technology, size, product differentiation) are hallmarks of multinationals and underlie many of their actions.

Their impact on the income distribution within nations varies within wide bounds, depending on the considerations mentioned and on whether home or host countries are concerned. Their effect on the income distribution among nations is also unclear but depends more on national policies toward taxation, employment, joint ventures, and the location of research-and-development activity. Finally, multinationals almost certainly undermine government independence and policy discretion. Whether this is good or bad depends on how ready the reader is to identify with the global (albeit corporate) perspective of most multinationals rather than the nationalistic and subnationalistic perspectives from which we have examined most problems of economic welfare in this book.

Key Terms

trade in "inputs"
immigration, emigration
Stolper-Samuelson Theorem
factor price equalization
brain drain
foreign direct investment:
    takeovers and green-field investment

wholly owned, joint-venture
    affiliates (subsidiaries)
cross-penetration
tax havens, tax deferral, and
    tax-credit arrangements
enclaves
transfer pricing
extraterritoriality

Key Concepts and Review

Similarities and differences between international migration and resource/technology transfer: (1) among unrelated sellers and buyers ("pure" input trade); (2) within multinational corporations.

Substitutability between input trade and output trade.

Feedback (reciprocal causation) between barriers to input trade and international income inequality.

Oligopolistic advantage, normal profits, and barriers to entry.

Similarities and differences between extractive and market-oriented, horizontally and vertically integrated multinationals.

Six (and more) causes of foreign direct investment.

The impact of multinational corporations on: income distribution; balances of payments; tax revenues; and government policy.

Supplement 13A
The Brain Drain

Across-the-board technological leadership by the United States, Canada, and Europe has raised incomes and standards of living so high in these regions that there are strong incentives for almost *all* resource owners to migrate there. The world's unskilled are obviously attracted, although most are excluded by strict immigration restrictions.[1] The less-developed world's skilled professionals and other owners of capital are also attracted. Although their relative scarcity in poorer countries tends to raise their incomes there, this advantage is not always strong enough to offset the higher incomes made possible by technological superiority in richer countries. The United Nations estimates that roughly 300,000 scientists, engineers, physicians, and surgeons emigrated permanently from less-developed to developed countries during the decade ending in the early 1970s and that the emigration has continued since then only at a slower rate.[2] This emigration is usually labeled the *brain drain*.

The United States, Canada, and Europe tolerate permanent immigration by skilled professionals, if not quite welcoming it. Their toleration and the exasperation of less-developed countries (LDCs) at the brain drain are opposite sides of the same coin. Both relate to the composite nature of brain-drain migration. More than just migration by labor, it is migration of both human capital and the potential for technological advancement (as embodied in the person migrating).

In LDCs, the loss of human capital and technological potential inevitably reduces the average endowment of capital and future technology for each person who remains. On average, these people end up less productive than they would have been, and their incomes and purchasing power are lower. From the government's point of view, the country as a whole is hurt; the clear gains to the migrants do not offset the losses to the stable inhabitants because the migrants have committed themselves to giving up their citizenship.

LDCs also suffer from their brain drain if it cuts off two other potential benefits. First, if skilled professionals had remained, they might have developed innovations that led to commodity or technology exports based on uneven technological gaps. Such exports would have been accompanied by temporary monopoly profits both to the innovator and to the LDC as a whole. Second, if skilled professionals had remained, their activities might well have had some unexpected

---

[1] Exclusion was not always the rule in the United States. During the nineteenth century, unskilled Irish and Chinese immigrants were welcomed and put to work building the nation's railroad system. Even today, Mexicans who enter the United States temporarily as seasonal field and factory workers are for the most part unskilled.

[2] *Wall Street Journal*, January 14, 1977.

external benefits.[3] For example, research and development oriented toward one industry might have spilled over into applications for others. Home-produced higher education that could have been administered by educated nonmigrants might have reduced the resource costs of primary, secondary, and vocational schooling.

If LDC governments try to alleviate the brain drain by restricting emigration, they create other problems. They are forced to limit the freedom of their most skilled, intelligent, and ambitious citizens. Any consequent disenchantment can dampen incentives and reduce productivity, having adverse effects on national economic performance similar to those of the brain drain itself. Besides, emigration barriers raise the awkward noneconomic question of whether there should be any universal human right to emigrate.

In light of these problems, it is not surprising that LDCs lobby for the developed world to alleviate the brain drain on their behalf. Proposed solutions include tighter *im*migration policies in developed countries, or a system of compensatory transfer payments from rich to poor nations for every professional migrant.

Developed countries do not necessarily support such proposals. For them, the brain drain is arguably beneficial. Immigrants to the United States, for example, including those from LDCs, are generally more skilled than "native" Americans, as Table 13A.1 suggests. Thus the average "native" American gains by ending up with more cooperative, productivity-enhancing capital and technological expertise than would have been possible with less immigration.

The brain drain also has distributional consequences that exasperate the governments of poorer countries. Because it transfers humanly embodied capital and technological potential to rich developed countries, it makes the international distribution of income more unequal. And within the LDCs, the bulk of the losses are borne by the poorest, lowest-skilled labor groups, an effect that most LDC governments find unattractive.

In developed countries the internal distribution is affected oppositely. Low-skill groups probably gain. Others tend to lose. Loud objections are sometimes even heard from professional organizations who correctly feel threatened by the influx of skilled immigrant competitors.[4]

In sum, the brain drain raises problems that are as thorny and multifaceted as those raised by multinational corporations, only on a smaller scale. Controversy arises in both cases because the people,

---

[3] See the discussion of *externalities*, p. 287.

[4] Belgian physicians, for example, called for a general strike in 1977 to dramatize the threat to them from an "imminent invasion" of low-paid British and Italian medical professionals. Their "plight" was fostered by a European Community decision to allow doctors from every member country to practice in every other member country (*European Community*, no. 199 (January–February 1977), p. 42).

TABLE 13A.1. *Education and Skill Mix of Employed "Native" Americans and U.S. Immigrants, 1970*

Occupation	Percent of "Native" Americans in each occupation	Percent of U.S. immigrants in each occupation
Professional, technical, and kindred workers	12.5	20.0
Managers and administrators, except farm	6.9	7.4
Service workers	11.0	20.0
Farmers, farm managers, craftsmen, and kindred workers	17.8	13.0
Sales, clerical, and kindred workers	25.0	19.9
Operatives and laborers	26.9	19.7

Source. U.S. Department of Commerce, Bureau of the Census, *1/1000 Sample 1970 U.S. Census of Population;* and U.S. Department of Justice, Immigration and Naturalization Service, *1974 Annual Report: Immigration and Naturalization Service,* Table 41A, p. 114.

resources, and knowledge that move internationally are mixed and complex and because the consequences of their movement are more than just economic.

Chapter 14

Controversy over the International Economic Order

Today's compelling issues in international trade almost all spring from heightened dissatisfaction with its pattern and organization. The dissatisfaction is not universal. It is associated primarily with less-developed countries (LDCs), often referred to as the "South," to distinguish them from the industrialized developed countries of the northern hemisphere (the "North").

LDC governments and sympathetic supporters see an international economic system which perpetuates the status quo at best. At worst, they believe, the system has the following effects:

It shifts economic power and wealth from South to North, away from those countries that have the least of them in the first place. It drains financial resources from the poorest countries by saddling them with increasingly burdensome debt service; it disenfranchises the South in international monetary affairs by ad hoc agreements made outside duly constituted international organizations and by passively allowing official reserves to be created in the form of Euro-currencies rather than SDRs (Supplements 2B, 3A, and Chapter 7). It creates pressures on prices of primary products that cause the terms of trade of LDCs to deteriorate over time, reducing even further their already low share of the benefits from international trade (Supplement 8A). It discourages meaningful LDC participation in GATT-sponsored trade liberalization by insisting on reciprocal concessions (Chapter 11), even when those might mean the extinction of an infant industry or an entire development program (Chapter 9). It moves the international distribution of income in a regressive direction in many ways: by sanctioning barriers to free international movement of technology; by encouraging the proliferation of oligopolistic multinational corporations that move abroad only when they can extract an oligopolistic profit from economically weak host countries; and by benignly approving the brain drain from South to North, thereby depriving LDCs of their meager endowment of technological expertise and human capital (all outlined in Chapter 13).

Southern dissatisfaction thrives even though the present system of international exchange is almost surely preferable to self-sufficiency, even for LDCs. But they foresee immense benefits to a fundamental restructuring of international exchange—the creation of a *new international economic order* to alleviate the features that they feel have victimized them. Much of the North's alleged historical advantage in international exchange is seen by the South as an arbitrary consequence of market power, perhaps even an "immoral" consequence insofar as the innocently poor could have been made richer (at the expense of the well-meaning, but neglectful rich).

These positions illustrate how in North-South conflict the domains of economics, politics, ethics, and religion overlap at many points. The economic proposals to be discussed in this chapter are only parts of a broader, brooding controversy over the organization of all relationships among nations—economic, political, military, cultural. There are several consequences of this overlap. One is that economic proposals are often prized for their symbolic or psychological value, even when poorly justified on their own economic merits. A second is that economic proposals are frequently couched in the form of manifestos, even harangues, and their defense appeals more to emotion than to economics. ("To be dispassionate about such matters is to be insensitive. To use rhetoric is at least to care.") A third is that a narrow economic introduction to these proposals, such as follows, will necessarily understate their attractiveness to proponents. While it may be appropriate to a textbook in international economics, it cannot place them in their most revealing and appealing context.

Three of the most prominent proposals for reordering international exchange concern organizing trade in primary products, encouraging Northern market access for Southern manufactured exports, and facilitating international technology transfer. Others concern international regulation of multinational corporations, increased interdependence among LDCs themselves, and cooperative international decision making on "common" resources, such as the environment and deep-sea minerals, and on "basic human needs," such as food and health.

Before discussing these, it is helpful to examine the goals and philosophy of those who advocate a new international economic order and to establish a few reasons why these ideas have become increasingly potent in the international economy.

Economic Goals and Philosophy of the New International Economic Order

The economic goals of less-developed countries have changed little in the recent past. They seek increased absolute prosperity, increased prosperity relative to the developed world, an increased share of global industrial production,[1] and increased access to modern but "appropriate" technology. Increased relative prosperity is defended on the grounds of equity, often in a rhetorical question: why should the rich get richer faster than the poor do? Increased industrial shares are sought to enjoy more favorable trends in the terms of trade (Supplement 8A) and also because production of manufactures instead of primary products is believed to enhance both growth and technological advancement (pp. 294–296). Indigenous industrialization, growth, and technological progress are also sought in order to create countervailing economic dependence of the North on the South and redress an imbalance of dependence that the South sees forced on it by the current international economic order.

"Dependence" is one key reason why Southern tactics have changed recently even though their economic goals have not. (OPEC, discussed below, is the other.) As the South sees it, economic relations among nations after World War II accomplished few of their goals, yet saddled them with the peculiar kind of economic dependence that so-called free or liberal market systems impose. When international markets are organized by competing private individuals and institutions, those who compete most successfully are rewarded with positions of market power (independence). Others are forced into dependency relationships, which may be materially gainful but which are costly in terms of responsibility, freedom of action, and participation in decision making. Graduating students sense this as they enter the job market for the first time. So do individual farmers and even farmers' cooperatives if they market their produce to large food processors. Coffee-, tea-, and cocoa-producing countries find themselves in exactly the same position. So do producers of bauxite as they confront the handful of economically powerful multinational aluminum companies.

Nor does the South see dependency limited to sellers without market power. Buyers of sophisticated equipment, armaments, and new technology itself are equally dependent on limited alternatives. Only their own market power assures them of the freedom to participate in design, pricing, and important decisions which otherwise are made solely by oligopolistic sellers.

---

[1] The specific target proposed is to raise their current 8 to 10 percent share of world industrial production to roughly 25 percent by the year 2000.

A familiar counterargument is that liberal, market-oriented economic systems allow everyone equality of opportunity (opportunity to obtain market power). But this advantage is usually dismissed by proponents of a new international economic order. "Equality of opportunity among unequals is not equitable" is a familiar response. The South believes cynically that market power is usually inherited, not built from scratch on the basis of superior merit, and is institutionalized in rigid corporate property rights that persist long beyond the meritorious action that justified the market power originally.

The South realizes, of course, that it is dependent on the North in all spheres—economic, military, political. But it seems to sense that the balance of power is least unfavorable in political spheres. The ongoing cold war between East and West (despite détente) enhances Southern political power, and international organizations such as the United Nations provide forums for them to assert it. It is broadly accurate to describe Southern demands for a new international economic order as attempts to politicize international economic exchange: to "organize" trade, to make it "orderly" and less subject to the "whim" of those with market power, to "guide" it and "direct" it in a way that responds to political pressure, on the apparent grounds that even dictators usually express society's will more representatively than corporate management.

Thoughtful advocates are aware of the potential economic costs of a move toward socialistic organization of international exchange. Private ambition and productive incentives may be dulled dramatically. Economic efficiency may be lost as fewer and fewer markets provide price signals to guide individual producers and consumers (pp. 283–287). Administrative resource costs may burgeon as political bureaucracies replace or overrule corporate bureaucracies. Furthermore, power relationships, involuntary action, and dependence will all persist, even though they change character. Bureaucratic whim will replace market whim, and could potentially be even more enslaving.

So the new international economic order is no panacea, even to its proponents. But in it they expect to realize their goals more fully than they did under the liberal international economic order of the 1950s and the 1960s. "Liberal trade" in their eyes is only slightly less cruel an illusion than "free trade." Actual international trade is neither globally free nor globally liberal (permissive). It is liberating only for those with market power. It is no surprise to LDCs that the United States, Canada, Europe, and Japan have always been the most ardent supporters of a liberal world economic order. Those with market power really *are* more independent in such a system.

Southern hopes are supported by the remarkable success of the Organization of Petroleum Exporting Countries (OPEC). OPEC's example invigorated what had been idealistic and feeble demands. Its seizure of market power and financial wealth from developed countries, and its subsequent willingness to use both to back Southern demands (in the fashion of a prosperous Robin Hood), have forced the industrialized Northern world finally to take these demands seriously. Plaintive pleas of powerless have-not nations have been transformed into sober proposals for reshaping international economic relations.

OPEC is also seen by the South as an alluring example of a new order of economic development. The strategy of OPEC success differed drastically from the development formulas that the North had always preached to LDCs. OPEC made no extraordinary effort to save or sacrifice; rather it simply insisted on a fair share (in its eyes) of the gains from international trade in petroleum. OPEC made no initial effort to build new wealth from investment in capital and technology; rather it simply claimed the wealth that others had amassed from the joint and cooperative contribution of foreign technology, foreign capital, and OPEC's own natural resource abundance. OPEC made no unusual effort to rationalize resource allocation and domestic production as a precondition for developing; diversification and industrialization came rather as a consequence of development based on oil prices. Finally, to Southern sympathizers, OPEC demonstrated conclusively that involuntary redistribution of income and wealth from rich to poor had none of the cataclysmic consequences for global incentives and productivity that are often invoked by the rich to defend the distributive status quo. The rich survived, albeit somewhat painfully, and at least some of the poor prospered.

Many poor LDCs also lost, of course, as a result of OPEC. Yet sympathy of outlook has been remarkably preserved among oil-importing LDC victims and OPEC itself. Only part of this solidarity is due to OPEC charity. Most is due to the intensity of conviction among LDCs that OPEC's model leads to development with fewer tears. The model is simple:

> Confront the market power of Northern corporations with the political power of collective LDC governments. Use collective political agitation to force the North to abandon its malign neglect of international equity. Pursue wealth transfers from rich to poor, not wealth creation, as the key to development.

The South has been remarkably successful in cultivating the solidarity necessary for such a program to succeed. More differences than those between OPEC and non-OPEC could potentially divide proponents of a new international economic order. LDCs differ dramatically from each other in income per person,[2] dependence on

---

[2] Income per person varies among LDCs alone by a factor of 20. The International Monetary Fund and the World Bank often use income per person to divide LDCs into subgroups. The least developed of them are sometimes described as the *fourth world*, to set them apart from *third-world* countries (other LDCs). The United Nations also distinguishes a class of "most seriously affected" LDCs, referring to the severity of the burden placed on them by higher oil, food, and raw-materials prices during the mid-1970s.

agriculture and mineral wealth, stage and diversity of industrialization, size, openness, and sociocultural characteristics. They differ much more dramatically among themselves than developed countries (DCs) do. Yet in the 1970s they presented a formidable common front in the periodic United Nations Conference on Trade and Development (UNCTAD),[3] in the 1975 through 1977 Conferences on International Economic Cooperation (CIEC),[4] and in other international forums, as well.

This collective solidarity, and also Southern goals, strategy, and slogans, find an echo in the labor union movement in the industrialized North.[5] And the arguments on both sides of the new international economic order bear a striking resemblance to those that divided management from labor during the early years of unions. The North plays a role analogous to managers and owners; the South, a role analogous to workers and their unions. The debate in both instances is over how to divide the gains (spoils) from mutually beneficial exchange. It is also over how widely to allow those with market power to buy and sell (hire and fire) freely, without rules and procedures to protect the weak—rules which must be administratively negotiated and bureaucratically enforced. LDCs look hopefully to the day when their proposed rules and procedures for a new international economic order will be accepted just as those governing labor relations are within DCs today.

---

[3] The first United Nations Conference on Trade and Development was held in 1964 under pressure from less-developed UN members and with the reluctant support of developed members. Since then, there have been UNCTADs once every four years, and the name UNCTAD has also come to stand for the conferences' permanent secretariat and staff, established by the General Assembly of the UN. The periodic conferences and the permanent secretariat both reflect the General Assembly's one-nation, one-vote philosophy. Since LDCs outnumber DCs in UNCTAD, the organization has been a powerful voice for Southern demands for a new international economic order, and a frequently acrimonious forum in which to confront the North with these demands. Many of the proposals discussed in this chapter originated in the workings of UNCTAD.

[4] The Conferences on International Economic Cooperation (CIEC) arose out of OPEC's oil-pricing policy. Developed nations had pressed OPEC for a series of meetings to negotiate future actions and assurances on oil pricing, embargos, and related energy matters. OPEC and a group of LDCs insisted on broadening the agenda to include global marketing and pricing of all raw materials as well as the problems of economic development and its financing. Representatives from 27 countries (8 DCs, 7 OPEC countries, and 12 other LDCs) convened at irregular intervals from December 1975 to June 1977. Agreement was reached in principle on a number of issues, but the conferences served more importantly as forums for airing divergent views.

[5] The analogy has been expanded by Jagdish N. Bhagwati in his editorial introduction to *The New International Economic Order: The North-South Debate* (Cambridge, Mass.: M.I.T. Press, 1977).

Organizing Trade in Primary Products

The most fundamental proposals for a new international economic order are for thoroughgoing "commodity policy"—proposals that markets for primary products (minerals, raw materials, and basic foodstuffs) be replaced or carefully regulated by administrative planning. These proposals would bring a significant portion of currently "liberal" world trade, and almost half of the export trade of LDCs,[6] under the direct day-to-day influence of governments.

Commodity policy is aimed at two goals. One of them, price stabilization, could conceivably benefit North and South alike. Thus some commodity agreements are envisioned to be cooperative, two-sided ventures between producing and consuming countries. The second goal, however, necessarily benefits the South at the expense of the North: improving the terms of trade of primary producers. In the absence of a strong Northern commitment to transfer economic welfare to the South in this way, commodity agreements might have to be collusive, one-sided arrangements among producing countries alone, following the OPEC model.

STABILIZING COMMODITY PRICES

Prices of primary products are notoriously volatile, as illustrated by Table 14.1. The price of rice more than doubled between 1972 and 1973, and the price of phosphate rock almost quadrupled between 1973 and 1974. Cocoa prices in 1977 were eight times higher than they had been in 1971! We, as outsiders, can sense the severity of the double-digit declines in many prices by comparing them to double-digit deflation of the prices closest to home for most of us—our own wages.

The causes of such volatility include the susceptibility of agricultural supply to freakish weather conditions, the hypersensitivity of raw-materials demand to global business fluctuations,[7] the long lag

---

[6] Many countries besides LDCs export significant amounts of primary products, notably Canada, South Africa, and Australia, but few are as dependent on them as the typical LDC is.

[7] See Chapter 6 for reasons why business fluctuations tend to be parallel worldwide. Demands for raw materials and semiprocessed inputs such as lumber, petrochemicals, and aluminum seem to be subject to an *accelerator cycle* that has sharper ups and downs than the underlying business cycle. As expectations of a general upturn in business solidify, purchasers of raw materials and semiprocessed inputs try to build up their inventories to meet anticipated future needs as well as current needs. The upturn in the demand for inputs leads and is generally more rapid than the corresponding upturn in the demand for outputs. The opposite happens with spreading expectations of an impending business slump. Demand for primary products can even fall to zero (a wildly improbable event for most other goods) as regular purchasers work off what they view as excessive inventories.

TABLE 14.1. *Year-to-Year Changes in Selected Commodity Prices*

Percent change in price

Year	Cocoa	Coffee	Copper	Phos-phate rock	Rice	Rubber
1969–1970	−26	31	−4	−2	−23	−19
1970–1971	−23	−12	−24	2	−10	−15
1971–1972	19	13	−1	2	14	1
1972–1973	96	23	67	20	138	95
1973–1974	58	9	15	297	55	13
1974–1975	−28	7	−40	23	−33	−25
1975–1976	61	96	14	−47	−30	32
1976–1977	93	61	−7	−14	7	5
Ratio of maximum price to minimum price 1969–1977	8.2	6.0	1.9	6.1	4.2	2.3

Sources: International Monetary Fund, *International Financial Statistics*, May 1977 and March 1978. Price quotations: cocoa, Ghana (London); coffee, "all coffee" (New York); copper, United Kingdom (London); phosphate rock, Morocco (Casablanca); rice, Thailand (Bangkok); rubber, all origins (New York).

between the decision to produce primary products and actual sales, which leads to frequent under- and oversupply, because of the unpredictability of the distant future,[8] and the competitive nature of markets for many primary products, which translates supply and demand shocks almost immediately into price variation.

The alleged consequences of primary-product price volatility underlie Southern demands for a new international commodity policy. These consequences are evaluated in greater detail in Supplement 14A, where their similarity to the controversial consequences of exchange-rate variation is even more apparent than here:

1. Above-average volatility of prices may confront a country with recurrent dislocation and adjustment costs (of retooling, retraining, refurbishing, and relocating resources—discussed in Chapter 10) as resources are induced to shift back and forth among sectors of the economy.
2. Price volatility may create business uncertainty that discourages long-range planning, research and development, and investment in additional capacity or advanced processing facilities. In

[8] Certain primary products may be influenced by sophisticated versions of the behavior that generates price-quantity cycling in *hog-cycle* or *cobweb* models.

economies that are highly dependent on one commodity (such as Bangladesh on jute, Ghana on cocoa, Malaysia on natural rubber), such uncertainty may reduce the aggregate stock of productive capital and rate of technological progress, leading therefore to lower standards of living (pp. 423–429).

3. Rapid upward movement in the price of a country's principal export commodity can be generally inflationary. This is especially true when it is caused by a boom in world demand (so that quantity exported, export revenues, and the balance of payments all rise rapidly, too) and when a country's monetary control is weak. When these commodity-price bubbles burst, substantial hardship can be caused by dislocation of workers and idling of plant and equipment. This is especially true when the "bust" is caused by a sharp decline in world demand. Then exports and the balance of payments will both plunge, and the government may be forced to turn to austerity programs, as did Chile and Jamaica in the mid-1970s in the face of depressed world demand for copper and bauxite.

The South argues that even the industrial countries might welcome agreements to stabilize primary product prices, because they too would have small gains. Price stabilization would then be *mutually* beneficial, with the global gains distributed progressively (most to poor countries, some to rich countries). Northern gains might arise for three reasons:

1. Instability of prices can cause some costly resource shifts in developed countries, too; commodity-price bubbles can be inflationary; commodity-price busts can be dislocating—all these for the same reasons as in LDCs.
2. Accelerating upward price spirals can cause harmful destabilizing speculation, such as that which plagued U.S. and world commodity markets in 1972–1974. Producers hold back supplies in order to wait for better future prices; users of raw materials stock up on copper, newsprint, and so on to avoid higher future prices; consumers add to hoards of storable foodstuffs. Temporary shortages may develop, which persist for some time if governments attempt to freeze prices. Fears of further shortages and of the removal of price controls aggravate the speculative panic hoarding, which causes even greater shortages, and so on in a vicious circle.
3. Recurrent global shortages can lead to costly misallocation of production. DC governments are tempted to subsidize their own meager and exorbitantly costly resources, minerals, and agricultural products in the naive belief that they can isolate their country from global commodity shortages and speculation.[9]

_____

[9] The belief is naive because "sheltered" domestic producers usually find ways to secure the world price to which they feel they are entitled, including the *export* of products that are usually imported! United States exports of a

Southern insistence on sweeping global price stabilization for primary products draws a mixed response from Northern countries. On balance, they remain unpersuaded. They were genuinely alarmed and injured by the unprecedented commodity-price inflation between 1972 and 1974 (see Table 14.1). But the fall-back in many commodity prices since then has been counterinflationary in the North, and in that respect welcome. And DCs such as Japan that are highly dependent on primary product imports do not suffer nearly so much from price instability as do the many LDCs that are dependent on only one or two primary products for export. Least sympathetic of all to commodity agreements aimed at stabilizing prices is the United States, which is closer to primary-product self-sufficiency than most other DCs, especially with respect to critical industrial materials.[10]

Developed countries furthermore doubt the feasibility of most proposals for commodity-price stabilization. History does not reassure them, as Table 14.2 reveals. Many international agreements to stabilize prices have been short-lived. They have temporarily ironed out the minor price fluctuations that didn't seem to hurt much anyway, and they have failed precisely at those times when upward price instability was most pronounced and harmful.

Table 14.2 reveals the three common means of implementing commodity-price stabilization: buffer stocks, export quotas and

---

number of normally imported raw materials jumped in 1973–1974 as a response to U.S. price controls, which did not apply to export sales. Such exports aggravated domestic shortages.

[10] The U.S. National Commission on Supplies and Shortages estimated that for the 1970s the United States imported only 15 percent of its critical industrial materials, compared to Europe's 75 percent and Japan's 90 percent (Morgan Guaranty Trust Company, *Morgan Guaranty Survey*, May 1977, p. 7). The list below summarizes U.S. import dependence on a number of critical materials in the mid-1970s:

	Percent of consumption imported overall (1976)	*Percent of consumption imported from LDCs (1974)*
Manganese	100	48
Chromium	90	29
Bauxite (for aluminum)	88	63
Tin	75	73
Nickel	61	6
Zinc	60	14
Iron	35	9
Copper	16	10
Phosphates	0	0

Sources: International Economic Report of the President, March 1976, p. 96; United Nations Association, *The Global Economic Challenge* (New York, 1978), p. xx.

FIGURE 14.1. *Methods for Stabilizing Commodity Prices*

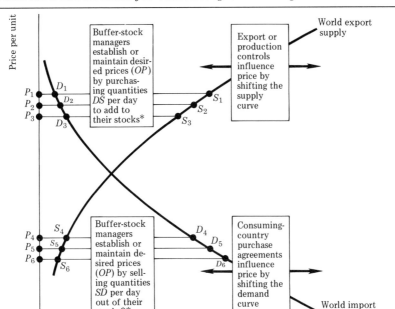

* The official buffer-stock facility is the residual demander of the excess private supplies (*DS*) at the target price.

** The official buffer-stock facility is the residual supplier of the excess private demand (*SD*) at the target price.

production controls, and special purchase arrangements with consuming-country governments. Figure 14.1 highlights how they work to influence prices.

The operational problems of stabilizing commodity prices through buffer stocks are similar to those of stabilizing exchange rates through official reserves (Chapters 2 and 3). In some ways buffer stocks of commodities present greater problems, involving physical space, storage facilities, maintenance personnel, and measures to prevent spoilage—resource costs that are minimal for currencies—as well as substantial transportation and brokerage costs—transactions costs that are minuscule for currencies. Nor are there opportunities for costless creation and lending of additional commodity stocks as there are for currency.[11]

[11] Examples are International Monetary Fund loans, creation of Special Drawing Rights, and Reciprocal Currency Arrangements discussed in Part I.

TABLE 14.2. *Some International Commodity Agreements for Price Stabilization among Producer and Consumer Countries*

	Cocoa	Coffee	Sugar	Tin
Implementation date of first commodity agreement after World War II	1973	1963	1953	1956
Implementation date of most recent commodity agreement	1976	1976	1978	1976
Number of (producer, consumer) country members	(18, 26)	(43, 24)	(26, 8) Provisionally	(7, 20)
United States participation	Yes, until 1976	Yes	Yes, except 1968–1977	Yes, since 1976
Method of implementation	Buffer stocks Export controls	Export controls with sanctions against violators	Buffer stocks Export controls	Buffer stocks Export controls with sanctions against violators

Success/failure record	No operations under 1976 agreement; prices have always exceeded target range; buffer stocks exhausted and no opportunity to rebuild; see also Table 14.1	Failure in early 1970s because of destruction of Brazilian crop; some success under 1976 agreement; see also Table 14.1	Unable to eliminate fluctuations that carried price from 1.4 cents per pound (January 1967) to 56.6 cents per pound (November 1974) to 7.1 cents per pound (October 1977)	Since 1956: failure to maintain prices above target floor about 5 percent of time; failure to maintain prices below target ceiling about 25 percent of time; revaluation of target prices on average once a year. No operations under 1976 agreement; prices have always exceeded target range; buffer stocks exhausted and no opportunity to rebuild

Sources: International Monetary Fund, *IMF Survey,* July 4, 1977, and November 21, 1977; Special Representative for Trade Negotiations, *Twenty-Second Annual Report of the President of the United States on the Trade Agreements Program—1977,* Washington, 1978; Louis M. Goreux, "The Use of Buffer Stocks," *Trade and Development* 15 (December 1978): 23–27; Jere R. Behrman, "International Commodity Agreements: An Evaluation of the UNCTAD Integrated Commodity Program," in *Policy Alternatives for a New International Economic Order: An Economic Analysis,* ed. William R. Cline (New York: Praeger, 1979).

Many commentators believe that the costs of creating and carrying really adequate buffer stocks of commodities would be astronomical and might well dominate any conceivable benefits from price stabilization. Pessimistic estimates suggest that official buffer stocks might have to maintain moderate activity on the same side of the market for as long as six years running. And in the case of commodities such as copper, the activity would have to be significant. Furthermore, developed-country critics point out that truly adequate buffer stocks of commodities might be much larger than can currently be estimated. They believe that a large number of private sellers and buyers in commodities markets already speculate in a profitable, price-stabilizing way, stocking up when commodity prices are low and living off accumulated stocks when prices are high. Similar purchases and sales by an official international buffer stock would reduce private profit from price stabilization, saddling the buffer-stock manager with the need to make transactions formerly made by private speculators, as well as those the stock planned to make, in order to bring prices fully within any target range.[12]

Developed countries also doubt the feasibility of export quotas and production controls. When prices are weak, member governments are tempted to pay only lip service to supranational orders to produce and export less, because they can gain competitively from cheating when other members don't, and they lose competitively from being honest when other members aren't.[13] Furthermore, the more tightly export and production controls bind, the more encouraged are nonmember producers to step up production and capture larger market shares, creating irresistible temptations for member countries to follow. (This problem has been notably destructive of the several international coffee agreements.) And when commodity prices come under severe or prolonged upward pressure, the removal of binding export and production quotas has only temporary dampening effects. Once they are fully removed, what holds down further price rises? Production and exports can be less easily encouraged than discouraged, especially over short periods. Consuming-nation members of commodity agreements feel cheated when price floors are successfully maintained but price ceilings are breached.

Finally, critics believe that the operational problems that under-

[12] Finally, developed-country critics believe that ill-designed governmental attempts to stabilize prices are the chief cause of the destabilizing speculation, shortages, and dislocation stressed on p. 465. Official stabilization efforts set up "one-way options" for speculators, who know which way the price would otherwise move and who speculate that collective speculation can overwhelm the official stabilization agency. (Each speculator has some chance for a large gain, and almost no chance for a significant loss, since the worst likely event is that prices will remain stable.) In this view, speculation, shortages, and gluts would all be less severe in unencumbered, unadministered commodity markets.

[13] This is another example of the famous *prisoner's dilemma* encountered in footnote 26 to Chapter 9.

mine official buffer stocks also doom arrangements whereby consumer-country governments make special purchases when prices are low and restrict purchases when prices are high. The problem is that consumer governments will inevitably act just like the buffer-stock facility, stockpiling unused purchases made solely in order to boost undesirably low prices, and drawing on stockpiles whenever forced to underpurchase in order to deflate undesirably high prices.

Developed countries also fear the political and administrative costs of any large-scale, integrated set of commodity agreements. They foresee acrimonious political confrontations among blocs of nations such as those that have afflicted the United Nations in recent years. They foresee a vast, costly international bureaucracy and fear wasteful conflict among it and national bureaucracies. The developed countries (particularly the United States) would prefer to lend their support, when desirable, on a case-by-case basis, temporarily, to selected price-stabilization agreements, without any universal or lasting commitment to them as a principle.

The South finds this attitude to be nationally self-indulgent, hypocritical, and insensitive. They observe that the United States in the past has been a major participant in price-stabilizing International Wheat Agreements, where its national production interests have been more directly served. They observe that the U.S. government itself maintains mammoth buffer stocks of almost 100 different materials, which it defends primarily on strategic grounds but has used occasionally to stabilize domestic U.S. prices (of copper, nickel, oil, and quinine). And they observe how almost all DCs rely on price-stabilizing buffer stocks in internal agricultural policy.

RAISING RELATIVE COMMODITY PRICES

Exasperation at Northern reluctance to participate cooperatively in international commodity agreements has helped attract some Southern producers toward "going it alone." So has emulation of OPEC, prompted by hope that concerted LDC action can bring about an improvement in their terms of trade. The most radical proposals are for collusion to create one-sided commodity cartels (no consumers) according to the OPEC model:

> Because these commodity cartels could successfully exert "commodity power" (a favorite slogan), they would not only stabilize commodity prices but raise them relative to manufactures prices. Concerted Southern market strength would increase bargaining power with the North and could reduce the dependence of any given Southern producer on traditional buyers for its goods. Cooperation with rich consuming countries would be unnecessary, even unwelcome: "solidarity rather than charity."

After the initial Southern euphoria, however, the scope for improv-

TABLE 14.3. One-Sided Producer Organizations

Name	Acronym
Organization of Petroleum Exporting Countries	OPEC
International Bauxite Association	IBA
Intergovernmental Council of Copper-Exporting Countries	CIPEC
Association of Iron-Ore Exporting Countries	—
Association of Natural Rubber Producing Countries	ANRPC
Café Mondial (Coffee)	—
Union of Banana Exporting Countries	UBEC
Asian Pepper Community	—

ing Southern welfare through one-sided producer associations began to appear quite limited. The only significant success seems to have been achieved by the International Bauxite Association (IBA), made up of major world producers of the ore of aluminum.[14] Other producer organizations, some of which are listed in Table 14.3, have become more activist, yet not more effective.

Political disparity weakens some organizations, such as the Association of Iron Ore Exporting Countries. Its members are diversely located and include several developed countries. By contrast, OPEC is organized around a geographically concentrated core of Middle Eastern countries, and almost all its members share a common Islamic tradition.

Economics is an even more important reason why one-sided producer cooperation has remained largely a vision. Few primary products face the dramatically growing world demand that petroleum did during the 1970s, which would have raised prices of oil relative to other products even in OPEC's absence. Few face the rapid rundown of proven global reserves that petroleum would have experienced within only decades at oil prices of the 1960s, which again would have caused oil prices to rise (eventually) even in the absence of OPEC. Unique long-term trends thus provided a firm foundation for OPEC's successful assertion of market power. Robust global demand reduced the casually perceived responsiveness of sales to price. And temporarily adequate, cheap oil reserves reduced the incentive to develop economically feasible energy substitutes. OPEC's success may also have been advanced by the multinational character of the oil companies, which found it not fully in their self-interest to resist OPEC advances.[15] Corporate spokespersons ended up serving in some measure

[14] Its members include Jamaica, Guyana, Suriname, Haiti, the Dominican Republic, Guinea, Sierra Leone, Yugoslavia, and Australia.
[15] This may also be true of the less dramatically successful IBA, which was able to deal with only a few large, multinational aluminum companies.

as a buffer between OPEC and consumer-nation governments. And corporate properties, including technology and long-term contracts, became potentially vulnerable hostages to make credible OPEC's price demands. Finally, no other primary products enjoy OPEC's luxury of a dominating set of producers (Saudi Arabia, Kuwait, and the United Arab Emirates) who are able and willing to alter production dramatically—with little injury to their tiny populations—in order to enforce the agreed level of prices.

INDEXING

Southern aspirations for both price stabilization and more favorable terms of trade are carried to their logical extreme in the proposal for *indexing* primary-product prices to manufactures prices. Indexing implies stabilizing primary commodity prices at a level that is "fair" relative to other prices:

> All products could potentially be covered, and indexed prices would be maintained by the cooperative actions of North and South alike. Fluctuations in price outside an internationally agreed range would justify compensating adjustments in other prices by injured countries. Inflation in the industrial world would not rob primary producers of their real purchasing power; recession in the industrial world would not impoverish primary producers through deterioration of their terms of trade.

Insurmountable problems face any thoroughgoing proposal for indexing. Not the least is the practical impossibility of agreeing on fair or just prices. Fair prices in a seller's eyes almost inevitably lie above fair prices in a buyer's eyes. Nor can every country simultaneously improve its terms of trade in moving toward a set of fair prices. Furthermore, a set of indexed "fair" prices would not guarantee equality of global production and global consumption. Administrative production and consumption controls and massive, universal buffer stocks would be required. Global production of overvalued commodities would have to be administratively restricted, consumption would have to be encouraged, and potentially wasteful stocks would have to be built up. Global production of undervalued commodities would have to be subsidized; consumption, constrained; and potentially valuable stocks, drawn down. The costs of the global planning required would be stupendous.[16]

Developed countries are violently opposed to indexing proposals, and even many less-developed countries see them as infeasible and

[16] Overvaluation and undervaluation refer to indexed prices that are respectively above and below those that would equate production and consumption. The problems that overvaluation and undervaluation create, multiplied many times over here, are familiar from Chapter 2's description of the foreign exchange market.

inflammatory. They remain, however, a revolutionary ideal and a rhetorical refrain in discussions of the new international economic order.

UNCTAD's INTEGRATED PROGRAM FOR COMMODITIES

The most carefully elaborated proposal for a new international economic order, which sprang from the fourth convening of UNCTAD, reflects the realities of feasible structural change. The Integrated Program for Commodities is most concretely a proposal for price stabilization[17] for a limited number of commodities. It makes no practical provision for long-term support of prices so as to alter any terms of trade. And it was formulated with almost purposeful suppression of any discussion of indexing.[18]

The centerpiece of the Integrated Program is the *Common Fund*, an international pool of financial resources on which individual commodity agreements could draw. Initially only agreements covering ten specific commodities, those most amenable to price stabilization, would have access to the Common Fund. Others might be granted access later.[19]

The Common Fund would be established by financial subscriptions and loans from Northern and Southern governments alike. The Fund in turn would encourage individual commodity agreements by making loans, which would be used primarily for the acquisition of buffer stocks as well as to cover certain costs of administrative control, modernization, and research. Since commodity prices do not vary together (see Table 14.1), there would be a complementarity gain, akin to the gain from portfolio diversification: the Common Fund would be smaller than the sum of ten unrelated funds financing the ten buffer stocks. Financial drains on the Common Fund from buffer-stock purchases of some commodities would be offset by repayment of loans from buffer-stock sales of others.

[17] Other important provisions of the Integrated Program for Commodities include (1) diversifying the production base of the South, especially by encouraging processing and fabrication of raw materials close to their source (instead of in the North), then promoting Southern involvement in their transportation and marketing; (2) assuring access to Northern markets for processed goods and for other Southern manufactures (in return for assuring the North of predictable access to crucial primary products in the South); and (3) improving the competitive position of natural products relative to synthetic substitutes. But no mechanisms were proposed to implement any of these provisions.
[18] Nevertheless, some commentators view the Integrated Program as a catalytic cutting edge in Southern demands for reshaping international exchange, with permanent terms-of-trade and indexing proposals to follow, after the pattern of North-South cooperation is firmly established with regard to price stabilization.
[19] The initial ten were coffee, cocoa, tea, sugar, cotton, rubber, jute, hard fibers, copper, and tin.

The South achieved one important political breakthrough in the Integrated Program for Commodities. Northern developed countries committed themselves in principle to supporting a linked group of international commodity agreements. In many cases the support was reluctant, and precise details of linkage remain to be worked out.[20] If the Integrated Program does end up successfully encouraging commodity agreements, it will more likely be because DCs support them directly, not because a Common Fund offers financial savings due to complementary price movements. As can be seen from Table 14.2, financial bankruptcy has never been the cause of the historically tarnished record of price stabilization through cooperative commodity agreements.

Northern Trade Preferences for Southern Products

Southern proposals for *preferential* treatment of their export products (*trade preferences*) entail a system of selective, unilateral trade liberalization by the North. Developed countries reduce or eliminate their import barriers on all products shipped from LDCs but maintain them on the same products shipped from other DCs. What LDCs gain from expanded business and more favorable terms of trade is obvious. Yet even DCs might possibly gain, despite terms-of-trade deterioration, through the familiar expansion of consumption possibilities that trade liberalization brings, especially in the long run after dislocation is eliminated and adjustment takes place.[21]

Northern trade preferences for Southern products require less radical changes in the current international economic order than integrated commodity policy. They even accord well with the liberal belief that diversifying outward toward world export markets is a more successful strategy for economic growth and development than turning inward toward domestic markets (through administratively directed import substitution). Yet preferential treatment of Southern products sets aside two of the most important principles of recent liberal trade relations: Most-Favored-Nation (MFN) treatment and reciprocity (Chapter 11). Liberalization is extended by DCs only to a group of favored LDCs, not to all countries equally. Nor need the favored LDCs reciprocate by reducing their own trade barriers. The

---

[20] For example, some developed countries would prefer that the Common Fund be abandoned for a "Common Clearing House," which would not have its own financial resources but would have powers to borrow from one individual commodity agreement and lend to another.

[21] See Chapter 10. That DC gains are not certain even in the long run, however, should be recalled from the discussion of trade diversion and the Theory of the Second Best in Chapter 11 and in Supplement 11C.

problem with both liberal principles, in the Southern view, is precisely that they *do* force equal treatment of trading partners (MFN) and equal concessions (reciprocity) in multilateral trade agreements. The South holds that such "equality" of treatment among rich and poor *un*equals can hardly be defended as equitable or just.

The South has long been dissatisfied with trade liberalization under the GATT. Ever since the 1950s Southern nations have pushed for *non*reciprocity, both in the name of international equity (not equality) and in order to preserve their trade policy to meet national goals. The North has been sympathetic to the point of extending all mutually agreed liberalization to LDCs, too, in accordance with MFN treatment, even though few reciprocal concessions were forthcoming. But little effort was made to incorporate the South in substantial phases of trade negotiations, since LDCs had little to offer reciprocally. Global import barriers have thus remained very high on products that loom large in Southern exports but small in Northern exports (textiles and apparel, footwear, tropical agricultural produce). On other goods global trade barriers have been dramatically reduced. Consequently, the benefits from recent GATT-sponsored trade liberalization have accrued in large measure to the already rich industrial world.

Since the early 1970s the North has reluctantly agreed to preferential treatment for Southern products. Carefully circumscribed *Generalized Systems of Preferences* (GSPs) have been adopted by almost all DCs, as described below. Yet this concession to Southern demands may turn out to be meaningless if historical GATT trade liberalization continues. The South opposes all such across-the-board, reciprocal, and even-handed reduction of global trade barriers because it reduces the preferential advantage that Southern export products currently enjoy in Northern markets. LDCs are willing to drop their opposition only if agreement can be reached that would compensate them, say by expanding further the still limited access of their manufactures and foodstuffs to developed markets. Any such agreement requires negotiation and may shift the determination of still more transactions from market to political forces.

GENERALIZED SYSTEMS OF PREFERENCES (GSPs)

Existing preferential arrangements of the more important developed countries are summarized in Table 14.4[22] Each is generalized in that it applies to almost all less-developed countries.[23] Each is

[22] Other countries that have implemented GSPs include Australia, Austria, New Zealand, and a number of Communist-bloc countries.

[23] They differ in this way from regionalized systems of preferences, such as those which the European Community maintains with a moderately large number of African, Caribbean, and Pacific countries under the *Lomé Convention*.

preferential in that tariffs are reduced or eliminated on LDC products by a proportion known as the "margin of preference." A 100 percent margin means elimination of any tariff on LDC products. A 50 percent margin means that tariffs on eligible LDC exports are only half those that confront other countries.

GSPs apply only to tariffs, not to increasingly important nontariff barriers to trade (Chapter 11). In fact, the degree to which any LDC can benefit from GSPs is carefully constrained by quotas. LDC exports beyond a maximum permissible amount are charged with the non-preferential tariff that more developed competitors face.[24]

Elimination of these quantitative barriers is a key LDC demand in their proposals for restructuring international trade. Increased product coverage is another. Most GSPs exclude entirely the very products in which the South is already most competitive and in which preferential treatment would be most valuable: textiles, clothing and other apparel, shoes and other footwear, and many foodstuffs. Furthermore, strict "rules of origin" make certain products ineligible if they were insufficiently fabricated, processed, or transformed in one particular LDC.

Northern governments have also been quick to alter the quantitative limitations and eligibility criteria and to invoke safeguard and escape-clause action (pp. 337–338) when competitive pressures from Southern exports build. Southern governments have had no international right to compensation to offset such unpredictable and sometimes capricious changes, because they have not reciprocally extended any concessions in return for GSPs. The Northern perspective is that liberalization without reciprocity is unilateral generosity. And unilateral generosity has its limits, especially when global stagnation aggravates the already formidable adjustment problems of their own weakest sectors (textiles and footwear and, increasingly, steel).

GSPs thus experience a highly tenuous and tentative existence.[25] Their uncertainty may undermine still further their potential benefits through its effect on investment by multinational and Southern producers. Long-term commitments of physical capital and innovation in products benefiting from GSPs could turn out to be unprofitable if preferences were unilaterally curtailed or withdrawn. Reluctance to invest because of the uncertain chance of loss cuts off with certainty the possibility for gain.

[24] Quantitative limits on exports at preferential rates thus make GSPs a system of concessional *tariff quotas,* described in Chapter 11.

[25] In fact, the GATT sanction of GSPs as an acceptable exception to MFN treatment (p. 366) was to expire in 1981 before being renewed in the Tokyo round. Furthermore, none of the concessional GSP rates has been "bound" under the GATT (see Supplement 11B). Thus the entire consultation/compensation/retaliation machinery of the GATT is irrelevant to GSPs, although it has contributed greatly to resolving conflicts under conventional GATT-sponsored liberalization.

TABLE 14.4. Selected Generalized Systems of Preferences (GSPs)

Country	Year of implementation	Margin of preference	Quantitative limitation on GSP access	Selected product exclusions
European Community	1971	100 percent for most manufactures; variable for most foodstuffs	Tariff quotas[a]	Textiles; apparel; some footwear; many foodstuffs
Japan	1971	100 percent on most; 50 percent on some	Tariff quotas[a]	Apparel; footwear; many foodstuffs
United States	1976	100 percent on most	Tariff quotas[a]	Textiles; footwear; watches; plywood; some chemicals; some steel products; many foodstuffs

Canada	1974	At least 33 percent	None	Textiles; apparel; footwear; some leather goods; color TVs; many foodstuffs
Finland, Norway, Sweden	1971, 1972	100 percent on most	None	Some textiles; some footwear; some handicrafts; some machinery; many foodstuffs
Switzerland	1972	100 percent on most; 30 percent on some	None, but other restrictions present	Some chemicals; some machinery; automobiles; many foodstuffs

ᵃ See footnote 24.

Sources: International Monetary Fund, *IMF Survey*, June 23, 1975, pp. 186–189; Zubair Iqbal, "The Generalized System of Preferences Examined," *Trade and Development* 12 (September 1975): 34–39; Robert E. Baldwin and Tracy Murray, "MFN Tariff Reductions and LDC Benefits Under the GSP," *Economic Journal* 87 (March 1977): 30–46; Mordechai E. Kreinin and J. Michael Finger, "A Critical Survey of the New International Economic Order," *Journal of World Trade Law*, November/December 1976.

Some Northern economists feel that Southern insistence on preferential treatment victimizes LDCs themselves. They believe that the South has never given enough credence to the benefits from traditional reciprocal trade liberalization.

It is not, they argue, that LDCs have tried reciprocity and found it wanting; it is that they have never tried it at all. Their unwillingness sacrifices the gains from stable, contractual, nonexclusive, and wide-ranging traditional trade liberalization for the sake of uncertain gains from volatile, selective, and tightly circumscribed GSPs. In addition, failure to adhere to the principle of reciprocity reduces trade and its benefits among LDCs themselves.

Defenders of preferential treatment respond that the best of all worlds for the South would feature stable, contractual, nonexclusive, and wide-ranging GSPs.

The North, they assert, should legally bind itself to permanent preferential margins and set up consultation and compensation mechanisms for any withdrawal of GSP benefits. Exclusion of selected products and countries should be abandoned, as should quantitative limits on exports under GSPs. The North should expand preferences to cover nontariff trade barriers as well as tariffs. They should implement preferential safeguard and escape-clause action, withdrawing trade concessions because of domestic injury from Northern producers only, not from Southern producers. They should make trade adjustment assistance more predictable and generous to offset any domestic injury caused by expanded Southern exports.

And why should the North do all this without any reciprocal concessions from the South? The Southern answer appeals to conscience. The imperatives from their standpoint are moral, not economic. Even futile pressure for preferential trade liberalization confronts the North continuously with the moral problem of simultaneous global poverty and prosperity.[26] In the Southern view, to abandon preferences and espouse reciprocity might be economically advantageous but would be

---

[26] The moral dilemma confronts LDCs among themselves as well. Present GSPs are most preferential toward exports of sophisticated manufactures from LDCs and least preferential toward exports of textiles, footwear, and agricultural products. The LDCs that gain the most from GSPs are therefore the most developed: Argentina, Brazil, Mexico, Venezuela, Korea, Singapore, Taiwan, and many Mediterranean countries. In brief, current GSPs probably alter the income distribution among LDCs *re*gressively, toward the "richer poor." The solution within a preferential context is, of course, to have a layered or graded set of preferences, with the widest preference margins available to the poorest LDCs and progressively narrower preference margins available to more prosperous LDCs.

morally reprehensible. It would be to accept the bribe that the rich offer to the poor to maintain the status quo.

Reordering International Technology Transfer

The South believes it realizes only small benefits from existing international technology transfer. Yet its program for restructuring it is still in a formative stage.[27] Southern skepticism about the benefits from technology transfer stems from its inherent link to multinational corporations. Much trade in technology occurs among closely related multinational corporate affiliates at negotiated (not "arm's-length") prices. The corporate superstructure also provides efficient channels for transferring the scientists, engineers, and managers in whom much technology is embodied. When a multinational affiliate in an LDC imports technology from its parent, therefore, residents of the LDC do not necessarily acquire the technology or directly realize its benefits. Ownership rights remain with, and profit on the transaction accrues directly to, the corporation. LDC residents benefit indirectly from their own enhanced productivity in cooperation with the imported technology.

LDC benefits from arm's-length imports of both technology and technology-intensive goods are also indirect. In these cases, LDC buyers usually find themselves arrayed against large, oligopolistic sellers anyway (whose market power may be supported by their technological superiority). The bargaining outcome is predictable. Sellers with market power price their technology, technical services, and products so as to reap most of the gains, leaving only enough to induce buyers without market power to make the purchase in preference to doing without altogether.

Southern countries find this "excessive pricing" inequitable. They also find that technology transfer is frequently accompanied by requirements that impose unwanted economic costs on them and that foster dependence. Corporate sellers of patent rights, machinery, or management services often insist on *tying* the sale to purchases of other products that are less desirable from an LDC perspective. They frequently impose territorial restrictions on subsequent exports of products embodying the transferred technology (and on resale of the technology itself) so as not to undermine their market power in third countries. For the same reason, they may demand ownership rights to any improvements or innovations made in the LDC on the particular product or process originally transferred.[28]

---

[27] The program will be sharpened considerably, however, as a result of the 1979 United Nations Conference on Science and Technology for Development.

[28] Provisions requiring that the ownership of new technology based on the old revert to the multinational parent company are known as "grant-back provisions."

One solution in principle to the South's perceived problems of technological inequity and dependence is to imitate. The Southern countries might develop their own technological base and become equal partners in the development and (oligopolistic) marketing of productive innovations. But this is a distant dream. Current technological progress almost always builds on past technological progress (such as educational advancement and learning-by-doing). And in the early 1970s less than 1 percent of all active patents worldwide were owned by nationals of LDCs.[29] Eliminating technological inferiority of this magnitude by imitation is at best a very long process, spanning several generations. Nor would it be welcomed by Northern owners and producers of current innovations, since it would compete away some of their oligopolistic advantage. Thus multinational corporations can be expected to resist the development of an indigenous technological base in the South, unless multinationals are themselves the agents of its development, as at present.[30]

LDC disenchantment with modes of transferring existing technology internationally has some economic support in terms of immediate global economic welfare. If existing productive knowledge were available to all, unrestricted by patents or by corporate instincts for self-preservation, global economic output would probably be larger in the short run. And it would almost certainly be distributed more evenly among nations. Freer dissemination of existing technology would thus alleviate both absolute global poverty and relative global poverty, as international technology gaps shrank to a "natural" level. These conclusions follow because existing technology is a perfect example of a *public good*. Use of it by one country or corporation for productive purposes does not reduce the amount of it available for productive use by other countries and corporations.

But that is not the whole story. The universal spread of technology at a price equal to the resource cost of conveying it would shrink drastically the returns that the innovating developer of that technology could realize, transforming them in many cases into economic losses. Competitive pressure would leave the developer no revenues to

<hr />

[29] United Nations Conference on Trade and Development, *Major Issues Arising From the Transfer of Technology to Developing Countries*, TD/B/AC, 11/10/Rev. 2 (New York: United Nations, 1975).

[30] Host-country regulation of multinational affiliates reflects an uneasy compromise of views. Many LDCs require some host-country ownership of multinational affiliates in order to profit directly from superior technology and management. Other common preconditions are local research and development and joint ventures with host-country firms. But it is unclear whether such regulations really lead to increased Southern gains from technology transfer. Many multinationals refuse to invest at all under these restrictions, and the potential indirect contributions of their technology are lost to LDCs. Coca-Cola, for example, left India rather than turn over the secret formula for its syrup to the Indian government in return for 40 percent ownership in a nationalized Indian soft-drink company (*Wall Street Journal*, August 10, 1977).

cover the large fixed costs of technological progress: false starts, experimental work to perfect design, permanent (and only infrequently "productive") research and development staffs. In fact, if there were no natural, oligopolistic, or governmental barriers to the free use of any innovation, economists predict quite confidently that little innovation would ever take place. Few persons or organizations ever choose voluntarily to lose. Technology would be static. Thus there is an inevitable trade-off in the long run between freer distribution of present technology and the amount of future technology.

Seen in this light, the current order for developing and disseminating technology is not so sinister. Governmentally sanctioned patent protection for innovating firms and individuals not only supports their oligopolistic advantage but guarantees their ongoing production of innovation. Large multinational (and domestic) corporations are a price the world may choose to pay to assure ongoing growth in global standards of living. And the reasons for Northern reluctance to endorse a new international economic order in technology transfer become apparent. They fear declines in the competitive positions of their multinationals not only because oligopolistic market power is nationally lucrative but also because its absence could lead to global disaster through technological stagnation.

The South accepts the need to protect the profitability of technological innovation, but it rejects the North's implied prescription that protection can be best arranged by the granting of temporary, exclusive patent rights to privately owned and controlled corporations. The South argues that:

> These corporations naturally, but unfortunately, capitalize their recurrent innovations into permanent oligopolistic profits that far exceed the minimum necessary to bring forth the innovations in the first place. Furthermore, profit-seeking firms naturally bias their innovations toward those that can be most easily patented or that are least vulnerable to competitive copy by reason of complexity or the high fixed costs of duplication. Some things therefore remain underproduced: simple (and easily stolen) techniques of mechanization; innovations most appropriate for small-scale enterprise (because they usually have small fixed costs of duplication); labor-intensive innovations (because acquaintance with the process will become widespread); and straightforward (but not easily patentable) "good ideas." These underproduced innovations are exactly the ones that would be most suitable to LDCs with small economic size but large populations. Northern technology may thus often be "inappropriate" for LDCs, and supplies of "appropriate" technology may not exist. Returns to private producers of appropriate technology cannot be adequately protected by the system of patents and oligopolistic advantage.

Better than the existing system, in the Southern view, would be greater governmental participation in research, development,[31] and dissemination of innovation. Supporters observe the important role that governments (including the U.S. government) already play in supporting advanced education and defense-oriented research, and they point to the prominent technological cooperation among DC governments in postwar reconstruction, and in current oil exploration, aircraft manufacture, and East-West détente. The South proposes a simple widening of the circle to include governments of have-not nations in technological planning, and increased regulation of international technology transfer. In the South's view, governments should strictly circumscribe "excessive pricing," tied package deals for technology, and territorial restrictions. Governments should also shorten the life of patents and actively encourage infant technology industries in Southern countries, insuring them adequate protection while preserving a "fair" (but nonoligopolistic) return for existing Northern innovators and multinational corporations.

The North is skeptical that the international politicization of technology creation and trade would have global economic benefits, and it is fairly sure that any such benefits would come at its own expense. Once again, the specter of a vast, inefficient, acrimonious, international bureaucracy looms forebodingly in Northern calculations. Thus Northern counterproposals have tended to be remedial rather than revolutionary: international institutes of research on appropriate technology; increased educational opportunities for Southern nationals in Northern institutions; and voluntary codes of conduct for multinational corporations and governments to circumscribe restrictive practices in international technology transfer.

Other Aspects of a New International Economic Order

The vision of a new international economic order includes a number of other possible developments.

DEESCALATED NORTHERN TARIFF STRUCTURES

The South finds inequity in the structure as well as in the level of protection in the North. Northern *tariff escalation* has discouraged

---

[31] The South is hopeful that governments will find it in their interest to develop "appropriate" technology even though oligopolistic private producers do not. The grounds for such optimism are shaky. Oligopolistic government enterprises may be just as dissuaded as oligopolistic private enterprises from producing easily pirated, hard-to-patent innovations. Huge losses to the national Treasury could be realized by paying the costs of research and development and then finding the returns competed away by imitative government and private enterprises in other countries!

processing of raw materials and fabrication of manufactures in the South.

Escalation of the tariff structure is a situation in which tariff rates are highest on imports of finished products, lower on imports of semi-finished products, and lowest of all on imports of raw materials and primary inputs into production activity. Almost every country in the world has an escalated tariff structure. One reason is political. There is usually an effective, organized lobby against import barriers to protect domestic producers of raw materials and intermediate products such as steel: user industries which are the "consumers" of such products and which are well aware that their costs will rise and profitability fall as a result of import barriers against their inputs. Lobbies against import barriers on final products, if they exist at all, are usually much less organized and effective; they tend to be made up of diverse and widely scattered consumers.

A second reason for escalated tariff structures is historical. In the early development of most Northern countries almost all goods were imported in their finished state. As development progressed, competitive domestic production began at the highest level of fabrication (such as final assembly) and was sheltered by import barriers justified on infant-industry grounds (Chapter 9). As development progressed, import barriers were usually invoked to protect more and more elemental stages in the production process (such as components manufacture and processing of raw materials). These import barriers, however, raised costs and lowered profitability for the established domestic assemblers of the final good, reducing their competitiveness and protecting them less effectively against imports of finished goods. When established assemblers used their reduced competitiveness as an argument to justify even higher tariffs, in order to restore their former level of protection, the tariff structure became escalated.[32]

[32] Economists sometimes calculate industry-by-industry measures of *effective protection* that take account of the higher costs that tariffs on imported inputs impose. The measures are *effective tariff rates* and can be calculated for a single industry as (1) the rise in output price per unit that producers can enjoy from tariffs on directly comparable imported products, minus (2) the rise in input costs per unit of output that producers face because of tariffs on imported inputs—the difference being expressed as a proportion of the producers' "value added" (revenue less cost of intermediate inputs) per unit of output. The measure illustrates how the effectiveness of protection for a given industry is undermined by higher tariffs on its imported inputs. In fact, if tariffs on imported inputs were high enough, producers might not be protected at all (negative effective protection). They would actually be *less* competitive relative to comparable imports than they would have been under completely free trade, with no tariffs at all on any product. The concept of effective protection has many useful applications. Among others, it illustrates how trade liberalization does not always reduce protection overall. For example, reducing barriers to steel imports reduces protection against imports for steel producers but *increases* protection against imports for automakers, machinery manufacturers, and all other industrial users of steel. It is entirely possible that the increased protection to the latter outweighs the reduced protection to the former.

Tariff escalation in DCs thus encourages LDCs to specialize production and exports on raw materials and goods at an elementary stage of processing.[33] Some economists believe that this cuts off LDC opportunities for diversified and sophisticated production, and that the results are comparatively unstable national income, export earnings, and terms of trade, comparatively smaller access to productivity-enhancing economies of scale and technological advance, less rapid growth overall, and reduced opportunity to differentiate national products so as to realize monopolistic market power in export markets.

The North resists Southern demands for deescalation of tariffs, seeing no prospect of mutual benefits. What the South might gain through altering its production mix more desirably, the North would lose through a corresponding but opposite production shift.

REGIONAL COOPERATION AMONG LESS-DEVELOPED COUNTRIES

Southern countries see increased economic integration among themselves as one of the most desirable ways to reshape global economic interchange. Included in the scope of such *South-South* cooperation are preferential liberalization of trade among LDCs themselves, joint planning of diversification to avoid overconcentration of the industrial base in the most-developed LDCs, and a common front with harmonized policies toward multinational corporations, resource exploitation, and technology transfer. All such policies replace dependence on the rich North with interdependence among "Southern brothers"; dependence is superseded by "collective self-reliance."

But South-South cooperation ranks low among feasible ways to reshape global economic exchange. Efforts in this direction in Latin America and the Middle East have been halting at best. Economic diversity among less-developed countries belies the commonality of their interests. Argentina, Brazil, Mexico, Venezuela, Nigeria, Iran, Korea, and Taiwan are (or are becoming) closer in many ways to the developed North than to the rest of the South. Geographical and ethnic diversity only aggravates the disparities. Historical insistence on nonreciprocity and emphasis on import substitution policies have left many LDCs indrawn and highly protected against each other's products. Tariffs, export taxes, and various taxes on foreign investors cannot easily be altered because in some countries they generate the bulk of government revenue and in others they are used flexibly and importantly to affect exchange rates and the balance of payments. Finally, global transportation and communications networks per-

---

[33] Tariff escalation in LDCs, of course, encourages DC exporters to follow suit. But the impact on the structure of production in DCs is small compared to that of DC tariff escalation on LDC production.

petuate the economic isolation of LDCs from each other and their dependence on DCs (Schema 12.1). While increased economic exchange among LDCs would motivate improved transportation and communication, high costs and primitive conditions are simultaneously formidable obstacles to such exchange.

GLOBAL PLANNING FOR COMMON RESOURCES

Individual and national property rights have not yet been extended to vast areas of ocean and airspace, nor for that matter to outer space. Yet many of these regions have alluring economic potential: nitrogen extraction from the air; mining of the deep seabeds for oil, manganese, and other valuable minerals; distillation of salt and other valuable substances from seawater itself; deep-sea farming of fish and edible plant life.

Southern activists have serious objections to allowing these frontiers to be developed according to liberal market incentives. Almost all potential economic activity on the remaining frontiers is technology intensive. In these activists' view, the North's technological monopoly would practically guarantee it most of the benefits from exploiting presently "common" resources under market-oriented development.

On this issue the North is somewhat more accommodating than on others. Vested interests in the private exploitation of ocean, air, and space resources have not yet been firmly established, although they are growing. Perceptions that U.S. producers would for some time be alone in their ability to mine the deep seabeds encouraged the United States to adopt a comparatively liberal market-oriented approach to common-resource proposals at the United Nations' Law of the Sea Conferences in the 1970s. But other developed countries without deep-sea mining technology were inclined more favorably toward exploitation by an international authority, say one chartered by the United Nations, with global distribution of the proceeds to all countries. Southern as well as Northern solidarity on this issue is broken by differences in perspectives between landlocked and coastal countries and between traditional minerals exporters and minerals importers.

FOOD AND HUNGER

Southern nations have particular aversions to a market-oriented international economic order for foodstuffs. Many of them depend on imports for basic staples such as grains and rice. When the normal flux of the market causes prices of these imports to rise, the result is not only inconvenience and deprivation (as occurs in *all* countries whenever the terms of trade deteriorate) but also malnutrition, starvation, and death. Global food shortages of the early 1970s have reinforced the moral judgment that market forces can acceptably preclude purchase of an appliance because people cannot afford it, but should not be allowed to starve people. The North usually subscribes to such moral values, which have motivated much humanitarian provision of food, medical supplies, and disaster-relief services.

In Southern eyes, however, charity demeans, and it fosters increased dependence on the North by reducing LDC agricultural incentives. Nor is charity always selfless. American food aid under the Food for Peace program has sometimes helped to reduce undesirably large storage costs of U.S. government stockpiles, and sometimes it has seemed politically motivated, as during the Vietnam War, when it was directed increasingly toward Southeast Asia.

For these reasons, LDCs generally favor a reordering of global trade in agricultural products. One aspect of the new order would be the use of governmentally supervised global reserves of grains and other storable staples on humanitarian rather than economic grounds.[34] A second would be internationally financed programs to encourage agricultural production in LDCs themselves.[35] Steps to reduce LDC dependence on food imports include the creation of the International Fund for Agricultural Development (IFAD), jointly financed by Northern and OPEC countries. Proposals to increase Southern exports of agricultural products usually include a deescalation of the Northern tariffs that discourage Southern production of processed foodstuffs.

Summary and Outlook

Southern militance and OPEC power make it likely that international economic relations will move toward the new order described in this chapter. Preferential treatment for Southern goods is now a firmly entrenched principle, but its practice is tightly circumscribed. There is an increasing international commitment to price-stabilization mechanisms for primary products, but good intentions will not necessarily make their implementation any more successful in the future than it was in the past. International technology transfer seems likely to become increasingly politicized—as the price multinational corporations must pay to secure entry to host countries or to avoid nationalization/expropriation.

But movement toward more radical aspects of the new international economic order is not at all certain. The inertia of the status quo

[34] It is important to ask, however, whether and why governments will be more likely to act on humanitarian principles, and less on motives of economic greed, than individuals. As we have seen frequently in this book, governments compete with each other and often respond to economic incentives as much as individuals do. The politicization of world agricultural trade might well *worsen* the incidence of global hunger and malnutrition.

[35] This goal is not necessarily consistent with that of increasing LDC production of sophisticated manufactures.

is a powerful force undermining indexing, South-South cooperation, and global planning for common resources. The present international distribution of income, wealth, and property rights is supported by two of the most powerful of motivating forces: materialism and nationalism. By comparison with the South, the North still has potentially overwhelming economic, political, and military power. Southern unity and commitment to the new international economic order may be shattered if LDCs themselves end up bearing a large part of its possibly significant global economic costs. The more enduring is the global stagnation of the 1970s, or the more pronounced it becomes, the more intransigent the North will be toward Southern demands. The developed communist world has yet to play any important role in the North-South conflict.

Even in any highly politicized new international economic order, most of Part II of this book will remain relevant. Nations will continue to trade goods and resources because it is nationally beneficial, and they will attempt to manage trade when possible to realize national advantage. The philosophical conflict between market organization of international exchange and government organization will persist. And the fundamental determinants of international exchange will remain intact, although their relative importance may change.

But the institutional structure of international trade would be altered radically by a new order. GATT and privately owned multinationals could disappear. Important new international bureaucracies would spring up. Value systems would be altered, too. Distributive issues of equity, fairness, and compensation would weigh even more heavily in national trade policy than they do now. And single-minded pursuit of maximal national consumption as a goal for trade policy would become less compelling. Even then, however, maximum *global* consumption as brought about by "free" trade would remain interesting as the benchmark against which to measure the global economic cost of the new international economic order as well as the distribution of that cost.

Key Terms

North and South
United Nations Conference on
   Trade and Development
   (UNCTAD)
Conference(s) on International
   Economic Cooperation (CIEC)
international commodity
   agreements
buffer stocks

Integrated Program for Commodities, Common Fund
margin of preference
public good
tariff escalation and de-escalation
effective protection, effective tariff rates

Key Concepts and Review

Dependence and market power.

Markets versus governments as administrators of economic activity.

The Organization of Petroleum Exporting Countries (OPEC) as a model.

The pros and cons of commodity-price stabilization.

Economic obstacles to the success of cartels and indexing.

Preferential versus reciprocal trade liberalization, Generalized Systems of (trade) Preferences (GSPs).

The trade-off between disseminating existing technology at cost and creating new technology.

Cooperation, common resources, and basic human needs.

Supplement 14A
Pros and Cons of Commodity-Price Stabilization

Supporters of a new international economic order, claiming that less-developed countries bear distinct social costs from the large price swings of the primary products they export, advocate commodity-price stabilization. The arguments they use are very much like those advanced in defense of exchange-rate stabilization in Chapter 3.

1. Above-average volatility of primary-product prices is alleged to cause economically costly shifts of resources back and forth among sectors of the economy. Since costs of production are thought to be less volatile than the commodity prices themselves, higher primary-product prices will attract resources from other sectors through higher profits. Lower commodity prices will then encourage their return. Both shifts of resources impose temporarily reduced productivity and increased resource costs for retooling, retraining, refurbishing, and relocating the resources that move (see Chapter 10). Such adjustment costs (and dislocation costs, too, in the case of price declines) might be avoided in principle by commodity-price stabilization.

The issue is controversial. If the interim period between high and low primary-product prices is long, the back-and-forth shift of resources may be warranted despite the adjustment and dislocation costs. To have stabilized prices so that resources did not move and were not allocated to their most productive use would have lost more for the nation than was saved by avoiding adjustment and dislocation. Furthermore, price-stabilization machinery itself is not costless. Stabilization agencies require resources: personnel, communications equipment, and physical facilities. The output sacrificed by diverting resources to stabilization activities may well exceed what must be sacrificed to facilitate back-and-forth shifts of resources between sectors.

2. Excessive price volatility is alleged to add an extra dimension of uncertainty to the normal uncertainties that face every business. On average, over a long series of ups and downs, this extra uncertainty may divert resources from the risky activities in which they would be most productive (for example, from production of cash crops for the market into production of subsistence crops for the home). And it may discourage technological progress and accumulation of productive capital in the economy as a whole, especially in LDCs that are highly specialized in the production of only one or a few primary products. Smaller endowments of technology and productive capital imply lower national standards of living (Chapter 13).

On the other hand, there is only very weak statistical evidence that price instability of export products has reduced the economic growth and welfare of primary producers. Some economists have even argued that extra business uncertainty may *increase* national capital accumulation. People and institutions may save more for precautionary reasons, and the increased propensity to save might sufficiently reduce the cost of accumulating capital to offset the reduced propensity to invest due to uncertainty.

3. Commodity-price bubbles are alleged to be generally inflationary. This is most plausible in those LDCs that depend heavily on primary production, and when the cause is a boom in foreign demand. Expanded export demand can be accompanied by a sense of euphoria and windfall gain. The monetary authorities are confronted with a more positive balance-of-payments position, which in the absence of sterilization can pump up the money stock (Chapter 5). Political pressures may keep them from tightening their monetary stance in order to rein in other prices enough to compensate for higher export prices, and inflation will spread.

Such monetary accommodation can even accompany upward price pressures that are due to supply shortfalls. Higher prices in the primary-products sector may induce imitative attempts to increase prices in other sectors out of jealousy or demands for equity (see p. 95). Supply shortfalls of foodstuffs especially generate pressure for higher nominal wages, both informally and contractually through cost-of-living clauses. Supply shortfalls may also bring about transitory unemployment of workers in the primary-product industry. Any of these possibilities may confront the monetary authorities with irresistible expansionary pressures.

On the other hand, periodic governmental attempts to stabilize commodity prices have usually failed when prices pressed too persistently against target ceilings rather than against target floors (see Table 14.2). Historical efforts to stabilize primary product prices may in fact have created more inflation than if prices had been left to the vicissitudes of the market: efforts to avoid low prices usually succeeded; efforts to avoid high prices often failed. When coupled with accommodating monetary policy, the net result of stabilization itself may have been higher, not lower, prices overall.

4. When commodity-price bubbles burst, the result can be substantial dislocation and hardship. This outcome, again, is most plausible for countries that depend heavily on primary production, and when the "bust" is due to declining business prosperity in customer countries. Demand for raw materials and semiprocessed inputs declines even faster (see footnote 7 in the text). Because of the inevitable downward rigidity in wages, rents, interest, and other contractual costs, the result is additional unemployment and excess capacity (Chapter 10).

Even when declining primary-product prices are due to increases in supplies brought about by favorable weather, increased investment, or technological advance, the result may be hardship and dislocation. If world demand facing the country's exporters is price inelastic (see Chapter 4), national export earnings will actually be lowered by increased export supplies, and unemployment and excess capacity may result (because of smaller aggregate income). The country's deteriorated terms of trade will only aggravate further the decline in real national output and consumption possibilities.[1]

5. Declines in the prices of primary products can cause acute balance-of-payments-deficit problems for countries that specialize in their export. Again this is especially plausible when prices fall because of declining foreign demand, but it will also occur when prices fall because of increased domestic supplies in the face of price-inelastic foreign demand. *Compensatory financing* for export shortfalls, such as that administered by the International Monetary Fund (see p. 73), alleviates this symptom of price volatility. But LDCs hold out the hope that commodity-price stabilization would eliminate the disease itself, especially if carried out through flexibly administered supply and export quotas.[2]

[1] Economists refer to this set of events as *immiserizing growth:* economic growth that (paradoxically) makes nations miserable by impoverishing them.

[2] Administratively restricting export supply could offset the price effects of a favorable harvest or technological advance and perhaps allow resources saved to be put to use elsewhere. This solution will be superior from a Southern perspective to compensatory financing of the export shortfall. Compensatory financing requires a future sacrifice of resources to produce the export surplus necessary to repay the loan. And export restriction will usually be better than supporting prices through purchases of the product by some governmentally administered buffer stock, which itself uses resources in its operation.

Further Reading

Chapter 1

Aliber, Robert Z. *The International Money Game.* New York: Basic Books, 1979.

Einzig, Paul. *A Textbook on Foreign Exchange.* New York: St. Martin's Press, 1969.

Kubarych, Roger M. *Foreign Exchange Markets in the United States.* New York: Federal Reserve Bank of New York, 1978.

Chapter 2

Grubel, Herbert G. *The International Monetary System.* Baltimore: Penguin, 1969. Especially Chapter 2.

International Monetary Fund. *Annual Report*, most recent issue.

International Monetary Fund. "The Fund Under the Second Amendment." *IMF Survey*, Supplement to the September 18, 1978, issue.

Solomon, Robert. *The International Monetary System, 1945–1976: An Insider's View.* New York: Harper and Row, 1977.

Chapter 3

Artus, Jacques R., and Crockett, Andrew E. "Floating Exchange Rates and the Need for Surveillance." *Essays in International Finance* No. 127, May 1978. Princeton University, Department of Economics, International Finance Section.

Cohen, Benjamin J. "International Reserves and Liquidity." In *International Trade and Finance: Frontiers for Research*, ed. Peter B. Kenen. New York: Cambridge University Press, 1975.

Friedman, Milton, and Roosa, Robert V. *The Balance of Payments: Free Versus Fixed Exchange Rates.* Washington, D.C.: American Enterprise Institute for Public Policy Research, 1967.

Whitman, Marina v. N. "The Current and Future Role of the Dollar: How Much Symmetry?" (and accompanying discussion by Richard N. Cooper, Robert Solomon, and others). *Brookings Papers on Economic Activity* 3 (1974), pp. 539–591.

Chapter 4

Bryant, Ralph C. *Money and Monetary Policy in an Open Economy.* Washington, D.C.: Brookings Institution, 1980.

Fried, Edward R., and Schultze, Charles L., eds. *Higher Oil Prices and the World Economy: The Adjustment Problem*. Washington, D.C.: Brookings Institution, 1975.

International Monetary Fund. Most recent *Annual Report on Exchange Restrictions*.

Staley, Charles E. *International Economics: Analysis and Issues*. Englewood Cliffs, N.J.: Prentice-Hall, 1970. Chapters 19–20.

Chapter 5

Dornbusch, Rudiger, and Krugman, Paul. "Flexible Exchange Rates in the Short Run" (and accompanying discussion by Richard N. Cooper, Marina v. N. Whitman, and others). *Brookings Papers on Economic Activity* 3 (1976), pp. 537–584.

Herring, Richard J., and Marston, Richard C. *National Monetary Policies and International Financial Markets*. Contributions to Economic Analysis No. 104. Amsterdam: North Holland, 1977.

Wanniski, Jude. "The Mundell-Laffer Hypothesis—A New View of the World Economy." *Public Interest* 39 (Spring 1975).

Chapter 6

Ando, Albert; Herring, Richard; and Marston, Richard. *International Aspects of Stabilization Policies*. Boston: Federal Reserve Bank of Boston, June 1974.

Meiselman, David I., and Laffer, Arthur B., eds. *The Phenomenon of Worldwide Inflation*. Washington, D.C.: American Enterprise Institute for Public Policy Research, 1975.

Whitman, Marina v. N. "International Interdependence and the U.S. Economy." In *Contemporary Economic Problems 1976*, ed. William Fellner. Washington, D.C.: American Enterprise Institute for Public Policy Research, 1977.

Chapter 7

Europe (formerly *European Community*) 209 (September/October 1978), and 211 (January/February 1979). Collected articles on the European Monetary System.

Lissakers, Karin. *International Debt, the Banks, and U.S. Foreign Policy*. A Staff Report prepared for the use of the Subcommittee on Foreign Economic Policy of the Committee on Foreign Relations of the United States Senate. Washington, D.C.: U.S. Government Printing Office, 1977.

Little, Jane Sneddon. *Euro-Dollars: The Money Market Gypsies*. New York: Harper and Row, 1975.

Williamson, John. *The Failure of World Monetary Reform, 1971–1974*. New York: New York University Press, 1977.

Chapter 8

Kindleberger, Charles P. *Foreign Trade and the National Economy*. New Haven: Yale University Press, 1962.

Vernon, Raymond, ed. *The Oil Crisis*. New York: Norton, 1976.

Yeager, Leland B., and Tuerck, David G. *Foreign Trade and U.S. Policy*. New York: Praeger, 1976. Chapters 1–5.

Chapter 9

Blackhurst, Richard; Marian, Nicolas; and Tumlir, Jan. *Trade*

Liberalization, Protection, and Interdependence. New York: Unipub, 1978.

Corden, W. M. *The Theory of Protection.* Oxford, Eng.: Clarendon Press, 1971.

Ingram, James C. *International Economic Problems.* New York: John Wiley, 1978. Chapters 2, 3, and 6.

Yeager, Leland B., and Tuerck, David G. *Foreign Trade and U.S. Policy.* New York: Praeger, 1976. Chapters 6–15.

Chapter 10

Baldwin, Robert E. "The Political Economy of Postwar U.S. Trade Policy." *The Bulletin,* 1976 (4). New York University, Graduate School of Business Administration, Center for the Study of Financial Institutions.

Frank, Charles R., Jr., with the assistance of Stephanie Levinson. *Foreign Trade and Domestic Aid.* Washington, D.C.: Brookings Institution, 1977.

Krauss, Melvyn B. *The New Protectionism: The Welfare State and International Trade.* New York: New York University Press, 1978.

Mayer, Wolfgang. "Short-Run and Long-Run Equilibrium for a Small Open Economy." *Journal of Political Economy* 82 (September/October 1974), pp. 955–967.

Chapter 11

Baldwin, Robert E. *Nontariff Distortions of International Trade.* Washington, D.C.: Brookings Institution, 1970.

Dam, Kenneth W. *The GATT: Law and International Organization.* Chicago: University of Chicago Press, 1970.

European Community 203 (September/October 1977). Collected articles on expansion of the European Community.

Swann, Dennis. *The Economics of the Common Market.* Baltimore: Penguin, 1972.

Chapter 12

Findlay, Ronald. *Trade and Specialization.* Baltimore: Penguin, 1970.

Hufbauer, G. C. "The Impact of National Characteristics and Technology on the Commodity Composition of Trade in Manufactured Goods." In *The Technology Factor in International Trade,* ed. Raymond Vernon. New York: Columbia University Press, 1970.

Ohlin, Bertil. *Interregional and International Trade.* Cambridge, Mass.: Harvard University Press, 1967.

Chapter 13

Bergsten, C. Fred; Horst, Thomas; and Moran, Theodore H. *American Multinationals and American Interests.* Washington, D.C.: Brookings Institution, 1978.

Bhagwati, Jagdish N., and Parrington, Michael, eds. *Taxing the Brain Drain—A Proposal.* Amsterdam: North Holland, 1976.

Ecevit, Zafer, and Zachariah, Kunniparampil C. "International Labor Migration." *Finance and Development* 15 (December 1978), pp. 32–37.

Vernon, Raymond. *Storm over the Multinationals: The Real Issues.* Cambridge, Mass.: Harvard University Press, 1977.

Chapter 14

Behrman, Jere R. *Development, the International Economic Order,* and *Commodity Agreements.* Reading, Mass.: Addison-Wesley, 1979.

Bhagwati, Jagdish N., ed. *The New International Economic Order: The North-South Debate.* Cambridge, Mass.: M.I.T. Press, 1977.

Kreinin, Mordechai E., and Finger, J.M. "A Critical Survey of the New International Economic Order."

Journal of World Trade Law, November/December 1976. Reprinted in Bela Balassa, ed., *Changing Patterns in Foreign Trade and Payments.* New York: Norton, 1978.

Murray, Tracy. *Trade Preferences for Developing Countries.* New York: Macmillan, 1977.

Index

Real-balance effects. *See* Wealth effects on spending
Reciprocal causation. *See* Feedback
Reciprocal currency arrangements. *See* Swap agreements
Reciprocity, 363–367, 457, 475–481
Recycling, 219, 221
Redlining, 221n
Reference (exchange) rates, 210
Reform, international monetary, 207–211
Regulation Q, 230n
Renegotiation (of debt), 224
Repatriation of earnings, 14n, 77, 146, 440n
Repurchases, IMF, 72, 214n
Rescheduling (of debt), 224
Reserve credit, 72, 107–108, 117
Reserve currency, 109–110
Reserve indicators, 210n
Reserve tranche, 72, 118
Resource endowments
  and commodity trade, 389–393, 400, 401–405
  and factor movements, 413, 415, 420, 426–427
  and multinationals, 439
Restitution, IMF gold, 76, 211
Retaliation, 146, 198, 300, 305–306, 307, 316, 337–338, 352, 355, 358n, 362, 370n, 371, 378, 380
Revaluation, 47–48
Reverse preferences, 370–371
Roosa bonds, 108
Runaway plants, 442
Rybczynski effect, 420n

Safeguard clause, 337–338, 477
Scale economies
  and commodity trade, 255, 292, 316n, 394, 398–400, 405–406, 409
  and Euro-banking, 215, 219, 229
  and multinationals, 436–437
  and prices, 89n
Scandinavian model, 96n, 196
SDRs (Special Drawing Rights), 58, 73–76, 107, 118, 207n, 210–211, 457, 467n
Second Best, Theory of, 287, 290, 301n, 329, 338, 369, 383, 475n

Seigniorage, 114, 119
Shadow prices, 284n
Simultaneous causation. *See* Feedback
Small countries, 305
Smithsonian Agreement, 204–205
Smuggling, 279
Snake in the tunnel, 212–213
Socialist planning, 284, 287, 451, 460
Soft and hard loans, 220n
South-South cooperation, 486–487
Sovereign debt, 218–224
Soviet Union and MFN, 366n
Specialization, 245–255, 296–298, 371–372
Speculation
  commodity, 465, 470n
  description, 15–17
  and Euro-banks, 217, 234
  forward, 31–34
  self-fulfilling, 16
Stand-by arrangements, 72–73, 117
State trading, 385–386n
Sterilization, 46, 71, 158–166, 492
Stocks, flows. *See* Investment, international financial
Stolper-Samuelson Theorem, 422
Subsidies
  to exports, 169, 293n, 358–362, 440n
  to production, 290–291
Substitutability of trade and factor movements, 408–410, 413–423
Substitution account, 211
Surcharge, import, 146, 198, 204, 308
Surplus, consumers' and producers', 286n
Surveillance, 207–210, 220, 231
Swap agreements, 111, 117–119, 467n
Swaps, forward, 162
Synchronization of business cycles, 178–201
Syndication of loans, 219, 229n

Takeovers, 429, 444–445
Tariff quota, 353, 477, 479
Tariffs
  ad valorem and specific, 270n, 353
  description, 269–271
  effects of, 277–282